LAW AND JUDICIAL DIALOGUE ON THE RETURN OF IRREGULAR MIGRANTS FROM THE EUROPEAN UNION

This volume examines the implementation of the Return Directive from the perspective of judicial dialogue. While the role of judges has been widely addressed in European asylum law and EU law more generally, their role in EU return policy has hitherto remained underexplored. This volume addresses the interaction and dialogue between domestic judiciaries and European courts in the implementation of European return policy. The book brings together leading authors from various backgrounds, including legal scholars, judges and practitioners. This allows the collection to offer theoretical and practical perspectives on important questions regarding the regulation of irregular migration in Europe, such as: what constitutes inadequate implementation of the Directive and under which conditions can judicial dialogue solve it? How can judges ensure that the right balance is struck between effective return procedures and fundamental rights? Why do we see different patterns of judicial dialogue in the Member States when it comes to particular questions of return policy, for example regarding the use of detention? These questions are more timely than ever given the shifting public discourse on immigration and the growing political backlash against immigration courts. This book will be essential reading for all scholars and practitioners in the fields of immigration law and policy, EU law and public law.

Volume 99 in the Series Modern Studies in European Law

Modern Studies in European Law

Recent titles in this series:

Illegally Staying in the EU: An Analysis of Illegality in EU Migration Law
Benedita Menezes Queiroz

Social Legitimacy in the Internal Market: A Dialogue of Mutual Responsiveness
Jotte Mulder

The EU Better Regulation Agenda: A Critical Assessment
Edited by Sacha Garben and Inge Govaere

Administrative Regulation Beyond the Non-Delegation Doctrine:
A Study on EU Agencies
Marta Simoncini

The Interface Between EU and International Law: Contemporary Reflections
Edited by Inge Govaere and Sacha Garben

The Rise and Decline of Fundamental Rights in EU Citizenship
Adrienne Yong

The Court of Justice and European Criminal Law: Leading Cases in a Contextual Analysis
Edited by Valsamis Mitsilegas, Alberto di Martino and Leandro Mancano

The EU as a Global Regulator for Environmental Protection: A Legitimacy Perspective
Ioanna Hadjiyianni

Citizenship, Crime and Community in the European Union
Stephen Coutts

Critical Reflections on Constitutional Democracy in the European Union
Edited by Sacha Garben and Inge Govaere

Constitutional Law of the EU's Common Foreign and Security Policy:
Competence and Institutions in External Relations
Graham Butler

The Juridification of Individual Sanctions and the Politics of EU Law
Eva Nanopoulos

Sixty Years of European Integration and Global Power Shifts:
Perceptions, Interactions and Lessons
Edited by Julien Chaisse

Fundamental Rights and Mutual Recognition in the Area of Freedom,
Security and Justice: A Role for Proportionality?
Ermioni Xanthopoulou

For the complete list of titles in this series, see 'Modern Studies in European Law' link at www.bloomsburyprofessional.com/uk/series/modern-studies-in-european-law

Law and Judicial Dialogue on the Return of Irregular Migrants from the European Union

Edited by
Madalina Moraru
Galina Cornelisse
and
Philippe De Bruycker

•HART•
OXFORD • LONDON • NEW YORK • NEW DELHI • SYDNEY

HART PUBLISHING

Bloomsbury Publishing Plc

Kemp House, Chawley Park, Cumnor Hill, Oxford, OX2 9PH, UK

1385 Broadway, New York, NY 10018, USA

HART PUBLISHING, the Hart/Stag logo, BLOOMSBURY and the Diana logo are trademarks of Bloomsbury Publishing Plc

First published in Great Britain 2020

A catalogue record for this book is available from the British Library.

Library of Congress Cataloging-in-Publication data

Names: Moraru, Madalina, editor. | Cornelisse, Galina, editor. | Bruycker, Philippe de, editor.

Title: Law and judicial dialogue on the return of irregular migrants from the European Union / edited by Madalina Moraru, Galina Cornelisse and Philippe De Bruycker.

Description: Oxford ; New York : Hart, 2020. | Series: Modern studies in European law; volume 99 | Includes bibliographical references and index.

Identifiers: LCCN 2020011764 (print) | LCCN 2020011765 (ebook) | ISBN 9781509922956 (hardcover) | ISBN 9781509922963 (Epub)

Subjects: LCSH: Illegal aliens—European Union countries. | Emigration and immigration law—European Union countries. | Asylum, Right of—European Union countries. | Repatriation—European Union countries. | European Parliament. Directive 2008/115/EC.

Classification: LCC KJE6050 .L39 2020 (print) | LCC KJE6050 (ebook) | DDC 342.2408/3—dc23

LC record available at https://lccn.loc.gov/2020011764

LC ebook record available at https://lccn.loc.gov/2020011765

ISBN: HB: 978-1-50992-295-6
ePDF: 978-1-50992-297-0
ePub: 978-1-50992-296-3

Typeset by Compuscript Ltd, Shannon

To find out more about our authors and books visit www.hartpublishing.co.uk. Here you will find extracts, author information, details of forthcoming events and the option to sign up for our newsletters.

ACKNOWLEDGEMENTS

This book is the result of multiple collaborations, the roots of which developed within the 'Odysseus' Academic Network for Legal Studies on Immigration and Asylum. The first of these was the CONTrol of DETENTION – CONTENTION project (2013–2014), funded by the European Return Fund, and implemented by the Migration Policy Centre (MPC) at the Robert Schumann Centre of Advanced Studies at the European University Institute in partnership with the Odysseus Network. A follow-up to CONTENTION was the Return directive DIALogue – REDIAL project (2014–2016). REDIAL was co-funded by the European Commission (DG Home) and coordinated by the Migration Policy Centre (MPC), in cooperation with the Centre for Judicial Cooperation (CJC) at the European University Institute and the Odysseus Network. The editors would like to express their gratitude to each of the national judges and academic experts who participated in CONTENTION and REDIAL for providing the contributors to this book with invaluable research data in their respective country reports. Special thanks go to Sergio Mananashivili and Géraldine Renaudiere for their research and coordination in these projects, and to Aurélie Boursier for her assistance in practical matters. We would also like to acknowledge the Faculty of Law of Masaryk University who provided the funds for a workshop organised by Madalina Moraru in September 2018 at Masaryk University in the Czech Republic, which was crucial for ensuring consistency in methodology and content of the chapters. Special thanks are due to Brid Ni Graihnne for her insightful comments and constructive criticism on the chapters in Part I. The volume has benefited enormously from meticulous proof-reading by Paul McDonough, Justin McCann and by Ellen Lefley, which has been made financially possible by Masaryk University, Odysseus Network and the VU Interdisciplinary Centre for European Studies (VICES). Last but not least, the editors would like to thank the contributors to this volume for their wonderful collaboration and their patience in addressing all the editors' suggestions.

We would like to conclude with a brief note on the contribution of each of the editors. The idea for this book and its scientific design were first conceived by Madalina Moraru. Galina Cornelisse and Madalina Moraru have subsequently worked in equal measure on editing individual chapters. This book would not have been possible without the academic input of Philippe De Bruycker, who has been at the very heart of both the CONTENTION and the REDIAL projects.

CONTENTS

PART 2
IMMIGRATION DETENTION IN THE EU: THE ROLE OF JUDGES IN SHAPING EFFECTIVE STANDARDS OF CONTROL
Edited by Galina Cornelisse

PART 3
RIGHTS AND SAFEGUARDS IN THE APPLICATION OF THE RETURN DIRECTIVE: THE ROLE OF JUDGES IN SAFEGUARDING PROCEDURAL AND FUNDAMENTAL RIGHTS PROTECTION
Edited by Madalina Moraru and Galina Cornelisse

LIST OF CONTRIBUTORS

Jacek Białas
Attorney-at-law and lawyer at the Helsinki Foundation for Human Rights, Poland

Adam Blisa
PhD candidate at the Department of Constitutional Law and Political Science, Law Faculty, Masaryk University, Czech Republic and clerk at the Supreme Administrative Court of the Czech Republic

Jonas Bornemann
Research Assistant at the Chair of Public, European and International Law at University of Konstanz, Germany

Ulrike Brandl
University of Salzburg, Department of Public, Public International and European Law, Austria

Jean-Yves Carlier
Professor at the University of Louvain (UCL) and at the University of Liège, Belgium

Galina Cornelisse
Associate Professor of EU Law and International Public Law at VU University Amsterdam, The Netherlands

Philippe de Brucyker
Coordinator of the Odysseus Academic Network for Legal Studies on Immigration and Asylum in Europe, Jean Monnet Chair for European Law on Immigration & Asylum at Université Libre de Bruxelles, Belgium and Avocat

Corina Demetriou
Senior Researcher, Centre for Fundamental Rights, University of Nicosia, Cyprus

Alessia Di Pascale
Associato di diritto dell'Unione europea, Università degli Studi di Milano, Dipartimento di Diritto pubblico italiano e sovranazionale, Italy

Harald Dörig
Professor at the University of Jena, Germany and former judge at the German Federal Administrative Court (Bundesverwaltungsgericht)

Jean-Baptiste Farcy
PhD Candidate at UCLouvain, Belgium

Cristina Gortázar Rotaeche
Full Professor of International Law and EU Law at Universidad Pontificia Comillas, Madrid, Spain

Carolus Grütters
Senior researcher at the Centre for Migration Law of the Faculty of Law of Radboud University in Nijmegen, The Netherlands

Valeria Ilareva
Head lawyer at the Foundation for Access to Rights (FAR) in Bulgaria

Irmantas Jarukaitis
Judge at the Court of Justice of the European Union, associate professor of Vilnius University Faculty of Law, Lithuania

Agnė Kalinauskaitė
Advisor of the Judicial Practice Department of the Supreme Administrative Court of Lithuania

Stergios Kofinis
PhD, Administrative Judge of First Instance Thessaloniki, Member of Independent Appeals Committee, Greece

David Kosař
Director of the Judicial Studies Institute (JUSTIN) at the Law Faculty, Masaryk University, Czech Republic

Luc Leboeuf
Avocat and Head of Research Group, Department of Law and Anthropology at the Max Planck Institute for Social Anthropology, Germany

Fabian Lutz
Senior Legal Expert, European Commission, DG Migration and Home Affairs, Brussels, Belgium

Madalina Moraru
Senior Research Fellow, Judicial Studies Institute (JUSTIN), Law Faculty, Masaryk University, Czech Republic and Centre for Judicial Cooperation, RSCAS, European University Institute, Italy

Aniel Pahladsingh
EU lawyer at the Dutch Council of State, researcher at the Radboud University of Nijmegen and deputy judge at the District Court of Rotterdam, The Netherlands

Angeliki Papapanagiotou-Leza
Administrative Judge of Appeal Athens, Member of the three-Member Board of Directors of the Administrative Court of Appeal of Athens, President of Independent Appeals Committee, Greece

Sylvie Sarolea
Professor in Migration Law, Private International Law and Human Rights at the UCL, Louvain la Neuve, Belgium

Serge Slama
Professeur de droit public, Université Grenoble-Alpes, CESICE, France

Nicos Trimikliniotis
Professor, School of Humanities and Social Sciences, Director of Centre for Fundamental Rights, University of Nicosia, Cyprus and barrister

Evangelia (Lilian) Tsourdi
Assistant Professor of European Union Law & Dutch Research Council (NWO) VENI grantee, Maastricht University, The Netherlands

Boštjan Zalar
Senior High Court Judge at the Administrative Court of the Republic of Slovenia, President of the European Chapter of the International Association of Refugee and Migration Judges (IARMJ-Europe), ad hoc Judge of the ECtHR

Prologue: The Genesis of the EU's Return Policy

FABIAN LUTZ*

European Commission, Directorate-General Migration and Home Affairs

I am very honoured and pleased to open this book, which is dedicated to the role of national courts and judicial interaction in ensuring the implementation of the Return Directive. The reader will find this publication interesting and useful since it gives an in-depth assessment of the changes brought about by the Return Directive ten years after its adoption in 2008 on very sensitive issues, such as detention, criminalisation of irregular stay, effective remedies and safeguards pending removal.

The editors asked me to summarise, in this prologue, the policy evolution of the EU's return policy from the early days of the elaboration of a Commission proposal until today. On the following pages, I will give a brief historic overview of its genesis, assess its impact on practices in Member States and present some considerations on possible future developments.

Return policy is, by its nature, likely to evoke emotions. Some readers may still remember the 'Directive of Shame' campaign,[1] which accompanied the first phase of adoption of the Return Directive in spring and summer 2008. Was this campaign justified? For those who are fundamentally opposed to enforcing migration rules, the emergence of common EU standards on return constituted, indeed, a further brick in the wall of fortress Europe since it harmonised repressive policy instruments, which had been hitherto used at national level, and upgraded and promoted their use at European level. Those who accept, in principle, the

* All views expressed in this article are purely personal and do not necessarily reflect the views of the European Commission. The author would like to thank Mauro Gagliardi and Simona Ardovino for valuable comments and contributions.

[1] The author was involved in the drafting of the Commission proposal for the Return Directive and its negotiation in the EP and Council. He published a book, *The Negotiations on the Return Directive* (Nijmegen, Wolf Legal Publishers, 2010), on which the historic overview given in this prologue is based; details on the 'Directive of Shame' campaign can be found in s 3 of this book.

need to enforce migration rules may come to a different assessment. For them, the decisive criterion is whether the EU return policy manages to achieve the dual objective of protecting the fundamental rights of persons affected by return procedures and promoting the legitimate interest of Member States in speedy and efficient return procedures. Any rational judgement on EU return policy (with the Return Directive as its key instrument) needs to be based on these two parameters. This book, with its rich empirical evidence on the impact of the substantive and procedural safeguards provided in the Return Directive, will give the reader a sound basis for understanding the complex realities. Some readers may even draw the conclusion that the impact of the Directive, brought about to a significant extent by the judicial interpretation of its provisions, allows it to be labelled, as it stands today, as a 'Directive of Protection'.

First Steps Towards a Common Return Policy in the Context of Schengen Acquis

The Schengen logic of abolishing checks at internal borders and introducing common standards of external border control also required Member States to agree on complementary measures to safeguard internal security and prevent illegal immigration. The Convention Implementing the Schengen Agreement (SIC) contained in its Articles 23 and 96 some basic provisions on return:[2] Article 23 (now replaced by Article 6 of the Return Directive) stated a basic rule that aliens who do not or who no longer fulfil the conditions for stay should normally be required to leave the territories of the Member States immediately. Article 96 SIC allowed Member States to enter migration- or return-related entry bans into the Schengen Information System. These rules were complemented by a number of Executive Committee Decisions covering certain technical aspects of return and readmission,[3] such as SCH/Com-ex(97)39 on means of proof and evidence for readmission, SCH/Com-ex(98)10 on cooperation in returning foreign nationals by air, and SCH/Com-ex(98)18 on documents required for expulsion. None of the broader return-related topics addressed by the Return Directive (detention, legal remedies, rights of returnees) had been harmonised at this stage yet.

[2] Convention implementing the Schengen Agreement of 14 June 1985 between the Governments of the States of the Benelux Economic Union, the Federal Republic of Germany and the French Republic on the gradual abolition of checks at their common borders [2000] OJ L239, 0019–0062.

[3] It is important to distinguish between return and readmission. The notion of *return* refers to the relationship between the returning Member State and the returnee. Its emphasis is on setting out rights of individuals in administrative procedures and the related legal safeguards, and details are now set out in the Return Directive. The notion of *readmission* refers to the relation between expelling Member State and receiving third country and details are regulated in readmission agreements between the EU (or its Member States) and countries of return, origin and transit. The Return Directive and readmission agreements complement each other: in each case of return covered by a readmission agreement, the legally binding safeguards contained in the Return Directive apply.

However, the fact that return was considered part of the Schengen acquis has had important ongoing practical consequences: the Schengen associated countries (Switzerland, Norway, Iceland and Liechtenstein) are bound by the EU's return acquis and the Commission is able to use the possibilities offered by the Schengen Evaluation Mechanism to evaluate Member States' compliance with the return acquis.

Designing the Shape of the EU's Return Policy (1999–2005)

In May 1999, the Treaty of Amsterdam entered into force. It provided, for the first time, a legal basis for the EC to adopt 'hard law' in the field of immigration and asylum. According to Article 63(3)(b) TEC, the Council was asked to adopt measures on immigration policy within the area of 'illegal immigration and illegal residence, including repatriation of illegal residents'. The October 1999 European Council Tampere Conclusions set out the broader political direction towards the creation of a common EU asylum and migration policy and underlined 'the need for more efficient management of migration flows at all their stages' (paragraph 22) as well as the political determination 'to tackle at its source illegal immigration' (paragraph 23), without, however, going into more detail on the issue of return.

In its ensuing Communication of 15 November 2001 on a Common Policy on Illegal Immigration,[4] the Commission pointed out that return policy is an integral and crucial part of the fight against illegal immigration. It also provided a first orientation on the substance of a Community return policy and set out that it

> should be based on three elements: common principles, common standards and common measures. Important common principles are, for example, the priority of voluntary return over forced return. … Another subject of further consideration should be the consequences of illegal entry and residence regarding each individual illegal resident, including the feasibility of exit controls.

The 10 April 2002 Green Paper on a Community Return Policy elaborated in more detail on the issue of return in order to trigger a broad debate among relevant stakeholders.[5] The ensuing 14 October 2002 Commission Communication on a Community Return Policy on Illegal Residents sketched a programme for further action.[6] Based on this Communication, the Council adopted its Return Action Programme,[7] in which it called for a trio of policy actions, consisting of improved operational cooperation among Member States (including exchange

[4] Commission Communication COM(2001) 672.
[5] Commission Communication COM(2002) 175.
[6] Commission Communication COM(2002) 564.
[7] Council document 14673/02 of 25 November 2002.

of information and best practices, common training, mutual assistance by immigration officers and joint return operations); intensified cooperation with third countries (both on return and readmission and on tackling root causes of irregular migration); and the establishment of common standards with the aim of facilitating operational cooperation on return.

At the end of 2002, most of the challenges to be addressed by a common EU return policy had already been identified and policy suggestions for addressing them were set out in the aforementioned Communications and Action Plan. It still took, however, more than five years until the main instrument of the EU's return policy, the Return Directive, was adopted. One factor explaining the relatively long period which elapsed between the adoption of the Council's Return Action Programme in November 2002 and the adoption of a Commission proposal in September 2005 may have been that the Commission preferred to wait for the December 2004 decision of the Council to switch to the co-decision procedure before submitting a proposal.[8] Based on experiences gained in negotiating the first generation of asylum and legal migration Directives,[9] the Commission was aware that it was easy for Member States to agree on a watered-down text with limited added value under the 'old' consultation procedure and may have hoped that the switch to co-decision might result in qualitative improvements of the text. Another possible factor was the change of the Commissioner in charge of Justice and Home Affairs and resulting adaptations of policy priorities.[10]

Negotiating the Return Directive (2005–2008)

Before the adoption of the Return Directive, Community legislation in the field of return had been limited to certain, mainly operational, issues chosen by Member States under their right of co-initiative, such as the organisation of joint flights for removal;[11] assistance in cases of transit for removal by air;[12] and the possibility of mutual recognition of expulsion decisions.[13] By contrast, the Return Directive was designed to be a horizontal piece of legislation, harmonising systematically

[8] Such a decision should have taken place – as foreseen by Art 67(2) TEC – by 1 May 2004, but the Council waited until December 2004 to take this step by means of Council Decision 2004/927/EC providing for certain areas covered by Title IV of Part Three of the Treaty Establishing the European Community to be governed by the procedure laid down in Article 251 of that Treaty [2004] OJ L396/45.

[9] Such as in particular the Family Reunification Directive 2003/86/EC, the Long-term Resident Directive 2003/109/EC, the Asylum Reception Conditions Directive 2003/9/EC, the Qualification Directive 2004/83/EC and the Asylum Procedures Directive 2005/85/EC.

[10] In November 2004, Franco Frattini took over the Justice and Home Affairs portfolio from Antonio Vitorino who had held this portfolio since September 1999.

[11] Decision 2004/573/EC [2004] OJ L261/28 on joint flights for removal.

[12] Directive 2003/110/EC [2003] OJ L321/26 on assistance in cases of transit for removal by air.

[13] Directive 2001/40/EC [2001] OJ L149/34 on mutual recognition of expulsion decisions.

and inclusively the standards and procedural safeguards in the Member States on return, removal, entry ban, detention, etc.

The Commission proposal was criticised by the Council as being too oriented towards protection and human rights. The main preoccupation expressed by Member States was the fear that the Directive would make return more difficult in practice. Member States asked, in particular, for the following changes to be made to the proposal:

- abandoning the allegedly 'over-bureaucratic' requirement of a two-step procedure (return decision and removal order in two subsequent and different steps);
- excluding 'persons rejected at the border' from the scope of the proposal;
- excluding persons who never had a right to stay ('illegal entrants') entirely from the scope of the proposal or from some of the safeguards provided in it;
- excluding persons falling under the scope of readmission agreements with third countries from the scope of the proposal;
- lowering the level of protection with regard to legal remedies and detention;
- deleting entirely the proposed chapter V, 'Apprehension in other Member States'.

Discussion within the Civil Liberties Committee (LIBE) of the European Parliament (EP) drifted diametrically away from discussion at the Council level and resulted in a number of draft amendments focused on protection-related suggestions, such as:

- an absolute prohibition on removing minors;
- suspensive effect of appeals in all cases;
- a prohibition on returning persons to countries of transit;
- an absolute prohibition on removing persons who can get better medical treatment in the EU than in their home countries.

The compromise solutions finally achieved on many contentious issues were inspired by the Council of Europe's 'Twenty Guidelines on Forced Return'.[14] These Guidelines had been formally accepted in 2005 as a legally non-binding instrument by the Committee of Ministers of the Council of Europe and reflected to a large extent a compilation of existing ECtHR case-law as well as standards established by the European Committee for the Prevention of Torture and Inhuman or Degrading Treatment (CPT). The fact that the Council of Europe had endorsed them was taken by the EP as a good sign for full human rights compliance. Member States were not always enthusiastic about converting these standards into

[14] Council of Europe document CM(2005)40 of 4 May 2005. Given that Recital 3 of the Directive explicitly refers to these guidelines, they may be considered a complementary tool for the interpretation of the Directive. This was expressly recognised by the CJEU in its judgment of 28 April 2011, Case C-61/11 PPU *El Dridi* EU:C:2011:268, para 43.

hard EU law, but they could not openly oppose Guidelines which had already been solemnly accepted by their ministers and therefore *nolens volens* accepted them as basis for compromise texts. This anecdote exemplifies how a court (in this case the ECtHR), with the convincing authority of its case-law, helped to shape soft law which subsequently spilled over into hard-law provisions.

The negotiations of the Return Directive provide evidence that the switch to the 'co-decision' procedure allowed for qualitative improvements which would not have been possible under the previous consultation procedure. This relates in particular to the provisions dealing with basic guarantees in border cases in Article 4(4); basic principles (*non-refoulement*, best interests of the child, family life, state of health) in Article 5; the right to a minimum period for voluntary departure in Article 7; forced return monitoring in Article 8(6); assistance for unaccompanied minors in Article 10; free legal aid in Article 13(4); minimum conditions of stay of non-removable returnees in Article 14; and detention conditions in Articles 16 and 17. All these provisions would not exist, or would have been watered down, if the Directive had been adopted by the Council under the consultation procedure.

First Decade of Application (2008–2018)

In its March 2014 implementation report the Commission presented a first overall picture on the impact of the Return Directive in the Member States.[15] According to this report, which was subsequently corroborated by further Commission Communications and findings of the Schengen Evaluation reports,[16] the Return Directive has positively influenced national law and practice regarding voluntary departure and has been a driver for change in forced return monitoring. It has contributed to a gradual convergence of detention periods across the EU. There has also been consistent movement towards a wider implementation of alternatives to detention across Member States. It has also delineated Member States' ability to criminalise mere irregular stay, and its procedural safeguards have contributed to more legal security. In the years 2012–2014, the Commission services carried out an organised programme of work on the correct transposition of the Return Directive, during which the Commission questioned Member States about any remaining issues with their transposition of the Directive. In technical bilateral meetings, details of identified shortcomings and possible solutions

[15] Commission Communication COM(2014) 199.

[16] Commission Communication COM(2015) 453 and COM(2017) 200. Scheval reports are 'restricted' documents and are not released to the public. The recommendations based on these reports are 'limited', hence they are not subject to the same strict rules of confidentiality, although they are also not published or publicly available. Some can nevertheless be found at websites such as Statewatch. See eg statewatch.org/news/2018/aug/eu-council-com-spain-returns-11339-18.pdf (accessed October 2018).

were discussed. These meetings and discussions proved to be very helpful and the majority of transposition issues were able to be settled without having to resort to formal infringement procedures. In those remaining cases in which it was not possible to find agreement and to obtain commitment from Member States to change their legislation in accordance with requests from the Commission, a limited number of EU Pilot procedures had to be launched.[17]

A series of rulings from the CJEU have clarified a number of key aspects of the Directive, for example on detention, entry bans, criminalisation of irregular stay, rights pending postponed return and the right to good administration including the right to be heard.[18] The rulings of these CJEU judgments, as well as the results of discussions with Member State experts on the interpretation of detailed aspects of the Directive, were compiled and operationalised in the Commission's Return Handbook,[19] published in 2015 and revised in 2017. The concern, expressed by some Member States at the time of adoption of the Directive, that its protective provisions would undermine the efficiency of return procedures has not materialised: experience has confirmed that the procedures foreseen in the Return Directive as well as the flexibility provided by this Directive allow for determined action when implemented correctly.[20] The main reasons for non-return relate to *practical* problems in the identification of returnees and in obtaining the necessary documentation from non-EU authorities as well as from limited or incorrect use of the flexibility provided by the Directive.

Joint ownership of and support for the key policy objectives of this new EU policy have gradually developed. All Member States now generally accept the main policy objectives of EU return policy including respect for fundamental rights, fair and efficient procedures, fewer cases in which migrants are left without clear legal status, the importance of effective implementation of entry bans for preventing irregular migration, the primacy of voluntary departure and the fostering of effective alternatives to detention. These positive changes have been confirmed at the international level by the United Nations International Law Commission's eighth report on the expulsion of aliens, in which the UN Special Rapporteur acknowledged that the EU's Return Directive 'contains extremely progressive provisions on such matters that are far more advanced than the norms found in other regions of the world'.[21]

[17] A detailed overview of enforcement action taken by the Commission can be found in part IV of Commission Communication COM(2014) 199.

[18] An exhaustive overview of this case-law with references to the main issues dealt with can be found on pp 88–89 of the Commission's revised Return Handbook C(2017) 6505.

[19] Commission Recommendation C(2015) 6250 establishing a common 'Return Handbook' amended by C(2017) 6505.

[20] See the assessment made by the Commission on the basis of a number of comparative studies in its first implementation report on the impact of the Return Directive in Member States' policies and practices COM(2014) 199, 12–29.

[21] Eighth report on the expulsion of aliens by Maurice Kamto, Special Rapporteur, A/CN/4/651, 22 March 2012, para 42.

Today's policy priorities in the field of return seem to have moved from the regulatory to the enforcement side. They are based on recognition of the fact that the main challenge of the EU's return policy is not to issue a return decision, but to enforce it. In view of EU return rates consistently below 40 per cent,[22] the focus is on finding tools for facilitating the identification of returnees and obtaining the necessary documentation from non-EU authorities. Today's priorities, as clearly emphasised by the 2017 Renewed Action Plan on Return,[23] as well as the 2017 Commission Recommendation on making returns more effective,[24] therefore relate to measures which directly contribute to identifying and documenting returnees, in particular through using more efficiently the discretion available to Member States under the Return Directive, a better use of the EU's large-scale IT systems for return purposes and an enhanced emphasis on overcoming the challenges of readmission by incentivising countries of return to better cooperate with the EU. Incentives under discussion draw on all relevant policy fields,[25] including home affairs (offering visa facilitation and opportunities for legal migration), neighbourhood policy, trade agreements and trade preferences as well as foreign policy, security and development assistance. At the same time increased emphasis is also given to return support and operational return activities of the European Border and Coast Guard Agency in both voluntary and forced return.[26] In the same vein, the September 2018 Commission proposal for a targeted revision of the Return Directive aims at reducing the length of return procedures, securing a better link between asylum and return procedures and ensuring more effective use of measures to prevent absconding.[27]

Future Developments?

This is not the place to discuss in detail the recently proposed targeted amendments or other possible future amendments to the Directive, but rather to recall the pros and cons of certain ideas against today's background. Some of these ideas – such as harmonising the reasons leading to expulsion and binding mutual recognition of return decisions – were already on the 2002 wish-list of the Council but were not included in the Commission proposal. Other issues were included in the Commission proposal but dropped during the negotiations due to insufficient support by the Council or EP; these included the creation of 'Dublin-like' rules for irregular migrants, a 'shall clause' on detention and the possibility of

[22] Commission Communication COM(2017) 558 of 27.9.2017 on the Delivery of the European Agenda on Migration, 9.
[23] Commission Communication COM(2017) 200.
[24] Commission Recommendation COM(2017) 1600.
[25] Commission Communication COM(2015) 453, 14.
[26] Commission Proposal COM(2018) 631 of 12.9.2018.
[27] Commission Proposal COM(2018) 634 of 12.9.2018.

return to a third country that is not the country of transit or origin. There are also issues no one thematised during the negotiations, such as the relation between return and criminalisation of irregular entry and stay (see the *El Dridi* case-law of the CJEU),[28] apprehension practices and possible firewall clauses,[29] and regularisation. Furthermore there are several aspects of the Directive which, based on experiences in the application of the Directive including Schengen evaluations as well as discussions on the Return Handbook, could be regulated in some more detail (such as grounds for detention, material detention conditions, approximation of the definition of risk of absconding,[30] conditions of stay of non-removable returnees,[31] rules for applying voluntary departure,[32] rules on forced return monitoring, border procedures, linking asylum procedures and return, practical modalities for 'taking back' returnees under existing bilateral arrangements between Member States, etc). I am limiting myself here to a selection of basic issues, which may (re)emerge in future policy debates.

Harmonising the Reasons Leading to Expulsion

In 2002, the Council called on the Commission to propose horizontal legislation making the 'expulsion' (ie withdrawal of a residence permit followed by subsequent return) of legally staying migrants who pose public order problems, in particular terrorists or hate preachers, mandatory. Such a provision was excluded by the Commission from the proposal for a Return Directive in 2005 for two main reasons. First, legal migration Directives as well as instruments in the asylum acquis already contained provisions on 'public order/security' which allow Member States to withdraw or not renew residence permits of third-country nationals and to return third-country nationals who constitute a threat to public policy or public security. Second, expelling a criminal or a suspected criminal may not always be in the interest of a Member State, as it may sometimes be preferable to bring criminal charges against such a person or to keep him or her under surveillance in a Member State rather than expelling him or her to a third country. The creation of a general obligation (a 'shall clause') to end the legal stay of specific categories of persons was therefore not aimed at. It cannot be excluded

[28] See more on this topic in G Cornelisse, 'The Scope of the Return Directive: How Much Space Is Left for National Procedural Law on Irregular Migration?', Chapter 1 in this volume.
[29] See the discussion of apprehension practices and respect of fundamental rights on pp 22–24 of the revised Return Handbook (C(2017) 6505).
[30] See more on this topic in M Moraru, 'Judicial Dialogue in Action: Making Sense of the Risk of Absconding in the Return Procedure', Chapter 5 in this volume.
[31] See more on this topic in B Zalar, 'Impact of Judicial Dialogue(s) on Development and Affirmation of the Right to Effective Legal Remedy from Articles 13 and 14 of the Return Directive', Chapter 16 in this volume.
[32] See more on this topic in U Brandl, 'Voluntary Departure as a Priority: Challenges and Best Practices', Chapter 3 in this volume.

that following serious crimes or terrorist acts committed by legally staying third-country nationals, action at EU level on this issue may be requested again in the future. The rational reasons quoted above for not doing so remain valid and may be used again.

Mutual Recognition of Return Decisions

In its 2002 Return Action Programme, the Council proposed that 'an expulsion decision issued by one Member State should … be enforced in another Member State without the latter having to issue a new expulsion decision'. Following this logic, one could have expected the Commission to propose a system of binding mutual recognition of return decisions. What were the reasons why the Commission did not propose such a system? Three main arguments played a role: in the first place, in spite of the harmonising Directives adopted in the field of migration, much is still regulated at national level, and administrative rules as well as case-law relating to the granting and ending of legal residence of third-country nationals differ significantly from one Member State to another. This absence of underlying full harmonisation would make it difficult to operate a system of binding mutual recognition. Second, return is closely linked to basic human rights guarantees, such as *non-refoulement*. It is difficult to imagine that Member States would be willing to blindly accept the return of a person to a third country based on a decision of another Member State without undertaking a reassessment of the case. Any proposal for a system of binding mutual recognition of return decisions would therefore have to provide for a series of important derogations. However, with every additional point to be checked before a return decision is recognised in the executing Member State, mutual recognition becomes more complicated and lengthier and the key benefit of mutual recognition – speed and simplicity based on trust – becomes ever more threatened. Third, one way to face these difficulties would be the creation of a single European forum for legal remedies in relation to return and removal. Taking into account the gradual development of a common European migration policy and the reluctance of Member States to give up sovereignty in this sensitive policy field, this may be a long-term vision. Given that today's real problem of EU return policy is not the regulatory aspect of issuance or recognition of return decisions but rather the enforcement angle (ie identification and documentation), there appears to be no strong policy leverage to move towards a binding mutual recognition system in the short term.

Dublin-Like System for Irregular Migrants

Under Article 6 of the Return Directive, the Member State of apprehension of an irregular migrant is in charge of carrying out the return procedure. If an irregular migrant absconds in a first Member State and is afterwards apprehended in a second Member State, this second Member State becomes competent and must carry out the return procedure. Article 16 of the Commission proposal had foreseen a 'Dublin-like' system for irregular migrants, allowing passing returnees back to a first Member State of entry, but this was unanimously rejected by Member States, which were reluctant to extend the Dublin logic from asylum seekers to additional groups of persons. However, Article 6(3) of the Return Directive offers a possibility for Member States to make use of existing bilateral readmission agreements between Member States. Since each Member State currently disposes of a large number (8–16) of such agreements,[33] covering the most important neighbouring countries, the practical relevance of Article 6(3) is very high. In principle, the Commission could revert to its 2005 proposal to replace the current piecemeal approach of bilateral agreements with a Dublin-like system. Such a proposal is, however, likely to be rejected by Member States for the same reasons as in 2005. Moreover, there is the valid argument that contrary to asylum seekers (who have a prospect of legal stay in the EU), returnees (who in principle have no prospect of legal stay) should be directly returned to third countries rather than transferred between Member States.

Status of Non-Removable Returnees and Regularisation[34]

The presence of a significant number of non-removable returnees in the EU poses concrete challenges. Even if it will be possible to increase return rates over the coming years, it is unlikely that the number of non-removable returnees will significantly decrease. The dilemma of how to address the issue of non-removability will therefore certainly remain very relevant in the years to come. It directly links to a number of issues addressed in different sections of this book. Currently, non-removable returnees benefit from some essential 'safeguards pending return'[35] listed in Article 14 of the Return Directive. According to the CJEU case-law,[36] enjoyment of the right to healthcare under Article 14 also gives rise to a concomitant requirement to make provision for the basic needs of the person. The current variety of differing approaches on granting further rights may constitute an incentive for secondary movements towards those Member States that offer de jure and de facto the best conditions of stay. A common approach among Member States concerning the rights of non-removable persons could prevent this from happening. In addition, the argument can be made that the existence of large numbers of

[33] 'Inventory of bilateral agreements linked to readmission', accessible online at www.jeanpierrecassarino.com/datasets/ra/.

[34] The following paragraphs presume elements which are set out in more detail in F Lutz, 'Non-Removable Returnees under Union Law, Status Quo and Possible Developments' (2018) 20 *European Journal of Migration and Law* 28.

[35] See more on this topic in JB Farcy, 'Unremovability under the Return Directive: An Empty Protection?' Chapter 19 in this volume.

[36] See Case C-562/13 *Abdida* EU:C:2014:2453.

'non-removables' with limited possibilities to work legally in order to earn their own living contributes to a negative public perception of migration and undermines the public acceptance of a sustainable EU migration policy as a whole. It also fuels the irregular labour market. Common standards that would grant at least certain categories of 'non-removables' a right to work could contribute towards alleviating this phenomenon.[37] However, it appears unlikely – from today's perspective with its emphasis on efficiency of return – that a legislative initiative at the EU level will further upgrade the rights of non-removable returnees in the foreseeable future.

Administrative Detention

Given the clear legal situation under the Return Directive and CJEU as well as ECtHR case-law which only allows the use of detention if there is a reasonable prospect of removal within the allowed maximum period of detention,[38] it seems unlikely that detention will become a more broadly used instrument for addressing cases of *long-term non-removability* (ie a prognosis that return is not possible within the maximum detention period prescribed by the Return Directive). Even if there were a political wish to change the provisions of the Return Directive and to allow for administrative detention of long-term non-removable returnees, this might not be a legally sustainable solution since the safeguards provided by the current text of the Return Directive are very similar to the existing ECtHR jurisprudence on Article 5(1)(f) ECHR, and any lowering of Return Directive standards in that respect would risk conflicting with this case-law. As regards *short-term non-removability* (ie a prognosis that return *is* possible within the maximum period of detention of 6 or 18 months allowed under the Return Directive), the Commission already recommended, both in its March 2017 Recommendation on making returns more effective[39] and in its 2017 recast of the Return Handbook,[40] to increase the efficiency of return by using detention as needed and by raising national detention periods to the maximum allowed under the Return Directive. Corresponding legislative changes may be justified in order to ensure that premature ending of detention and ensuing absconding do not undermine legitimate removal efforts. In its September 2018 proposal for a recast of the Return Directive, the Commission indeed proposed to require national legislation to provide for not less than 3 months as an initial minimum period of detention, in order to more appropriately reflect the time needed to successfully carry out return and readmission procedures with third countries.

[37] Such practices already exist in some Member States, the most prominent being the German *Duldung* legal instrument.

[38] See more on this topic in E Tsourdi, 'Alternatives to Immigration Detention in International and EU law: Control Standards and Judicial Interaction in an Heterarchy', Chapter 7 in this volume.

[39] Commission Recommendation (EU) 2017/432 of 7 March 2017 on making returns more effective, point 10.

[40] s 14.1.

Imprisonment as Criminal Law Sanction

Commission Recommendation (EU) 2017/432 expressly referred to the leeway left to Member States by the CJEU's *Achughbabian* judgment and suggested that 'in relation to illegally staying third-country nationals who intentionally obstruct the return processes, Member States should consider using sanctions in accordance with national law'.[41] It is possible that alongside encouraging such national rules and practices, reflections may start, at a certain stage, on possible legislative harmonisation according to which Member States would be obliged to impose penal sanctions on non-cooperating non-removable third-country nationals. The most important issue to be considered in this context will be the dissuasive effect of such measures: would the prospect of – possibly repeated – imprisonment under criminal law make non-cooperating returnees cooperate? Or would such measures rather be perceived by the migrants concerned as yet another, surmountable, obstacle on the long and burdensome way to regularisation?[42] Another open question is the extent to which national and European courts would find such enhanced criminalisation proportionate. In its September 2018 proposal for a recast of the Return Directive, the Commission proposed to create an express obligation to cooperate. According to this proposal, non-compliance with this obligation would have an impact on the determination of the risk of absconding, the granting of a period for voluntary departure and the possibility to impose detention. It remains to be seen to what extent this proposed harmonisation of an obligation to cooperate will leave leeway to Member States also to impose penal sanctions on non-cooperating returnees.

Continued Encouragement of Return

The obligation on Member States under the Return Directive to take all necessary measures to return irregular migrants also covers situations of protracted irregularity. It implies an obligation to regularly reassess the situation and to take the necessary measures to make return happen. It is likely that, in the future, increased policy attention will be paid to continued encouragement of voluntary departure (or removal),[43] flanked by enhanced readmission cooperation as well as policies of regular reassessment of the situation of returnees (in parallel to the proposed obligatory review of international protection needs in the area of asylum). It is also likely that the issue of involuntary return to a third country that is neither the country of transit or origin but nevertheless willing to accept a returnee (an option

[41] Case C-329/11 *Achughbabian* EU:C:2011:807, para 48; Commission Recommendation (EU) 2017/432 of 7 March 2017 on making returns more effective, point 11.

[42] See the thought-provoking quote 'Prison is Better than Iran' in C Gosme, 'Trapped Between Administrative Detention, Imprisonment, and Freedom in Limbo' in MJ Guia et al (eds), *Immigration Detention, Risks and Human Rights: Studies on Immigration and Crime* (Amsterdam: Springer Publishing, 2016) 117.

[43] See, for instance, Art 14(3) of the proposed recast of the Return Directive.

which had already been proposed by the Commission in 2005) may be discussed again in the coming years.

Pathways to Legal Stay

Currently there is no general obligation under EU law to grant a permit to non-removable returnees, but Article 6(4) of the Return Directive clarifies that Member States are free to do so at any moment. In order to avoid pull factors stemming from national large-scale regularisation measures, Member States committed themselves politically in the 2008 European Pact on Immigration and Asylum to use only case-by-case regularisation.[44] Currently most Member States have provisions in place allowing for case-by-case regularisation in order to tackle the practical and social problems resulting from non-removability. An arguable case can be made, using the level playing-field argument as well as considerations related to avoidance of secondary movements, that it would be in the common European interest to develop a more harmonised approach on this issue. In spite of these valid arguments, Member States have so far preferred to tackle the issue at the national level only. In its Return Handbook,[45] the Commission recommended a number of assessment criteria as regards the conduct of case-by-case regularisations: the cooperative or uncooperative attitude of the returnee; the length of stay of the returnee in the Member State; integration efforts made by the returnee; the personal conduct of the returnee; family links; humanitarian considerations; the likelihood of return in the foreseeable future; the need to avoid rewarding irregularity; the impact of regularisation measures on migration patterns of prospective (irregular) migrants and the likelihood of secondary movements within the Schengen area. These criteria, which take into account both individual and state interests, could be the starting point for future work in this field. The issue is also a subject of the ongoing Regulatory Fitness Check of the EU's legal migration acquis. Further work in this field is certainly required.

Towards a Policy of 'Hostile Environment'?

In recent years, the notion of 'hostile environment' has been rising in the political debate of some Member States.[46] The idea behind this concept is to convince irregular migrants, including non-removable returnees, that they will not be able to find a sustainable situation in the EU by granting them only very limited rights and by closing the road to regularisation. This approach – so the argument

[44] Council document 13440/08, 7.
[45] Return Handbook (both 2015 and 2017 versions) s 13.2.
[46] This notion was notably promoted by UK Home Secretary, Theresa May, in preparing changes in the UK Immigration Law in 2012.

goes – would then limit irregular migration flows and increase the number of those who accept voluntary departure offers. The main counterargument against such an approach is that it may increase situations of destitution and lead to a loss of contact between authorities and returnees, affecting the feasibility of possible future return. Moreover, given the devastating situation in certain countries of origin, returnees may still prefer to live underground as irregular migrants in the EU over going home. The effectiveness of such a policy approach is questionable, but it still cannot be excluded that it will find further support in the future. A rational analysis of pros and cons is therefore needed. In its September 2017 Communication on the Delivery of the European Agenda on Migration the Commission announced a launch of consultations with Member States and other players, to catalogue factors contributing to irregular entry and stay of migrants on EU territory.[47] This will imply collecting and sharing what Member States currently recognise as the main pull factors attracting irregular migrants and finding out about policy practice which might help to counter these pull factors and make irregular entry and stay a less attractive option. The results of these consultations will be important for further shaping EU policy in the field of irregular migration in general, including return.

Apprehension Practices and Firewall Provisions

A closely related issue concerns the obligation under Article 6(1) of the Return Directive for Member States to issue a return decision to any third-country national staying illegally on their territory. According to this provision, Member States are not allowed to tolerate in practice the presence of illegally staying third-country nationals on their territory without either launching a return procedure or granting a right to stay.[48] The obligation on Member States to issue a return decision to any third-country national staying illegally on their territory is, however, subject to respect for fundamental rights, including the principle of proportionality. The legitimate aim of fighting illegal migration may be balanced against other legitimate state interests, such as general public health considerations, the interest of the state in fighting crime, the interest in having comprehensive birth registration, respect for the best interests of the child, the Geneva Convention, and other rights recognised by the Charter of Fundamental Rights of the EU. Should irregular migrants be apprehended at any cost or are there situations in which other interests prevail? On this tricky question, the Commission expressly refers, in section 5 of its Return Handbook, to the considerations set out in the 2012 Fundamental Rights Agency document 'Apprehension of Migrants in an Irregular Situation – Fundamental Rights Considerations' as guidance on how apprehension

[47] Commission Communication COM(2017) 558, 10.

[48] See more on this topic in CG Rotaeche, 'Return Decisions and Domestic Judicial Practices: Is Spaindifferent?', Chapter 2 in this volume.

practices can be carried out in respect of the fundamental rights of third-country nationals while ensuring effective return procedures.[49] The Commission affirms that Member States' practices that respect certain 'firewalls' can be considered as not affecting the obligation under Article 6(1) of the Return Directive to issue return decisions to third-country nationals staying illegally. The most important examples listed in the Return Handbook relate to the following factors:

- Public health: migrants in an irregular situation seeking medical assistance should not be apprehended at or beside medical facilities; medical establishments should not be required to share migrants' personal data with immigration law enforcement authorities for eventual return purposes.
- Access to education: migrants in an irregular situation should not be apprehended at or beside the school that their children are attending; schools should not be required to share migrants' personal data with immigration law enforcement authorities for eventual return purposes;
- Freedom of religion: migrants in an irregular situation should not be apprehended at or beside recognised religious establishments when practising their religion.
- Birth registration: migrants in an irregular situation should be able to register the birth and should be able to obtain a birth certificate for their children without risk of apprehension; civil registries issuing birth certificates should not be required to share migrants' personal data with immigration law enforcement authorities for eventual return purposes.
- Access to justice: in the interest of fighting crime, Member States may introduce possibilities for anonymous, or semi-anonymous, or other effective reporting facilities and offer victims and witnesses of serious crimes the possibility to turn to the police via third parties such as a migrant's ombudsman, specially designated officials or entities providing humanitarian and legal assistance.

***

I will now conclude and leave the patient reader the pleasure of entering into the details of the wide range of topics covered by this book. Browsing through the rich national and supranational case-law on the subjects addressed in this publication, the reader will be reassured to realise that whatever direction EU return policy and legislation will take in the future, one thing is sure: national and European courts will accompany this development and will, as they have already successfully done over the last decade, interpret legal provisions in the light of their *effet utile* and fundamental rights. This important role played by the courts will further contribute to shaping EU return policy along the lines of how it was intended to be from the outset: based on the rule of law, firm but proportionate, humane not hostile.

[49] Council document 13847/12.

Introduction: Judicial Dialogue on the Return Directive – Catalyst for Changing Migration Governance?*

GALINA CORNELISSE AND MADALINA MORARU

This book analyses how courts and judicial dialogue shape return policies in the European Union. The way in which states have traditionally dealt with irregular migration has for many decades been characterised by extensive executive discretion, with a very limited role for the judiciary.[1] This book argues that in the European Union, the adoption of the Return Directive[2] brought a significant change to the physiognomy of immigration law in this respect. In particular, it has brought expulsion procedures under judicial scrutiny and thus within the rule of law.[3] Indeed, seeing that EU law enforcement is decentralised and relies for a large extent on the bottom-up engagement of individuals claiming their rights, the Directive empowered domestic courts to venture into a field that had hitherto been dominated by the executive. With domestic judges able to assume the position of 'natural judges'[4] of the Directive, it was predictable that the deference shown by domestic courts to the executive would wane. And certainly, in many

* The chapters of the volume were concluded in 2019 and were largely based on the data collected within the REturn Directive DIALogue – REDIAL project (2014–2016).

[1] While other areas of migration law, most significantly asylum and family related migration, have over the past decades witnessed the institutionalisation of important limits to the state's exclusionary powers by the judiciary, the return and removal of irregular migrants has remained until recently largely outside the purview of courts. See G Cornelisse, *Immigration Detention and Human Rights: Rethinking Territorial Sovereignty* (Leiden and Boston, MA, Brill, 2010), in particular ch 5. See also G Cornelisse, 'Case C-357/09 PPU, Proceedings Concerning Said Shamilovich Kadzoev (Huchbarov), Judgment of the European Court of Justice (Grand Chamber) of 30 November 2009" (2011) 48 *CML Rev* 925, 941; M de Somer, *Precedents and Judicial Politics in EU Immigration Law* (Basingstoke, Palgrave, 2019); C Costello, *The Human Rights of Migrants and Refugees in European Law* (Oxford, Oxford University Press, 2015).

[2] Directive 2008/115/EC of the European Parliament and the Council, of 16 December 2008, on common standards and procedures in Member States for returning illegally staying third-country nationals [2008] OJ L348 ('Return Directive').

[3] For judicial scrutiny as an important component of the rule of law, see RS Summers, 'The Principles of the Rule of Law' (1999) 74 *Notre Dame Law Review* 1691, 1694.

[4] The term was first used by Tzanakopoulos in relation to judges implementing international law. See A Tzanakopoulos, 'Domestic Courts as the "Natural Judge" of International Law: A Change in Physiognomy' in J Crawford and S Nouwen (eds), *Select Proceedings of the European Society of International Law*, vol 3 (Oxford, Hart Publishing, 2010) 155–68.

Member States, domestic courts' application of the Directive has constrained the executive in unforeseen ways, especially when these courts started to engage in judicial dialogue with the Court of Justice of the EU (CJEU) to ensure its correct interpretation and implementation. Cases such as *Kadzoev*,[5] *Zh and O*,[6] *El Dridi*,[7] *Mahdi*,[8] *Affum*[9] and *Arib*[10] exemplify how such dialogue has strengthened the role of courts in scrutinising the choices made by governments on border control and expulsion, even under conditions of highly mediatised political pressures.[11] Judicial dialogue on the implementation of the Return Directive has produced very real effects at both the EU and domestic level, such as limiting the criminalisation of irregular migration, prioritising voluntary departure over pre-removal detention, and providing for more judicial control over administrative detention and other coercive measures of immigration law enforcement. As such, it has ensured the checks and balances of state powers that usually exist in other fields of law, but were less present in immigration law before the entry into force of the Directive.

More generally, by clarifying the direct effect of certain provisions of the Return Directive, emphasising the EU principle of proportionality, and applying several rights guaranteed by the Charter of Fundamental Rights of the EU ('the Charter'), the engagement of and interaction among judges has brought into sharp focus that the exercise of migration control by the state (also when it concerns irregular migrants) impinges on the rights of individuals, and needs proper constitutional scrutiny.[12] Judicial dialogue has thus enhanced procedural safeguards and the protection of individuals' fundamental rights. However, the extent to which the Return Directive has been able to shift the institutional configuration of the Member States when it comes to the enforcement of immigration powers shows diverse patterns, with some Member States' judiciaries having seized more control over administrative decision-making than others, and some more inclined to interact with EU law, the CJEU and other national courts than others.

[5] Case C-357/09 PPU *Kadzoev* ECLI:EU:C:2009:741.

[6] Case C-554/13 *Zh. and O* ECLI:EU:C:2015:377.

[7] Case C-61/11 PPU *El Dridi* ECLI:EU:C:2011:268.

[8] Case C-146/14 *Mahd*, ECLI:EU:C:2014:1320.

[9] Case C-47/15 *Affum* ECLI:EU:C:2016:408.

[10] Case C-444/17 *Arib* ECLI:EU:C:2019:220.

[11] See the attack by Italy's former interior minister, Matteo Salvini, on three individual judges over their rulings in immigration cases, *The Guardian* (6 June 2019) www.theguardian.com/world/2019/jun/06/salvini-steps-up-attacks-on-italian-judges-who-challenge-him; see also Viktor Orban's attack on the European Court of Human Rights (ECtHR), see Euractiv (30 March 2017) www.euractiv.com/section/global-europe/news/orban-attacks-the-european-court-of-human-rights-at-epp-congress/. The *Affum* and *Arib* cases were decided within the context of the 'Schengen crisis', see TA Börzel and T Risse, 'From the Euro to the Schengen Crises: European Integration Theories, Politicization, and Identity Politics' (2018) 25 *Journal of European Public Policy* 83–108.

[12] G Cornelisse, 'The Constitutionalisation of Immigration Detention: Between EU Law and the European Convention on Human Rights', Global Detention Project Working Paper No 15 (October 2016).

The chapters in this volume focus on the role of the judiciary in the implementation of the Return Directive in the Member States. Specifically, they zoom in on judicial interactions when courts decide cases that fall within the scope of the Directive. The book thus aims to shed light on the role played by the judiciary in one of the most important strongholds of national executives, and one of the most politically sensitive fields of EU law: return policy.[13] A key question throughout the book is how domestic judges have exercised their role as ordinary judges of EU law, bound to give effect to sometimes opposing policy objectives, namely an effective return policy *and* the protection of fundamental rights, while also being obliged to act in accordance with general principles of EU law. In such a politically loaded area, it is inevitable that national courts face struggles when giving effect to the Directive, brought about by an awareness of the domestic and European political implications of their decisions. Furthermore, judges in Europe deciding in return cases manoeuvre an area that is not only characterised by the interaction between EU law and domestic law, but that is also subject to regulation from other legal orders, both global (UN), and regional (eg the ECHR). The chapters in this book will show that there are crucial differences in the way in which these courts and judges perceive their responsibility to ensure the effectiveness of EU law in this complex legal configuration, not only among the Member States' judiciaries, but also among the branches of the judiciary within single Member States.[14] These differences have implications for the way in which the rights of irregular migrants are protected in Europe. Moreover, they raise pertinent questions as regards the role of the judiciary in the European legal constellation, which are not only relevant for assessing law and policy in the area of irregular migration, but also have wider implications for European integration at a time when European institutional dynamics are under increasing pressure.[15] We will revisit these issues below.

In this introduction, we briefly explain the necessity of in-depth research into the role of courts and judicial dialogue in relation to the implementation of the Return Directive (section I). Second, we define 'judicial dialogue' as used in this volume, and explain our research design and the questions this book aims to

[13] ibid.

[14] See S Slama, 'Trois hautes juridictions nationales pour une directive: une interaction judiciaire en trompe l'œil', Chapter 14 in this volume.

[15] For a detailed discussion of such implications in the case of Schengen integration (drawing a parallel with monetary policies), see G Cornelisse, 'What's Wrong with Schengen? Border Disputes and the nature of Integration in the Area without Internal Borders' (2014) 51 *CML Rev* 741. For a discussion of how configurations of political authority are changing as a result of the partial transfer of lawmaking competence in immigration policy from the national to the EU level, see G Cornelisse, 'Legal Pluralism in the European Regulation of Border Control: Disassembling, Diffusing, and Legalizing the Power to Exclude' in G Davies and M Avbelj (eds), *Research Handbook in Legal Pluralism and EU Law* (Cheltenham, Edward Elgar Publishing 2018). For a discussion of challenges posed by the 'refugee crisis' and return policies to the EU integration project, see P Vimont, 'The European Project in Crisis: Myths and Realities', in *IEMed Mediterranean Yearbook 2017*, https://carnegieeurope.eu/2017/11/17/european-project-in-crisis-myths-and-realities-pub-74770.

answer (section II). Third, we contextualise some of the key findings of the individual chapters as regards the contribution of courts and judicial dialogue to the implementation of the Return Directive, paying specific attention to future challenges of courts and judicial dialogue in return proceedings (section III).

I. Research Agenda: Why Courts, Why Return, Why Judicial Dialogue?

More than ten years after the adoption of the Return Directive, an in-depth analysis of the role of courts and judicial dialogue in return proceedings is timely. The Directive is one of the most controversial instruments of EU immigration policy, being one of the longest negotiated,[16] most criticised[17] and most litigated instruments of European migration management.[18] Nonetheless, an instrument that started out as the 'Directive of Shame'[19] has in some respects become a normative example for legal orders around the globe,[20] due to its unexpected protective effect for the rights of irregular third-country nationals in practice. It is significant that the 'protective' potential of the Directive has been gradually built by European and national courts, which have acted – often in dialogue with each other – as gatekeepers for the human rights protection of irregular migrants and the effective implementation of the Directive.[21] Their task has been far from easy,

[16] For more details on the negotiation procedure, see F Lutz, *The Negotiations on the Return Directive* (Nijmegen, Wolf Legal Publishers, 2010).

[17] A Baldaccini, 'The Return and Removal of Irregular Migrants under EU Law: An Analysis of the Returns Directive' (2009) 11 *European Journal of Migration and Law* 1 (citing international organisations, third countries and other officials criticising the Directive); E Guild, 'Illegal Migrants: Proposals for a Common EU Policy on Returns', 32nd Report of Session 2005–06, 121 (Q384); D Acosta Arcarazo, 'The Returns Directive: Possible Limits and Interpretation' in K Zwaan (ed), *The Returns Directive: Central Themes, Problem Issues, and Implementation in Selected Member States* (Nijmegen, Wolf Legal Publishers, 2011); V Mitsilegas, *The Criminalisation of Migration in Europe: Challenges to Human Rights and the Rule of Law* (Springer, London, 2015) 93–107; S Carrera, *Implementation of EU Readmission Agreements: Identity Determination Dilemmas and the Blurring of Rights* (Springer, London, 2016), 56.

[18] Of all the EU immigration instruments, the Return Directive has been the object of the highest number of preliminary rulings delivered by the CJEU, 30 in a period of 10 years (last checked 31 October 2019).

[19] Or 'a draconian policy towards migrants', see V Mitsilegas, 'Immigration Detention, Risk and Human Rights in the Law of the European Union. Lessons from the Returns Directive' in N Guia, R Koulish and V Mitsilegas (eds), *Immigration Detention, Risk and Human Rights* (Springer, Cham, 2016) 27.

[20] See the statement of the UN Special Rapporteur on the expulsion of aliens acknowledging that the Return Directive 'contains extremely progressive provisions on such matters that are far more advanced than the norms found in other regions of the world'. in Communication from the Commission to the Council and the European Parliament on the EU Return Policy, Brussels, 28.3.2014 COM(2014) 199 final, 30; MJ Flynn, 'Conclusion: The Many Sides to Challenging Immigration Detention' in MJ Flynn and MB Flynn (eds), *Challenging Immigration Detention Academics, Activists and Policy-makers* (Cheltenham, Edward Elgar Publishing, 2017).

[21] By 'protective' this book refers to human rights, but also to other rights and procedural safeguards such as legal certainty, transparency, primacy of voluntary departure and good administration.

since it involves striking the right balance between at times competing objectives: effective returns and protection of human rights. Furthermore, as shown by the chapters in this volume, domestic courts have had to overcome constitutional, legislative and executive hurdles limiting judicial intervention and scrutiny of administrative decision-making in matters of immigration.[22] The Return Directive has thus enabled removal cases to be litigated before courts and empowered domestic judges to exercise a degree of control which they lacked before. However, this nascent reordering of the balance between state powers has been under threat since the 'refugee crisis', with both supranational and domestic courts facing immense pressures from governments in immigration cases.[23] This book analyses how such challenges have played out in courts' scrutiny of return-related measures.

Moreover, the discourse of crisis and threat[24] has also led to proposed changes in the legislative framework governing migration and asylum at the European level. In September 2018 the European Commission put forward a proposal for amending the Return Directive.[25] The Proposal has been criticised for betraying a shift in the EU's immigration agenda by prioritising speedy returns, increasing possibilities for the use of pre-removal detention, and limiting judicial scrutiny, thus overlooking important human rights and procedural guarantees developed by European and domestic courts.[26] Within this highly charged political context of attempts to curb the powers of national courts in this area (with governments at times even holding courts responsible for the inefficiency of return policy),[27] it is particularly important to assess the contribution of courts to the implementation of the Directive across the Member States. Now that the value and usefulness of existing legal instruments such as the Return Directive are being debated and changes proposed, taking a closer look at the way in which the

[22] For additional constitutional limitations as regards the judicial review of pre-removal detention, see M Moraru and G Renaudiere, *REDIAL Research Report 2016/05*, available at http://euredial.eu/. More broadly, outside the EU, see M Giannacopoulos, M Marmo and W De Lint, 'Irregular Migration: Emerging Regimes of Power and the Disappearing Human' (2012) 22 *Griffith Law Review* 559.

[23] See the press releases of Salvini and Orban (n 11). See also the 2017 Minitti Decree limiting the hearing powers of immigration courts in Italy (Decreto-legge 13 of 17 February 2017, see further amendments in Decreto-legge 53 of 14 June 2019); as regards the pressure exercised by governments on the ECtHR, see the Separate Opinion of Judge Alburquerque in *MA and others v Lithuania*, Appl No 59793/17, Judgment of 11 March 2019, and the Draft Copenhagen Declaration, of 5 February 2018, points 25 and 26.

[24] See the EU's strategic agenda for 2019–2024, European Council, 20–21 June 2019.

[25] See Proposal for a Directive of the European Parliament and of the Council on common standards and procedures in Member States for returning illegally staying third-country nationals (recast) Brussels, 12.9.2018 COM(2018) 634 final 2018/0329 (COD) ('the Proposal').

[26] Such as: the principle of *non-refoulement*, the right to be heard, priority of voluntary departure, due-diligence obligations. See Opinion from the Fundamental Rights Agency (FRA Opinion – 1/2019 [Return], Vienna, 10 January 2019, 'The recast Return Directive and its fundamental rights implications'; and ECRE Comments on the Commission Proposal for a Recast Return Directive COM(2018) 634, November 2018.

[27] See 2017 EMN Report on the effectiveness of return in the EU Member States, 3.

Directive has been applied by courts in the Member States over the last ten years seems timely and necessary.

While a focus on the role of courts when investigating the implementation of the Return Directive is clearly necessary in light of national and European institutional and political dynamics, the chapters in this volume do not merely address the role of courts. They also use the concept of *judicial dialogue* to analyse the regulation of irregular migration in Europe and the implications of such regulation for individual rights and institutional settings. A focus on dialogue between judges is warranted for several reasons. First, a very high number of preliminary references have been sent by national courts from both old and new Member States on the Return Directive.[28] An analysis of the dynamics within domestic judiciaries leading to such references and their subsequent impact on national practice can show under which conditions EU law can lead to shifts in the balance of powers within Member States and within the EU as a whole, and illustrate the extent of the Directive's effectiveness.

Second, the specific characteristics of EU law, such as the decentralised system of implementation relying on national courts (and individuals claiming their rights) for the enforcement of EU law,[29] the obligation of uniform application of EU law, and differences between the judicial roles of the CJEU and domestic judiciaries, mean that an analysis of the role of courts in implementing the Return Directive needs to be mindful of the wider legal and discursive framework in which that role is carried out. More specifically with regard to the way in which the characteristics of EU law could affect the balance of powers in the area of immigration law enforcement, it is significant that the preliminary reference procedure in Article 267 TFEU may provide domestic courts with opportunities to circumvent domestic courts' hierarchy, as *every* court in the EU may refer questions to the CJEU.[30]

Finally, judges adjudicating the Return Directive are not only 'ordinary judges of EU law' but act in an area that is increasingly regulated by a multiplicity of legal orders, including the ECHR and global legal norms. Norms emanating from these orders may at times be complementary or mutually reinforcing, or they may be in tension or even conflict with each other. If we want to know more about the judicial role in adjudicating irregular migration and its effects on individual rights and institutional balance, we need to pay close attention to the ways in which courts navigate these different legal orders. Such a perspective inherently requires addressing the question of whether judges from different legal orders

[28] eg Belgium, Bulgaria, the Czech Republic, France, Germany, Italy and the Netherlands.

[29] JHH Weiler, 'Van Gend en Loos: The Individual as Subject and Object and the Dilemma of European Legitimacy' (2014) 12 *International Journal of Constitutional Law* 94.

[30] G Cornelisse, 'Immigration Detention: An Instrument in the Fight Against Illegal immigration or a Tool for its Management?' in M Joao Guia, V Mitsilegas and R Koulish (eds), *Immigration Detention, Risk and Human Rights* (Cham, Springer, 2016) 73, 88. See also A Dyevre, 'Judicial Non-Compliance in a Multi-Level, Nonhierarchical Legal Order: Isolated Accident or Omen of Judicial Armageddon?' [2012] *Max Planck Institute for International and Comparative Law*.

interact with each other when dealing with complementarity or conflict. Indeed, the perspective of judicial dialogue can elucidate how the judiciary approaches issues such as uniform interpretation, normative clarification and conflict resolution when adjudicating issues that are regulated by a plurality of legal orders, and the implications thereof for the protection of individual rights and increasing scrutiny of executive power.

While the role of courts and judicial dialogue has been the subject of a vast literature covering numerous fields of law and political science,[31] this book is the first to analyse the implementation of the Return Directive from the perspective of courts and judicial dialogue. Interaction between judges when applying or interpreting the Return Directive has impacted on the vertical and horizontal delimitation of competences in the EU when it comes to migration. This interaction has affected the state's immigration powers, by limiting its coercive powers of removal, the use of pre-removal detention, and criminalisation of illegal entry or stay. In addition, judicial interaction has redefined the relation between law and policy on irregular immigration and the reinstitution of internal border controls, and has had significant effects on individual rights, including the rights of children and their families and procedural guarantees in return procedures.

However, patterns of judicial dialogue differ depending on the type of return-related measure and the Member State. Broadly speaking, at one end of the spectrum are cases where ample opportunities already exist for judicial scrutiny of executive power (either because domestic courts are already endowed with significant powers of judicial control, or because the norms from one legal order provide particularly robust guarantees). In such cases, there is relatively little dialogue between judges. At the other end of the spectrum, where national courts are strongly constrained in exercising control (which can be for a variety of reasons ranging from traditional, deeply entrenched views on the judicial role to more prosaic constraints such as time limits), dialogue is also much less likely to flourish. Accordingly, most dialogue is seen in the cases that sit between these two poles. In these cases, the interaction between judges has opened up space for contestation of domestic immigration law and changes in institutional configurations. In section III we will present the main findings of the book on the outcomes of judicial dialogue and discuss challenges to its future development. Before doing so, we explain what we understand by the term *judicial dialogue* and set out the research design of this book.

[31] AM Slaughter, 'A Global Community of Courts' (2003) 44 *Harvard International Law Journal* 191; by the same author, *A New World Order* (Princeton, NJ, Princeton University Press, 2004); D Baldinger, *Vertical Judicial Dialogues in Asylum Cases: Standards on Judicial Scrutiny and Evidence in International and European Asylum Law* (Leiden, Brill, 2015); A Müller, *Judicial Dialogue and Human Rights* (Cambridge, Cambridge University Press 2017); P Lobba and T Mariniello, *Judicial Dialogue on Human Rights: The Practice of International Criminal Tribunals* (Leiden, Brill, 2017); B de Witte, JA Mayoral, U Jaremba, M Wind and K Podstawa, *National Courts and EU Law, New Issues, Theories and Methods* (Cheltenham, Edward Elgar Publishing, 2016).

II. Research Design: What Do We Mean When We Talk About 'Judicial Dialogue'?

In the last decade, judicial interactions among national and European judges have significantly increased.[32] Whether direct (eg preliminary reference), indirect (eg citation of European or foreign judgments), informal (eg meetings between national judges, circulation of legal enquiries or questionnaires on the application of certain EU legal provisions), they have contributed immensely to the implementation of EU law. The added value of these interactions is to offer an opportunity to national judges to discuss the development of jurisprudence, tackling problems of interpretation and application in diverse areas of law. Consequently, several disciplines have attempted to develop a general theory of judicial dialogue.[33]

In academic writing, the term 'judicial dialogue' has been given various meanings and qualifications, such as a vehicle for transplants of legal reasoning;[34] an informal way of communication between judicial and political bodies;[35] a new paradigm of judicial relations between actors of different legal orders;[36] a source of communication in which common solutions are built by courts in non-formalised institutional contexts;[37] ongoing exchange of arguments in order to reach common understandings;[38] exchange of arguments for the purpose of achieving a specific outcome;[39] and mutual references to case-law, including cross-citation leading to positive impact as well as to debate or opposite judicial solutions.[40]

[32] Anne-Marie Slaughter suggested that courts and other quasi-judicial bodies are increasingly entering into a dialogue among themselves (see 'A Global Community of Courts' (n 31)); see also the other authors cited in n 31.

[33] For a legal perspective, see, among others, Slaughter, 'A Global Community of Courts' (n 31) 191; AT Pérez, *Conflicts of Rights in the European Union: A Theory of Supranational Adjudication* (Oxford, Oxford University Press, 2009) ch 5; A Arnull, 'Judicial Dialogue in the European Union' in J Dickson and P Eleftheriadis (eds), *Philosophical Foundations of European Union Law* (Oxford, Oxford University Press, 2012); for a political science perspective, see E Voeten, 'Borrowing and Nonborrowing among International Courts' (2010) 39 *Journal of Legal Studies* 547; U Sadl and Y Panagis, 'The Force of EU Case Law: An Empirical Study of Precedential Constraint' (JURIX Proceedings, Foundation for Legal Knowledge Based Systems, 2015); U Sadl and H Palmer, 'Can Quantitative Methods Complement Doctrinal Legal Studies? Using Citation Network and Corpus Linguistic Analysis to Understand International Courts' (2017) 30 *Leiden Journal of International Law* 327.

[34] EF Mac-Gregor, 'What Do We Mean When We Talk about Judicial Dialogue: Reflections of a Judge of the Inter-American Court of Human Rights' (2017) 30 *Harvard Human Rights Journal* 89.

[35] In particular in the US literature, see eg MC Miller, *Exploring Judicial Politics* (Oxford, Oxford University Press 2009).

[36] Arnull (n 33) 133; A Rosas, 'The European Court of Justice in Context: Forms and Patterns of Judicial Dialogue' (2007) 1 *European Journal of Legal Studies*.

[37] M Claes and M de Visser, 'Are You Networked Yet? On Dialogues in European Judicial Networks' (2012) 8(2) *Utrecht Law Review* 100; D Sarmiento, 'The Silent Lamb and the Deaf Wolves. Discursive Pluralism, Preliminary References and Empty Judgments in a Brave New World', paper presented at the conference 'Constitutional Pluralism in the EU and Beyond', Oxford, 20–21 March 2009.

[38] See Pérez (n 33) 112–13.

[39] LB Tremblay, 'The Legitimacy of Judicial Review: The Limits of Dialogue between Courts and Legislatures' (2005) 3(4) *International Journal of Constitutional Law* 617.

[40] European Commission, Democracy through Law (The Venice Commission), 'Report on the Implementation of International Human Rights Treaties in Domestic Law and the Role of Courts' (8 December 2014).

Other scholars have defined judicial dialogue by its purposes and effects rather than by its characteristics. Those purposes and effects purportedly lie in enhancing the effectiveness, persuasiveness and legitimacy of supranational law through the creation of a process of collective deliberation, cross-fertilisation of case-law and domestication of international obligations.[41] Several scholars argue that for a robust dialogue to develop, several prerequisites have to be fulfilled, of which reciprocity and mutual recognition, respect between the actors engaging in dialogue, and continuity over time are key features.[42] A closer look reveals that legal scholars habitually adopt three meanings of judicial dialogue. They employ a narrow understanding when judicial dialogue would require reciprocity between the courts engaged in dialogue.[43] A broader sense of judicial dialogue can be seen when it is defined as a set of various interactions among courts, which do not necessarily involve reciprocity and continuity over time.[44] A last, broadest understanding of judicial dialogue not only looks at formal judicial interactions, but also includes informal communications among judges outside the courtroom.[45] This book uses the second meaning of judicial dialogue as *the use of judicial reasoning from one court by another court, for the purpose of constructing a better interpretation of a legal norm, without necessarily involving reciprocity or continuity over time.*

In this book, then, judicial dialogue refers to the various techniques that courts and judges resort to in order to solve issues of normative or judicial interpretation incompatibility in a way that ensures coherence and coordination among different judicial systems in the safeguard of effectiveness of EU law and legal obligations stemming from other legal orders (including but not limited to European and global human rights law). Judicial interactions may differ from each other in intensity, outcome and typology. Notably, within the EU there can be a dialogue along three dimensions. First, judicial interactions habitually occur between national judges and the CJEU, most notably in the preliminary reference procedure, but also when national judges engage in other ways with CJEU case-law. This we call *vertical judicial dialogue*. This term we use also for engagement by national judiciaries with ECtHR case-law. Second, there will often be interactions between judges within the same Member State, which we call *horizontal judicial dialogue*. Third, national judges may engage with the case-law of other Member States' courts, which we call *transnational judicial dialogue*. The term *transnational judicial dialogue* can also describe interactions between the CJEU and the ECtHR. As we employ a broad understanding of the concept, judicial dialogue can take various forms, of which the most important are the duty of consistent interpretation of national law with EU legal obligations as interpreted by the CJEU; the preliminary reference

[41] AM Slaughter, 'A Typology of Transjudicial Communication' (1994) 29 *University of Richmond Law Review* 99.
[42] See, in particular, Pérez (n 33); Slaughter, 'A Global Community of Courts' (n 31).
[43] Pérez, Slaughter, ibid.
[44] MacGregor (n 33).
[45] Claes and de Visser (n 37).

procedure; mutual recognition of foreign judgments; comparative reasoning with national legislation and jurisprudence from other Member States; disapplication of national law due to violation of EU law as explained by the CJEU; and engagement with judgements from the ECtHR by national judiciaries.[46]

The premise of this book is that judicial dialogue can answer complex legal questions relating to the implementation of the Return Directive. Throughout its chapters, the book will analyse the impact of various forms of judicial dialogue on return procedures, and take stock of the effect on the rights of the returnees and the institutional configuration within the Member States and the EU when it comes to regulating migration control. Three overarching questions accordingly guide the assessment of judicial dialogue in this volume. First, has judicial dialogue contributed to a more coherent application of the Return Directive across Europe, or has it resulted in an even more complex legal situation than before such dialogue took place? Second, can judicial dialogue resolve the tension between the requirements of the Directive and the legal and institutional configuration regulating immigration powers in the Member States, and under which conditions is this so? Third, have judicial interactions enhanced the protection of the fundamental rights of individuals, and if so, in what way?

To comprehensively address these questions, the book brings together leading authors from various backgrounds, including scholars, lawyers, judges and policy officers.[47] This allows the collection to offer both theoretical and practical perspectives on the relationship between judicial dialogue and the implementation of the Return Directive. Jurisprudence by courts from all levels of jurisdiction is covered and has been primarily collected within the Return Directive DIALogue (REDIAL) Project.[48] An additional innovative contribution of the book to the field of immigration governance is that of engaging the actual protagonists of judicial dialogue – judges – in the research design. While writing their chapters, all contributors were invited to consider a common list of questions, such as: which types of judicial dialogue were used to solve a conflict or unclarity regarding the implementation of the Return Directive? Are there preferences for a certain type of judicial dialogue within particular states? What are the reasons for not using judicial dialogue? What challenges do judges face in using judicial dialogue? And what is the impact of judicial dialogue on national case-law, legislation and administrative practice?[49] In the next section we will present the

[46] For a more in-depth analysis of 'Judicial Interaction Techniques', see M Moraru, 2017 ACTIONES Module of Judicial Interaction Techniques, published by the Centre for Judicial Cooperation of the European University Institute, available on the website of the CJC, see https://cjc.eui.eu/wp-content/uploads/2019/03/D1.1.b-Module-2.pdf.

[47] Seventeen scholars and 11 practitioners (judges, lawyers and policy officers) have contributed to this book. For more details on the REDIAL Project, see http://euredial.eu/.

[48] The jurisprudence is included in the REDIAL database and is analysed in the National Reports, European Synthesis Reports and Electronic Journals, available http://euredial.eu/.

[49] The jurisprudence analysed by the authors consists primarily of that collected within the REDIAL database and analysed in the National Reports, European Synthesis Reports and Electronic Journals, available at http://euredial.eu/.

key findings of the individual chapters, relating them to the three overarching research questions.

III. The Return Directive and Judicial Dialogue: Is the Genie Out of the Bottle?

This volume is divided into three parts, dealing with termination of illegal stay (Part I), pre-removal detention (Part II) and procedural safeguards (Part III). These correspond largely to the structure of the Return Directive which starts out with a chapter on general provisions, moves on to the procedure to be followed in the case of illegal stay, then deals with procedural safeguards and contains a separate chapter on the use of detention in removal procedures. In this section we briefly present the three parts and their individual chapters, contextualising their key findings against the overarching themes: to what extent has judicial dialogue on the implementation of the Directive brought more coherence and uniformity with regard to return procedures within Europe, and how has it impacted the rights of irregular migrants and affected the institutional balance within the EU and the Member States?

The aim of Part I is to offer a comparative overview of the contribution of courts and judicial dialogue to the scope of application of the Return Directive and the order of measures to be followed by administrative authorities in return proceedings. Perhaps one of the most difficult tasks of domestic courts in the implementation of the Return Directive is the determination of the Directive's scope of application when other legal fields are partially overlapping, such as EU legal migration, asylum, citizenship and/or domestic criminal law.[50] For instance, in Chapter 1, Galina Cornelisse analyses courts' contributions in resisting the persistent attempts of governments to withdraw immigration proceedings from the scope of the Return Directive into that of domestic law. She argues that the vertical judicial dialogue started by domestic courts from different Member States has led to a process of creeping competences of the EU over immigration which is an inevitable, although at times unintended, result of procedural harmonisation; and which will not stop soon. Judicial dialogue on the vertical delimitation of competences arguably resembles a snowball, with one preliminary question paving the way for the next, implicating ever more areas of European regulation, and leaving ever fewer issues within the sole discretion of the Member States.

The next challenge in the implementation of the Return Directive has been the determination of the order of return-related measures. Again, vertical judicial

[50] Since the entry into force of the Return Directive, the scope of application of the Directive has been the persistent object of preliminary questions addressed to the CJEU, starting with *Arslan* (Case C-534/11 ECLI:EU:C:2013:343) and continuing with most recent *MA and others* (Case C-673/19 registered on 11 September 2019), see more in G Cornelisse, 'The Scope of the Return Directive: How Much Space Is Left for National Procedural Law on Irregular Migration?', Chapter 1 in this volume.

dialogue has clarified the guiding principle of return proceedings – that is, the sliding scale of measures according to which the Member States should first issue a return decision,[51] then consider allowing a period for voluntary departure,[52] and only if this is not possible to proceed with removal. The subsequent chapters in Part I analyse the processes of judicial dialogue leading up to the now settled principle of 'gradualism' dictating the choice of the appropriate return measure.[53]

First, the challenges of making a return decision the first step of a return procedure are analysed by Cristina J Gortázar Rotaeche, in particular within Spain. Chapter 2 shows that vertical judicial dialogue might not immediately lead to the systemic reform of a domestic expulsion system (in the case of Spain, to issuing a return decision instead of imposing financial penalties). Her chapter shows that even when judicial dialogue is used, its domestic effects need time to develop uniformly. Unclear transposition may contribute to this lagging, especially when the legislature uses terms and notions in implementing legislation that have established connotations in prior administrative practice.[54]

The next stage in the return procedure is the voluntary departure measure. In Chapter 3, Ulrike Brandl shows how judicial dialogue has been significant in clarifying key guarantees in the implementation of voluntary departures, such as pertaining to the starting point of the period for voluntary return, circumstances where extension of the voluntary departure period is necessary and the importance of hearing irregular third-country nationals before deciding whether to grant voluntary departure. The concept of voluntary return and the judicial dialogue it spurred provide a particularly apt example of how legal norms formulated at the EU level have been able to open space for contestation by turning the human interests of irregular migrants into rights that are justiciable and enforceable by domestic courts, a dynamic exemplified by the CJEU judgment in *Zh and O*.[55]

In Chapter 4, Aniel Pahladsingh analyses the legal requirements of the entry ban set out in the Return Directive and the role of vertical judicial dialogue in clarifying their application. He argues that vertical judicial dialogue filled the gaps left by EU legislation or eliminated incompatibilities between national legislation and provisions of the Return Directive, by bringing in fundamental rights such as respect for private and family life (Article 7 Charter) and the best interests of the

[51] Art 6 of the Return Directive.

[52] Art 7 of the Return Directive.

[53] The term 'gradualism' is expressly mentioned by the CJEU in Case C-61/11 PPU *El Dridi* ECLI:EU:C:2011:268, para 41.

[54] This conclusion as regards the Member States' lagging behind the reform of their return procedure according to the principle of gradualism and prioritisation of voluntary departure can be found also in some of the chapters in Part II, eg A Di Pascale, 'Can a Justice of the Peace Be a Good Detention Judge? The Case of Italy', Chapter 13 in this volume; S Slama, 'Trois hautes juridictions nationales pour une directive: une interaction judiciaire en trompe l'œil', Chapter 14 in this volume; and S Sarolea, 'Detention of Migrants in Belgium and the Criminal Judge: A Lewis Carroll World', Chapter 11 in this volume.

[55] Case C-554/13 *Zh and O* ECLI:EU:C:2015:377.

child (Article 24(2) Charter). He shows that in the Netherlands, horizontal judicial dialogue has also played a crucial role in diffusing legal uniformity domestically regarding issues such as the grounds for an entry ban or the definition of serious threat to public security and national security, but argues that more effort is needed by way of national courts playing a more active role in improving the quality, effectiveness and uniform application of EU legislation.

The mixed story of successes and failures of judicial dialogue continues in Chapter 5, which analyses the implementation of one of the most problematic notions introduced by the Return Directive: 'the risk of absconding'.[56] Madalina Moraru shows how national courts have used judicial dialogue (vertical, transnational and horizontal) to unveil the meaning of the risk of absconding in an attempt to determine the correct return measure to adopt when such a risk is present. Indirectly, the unfolded judicial dialogue has succeeded in strengthening courts' position vis-a-vis domestic administrative authorities in an attempt to ensure the *effet utile* of the Return Directive. While judicial dialogue has widely contributed to the legality and transparency of objective criteria (ie definition in national legislation), the number and content of objective criteria have mostly remained as before the entry into force of the Directive. On this issue, the intervention of courts has been quite conservative and did not lead to a systemic reform of the long domestic lists of objective criteria along the lines of the CJEU jurisprudence.

While the first five chapters identify multidimensional instances of judicial dialogue, and indicate an overall positive impact on the effective enforcement of Return Directive, fundamental rights protection and procedural safeguards for irregularly present third-country nationals, Chapter 6 illustrates how a particular legal-political context can severely limit the possibilities for judicial dialogue to develop. Corina Demetriou and Nicos Trimikliniotis highlight the critical role of the Cypriot courts in ensuring (or undermining) effective implementation and engaging with gaps and weaknesses in the outcomes. They argue that the problems encountered in accessing rights under the Directive partly stem from the failure of the domestic judicial tradition to learn from European and foreign courts and to embrace a rights-based approach. Mostly, however, these problems arise from flaws in the Cypriot judicial system itself. The reluctance to afford primacy to the protection of fundamental rights as enshrined in the Charter, and to interpret all laws transposing the EU acquis in a manner compliant with the Charter, remains a key issue for Cypriot courts. In most cases, the (incorrect and partial) transposition of the Return Directive has brought little change to administrative policies and practices, and to judicial approaches.

The chapters of Part I show that judicial dialogue has triggered a process of reform of domestic expulsion procedures, requiring a change of notions, definitions, chronological order of return measures, and, most importantly, of their 'securitisation' or 'criminalisation' approaches for managing irregular migration.

[56] The risk of absconding is defined in Art 3(7) of the Return Directive.

Nevertheless, the process of reform requires more sustained efforts, first to ensure that the application of the Return Directive becomes the norm, instead of circumventing its application by recourse to criminal sanctions for return related offences, and second to prioritise voluntary departure instead of removal and entry bans.

Part II of the volume addresses judicial dialogue on pre-removal detention under the Return Directive. The norm of judicial control of a deprivation of personal liberty was part of the constitutional traditions of the Member States, international human rights law including the ECHR, and the Charter long before it was codified in Article 15 of the Return Directive. Moreover, in contrast to other human rights, the procedural guarantee of judicial control forms an inherent part of the right to personal liberty itself.[57] Theoretically, then, the robust guarantee of judicial control when it comes to any deprivation of personal liberty stands in stark contrast to the traditional deference shown to the executive in matters of immigration. The conflicting forces which accordingly regulate the role of the judiciary when deciding on *immigration detention*, taken together with the multiplicity of legal instruments that require their intervention, turn pre-removal detention into a particularly apt case study for analysing the role of judges in implementing the Return Directive, and their use of judicial dialogue when doing so. The chapters in this part of the book show that the Return Directive has generally led to increased protection of the rights of detained irregular immigrants, for example through a stronger insistence on the use of alternative measures.[58] Moreover, judicial dialogue on the scope of judicial review under Article 15 of the Return Directive has empowered (or required) courts in the Member States to extend their powers significantly vis-a-vis administrative discretion. However, the chapters also show the limitations of judicial dialogue and courts' intervention, which have not fully succeeded in fundamentally reforming domestic return systems that rely on pre-removal detention as a normalised part of return procedures.

Part II starts with two chapters that provide a solid basis for understanding the impact of courts and judicial dialogue on pre-removal detention. In Chapter 7, Lilian Tsourdi analyses how alternatives to immigration detention have featured in diverse legal regimes in order to uphold the prohibition of arbitrary deprivations of liberty. She does so by engaging with decisions by the UN Human Rights Committee and judgments by the ECtHR and the CJEU on immigration detention, and explores how these bodies have interacted with each other. The chapter shows that specific instruments of EU law and the case-law of the CJEU

[57] See, amongst many examples in all major human rights documents, Art 5(4) ECHR and Article 9(3) ICCPR.

[58] See, in particular, I Jarukaitis and A Kalinauskaitė, 'The Administrative Judge as a Detention Judge: The Case of Lithuania', Chapter 9 in this volume; A Di Pascale, Can a Justice of Peace Be a Good Detention Judge? The Case of Italy', Chapter 12 in this volume; and S Slama, 'Trois hautes juridictions nationales pour une directive: une interaction judiciaire en trompe l'œil', Chapter 14 in this volume.

have paved the way for a more stringent requirement that immigration detention always be a proportionate measure. Tsourdi also highlights an instance of transnational judicial dialogue gone awry: the selective reading by the CJEU of the ECtHR case-law when public order prerogatives and immigration detention interact.[59] Next, Chapter 8 zooms in on national models of judicial scrutiny of detention, with a particular focus on the relationship between institutional design and scope of review. David Kosar and Adam Blisa expose significant institutional diversity in the domestic design of judicial review of detention under the Return Directive. This diversity exemplifies the fact that while the procedural requirement of judicial control of detention has been part of the constitutional tradition of individual Member States, the historical development of the judiciary and its position versus the executive has followed vastly differing trajectories in the Member States. Kosar and Blisa show that differing institutional setups across the EU have substantial impact on the quality of the control of pre-removal detention. They identify relevant factors in reducing what they call the 'detention roulette'.

Part II continues with six chapters that further detail the legal and institutional framework of judicial control of pre-removal detention by focusing on its main models and their implications for judicial dialogue. Chapter 9 analyses the German model, where the transposition of the Return Directive affirmed the central role accorded by the German Constitution to the civil judge as the principal administrator of pre-removal detention. Jonas Bornemann and Harald Dörig show that the constitutional requirement of full review of the legality of detention means that German civil judges are not inclined to engage in judicial dialogue in this area. Nonetheless, they identify a crucial instance of vertical judicial dialogue on the implementation of return detention in prisons, which resulted in a significant decline in detention orders, thereby illustrating the receptivity of the German model to additional safeguards from other legal orders, if required. Chapter 10 examines the role of administrative judges in Lithuania in reviewing pre-removal detention. Irmantas Jarukaitis and Agnė Kalinauskaitė note that in contrast to other areas of law, vertical judicial dialogue on pre-removal detention is limited. They argue that this may be the result of a trade-off between the requirement of a speedy judicial review of any deprivation of liberty, and the completeness of legal reasoning in the sense of reliance on EU law. Importantly, the authors remind us that judicial dialogue is not an end in itself: just as in Germany, in Lithuania its use may be limited because full powers of review are already exercised as a result of domestic legal requirements.

The remaining chapters in Part II reveal more problematic systems of judicial control of detention, when assessed against checks on the exercise of executive power and the protection of individual rights. In Chapter 11, Sylvie Sarolea argues that the Belgian model, where a criminal judge reviews pre-removal detention, is

[59] Case C-601/15 PPU *JN* ECLI:EU:C:2016:84.

fundamentally flawed because criminal judges have limited power to review the legality of return and removal, resulting in ineffective review of detention. Her contribution draws attention to the absence of horizontal *and* vertical judicial dialogue when judges control the lawfulness of pre-removal detention,[60] caused by a particular institutional setup upon which the Return Directive has had surprisingly little impact. Similarly, in Chapter 12, Angeliki Papapanagiotou-Leza and Stergios Kofinis highlight constraints inherent in the legal remedy provided for by Greek legislation, to explain the lack of direct vertical and transnational judicial dialogue on pre-removal detention. They draw attention to the limited opportunities for judicial reasoning, the absence of specific procedural rules, and the lack of second-level jurisdiction in detention cases. In Chapter 13, Alessia Di Pascale assesses a particular model of judicial control, exercised by justices of the peace. She argues that the attribution of jurisdiction to the justice of the peace has not provided an opportunity for careful control of the lawfulness of detention, nor for vertical judicial dialogue, a situation which may be partially remedied through the engagement of the Italian Court of Cassation. Part II concludes with a controversial story of intricate instrumentalisation of judicial dialogue. In Chapter 14, Serge Slama argues that when it comes to reviewing detention, French courts conduct a judicial interaction 'a trompe l'oeil': an instrumental use of judicial dialogue between themselves and with the CJEU. The aim is, essentially, to protect the domestic courts' margin of appreciation and those of the administration, without necessarily ensuring the effectiveness of return procedures or protecting the fundamental rights of third-country nationals.[61]

Part III of the volume assess the judicial implementation of procedural safeguards and rights of irregularly present third-country nationals throughout the various stages of return procedures, touching in particular on the provisions of Chapter III of the Return Directive. These provisions allow a substantial margin of discretion to the Member States, which the authors argue has been shaped by courts and judicial dialogue in prominent judgments. A common thread in this part is the crucial role played by the Charter, the ECHR and general principles of EU law in gap-filling on procedural safeguards in return procedures at both EU and domestic levels, and as legality parameters for national legislation on access to social benefits pending removal. Reading these chapters, it becomes evident that return proceedings are, in practice, closely linked to other migration-related proceedings, such as asylum or visa/residence procedures. Therefore, as

[60] It is important to highlight that other areas relating to the rights of irregularly staying third-country nationals may be much less characterised by the absence of judicial dialogue. Thus, the case-law of the CJEU on the right to be heard has led to significant developments in the jurisprudence of Belgian courts. For instance, the Council of Alien Law Litigation (CALL) now consistently applies the right to be heard as a general principle of EU law, which has also substantially affected administrative practice. See M Moraru and G Renaudiere, 'European Synthesis Report on the Judicial Implementation of Chapter III of the Return Directive Procedural Safeguards' *REDIAL Research Report 2016/03*, 12.

[61] Here a similar qualification should be made as with regard to the situation in Belgium; especially salient in this respect is that judicial dialogue on the right to be heard originated in France.

mentioned in Part I, a return judge must have a proper understanding of other migration-related issues and procedures in order to deliver a just judgment. This conclusion takes shape in the first chapter of Part III, where Valeria Ilareva shows how the right to be heard in return procedures is closely linked to the right to be heard in asylum and other migration-related procedures, and how deciding on the right to be heard in one of these procedures has implications for the right to be heard in return procedures. She also argues that while other EU migration provisions regulate in more detail the right to be heard of third-country nationals, the right to be heard in return procedures is primarily a court- and judicial-dialogue-driven construct. Analysis of the case-law reveals the potential judicial dialogue has in forging effective standards that correspond to the practical issues arising in the implementation of the right to be heard.

Equally important is the right to an effective remedy. Unlike with the right to be heard, the Directive includes express standards on the right to an effective remedy. Nevertheless, practice has shown the need for further clarification of these standards. In Chapter 16, Boštjan Zalar shows the multiple contributions of judicial dialogue leading to the enhancement of the right to an effective remedy, as enshrined in Article 13 of the Return Directive. After an in-depth analysis of the preliminary questions addressed by domestic courts on the right to effective remedy in return procedures and the answers given by the CJEU, the author claims that the preliminary reference procedure, although it plays an essential role for judicial dialogue between courts of Member States and the CJEU, needs to be complemented by alternative modes of judicial dialogue, as potential means for enhancing the rule of law in relation to the Return Directive. Such alternative judicial dialogues would need to be meaningfully integrated in the knowledge-management and quality-management systems of national judiciaries.

Both the right to be heard and the right to an effective remedy have been increasingly limited in circumstances of national security. In Chapter 17, Jacek Białas shows such an example of intrusive limitations pursued by Polish law, which provides that in return cases involving national security, the third-country national has no access to the classified case files and the justification of the decision is limited. His chapter analyses the litigation strategies pursued by lawyers for the purpose of triggering legislative reform ensuring the application of the Return Directive and CJEU standards. Unfortunately, most of these strategies have remained unsuccessful due to the Polish administrative courts' reluctance to use the relevant ECtHR or CJEU case-law or engage in judicial dialogue.

The next chapter focuses on the role of courts and judicial dialogue regarding the rights of children in return procedures (Chapter 18). Carolus Grütters comparatively analyses the contribution of the European and domestic judiciaries to the enhancement of the rights of children. First, he argues that, so far, judicial dialogue on the rights of children in return procedures has concentrated on: (a) detention of children as a last resort; and (b) detention conditions of children. Second, he argues that unlike other provisions of the Return Directive, the rights of children have so far been advanced mostly by the ECtHR, which has increasingly developed child-friendly judgments. While judicial dialogue is in an incipient stage on the rights of children in return proceedings, the ECtHR case-law might, nevertheless, affect CJEU jurisprudence in the future.

While the Return Directive prescribes clear steps to be followed in the return procedure, it also acknowledges there might be circumstances were the removal of irregular third-country nationals may or must be postponed for technical or legal reasons. In Chapter 19, Jean-Baptiste Farcy addresses legal impediments to removal as well as the rights of third-country nationals whose removal is postponed. The analysis shows that the case-law of the CJEU regarding 'postponement of removal' and that of the ECtHR have led to congruent judicial standards, in particular with respect to the principle of *non-refoulement*. However, these courts have yet to engage in a mutual dialogue on the issue of safeguards pending return. While the CJEU gave an extensive reading of the Return Directive's provisions on safeguards pending return, the ECtHR does not offer meaningful remedies to unremovable migrants who may be left in a state of rightlessness. As a result, the status and rights of third-country nationals whose removal is postponed are regulated at national level. Considering the diversity of Member States' practices, the chapter argues that judicial interactions between domestic courts could play a positive role in fostering a shift towards the judicialisation of regularisation. Regularisation would then be based on judicial standards rather than administrative discretion.

The book concludes with Chapter 20, dealing with one of the most politically sensitive issues in return proceedings and more generally immigration – the prohibition of collective expulsion. Jean-Yves Carlier and Luc Leboeuf start from the observation that the prohibition of collective expulsion as interpreted by the ECtHR has not instigated major developments or controversies before the CJEU and domestic courts so far. They reflect on the potential reasons why there does not seem to be a vivid judicial dialogue on the interpretation of that prohibition. They argue that its absence can be explained by the constitutive elements of a collective expulsion as established by the ECtHR, which may be contained already in other provisions established in EU law. They show that the prohibition of collective expulsion evolved from the prohibition of discriminatory policies targeting a given group of aliens on the basis of ethnic criteria, to a broader procedural protection requiring the examination of each individual's situation prior to removal. This requirement is then compared to existing guarantees under EU asylum and migration law, which contains numerous similar procedural and substantive protections requiring the assessment of the situation of each third-country national.

Taken together, the chapters show that formulating clear and unambiguous answers to our research questions is far from easy. Indeed, focusing on the main findings risks not doing justice to the individual chapters, which each in their own way illustrate complexity and instances of judicial conflict, occasional incoherence and disagreement. Our concluding remarks attempt to reconcile the need for clear conclusions on the role of the judiciary in the implementation of the Return Directive, with the equally important requirement of doing justice to the picture of nuance and even incoherence, ineffectiveness and conflict that the chapters have brought forward.

First, judicial dialogue has doubtless provided the judiciary in the Member States with more opportunities to control administrative decision-making, thus ensuring the rule of law. Such dialogue has also led to a beneficial exchange of views among judicial authorities, resulting in more elaborate or progressive judicial reasoning. Second, judicial dialogue on the Return Directive has led to enhanced protection of fundamental rights and provided a counterbalance to restrictive or criminalisation approaches advanced by national administrations. As such, judicial dialogue has offered judges opportunities to resist the securitisation paradigm (with its accompanying threats to the rule of law), which has increasingly dictated policy choices made at Member State and EU level in immigration governance.[62] Third, by filling gaps in European legislation, judicial dialogue has led to a more coherent application of the Directive across the Member States, which has been coupled with an extension of EU competences on irregular immigration.

These three key findings need to be contextualised against three other significant threads emerging from the chapters. The first thread is that judicial dialogue has developed unevenly across the Member States. While in many of these, national courts have started to engage in an extensive and careful dialogue, either directly with the CJEU or indirectly by applying preliminary rulings, or with other courts abroad, in other states the judiciary has been reticent to partake in such dialogue. At times this can be explained by the argument that judicial dialogue is not an aim in itself: if effective protection already exists at the national level, for example because domestic courts have traditionally been endowed with significant powers of review, or if effective implementation of the Return Directive is ensured by other means, then the need for dialogue diminishes. Moreover, a lack of explicit references can also be due to judicial economy considerations: the interpretation provided in CJEU preliminary rulings might be followed without citing the relevant case-law. More often, however, the lack of dialogue has more insidious causes, such as an inward-looking judiciary or a judiciary constrained by institutional or procedural limitations. Even the reactions of referring courts to preliminary rulings by the CJEU have differed: some have readily set aside conflicting national legislation (eg Italian courts following the *El Dridi* judgment), while others take more time to implement a preliminary ruling (eg Spain, post-*Zaizoune*). Moreover, transnational judicial dialogue seems to be still in its infancy, with courts showing limited interaction with domestic courts from other Member States. This is unfortunate,

[62] See S Carrera, A den Hertog, M Panizzon and D Kostakopoulou (eds), *EU External Migration Policies in an Era of Global Mobilities: Intersecting Policy Universes* (Leiden, Brill, 2019); S Carrera, 'An Appraisal of the European Commission of Crisis: Has the Juncker Commission Delivered a New Start for EU Justice and Home Affairs?', CEPS paper (2018). On how the Proposal to recast the Return Directive prioritises speedy returns over humane return standards, see J Kilpatrick, 'The Revised Returns Directive: A Dangerous Attempt to Step Up Deportations by Restricting Rights', *Statewatch Analysis* (September 2019); and FRA Opinion – 1/2019 [Return] (n 26).

as such dialogue can illustrate the need for vertical judicial dialogue, seeing that diverging interpretations of EU law across the Member States ultimately require the engagement of the CJEU.

A second thread is that judicial dialogue, even when used, does not necessarily bring about effective changes or guarantee the uniform application of EU law. This lack of *effet utile* of judicial dialogue can be explained by courts using it instrumentally, for example to protect the prerogatives of the administration as they have traditionally done, or by viscous institutional settings and legal-political configurations that need time and effort to change. Moreover, the enforcement of domestic or European judgments depends on the effective collaboration of the other branches of state powers. The legislature might delay amendment or incorrectly implement the outcomes of judicial dialogue; the executive might delay the revision of its return-related practices or restrictively interpret judgments favourable to irregular third-country nationals. Ten years after the entry into force of the Return Directive, incorrect implementation is still widespread across the EU. In some instances only a systemic reform of return procedures would bring domestic immigration law into conformity with the Directive and the rule of law.

A third thread is that judicial dialogue has led, to a certain extent, to increased (administrative) complexity in return procedures.[63] This is partly caused by the plurality of legal orders regulating return and removal and intersection with other legal fields. Instances of conflicting interpretations of legal obligations at the EU level and the ECHR are emblematic for this increasing complexity. These legal and jurisprudential overcomplexities make the task of *national* judges by far the most difficult among the European judiciaries, as they have to manoeuvre all legal orders when deciding in concrete cases. While judicial dialogue in turn could also help national judges to carry out this complex task, its use in practice is fragmented and certain forms remain minimal. Moreover, as argued by Bostjan Zalar, the academic expectations of judicial dialogue might have been overly optimistic by failing to take account of the professional environment in which judges function. Judicial dialogue, in all its forms and dimensions,

> will continue to be limited as long as leading actors within judicial systems do not comprehend that the quality of judicial services is a complex matter that cannot be dealt with simply by monitoring the numbers of judgments upheld or quashed in appeal procedures, and that complex models of quality management must be incorporated into all major aspects of regulation of selection, promotion, evaluation, disciplinary procedure and tenure.[64]

Finally, it is worth reflecting on the future of judicial dialogue in return proceedings and the possible impact on the interpretation of immigration rules in the

[63] See more in G Cornelisse, 'The Scope of the Return Directive: How Much Space Is left for National Procedural Law on Irregular Migration?', Chapter 1 in this volume.

[64] See B Zalar, 'Impact of Judicial Dialogue(s) on Development and Affirmation of the Right to Effective Legal Remedy from Articles 13 and 14 of the Return Directive', Chapter 16 in this volume.

age of migration control,[65] expedited returns[66] and overcomplexity of procedures. Given the increase of actors competent to act and take decisions in return proceedings (eg European Border and Coast Guard Agency[67]), coupled with a persistent absence of experienced legal aid lawyers, and states' efforts to avoid the application of the Return Directive and criticising, at times even curbing, judicial scrutiny powers,[68] the role of courts in preserving the rule of law in return proceedings is set to become ever more difficult. Against this background, judicial dialogue may provide these courts with the critical tools needed to ensure that EU return policy is shaped as it was intended to be from the outset: based on the rule of law, firm but proportionate, humane not hostile.[69]

[65] See the Interoperability regulations: Regulation (EU) 2019/817 of the European Parliament and of the Council of 20 May 2019 on establishing a framework for interoperability between EU information systems in the field of borders and visa, and Regulation (EU) 2019/818 of the European Parliament and of the Council of 20 May 2019 on establishing a framework for interoperability between EU information systems in the field of police and judicial cooperation, asylum and migration; see also 'Interoperability and Fundamental Rights Implications – Opinion of the European Union Agency for Fundamental Rights', 11 April 2018, 19.

[66] JP Cassarino, 'Informalizing EU Readmission Policy' in AR Servent and F Trauner (eds), *The Routledge Handbook of Justice and Home Affairs Research* (London, Routledge, 2018) ch 7; J Slagter, 'An "Informal" Turn in the European Union's Migrant Returns Policy towards Sub-Saharan Africa', *MPI Policy Brief* (January 2019).

[67] Regulation (EU) 2019/1896 of the European Parliament and of the Council of 13 November 2019 on the European Border and Coast Guard and repealing Regulations (EU) No 1052/2013 and (EU) 2016/1624 PE/33/2019/REV/1 [2019] OJ L295, 1–131.

[68] For example, Art 16(1) of the proposal for the recast Return Directive imposes a single level of jurisdiction against the return decision where it is based on a decision rejecting an asylum application when that decision has already been subject to an effective judicial review according to Art 53 of the (not yet finalised) Asylum Procedure Regulation. Furthermore, a very tight deadline was proposed by the EC for appealing before a court (see Proposal, Art 16(3)).

[69] F Lutz, 'Prologue', in this volume.

PART 1

Stages of the EU Return Procedure: The Role of Judges in Ensuring an Effective Implementation of the Return Directive

EDITED BY MADALINA MORARU

1

The Scope of the Return Directive: How Much Space is Left for National Procedural Law on Irregular Migration?

GALINA CORNELISSE

I. Introduction

This chapter analyses the impact of vertical judicial dialogue on the scope of the Return Directive. It focuses on questions of delimitation of the Directive, both versus other areas of EU law as well as versus the national legal orders of the Member States. Logically, questions relating to the scope of the Directive brought before the Court of Justice of the EU (ECJ) in the preliminary reference procedure have mainly surfaced when the Directive intersects either with other areas of law such as asylum law, the legal regulation of free movement and external border control, and criminal law.[1] Some of these substantive areas of law, for example asylum law and free movement, are currently for a large part covered by EU law, while others, such as criminal law, still fall largely within the competence of Member States.

In this chapter we will see that judges interpreting and deciding on the scope of the Directive, often in dialogue with each other, therewith inevitably also rule on the division of competences between the EU and the Member States with regard to regulating irregular migration and return. This is most notably the case with regard to judicial questions regarding Member States' use of criminal law to deal with illegally staying immigrants, but questions impacting on the vertical division of competences in the EU have also featured in a recent ruling addressing the intersection of the external border control, reinstatement of internal border

[1] A significant area where intersection may occur is also with regard to the Dublin Regulation, see the Commission Return Handbook, 26–28. However, as this particular intersection has so far not been dealt with in the preliminary reference procedure, delimitation of the Directive vis-a-vis the Dublin Regulation will not be addressed in this chapter.

controls and return of irregular migrants.[2] The main finding of the chapter is that the preliminary reference procedure leads to an extension of the regulatory questions that are covered by EU law, the nature and extent of which is at times unforeseen by national judges and the ECJ alike. I claim that, because of the growing density of the legal regimes covering the return of irregular migrants in the EU, it is important that judges, while interpreting and/or applying the law, are aware of their distinctive place as defined by the respective legal orders in which they carry out their judicial functions.

In the remainder of this introduction I will set the stage by introducing what is understood by the concept of scope and its implications for the delimitation of the Directive with other areas of law. Section II then delves deeper into the way in which the Directive relates to other areas of EU law, focusing more specifically on asylum law and the regulation of free movement of EU citizens and their family members. In Section III the relationship of the Directive with national law is addressed. Particular attention is paid to the way in which preliminary rulings have led to an incremental increase in EU competences over irregular migration. The conclusions (Section IV) focus on the implications of 'creeping competences' in this field, and elaborate upon the role of national judges in particular.

Article 2 defines the scope of the Directive as follows: 'This Directive applies to third-country nationals staying illegally on the territory of a Member State.' The second paragraph of Article 2 then grants Member States the possibility to limit the application of the Directive in two well-defined cases, and Article 3 provides definitions of the concepts of third-country national and illegal stay. Before addressing these provisions and definitions in more detail below, it needs to be pointed out that questions relating to the material scope of the Directive cannot be examined in isolation from Article 1, which defines its subject matter as setting out 'common standards and procedures to be applied in Member States for returning illegally staying third-country nationals'. According to the ECJ, this means that the Directive is not meant to harmonise in its entirety national rules on illegally staying nationals, but only aims to set common standards and procedures with regard to the adoption and the implementation of return decisions.[3]

When discussing the scope of a particular piece of legislation we may distinguish between four aspects. In the first place we can point at *territorial scope*. The territorial scope of the Directive is clear from the general structure of the Treaties and the terms used in Article 2: the Directive applies 'on the territory of the Member States'.[4] A second element is *temporal scope*. The Directive entered into force in 2008, and the Member States were obliged to transpose (most of) its

[2] Case C-444/17 *Arib* ECLI:EU:C:2019:220.

[3] C-329/11 *Achughbabian* ECLI:EU:C:2011:807.

[4] Note that as the Directive is part of the Schengen *acquis*, its territorial scope does not equal the territory of the EU. Thus, all EU Member States except the UK and Ireland, plus the four Schengen-associated countries, ie Switzerland, Norway, Iceland and Liechtenstein, are bound by the Directive.

provisions by 24 December 2011. By this date the provisions of the Directive also apply to the effects of situations that arose under previous, national rules.[5]

The third and fourth aspects are *personal scope* and *material scope*, respectively defining who is covered by the Return Directive, and in which situations it applies. Article 3 defines a third-country national as

> any person who is not a citizen of the Union within the meaning of Article 17(1) of the Treaty and who is not a person enjoying the Community right of free movement, as defined in Article 2(5) of the Schengen Borders Code.

Illegal stay, according to that same provision, means

> the presence on the territory of a Member State, of a third-country national who does not fulfil, or no longer fulfils the conditions of entry as set out in Article 5 of the Schengen Borders Code or other conditions for entry, stay or residence in that Member State.

In *Affum*, the ECJ ruled that the duration of the stay and the intention of the third-country national are irrelevant to establishing whether a third-country national falls under the scope of the Directive. Thus, a third-country national who is present on the territory of the Member States 'without fulfilling the conditions for entry, stay or residence there is, by virtue of that fact alone, staying there illegally' regardless of whether 'such presence is merely temporary or by way of transit'.[6]

The preamble of the Directive states that third country-nationals who have applied for asylum should not be regarded as 'staying illegally'. Hence, the personal and material scope of the Directive cannot be established in isolation from, inter alia, EU asylum law and the regulation of the right of free movement in the EU, which I will address in Section II. In the remainder of this chapter, I will not always make a clear distinction between personal and material scope, as the questions regarding who is covered by the Directive and in which situations it applies are often conflated.

Paragraph 2 of Article 2 allows Member States *not* to apply the Directive to

> third country nationals who are subject to a refusal of entry in accordance with Article 13 of the Schengen Borders Code, or who are apprehended or intercepted by the competent authorities in connection with the irregular crossing by land, sea or air of the external border of a Member State and who have not subsequently obtained an authorisation or a right to stay in that Member State

Moreover, Member States are allowed to decide not to apply the Directive to persons 'who are subject to return as a criminal law sanction or as a consequence of a criminal law sanction, according to national law, or who are the subject of extradition procedures'. As the interpretation of these exceptions primarily involves the

[5] Case C-357/09 PPU *Kadzoev* ECLI:EU:C:2009:741, para 38; and Case C-297/12 *Filev and Osmani* ECLI:EU:C:2013:569, paras 40 and 41. See also A Pahladsingh, 'The Legal Requirements of the Entry ban: The Role of National Courts and Dialogue with the Court of Justice of the European Union', Chapter 4 in this volume.

[6] Case C-47/15 *Affum* ECLI:EU:C:2016:408, para 48.

relationship of the Directive with national law, relating either to external border control, or to criminal law, they will be addressed in further detail in Section III below.

II. Establishing the Scope of the Return Directive versus Other Areas of EU Law

The Return Directive does not harmonise the conditions under which the stay of a third-country national becomes illegal. As illegal stay is, however, a necessary and sufficient condition for the Directive's application, establishing its scope will accordingly be contingent on the way in which either EU law or national law defines the conditions for lawful entry, stay or residence.[7] In this section I will first address the intersection of the Directive with EU asylum law, after which I turn to the way in which it relates to free movement rights of EU citizens and their family members.

A. How Does EU Asylum Law Affect the Scope of the Directive?

The difficulty of distinguishing between personal and material scope is perhaps best illustrated by Recital 9 in the Directive's preamble, which stipulates that:

> [A] third-country national who has applied for asylum in a Member State should not be regarded as staying illegally on the territory of that Member State until a negative decision on the application, or a decision ending his or her right of stay as asylum seeker has entered into force.

The question whether and to what extent asylum seekers may nevertheless fall under the Return Directive has been the topic of ongoing judicial dialogue of domestic courts with the ECJ, and it is a question of continuing relevance in domestic litigation. In fact, the very first preliminary ruling by the ECJ regarding the Directive concerned (amongst other issues) the intersection of the Directive with EU asylum law.

The facts are well known: Kadzoev, a third-country national who had been detained after being served with an order for removal, applied for asylum while in detention. The Bulgarian referring judge asked the ECJ (amongst other questions) to clarify whether the period that Kadzoev had spent in detention while his application for asylum was pending should be taken into account for calculating the maximum duration of detention under Article 15 of the Return Directive. Without explicitly ruling on the scope of the Directive, the Court recalled Recital 9 of the preamble and stated that the detention of asylum seekers and detention for the

[7] See Art 3 of the Return Directive.

purpose of removal fall under different legal rules, namely: asylum seekers under the Reception Conditions Directive,[8] and detention for the purpose of removal under Article 15 of the Return Directive.

Two years later, the delimitation between asylum law and the Return Directive was addressed once again in *Arslan*.[9] In that judgment, also concerning the situation of a third-country national detained in the context of removal proceedings, who subsequently applied for asylum, the ECJ was explicitly asked by the Czech judge to rule on the scope of the Return Directive. Interestingly, the French government had argued in the proceedings before the Court that the question as regards the applicability of the Return Directive to asylum seekers was not admissible. It held that it was a hypothetical question, because Arslan had never brought forward this argument, but merely that extension of his detention was contrary to Article 15, because the length of asylum proceedings in the Czech Republic was such that his removal could not be carried out within the maximum period of detention. The ECJ dismissed this argument swiftly: '[I]n order to determine whether extension [of the detention] breaches Article 15 … the referring court must first determine whether that directive is still applicable to Mr Arslan's situation after his application for asylum has been made.'

The Court then explicitly referred to the right to remain for asylum seekers until a decision in first instance was taken according to the Procedures Directive,[10] *and* the possibility for individual Member States to extend the right to stay pending the outcome of an appeal against a negative decision on the asylum application in first instance. It concluded that it is 'clearly apparent from the wording, scheme and purpose' of the Procedures Directive and the Return Directive that an asylum seeker 'has the right to remain in the territory of the Member State concerned at least until his application has been rejected at first instance, and cannot therefore be considered to be "illegally staying" within the meaning of the Return Directive'. It clearly delimited the scope of asylum law and the Return Directive by excluding asylum seekers from the scope of the latter 'during the period from the making of the application to the adoption of the decision at first instance on that application or, as the case may be, until the outcome of any action brought against that decision is known'.

The ruling in *Arslan* meant that the precise delimitation of the asylum acquis and the Return Directive could differ per Member State, because the Procedures Directive in force at that time left it up to individual Member States to determine whether asylum seekers had a right to stay on the territory during the appeal against a negative decision on their application. The recast Procedures Directive, however, has changed this: asylum seekers have a right to remain in the territory of the Member States, not only until they have received a decision at first instance, but

[8] The Reception Conditions Directive then in force: Directive 2003/9/EC of 27 January 2003 laying down minimum standards for the reception of asylum seekers [2003] OJL31/18.

[9] Case C-534/11 *Arslan* ECLI:EU:C:2013:343.

[10] The Procedures Directive then in force: Directive 2005/85 of 1 December 2005 on minimum standards on procedures in Member States for granting and withdrawing refugee status [2005] OJ L326/13.

generally also pending the outcome of their appeal against a negative decision.[11] Following *Arslan*, this would presumably mean that asylum seekers would usually be excluded from the scope of the Return Directive until their appeal against a negative decision is rejected.

However, in *Gnandi*, the Court seemed to depart from its position on the delimitation of the Return Directive and the asylum acquis,[12] with the curious outcome that a third-country national can fall under the scope of both bodies of law, which – perhaps even more curious – may in some cases add to their protection, as we will see below. First a bit more background regarding *Gnandi*: the Belgian court had asked the ECJ whether a return decision in the sense of Article 6 of the Return Directive could be adopted immediately after the rejection of an asylum application, before the conclusion of appeal proceedings. In its question, the Belgian court had referred to the right to an effective remedy and the obligation to respect the principle of *non-refoulement* in the Return Directive itself. The ECJ, however, tackles the question by focusing on the *scope* of the Directive: it holds that in order to determine whether a return decision may be adopted in such a case, it needs to be examined whether an asylum seeker can be regarded as staying illegally on the territory of the Member State that rejected the application in first instance, within the meaning of the Directive.

The Court then points to Article 7 of the Procedures Directive (2005/85) and explains that the fact that it grants the asylum seeker a right to remain until a decision in first instance is taken precludes an asylum seeker from being regarded as staying illegally in the sense of the Return Directive. However, the wording of Article 7 of the Procedures Directive makes clear that the right to remain ends upon the adoption of a first-instance decision rejecting the asylum application, and accordingly, the Court adds, the stay of the asylum seeker becomes illegal from that moment onwards. This conclusion is not altered by the existence of domestic laws that provide for a right to stay pending the outcome of an appeal. Hence, an asylum seeker falls under the scope of the Return Directive 'as soon as his application for international protection is rejected at first instance by the determining authority, irrespective of the existence of an authorisation to remain pending the outcome of an appeal against that rejection'. The Court finds that a return decision may be adopted against such a third-country national, either after rejection of the asylum application, or together with it in a single administrative act.[13]

[11] Recast Procedures Directive (Directive 2013/32 of 26 June 2013 on common procedures for granting and withdrawing international protection (recast) [2013] OJ L180/60, Art 2 under (p), Art 9 and Art 46, para 5. For exceptions, see Art 41 (cases of subsequent applications) and Art 46, para 6 (exceptions to the right to remain during appeal proceedings).

[12] Case C-181/16 *Gnandi* ECLI:EU:C:2018:465.

[13] There seems to be no *obligation* to adopt a return decision as is usually the case for illegally staying third-country nationals (Case C-38/14 *Zaizoune* ECLI:EU:C:2015:260), in view of the possibility to grant an authorisation to stay in Art 6(4) of the Return Directive. It could be argued that the term 'may' could also be read to refer to the discretionary power of the Member States to choose the type of administrative return procedure: separate decisions or combined; and not to the obligation to issue a return decision as such.

Importantly however, the Court refers to its earlier case-law in *Abdida* and *Tall*, affirming that while an appeal against the rejection of an application for international protection does not need to have suspensory effect, the requirements arising from the principle of *non-refoulement* and Article 47 of the Charter of Fundamental Rights of the EU ('the Charter') necessitate that an appeal in first instance against the return decision has automatic suspensory effect. In *Abdida* notably, the Court had excluded from the scope of EU asylum law third-country nationals suffering from a serious illness who, when returned, would be exposed to a serious risk of grave and irreversible deterioration in their state of health.[14] However, by bringing their situation within the scope of the Return Directive, it had imposed upon Member States an obligation to grant suspensory effect of the appeal against a decision ordering them to leave the territory of a Member State, and to provide for the basic needs of such persons during that period, when there is a risk of violation of the principle of *non-refoulement*.[15]

Similarly, in *Gnandi*, the Court reiterates that all the legal effects of the return decision should be suspended during the time that appeal before at least one judicial instance is possible or until such an appeal is resolved.[16] This does not only imply that such a decision cannot be enforced (removal), but also that the period for voluntary departure cannot begin to run, and that detention on the basis of the Return Directive cannot be applied.[17] Moreover, during this time the asylum seeker is entitled to enjoy the rights granted to him under the Reception Conditions Directive.

Although the ruling in *Gnandi* relates to the previous Procedures Directive, the order by the ECJ in Case C-269/18 PPU shows that it also applies to asylum applications decided under the recast Asylum Directives.[18] It seems partly motivated by the Court's wish to allow Member States to continue making use of the possibility to couple the rejection of the asylum application with a return decision, as provided for in Article 6(6) of the Return Directive, and as such to facilitate the establishment of an effective return and repatriation policy.[19] It is questionable whether the reasoning of the Court in this respect is legally sound: it

[14] Case C-562/13 *Abdida* ECLI:EU:C:2014:2453.

[15] See JB Farcy, 'Safeguards Pending Return and Access to Rights for Non-Removable Migrants', Chapter 19 in this volume.

[16] Note that EU law only prescribes an effective remedy before *one judicial instance*, both as regards appeals against decisions refusing an application for international protection and appeals against return decisions. Suspensory effect during a possible second instance appeal provided by national law is thus not required either under the Procedures Directive or the Return Directive. See Case C-175/17 *X* ECLI:EU:C:2018:776.

[17] Thus, the asylum seeker is not under an obligation to leave the territory of the Member States, which was one of reasons AG Mengozzi argued *against* including this group under the scope of the Return Directive (see additional opinion of AG Mengozzi, delivered on 22 February 2018, ECLI:EU:C:2018:90). Note that detention can still be applied on the basis of the current Reception Conditions Directive.

[18] Case C-269/18 PPU *C and J and S* ECLI:EU:C:2018:544.

[19] *Gnandi* (n 12) para. 49.

seems nonsensical to determine the scope of the Return Directive by referring to a procedural rule which allows states to couple a return decision with a decision ending legal stay, because the question whether legal stay of an asylum seeker is ended by the rejection in first instance is precisely the question that the Court needed to answer.[20]

That being said, the effect of the ruling is that a rejected asylum seeker's appeal will result in automatic suspension of 'all of the effects of the return decision' during the appeal, also in those cases in which EU asylum law has not provided for automatic suspensory effect, for example in case of asylum applications which are manifestly unfound.[21] It puts an end to the practice of many Member States of imposing an enforceable obligation to return for the asylum seeker whose application for asylum has been rejected in first instance, and hence prohibits the detention of these persons with a view to deportation.[22] Moreover, it entitles the asylum seekers to continue to benefit from the rights under the Reception Conditions Directive.

The Court's decision in *Gnandi* thus shows that defining the scope of the Return Directive as in some cases *overlapping* with the asylum acquis has the result of harmonising thorny issues that were previously excluded from explicit EU law guarantees. Even though it could be argued that such guarantees were implicitly present in EU law through the applicability of the Charter, these were not applied as such in national judiciary practice. This aspect of *Gnandi* has spurred domestic litigation, at least in the Netherlands, for example regarding the question whether the principles formulated by the Court also apply in cases of subsequent asylum applications.[23] More crucially, it has resulted in the Dutch Council of State ruling that there is no longer a valid ground for the detention of asylum seekers whose applications have been rejected in the border procedure in first instance, because in Dutch law, such detention is based upon a provision implementing the Return Directive. As such, these asylum seekers have to be granted entry to Dutch territory until the Dutch legislator creates a legal basis for detention for these asylum seekers in line with the Reception Conditions Directive.[24] Although the judgment in *Gnandi* has been criticised, inter alia by referring to a possible risk of violating

[20] For a critical perspective on the notion of a sharp binary between legal and illegal migration, see C Costello, *The Human Rights of Migrants and Refugees in European Law* (Oxford, Oxford University Press, 2016) 63–102. See also S Da Lomba, *The Right to Seek Refugee Status in the European Union* (New York, Intersentia, 2004) 16, arguing that asylum policies in the EU are increasingly under threat of being engulfed by migration policies.

[21] For all the exceptions, see Art 46, para 6 of the recast Procedures Directive. See also Case C-269/18 PPU *C and J and S* (n 18).

[22] For an overview of how different Member States apply the Return Directive to rejected asylum seekers, see G Strban et al, 'Return Procedures Applicable to Rejected Asylum-Seekers' (2018) *Refugee Survey Quarterly*, 71.

[23] See eg District Court The Hague, Judgment of 11 December 2018, ECLI:NL:RBDHA:2018:15612.

[24] Council of State, Judgment of 5 June 2019, ECLI:NL:RVS:2019:1710.

the principle of non-refoulement,[25] I would argue there is also another side to the judgment: defining the scope of EU asylum law and the Return Directive as overlapping has in national judicial practice brought about *more* protection for these persons, not less.

B. How Does the Return Directive Relate to Free Movement Rights and EU Citizenship?

The question as to how the Return Directive relates to free movement rights and EU citizenship is addressed in Articles 2(3) and 3(1) of the Directive. These provisions stipulate that the Directive does not apply to 'persons enjoying the Community right of free movement as defined in Article 2(5) of the Schengen Borders Code' and that third-country nationals in the sense of this instrument do not include this category either. Nor does it include 'citizens of the Union within the meaning of Article 17(1) of the Treaty'. In Article 2(5) of the Schengen Borders Code persons enjoying the right of free movement under EU law are defined as

> Union citizens within the meaning of Article 20(1) TFEU, and third-country nationals who are members of the family of a Union citizen exercising his or her right to free movement to whom Directive 2004/38/EC of the European Parliament and of the Council applies.[26]

A Greek court, seized with a case of an EU citizen (a Romanian national) who had been the subject of an exclusion order because he posed a risk to public policy, asked the ECJ whether EU law precludes a decision to return the person from being adopted by the same authorities, and according to the same procedure, as a decision to return an illegally staying third-country national, referred to in Article 6(1) of the Return Directive. The Court answers in the negative, pointing to the procedural autonomy of states, adding that, if the Citizenship Directive (Directive 2004/38) contains more favourable provisions, these have to be applied.[27]

A more complicated concern arose in the case of *KA and others*.[28] Belgium had adopted return decisions and entry bans in relation to a number of third-country nationals. These persons argued that they could rely on a derived right of residence in Belgium, because otherwise their EU citizen family members would be forced

[25] See M Moraru, *Lawyers Voice – The Return Directive and Irregularity: The Gnandi Case (C-181/16) and the Recast Return Directive* (blog, 2018) available at: https://picum.org/redrawing-the-boundaries-of-the-return-directive-and-irregularity-the-gnandi-case-c-181-16-and-the-proposed-recast-return-directive/.

[26] And it includes also third-country nationals and their family members, whatever their nationality, who, under agreements between the Union and its Member States, on the one hand, and those third countries, on the other hand, enjoy rights of free movement equivalent to those of EU citizens.

[27] Case C-184/16 *Petrea* ECLI:EU:C:2017:684.

[28] Case C-82/16 *KA and others* ECLI:EU:C:2018:308.

to leave the territory of the EU as a whole. This particular construction provides a basis for (derived) rights of residence for family members of EU citizens who have never exercised their free movement rights under the Citizenship Directive since the judgment in *Zambrano*.[29] The Belgian government, however, argued that it could not examine the applications for residence for the purposes of family reunification because the third-country nationals were each subject to an entry ban. According to the authorities, they should first leave Belgium and make an application for the removal or suspension of the entry ban from outside the EU before they could submit their application for family reunification.

The Court ruled firmly that such a practice is not in conformity with Article 20 of the Treaty on the Functioning of the European Union (TFEU): the third-country national cannot be compelled to leave the territory of the EU for an indefinite period of time in order to ask for a withdrawal or suspension of the entry if it has not been ascertained by the Member State

> that there does not exist, between that third-country national and a Union citizen who is a family member, a relationship of dependency of such a nature that the Union citizen would be compelled to accompany the third-country national to his or her country of origin, even though, precisely because of that relationship of dependency, a derived right of residence ought, as a general rule, to be granted to that third-country national under Article 20 TFEU.

Such applications for family reunification need to be examined by the authorities and entry bans cannot be held against them. Instead, authorities 'must withdraw or, at the least, suspend the return decision and the entry ban to which that third-country national is subject'.[30]

It is somewhat surprising that the Court does not begin its answer with explicit reflections on the scope of the Return Directive. Obviously, seeing that the residence rights at issue derive directly from the TFEU, persons who benefit from these could not be regarded as illegally staying on the territory of the Member States, regardless of how national states qualify their situation. Two reasons could explain the relative lack of emphasis on scope in the judgment. In some of the cases at issue in *KA*, return decisions and entry bans had been issued *before* the family ties came into existence, and in all of the cases those decisions were issued *before* the third-country nationals applied for family reunification. The entry ban thus preceded (possible) residence rights in some instances,[31] and in all cases the authorities did not know that the third-country nationals were invoking a right to lawful stay at the moment that they adopted a return decision. Accordingly,

[29] C-34/09 *Zambrano* ECLI:EU:C:2011:124.

[30] *KA* (n 28) para 57.

[31] Note that it is immaterial for an appeal to derived residence rights that the relationship of dependency relied on by a third-country national in support of his application for family reunification comes into being after the imposition on him of an entry ban, or the fact that it has become final. My observations above solely concern the question as to why the Court does not underline the issue of scope much more in its answer.

the issue of scope becomes less pertinent than, for example, in a case where the authorities would have adopted a return decision or entry ban with regard to a person who has previously invoked or simultaneously invokes a derived right of residence on the basis of Article 20 TFEU. In such a case, the authorities would certainly be obliged to carry out an assessment of the relationship of dependency of the third-country national with the EU citizen *before* adopting a return decision and/or an entry ban.[32]

The Court does, however, explicitly mention the scope of the Return Directive later in the judgment, when it addresses the question as to whether it makes a difference if the entry ban was imposed for reasons of public order or for failure to voluntarily leave the territory. Notably, it underlines that a third-country national enjoying the right of residence on the basis of Article 20 TFEU cannot be considered staying illegally in the territory of the Member State, within the meaning of Article 3(2) of the Directive, from the moment that the relationship of dependency came into being and for as long as that relationship of dependency lasts.

III. The Return Directive and National (Criminal Law) Competences

The previous section addressed the relationship of the Return Directive with other areas of EU law. My analysis of the case-law of the ECJ showed that defining the scope of different bodies of law in this area is not merely a technical exercise of delimiting the scope of various EU legal instruments vis-a-vis each other, but has crucial implications for the question as to which precise issues are actually regulated by EU law. A much more explicit emphasis on delimiting national law versus EU law is apparent in preliminary references that have addressed the relationship of the Return Directive with national *criminal* law. The case-law of the ECJ regarding the way in which the Return Directive impacts on Member States' power to use criminal law to deal with irregular migration is extensively documented in the academic literature.[33] The Return Directive does not preclude the Member States from having competence in criminal matters in the area of illegal immigration – as

[32] Which will also impact on the right to be heard as guaranteed by Art 47 of the Charter before the authorities adopt these measures. See Cases C-163/13 *Mukurabega* ECLI:EU:C:2014:2336; C-249-13 *Boudjlida* ECLI:EU:C:2014:2431; and C-383/13 *M and R* ECLI:EU:C:2013:533. See also V Ilareva, 'The Right to Be Heard: The Underestimated Condition for Effective Returns and Human Rights Considerations', Chapter 15 in this volume.

[33] R Raffaelli, 'Criminalizing Irregular Immigration and the Returns Directive: An Analysis of the El Dridi Case' (2011) 13 *European Journal of Migration and Law* 467; M Savino, 'Irregular Migration at the Crossroads, Between Administrative Removal and Criminal Deterrence: The *Celaj* Case' (2016) 53 *Common Market Law Review* 1419; A Kosińska, 'The Problem of Criminalisation of the Illegal Entry of a Third-Country National in the Case of Breaching an Entry Ban – Commentary on the Judgment of the Court of Justice of 1 October 2015 in Case C 290/14, Skerdjan Celaj' (2016) 18 *European Journal of Migration and Law* 243.

it was never meant to harmonise the entirety of rules dealing with irregular migration, but only sets common standards and procedures with regard to the adoption and implementation of return decisions.[34] Nevertheless, the application of national criminal law in this area may not interfere with effective return procedures.[35] The duty of loyal cooperation and the principle of effectiveness thus set crucial limits to the use of criminal law by Member States to fight irregular migration.

Thus, according to a series of well-argued judgments by the Court, imprisonment of illegally staying third-country nationals on the basis of criminal law is only permitted if the return procedure has been applied, and the person either remains on national territory without a valid ground for not returning, or re-enters in breach of an entry ban.[36] As such, it has significantly limited Member States' powers in this area. Therefore, it is not surprising that some of those states have attempted to exclude certain categories of illegally staying third-country nationals from the scope of the Directive, so that they may continue using their criminal laws in the way they did before the entry into force of the Directive. This in turn has led to other preliminary references, such as in *Affum* and *Arib*, in which France invoked the possibility granted to Member States in Article 2(2)(a) of the Directive *not* to apply the Directive to third-country nationals who are arrested in connection with the irregular crossing of the external border of a Member State.

Below I will first deal with the way in which the Court has interpreted this what I will call the 'external border control exception'. After that I will flesh out how judicial dialogue has shaped national criminal law and policy with regard to irregular migration in a particular Member State, the Netherlands, focusing specifically on the significant impact of the judgment in *Ouhrami* on national practice with regard to criminalising irregular stay.[37]

A. The Return Directive and External Border Control

As mentioned above, Article 2(2) grants Member States the possibility to exclude from the scope of application of the Directive third-country nationals who are refused entry or intercepted in connection with the irregular crossing of the external border, as well as those who are subject to return as (a consequence of) a criminal law sanction or subject to extradition procedures. France in particular has been keen to invoke what I call the external border control exception before the ECJ, in order to justify imposing a sentence of imprisonment for irregular entry.

[34] Case C-329/11 *Achugbabian* ECLI:EU:C:2011:807.

[35] Case C-61/11 PPU *El Dridi* ECLI:EU:C:2011:268.

[36] In addition to *El Dridi* and *Achughbabian*, see also Case C-430/11 *Sagor* ECLI:EU:C:2012:777; and Case C-290/14 *Celaj* ECLI:EU:C:2015:640.

[37] C-225/16 *Ouhrami* ECLI:EU:C:2017:590. I have chosen to focus on just one Member State in the remainder of this chapter as this will allow for a more detailed look at the intricate way in which national and EU law interact in this area, and at accompanying complexities.

The case of *Affum* is a case in point. Affum was a third-country national transiting through French territory from Belgium to the UK, and the authorities wanted to sentence her to imprisonment on account of her illegal entry into France. The French court referred the matter to the ECJ because it was not sure if such imprisonment would be allowed. In the proceedings the French government relied on the external border control exception, arguing it applied to the illegal crossing of an external border of a Member State both on entry into and on exit from the Schengen area. The ECJ, however, pointed out that the external border control exception relates exclusively to the crossing of a Member State's external border, as defined in Article 2(2) of the Schengen Borders Code, and therefore Member States cannot exclude from the scope of the Directive persons crossing *internal* borders. Furthermore, it held that it does not apply to persons who seek to *leave*.[38] As a consequence such a person could not be excluded from the scope of the Directive, which, the Court then logically ruled, impeded their imprisonment merely on account of irregular entry across an internal border, if the return procedure had not been applied.[39]

The ruling in *Arib* developed the case-law on the external border control exception further.[40] In this case a third-country national, Arib, was apprehended close to the border between France and Spain, after France had reinstalled border control at the internal border on account of a serious threat to public policy and internal security, as provided for in Article of the Schengen Borders Code. Arib was held in detention upon his arrest. The court ruling in first instance on his detention annulled this measure, seeing that he fell under the scope of the Return Directive and could therefore not be detained under the conditions laid down in domestic law. This decision was upheld by the Court of Appeal, upon which the Court of Cassation decided to refer the case to the ECJ. It wanted to know whether a state that has reinstalled border control at the internal border may rely on the external border control exception in Article 2 of the Directive, to exclude from its scope a third-country national who had crossed that border but not yet stayed in national territory. It invoked Article 32 of the Schengen Borders Code, which stipulates that when internal border controls are introduced, the provisions on external border control in Title II of the Code apply mutatis mutandis to these border controls.

The ECJ recalls that in order for a state to invoke the external border control exception, there must be a 'direct spatial and temporal link' between the apprehension of the third-country national and the crossing of an external border. It underlines that exceptions to the scope of the Directive need to be narrowly interpreted, and it then applies a textual and teleological interpretation of Article 2(2)(a). First it emphasises that this provision only uses the words external border, and makes no mention of internal borders at which controls have been reinstalled,

[38] *Affum* (n 6) paras 71–72, 78.
[39] ibid, para 93.
[40] *Arib* (n 2).

despite that fact that when the Return Directive was adopted, the Schengen Borders Code already contained the possibility to reintroduce internal border control. It also recalls the purpose of the external border control exception, which is to enable states to continue to apply simplified *national* return procedures at their external borders, in order to return persons more swiftly, just as in the case of persons who have been refused entry. As such, its purpose is to prevent persons, who have been refused entry or have been intercepted just after crossing the external border, from staying on the territory of the Schengen area. This rationale does not apply when it concerns an internal border at which controls have been reinstalled according to the Court, and so persons intercepted there cannot be excluded from the scope of the Directive. The Court also stresses that the Directive does not preclude imprisonment to punish offences other than those stemming from illegal entry, including the case of a person suspected of having committed an offence that poses a threat to public policy of internal security.

The Court also highlighted that, if Member States choose to exclude from the scope of the Directive, in accordance with Article 2(2), third-country nationals who would otherwise be covered by it, certain guarantees remain applicable. Thus, Article 4(4) determines that they should receive protection at least equivalent as the protection provided in the provisions dealing with limitations on use of coercive measures, postponement of removal, emergency healthcare, the needs of vulnerable persons, detention conditions and *non-refoulement*.[41]

Interestingly, judicial dialogue has featured with regard to the external border control exception in another – much less expected – manner as well. Thus, the Netherlands, like many other countries, applies the exception for those who have been refused entry. These persons do not have to be issued with a return decision, and they are not granted a period of voluntary return, and as such detention is more easily applied. After the judgement in *Mahdi*,[42] courts in the Netherlands started to require that the authorities provided reasons in fact and law for the measure of detention as elaborated upon by the Court in that judgment, which goes further than what was previously required in the Netherlands.[43] Courts did so not only for detention under the Return Directive, but for *all* instances of immigration detention that were regulated by EU law, such as under the Dublin Regulation and the Reception Conditions Directive. However, and significantly, some lower courts also extended these requirements to cases that fell *outside* the scope of these EU instruments, namely with regard to the detention of third-country nationals who were refused entry and were thus excluded from the scope of the Return Directive. The Council of State confirmed this approach, justifying the application of the

[41] Art 8(4) and (5), Art 9(2)(a), Art 14(1)(b) and (d), and Arts 16 and 17. Note that in *Affum* as well, the Court had called attention to these requirements explicitly with regard to conditions of detention.

[42] C-146/14 *Mahdi* ECLI:EU:C:2014:1320.

[43] See G Cornelisse, 'Van de Magna Carta tot Mahdi: Reikwijdte en intensiteit van de rechterlijke toetsing van vreemdelingendetentie' (2015) 5/6 *Asiel & Migrantenrecht* 199.

'Mahdi' obligation to state reasons to detention cases that fall outside of EU law by referring to the principles of equality before the law and clarity of the law.[44]

B. Judicial Dialogue and National Criminal Law Competences

As mentioned above, judicial dialogue addressing the compatibility of detention on the basis of national criminal law with the Return Directive has had a large impact on domestic legal practice. The Court's judgments in *El Dridi*, *Achughbabian*, *Sagor* and *Affum* have significantly restricted the ability of Member States to use criminal law with regard to irregularly staying third-country nationals. The ECJ has ruled that the obligation imposed on the Member States by Article 8 of the Directive to carry out the removal must be fulfilled as soon as possible.[45] Criminal sanctions for illegal stay, such as home arrest or the execution of a prison sentence, are measures that do not contribute to such swift removal, and can therefore not be understood as a 'measure' or a 'coercive measure' within the meaning of Article 8 of the Directive.[46]

In the Netherlands, mere illegal entry or stay as such is not a criminal offence. While transposing the Return Directive, the Dutch legislature instead chose to criminalise a qualified form of illegal stay, as there was no political consensus on making mere illegal stay a criminal offence. As such, the Dutch Criminal Code now determines that an alien who stays in the Netherlands while they know or should know that an entry ban has been issued is punishable by a fine or imprisonment of a maximum of six months (Article 197 of the Dutch Criminal Code).

Until recently, the Dutch Supreme Court[47] has interpreted the Directive in line with the case-law of the ECJ by ruling that it does not preclude the sentencing of a third-country national on the basis of 197 Criminal Code, if three conditions are met: (1) the third-country national concerned does not have a valid reason for his non-return; (2) all the steps of the return procedure as foreseen in the Directive have been applied to him; and (3) the judgment provides well-argued reasoning that the return procedure has been applied in the individual case.[48] This case-law concerns cases in which a third-country national is sentenced for the criminal offence of staying in the Netherlands while an entry ban applies, and has not yet left the EU after the issuing of the return decision (and accompanying entry ban). This situation should be distinguished from the case in which they have left the

[44] Council of State, Judgment of 27 June 2015, ECLI:NL:RVS:2015:2534.

[45] See, inter alia, *Achughbabian* (n 3) para. 45.

[46] See eg *Sagor* (n 36) para 44; and *Achughbabian* (n 3) para 37.

[47] In the Netherlands, the Supreme Court is the highest court when it comes to criminal law cases, while the Council of State is the highest court in administrative law cases, ie immigration law litigation.

[48] Supreme Court, Judgment of 21 May 2013, ECLI:NL:HR:2013:BY3151. See also Supreme Court, Judgment of 3 December 2013, ECLI:NL:HR:2013:1563.

EU after the issuing of a return decision, but have re-entered in spite of the accompanying entry ban. In this latter case, even before the ruling in *Celaj*, the Supreme Court did not require that either before the departure of the third-country national concerned, or after his re-entry, all the steps of the return procedure as laid down in the Return Directive had been applied.[49] In such cases the criminal judge may accordingly sentence the third-country national to a prison sentence, without examining whether the return procedure has been completed.

The Return Directive requires that an entry ban has a limited temporal validity, of five years as a rule. Accordingly, in Dutch courts, a recurrent issue has been the question from which moment the period of the entry ban starts running – whether this would be the moment of its issuance, or the moment that the third-country national had left the territory of the Member States.[50] In *Ouhrami*, referred to the ECJ by the Dutch Supreme Court, the ECJ ruled that the entry ban starts to run from the moment that the third-country national has left the territory of the Member States. This was in line with the way in which national judges, both criminal and administrative, had so far applied the law before the case was referred to the ECJ.

However, *Ouhrami* has had another, unforeseen, effect on Dutch case-law and legal practice. In the judgment, the Court drew a clear distinction between the entry ban and the return decision, explaining that the return decision covers the unlawful stay of the third-country national until that person 'has … actually gone back to his country of origin, to a country of transit or to another third country'.[51] The entry ban only produces its effects after that point in time, 'by prohibiting the person concerned, for a certain period of time following his return, from again entering and staying in the territory of the Member States'.[52] In the Netherlands, however, Article 197 of the Criminal Code criminalises the stay of a third-country national who knows or should know that an entry ban has been issued against them. Over the years this provision has provided the legal basis for prosecutions and convictions of third-country nationals, also those who had never left the Netherlands (or the EU for that matter). Seeing that the Court in *Ouhrami* explained that the entry ban does not cover the illegal stay of the third-country national *until* they have left the territory of the EU, it is unclear which individual conduct is precisely criminalised in Article 197 of the Dutch Criminal Code.

This implication of *Ouhrami* was not picked up in Dutch legal practice until I wrote about it in two articles, arguing that in view of the judgment, there is no legal basis for the prosecution of a foreign national who has not left the European Union after the entry ban has been issued.[53] I claimed that the principle of legality

[49] Supreme Court, Judgment of 4 November 2014, ECLI:NL:HR:2014:3091.

[50] For a more elaborate overview of the litigation, see Pahladsingh (n 5).

[51] *Ouhrami* (n 37) para 49.

[52] ibid.

[53] G Cornelisse, 'Inreisverboden die (nog) geen rechtsgevolgen hebben' (2017) 38 *Nederlands Juristenblad* 2814, and G Cornelisse in H Battjes et al, 'Kroniek van het migratierecht' in (2017) 35 *Nederlands Juristenblad* 2594, 2602.

requires a clear legal basis for criminal liability, and the wording of Article 197 does not refer to illegal stay as such, but merely to the 'stay' of an alien while he knows or should know that an entry ban has been issued. This argument has subsequently been brought forward in criminal law litigation, culminating in a recent ruling by the Supreme Court, in which it decided to refer the matter to the ECJ. It asks the Court to rule on the compatibility with EU law of prosecutions on the basis of Article 197 of the Dutch Criminal Code while the third-country national concerned has not yet left the EU.[54] Seeing that the Court in Luxembourg will take some time to answer, the public prosecutor has now requested courts to determine that there is no reasonable basis to proceed with prosecutions already brought before these courts.[55]

IV. Conclusions

This chapter has zoomed in on judicial dialogue in the European Union regarding the scope of the Return Directive versus other instruments of EU law and versus national law. We have seen that in the judgments issued by the ECJ, questions on the relationship of the Directive with other instruments of EU law habitually intersect with questions on the delimitation of national and EU law. In other words, and perhaps unexpectedly, establishing the scope of the Return Directive versus other areas of EU law critically influences the question as to how much scope is left for *national* procedural choices. The ruling in *Gnandi* illustrates this well: while deciding on the way in which the scope of the Return Directive relates to the asylum acquis, the Court actually extends the grip of EU law on national procedural law.

This also means that judicial dialogue on the Return Directive's scope has resulted in increasing complexity with regard to the question of which precise situations fall under EU law, and the exact requirements that national procedures as a result need to satisfy.[56] Indeed, in many, if not most, instances the answers by the ECJ on the questions posed to it by national judges have resulted in an even more dense covering by EU law of the diverse national procedural practices applied to third-country nationals who are regarded as illegally staying by the Member States. Some of these rulings, eg those in *Gnandi* and *KA*, thus exemplify an intricate legal configuration of diverse, overlapping and intersecting legal regimes, in which, slowly and surely, little decision-making power of administrative authorities is solely regulated by national law. An increase in legal questions potentially covered by EU law is also exemplified in cases brought before the ECJ in which Member States have resorted to their criminal laws to 'regulate'

[54] Supreme Court, Judgment of 27 November 2018, ECLI:NL:HR:2018:2192.
[55] Court of Appeal Amsterdam, judgment of 24 May 2019, ECLI:NL:GHAMS:2019:1736. The Court of Appeal dismissed all 39 cases pending before it.
[56] See, for example, on detention: Council of State, Judgment of 13 May, ECLI:NL:RVS:2019:1528.

irregular migration. In this particular area we see that previous rulings regarding the delimitation of EU law and national law by the ECJ have spurred new preliminary questions, which – no matter how technical the court keeps its approach – will inevitably draw into the sphere of EU law questions that were previously reserved for national administrative, criminal or constitutional courts.[57]

In a way, the process of dialogue described in this chapter thus resembles a snowball. This incremental and often unforeseen process is exemplified by the dialogue between national judges and the ECJ in *Ouhrami* and the ensuing current questions posed by the Dutch Supreme Court: in order to answer these questions, the ECJ will need to reflect more thoroughly on national choices regarding criminal procedural law than it has done so far in its case-law regarding the Return Directive. A pertinent question is whether the Court will deem it fit to evaluate these choices in light of the Charter of Fundamental Rights – which, I would argue, is squarely applicable to the use by the Member States of their criminal laws to sanction irregular stay.[58] No matter how the Court draws the line between the precise scope of the Return Directive and national criminal law, a Member State that chooses to use criminal law to carry out its obligations under EU law more effectively[59] needs to ensure that the application of these laws is in conformity with the Charter.[60] In this case, the relevant provisions of the Charter are, inter alia, Articles 48, 49 and 50.

As we have seen, the text of the Dutch Criminal Code criminalises the stay of an alien against whom an entry ban has been issued – not the *illegal* stay of such a person. The fact that an entry ban can only be issued when a return decision has been taken (and so the Code factually criminalises *illegal* stay and not the

[57] That in itself can be said to have a constitutionalising effect, therewith relativising the distinction drawn by Daniel Thym between an administrative mind-set and a constitutional one. See D Thym, 'Between "Administrative Mindset" and "Constitutional Imagination": The Role of the Court of Justice in Immigration, Asylum and Border Control Policy' (2019) 44 *European Law Review* 139.

[58] C-617/10 *Akerberg Fransson* ECLI:EU:C:2013:105.

[59] This was the reasoning brought forward by the Dutch government for the criminalisation of stay in breach of an entry ban in the implementing legislation. In the explanation accompanying this legislation it argues as follows: 'Nonetheless, the principle of loyal cooperation implies that the effectiveness of [the Return] Directive must be guaranteed and, in that context, a sanction is imposed for violating the European entry ban.' Kamerstukken II 2010/11, 32420, 9, 3. Note that the implementing legislation clearly talks about *violating* the entry ban – which is difficult to do if its legal effects have not yet started to produce effects.

[60] A similar argument can be made regarding a case which is currently pending before the ECJ (Case C-673/19 *MA and others*, registered on 11 September 2019). The Dutch Council of State is not sure whether third-country nationals who stay illegally in one Member State but enjoy international protection status in another Member State fall under the scope of the Directive. More specifically, it asks the ECJ to clarify whether detention under the Directive of these individuals is precluded if a return decision has not been taken. In light of the case-law of the ECJ it seems justified to conclude that these individuals fall under the scope of the Directive, but that their detention cannot be based on Art 15. However, even if such detention is based upon national law because the EU legislature did not foresee this situation, it still needs to be in conformity with Arts 6 and 52 of the Charter. See also Council of State, Judgment of 4 September 2019, ECLI 201808499/1/V3.

breach of the entry ban),[61] does not make the application of Article 197 of the Dutch Criminal Code foreseeable, even less so seeing the complex legal configuration characterising contemporary return procedures. As we have seen above, this complexity has become more profound because of recent rulings such as *Gnandi* and *KA*. While third-country nationals in a comparable situation as the family members of the EU citizens in *KA* would not be staying illegally, they would be acting in contravention of Article 197 of the Dutch Criminal Code. That seems hardly in conformity with fundamental principles of criminal law, most notably legality, protected in the constitutional traditions of the Member States, the European Convention on Human Rights (ECHR) and the Charter. How the Court in Luxembourg will tackle these issues remains to be seen. Nevertheless, I am sure that from there, it is only a matter of time until national courts will start to ask it to rule on the compatibility of national criminal law on illegally staying nationals with other instruments of European law, such as relating to criminal procedures, and how the administrative procedures instigated against these individuals relate to their fair trial guarantees in these instruments (and, obviously, the ECtHR).[62]

To conclude, I would like to underline how important it is to distinguish between the positions of the various judges in Europe who, adjudicating from very different places, may deal with the same concrete case. Depending on where these judges are located in the intersecting legal orders that characterise the return of irregular migrants in Europe, the legal questions that they can pose may differ greatly, as well as the answers they formulate. While the ECJ in the preliminary reference procedure only rules on the interpretation and validity of EU law, national judges will have to *apply* these laws, as well as interpret and apply *national laws*. This means that the task of the national judge is by far the most complex one. Such a judge, when adjudicating a return case, will obviously need to guarantee conformity of national decision-making with EU law. But in addition, she will also have to rule on how national legislation – including legislation that implements EU legal instruments – relates to national constitutional law and

[61] Which seems to be the argument of the Attorney General at the Supreme Court (who advised the Court to refer the case to the ECJ), see Additional Conclusion of PG Silvis of 18 September 2018, ECLI:NL:PHR:2018:1019. This argument bypasses the way in which criminalisation in Article 197 Criminal Code was presented to the Dutch Parliament when the implementing legislation was negotiated. See also n 54.

[62] See the following instruments: Directive 2010/64/EU of 22 May 2012 on the right to interpretation and translation in criminal proceedings [2010] OJ L280/1; Directive 2012/13/EU of 22 May 2012 on the right to information in criminal proceedings [2012] OJ L142/1; Directive 2013/48/EU of 22 October 2013 on the right of access to a lawyer in criminal proceedings and in European arrest warrant proceedings, and on the right to have a third party informed upon deprivation of liberty and to communicate with third persons and with consular authorities while deprived of liberty [2013] OJ L294/1; Directive (EU) 2016/343 on the strengthening of certain aspects of the presumption of innocence and of the right to be present at the trial in criminal proceedings [2016] OJ L 65/1; Directive (EU) 2016/800 of 11 May 2016 on procedural safeguards for children who are suspects or accused persons in criminal proceedings [2016] OJ L132/1; Directive (EU) 2016/1919 of 26 October 2016 on legal aid for suspects and accused persons in criminal proceedings and for requested persons in European arrest warrant proceedings [2016] OJ L297/1.

the ECHR. These particular issues cannot be addressed in the dialogue that is constituted by the preliminary reference procedure as conceived by Article 267 TFEU. Hence, judges engaging in this particular dialogue need to be aware that it is characterised by an asymmetry that goes beyond the mere fact that the position of the ECJ is the more authoritative one when it comes to interpreting EU law. Instead, it is also limited by the institutional constraints in which each of the participants operate.

This perspective is crucial for national judges when formulating questions to be answered in the preliminary reference procedure. Thus, the Dutch Supreme Court and its Attorney General in the case discussed in this chapter seem to focus exclusively on the way in which criminalisation of illegal stay in the Dutch Criminal Code relates to the Return Directive. Nonetheless, a more detailed awareness of the intersecting legal orders and areas of law that regulate this issue, and in which this particular court operates, would have brought to light two important points. In the first place: it is an *acte éclairé* that the entry ban cannot be violated before the third-country national has left the EU. Secondly, from this conclusion it follows that the sole remaining question in this particular case is whether the legal basis provided by the Dutch legislature for prosecuting illegally staying third-country nationals is in conformity with: (1) its own constitutional requirements regarding the principle of legality in criminal procedures;[63] (2) those of the ECHR; and (3) the Charter of Fundamental Rights of the EU and possibly EU law on criminal procedures. Only the third aspect of this question can be answered by the Court in Luxembourg.[64]

A final remark on scope. Scope as a legal concept resonates deeply with the very substance of this book – irregular migration. For a long time, a large part of state action in the area of irregular migration simply fell outside the scope of legal regulation. Deportation could not be contested if there was no underlying interest implicated (such as family life, or *non-refoulement*). Seen from this perspective, no matter how restrictive some laws may be, the very fact that state action becomes legally regulated 'normalises' the discourse that is applied to it. Before the entry into force of the Return Directive, concepts such as voluntary departure and public order either did not exist, or they were not treated as *legal* concepts in the practice of many Member States. As a result, the implications of state action for the individual could not be contested in a court, let alone that there was a judicial space where the individual interests at stake could become visible.[65] The very notion of *what* is actually regulated by law has significantly shifted with the entry into force of the Return Directive. The legalisation of the exercise of state

[63] Art 16 Constitution, Art 1 Criminal Code.

[64] Which is not to say that fundamental rights as protected in these other legal orders cannot feature its case law. See Art 6 TEU and Art 52(3) TFEU.

[65] G Cornelisse, *Immigration Detention and Human Rights: Rethinking Territorial Sovereignty* (Leiden, Brill, 2011).

power that this instrument has brought about means that it has become possible to contest its concrete manifestation in an increasing number of areas. More judicial engagement, possibly in dialogue, would certainly be warranted with regard to some of the more striking instances of the exercise of state power in this area, such as the coercive measures that Member States use to carry out the removal of third-country nationals. Hopefully it is a matter of time before courts in Europe start to apply the strict legal requirements set out in the Return Directive[66] in this area too.

[66] Article 8(4) RD.

2

Return Decisions and Domestic Judicial Practices: Is Spain Different?

CRISTINA GORTÁZAR ROTAECHE

I. The Return Directive and its (Un)Satisfactory Application

The Return Directive[1] provides for common standards and procedures obliging EU Member States[2] to return third-country nationals who do not comply or no longer comply with the conditions for residence in a Member State. The Directive sets out to accomplish this obligation as soon as possible by requiring the issue of a return decision.[3] If voluntary departure is not an option or the third-country national does not voluntarily depart, the Return Directive requires the removal of an irregularly staying third-country national to their country of origin or transit.

The return decision should offer an appropriate period for voluntary departure of between 7 and 30 days. Member States should, where necessary, extend this period taking into account the specific circumstances of each case (the length of stay, the existence of children attending school or of other family and social links).[4] However, Member States may decide not to apply the period for voluntary

[1] Directive 2008/115/EC of 16 December 2008 on common standards and procedures in Member States for returning illegally-staying third-country nationals [2008] OJ L348/98. Hereinafter 'the Return Directive'. The Commission has proposed a targeted revision of the Directive in order to achieve a more effective and coherent European return policy. See Commission, 'Proposal for a Directive of the European Parliament and of the Council on common standards and procedures in Member States for returning illegally staying third-country nationals' (recast) 12.9.2018 COM(2018) 634 final. Hereinafter '2018 Proposal for a Return Directive'.

[2] Currently, all EU Member States except the UK and Ireland are governed by the Return Directive, which also binds Switzerland, Norway, Iceland and Liechtenstein. The latter four states are only bound to the EU directives in conformity with the general principles of public international law, and therefore they are not bound by the CJEU jurisprudence regarding transposition.

[3] Art 6(1) of the Return Directive.

[4] Art 7(4) of the Return Directive establishes that the third-country national can receive a period shorter than seven days for voluntary departure or even be refused the period in some cases. The 2018 Proposal for a Return Directive does not make it mandatory anymore to grant a minimum of seven days. Member States will be allowed to decide *in general terms* on a shorter period. See 2018 Proposal for a Return Directive, 7. For a detailed analysis of the voluntary departure measure, see U Brandl, 'Voluntary Departure as a Priority: Challenges and Best Practices', Chapter 3 in this volume.

return to third-country nationals in cases, inter alia, of interception at the border in connection with the irregular crossing.[5] Moreover, the Directive also establishes that Member States are not obliged to issue a return decision when the exceptions laid down in Article 6(2)–(5) apply. Article 6(4) provides that:

> Member States may at any moment decide to grant an autonomous residence permit or other authorisation offering a right to stay for compassionate, humanitarian or other reasons to a third-country national staying illegally on their territory. In that event no return decision shall be issued.

The Return Directive is justified by the intention to reduce irregular staying situations within the EU, while supporting ordered, legal immigration, as well as to prevent abuse or exploitation of irregularly staying third-country nationals in vulnerable situations. Nonetheless, eight years since the entry into force of the Directive, practice shows that the effective fulfilment of its noble objectives is quite low.[6] The number of third-country nationals irregularly staying in the territory of any EU Member State is still a cause for deep concern for both the Member States and the EU as a whole due to the fact that the rate of irregularly staying third-country nationals who leave the territory of the EU Member States, either in a voluntary or a forced manner, remains quite modest.[7]

Many questions regarding the lack of effectiveness of the Return Directive merit discussion. Perhaps Member States have not made sufficient efforts to complete return procedures for budgetary or technical reasons, or even due to mere indolence. The Directive might be insufficiently thorough in addressing the actual problems states might face when applying return procedures. Deficiencies in its application may be attributable both to causes arising from inaccurate application by states and to a certain degree of naivety or lack of specificity in the Directive.[8]

This chapter focuses on one of the main difficulties encountered by the Member States when implementing the Return Directive: the obligation to issue a return decision to third-country nationals irregularly staying or entering the EU. In fact, the 2018 proposal for the amendment of the Directive lists as one of its main goals the necessity to provide 'clearer and more effective rules on the issuing of return decisions and on the appeals against such decisions'.[9]

[5] Art 2(2) of the Return Directive. This provision has been criticised by a number of authors. See eg E García Coso, *La regulación de la Inmigracion Irregular. Derechos humanos y control de fronteras en la Unión Europea* (Pamplona, Thomson Reuters Aranzadi, 2014) 85.

[6] The European Commission recently recognised the '[s]low progress on improving the EU's effective return rate (2014; 36.3%; 2015: 36.8%; 2016: 45.8%; 2017: 36.6%)', in 'Managing Migration in All its Aspects' Commission Note ahead of the June European Council 2018.

[7] In 2016, 493,785 non-EU citizens were ordered to leave the Member States, but only 226,150 were actually returned. Eurostat, 'Statistics on enforcement of immigration legislation data' at ec.europa.eu/eurostat/statistics explained/index.php/Statistics_on_enforcement_of_immigration_legislation.

[8] For example: has the Return Directive foreseen situations where the persons may not be returned but, at the same time, there is no reason a priori why they may be granted a residence permit?

[9] See 2018 Proposal for a Return Directive, 7.

The chapter also investigates whether there is a correlation between the Return Directive's modest effectiveness rate and the problems encountered by the Member States when issuing return decisions. Do these difficulties stem from poor transposition of the Directive into domestic law? If so, a further question arises: how have national judges reacted to inconsistencies on the part of Member States on the matter? This chapter argues that the Spanish practice illustrates well the foregoing problems and could inspire solutions for these questions.

The first part of the chapter discusses general concerns regarding Member States' sanctions for unlawful stay in order to emphasise that these have nothing to do with the obligation to issue return decisions. It then addresses voluntary departure as a preferred option. It concludes by addressing the respect for the fundamental rights and dignity of irregularly staying third-country nationals during return proceedings consequent to the sometimes complex act of issuing a return decision.

As an example of national courts' difficulties regarding the oversight of the obligation to issue return decisions, the second part of the chapter explores the curious misunderstanding caused among the Spanish judges by the CJEU ruling in the case of *Samir Zaizoune*.[10] Only three years after the delivery of the CJEU's preliminary ruling did the Spanish Supreme Court establish its consequences on the Spanish jurisprudence.[11] The ruling in *Zaizoune* was widely discussed and caused Spanish judges to adopt different, sometimes inconsistent approaches.[12] Arguably, the misunderstanding itself comes from an unclear transposition of the Return Directive in Spain, specifically from the use by lawmakers of different terms than those used by the Directive, although with similar meanings.

II. Shortcomings in Ensuring Conformity with the Return Directive Objective – Effective Return in Compliance with Human Rights

A. Member States' Sanctions for an Unlawful Stay

One of the most controversial issues national courts face regarding the implementation of the Return Directive is the conformity of the sanctions imposed by some Member States on irregularly entering or staying third-country nationals. The conformity of imprisonment and economic sanctions with the Directive were referred by national courts to the CJEU for preliminary ruling by several judges. The CJEU stated that Member States are free to lay down

[10] Case C38/14 *Subdelegación del Gobierno en Gipuzkoa – Extranjería v Samir Zaizoune* ECLI:EU:C:2015:260.

[11] STS 980/2018 (3rd Room, 5th Section) of 12 June 2018.

[12] See below section I.C.iv.

effective, proportionate and dissuasive sanctions, including imprisonment as a criminal sanction, in relation to infringements of migration rules, provided such measures *do not compromise the application of the Return Directive* and ensure the full observance of fundamental rights, particularly those guaranteed by the Charter interpreted in accordance with the corresponding provisions of the ECHR.[13]

Shortly after the Return Directive's transposition deadline passed, the CJEU answered on the issue of detention sanctions for an unlawful stay in the preliminary ruling delivered in the *El Dridi* case.[14] The CJEU established that Articles 15 and 16 of the Directive prohibit Member States from keeping third-country nationals in detention solely for illegal stay in their territory, and when *such penalty delays efficient compliance with the Directive provisions*, that is, returning the illegally staying migrant.[15]

Financial sanctions are treated differently. The imposition of a fine by Member States as a sanction for irregular stay, according to their own criminal laws (or administrative laws, as is the case in the Spanish legal framework), is compatible with the Directive since it does not challenge its goal to have the third-country national regularise their situation or leave the Schengen Area.[16] However, a financial sanction can never replace a removal order. With regard to this, the longstanding Spanish practice of imposing a fine, apparently *instead of* an administrative sanction of removal, is a particularly confusing practice to which I will devote the second part of this chapter.

B. Voluntary Departure

As mentioned by the 'ReDial European Synthesis Report on the Termination of Illegal Stay', according to Article 6(1) of the Directive and the CJEU jurisprudence,[17] after issuing the return decision, Member States should give priority to the voluntary departure of irregular third-country nationals. Only if it is not possible or if it is unsuccessful can the national authorities order the person's forced removal:

> In practice the issue of the return decision is closely linked to the conferral of voluntary departure. This is so, because according to the Directive's definition of voluntary

[13] Case C-329/11 *Alexandre Achughbabian v Préfet du Val-de-Marne* ECLI:EU:C:2011:807 (emphasis added). In July 2012, the French Court de cassation issued a judgment in line with the *Achugbabian* ruling See M Moraru, 'REDIAL Electronic Journal on Judicial Interaction and the EU Return Policy Third Edition: Articles 15 to 18 of the Return Directive 2008/115', REDIAL Research Report 2017/01, 15.

[14] Case C-61/11 PPU *El Dridi* ECLI:EU:C:2011:268. *El Dridi* is one of the most quoted CJEU judgments by Member States' judges. Only three days after it was issued, the Italian Corte di cassazione issued a ruling confirming the jurisprudence of the CJEU. In June 2011, Italy also enacted a new law to ensure that Italian laws were compliant with the Return Directive and the *El Dridi* ruling. Moraru (ibid) 13.

[15] Emphasis added.

[16] Case C-430/11 *Md Sagor* ECLI:EU:C:2012:777.

[17] See eg *El Dridi* (n 14) and *Achughbabian* (n 13).

> departure, the obligation to voluntary depart within a time limit is fixed in the return decision.[18]

Unfortunately, in some Member States, the return procedures where no possibility of voluntary departure is offered or when forced return is preferred to voluntary departure are far more than the Directive seems to provide.[19] In Spain, removal of a third-country national may be carried out through two different procedures outlined in the Act on Aliens 4/2000: the ordinary procedure and the preferential procedure.[20] Only the *expulsion* (Spanish legal expression used instead of removal) ordinary procedure offers the third-country national the opportunity to prepare for their voluntary departure within a reasonable period of time and in particular to avoid forced removal and the corresponding entry ban.[21]

Regarding the *expulsion* preferential procedure, where voluntary departure is not provided, Article 63 of the Act on Aliens 4/2000 and Articles 234 to 237 of Royal Decree 577/2011[22] establish that this summary procedure is only to be applied to third-country nationals irregularly staying in Spain when: (a) there is risk of failing to appear; (b) the person prevented or obstructed their own removal; or (c) the person represents a risk to public order, public security or national security.[23] However, in practice the preferential procedure has often been applied without demonstrating a risk of failing to appear, or a danger to public order or national security. In some judicial cases, the appellant disputed the use of the preferential procedure on this basis, stating that the circumstances did not justify application of a procedure with limited guarantees protecting the person concerned.[24]

[18] Ph De Bruycker, M Moraru and G Renaudiere, 'European Synthesis Report on the Termination of Illegal Stay (Articles 7 to 11 of Directive 2008/115/EC)', REDIAL Research Report 2016/01, 8.

[19] For instance, in Italy, the national removal procedure gave preference to forced return over voluntary departure. See R Raffaelli, 'Criminalizing Irregular Immigration and the Return Directive: An Analysis of the El Dridi Case' (2011) 13 *European Journal of Migration and Law* 474.

[20] Organic Act 4/2000, of 11 January, on the rights and freedoms of foreign nationals in Spain and their social integration (amended by Organic Acts 8/2000, 11/2003, 14/2003, 2/2009, 10/2011, 4/2013 and 4/2015 and by Royal Decree-Act 16/2012).

[21] Art 63 bis of the Act on Aliens 4/2000 states:

> 1. When removal proceedings are carried out in situations other that those provided by article 63, the procedure of choice shall be the ordinary proceedings. 2. The decision ordering a removal carried out by means of the ordinary procedure shall include a term for voluntary compliance in which the affected person may voluntarily leave the national territory. The length of this term shall range from seven to thirty days and shall be counted from the moment that the aforementioned decision is notified.

[22] Royal Decree 557/2011 of 20 April, on the approval of the Regulation to Organic Act 4/2000 of 11 January on rights and freedoms of aliens in Spain and on their social integration, as modified by organic Act 2/2009.

[23] Art 235 of Royal Decree 577/2011 states:

> The decision, considering the preferential and summary nature of the procedure, shall be issued immediately. Such decision must be duly justified and solve all the questions arising in the proceedings … without excluding the right to effective remedy by the legitimate parties, *notwithstanding the immediate nature for the removal and the inappropriateness of declare any administrative suspensive effect against it.* (emphasis added)

[24] See Judgment of the High Court of Justice of Andalusia (STSJ 2358/2014.JUR\2015\73548. 28/11/2014). In this case, the third-country national filed a lawsuit against a removal before the High

There are no official data about how many illegally staying third-country nationals have left Spain by virtue of the ordinary procedure and, therefore, have had the opportunity to depart voluntarily.[25]

C. Respect for the Fundamental Rights and Dignity of Irregularly Staying Third-Country Nationals During the Return Process

Correct and efficient implementation of the Directive entails that the return of third-country nationals is carried out with full respect for fundamental rights and dignity.[26] For instance, a relevant question is where the third-country national is to be kept in detention in order to prepare their return proceedings. Although not specified in the Directive, the European Commission in the Return Handbook addressed concerns raised by non-governmental organisations and civil society which question the legality or adherence to human rights standards and good practices in places where third-country nationals are detained pending removal.[27] This section will, however, focus only on questions related to the issue of return decisions. In Spain, for instance, as the transposition of *what a return decision means* has been confusing, some important third-country national rights have been affected.

i. The Enforcement of a Return Decision Adopted at an Earlier Stage

Another concern from judicial practice with regard to return decisions is that they cannot be subject to time restrictions. Therefore, the authorities may enforce a

Court of Justice of Andalusia (appeal proceedings no 724/2012). Their legal representative presented a complaint against the preferential procedure stating that the risk of absconding was not proved.

[25] I asked a member of the Congress of Deputies to require information on this matter through two written requests. The term for the Spanish government (Ministry of Internal Affairs) to reply ended without having received any reply. In its original language, the text states: 'I ¿Cuántas expulsiones de nacionales de terceros países en situación irregular se han llevado a cabo en el Estado siguiendo el procedimiento ordinario en 2014 y que porcentaje del total de expulsiones supone? 2 ¿Con qué criterios en la práctica – si los hubiere – se aplica a tal efecto (utilizar el procedimiento preferente en lugar del ordinario) el riesgo de fuga o la amenaza al orden, seguridad o salud públicos? Congreso de los Diputados, 1 de julio de 2015.'

[26] Art 8(4) of the Directive.

[27] According to the European Commission criteria, the places where illegally staying third-country nationals may not be kept in detention include healthcare centres and their surroundings, schools and their surroundings, religious premises, civil registries where third-country nationals may go (to register the birth of a child, for example) and unions or other institutions which provide third-country nationals with legal assistance; they may not also be kept in detention in the premises where they request international protection, when this is the case. Healthcare centres, schools and civil registries are not obliged to share with the police personal data of migrants pursuant to return. The criteria for granting residence permits to victims or witnesses of a crime, as well as victims of domestic violence, pursuant to the Directive are also set forth. Return Handbook included in 'Commission Recommendation (EU) 2017/2338 of 16 November 2017 establishing a common "Return Handbook" to be used

return decision issued a long time ago without having to restart the return procedure. In Spain, this question may give rise to dubious practices, especially when a long time has elapsed since the return decision was issued, during which the personal situation of the third-country national may have changed substantially. In this sense, even if there was no reason to grant a stay permit to the third-country national at the time of the return decision,[28] by the time of the forced removal humanitarian or social reasons might be relevant. In such circumstances, would the Member State be obliged to reassess the personal and family circumstances?

In the case *Khaled Boudjlida*, the CJEU examined the right of a third-country national to be heard before a return-related measure is adopted. The Court held that the right to be heard in all procedures pursued in the context of the Return Directive and, particularly, its Article 6, must be construed to include the right of the third-country national to have their say on the legality of their situation, on the possible implementation of Articles 5 and 6(2)–(5) of the Return Directive, and on the details of their removal agreements before a return decision is issued. The right to be heard must be construed so that irregularly staying third-country nationals can seek legal assistance before the return decision is issued. This assistance may include addressing the competent authority, 'provided that the exercise of that right does not affect the due progress of the return procedure'.[29] Nevertheless, what happens if years elapsed between the issuance of the return decision and its implementation? Does the third-country national deserve a new opportunity to be heard?

In Spain, at least until the CJEU issued its preliminary ruling in the *Zaizoune* case, most people subject to a fine for staying unlawfully (always with an attached order of compulsory departure in 15 days) continued to live in Spain without supervision by the administration regarding their disobedience of the compulsory departure. Some of them later had a chance to obtain a residence permit on the grounds of integration.[30] Others were identified again as irregularly staying (and having disobeyed the departure order). Although years may have passed and personal circumstances may have radically changed, these changed circumstances are not taken into account. Article 64(1) of the Spanish Act on Aliens 4/2000 establishes that if under the ordinary procedure the third-country national has not left the national territory within the period of voluntary departure, or, *in all cases where the preferential procedure has been followed*, the third-country national is to be forcibly removed within 72 hours, unless removal is not possible, in which case they will be kept in detention. In my view, enforcement of this period can only be proportionate when forced return is carried out immediately after the failure to comply with the term given for voluntary departure, not when it is carried out months or even years afterwards.

by Member States' competent authorities when carrying out return-related tasks' [2017] OJ L339/83, 101–02.

[28] See Art 6(4) of the Return Directive.

[29] Case C-249/13 *Khaled Boudjlida v Préfet des Pyrénées-Atlantiques* ECLI:EU:C:2014:2431.

[30] In some cases, after paying the fine, the third-country national succeeds in regularising their situation on grounds of social integration (Art 124.2 of Royal Decree 557/2011) which affords, when certain conditions are complied with, the possibility of obtaining a residence permit after staying illegally.

ii. Effective Remedy in Case of Risk of Refoulement

The CJEU has gradually stated other obligations of Member States with respect to illegally staying third-country nationals to whom a return decision must be issued. On 18 December 2014, the CJEU addressed the issue in a preliminary ruling in the *Moussa Abdida* case.[31] The CJEU stated that Article 5 of the Return Directive establishes that Member States must consider the health of the third-country national in applying the principle of *non-refoulement*.[32] In the new scenario created in Spain after the *Zaizoune* ruling, where there is clarity regarding the impossibility *to substitute* a removal with a fine, Article 5 of the Directive and full respect for *non-refoulement* acquire crucial importance.[33]

III. The Unclear Transposition of the Obligation to Issue a Return Decision in Spain

A. The Case of Samir Zaizoune

In October 2011, Mr Samir Zaizoune, a Moroccan national, was arrested while illegally staying in Irun, Spain. The Central Government Delegate in the Basque Country sanctioned him with *expulsion* (the Spanish legal term) from the national territory as well as with a five-year Schengen entry ban. This decision was based on Articles 53(1)(a)–57(1) of the Spanish Act on Aliens 4/2000,[34] as construed by

[31] Case C-562/13 *Centre public d'action sociale d'Ottignies-Louvain-La-Neuve v Moussa Abdida* ECLI:EU:C:2014:2453.

[32] See also ECtHR, GC, 13 December 2016, *Paposhvili v Belgium*, Appl No 41738/10: the referral to the Grand Chamber came after the Fifth Section of the Court found that the removal of a Georgian national suffering from chronic lymphocytic leukaemia and tuberculosis would not encroach upon his Arts 3 and 8 rights under the ECHR. Recalling that, since ECtHR, GC, 27 May 2008, *N v United Kingdom*, Appl No 26565/05, in only very exceptional cases will Art 3 be breached in removal cases of seriously ill persons, the Court found that the definition of 'very exceptional' needed to be clarified. The Court found that the Belgian Aliens Office had not examined the applicant's medical conditions in light of Art 3 in the context of his regularisation, nor his proposed removal, and as a result violated Art 3. With regards to Art 8, the Chamber emphasised the positive obligations on Belgium, especially in light of the facts of the case. Much like the lack of assessment on Art 3, the authorities did not examine the degree of the applicant's dependence on his family or the impact of removal on his family life. The Grand Chamber thus found Art 8 also to have been breached.

[33] STS (3rd Room, 5th Section) of 12 June 2018.

[34] See n 20 above. Art 53(1), last amended when Act 2/2009 was enacted, reads:

> The following shall be considered serious infringements: a) illegally staying in the Spanish territory after their residence permit has not been extended, was never granted on the first place or has expired more than three months ago, and provided that the relevant foreigner has not requested the renewal of such permit in the period established for it by the relevant regulations.

the Supreme Court,[35] which states that the main sanction for irregular stay is a fine but that this may be replaced by removal under certain circumstances. According to the Representation, Mr Zaizoune fell within this last category. For this reason, a sentence of removal was adopted instead of a fine. Mr Zaizoune sought a review before Administrative Court no 2 of San Sebastian, which admitted the procedure and issued a judgment replacing the sanction of removal with a financial penalty. However, the Provincial Government Representation appealed this decision before the High Court of Justice of the Basque Country. Before issuing a decision on the appeal, that court submitted a preliminary question to the CJEU:

> In the light of the principles of sincere cooperation and the effectiveness of directives, must Articles 4(2), 4(3) and 6(1) of Directive 2008/115/EC (1) be interpreted as meaning that they preclude legislation, such as the national legislation at issue in the main proceedings and the case-law which interprets it, pursuant to which the illegal stay of a foreign national may be punishable just by a financial penalty, which, moreover, may not be imposed concurrently with the penalty of removal?[36]

The CJEU's reply focused on how Articles 6(1) and 8(1) of the Return Directive, read together with Article 4(2) and (3), were to be construed.[37] Thus, the CJEU ruled that the main goal of the Return Directive was to ensure an effective removal and repatriation policy. It referred to *El Dridi* and *Achughbabian* to establish that Article 6(1) of the Directive sets out the obligation of issuing a return decision against any third-country national found irregularly staying in a Member State, notwithstanding any exceptions described in paragraphs (2)–(5) of Article 6 (on regularisation options). Furthermore, as set forth in the *Sagor* judgment, the obligations imposed by Article 8 for removing a third-country national must be complied with as soon as possible.

Finally, the CJEU stated that none of the provisions of the Return Directive, not even Article 4(2), allows a Member State to choose between a financial sanction and a removal order depending on the circumstances of the case. Pursuant to Article 4(3) of the Directive, the Court declared that although it is possible for a Member State to adopt more favourable national provisions, they must be

[35] Article 57(1), last amended when Act 2/2009 was enacted, reads:

> Expulsion from the Spanish territory: 1. When offenders are foreigners and incur in behaviours described as very serious or serious in paragraphs a), b), c), d) and f) of article 53.1 of this Organic Act, the imposed sanction *may be, instead of an financial sanction, removal from the Spanish territory*, provided that the respective administrative proceedings have been completed and by virtue of a justified decision which takes into account of the facts that make up the offence and respect the principle of proportionality. (emphasis added)

[36] Case C-38/14 *Subdelegación del Gobierno en Gipuzkoa – Extranjería v Samir Zaizoune*, ECLI:EU:C:2015:260.

[37] The CJEU reformulated the question, referring also to Art 8 of the Return Directive, which the referring court did not cite.

compatible with the Return Directive. Here, such compatibility was absent.[38] Once the preliminary ruling was received, the High Court of Justice of the Basque Country issued a judgment stating that there are no circumstances to justify an exception, so Mr Zaizoune must be returned to his country of origin.[39]

B. The Spanish Transposition of the Return Directive

Many of the inconsistencies raised by Spanish judges in relation with the CJEU ruling in the *Zaizoune* case arise from the fact that the Act on Aliens 4/2000 and the regulations governing its application do not use the same terms as the Directive when dealing with the return of irregularly staying third-country nationals.[40] Thus, the Act had not included the definition for return decision provided by the Directive as 'an administrative or judicial decision or act, stating or declaring the stay of a third-country national to be illegal and imposing or stating an obligation to return'.[41] Neither does the Act include a definition of removal as the enforcement of the obligation to return, namely the physical transportation out of the Member State.[42] The Act only uses the expression 'expulsion from the Spanish territory'. Spanish laws on aliens continue to use the same terms as before the Return Directive entered into force.[43]

Thus, according to the Spanish Supreme Court, in their ruling of 28 November 2008, under the regime created by the (former) Act on Aliens 7/1985, removal of

[38] In the *El Dridi* case, the CJEU, stated at para 33:

> [A]lthough Article 4(3) allows Member States to adopt or maintain provisions that are more favourable than Directive 2008/115 to illegally-staying third-country nationals provided that such provisions are compatible with it, that directive does not however allow those States to apply stricter standards in the area that it governs.

With regard to compatibility of more favourable national provisions with the Directive, see the contributions of D Acosta and A Romano, 'The Returns Directive and the Expulsion of Migrants in an Irregular Situation in Spain' (2 May 2015) at eulawanalysis.blogspot.com.es/2015/05/the-returns-directive-and-expulsion-of.html.

[39] High Court of Justice of the Basque County, Administrative Court, section 3 STSJ 428/2015 (Id Cendoj: 48020330032015100388).

[40] The High Court of Justice of Madrid, Judgment 31 October 2017, TSJ Madrid, Contentious-Administrative Chamber, Judgment 732/2017, 31 October Appeal 184/2017 (LAW 178624/2017), states:

> The failure to incorporate Directive 2008/115 into domestic law prevents the expulsion of foreigners in an irregular situation. … The Spanish State is not entitled to claim the inverse vertical effect of Directive 2008/115, since it has been the State itself that has decided not to incorporate the mandates of the same into domestic law. Moreover, [Spanish domestic legislation] turns out to be more advantageous for the alien who is in Spain in an irregular situation than the application of the said Return Directive.

[41] Art 3(4) of the Return Directive.

[42] Art 3(5) of the Return Directive.

[43] Spanish Supreme Court, 28 November 2008 (Rec 9581/2003).

a third-country national was not considered an administrative sanction (but only the consequence of irregularly staying). However, when the Act on Aliens 4/2000 was enacted, lawmakers changed the governing criteria, and thus the removal (*expulsion* under Spanish law) of third-country nationals began to be considered an administrative sanction. Therefore, when Act 4/2000 was enacted, principles and guarantees related to administrative infringements and corresponding sanctions procedures included in the Spanish administrative laws started to apply to removal, among them the principle of proportionality. Due largely to the application of such principles, the Spanish Supreme Court construed the Act on Aliens 4/2000 so as to declare that:

> [W]hen a removal (expulsion) is enforced, the Administration must state which are the reasons for proportionality, the degree of subjectivity, damage or risk arising from the relevant infringement, and in general, which factual or legal circumstances that justify an expulsion and an entry ban, which is a harsher sanction than a fine.[44]

Although the Organic Act 2/2009, which modifies the Act on Aliens 4/2000, expressed that one of its goals was the transposition of the Return Directive, only minor changes in this sense were made. Under Article 53(1)(a) of the Act on Aliens 4/2000, unlawful stay in the Spanish territory constitutes a serious infringement. Article 57(1) of the same Act applies sanctions in the following terms:

> [W]ith respect to the principle of proportionality, a financial sanction *may be substituted by removal* from the Spanish territory, after the corresponding administrative procedure has been filed and in virtue of a justified decision.[45]

One obvious problem arising in this transposition of the Return Directive is that the most widespread sanction imposed on a third-country national irregularly staying in Spain had been a financial sanction, with further circumstances necessary to justify a removal order.[46] Between 2005 and 2008, the Spanish Supreme Court interpreted Article 57(1) of the Act on Aliens in this way. Circumstances envisioned included failure to produce valid documents; being arrested for participation in a criminal offence;[47] being homeless or lacking roots in Spain; failure to comply with a compulsory departure order without trying to regularise their situation; or being subject to a Schengen entry ban. Absent any of these circumstances, the appropriate sanction would be a fine. The Act on Aliens 4/2000 has

[44] ibid.

[45] Emphasis added.

[46] The Supreme Court has stated: '[I]llegal stay of a third country national is to be sanctioned with an economic sanction and, only when other negative circumstances concur, removal from the Spanish territory shall apply' (see eg judgments of 28 November 2008, Rec 9581/2003; of 9 January 2008, Rec 5245/2004; and of 19 July 2007, Rec 1815/2004).

[47] For failing to produce valid documents (see Supreme Court, 30 June 2006; 31 October 2006; 29 March 2007); having been arrested for taking part in a criminal offence (see Supreme Court, 19 December 2006); failing to produce proof of a home or roots in Spain (see Supreme Court, 28 February 2007); or being subject to an entry ban to the Schengen Area (see Supreme Court, 4 October 2007).

been amended several times,[48] but the provision on the generally imposed sanction has not changed. The opinion of the Supreme Court with respect to the 'fine doctrine' was not changed until 2013, some months before the *Zaizoune* ruling.

The Supreme Court doctrine favouring the fine instead of expulsion was developed before the Return Directive entered into force.[49] Once the period for transposition of the Directive had elapsed, the Supreme Court did not have the chance to reconsider the doctrine favouring financial sanctions, since the Spanish legal framework was reformed in 2008. Competences on judicial remedies against administrative acts regarding removal of third-country nationals were transferred to administrative courts and appeals to the High Court of Justice of each autonomous region. However, such courts have generally followed the doctrine of the Supreme Court in the sense of considering that a fine could substitute for removal.[50]

In addition, on 22 October 2009, the CJEU issued a judgment on the question submitted to it for preliminary ruling in the *Zurita García y Choque Cabrera* case, which referred to persons in similar situations as in the later *Zaizoune* case. The CJEU opinion was that where a third-country national is unlawfully present on the territory of a Member State because he or she does not fulfil, or no longer fulfils, the conditions of duration of stay applicable there, that Member State is not obliged to adopt a decision to expel that person.[51]

However, that CJEU answer referred to Articles 5, 11 and 13 of the Schengen Borders Code,[52] not to the Return Directive, whose period for transposition (up to 24 December 2010) had not yet elapsed. Three years later, when the Return Directive was enforceable, the *Md Sagor* case revealed that 'the imposition of a fine does not in any way prevent a return decision from being made and implemented in full compliance with the conditions set out in Articles 6 to 8 of Directive 2008/115'.[53]

[48] See n 20 above.

[49] Also in Pascual Aguelo Navarro y Hipólito-Vte Granero Sánchez 'Comentarios a vuelapluma sobre la sentencia del TJUE de 23.04.2015', *Abogacía Española* (27 April 2015).

[50] See eg Castile-La Mancha, no 10016/2015 of 28 January 2015; Andalusia, no 2225/2014 of 30 December 2014; Galicia, no 751/2014 of 17 December 2014; Castile-La Mancha, no 318/2014 of 15 December 2014; Autonomous Region of Valencia, no 1174/2014 of 12 December 2014; Castile-La Mancha, Judgment no 10278/2014 of 26 November 2014; Castile-La Mancha, Judgment no 10229/2014 of 17 June 2014. Judgment no 1910/2014 of 7 October 2014 of the High Court of Justice of Andalusia stated (para 4, FJ 4) that, after a fine has been imposed, it is necessary that the third-country national 'regularises their situation with regard to the administration, or a return decision shall be applied'. Other judgments of the Courts of Justice where the *doctrine favouring financial penalties* is applied did not include this reasoning, High Court of Justice of Madrid 565/2014, 18 July 2014 and 565/2014, 17 July 2017.

[51] See Joined Cases C-261/08 and C-348/08 *María Julia Zurita García Aurelio Choque Cabrera v Delegado del Gobierno en la Región de Murcia* ECLI:EU:C:2009:648, para 67.

[52] At that time: Regulation (EC) no 562/2006 of the European Parliament and of the Council of 15 March 2006 establishing a Community Code on the rules governing the movement of persons across borders [2006] OJ L105, 1.

[53] *Md Sagor* (n 16). In para 35, the CJEU does not exclude that an illegally staying third-country national may be fined for unlawful stay and that the fine may be replaced by a removal order; however,

On 12 March 2013,[54] the Supreme Court introduced, for the first time, a significant change in the doctrine favouring financial sanction.[55] This decision established that, pursuant to the Return Directive, the first stage should be to afford the third-country national the possibility of a voluntary departure (Article 7 of the Return Directive). Forced removal should only be enforced if the third-country national did not comply with voluntary departure. Therefore, it concluded that the Return Directive entailed a significant change with regard to the previous Spanish practice. The Court stated that the Directive significantly reinforces the obligation of Member States to guarantee the effectiveness of return procedures, and that such a change, if implemented at European level, may pose a challenge 'for current interpretation and enforcement of Spanish laws which allow, under certain circumstances, to choose between sanctions of fine or removal for illegally staying foreigners'.[56] Despite this significant opinion, Spanish courts and judges continued to apply the doctrine favouring financial sanction to replace removal. Only the High Court of Justice of Castile-Leon took into consideration the new position of the Supreme Court and, in almost all cases, imposed removal (Spanish expulsion) instead of a fine on the third-country national, but provided that aggravating circumstances are present, in addition to unlawful stay.[57]

it does exclude sanctions in the form of home detention unless such home detention ends as soon as it is possible to enforce removal. After the *El Dridi* ruling, Italy kept considering unlawful stay as a criminal offence but sanctioned with fines. After the *Sagor* case, Italy modified its Act on Aliens to make unlawful entry or stay an administrative offence (not a criminal offence). Moraru (n 13)16.

[54] Some months before the referral of the preliminary question in the *Zaizoune* case.

[55] The judgment of the Supreme Court was possible due to an appeal submitted by some non-governmental organisations against several provisions of Royal Decree 557/2011; see n 22.

[56] Supreme Court, 13 March 2013, Roj: STS 988/2013-ECLI:ES:TS:2013:988. Para 7 (FJ 7) reads:

> [A]nalysis of this situation cannot leave out the significant change that has entailed the implementation of a harmonised policy at European level regarding return of illegally staying third country nationals. Approval of Organic Act 2/2009 involves incorporating Directives passed after the last amendment to Act 4/2000 (that is, the one carried out in 2003) to the Spanish legal framework. The most relevant of these Directives is precisely the aforementioned Directive 2008/115/CE. … Besides, Directive 2008/115/CE has been construed by the Court of Justice of the European Union in terms that considerably reinforce the duty of states to proceed as soon as possible to ensure effectively of illegally staying foreigners return procedures; this effectively implies, for member states 'a requirement to carry out the removal by taking all necessary measures' (judgments of 28 April 2011 (CJEC 2011, 111) for case C-61/11 PPU; of 6 December 2011 (CJEC 2011, 390), for case C-329/11 and of 6 December 2011 (CJEC 2012, 369) for case C-430/11). This case law of the Court of Justice shall probably cause to modulate the interpretation dominant until now, and the application of legal standards which under certain situations allow choosing between removal and a financial penalty for illegally staying foreigners.

[57] See High Court of Justice of Castile-Leon (Valladolid): 996/2014 of 16 May 2014. On 22 November 2013, the Administrative Court no 1 of Salamanca rejected the appeal of Mr Mario, a Moroccan national, against the decision of the Provincial Representation of the Government in Salamanca, which ordered his removal and a five-year entry ban for illegal stay. Mr Mario appealed to the High Court of Justice of Castile-Leon. Besides being found illegally staying in Spain, Mr Mario had been sentenced by the Criminal Court no 6 of Tenerife to two years' imprisonment for an offence of bodily injury, and to two years and four months imprisonment for a violent robbery. Finally, the High Court decided that unlawful stay may be (when other negative circumstances concur) grounds for removal (instead

C. After *Zaizoune*: Memorandum of the General Spanish Bar Association

Soon after the CJEU preliminary ruling on *Zaizoune*, on 25 May 2015, the Subdirectorate on Alien Law of the General Spanish Bar Association published an opinion on the new scenario created by the CJEU ruling.[58] This is addressed to Spanish courts and maintains that the *Zaizoune* decision does not affect the doctrine of the Supreme Court, and therefore does not prevent the High Courts of Justice from imposing a fine as a sanction for illegally staying in Spanish territory.

In the Bar Association's opinion, the Spanish Act 4/2000 and the regulations governing its application state that the sanction of compulsory removal has to be imposed on all foreigners without authorisation to stay in Spain. Such scenarios include imposing a fine, which must be linked to an order to depart the country within 15 days.[59] Thus, there are no inconsistencies with the Directive.[60] The statements in this Memorandum reflect an assertion often repeated by Spanish barristers and scholars.[61] From their perspective, the key issue is that the question submitted by the High Court of Justice of the Basque County was ill conceived. Tying the fine to a compulsory departure order implies full compliance with

of a fine) and entry ban sentence. This ruling is notable because the High Court *brings up the Supreme Court's doctrine favouring financial sanctions* (Supreme Court 2005–2008) but *also highlights the new position of the Supreme Court as established in their decision of 12 March 2013*. See other judgments by High Court of Justice of Castile-Leon: 6/2015, of 8 January (Administrative Court, Section 3) (JUR 2015\37136); 8/2015, of 8 January (Administrative Court, Section 3) (JUR 2015\34346); 2390/2014, of 25 November (Administrative Court, Section 3) (JUR 2015\29080); 2391/2014, of 25 November (Administrative Court, Section 3) (JUR 2015\29798); 2360/2014, of 21 November (Administrative Court, Section 3) (JUR 2015\29079); 2338/2014, of 19 November (Administrative Court, Section 3) (JUR 2015\27364); 2301/2014, of 14 November (Administrative Court, Section 3) (JUR 2015\28109); 1786/2014, of 15 September (Administrative Court, Section 3) (JUR 2014\265407); 996/2014, of 16 May (Administrative Court, Section 3) (JUR 2014\174659); 367/2014, of 21 February (Administrative Court, Section 3) (JUR 2014\90399); 189/2014, of 31 January (Administrative Court, Section 3) (JUR 2014\70965); 142/2014, of 27 January (Administrative Court, Section 3) (JUR 2014\46672).

[58] Memorandum no 43/2015 *Argumentario a la sentencia de 23 de abril de 2015 del TJUE*. Subdirectorate on Alien Law of the General Spanish Bar Association, at: icalorca.es/wp-content/uploads/RS_06273_15.pdf.

[59] The order of compulsory departure is governed in the Spanish laws on aliens and is provided for those cases where residence permit is denied and also tied to a financial penalty for irregularly staying third-country nationals. Although Spanish jurisprudence mentioning *voluntary departure* (Art 7 of the Return Directive) is scarce, an *order of compulsory departure* appears in several judgments, although *never* with regard to Art 7 of the Return Directive. See eg High Court of Justice of the Balearic Islands, 222/2015, of 31 March (JUR 2015\107397). In this case, an illegally staying third-country national was arrested while driving under the influence of alcohol and other drugs. He was sanctioned with a fine and an order of compulsory departure. He appealed this decision on grounds of integration, since he has a life partner in Spain. The Court decided to suspend the order of compulsory departure and sanction him only with a fine.

[60] Dissenting vote of Magistrate Francisca Rosas Carrión to judgment no 638/2015 of 14 October 2015 issued on appeal to the ruling on case 253/2015 under the records of this Section. Roj: STSJ M 11877/2015 – ECLI:ES:TSJM:2015:11877.

[61] Comments: Francisco Solans, Primeras reflexiones tras la sentencia sobre expulsiones y multas del tribunal de la UE; Pascual Aguelo Navarro and Hipólito-Vte Granero Sánchez, Comentarios a

the Directive, since potential removal and financial penalties are not mutually exclusive.

In this sense, the Bar Association considers that imposing a fine and a departure order are equivalent to what the Return Directive considers a return decision.[62] Should the person fail to depart in 15 days, they would be forcibly removed. The Memorandum also encouraged the courts to submit the following issue to the CJEU for preliminary ruling:

> When the law allows to sanction the mere fact of unlawful stay with a financial fine and the legal obligation to depart the national territory within 15 natural days, with the warning that a sanction of removal may be imposed in the event that such obligation to depart was not fulfilled: Is it consistent with the provisions of articles 4(2) 4(3) and 6(1) of Directive 2008/115/CE?

In the view of the General Bar Council, the Act on Aliens and the regulations governing its application remain lawful. However, the Memorandum argues that the decision of the CJEU with regard to the *Zaizoune* case had a non-retrospective nature, which results from the case-law established by the European Court of Human Rights (ECtHR) with regard to the *Del Río Prada v Spain* case. But the CJEU has established that national courts may not restrict in time the enforcement of CJEU judgments,[63] only the CJEU is entitled to do this.[64] In addition, this aim of the Memorandum is not consistent with the other arguments proposed, since Spain's General Bar Council states that financial sanctions and removal are not mutually exclusive. Therefore, if (in their view) the Return Directive has not been incorrectly transposed and no new situation has arisen from the preliminary ruling on *Zaizoune* which damages any individual right, why even mention non-retroactivity?

vuelapluma sobre la sentencia del TJUE de 23.04.2015; José Ramón Chaves, El gran embrollo: Expulsión de extranjeros tras la Sentencia del Tribunal de Justicia de 2015; Alfredo Herranz, La expulsión de inmigrantes irregulares: la sentencia de 23 de abril de 2015 del TJUE; Javier Sánchez Riba, El Tribunal de Justicia de la Unión Europea establece que no se puede sancionar con multa a los inmigrantes en situación irregular; Julian Lopez, Expulsión o multa a extranjero en situación irregular: nueva polémica tras la sentencia del TJUE; Alejandro Peña Pérez, STJUE of 23 April 2015: Una interpretación alternativa; Andrea Romano, 'The Returns Directive and the Removal of Migrants in an Irregular Situation in Spain'; Cristina J. Gortázar Rotaeche and Nuria Ferré, 'A Fine or Removal? The Impact of the ECJ's Zaizoune Judgment on the Spanish Doctrine'.

[62] The Directive allows the order of removal to be issued together with the return decision (single procedure) or separately (two-stage procedure). When the decision and the order are issued in a single procedure, if a term for voluntary departure is allowed, it must be clear that removal will only be enforced if the obligation to depart is not complied with within that term. In Spain administrative offences are sanctioned either with a fine or with removal, but this may be understood as a two-stage removal decision. In the first stage, the illegally staying third-country national is fined and invited to leave the Spanish territory (and Schengen Area) by their own means. Only when this person does not leave in the established period, is the second stage triggered with the issuance of a return decision and an order of removal.

[63] See Case C-199/82 *Amministrazione delle Finanze dello Stato v SpA San Giorgio* ECLI:EU:C:1983:318; Case C-13/08 *Stamm and Hauser* ECLI:EU:C:2008:774.

[64] See Case C-263/10 *Iulian Nisipeanu v Direcţia Generală a Finanţelor Publice Gorj and Others* ECLI:EU:C:2011:466.

D. Different Judicial Reactions to the CJEU Preliminary Ruling in *Zaizoune*

After the *Zaizoune* ruling, as a consequence of the end of the doctrine favouring financial sanctions over removal, many irregularly staying third-country nationals, who in the past would have been fined, are encouraged to leave the country voluntarily or to be forcibly returned (when possible) in all cases where an extraordinary stay permit does not apply.[65]

A positive consequence of the *Zaizoune* preliminary ruling is that Spanish judges have started to claim that third-country nationals have the right to be offered a chance for voluntary departure before the enforcement of return, not only by virtue of the Directive but also for a rightful application of the principle of proportionality included in the Spanish Constitution. Since voluntary departure does not entail an entry ban, the third-country national may remedy any unlawful situation in their country of origin and come back lawfully to the Schengen Area.

Therefore, the Spanish High Courts of Justice have understood that the *Zaizoune* preliminary ruling established 'a new framework in which it is no longer possible to replace removal from the Spanish territory, and it is key to afford the illegally staying third-country national an opportunity of voluntary departure'.[66] The Administrative Court no 1 of Ourense (Galicia) partially admitted the appeal filed by a Uruguayan national to the decision ordering his removal and a three-year entry ban. The court cancelled the removal order and replaced it with a fine of €501, with the warning that he must start the procedure for regularisation if he fulfils the established requirements or 'voluntarily leaves the Spanish territory within 30 days'.[67]

[65] However, even after the *Zaizoune* case, the situation took long to be understood. For example, the High Court of Justice of Madrid, no 227/2015 of 27 May 2016 JUR 2015\158468 states:

> [H]owever, a financial penalty is a penalty that does not *change* the situation of the third-country national. … If the third-country national does not voluntarily leave the Spanish territory, they *run the risk* of being imposed a new sanction which *might* entail removal from the Spanish territory. (emphasis added)

However, some judges have continued to defend the old doctrine of the fine even after *Zaizoune* ruling:

> When a national rule is contradictory to a Directive, the lack of transposition, or the deficient or insufficient transposition, the national standard is interpreted in accordance with the other rules of the EU order. The fact that the Spanish regulations are more advantageous for foreigners in Spain in an irregular situation prevents, on its own, the direct application of the Return Directive. Therefore, the TSJ confirms the adaptation to the right of the sanction of the fine imposed, in substitution of the expulsion, applying the national rule that allows to choose between the expulsion or the fine. The fine has been imposed in accordance with the aforementioned principle of proportionality.

TSJ Madrid. See n 40 above.

[66] High Court of Justice of Murcia, no 422/2015, of 22 June Roj: STSJ MU 1635/2015 – ECLI:ES:TSJMU:2015:1635. In this case, since the removal was decided according to the preferential procedure, the High Court of Justice stated that a return decision has to be enforced, and established a period between seven and 30 days for voluntary departure.

[67] Administrative Court of Ourense, section 1, no 6/2016, Rec 130/2015 of 14 January 2016.

Another positive consequence of the *Zaizoune* ruling is that Spanish courts have started referring to regularisation of third-country nationals as a desirable alternative to enforcement of a return decision. Thus, for example, a decision of the High Court of Justice of Murcia issued after the *Zaizoune* ruling revoked a removal order and six-year entry ban by virtue of the application of Article 5 of the Directive regarding the 'best interests of the child', who was born in Spain.[68]

Three years after *Zaizoune*, the Spanish courts still do not hold a homogeneous position regarding the doctrine favouring financial penalties and their replacement by removal orders. Thus, for example, a ruling of the High Court of Justice of the Basque Country on 25 April 2017 nullified a sanction of removal imposed on a Ghanaian national illegally staying in Spain because 'such a removal order may not be considered as a single return decision', and replaced the order with a fine of €501, stating even that 'the legal type of irregular stay remains unchanged'.[69]

E. The Supreme Court Decision of 12 June 2018

In this rich but confusing judicial scenario, the Spanish Supreme Court recently established a final doctrine on the application of the *Zaizoune* case.[70] The case reached the Supreme Court on the appeal of a third-country national against the decision of the High Court of Madrid to expel them from Spanish territory together with the imposition of a two-year entry ban. The appellants argued that the appropriate sanction according to the Spanish legislation was a fine, as there were no negative factors apart from their irregular situation.

The Supreme Court ruled that there is no cassation and that the High Court of Madrid judgment (and the first-instance court) had applied correctly the *Zaizoune* doctrine. Following the ruling of the CJEU in *Zaizoune*, 'there is no possibility to change a removal with a fine'. The Supreme Court considered that there is a link between the Spanish courts and the CJEU on the obligation to apply EU law with preference over domestic legislation.[71] The Supreme Court also stated that Article 57(1) of the Act on Aliens 4/2000 should be interpreted as a removal decision (in

[68] Judgment of the TSJ of Murcia, 6 October 2017, which confirms the need for ordinary expulsion record or a prior voluntary departure when no circumstances are given in the record that are pursuant to Art 7(4) of the Return Directive: STSJ MU 1648/2017 – ECLI:ES:TSJMU:2017:1648.

[69] Sentence of the High Court of Justice of the Basque Country, section 2 of Administrative Courts no 200/2017 of 25 April, ECLI:ES:TSJPV:2017:1421.

[70] STS (3rd Room, 5th Section) of 12 June 2018. In order to understand the question mark, see the following note.

[71] Since the *Simmenthal* case, 9 March 1978 onwards (Case C-106/77 *Finanze dello Stato v Simmenthal SpA* ECLI:EU:C:1978:49). However, this consideration has already been seriously contested by a Spanish specialist based on the following argument: Spain has badly transposed the Directive and the EU law preference over domestic legislation is only applied in cases of direct effect, which is not the present case. D Acosta, 'Derecho Europeo de Inmigración, Directivas y Efecto Directo', XIV Congreso de la Abogacía, Málaga, 18–19 October 2018.

the sense of the Return Directive) unless exceptions quoted at Article 6(2)–(5) of the Directive apply. It stated that when Article 5 of the Return Directive is applicable (higher interests of the child, family life, health, *non-refoulement*), the removal will not take place and a permit to stay will be issued.

IV. Concluding Remarks

The 2018 Proposal for the amendment of the Return Directive lists as one of its main targets the necessity to provide clearer and more effective rules on the issuing of return decisions.[72] This chapter has tried to determine whether there is a correlation between the Return Directive's modest effectiveness rate and the problems encountered by the Member States when issuing return decisions, throughout the Spanish practice. It is difficult to know how many irregularly staying third-country nationals have remained in Spain between 2010 and 2018 after being identified and punished with a fine (which included a compulsory exit that was not supervised). In the Spanish case, it seems to correspond more with an unclear transposition of some provisions than to the lack of clarity of the Directive itself. However, there may have been a combination of both causes.

The *Zaizoune* ruling significantly affected Spanish judicial practice regarding the correct interpretation of the Return Directive on the obligation to issue return decisions. Before the ruling, Spanish judges were not very prone to refer to the Return Directive, nor to refer to CJEU jurisprudence regarding the correct interpretation of this Directive.[73] The principle of proportionality in the Spanish Constitution and the jurisprudence of the Supreme Court interpreting it were the main legal sources used in cases concerning removals of irregularly staying third-country nationals. This relative lack of attention to the Directive and the CJEU case law changed after the *Zaizoune* ruling.

Although financial sanctions on irregularly staying third-country nationals are tied to an order of compulsory departure within 15 days, before the *Zaizoune* ruling such an order of compulsory leave was not sufficiently monitored. Some of the persons concerned achieved regularisation on grounds of integration. Others were arrested (sometimes after years) and removed from the country within 72 hours without having the opportunity of being heard regarding their current personal and family circumstances.

The clarification by the Supreme Court in 2018 on the interpretation of Spanish law in light of the *Zaizoune* ruling tries to put an end to the puzzle created by an unsatisfactory transposition into Spanish law of different Return Directive provisions, although in all likelihood the Court is using the EU law primacy doctrine wrongly.[74]

[72] See 2018 Proposal for a Return Directive, 7.
[73] See the ReDial Case Law database on Spain, available at http://euredial.eu/national-caselaw/.
[74] See n 71.

Nonetheless, many issues continue to be obscure: the lack of precision regarding what a return decision is; how third-country national voluntary departure works; when is it possible to issue an autonomous permit; and in which circumstances the *non-refoulement* principle applies to prevent a return decision from being issued.

This chapter explained the consequences of an unclear transposition of the Return Directive into Spanish legislation. Spain exemplifies the difficulties and weaknesses of judicial systems in the Member States in ensuring effective enforcement of the Directive. This is evidenced with regard to the *Zaizoune* preliminary ruling of the CJEU. Years of sometimes contradictory domestic judicial decisions damaged human rights and the expectations of persons irregularly staying in the EU. A modification of Spanish national legislation is still necessary. The Spanish judges involved are now, however, much more familiar with EU law and CJEU case-law.

3

Voluntary Departure as a Priority: Challenges and Best Practices

ULRIKE BRANDL

I. Introduction

The Preamble of the Return Directive clearly emphasises the priority of voluntary departure over forced removal.[1] This precedence is also explicitly mentioned in a number of Commission documents, including the renewed 2017 Commission Action Plan[2] and the Return Handbook,[3] highlighting that the promotion of voluntary departure is one of the key objectives of the Return Directive. The Handbook also recommends several restrictions – for instance, that Member States should require an application for voluntary departure – and thus tries to find a compromise between voluntarism and effectiveness of return procedures.[4] The CJEU confirms in its constant jurisprudence that voluntary departure has priority over other forms of return of irregular migrants.[5] The Proposal for a recast of the Return Directive published by the Commission on 12 September 2018[6] does not deviate from the priority of non-enforced return in general, but does impose

[1] Directive 2008/115/EC of 16 December 2008 on common standards and procedures in Member States for returning illegally staying third-country nationals [2008] OJ L348, 98, Recital 10 of the Preamble.

[2] Commission, 'Communication from the Commission to the European Parliament and the Council on a More Effective Return Policy in the European Union – A Renewed Action Plan' COM(2017) 200 final, 7.

[3] Commission, Annex to 'Commission Recommendation Establishing a Common "Return Handbook" To Be Used by Member States' Competent Authorities when Carrying Out Return Related Tasks' 27 September 2017, C(2017) 6505. Annex available at ec.europa.eu/home-affairs/sites/homeaffairs/files/what-we-do/policies/european-agenda-migration/proposal-implementation-package/docs/return_handbook_en.pdf.

[4] ibid, 34.

[5] See eg Case C-61/11 PPU *Hassen El Dridi, alias Karim Soufi* ECLI:EU:C:2011:268, para 36: 'As part of that initial stage of the return procedure, priority is to be given, except where otherwise provided for, to voluntary compliance with the obligation resulting from that return decision.'

[6] Commission, 'Proposal for a Directive on Common Standards and Procedures in Member States for Returning Illegally Staying Third-Country Nationals (Recast)' COM(2018) 634 final.

several restrictions and establishes a number of cases where it becomes mandatory not to grant a period for voluntary departure.

From the various measures and gradual steps established by the Return Directive, voluntary departure is the least contentious option, widely welcomed by the Commission[7] and academics.[8] The practical enforcement of voluntary departure, however, raises several important questions including compatibility with human rights obligations.[9] The critical issues are: the length of the time limit for voluntary departure; the possibility to prolong this period; the start of the period; the question whether the conditions in the departure country or in the country of return allow a return within the prescribed period; and family life protection during preparation of departure or after the departure. Furthermore, supervision of voluntary return and measures against absconding may affect human rights guarantees. This chapter aims to analyse gaps and ambiguities in the interpretation and application of the provisions on voluntary return in the Return Directive. They mirror the difficult balance between protection of the rights of individual returnees and Member States' intentions to make return procedures more effective.

This chapter comprises five sections.[10] Following the introduction, the second section deals with the provisions on voluntary departure in the Return Directive and analyses national practice and jurisprudence with regard to gaps and deficiencies in their implementation. It covers the granting and calculation of a time limit for voluntary departure, the extension and revocation of the time limit, and the provisions allowing Member States to grant no time limit (Article 7(4) Return Directive). Section III deals with international jurisprudence with regard to voluntary departure and elaborates if and how far international jurisprudence has had an influence on national practice and jurisprudence, focusing on key examples of judicial dialogue and on areas where such a dialogue could lead to positive influences on the practices of other Member States. Section IV discusses measures to support voluntary return including incentives, and section V concludes.

[7] See nn 2 and 3, and the Return Handbook (n 3) at 34: 'The promotion of voluntary departure is one of the key objectives of the Return Directive. Voluntary compliance with an obligation to return is preferable to removal for the threefold reason that it is a more dignified, safer, and frequently a more cost-effective return option.'

[8] cf D Acosta Arcarazo, 'The Returns Directive: Possible Limits and Interpretation' in K Zwaan (ed), *The Returns Directive: Central Themes, Problem Issues, and Implementation in Selected Member States* (Nijmegen, Wolf Legal Publishers, 2011) 7–24, 12; A Baldaccini, 'The Return and Removal of Irregular Migrants under EU Law: An Analysis of the Returns Directive' (2009) 1 *European Journal of Migration and Law* 1, 7–8.

[9] Art 1 of the Return Directive points to the general aims of the Directive: that illegally staying third-country nationals leave the Member State, that common standards and procedures are applied in Member States for returning illegally staying third-country nationals and also that their fundamental rights are respected. See also F Lutz, 'Prologue: The Genesis of the EU's Return Policy', in this volume.

[10] The findings in this chapter are based on the national synthesis reports and the database set up in the context of the REDIAL Project, which collects data up until 2017, accessed at euredial.eu/publications/national-synthesis-reports/ and euredial.eu/national-caselaw/.

II. Voluntary Departure in the Return Directive: Gaps and Ambiguities in State Practice and Jurisprudence

This section deals with the provisions about voluntary return in the Return Directive, identifies where states have scope for implementation and how they use it in diverging ways. It also discusses where Member States did not or still do not fulfil the obligations contained in the Return Directive and where national jurisprudence either corrected this practice or clarified issues for which the provisions did not specifically regulate. The section also covers the proposed changes to the Return Directive and analyses whether they are a result of already existing practice.

A. Voluntary Return and the Role of National Courts

'Voluntary departure' is defined in Article 3(8) of the Return Directive as 'compliance with the obligation to return within the time-limit fixed for that purpose in the return decision'. The return decision[11] and the period for voluntary departure create the obligation for the third-country national to depart during the prescribed period. Member States still retain the sovereign right to grant autonomous residence to third-country nationals without a right to reside for compassionate, humanitarian or other reasons at any stage of the procedure, according to Article 6(4) Return Directive.

An analysis of the decisions and judgments contained in the REDIAL (REturn Directive DIALogue) database and referred to in the REDIAL national reports reveals that national courts have seldom decided cases in which issues of voluntary departure and the time limit for departure were raised.[12] Cases have more often reached national courts for judicial review regarding the determination of a risk of absconding and also in connection with detention and forced removal. The main reason for this is the concept of the Return Directive. The conferral of a time limit for voluntary departure is either included in the return decision or in the removal order, depending on national procedural law.[13] Requests for judicial review are consequently directed against these decisions and do not especially address the provisions on voluntary departure. Persons concerned ask the courts

[11] The return decision is the first step in the successive stages in the return procedure. According to Art 6 of the Return Directive, Member States are obligated to issue a return decision if a third-country national is staying illegally on their territory. There are exceptions to this general rule as enumerated in Art 6(2)–(5). See more in C Gortázar Rotaeche, 'Return Decisions and Domestic Judicial Practices: Is Spain Different?', Chapter 2 in this colume.

[12] cf Ph De Bruycker, M Moraru and G Renaudiere, 'European Synthesis Report on the Judicial Implementation of Chapter III of the Return Directive Procedural Safeguards', REDIAL Research Report 2016/03, 9. See for the REDIAL national reports and the database (n10).

[13] See Ph De Bruycker, M Moraru and G Renaudiere, 'European Synthesis Report on the Termination of Illegal Stay (Articles 7 to 11 of Directive 2008/115/EC)', REDIAL Research Report 2016/01.

for a revocation of the return decision or the removal order and do not direct their applications against the non-conferral of a time limit or against the length of a time limit. However, in several cases where applications *were* directed against return decisions, national courts also addressed voluntary departure and interpreted provisions of the Return Directive.[14] Conversely, when return decisions are issued without indicating the reasons in sufficient clarity, as is current practice in Croatia,[15] there is little or no court practice reviewing the legality of the return decision. As there is no or no substantial reasoning included in the decisions, there are no possibilities to bring cases to courts as there are no legal arguments that can be deduced from these decisions.

B. Priority of Voluntary Return and the Time Limit for Voluntary Return

Article 7 of the Return Directive does not repeat the Preamble's explicit reference to the priority of voluntary departure, but does contain the obligation to grant a time period for leaving the country voluntarily. Exceptions may only be based on Article 7(2) or (4). The appropriate period may be determined from 7 to 30 days. The Return Directive does not provide criteria for the initial calculation. Member States may allow fixed periods or periods determined in individual cases.

Inspiration for criteria by which the length of the appropriate voluntary departure period is calculated could be taken from Article 7(2), which provides criteria for the extension of the initial period. National laws in the Member States make use of the possibilities offered by the Return Directive[16] and either stipulate a fixed

[14] In a Lithuanian case the remedy was directed against the return decision as such and not against the time limit for voluntary return. The case is, however, also interesting with regard to voluntary departure. The applicant argued her and her son's particular situation had not been taken into account as her son was born in Lithuania and had never been to Vietnam. The authority argued that under the law on the Legal Status of Aliens there is no obligation to evaluate, if there are circumstances precluding the return at the voluntary departure stage. These circumstances should be evaluated only if the alien does not leave the territory voluntarily and a decision ordering forced expulsion should be adopted. The Court ruled that although the law *expressis verbis* does not establish the obligation to evaluate relevant circumstances at the stage of adoption of the decision ordering the alien to depart from Lithuania, provisions of the Return Directive favour voluntary departure and require evaluation of all relevant circumstances before adopting a return decision, see Supreme Administrative Court of Lithuania, A858-2332/2011 17 October 2011. See also I Jarukaitis, 'REDIAL National Synthesis Report – Lithuania, Procedural Safeguards'.

[15] The entry into force of an amendment of Croatian legislation on 27 June 2013 led to the consequence that return decisions are issued without indicating the reasons in sufficient clarity. See ŽZ Ježekl and I Goldner Lang, 'National Synthesis Report – Croatia, Termination of Illegal Stay'.

[16] For national legislation and practice, see European Migration Network, 'The Effectiveness of Return in EU Member States', Synthesis Report for the EMN Focussed Study, 2017.

time limit[17] or leave the determination to the authorities, who have certain discretion to determine the period within a time frame.[18]

According to the Commission Proposal for a recast of the Return Directive, there is a need to adapt the rules for granting a period for voluntary departure.[19] Article 9 of the Proposal regulates that the appropriate period for voluntary departure is a period of up to 30 days. The Proposal eliminates the seven-day minimum period and allows Member States to decide on a shorter period. Whereas the Return Directive does not provide criteria to calculate the period for voluntary departure, the Proposal requires that Member States establish the period with due regard to the specific circumstances of the individual case, taking into account in particular the prospect of return. The text does not mention criteria for the reasons which might establish such a prospect.

The Proposal identifies a number of cases in which it becomes mandatory not to grant a period for voluntary departure at all.[20] These are the same situations for which the Return Directive currently in force allows no period or a shorter period than seven days for voluntary departure. In general, the Proposal reveals the intention still to focus on the priority of voluntary departure, but also to tighten the criteria for it.

According to the Return Directive, Member States may only grant a period shorter than seven days if there is a risk of absconding, if the person concerned poses a risk to public policy, public or national security, or if an application for a legal stay has been dismissed as manifestly unfounded or fraudulent. If it emerges during the period for voluntary departure that there is such a risk, the return decision can be enforced before the expiry of the period granted for voluntary departure.[21] In the present Return Directive – in contrast to the Proposal – there are no mandatory reasons for an exclusion of voluntary departure.

The only procedural requirement Member States may impose is the formal application for a period for voluntary departure.[22] If such an application is necessary, the third-country nationals concerned have to be informed about this possibility. The Return Directive itself does not regulate how this information has to be communicated. Concrete interpretative guidelines are provided by the Return Handbook, which requires that Member States inform the persons concerned individually. General information sheets are considered to be insufficient as an individual guarantee.[23]

[17] As an example for a fixed period, see Austria, where the time limit is 14 days from the date when the return decision becomes final (Art 55(2) Aliens Police Act).

[18] This is the case for Croatia, where the deadline for leaving may not be less than 7 or more than 30 days. The Croatian report shows that the governing body usually specifies the maximum limit of 30 days. National Synthesis Report – Croatia (n 15).

[19] Proposal (n 6).

[20] ibid.

[21] cf Return Handbook (n 3) 30.

[22] cf REDIAL Research Report 2016/03 (n 12).

[23] Return Handbook (n 3) 35.

If no period for voluntary departure is granted in a return decision or if the obligation to return has not been complied with, an entry ban has to be issued according to Article 11 of the Return Directive. Such an entry ban is a serious consequence for the returnee. Thus, the decision whether a period for voluntary departure is granted is also decisive of the possibility to re-enter the state.

C. Gaps and Ambiguities in the Interpretation and Application of the Provisions About Voluntary Return

There is a difficult balance between the protection of individual rights and Member States' legitimate intention to make return procedures more efficient. This has led, on the one hand, to the fact that the Commission issued recommendations to speed up return procedures. On the other hand, national legislation and administrative and/or judicial practice have violated provisions of the Return Directive or interpreted them in a restrictive way. Member States have considered the absence of both mandatory reasons for not granting a period for voluntary departure and obligations for an application for such a period as an impediment to effective return.

In 2017, the Commission reacted and published a Recommendation to make returns more effective, limiting the procedural discretion of Member States and adding interpretative guidelines on the enforcement of voluntary departure for the provisions contained in the Return Directive.[24] The Recommendation stipulates that Member States should only grant the shortest period necessary for the organisation of voluntary departure, but does not suggest what criteria are relevant for such organisation.[25] This recommendation interprets the calculation of the time limit in a way that does not sufficiently take into account the interests of returnees, and instead recommends Member States use their discretion to interpret and apply the provisions on voluntary return in the most restrictive way.

Paragraph 17 of the Recommendation indicates that Member States should require an application for voluntary departure, intending to limit their current procedural discretion whether or not to require an individual application. Thus, the Recommendation contradicts the general prioritisation of voluntary departure, intending that Member States use their discretion to interpret and apply the provisions on voluntary return in a restrictive way. The Proposal for a recast of the Return Directive follows the Recommendation and contains mandatory reasons for not granting a period for voluntary departure. The Proposal, however, does not oblige Member States to require an application for a period for voluntary departure, but leaves this option to the Member States.[26]

[24] European Commission, 'Commission Recommendation of 7 March 2017 on Making Returns More Effective when Implementing the Directive 2008/115/EC of the European Parliament and of the Council' COM(2017) 1600 final.

[25] ibid.

[26] Proposal (n 6).

Practice in some Member States has not been in line with the provisions of Article 7(1) of the Return Directive. In Italy, for instance, third-country nationals must prove they have adequate economic resources from legal sources proportionate to the time granted for voluntary departure.[27] This automatic addition of an obligation to prove economic resources is incompatible with the Return Directive, which does not impose financial or similar prerequisites for the conferral of voluntary departure. So far, however, jurisprudence has not corrected this violation.

In Cyprus, the law provides that the return decision sets out a mandatory time frame for voluntary return ranging between 7 and 30 days.[28] Cypriot practice, however, reveals that a period for voluntary return is not granted.[29] The administrative decision offering the possibility of voluntary departure is not even considered an administrative act. It is a mere request that cannot be reviewed by courts. Already in 2013, the Cypriot Supreme Court found that:

> [T]he standard letter which the immigration authorities customarily send to all TCNs [third-country nationals] in an irregular situation requesting them to depart by themselves does not constitute an executive administrative act but a mere request of no legal consequence and as such it cannot be subjected to judicial review or be suspended through an interim order.[30]

The Court did not recognise the immigration authorities' practice of requesting the applicant to depart as a voluntary departure decision within the meaning of the Return Directive, and there is no procedure and no time frame prescribed in law for applications for voluntary departure. The courts so far have not corrected the practice violating obligations contained in the Directive.

In Spain, even the judgment of the CJEU – the *Zaizoune* case[31] – and an amendment of Spanish legislation could neither end divergent practice nor the legal dispute surrounding the correct interpretation of provisions of the Return Directive. Initially many cases were decided in urgent proceedings (*procedimiento preferente*) due to the situation as perceived by the authorities: that third-country nationals concerned

[27] The amount is from one to three times the amount of the monthly welfare payment. This payment amounted to €453 in 2018. See A di Pascale, 'REDIAL National Synthesis Report – Italy, Termination of Illegal Stay' and REDIAL Research Report 2016/03 (n 12).

[28] See N Trimikliniotis and C Demetriou, 'REDIAL National Synthesis Report – Cyprus, Termination of Illegal Stay'.

[29] ibid. In practice, once the authorities have located the whereabouts of a third-country national illegally staying in Cyprus, they serve him/her with the standard letter which does not grant a voluntary departure period and which places the person under arrest, in order to avoid the risk of absconding. The Cypriot report refers to the fact that none of the stakeholders consulted for the purposes of the report were aware of any voluntary departure periods granted in any case. There is no administrative procedure in place to appeal against a negative decision for an application for voluntary departure. In theory, all decisions of the administration can be appealed against, under Art 146 of the constitution. In such a case, however, the voluntary return procedure is not automatically suspended as a result of filing such an action. This is based on practice and was confirmed by a court decision.

[30] See REDIAL National Synthesis Report – Cyprus (n 28) and *Tatsiana Balashevich v Republic*, Cypriot Supreme Court case no 5635/2013, 10 July 2013.

[31] Case C-38/14 *Subdelegación del Gobierno en Guipuzkoa – Extranjeria v Samir Zaizoune* ECLI:EU:C:2015:260, para 33.

were illegally present and the authorities decided that there was a risk of absconding. In urgent proceedings, no period for voluntary departure could be granted. These proceedings reduced the rights of third-country nationals and deprived them of the opportunity to exit the country voluntarily and consequently avoid an entry ban. The Spanish Supreme Court established a specific interpretation of the Spanish Immigration Act, according to which a fine was the main sanction for illegal stay, and the so-called 'doctrine of the fine' was applied until 2013. Following the CJEU judgment in the *Zaizoune* case, Spanish legislation was amended; however, some Spanish judges have continued to defend the old doctrine of the fine even after the *Zaizoune* ruling.[32] The judgment clarified that Member States have to issue a return decision; however, this vertical judicial dialogue could not finally solve the conflict. It only led to a partial change of Spanish practice.

In Italy, a national court decided that the relevant provision of the Return Directive was sufficiently clear to be directly applicable. Italian legislation did not transpose the obligations deriving from the Return Directive within the period required. After the end of the period for transposition, the Justice of the Peace of Alessandria decided that the provisions on voluntary departure in the Directive were directly applicable in Italian law.[33] The conclusion that the voluntary departure provisions were sufficiently clear and unconditional? was mainly due to the granting of a period for voluntary departure between 7 and 30 days and the limited exceptions. This interpretation is convincing and would be a good example for other national courts in Member States where the provisions of the Return Directive are not, or not fully, transposed or where national administrative practice violates obligations contained in the Directive.

These examples show how some national courts interpreted the provisions of the Return Directive and national law in a way that contradicted the obligations deriving from the Directive, whereas others interpreted the Directive in a way that obliged authorities to implement its provisions in a correct way.

D. Start of the Period for Voluntary Departure

The moment when the period for voluntary departure starts to run is not specified in the Return Directive; however, this determination is important for the calculation of the period. In addition, most national laws do not determine the start of the period either. Czech legislation is an exception and explicitly provides that, in cases where the voluntary departure period starts during the detention, its factual application will be postponed.[34] Similarly, if the third-country national is detained

[32] See also Gortázar Rotaeche, 'Return Decisions and Domestic Judicial Practices' (n 11).

[33] Italy, Justice of the Peace of Alessandria, 10 May 2011. See later Italian Supreme Court n 10243/2012, 20 June 2012.

[34] See D Kosař and S Sládeková, 'REDIAL National Synthesis Report – Czech Republic, Termination of Illegal Stay'.

during the voluntary departure period, the period has to be suspended until the end of the detention period.

A Czech court quashed the administrative order for removal because the authorities did not provide adequate reasons for refusing first to impose voluntary departure with attached obligations prior to deciding to impose a removal order.[35] According to the Court, interpreting the provisions of the Return Directive leads to the conclusion that the voluntary departure period only starts when the third-country national is free to make the necessary return arrangements. In the specific case, the period was interpreted as starting to run only after the release from detention.

In a similar way, the Cour administrative d'appel de Paris quashed an administrative decision that did not take the existence of criminal sanctions into account for the calculation of the period for voluntary departure and thereby adapt the start of the period for voluntary departure accordingly.[36]

In this respect, national jurisprudence clarified the provisions of the Return Directive and established precise criteria for returnees, the time limit only starting when the person is ready to be engaged in the preparation of his or her departure.

E. Extension of the Period for Voluntary Return

Article 7(2) of the Return Directive provides for the obligatory extension of the initial period in cases where the extension is necessary due to specific circumstances, such as the length of stay, the existence of children attending school or the existence of other family and social links.[37] This list of reasons is not exhaustive and the provision does not set a fixed time frame for the extension. Member States thus have a considerable margin of discretion to determine the length of the prolongation period. National laws either refer to the circumstances mentioned in Article 7(2), enumerate additional criteria or just grant the discretion to authorities without giving reasons.[38] Article 7(2) only comprises reasons in the relevant Member State; other reasons, especially reasons that occur in the country of return, are not explicitly mentioned. However, jurisprudence in some countries also takes these reasons into account.

[35] ibid.

[36] See H Labayle and M Garcia, 'REDIAL National Synthesis Report – France, Termination of Illegal Stay', Cour administrative d'appel de Paris, 22/03/2013, no 12PA03710.

[37] cf Return Handbook (n 3): 'The term "where necessary" refers to circumstances both in the sphere of the returnee and in the sphere of the returning State. Member States enjoy discretion relating to the substance and the regulatory depth of their national implementing legislation on this issue.'

[38] In Austria, Art 55 Aliens Police Act neither enumerates such reasons nor does it specify details. According to the Government Proposal (legislative document) Art 55(3) Aliens Police Act transposes Art 7(2) of the Return Directive. The government proposal also refers to examples. These are the previous length of stay of the third-country national, the necessity that a child completes a semester at an Austrian school or similar and equivalent reasons. See U Brandl, 'REDIAL National Synthesis Report – Austria, Termination of Illegal Stay'.

Austrian jurisprudence is particularly interesting in this respect. The Austrian High Administrative Court decided, based on an analysis of Article 7 of the Return Directive and its transposition into Austrian law, that not only circumstances existing in Austria might create the necessity to prolong the period for voluntary return, but also circumstances in the country of origin.[39] The applicants had stated that they did not have a social net in Byelorussia and their house had been taken by relatives. There were no possibilities for them to move to their country of origin in winter because it would be impossible to find a place to live with (adequate) heating. Furthermore, their son was born in Austria and was not registered in Byelorussia.[40]

In another case, the court decided that the expected conditions in the home country (in this case a return with a three-year old child without a place of accommodation) necessitated the extension of the period for voluntary departure.[41] The same applied to the need to obtain a travel document for the child.[42]

A German judgment[43] referred to the reasons for prolonging the period for voluntary departure under Article 7(2) of the Return Directive and section 59 of the German Residence Act. The Higher Administrative Court of Nordrhein-Westfalen decided not to extend the period for voluntary departure. The court stated that Article 7(2) of the Return Directive has the purpose of mitigating the consequences of the termination of sojourn. No other factors, such as future developments, have to be taken into account.[44] This decision is an example of the diverging interpretations of the Return Directive by national courts, since the German court did not take circumstances existing in the country of origin into account. The Austrian court's interpretation would thus be a good example of such a dialogue leading to positive effects in other Member States.

A French judgment justified the use of the possibility of extending the period for voluntary departure, subject to specific circumstances and exceptional cases. In this particular case, pending divorce proceedings were not considered to justify prolonging the period for voluntary departure beyond the initial period of 30 days.[45]

[39] Austrian High Administrative Court 2012/21/0072, 16 May 2013.

[40] ibid. The Court then referred to the necessity to interpret the personal circumstances in a broad way. This wide interpretation is also stated in the legislative documents relating to Art 55 Aliens Police Act. The authorities have to reach a fair balance between the personal and public interests. The circumstances in the country of origin not allowing a return have to be temporary. Their termination must be predictable.

[41] Austrian Federal Administrative Court, GZ 2012/, 21/007216.5.2013.

[42] ibid.

[43] See K Hailbronner and D Thym 'REDIAL National Synthesis Report – Germany, Termination of Illegal Stay'. Higher Administrative Court Nordrhein-Westfalen, case no 18 B 779/15, 23-07-2015.

[44] ibid.

[45] France, case no 14NT0149, 26 February 2015.

According to evaluations, the most common grounds considered to justify prolonging the voluntary departure period are health issues[46] and children of the third-country national attending school.[47] Organising travel documentation is taken into consideration in a few cases, but not generally.

F. No Time Limit for Voluntary Return and Revocation of the Time Limit

Article 7(4) enumerates circumstances where Member States may decide not to grant a period for voluntary departure or the period may be shorter than seven days. The reasons are: an existing risk of absconding; an application for a legal stay that has been dismissed as manifestly unfounded or fraudulent; or a risk to public policy, public security or national security. The Proposal for a recast of the Return Directive stipulates that these reasons are mandatory.[48] No other reasons may be invoked for refraining from granting a period for voluntary departure.

Revocation of the period for voluntary departure is often based on the same reasons that allow the denial of the voluntary departure period. States especially withdraw the period for voluntary departure when the reasons did not exist when the decision was rendered but only developed later, or when the reasons were only disclosed later.[49]

i. Risk of Absconding

Article 7(4) requires that a risk of absconding has been established on the basis of objective criteria. The following grounds are contained in national legislations

[46] The Austrian Federal Administrative Court referred to this reasoning with regard to a case concerning a Macedonian citizen, who already had a surgery on his eye and was on the waiting list for a transplantation of the cornea in his right eye. The Court decided that he had a time limit of one year to leave the country. In such a case, complications may occur and it was thus seen as necessary to grant a period of one year. In this case, medical aspects and possible consequences of a complex eye surgery were taken into account. See Austrian Federal Administrative Court, W196 2015947-1, 28.1.2015.

[47] EMN study (n 16). See an evaluation carried out in 2013. European Commission, Evaluation on the application of the Return Directive (2008/115/EC), Final Report, 22 October 2013, 13, 81, 88, 190.

[48] Art 9(4) Proposal (n 6): 'Member States shall not grant a period for voluntary departure in following cases: (a) where there is a risk of absconding determined in accordance with Article 6; (b) where an application for a legal stay has been dismissed as manifestly unfounded or fraudulent; (c) where the third-country national concerned poses a risk to public policy, public security or national security.'

[49] In a Dutch case, the Council of State decided that following an interpretation of Arts 1, 2 3, 6 and 7, the goal of the Return Directive is to ensure the effective return of a third-country national. Therefore, the revocation was seen as similar to the dismissal of an application for the granting of a period for voluntary departure that was done on the basis of fraudulent information (the residence permit was revoked because it was obtained by fraud). Dutch Council of State case 201309038/1/V1, 10 July 2014. Administrative and judicial practice in other states seems to follow the same approach.

as objective criteria for an existing risk: lack of documentation, absence of cooperation to determine identity, use of false documentation or the deliberate destruction of existing documents, failing repeatedly to report to the relevant authorities, explicit expression of intent of non-compliance, existence of a conviction for a criminal offence, non-compliance with existing entry bans and the violation of a return decision.[50] In certain Member States, the list of objective factors indicating a risk of absconding is not exhaustively provided by the national legislation (eg Bulgaria). This is not in line with the provisions of the Return Directive and the jurisprudence of the CJEU.[51]

Several national reports reveal that there are distinctions to be made when establishing the risk factors. Dutch legislation offers detailed criteria, providing 16 grounds for finding a 'risk of absconding'.[52] These criteria are divided into substantial and non-substantial grounds. If at least two substantial grounds exist, the period for voluntary departure is refused. The Return Directive, however, requires an individual assessment of each case. Non-substantial grounds may not in themselves lead to the conclusion that there is such a risk. Therefore the authorities are obliged to give further explanation.

The Dutch Council of State ruled that the Return Directive only requires that these criteria are laid down in law, and that the Directive does not prescribe the material conditions the criteria have to meet.[53] It has been argued before the Council of State that the criteria to assume a risk of absconding are so widely formulated in Dutch law that the administrative authorities will quickly assume that there is a risk of absconding and accordingly are not obliged to grant the (full) period for voluntary departure. In the light of the subsequent judgment of the Court of Justice in *Zh and O*, it is questionable whether the factual reversal of the burden of proof[54] when the authorities invoke the so-called substantial grounds is in conformity with the strict requirements that the Court sets to the invocation of Article 7(4) of the Return Directive.

An amendment to the Austrian legislation included a definition of the risk of absconding with regard to transfers under the Dublin III Regulation.[55] The definition also applies to the risk of absconding during the voluntary departure phase.

A positive evolution in the application of the principle of gradualism has recently emerged in Czech jurisprudence.[56] The lack of adequate reasons for determining

[50] See REDIAL Research Report 2016/03 (n 12).

[51] For a detailed analysis on the risk of absconding, see more in M Moraru, 'Judicial Dialogue in Action: Making Sense of the Risk of Absconding in the Return Procedure', Chapter 5 in this volume.

[52] See G Cornelisse and J Bouwman, 'REDIAL National Synthesis Report – Netherlands, Termination of Illegal Stay', 2.

[53] Dutch Council of State, case 201201202/1/V4, 15 June 2012.

[54] See 'REDIAL National Synthesis Report – Netherlands' (n 52).

[55] See para 76(3) Aliens Police Act as amended by FLG I No 70/2015. Austrian High Administrative Court Ro 2014/21/0075, 19 February 2015.

[56] See REDIAL Research Report 2016/03 (n 12).

a risk of absconding for refusing to allow voluntary departure is recognised as a legitimate ground for quashing the administrative order for removal.[57]

Several Member States consider the lack of a passport or the lack of identity documents in general as a reason justifying the existence of a risk of absconding. In the case of *Re Rita Kumah*, a Cypriot court even confirmed the consequence that 'that detention is necessary for as long as there is a risk of absconding and there is a risk of absconding in this case because the applicant did not have a passport or a residence permit'.[58] In Cyprus, it is extremely rare that third-country nationals are granted voluntary departure as an inherent risk of absconding is supposed. The law does not specify objective criteria in order to determine the risk of absconding or other factors that may restrict or condition the voluntary return. A French judgment concluded that if a third-country national has already been subject to a removal order, he or she cannot benefit from a period for voluntary departure.[59] The Bulgarian Supreme Court decided that irregular entry and the lack of personal identification documents justifies not granting a period for voluntary departure.[60] Hungarian case-law reveals that the lack of a travel document and return ticket, or the financial means to buy a ticket, justifies not granting a period for voluntary departure.[61] These court cases show that national courts have not interpreted the requirements established by the Return Directive for the existence of a risk of absconding in a way which is in conformity with the Directive.

The Proposal for a recast of the Return Directive mentions in the Preamble that the new Directive should set out specific criteria establishing a ground for a rebuttable presumption of an existing risk of absconding. Union-wide objective criteria should apply for the determination whether a risk exists. The determination should ensure 'clearer and more effective rules for granting a period for voluntary departure and detaining a third-country national'.[62] The criteria are enumerated in the proposed Article 6. Many criteria already established by national law are included in the list. Non-compliance with a return decision, including an obligation to return within the period for voluntary departure, is one criterion mentioned. When these criteria are included into the final text, their transposition and implementation in national law will be a future challenge for human rights protection.

[57] See 'REDIAL National Synthesis Report – Czech Republic' (n 34).

[58] Cypriot Supreme Court, *Re the application of Rita Kumah*, civil application no 198/2013 29 November 2013. See also 'REDIAL National Synthesis Report – Cyprus, Termination of Illegal Stay' (n 28).

[59] See 'REDIAL National Synthesis Report – France, Termination of Illegal Stay' (n 36), CAA Lyon, 14LY01175, 6 January 2015.

[60] Bulgarian Supreme Administrative Court, *Salar Zangenhe v District Directorate of Border Police – Smolian*, 5673/2010, 10 January 2011.

[61] See B Nagy, 'REDIAL National Synthesis Report – Hungary, Termination of Illegal Stay', Hungarian Administrative and Labour Court of Budapest case 15.K.31.371/2013/5, 30 May 2013.

[62] Proposal (n 6).

ii. Application for a Legal Stay Dismissed as Manifestly Unfounded or Fraudulent

The reason that an application for a legal stay has been dismissed as manifestly unfounded or fraudulent does not play a crucial role in national practice.[63] National reports reveal that the judgments are mainly based on risk of absconding and national security. The conclusion that an application is manifestly unfounded or fraudulent is, however, taken into account when determining that the two other reasons are established, especially that a risk of absconding exists.

iii. Risk to Public policy, Public Security or National Security

In the case *Z Zh v Staatssecretaris van Veiligheid en Justitie and Staatssecretaris van Veiligheid en Justitie v I O*,[64] the CJEU was asked to clarify the notions risk to public policy, public security or national security. The court interpreted Article 7(4) of the Return Directive and concluded that national practice whereby an illegally staying third-country national is deemed to pose a risk to public policy on the 'sole ground' that he is 'suspected, or has been criminally convicted, of an act punishable as a criminal offence under national law cannot, in itself, justify a finding that that national poses a risk to public policy'.[65] According to this judgment, other factors, such as the nature and seriousness of the act, the time which has elapsed since it was committed and the fact that that national was in the process of leaving the territory of that Member State when he was detained by the national authorities, may be relevant in the assessment of the risk to public policy. Any matter which relates to the reliability of the suspicion is relevant to that assessment. According to the CJEU, legislation or practice of a Member State has to ensure that a case-by-case assessment is conducted of whether the refusal to grant a period for voluntary departure is compatible with that person's fundamental rights.[66]

The answers that the CJEU provided in the judgment *Z Zh* concerning the interpretation of the 'risk to public policy' made clear that Dutch law and policy with regard to the refusal of a period for voluntary departure contradicted Article 7(4) of the Return Directive.

[63] Hungarian jurisprudence shows that the fact that the applicant has made 'a series of applications in order to legalize his stay' was seen to justify forced removal as the person refused to leave the territory voluntarily and did not possess the financial means necessary to travel home and had no recourse to any means in order to be allowed to stay. Although the dismissal was not especially based on the reason manifestly unfounded or fraudulent, the reasoning was based on a similar consideration. See 'REDIAL National Synthesis Report – Hungary, Termination of Illegal Stay' (n 61), Hungarian Administrative and Labour Court of Budapest case 17.K.33.554/2013/2 29 November 2013.

[64] Case C-554/13 *Z Zh Staatssecretaris voor Veiligheid en Justitie and Staatssecretaris voor Veiligheid en Justitie v IO* ECLI:EU:C:2015:377.

[65] ibid, para 50.

[66] ibid, para 70.

G. Obligations During the Period for Voluntary Departure

Article 7(3) of the Return Directive provides for certain obligations that should secure voluntary departure and minimise the risk of absconding during voluntary departure.[67] These are regular reporting to the authorities, the deposit of an adequate financial guarantee, the submission of documents or the obligation to stay at a certain place. The purpose of imposing additional obligations is to allow a period for voluntary departure in cases that otherwise would not qualify for voluntary departure.[68] Preserving the voluntary departure measure, while requiring the third-country national to fulfil certain obligations during this period, is a compromise between ensuring the fulfilment of the objective of the Return Directive – effective removal – and the principles of 'voluntarism' and proportionality which govern the return procedure.[69] The possibility to impose additional obligations is contained in most national legislations. The Return Directive also provides for more lenient alternatives to detention if these measures are sufficient to secure the departure.[70] These measures may also be imposed in other phases of the return procedure. For instance, the risk of absconding is a reason for the supervision of voluntary departure but also for detention.

According to Italian legislation and practice, third-country nationals who are granted a period for voluntary departure have to comply with at least one obligation during that period.[71] National authorities do not need to prove a 'risk of absconding', since the risk is presumed ab initio when voluntary departure is conferred.[72] This practice contradicts the provisions of the Return Directive.

H. Facilitation of Voluntary Return by Member States

The Return Directive does not contain details on how the obligation to confer voluntary departure measures as the first step in return proceedings should be facilitated by Member States. Furthermore, the jurisprudence of the CJEU does not reveal further details, though – as mentioned above – the Court constantly stresses that voluntary departure should be the first step in return proceedings and should have priority.[73] Measures could comprise: issuance of a travel document and/or a *laissez passer*; contact and cooperation with countries of origin and third countries in order to support the issuance of return certificates or other

[67] See REDIAL Research Report 2016/03 (n 12).
[68] ibid.
[69] ibid.
[70] Art 15 of the Return Directive.
[71] See 'REDIAL National Synthesis Report – Italy' (n 27) and REDIAL Research Report 2016/03 (n 12).
[72] See A di Pascale, 'Can a Justice of Peace be a Good Detention Judge? The Case of Italy', Chapter 13 in this Volume.
[73] *El Dridi* (n 5).

documents; organisation and preparation of the return and also the investigation of whether the person will be accepted and has the possibility to live in the country of origin in a humane surrounding and in dignity at the time of return. Incentives for voluntary departure could also be a possibility to assist third-country nationals in preparation for the return and helping them to adapt to the life in the country of origin again.

The Return Handbook refers to some questions concerning these practical arrangements of voluntary return, mainly with regard to the transit through other Member States. The Commission recommends that Member States should recognise the return decision issued by another Member State and the period for voluntary departure granted in that decision. Neither the issuance of a (transit) visa nor of a *laissez passer* are considered to be suitable options for the facilitation of transit through another Member State.[74] The Commission draws the conclusion that returnees intending to transit through another Member State whilst leaving the territory of the EU by land run the risk of being apprehended by the police of this Member State. This consequence runs contrary to the policy objective to encourage voluntary departure.

As the Return Directive prioritises voluntary return, Member States have to facilitate the return by issuing the necessary documentation. As such, binding provisions should be adopted to achieve the aim of voluntary return by facilitating transit through EU Member States. The Proposal for a recast of the Return Directive, however, does not establish such obligations and misses the opportunity to extend the possibilities for voluntary return.

III. Jurisprudence of the CJEU and Judicial Dialogue with National Courts

National courts have brought questions with regard to the interpretation of provisions related to the return decision to the CJEU; referring courts have not directly asked for an interpretation of the norms on voluntary departure. The CJEU has confirmed in several judgments that voluntary departure is the preferred aim and has priority over forced return.[75] In its jurisprudence, the Court interpreted the

[74] See Return Handbook (n 3) 38: 'Issuing a transit visa to the returnee would be an inappropriate and inadequate solution, since granting a visa to illegally staying third-country nationals who are obliged to leave would be contrary to EU rules on visa. Moreover transit Member States do not seem to have any incentive to issue such kind of visa (risk that persons may abscond and/or cause removal costs) and would in practice therefore frequently refuse issuing the visa. Providing for a "European laissez-passer" for the returnee does not offer a solution either: In the absence of a clearly defined legal nature and legal effects of such a "laissez-passer" the returnee would – strictly legally speaking – still be considered as "illegally staying" in the transit State and might therefore be subject of a new return decision in accordance with Article 6(1).'

[75] *El Dridi* (n 5) para 36: 'priority is to be given, except where otherwise provided for, to voluntary compliance with the obligation resulting from that return decision.'

Return Directive, clarified its purpose, and also stressed that rights of persons in the return proceedings must be assessed in the light of the objective of the Directive. In initial judgments, reference was mainly made to the objective to guarantee effective return.[76] In later judgments, the Court made more nuanced statements[77] with regard to human rights obligations of Member States and pointed to the underlying value of human dignity. The CJEU explicitly referred to Recitals 2 and 11 of the Preamble[78] and constantly emphasises the importance of human rights with regard to all measures in connection with return whilst also pointing to the objective of effective return. However, this effectiveness is understood as limited and governed by human rights safeguards.

Only few judgments of the CJEU refer to and interpret Member States' obligations directly related to voluntary return. The most important judgment with regard to procedural rights in connection with voluntary departure is the case of *Khaled Boudjlida v Préfet des Pyrénées-Atlantiques*.[79] In this judgment, the Court considered the circumstances for voluntary return in the course of examining questions with regard to the scope of the right to be heard.[80] The Court's conclusions are of general importance for the voluntary departure period. The Court decided that the authority must observe the obligations imposed by Article 5 of the Return Directive and hear the person concerned before a return decision is issued.[81] The CJEU specified that the right to be heard has to enable the person concerned to express his or her point of view on the detailed arrangements for the return, such as the period allowed for departure and whether return is to be voluntary or coerced. The Court drew this conclusion by interpreting Article 7 of the Return Directive in connection with the issuance of a return decision and procedural guarantees in this procedure.[82] The Court also referred to the EU Charter of Fundamental Rights (EUCFR).[83] This judgment makes clear that procedural guarantees also apply during the voluntary return phase and have to be guaranteed in all phases of the return procedure. The right to be heard should thus include the right of the returnee to express his or her opinion about the conditions and time limit for voluntary departure.

[76] C-249/13 *Khaled Boudjlida v Préfet des Pyrénées-Atlantiques* ECLI:EU:C:2014:2431, para 45. For the object and purpose of the Return Directive, see also case C-329/11 *Alexandre Achughbabian v Préfet du Val-de-Marne* ECLI:EU:C:2011:807, para 30 and *Zaizoune* (n 31) para 33.

[77] *Z Zh Staatssecretaris voor Veiligheid en Justitie* (n 64) para 47. See also C-146/14 PPU *Bashir Mohamed Ali Mahdi* ECLI:EU:C:2014:1320, para 38.

[78] *Mahdi*, ibid, para 38.

[79] *Khaled Boudjlida* (n 76) para 51.

[80] ibid, para 45. For the scope of the right to be heard in return procedures, see also C-166/13 *Sophie Mukarubega v Préfet de police and Préfet de la Seine-Saint-Denis* ECLI:EU:C:2014:2336, para 62. See also V Ilareva, 'The Right to Be Heard – The Underestimated Condition for Effective Returns and Human Rights Consideration', Chapter 15 in this volume.

[81] *Khaled Boudjlida* (n 76) paras 51–52.

[82] ibid, para 51.

[83] ibid, para 31: 'The right to be heard in all proceedings is now affirmed not only in Articles 47 and 48 of the Charter, which ensure respect for both the rights of the defence and the right to fair legal process in all judicial proceedings, but also in Article 41 of the Charter, which guarantees the right to good administration.'

The Court also mentioned the obligation of third-country nationals to cooperate. Only if all relevant information is provided the authority is able to decide by taking all relevant information into account. This information is necessary for the calculation and extension of the time limit for voluntary departure. It should include facts about the personal and family situation and, in particular, about any circumstance which might justify a return decision not being issued.[84] The obligation to cooperate is explicitly established in Article 7 of the Proposal for the recast of the Return Directive.[85]

The Return Directive does not provide for special procedural guarantees for the voluntary departure period. National laws have set up further standards and national jurisprudence has also referred to other procedural guarantees in return procedures. These are the right to a fair trial and also the right to an effective remedy in cases where international obligations or national law require such a remedy.[86] Furthermore, the authorities have to provide a substantiated reasoning for all decisions related to return including the period for voluntary departure. The use of standard forms and templates without adequate translation is a violation of procedural guarantees. Other legislations require free legal aid and assistance, qualified interpreters and a translation of decisions in a language understandable/spoken by the applicant.[87]

The other judgments by the CJEU with regard to voluntary departure deal with questions of admissible restrictions. The judgment *Z Zh v Staatssecretaris van Veiligheid en Justitie and Staatssecretaris van Veiligheid en Justitie v IO*[88] – as mentioned above – is of particular significance as it again stressed the importance of the human rights compatibility of legislation and measures in the return procedure. Furthermore, the Court pointed to the necessity for an individual assessment of all circumstances. Following this interpretation, a general rule that certain criminal offences stipulated in domestic law allow a forcible return without granting a period for voluntary departure is not allowed.

According to the Return Directive, the risk of absconding is a reason for attaching certain obligations to be complied with during the voluntary departure period, for shortening the voluntary departure period or refusing to confer a period for voluntary departure. The risk is also a reason for detention according to Article 15 of the Return Directive and is furthermore contained in the Dublin III Regulation. With regard to the latter, the CJEU found that detention in the absence of objective criteria determining the risk of absconding is not lawful.[89] The Court continued that measures on deprivation of liberty must be accessible, precise and foreseeable, as required by Article 6 of the EUCFR, interpreted in

[84] ibid, para 50.
[85] Proposal (n 6).
[86] See REDIAL Research Report 2016/03 (n 12).
[87] ibid.
[88] See *Z Zh* (n 64).
[89] Case C-528/15 *Policie ČR, Krajské ředitelství policie Ústeckého kraje, odbor cizinecké policie v Salah Al Chodor, Ajlin Al Chodor, Ajvar Al Chodor* ECLI:EU:C:2017:213.

light of the case-law of the ECtHR.[90] The Court concluded that Member States are required to establish objective criteria underlying the reasons for believing that a person may abscond.[91] As the system of the Return Directive is comparable to that of the Dublin III Regulation with regard to the consequence that the person has to leave the Member State, it is legitimate to draw the conclusion that the risk also has to be defined by objective criteria with regard to measures imposed based on the Return Directive.

The CJEU's clear statement with regard to the precedence of voluntary departure has had a considerable influence on national jurisprudence. It is a telling example of a direct and indirect vertical judicial dialogue. In 2011, shortly after the *El Dridi* judgment was published, the Italian Supreme Court of Cassation decided that a particular form of administrative expulsion containing a period of five days for voluntary departure might no longer be imposed.[92] According to the Italian court, such measures did not comply with the principles underlying the Directive, which was intended to facilitate voluntary departure and the gradual adoption of coercive measures. The Court referred to the CJEU's *El Dridi* judgment and ended administrative practice which was contradicting obligations contained in the Return Directive.[93]

The Bulgarian Supreme Administrative Court referred to the *El Dridi* judgment in the same way. Bulgarian law provides for a period for voluntary departure between 7 and 30 days. In practice, however, in the most common orders, called 'orders for coercive taking to the border', no time limits were granted.[94] In the case of *Dorofeev*, the Bulgarian Supreme Administrative Court decided that this was 'a violation of the material requisites of the law' and declared the order unlawful. The Court confirmed this conclusion in another case and specifically pointed to the fact that there were no reasons given and no reference to any of the grounds provided in national law for refraining from granting a period for voluntary departure.[95] The reasoning was based on the reasoning in the *El Dridi* judgment. The case is a further example of a judicial dialogue and an adaption of national practice extending the rights of returnees.

[90] ibid, para 28: 'This is the case with regard to Article 2(n) of the Dublin III Regulation, which explicitly requires that objective criteria defining the existence of a risk of absconding be "defined by law". Since those criteria have been established neither by that regulation nor in another EU legal act, the elaboration of those criteria, in the context of that regulation, is a matter for national law.'

[91] ibid, para 47.

[92] See Italian Supreme Court No 18481/2011, 8 September 2011.

[93] *El Dridi* (n 5).

[94] See V Ilareva, 'REDIAL National Synthesis Report – Bulgaria, Termination of Illegal Stay'.

[95] Bulgarian Supreme Administrative Court, *Hossam Eldin Elsaid Mohamed Hamada v The Director of Directorate "Migration" – Ministry of Interior*, case no 6339/20117 March 2012. Bulgarian Supreme Administrative Court, *Dorofeev v District directorate of Ministry of Interior – Vratza* case no 15505/2010 12 December 2011. Mr Dorofeev had served a punishment of imprisonment for crimes under the Penal Code with a cumulative penalty of three years and six months and therefore posed a risk to the public security. The decision, however, did not mention these reasons and thus the Court ruled that the lack of a period for voluntary compliance was in violation of the law.

A Greek decision[96] explicitly referred to the CJEU's reasoning in the *Khaled Boudjlida* judgment.[97] The Greek court decided that the applicant had not been heard in the procedure for a renewal of the residence permit, and this could have had an influence on the return decision. The Return Directive requires that the competent national authorities hear the view of third-country nationals concerning the right to family life and the obligations imposed by Article 5 of the Return Directive. In the Netherlands, the *Boudjlida* judgment has led to the expansion of the standard list of questions in hearings preceding the return decision.[98]

The Belgian Council for Alien Law Litigation requires that the right to be heard is respected in relation to each of the return-related decisions adopted by the administration.[99]

In Spain, the application of the rules for urgent proceedings reduced the rights of third-country nationals and deprived them of the opportunity to exit the country voluntarily and consequently avoid an entry ban. Only following the CJEU judgment in the *Zaizoune* case[100] and the subsequent amendment of Spanish legislation the situation changed. The *Zaizoune* judgment, however, only led to a slow and still incomplete change of practice.[101]

These examples clearly reveal that national courts have followed the interpretation developed in the jurisprudence of the CJEU with regard to the priority of voluntary departure and procedural guarantees. Judicial dialogue has led to an increase in protection of returnees.

IV. Measures to Support and Incentives for Voluntary Return

The Preamble of the Return Directive not only points to the fact that voluntary return should be promoted but also suggests that Member States should provide for enhanced return assistance and counselling as well as making best use of the relevant funding possibilities offered under the European Return Fund.[102] In contrast to the text of the Preamble, there are no obligations specified in the Articles dealing with voluntary return. National practice reports reveal that only a few Member States have provided for return support assistance programmes.[103]

[96] Greek Administrative Court of First Instance of Thessaloniki, *Leonard Koleci v Minister of Interior*, 717/2015, 27 April 2015.

[97] *Khaled Boudjlida* (n 76) para 51. The Return Handbook (n 3) also refers to the right to be heard.

[98] ibid. EMN study (n 16) 71.

[99] Belgium Council for Alien Law Litigation, 128.272 of 27.8.2014. See also L Leboeuf and H Gribomont 'REDIAL National Synthesis Report – Belgium, Termination of Illegal Stay'.

[100] *Zaizoune* (n 31).

[101] See C Gortázar Rotaeche, 'REDIAL National Synthesis Report – Spain, Termination of Illegal Stay'. See by the same author, 'Return Decisions and Domestic Judicial Practices' (n 11).

[102] As the focus of this contribution is judicial dialogue regarding voluntary return, support programmes are not dealt with in detail.

[103] Initially Member States made little use of available funds and did not use the money for creating an environment for encouraging voluntary departure. Only recent developments and initiatives launched

Several Commission documents propose measures which should support voluntary return and make it more attractive. For instance, the 2017 renewed Commission Action Plan highlights the importance of measures, projects and programmes for voluntary return. The Action Plan also identifies that the effectiveness of return programmes requires common standards and should not be left to the discretion of Member States. A set of common standards was summarised in the Guidelines on the use of Assisted Voluntary Return and Reintegration Programmes, endorsed by the Council on 9 June 2016.[104]

The Proposal for a recast of the Return Directive focuses on an extended support for voluntary return and sets an obligation for Member States to establish voluntary return programmes. The text provides for establishing a framework for the granting of financial, material and in-kind assistance to create incentives for voluntary return and support return.[105] The establishment of such return programmes has the potential to make voluntary return more attractive and to support the reintegration of third-country nationals in the country of origin. Such return programmes are to be preferred over enforced return.

V. Concluding Remarks

Although the primary role of voluntary departure within return proceedings is clearly outlined in the Preamble, the text of the Return Directive shows the compromise reached during negotiations. Namely, the Directive prioritises voluntary return but equally stresses that an effective enforcement of return decisions should be secured. The jurisprudence of the CJEU has interpreted the aims of the Directive and has clearly established that the Directive provides for stages in the return, starting from voluntary departure 'to measures which restrict that liberty the most, namely detention in a specialised facility'.[106] On the other hand, the jurisprudence also stresses the obligations of third-country nationals to cooperate.

Procedural guarantees, eg the right to be heard, are not explicitly mentioned in the Return Directive with regard to the voluntary departure phase. The CJEU, however, has clearly established the obligation of Member States to allow the returnee to express his or her opinion about all decisive elements with regard to voluntary return, such as the time limit, the personal situation, and the obligations

by the Commission led to the establishment of new programmes, projects and incentives for return. The REDIAL National Synthesis Reports, First Package of the REDIAL Project from 2016, revealed that only a few of the Member States provided for return support assistance.

[104] Council of the EU, 'Non-Binding Common Standards for Assisted Voluntary Return (and Reintegration) Programmes Implemented by Member States' 11 May 2016, Council document 8829/16. These standards were endorsed by the Council in its 'Conclusions on the Return and Readmission of Illegally Staying Third-Country Nationals', 9 June 2016.

[105] Proposal (n 6).

[106] *El Dridi* (n 5) para 41.

imposed during the period allowed for voluntary return. The Court has decided that the authority must observe the obligations imposed by Article 5 of the Return Directive and hear the person concerned before a return decision is issued.[107] These conclusions are of general importance for the voluntary departure period.[108] However, the Proposal for a recast of the Return Directive does not explicitly include procedural guarantees with regard to voluntary departure and misses the opportunity to follow the requirements established by the jurisprudence. On the other hand, the obligation of third-country nationals to cooperate with regard to the facilitation of their voluntary return, which was also elaborated by jurisprudence, is now explicitly established in Article 7 of the Proposal for the recast of the Return Directive.[109]

National jurisprudence has clarified the provisions of the Return Directive with regard to the start of the period for voluntary departure and has established clear conditions for returnees, as the time limit only starts when the person is able to prepare departure. There is, however, no indication of a formal judicial dialogue between national courts. The Proposal for a recast of the Directive does not define the start of the period either.

This chapter referred to national practice and showed that such practice is not, or has not been, in line with the concept of the Return Directive, even violating Directive obligations. National courts have interpreted the Return Directive and decided that national law violates provisions of the Directive, whereas others have confirmed an interpretation which contradicts obligations contained in the Directive. A number of alleged violations still need to be brought before national courts and/or referred to the CJEU. Several national courts have decided that the provisions of the Return Directive require an amendment of law or practice, revealing that national jurisprudence can have a considerable influence on national legislation and on the correct transposition and implementation of this Directive.

[107] *Khaled Boudjlida* (n 76) paras 51–52.

[108] ibid, para 45. For the scope of the right to be heard in return procedures, see also *Mukarubega* (n 80) para 62.

[109] Proposal (n 6).

4

The Legal Requirements of the Entry Ban: The Role of National Courts and Dialogue with the Court of Justice of the European Union

ANIEL PAHLADSINGH

I. Introduction

This chapter analyses the legal requirements of the entry ban set out in Directive 2008/115/EC (the Return Directive)[1] and the role of courts in interpreting this Directive and filling any gaps it contains. According to Article 3(6) of the Return Directive, an entry ban is 'an administrative or judicial decision or act prohibiting entry into and stay on the territory of the Member States for a specified period, accompanying a return decision'. Pursuant to Article 11(1) of the Directive, return decisions must be accompanied by entry bans if: (i) no period for voluntary departure has been granted; or (ii) the obligation to return has not been complied with. In all other cases, return decisions may be accompanied by entry bans.

Article 11(2) of the Directive provides that the length of entry bans should be determined based on all relevant circumstances of the individual case of the third-country national concerned and should not, in principle, exceed five years.[2] Exceptionally, this period may be extended where a third-country national represents a serious threat to public policy, public security or national security. An entry ban is intended to have preventive effects regarding the illegal stay of third-country nationals and to foster the credibility of EU return policy by sending a clear message to those who disregard migration rules in EU Member States that they will not be allowed to re-enter any EU Member State for a specified period.[3]

[1] [2008] OJ L348, 24 December, 98.

[2] See also Recital 14 of the preamble of the Return Directive.

[3] Commission Recommendation (EU) 2017/2338 of 16 November 2017 establishing a common 'Return Handbook' to be used by Member States' competent authorities when carrying out return-related tasks, C/2017/6505 [2017] OJ L339, 42.

The text of the Directive saw a number of significant changes during the often polemic negotiating process, which lasted for more than three years and attracted fierce criticism from various non-governmental organisations as well as several governments of Latin American countries.[4] Not all aspects regarding the entry ban made it into the Directive's provisions.[5] Among the issues not covered by the Return Directive, the following can be mentioned: the legal consequences of breaching an entry ban;[6] the time from which an entry ban takes effect; and the relationship between the Return Directive and other EU instruments regarding the entry ban. Specific questions also arose regarding the interpretation of terms mentioned in Article 11 of the Return Directive, such as the duration of the entry ban and the interpretation of 'serious threat to public policy, public security or national security'. However, as these issues were raised in practice, they had to be resolved by national courts. National courts initiated a prolific vertical dialogue with the CJEU on these issues via the preliminary ruling procedure. The national courts play a crucial role in interpreting and applying EU law and have a responsibility to ensure that the preliminary ruling procedure works as efficiently and effectively as possible.[7] In this chapter, Dutch case-law is preponderant as the national courts in the Netherlands were very active in entering into direct dialogue with the CJEU on the entry ban provisions of the Return Directive.

This chapter analyses the role of national courts, sometimes in cooperation with the CJEU, in the interpretation of the entry ban mentioned in the Return Directive.[8] Interpretation is crucial for the application of law.[9] Judicial dialogue

[4] See K Hailbronner (ed), *EU Immigration and Asylum Law – Commentary, Germany* (Munich, Verlag CH Beck, 2010) 1506. For an overview of the Latin-American reactions, see http://aei.pitt.edu/15101/1/latin-american-reactions-adoption-returns-directive.pdf. See also F Lutz, 'Prologue: The Genesis of the EU's Return Policy', this volume.

[5] For a more detailed description, see: F Lutz, *The Negotiations on the Return Directive. Comments and Materials* (Nijmegen, Wolf Legal Publishers, 2010) 17–80; D Acosta, 'The Good, the Bad and the Ugly in EU Migration Law: Is the European Parliament Becoming Bad and Ugly? (The Adoption of Directive 2008/15: The Returns Directive)' (2009) 11(1) *European Journal of Migration and Law* 31.

[6] On the penalising breach of entry bans, see G Cornelisse, 'The Scope of the Return Directive: How Much Space is left for National Procedural Law on Irregular Migration?', Chapter 1 in this volume. See also J Waasdorp and A Pahladsingh, 'Expulsion or Imprisonment? Criminal Law Sanctions for Breaching an Entry Ban in the Light of Crimmigration Law' (2016) 4(2) *Bergen Journal of Criminal Law and Criminal Justice* 247 A Pahladsingh and J Waasdorp, 'Criminal Law Sanctions and the Return Directive: The Position of Illegally Staying Third-Country Nationals in the European Union' [2017] no 1 *Crimmigratie & Recht* 20.

[7] S Prechal, 'Communication Within the Preliminary Rulings Procedures – Responsibilities of the National Courts' (2014) 21 *Maastricht Journal of European and Comparative Law* 757.

[8] More about CJEU case-law and the entry ban: A Pahladsingh and J Waasdorp, *Crimmigration Law in the European Union: The Return Directive and the Entry Ban* (Oisterwijk, Wolf Legal Publishers, 2016).

[9] See J d'Aspremont, 'The Systemic Integration of International Law by Domestic Courts: Domestic Courts as Architects of the Consistency of the International Legal Order' in OK Fauchald and A Nollkaemper (eds), *The Practice of International and National Courts and the De-Fragmentation of International Law* (Oxford, Hart Publishing, 2012) 141, 141 with further references. According to G Scelle, 'il n'y a pas d'application sans interprétation', see *Précis de droit des gens: principes et systématique*, vol 2 (Paris, Sirey, 1934) 488.

has been hailed as an important tool for regulating competing jurisdictions between courts, both domestic and international,[10] as well as for the interpretation of international law in national courts.[11] This chapter discusses the following legal requirements of the entry ban, in which the judicial dialogue of the courts played an important role: the grounds for an entry ban (section II); the starting point of the validity of an entry ban (section III); the duration of an entry ban (section IV); the sanctions for breaching an entry ban (section V); and the relation between the entry ban and other instruments (section VI); followed by conclusions (section VII).

II. Grounds for Issuing an Entry Ban

Article 11(1) of the Return Directive provides that an entry ban must be issued if: (1) no period for voluntary departure has been granted, as set out by Article 7(4) of the Directive, where the person concerned represents a risk to public policy, public security or national security, if there is a risk of absconding, or if an application for a legal stay has been dismissed as manifestly unfounded or fraudulent; or (2) if the obligation to return has not been complied with (ie if return has not taken place within the period for voluntary departure set by Article 7(1)).

In all other cases an entry ban may accompany a return decision.[12] The Return Directive distinguishes between mandatory and optional entry bans.[13] This implies that an entry ban may also be foreseen even if the person departed voluntarily. However, Member States enjoy discretion in this respect and are encouraged to exercise this discretion in a way that encourages voluntary departure.[14] A majority of Member States impose entry bans automatically in the cases foreseen by Article 11(1) of the Directive.[15] The legislation of most Member States imposes an

[10] See generally CPR Romano, 'Deciphering the Grammar of the International Jurisprudential Dialogue' (2009) 41 *New York University Journal of International Law & Policy* 755.

[11] A Tzanakopoulos, 'Judicial Dialogue as a Means of Interpretation', Oxford Legal Studies Research Paper 71/2014, 72.

[12] More about CJEU case-law and the return decision: A Pahladsingh, *Crimmigration Law in the European Union (Part 2). The Return Directive: Return Decision and Detention* (Oisterwijk: Wolf Legal Publishers, 2016).

[13] In the Netherlands there is a distinction between what is in administrative practice called a 'heavy' and a 'light' entry ban. A 'heavy' entry ban relates to the 'dangerousness of the public order threat', while 'light' entry bans are all the other entry bans taken for another reason. This distinction is interesting because it has consequence for the power of the administration. The administration is obliged to order a light entry ban, but regarding a heavy entry ban there has to be a weighing of the interests. See M Moraru and G Renaudiere, 'REDIAL Electronic Journal on Judicial Interaction and the EU Return Policy: First Edition: Articles 7 to 11 of the Return Directive', REDIAL Research Report, 2016/02.

[14] See Case C-61/11 PPU *El Dridi* ECLI:EU:C:2011:268.

[15] The effectiveness of return in EU Member States, Synthesis Report for the EMN Focussed Study, 2017: BE, EL, ES, FI, FR, HR, LT, NL, SE, SI, SK, while four Member States (CZ, EE, ES, HR, and IT) automatically imposed an entry ban with all return decisions issued.

entry ban if the person concerned presented a risk of absconding.[16] The wording of the grounds for issuing an entry ban are clear in the Directive. The shortcoming in practice is related to inadequate implementation at the domestic level.

The proposal of the European Commission to amend the Return Directive includes a new Article 13 which allows Member States to impose an entry ban without issuing a return decision following a case-by-case assessment and taking into account the principle of proportionality.[17] The question in practice is whether police or border guards will be competent and able to carry out such assessments.

A. Risk to Public Policy, Public Security or National Security

Article 11(2) of the Return Directive, regarding the entry ban, does not define the term 'serious threat to public policy, public security or national security'. According to the European Commission, the CJEU case-law on the use of this term in other migration directives and in the free-movement context does not directly apply here, since the issues at stake and the context are different.[18]

The term 'serious threat to public policy, public security or national security' was not included in Dutch legislation as a ground for imposing an entry ban. If a third-country national poses a serious threat, however, the Dutch authorities may decide not to award a period for voluntary departure. This means that the person must leave the Netherlands immediately and that an entry ban will be imposed. In the Netherlands there has been a discussion in the case-law when an entry ban is imposed for five years or longer and the third-country national poses a serious threat to public policy, public security or national security as to how this criteria should be interpreted. The public order concept is important regarding the entry ban for two reasons. First, the existence of a such a threat is a reason for not conferring a period for voluntary departure, thus leading to a mandatory entry ban. Second, an entry ban, normally limited to a maximum of five years,

[16] The effectiveness of return in EU Member States, Synthesis Report for the EMN Focussed Study, 2017: BE, CZ, EE, EL, FI, FR, HR, LU, MT, NL, SI, SE, and SK. In other Member States, the risk of absconding, whilst not being explicitly mentioned in national legislation as grounds for imposing an entry ban, can be taken into account indirectly when assessing the individual circumstances of the case (AT, LT) or when adopting a return decision which is accompanied by an entry ban (LV).

[17] European Commission, Proposal for a Directive of the European Parliament and of the Council on common standards and procedures in Member States for returning illegally staying third-country nationals (recast), COM(2018) 634 final, 8. Art 13(2): 'Member States may impose an entry ban, which does not accompany a return decision, to a third-country national who has been illegally staying in the territory of the Member States and whose illegal stay is detected in connection with border checks carried out at exit in accordance with Article 8 of Regulation (EU) 2016/399, where justified on the basis of the specific circumstances of the individual case and taking into account the principle of proportionality' (hereinafter 'Proposal').

[18] Commission Recommendation (EU) 2017/2338 of 16 November 2017 establishing a common 'Return Handbook' to be used by Member States' competent authorities when carrying out return-related tasks, C/2017/6505 [2017] OJ L339, 44 (hereinafter 'Return Handbook').

can only be extended if there is a 'serious threat' to public policy, public security or national security. According to the CJEU in *Zh and O*, the concept of public order in Article 7(4) 'presupposes, in any event, the existence, in addition to the perturbation of the social order which any infringement of the law involves, of a genuine, present and sufficiently serious threat affecting one of the fundamental interests of society'.[19]

The Court of Appeal in Amsterdam, when judging the criminal consequences of the breach of an entry ban, assumes that the interpretation given by the CJEU of Article 7 (4) of the Return Directive is guiding for the interpretation of Article 11(2) of that Directive.[20] The administrative courts were divided on whether the judgment of the CJEU in *Zh and O*[21] also applies to the interpretation of the term 'serious threat to public order' applicable to entry bans.[22] On 2 June 2016, in higher appeal, the Council of State considered that the interpretation of the judgment in *Zh and O* also applies to the issuance of an entry ban for more than five years.[23] The highest administrative court reached the same outcome as the criminal appeal court. Later, this view was confirmed also by the Supreme Court in criminal cases.[24] In an exercise of *horizontal* dialogue, the administrative and criminal courts in the Netherlands concluded from the judgment in *Zh and O* that an entry ban issued on the ground of public order requires that there is a real, current and sufficiently serious threat to a fundamental interest of society. They did not address a preliminary reference on this matter to the CJEU as they considered it was clear in the case-law of the CJEU.[25]

[19] Case C-554/13 *Zh and O* ECLI:EU:C:2015:377, para 60.

[20] Gerechtshof Amsterdam, 17 November 2015, ECLI:NL:GHAMS:2015:4751; Gerechtshof Amsterdam, 16 December 2015, ECLI:NL:GHAMS:2015:5264.

[21] In *Zh and O* the CJEU has ruled on the concept of 'danger to public order' for return decisions, as referred to in Art 7(4) of the Return Directive. According to the CJEU this concept must be interpreted as meaning that the personal conduct of the foreign national concerned must represent a genuine, current and sufficiently serious threat that is detrimental to society's fundamental interests. In the Netherlands, the *Zh and O* CJEU ruling has had consequences on the periods for voluntary departure and issuance of entry bans. When imposing an entry ban of more than two years, the additional criterion must also be taken into consideration of a 'genuine, present and sufficiently serious threat affecting one of the fundamental interests of society'. The threshold for imposing entry bans of over two years has thus become higher.

[22] Rb Den Haag, zp Roermond, 13 October 2015, ECLI:NL:RBDHA:2015:11719; Rb Den Haag, 10 December 2015, ECLI:NL:RBDHA:2015:14353. For more about this subject, see J Waaasdorp and A Pahladsingh, *Het inreisverbod, over de doorwerking van deze Unierechtelijke maatregel in het vreemdelingenstrafrecht* (Den Haag, SDU uitgeverij, 2018) 135–37.

[23] Afdeling Bestuursrechtspraak van de Raad van State (ABRvS), 2 June 2016, ECLI:NL:RVS:2016:1550. For more about public order in Dutch migration law, see ACVZ, *Gewogen gevaar. De belangenafweging in het vreemdelingenrechtelijke openbare-ordebeleid* (Den Haag, 2018) available at www.acvz.nl; A Pahladsingh, '25 jaar Unieburgerschap, De complexiteit van openbare orde' [2018] July *Asiel &MigrantenRecht* 322.

[24] Hoge Raad (HR), 14 February 2017, ECLI:NL:HR:2017:239. See also HR 28 March 2013, ECLI:NL:HR:2017:527.

[25] A Pahladsingh and J Waasdorp, 'Het inreisverbod en de openbare orde: een interne rechtsvergelijking tussen het vreemdelingenrecht en het strafrecht' [2016] *Journaal Vreemdelingenrecht* 81.

III. Starting Point Validity of an Entry Ban: The CJEU Judgment in the Case of *Ouhrami*[26]

The Return Directive does not specify the starting point for calculating the period of application of the entry ban. In the Netherlands, the Council of State – the highest administrative court – judged that it starts only when the illegal third-country national has fulfilled his obligation to return to a third country.[27] This requires departure from the territory of the Member States.[28] The Supreme Court also had to pronounce on the matter as breaches of entry bans are a criminal offence in the Netherlands.[29] The Supreme Court initially followed this view, in a horizontal dialogue with the Dutch Council of State.[30] However, the Supreme Court decided on 29 March 2016 to make a reference to the CJEU on the starting point, based on an opinion of Advocate General Spronken. She argued that there was no clarity in Dutch literature about this question,[31] and compared six Member States' legislation and practice, which showed different points for the beginning of the entry ban period.[32] The case originated in criminal proceedings against Mr Mossa Ouhrami, an Algerian national who was declared undesirable in 2002 and thus under an obligation to leave the Netherlands, failing which he could be removed, and barred from re-entering for 10 years. Mr Ouhrami submitted, on appeal to the Supreme Court, that the lower court had erred in convicting him, because the decision declaring him undesirable had ceased to produce legal effects. Therefore, it had to be regarded as equivalent to an entry

[26] Case C-225/16 *Ouhrami* ECLI:EU:C:2017:590.

[27] Pursuant to Art 66a(4) of the Vreemdelingenwet 2000, the duration of the entry ban is calculated with effect from the date on which the foreign national has actually left the Netherlands.

[28] ABRvS 6 February 2013, ECLI:NL:RVS:2013:BZ2342; ABRvS 16 April 2014, ECLI:NL:RVS:2014:1434; ABRvS 31 July 2014, ECLI:NL:RVS:2014:2960.

[29] See Art 197 Criminal Code.

[30] HR 21 May 2013, ECLI:NL:HR:2013:BZ3930.

[31] According to the first stream, the duration of the entry ban starts at the moment the entry ban is established or promulgated: P Boeles, *Jurisprudentie Vreemdelingenrecht* 2014/388; A Klip, *Nederlandse Jurisprudentie* 2015/24; J Altena-Davidsen, 'Europees strafrecht' [2015] *Delikt & Delikwent*; GML Sieben, *Kroniek van het strafrecht* (Deventer, Kluwer, 2014); N Ros, 'De jurisprudentie van de Hoge Raad over de strafvervolging en strafoplegging wegens overtreding van artikel 197 Sr beoordeeld in het licht van het Europese recht' [2015] *Tijdschrift Praktijkwijzer Strafrecht*. The second movement is based on the view that the duration of the entry ban only starts when the foreign national has actually returned to a third country: J Waasdorp and A Pahladsingh 'Rechtseenheid in het vreemdelingenstrafrecht? Over (de aanvang van) de duur van het inreisverbod' [2015] *Nederlands Juristenblad*; J Waasdorp and A Pahladsingh, 'Effectief terugkeerbeleid. Wanneer vangt de duur van een inreisverbod aan?' [2016] *Nederlands Juristen Blad*.

[32] Opinion Spronken PHR 17 March 2015, ECLI:NL:PHR:2015:776. For example, the duration of an entry ban in France and Belgium will start on the date of service on the illegal third-country national. In the Czech Republic, the date of commencement must be stated in the entry ban, failing which the duration will start at the moment that the entry ban has become irrevocable. In the Netherlands, Germany and Switzerland the term starts to run when the illegal third-country national has actually left the territory. In Denmark there are even different moments. See more MF Wijngaarden, 'Ouhrami: Hoe een vasthoudende advocaat-generaal de wetgever liet verrassen' [2018] *Crimmigratie & Recht*.

ban, which could not exceed five years pursuant to Article 11(2) of the Return Directive.

The CJEU disagreed with the argument of Denmark that the determination of the starting point of the entry ban period should be left to the discretion of each Member State.[33] According to the CJEU, as is apparent from Recital 14 of the Directive, the purpose of introducing an entry ban applicable in all Member States is to give a European dimension to the effects of national return measures.[34]

With reference to the wording, general scheme and objectives of the Return Directive, the CJEU held that issuing a return decision and issuing an entry ban must be regarded as separate decisions.[35] Consequently, until the return is voluntarily complied with or enforced, the illegal stay of the person concerned is governed by the return decision and not by the entry ban. Only when the person concerned has left the territory of the Member States must the entry ban period begin.[36] If it were to begin before then, a third-country national who refuses to cooperate in a removal procedure could avoid, in whole or in part, the legal effects of an entry ban.[37]

The CJEU reiterated that as Mr Ouhrami did not leave the Netherlands following the adoption of the decision declaring him undesirable, consequently the obligation to return prescribed by that decision was never fulfilled.[38] Therefore, his unlawful situation was a consequence of an initial illegal stay and not of a subsequent illegal stay which resulted from breaching an entry ban.[39]

In the *Ouhrami* judgment, the CJEU replied that an entry ban starts at the moment the person concerned actually complies with his return obligation. This confirms the settled case-law of the Council of State and the Supreme Court discussed above. In the final judgment of 14 November 2017, the Supreme Court followed the judgment of the CJEU and sentenced Ouhrami to two months in prison.[40]

This ruling will have to lead to legislative changes in a number of Member States. It also prompts questions about which party will have to bear the burden of proof: either third-country nationals or the national authorities will have to prove that the person concerned has left the territory on a specific date to calculate whether the entry ban is still valid. Finland and Sweden added that they are currently working on adapting their practices to the *Ouhrami* judgment.[41]

[33] *Ouhrami* (n 26) para 40.
[34] ibid, para 41.
[35] ibid, para 50.
[36] ibid, para 51.
[37] ibid, para 52.
[38] ibid, para 55.
[39] ibid, paras 56–57.
[40] HR 14 november 2017, ECLI:NL:HR:2017:2862.
[41] The effectiveness of return in EU Member States, Synthesis Report for the EMN Focussed Study, 2017, 83.

In Belgium too the immigration law has to be changed so that the entry ban enters into effect the day on which the decision regarding the entry ban is served.[42]

After the *Ouhrami* judgment, the question was raised in the Netherlands as to whether prosecution is still possible of a suspect against whom an entry ban has been issued but who has never actually left.[43] The clear distinction made by the CJEU between the return decision and the entry ban means, according to Cornelisse,[44] that the criminal prosecution of an illegally staying third-country national who has not yet left the Netherlands cannot be based solely on the existence of an entry ban, which at that time had no legal effects.[45] The Procureur Général at the Supreme Court recently advised the Court to ask a preliminary question regarding the criminalisation of breaches of entry ban.[46] The Supreme Court made this reference to the CJEU on 27 November 2018.[47] When transposing the Return Directive, the Dutch legislator opted not to make illegal stay as such a criminal offence, but only illegal stay when an entry ban has been issued.

IV. Duration of an Entry Ban: The Impact of the *Filev and Osmani* Preliminary Ruling[48]

Article 11(2) of the Return Directive provides that the length of entry bans should be based on all relevant circumstances of the individual case and should not, in principle, exceed five years. Exceptionally, this period may be extended where a third-country national represents a serious threat to public policy, public or national security.

The Amtsgericht Laufen in Germany made a request during criminal proceedings against Messrs Filev and Osmani, nationals of the former Yugoslav Republic of Macedonia and of the Republic of Serbia, respectively. Filev and Osmani were expelled from Germany in the 1990s and received entry bans of unlimited

[42] A Pahladsingh, 'Note CJEU 26 July 2017, Case 225/16, *Ouhrami*' [2018] no 3 *Tijdschrift voor Vreemdelingenrecht* 270–74: Art 74/11, § 3 Verblijfswet has to be changed.

[43] G Cornelisse, 'Inreisverboden die (nog) geen rechtsgevolgen hebben. Geen wettelijke grondslag voor de strafvervolging van een vreemdeling die Nederland nog niet verlaten heeft' [2017] *Nederlands Juristenblad* 2818; H Battjes et al, 'Kroniek van het migratierecht' [2017] *Nederlands Juristenblad* 2602; TNBM Spronken and M ter Heide, 'Is de ene vraag beantwoord, doemt er weer een andere op – De Terugkeerrichtlijn' [2017] *NBSTRAF*. See also Opinion AG Spronken PHR 17 October 2017, ECLI:NL:PHR:2017:1240; Opinion AG Vellinga PHR 21 November 2017 ECLI:NL:PHR:2017:1449.

[44] Cornelisse, ibid. For another view, see F Heinink and M Bouma, 'Inreisverbod-rechtens relevant vanaf uitvaardiging' [2018] no 3 *Journaal Vreemdelingenrecht* 34.

[45] I also note that in the Dutch Aliens Act, Art 108(6) Vw 2000, there is the possibility for prosecution in the situation of a light entry ban. The same question can arise then before the aminsitrative courts.

[46] See opinion PG Silvis 18 September 2018, ECLI:NL:PHR:2018:1019.

[47] HR 27 November 2018, ECLI:NL:HR:2018:2192. This reference is still pending at the CJEU and is registered there as Case 806/18, *JZ*.

[48] Case C-297/12 *Filev and Osmani* ECLI:EU:C:2013:569. See more in the REDIAL Research Report, 2016/02 (n 13) 13.

duration. Although they were informed of their right under German law to apply for a time limit to the entry bans, they did not exercise this right. They returned to Germany in April 2012 and were prosecuted for breach of their entry bans.

Article 11(2) of the Return Directive had direct effect in Germany between 24 December 2010, the deadline laid down in Article 20(1) for its transposition into national law, and 26 November 2011, when the law of 22 November 2011 implementing the Directive took effect. Accordingly, expulsion or removal orders made more than five years before 24 December 2010 could no longer serve as a basis for a criminal conviction pursuant to Article 95 of the Aufenthaltsgesetz. The Amtsgericht Laufen also noted that Article 11(1) of that law does not provide for the effects of such orders to be limited in time, but only for the interested party to make an application seeking such a limit. The referring court stated that Mr Filev does not appear to pose a serious threat to public policy, public security or national security within the meaning of the second sentence of Article 11(2) of the Return Directive. However, he did not apply for the expulsion and removal orders made against him to be limited in time, as a consequence of which those orders have been producing effects for close to 20 years. The referring court noted that Article 95(2) of the Aufenthaltsgesetz makes Mr Osmani subject to sanctions as a result of his entry into Germany following his expulsion in 1999 or his removal in 2004, and that Article 2(2)(b) of the Return Directive permits Member States to decide not to apply that Directive where a person's return is consequent to a criminal sanction. However, the court noted that no derogation was adopted in German law pursuant to that provision while the Directive had direct effect in Germany, but that one was introduced by Article 11(1) of the Aufenthaltsgesetz as amended by the law of 22 November 2011.

First, the CJEU concluded that Article 11(2) of the Return Directive must be interpreted as precluding a provision such as Article 11(1) of the Aufenthaltsgesetz, which makes the limitation of the length of an entry ban conditional on applying for it. Second, the CJEU ruled that Article 11(2) must be interpreted as precluding a breach of an entry ban in the territory of a Member State that was issued more than five years before the date either of the re-entry into that territory of the third-country national concerned or of the entry into force of the national legislation implementing that Directive from giving rise to a criminal law sanction, unless that national constitutes a serious threat to public order, public security or national security.[49]

According to Article 2(2)(b), Member States may decide not to apply the Return Directive to third-country nationals who are subject to return as a criminal law sanction or as a consequence of a criminal law sanction, according to national law, or who are the subject of extradition procedures. In the *Filev and Osmani* case the order was based on a criminal law sanction within the meaning of Article 2(2)(b). Germany exercised its discretion under that provision.[50]

[49] *Filev and Osmani*, ibid, paras 44–45.
[50] ibid, paras 50–52.

The consequence of the use by the Member States of the discretion provided for in Article 2(2)(b), at the latest upon expiry of the period for implementing that directive, is that third-country nationals referred to therein will not at any time fall within the scope of that Directive. In contrast, in so far as a Member State has not yet made use of that discretion after expiry of the said time period for implementation, in particular because of the fact that it has not yet implemented the Return Directive in national law, then it may not avail itself of the right to restrict the personal scope of application of the Directive.[51]

The CJEU clarified that the Return Directive precludes a provision of national law, such as the one in Germany, which subjected the limitation of the length of an entry ban to an application by the third-country national. Legal amendments were necessary after the judgment in the case of *Filev and Osmani* in Germany such as the obligation to limit entry bans ex officio instead of limiting them only upon application.[52]

Furthermore, historic entry bans issued before the Directive became applicable (24 December 2010) had to be adapted in line with the standards fixed in Article 11 (maximum of five years and subject to an individual assessment), if they were still applicable after 24 December 2010 and if they were not in line with the safeguards of Article 11 of the Return Directive.[53]

The *Filev and Osmani* case also affected Dutch jurisprudence. In the Netherlands, criminal courts used to have divergent intepretations of whether a historic entry ban for an unlimited time has consequences under the Return Directive.[54] Following the *Filev and Osmani* case, the Supreme Court reconsidered its approach on the legal consequences of the historic entry bans in light of the requirements set out by the CJEU judgement.[55] According to the Supreme Court, a historic entry ban (in the Netherlands declaring the third-country national undesirable)[56] is to be equated with an entry ban as provided in Article 3(6) of the Return Directive. This means that the entry ban has the maximum duration of five years referred to in Article 11 (2) unless there is serious threat to public policy, public security or national security.[57] The legislation has not changed, but the Supreme Court directly applies this rule regarding historic entry bans in criminal cases.

[51] In particular, with regard to those persons who were already able to avail themselves of the effects of that directive, see Filev and Osmani, ibid, para 53.

[52] See more in OH Zlotnikm, 'Return Policy in Germany in the Context of EU Rules and Standards Focussed Study by the German National Contact Point for the European Migration Network (EMN)', Working Paper 77 (2017); the breach of an entry ban is a criminal offence which may be punished by up to three year's imprisonment or a fine; the attempt is equally punishable (section 95 subs 2 no 1 and subs 3 of the Residence Act).

[53] *Filev and Osmani* (n 48) paras 39–41.

[54] A Pahladsingh and J Waasdorp, 'De duur van het inreisverbod in Nederland' [2015] *Asiel &MigrantenRecht* 212.

[55] See note by Cornelisse in JV 2013/376 about the judgment in *Filev and Osmani* in which she gives an overview of statements of the criminal chambers showing that the criminal judges dealt with this issue in a divided way.

[56] The 'undesirable declaration' (Art 67 Vw 2000) in the Netherlands is an historic entry ban.

[57] HR 4 November 2014, ECLI:NL:HR:2014:3093; HR, 29 March 2016, ECLI:NL:HR:2016:515.

V. Sanctions for Non-Respect of an Entry Ban: The CJEU Judgment in the Case of *Celaj*[58]

According to the European Commission, non-respect of an entry ban should be taken into account by Member States when considering the length of a subsequent entry ban.[59] The question is whether Member States can take administrative or criminal measures against a breach of an entry ban. This is not regulated in the Return Directive.

The CJEU concluded in *Celaj* that the Return Directive must be interpreted as not, in principle, precluding Member State legislation which imposes a prison sentence on an illegally staying third-country national who, after having been returned to his country of origin in the context of a return procedure, re-enters the territory of that state in breach of an entry ban.

In *Celaj*, the criminal proceedings at issue involved an illegally staying third-country national to whom the common standards and procedures established by the Return Directive were already applied. The referring court is asking whether Directive 2008/115 must be interpreted as precluding legislation of a Member State which provides for the imposition of a prison sentence on an illegally staying third-country national who, after having been returned to his country of origin in the context of an earlier return procedure, unlawfully re-enters the territory of that State in breach of an entry ban.In its judgment, the CJEU did not follow the Opinion of Advocate General Szpunar.[60] The Advocate General invited the CJEU to declare that imprisonment for a breach of entry ban, as a criminal penalty, is incompatible with the Directive because it would delay the return of the person concerned. The Advocate General based his Opinion on the effectiveness of returns as the main objective of the Directive. This brought the CJEU to distinguish the circumstances of *Celaj* from those of *El Dridi*[61] and *Achughbabian*,[62] in which illegally staying third-country nationals were subject to a first return procedure in a Member State.[63] Thus, the CJEU suggests that authorities should differentiate between the first entry and subsequent entries in applying the Directive. The CJEU approved the possibility for Member States to lay down criminal sanctions against illegally staying third-country nationals for whom the application of the

[58] Case C-290/14 *Celaj* ECLI:EU:C:2015:640. See more detailed information on this case in REDIAL Research Report 2016/02 (n 13) 15.

[59] See the Return Handbook (n 18) 83–159.

[60] Opinion of AG Szpunar of 28 April 2015, ECLI:EU:C:2015:285.

[61] *El Dridi* (n 14).

[62] Case C-329/11 *Achughbabian* ECLI:EU:C:2011:807. See more in R Raffaelli, 'Case Note: The *Achughbabian* Case: Impact of the Return Directive on National Criminal Legislation' [2012] no 2 *Diritto Penale Contemporaneo*.

[63] The 'distinction' argument had been advanced by the European Commission and intervening governments during the proceedings. They stressed that the circumstances in re-entry cases are distinct because penal sanctions could be imposed to dissuade migrants from breaching re-entry bans (Opinion of AG Szpunar of 28 April 2015, *Celaj* (n 58) point 46). For more criticism of the distinction argument, see I Majcher, 'The CJEU's Ruling in *Celaj*: Criminal Penalties, Entry Bans and the Returns Directive', http://eulawanalysis.blogspot.nl/2015/10/the-cjeus-ruling-in-celaj-criminal.html.

procedure established by that Directive resulted in them leaving and who then re-enter a Member State in breach of an entry ban.

According to certain scholars, the ruling in *Celaj* seems to compromise the effectiveness of the Return Directive in order to allow Member States discretion to apply domestic criminal provisions to deter and punish migrants for breaching an entry ban.[64] Furthermore, in the dialogue between the Italian referring court and the CJEU, the referring court made clear in its preliminary reference that it considers the Italian legislation as not fully complying with the Return Directive. In spite of the difference of opinions, the referring court closely followed the judgment of the CJEU and approved the criminal sanction of eight months ordered by the Prefect of Firenze.[65]

It is interesting to note that a legislative framework that is similar to the Italian one exists in the Netherlands.[66] Before the CJEU gave a judgment in the case of *Celaj*, the Dutch Supreme Court came to a similar conclusion in a judgment of 4 November 2014.[67] One difference is that the Dutch Supreme Court does not require the authorities to check whether the return procedure had been fully applied, since it considers that the Directive was not applicable to sanctions for non-respect of an entry ban.[68] The *Celaj* judgment did not have a major impact in criminal cases. In administrative law cases there is a judgment of the Council of State which explicitly referred to the *Celaj* judgment to conclude that the duration of an entry ban has not fully expired if an illegal third-country national, after having departed from the EU, returns to the territory of the EU within the duration of that re-entry ban.[69]

VI. Relation with Other Return Related Measures

The entry ban is directly connected with other return-related measures, such as the return decision or removal, but also with other international instruments,

[64] See Majcher, ibid. Of a similar opinion is also AM Kosińska, 'The Problem of Criminalisation of the Illegal Entry of a Third-Country National in the Case of Breaching an Entry Ban – Commentary on the Judgment of the Court of Justice of 1 October 2015 in Case C 290/14, Skerdjan Celaj' (2016) 18(3) *European Journal of Migration and Law* 243.

[65] For a detailed analysis, see A Pascale, 'Can a Justice of Peace be a Good Detention Judge? The Case of Italy', Chapter 13 in this volume.

[66] See REDIAL Research Report 2016/02 (n 13) 30.

[67] HR 4 November 2014, ECLI:NL:HR:2014:3093.

[68] De Jonge van Ellemeet JV 2015/309. According to De Jonge van Ellemeet, this judgment confirms the line set out by the Supreme Court on 4 November 2014, in the sense that the CJEU rules that the Return Directive does not preclude a Member State from imposing criminal sanctions on a suspect who has been returned from his previous return procedure to his country of origin and then, in spite of an entry ban, has returned to the Member State. I have to add that the judgment of the Supreme Court has the same outcome as in the CJEU in *Celaj*, but the main difference is that for the CJEU the Directive is applicable in such a situation and for the Supreme Court the Directive was not applicable.

[69] ABRvS 21 February 2018, ECLI:NL:RVS:2018:622.

such as the Convention Implementing the Schengen Agreement (CISA).[70] Where a Member State is considering issuing a residence permit or other authorisation to stay to a third-country national who is the subject of an entry ban issued by another Member State, it must first consult that Member State and take account of its interests in accordance with Article 25 of the CISA. Questions have arisen as to issuing entry bans to persons who requested legal stay on the basis of family reunification. This section will analyse the effects of the CJEU judgments in the cases of *E* and *K and others* on whether an entry ban precludes the applicability of a resident permit in another Member State or an application for family reunification.

A. CJEU Judgment: The Case of *E*[71]

On 16 January 2018, the CJEU ruled in the case of *E*, which involved a third-country national with a residence permit in Spain. This case concerned the interpretation of Article 25(2) of the CISA and the validity of the decision by the Finnish National Immigration Service to return E to his home country and to ban him from entering the Schengen Area. According to Article 25(2), first subparagraph, of the CISA, only where an alert for the purposes of refusing entry has been entered in the Schengen Information System for an alien who holds a valid residence permit issued by one of the Contracting Parties must the Contracting State entering the alert consult the Contracting State which issued the permit. Article 25(2) of the CISA states that if the residence permit is not withdrawn, the first state must withdraw the alert for the purposes of refusing admission.

The main proceeding concerned a Nigerian national holding a residence permit issued by Spain who was sentenced to prison in Finland for narcotics offences. The Finnish authorities issued a return decision accompanied by an entry ban for the Schengen Area. The Supreme Administrative Court in Finland asked the CJEU about the effects of the consultation procedure laid down in Article 25(2) of the CISA.

First, the CJEU ruled that, as is clear in most of the language versions of Article 25(2) of the CISA, the consultation procedure must, in principle, be initiated only after an alert for the purposes of refusing entry has been entered in the Schengen Information System.[72] However, that provision does not prohibit a Contracting State from initiating the consultation procedure, which it lays down, before the issue of a return decision accompanied by an entry ban.[73] It seems

[70] The Schengen *acquis* – Convention implementing the Schengen Agreement of 14 June 1985 between the Governments of the States of the Benelux Economic Union, the Federal Republic of Germany and the French Republic on the gradual abolition of checks at their common borders [2000] OJ L239, 19.

[71] Case C-240/17 *E* ECLI:EU:C:2018:8.

[72] ibid, para 34.

[73] ibid, para.37.

thus that the CJEU prioritises the Return Directive's objectives over those of the CISA.

Second, the CJEU found that Article 25(2) allows a return decision accompanied by an entry ban to be enforced while the consultation procedure is still ongoing if the third-country national is regarded as presenting a threat to public order or national security.[74] A Member State must assess the 'risk to public policy' within the meaning of Article 7(4) of the Return Directive on a case-by-case basis,[75] in order to ascertain whether the conduct of the person concerned poses a genuine and present risk, bearing in mind that the mere fact of criminal conviction is not sufficient to prove such a risk.[76] The CJEU is thus providing a uniform interpretation of the concept of 'risk to public policy' as set out by different migration law instruments which binds the Member States at the domestic level.[77] However, E is entitled to go to the territory of the Contracting State which issued his residence permit.[78]

Third, the CJEU found that after a reasonable time from the initiation of the consultation procedure, and in the absence of a response from the Contracting State consulted, the Contracting State issuing the alert must withdraw it and, if necessary, put the third-country national on its national list of alerts.[79] Finally, the CJEU ruled that a third-country national may rely before the national courts on the legal effects resulting from the consultation procedure laid down in Article 25(2) of the CISA.[80] This is an improvement in the legal protection for the third-country national.

It is essential to inform other Member States about all entry bans which have been issued. Entering an entry ban alert into the SIS in application of Article 24(3) of the SIS II Regulation is the main – but not the exclusive – means for informing other Member States of an entry ban and for ensuring its successful enforcement. As regards those Member States which have no access to SIS, information exchange may be achieved through other channels such as bilateral contacts. Under current legislation, Member States may register alerts related to entry bans issued in accordance with the Return Directive in the SIS, but are not obliged to do so. However, in order to give full effect to the European dimension of entry bans issued under the Return Directive, Member States should systematically do so.[81]

[74] ibid, para. 48.

[75] See *Zh and O* (n 19).

[76] *E* (n 71) para 49.

[77] See cases from the Dutch Council of State to the CJEU about the interpretation of the term public order in Art 6 of the Schengenbordercode, Art 6(1) and (2) of Directive 2003/86/EC (family reunification). The cases are registered at the CJEU as follows: C-380/18, *EP*; C-381/18, *GS*; and C-382/18, *VG*. On 12 December 2019 the CJEU delivered the judgments in these three cases C-380/18, ECLI:EU:C:2019:1071; joined cases C-381/18 and C-382/18, ECLI:EU:C:2019:1072.

[78] *E* (n 71) para 50.

[79] ibid, para 54.

[80] ibid, para 60.

[81] See European Commission, Proposal (n 17) preamble point 37.

The CJEU confirms, like the courts in the Netherlands already did, that an entry ban which is provided for the public order and national security has to be justified as in the CJEU judgment of 11 June 2015 in the case of *Zh and O.*

B. CJEU Judgment in the Case of *K and Others*[82]

K and others concerns EU citizens who have never exercised their rights to freedom of movement ('static EU citizens'),[83] and their family members, third-country nationals, who have lodged applications for family reunification. The applications are not examined by the Immigration Office, because the persons concerned are subject to an entry ban which is both valid and final, and the applications are not lodged from outside the territory of the European Union. According to the CJEU, national measures which have the effect of depriving EU citizens of the genuine enjoyment of the substance of the rights conferred by virtue of their status are prohibited.[84] This is only the case if there exists a relationship of dependency of such a nature that the EU citizen would be compelled to accompany the third-country national concerned. If this is the case, the obligation to leave the territory of the EU in order to contest the entry ban is also liable to undermine the effectiveness of Article 20 TFEU.[85]

It follows, therefore, that national authorities cannot refuse to examine an application for family reunification solely because the third-country national is the subject of a ban on entering that Member State. It is the duty of those authorities to examine that application and to assess whether there exists a relationship of dependency such that a derived right of residence must, as a general rule, be accorded to that third-country national under Article 20 TFEU.[86] In such circumstances, the Member State concerned must withdraw or suspend the return decision and the entry ban to which that third-country national is subject.[87]

The CJEU has clarified the degree of dependence capable of justifying a derived right of residence under Article 20 TFEU. In the case of adults, such a relationship of dependency is conceivable only in exceptional cases, where, having regard to all the relevant circumstances, there could be no form of separation of the individual concerned from the member of his family on whom he is dependent.[88]

In the case of children, the competent authorities must take primary account of the right to respect for family life, as enshrined in Article 7 of the EU Charter of Fundamental Rights (EU Charter) and the obligation to take into consideration

[82] Case C-82/16 *KA and others* ECLI:EU:C:2018:308.
[83] Art 20 TFEU.
[84] *KA and others* (n 82) para 49.
[85] ibid, para 51.
[86] ibid, para 57.
[87] ibid, para 55.
[88] ibid, paras 64–65.

the best interests of the child (Article 24(2) EU Charter).[89] Account must be taken of all the specific circumstances, including age, physical and emotional development, the extent of emotional ties to the EU citizen parent and to the third-country national parent, and the risks which separation from the latter might entail for that child's equilibrium.[90] Cohabitation is not a prerequisite but is a relevant factor to be taken into account. Similarly, the existence of a family link, whether natural or legal, cannot be sufficient to justify the grant of a derived right of residence.[91]

The CJEU also ruled that it is immaterial that the relationship of dependency came into being after the imposition of the entry ban.[92] It is also immaterial that the entry ban has become final at the time the third-country national submits an application for family reunification.[93] With regard to the justification for derogating from the right of residence of EU citizens or members of their families, the CJEU ruled that the concepts of 'public policy'[94] and 'public security' must be interpreted strictly.[95] That assessment must take account of the personal conduct of the individual, the length and legality of his residence on the territory of the Member State, the nature and gravity of the offence committed, the extent to which the person concerned is currently a danger to society, the age of any children at issue and their state of health, and their economic and family situation.[96] The CJEU is thus applying its established case-law on EU citizenship rights derived from Article 20 TFEU to cases concerning assessment of entry ban grounds. It follows that when the competent national authority is contemplating the adoption of a return decision, it must observe the obligations imposed by Article 5 of the Return Directive and hear the person concerned on that subject.[97] The person must cooperate with the competent national authority in order to provide all relevant information on his personal and family situation, in particular information that might justify a return decision not being issued.[98]

In this judgment a clear distinction is made between two legal issues: the potential application of Article 20 TFEU, and the potential application of family

[89] ibid, para 71.
[90] ibid, para 74.
[91] ibid, para 76.
[92] ibid, para 81.
[93] ibid, para 84.
[94] A Pahladsingh, 'Welke mogelijkheden hebben de lidstaten om de openbare orde te beschermen tegen de criminele burger van de Unie? Een nadere analyse van de excepties van de Unierechtelijke openbare orde', [2018] no 1 *Tijdschrift voor Vreemdelingenrecht (Belgium)* 29.
[95] *KA and others* (n 82) para 91: '"public policy" presupposes, in any event, the existence of a genuine, present and sufficiently serious threat affecting one of the fundamental interests of society. Secondly, as regards the concept of "public security", that concept covers both the internal security of a Member State and its external security, and, consequently, a threat to the functioning of institutions and essential public services and the survival of the population, as well as the risk of a serious disturbance to foreign relations or to peaceful coexistence of nations, or a threat to military interests.'
[96] ibid, para 94.
[97] ibid, para 100.
[98] ibid, para 103.

reunification rules when Article 20 is not applicable. In the first situation, in order to ensure that Article 20 TFEU has practical effect, it is necessary to withdraw or suspend such an entry ban, even when that ban has become final, if there exists, between that third-country national and an EU citizen who is a member of his family, such a relationship of dependency as to justify according to that third-country national a derived right of residence, under Article 20, in the territory of the Member State concerned. It is immaterial that the entry ban has become final at the time when he submits his application. In the second situation the person is subject to a duty of honest cooperation with the competent national authority. He or she is obliged, as soon as possible, to inform that authority of any relevant changes in his or her family life. The right of a third-country national to expect that changes in his or her family situation will be taken into account before a return decision is adopted cannot be used to reopen or extend indefinitely the administrative procedure. The competent national authority cannot be criticised for failing to take those details into account, in the course of a subsequent return procedure, since those details ought to have been put forward by the person concerned at an earlier procedural stage.

The judgment in *KA and others* has had a major impact on the Belgian legal order as the legislation has to be changed.[99] The practice in Belgium of not examining an application based on Article 20 TFEU solely on the ground of a final entry ban is thus precluded by the CJEU interpretation of Articles 5 and 11 of the Return Directive. The CJEU also secures the fundamental rights in the situation of children because the competent authorities must take primary account of the right to respect for family life (Article 7 EU Charter) and the obligation to take into consideration the best interests of the child (Article 24(2) EU Charter). An interesting question is whether this obligation for the Member State can also be applied in cases which fall under the Family Reunification Directive (2003/86/EC).[100]

The CJEU apparently believes that an entry ban can be 'valid', even if its duration has not yet begun by the person's departure from the EU, as follows from the *Ouhrami* judgment. It is not clear what this exactly means. It must be assumed that the CJEU deliberately uses the term 'valid', since the Advocate General explicitly raised this problem.[101]

[99] See P. Boeles JV 2018/108.

[100] See P Boeles JV 2018/108.

[101] Opinion of AG Sharpston of 26 October 2017, ECLI:EU:C:2017:821, para 83: 'I shall start with some general comments concerning entry bans which are the focus of the fourth question. Under national rules, an entry ban applies from the date of notification, rather than the date when the third-country national concerned leaves the Belgian territory. However, the Court has ruled that such bans are intended to supplement return decisions. It has also held that the period of application of an entry ban begins to run from the date on which the person concerned has actually left EU territory. The illegal stay of the third-country national concerned is governed by the return decision rather than the entry ban. The national rules as described in the order for reference do not appear to reflect the wording, purpose and scheme of the Return Directive in that respect.'

VII. Conclusion

Judicial dialogue and interactions have contributed in a positive way to the implementation of the Return Directive's entry ban provisions. For instance, the CJEU filled the gaps left by the EU legislator (*Zh and O*, *Filev and Osmani*, *Ouhrami* and *Celaj*); or eliminated incompatibilities between national legislation and the Return Directive provisions (*KA and others*). Judicial dialogue has also resulted in a common judicial interpretation and understanding of the sometimes abstract and general provisions of the Return Directive (*Zh and O*). The CJEU followed at times the arguments of the national court (*Ouhrami*), while in other cases chose a different approach (*Celaj*).

The case-law of the CJEU regarding the starting point of the validity of an entry ban and the relationship between the Return Directive and other EU instruments will also lead to changes in the legislation and practice of several Member States. The reason therefore is that certain legislation and practice in Member States is not compatible with the judgments of the CJEU in the cases of *Ouhrami* and *K and others*. In this case-law, the CJEU has paid attention to human rights such as the respect of private and family life (Article 7 EU Charter) and the best interests of the child (Article 24(2) EU Charter).

The entry ban has an EU-wide effect as it prohibits entry and stay on the territory of all Member States. The EU-wide effect is one of the key European added values of the Return Directive.[102] On some topics, such as the grounds for an entry ban and the definition of a serious threat to public policy, public security and national security, *horizontal* dialogue in the Netherlands has led to legal uniformity without making a reference to the CJEU. The results of *vertical* and *horizontal* dialogue between national courts in the Member States can deliver useful information about the interpretation of the Directive. National courts could play a more active role in improving the quality and effectiveness of European legislation as Commissioner Timmermans stated on 15 May 2017.[103] The ACA Europe[104] is starting a project called 'Better Regulation' in which the national courts or the judiciary play a role to differing degrees to improve EU legislation: an independent evaluation of the legal quality of (proposed) legislation or procedures to signal judicial bottlenecks in existing legislation to the European Commission. An interesting topic to signal judicial bottlenecks in existing legislation to the European Commission could be the area of asylum and migration, especially the Return

[102] Commission Recommendation (n 3) 42.

[103] www.aca-europe.eu/index.php/en/evenements-en/529-the-hague-15-may-2017-seminar-better-regulation.

[104] ACA-Europe is a European association composed of the CJEU and the councils of state or the supreme administrative jurisdictions of each of the members of the European Union. The jurisdictions and institutions similarly empowered of states which are engaged in negotiations with a view to their actually joining the European Union can be admitted as ibservers.

Directive. Another option is to share national case-law with other national courts and the CJEU in the Judicial Network of the European Union.[105] In this way the *vertical*, *transnational* and *horizontal* dialogue between the national courts and the CJEU can be improved.

[105] www.curia.europa.eu/jcms/jcms/p1_2170125/en/ : The Judicial Network of the European Union (JNEU) is managed by the CJEU. It is designed to promote the exchange of information on jurisprudence between the participating national courts and the CJEU. The main objective of this area is to share and centralise information and documents relevant to the application, dissemination and study of EU law, as interpreted and applied not only by the Court of Justice of the European Union but also by national courts and tribunals. It also aims to promote mutual knowledge and understanding of the laws and systems of the Member States from a comparative law perspective that can facilitate consideration of the legal traditions of each Member State.Also the follow-up judgments to the preliminary references are included. The website has been online since 1 January 2018, but is only accessible to members and not the general public.

5

Judicial Dialogue in Action: Making Sense of the Risk of Absconding in the Return Procedure

MADALINA MORARU

I. Introduction

This chapter analyses the contribution of courts and judicial dialogue to the implementation of the 'risk of absconding',[1] which has proved to be one of the most problematic notions introduced by the Return Directive.[2] The meaning of the 'risk of absconding' has been surrounded by confusion from the very start of the negotiations on the Return Directive.[3] Initially, the European Commission's proposal for a Return Directive did not provide a definition of this notion. Instead, a definition was introduced in Article 3(7) following a compromise reached between the opposing views of the Commission, Council and Parliament.[4] The compromise definition used a very broad phrasing and did not provide for a harmonised list of circumstances that could lead to finding a risk of absconding. According to the Return Directive, Member States are required only to provide for objective criteria in national laws. The number and content of 'objective criteria' is not harmonised at EU level; instead Member States have retained the power to set these circumstances. This freedom has been wrongly interpreted as being unrestricted by EU legal guarantees, so much so that certain Member States listed so many and broad circumstances that a risk of absconding would almost always

[1] See Art 3(7) of the Return Directive.

[2] Directive 2008/115/EC of the European Parliament and of the Council of 16 December 2008 on common standards and procedures in Member States for returning illegally staying third-country nationals [2008] OJ L348, 98.

[3] See also the 2017 European Migration Network (EMN) Report on the effectiveness of return in the EU Member States (hereinafter '2017 EMN Report') 3.

[4] See F Lutz and S Manashvili, 'Commentary on the Return Directive' in K Hailbronner and D Thym (eds), *EU Asylum and Immigration Law*, 2nd edn (Munich and Oxford, CH Beck and Hart Publishing, 2016) 693.

be presumed to exist,[5] thus endangering the effective fulfilment of the Directive's objectives.[6]

The implementation of the risk of absconding has been a constant challenge for national authorities.[7] The first problem consisted of partial domestic transposition of this concept, particularly during the first four years after the Directive's entry into force.[8] Even when the notion was later on domestically transposed, administrative practices varied widely across the Member States in terms of: types of legal acts implementing the risk of absconding; scope of objective criteria on the basis of which a risk of absconding would be presumed; standards for the burden of proof; and the level of individual assessment that should be carried out before finding the existence of a risk of absconding.[9] More recently governments have mentioned challenges to complying with the high standards imposed by national judicial authorities interpreting the notion of risk of absconding.[10]

Within this context of minimal harmonisation of the 'objective criteria', and arrogated unfettered Member States' powers to define them, national courts have been consistently seized with requests of clarification of the notion of risk of absconding. Domestic courts across the EU were faced with similar questions regarding the interpretation and application of the risk of absconding, namely: in what type of legal act should the risk of absconding be defined? What circumstances can be considered as objective criteria and how many objective criteria can be included within the risk of absconding definition? Is the existence of objective criteria sufficient to find a risk of absconding or other circumstances, and which ones should be taken into consideration in the assessment? What type of return-related measure should be chosen when a risk of absconding is identified? In addition to these questions, which the competent administrative authorities must also address, courts initially faced an additional challenge which results from their limited powers of review and remedy in immigration cases. Due to the fact that the Return Directive had not harmonised procedural aspects regarding the division of competences between courts and administration, nor the domestic judicial design over return proceedings,[11] a varied configuration of courts with different reviewing and remedial judicial powers had developed in the EU.[12]

[5] eg Italy, Netherlands, Slovenia; for more details, see section II.

[6] ie according to Art 1: effective return and respect of fundamental rights.

[7] According to Communication from the Commission to the Council and the European Parliament on EU Return Policy, COM(2014)0199 final (hereinafter '2014 EC Evaluation of the Implementation of the Return Directive'); P de Bruycker, M Moraru and G Renaudiere, 'Report on Effective Returns, and European Synthesis report on the Termination of Illegal Stay', REDIAL Research Report 2016/01, 17 et seq, available at https://cadmus.eui.eu/handle/1814/41206.

[8] Namely, not all Member States transposed the Return Directive, and in particular Art 3(7) of the Directive; see 2014 EC Evaluation of the Implementation of the Return Directive, ibid, 12.

[9] According to data collected within the REDIAL Project; see more in the national reports available at http://euredial.eu/.

[10] According to the 2017 EMN Report (n 3) 3.

[11] These procedural aspects commonly fall under the procedural autonomy of the Member States.

[12] For an accurate mapping of the judicial competences in return procedures across the EU, see D Kosar and A Blisa, 'Scope and Intensity of Judicial Review: Which Power for Judges Within the Control of Immigration Detention?' Chapter 8 in this volume.

This has contributed to a divergent practice, especially as regards the choice of different types of return measures being adopted for similar risks of absconding.[13] This varied judicial design added another source for divergent interpretation and implementation of the risk of absconding,[14] at least up until the CJEU delivered its judgment in the *Mahdi* case.[15]

This chapter argues that courts, with the help of vertical and transnational judicial dialogue, have played a crucial role in clarifying key aspects of the EU law notion of 'risk of absconding'. For instance, multidimensional judicial dialogue has widely contributed to the legality and transparency of 'objective criteria' (ie definition in national legislation) and establishing individual assessment as a mandatory requirement for establishing the appropriate return measure when a risk of absconding is present. On the other hand, the number and content of 'objective criteria' have mostly remained those existent before the entry into force of the Directive.[16] On this issue, the domestic courts' approach has been quite conservative, as they neither addressed a preliminary reference to the CJEU asking for guidelines on how to interpret the requirement of 'objective criteria', nor disapplied national legislation providing numerous objective criteria that would revert the Directive mandatory order of return stages. This chapter thus argues that more efforts are needed both from domestic judiciaries and legislatures to remedy the domestic lists including numerous objective criteria, especially those originating from before the entry into force of the Directive,[17] along the lines of the CJEU jurisprudence.

The chapter builds this argument in two main sections. First, it will map out the main problems in the implementation of the EU notion of the 'risk of absconding' in section II. Second, it will analyse the contribution of the courts and judicial dialogue in tackling these various problems in section III.[18] The chapter concludes by finding that, through the use of judicial dialogue (vertical, transnational and horizontal), national courts have ultimately strengthened their position vis-a-vis domestic administrative authorities in an attempt to ensure the *effet utile* of the Return Directive. Seeing their immigration powers gradually constrained by judicial principles, domestic governments are increasingly challenging the judiciary's understanding of immigration issues and, thus, implicitly, also the legitimacy of the judicial scrutiny of the Return Directive's

[13] See, in particular, Chapters 1, 6 and 11–14 in this volume.

[14] See the results of the comparative analysis presented by M Moraru and G Renaudiere, REDIAL Research Report 2016/05, available at http://euredial.eu/.

[15] Case C-146/14 *Mahdi* ECLI:EU:C:2014:1320.

[16] eg Spain (see Chapter 1 in this volume), Netherlands (G Cornelisse and J Bouwman, 'REDIAL National Synthesis Report on Termination of Illegal Stay', 2–4, available at http://euredial.eu/docs/publications/national-synthesis-reports/NETHERLANDS.pdf) and Slovenia (REDIAL Research Report 2016/01 (n 7) 17 et seq).

[17] See, in particular, Spain, according to CG Rotaeche, 'Return Decisions and Domestic Judicial Practices: Is Spain Different?', Chapter 2 in this volume.

[18] The case-law used for this chapter comes from the REDIAL database and other chapters in this volume.

administrative implementation.[19] In addition, the Commission proposal for a Recast of the Return Directive puts forward highly challengeable proposals on the risk of absconding from the perspective of their compliance with judicially developed standards.[20] A new Article 6 is proposed, which includes a non-exhaustive list of objective criteria, which are divided in two categories: rebuttable and indicative criteria, which challenge the foundational principle of individual assessment governing return proceedings.[21] This very broad definition of the risk of absconding, including criteria contrary to the CJEU jurisprudence,[22] has attracted heavy criticism from the Council of Europe's Human Rights Commissioner, the EU's Fundamental Rights Agency and OSCE. These institutions argued that the Commission-proposed definition of the risk of absconding is 'likely to lead to human rights violations without furthering other goals, such as facilitating the processing of asylum claims or promoting dignified returns'.[23] It is thus timely to question what are the red lines developed by European and domestic courts on the content and effects of the risk of absconding in return procedures, which should be respected at both EU and domestic level.

II. Diagnosing the Implementation of the Risk of Absconding: Problems and their Sources

The Return Directive defined the risk of absconding as 'existence of reasons in an individual case which are based on objective criteria defined by law to believe that a third-country national who is the subject of return procedures may abscond'. Notably, the definition includes two cumulative requirements: (1) an objective, general requirement ('objective criteria defined by law'), which must be defined in the laws of the Member States; and (2) a fact-based requirement

[19] See B Nagy, 'Restricting Access to Asylum and Contempt of Courts: Illiberals at Work in Hungary', 18 December 2017, OMNIA blog; 'Italy's Far-Right Interior Minister, Matteo Salvini, Escalates Attack on Judges', *The Guardian*, www.theguardian.com/world/2019/jun/06/salvini-steps-up-attacks-on-italian-judges-who-challenge-him; M Marmo and M Giannacopoulos, 'Cycles of Judicial and Executive Power in Irregular Migration' (2017) 5(1) *Comparative migration studies* 16; and 2017 EMN Report (n 4) 3.

[20] See Proposal for a Directive of the European Parliament and of the Council on common standards and procedures in Member States for returning illegally staying third-country nationals (recast) Brussels, COM(2018) 634 final 2018/0329 (COD) ('the Proposal').

[21] See proposed Art 6. The 'individual assessment' is a mandatory requirement under both current version of the Return Directive (eg Recitals 10, 14, Arts 3(7), 7, 15) and recast version (eg Recitals 12, 13, 17, 19, 24, 28, Arts 3(7), 7(2)).

[22] Such as: lack of documentation proving the identity, illegal entry into the territory of the Member States.

[23] See FRA Opinion – 1/2019 [Return], Vienna, 10 January 2019, 'The recast Return Directive and its fundamental rights implications, and the public statement of Council of Europe's Commissioner for Human Rights, Nils Muižnieks, www.facebook.com/CommissionerHR/posts/753609061481673; OSCE PA Ad Hoc Committee on Migration, 'Briefing on Effective and Humane Return Policy', 2 April 2019.

('in an individual case'), whereby competent authorities – namely the administrative or judicial authorities – are required to examine on a case-by-case basis all the individual, specific circumstances that characterise each applicant's situation.[24] Although this definition is a step forward compared to the initial proposal of the Commission which did not include any definition of the risk of absconding, it leaves key questions unanswered: in particular, the type and number of objective criteria, and the level of certainty required to find a risk of absconding. In practice, the Member States have arrogated unfettered powers to define these aspects, often overlooking key EU legal guarantees introduced by Article 3(7), the preamble of the Directive and general EU legal principles, such as proportionality and rule of law.

This section argues that six common issues have transnationally developed in the domestic implementation of the risk of absconding: (1) delayed domestic transposition of the notion of 'risk of absconding'; (2) incorrect transposition of the notion of 'law' solely in administrative practice or acts which lack the essential requirements of legality as defined by the ECtHR and CJEU;[25] (3) a broad list of objective criteria establishing a risk of absconding in almost all cases of irregularity; (4) inclusion of challengeable circumstances, such as illegal stay, entry, lack of documentation and financial resources as objective criteria for finding a risk of absconding; (5) the automatic assumption of a risk of absconding solely based on existence of one of the objective criteria; and (6) a preference for establishing forced return measures over less coercive measures when a risk of absconding is identified.

These practices of incorrect and inconsistent domestic implementation of the risk of absconding have mostly resulted from a combination of factors, such as: the minimum harmonisation introduced by the Directive as regards the definition of the risk of absconding, which was wrongly interpreted by the Member States as leaving them unfettered powers of regulation; the persistent resistance of the Member States to adapt their return procedures to the common procedure established by the Directive; the incorrect implementation of key principles guiding the entire return procedure, such as individual assessment, proportionality and fair procedures; and limited domestic judicial scrutiny and remedial powers in return proceedings.

First, several Member States have long delayed the transposition of the risk of absconding in their domestic laws,[26] and some still do not provide a legal definition of the risk of absconding within the scope of return proceedings.[27] Similar to other specific notions, such as 'return decision' and pre-removal 'detention',

[24] See also AG Opinion in the *Al Chodor* case, ECLI:EU:C:2016:865, points 59 and 60.

[25] ie precision, transparency, foreseeability, offers of additional assurances in terms of external control of the discretion of the administrative and judicial authorities responsible for assessing the risk of absconding.

[26] Austria in 2014, Czech Republic in 2015, Germany in 2016; more detailed information will follow in section III.

[27] eg Malta, according to data available up until January 2019.

the risk of absconding was transposed with delays due to the reticence of certain Member States to adapt their immigration procedures to the specific terminology introduced by the Return Directive.[28] Instead, some of the Member States retained their previous expulsion-related terminology or introduced broader concepts than the risk of absconding.[29]

Even when the Member States did transpose the risk of absconding at the domestic level, a second problem resulted from the fact that not all Member States defined the risk of absconding in a domestic 'law' in the sense of Article 3(7). Some Member States have provided a definition in administrative acts (eg Belgium, Hungary and the Netherlands), instead of laws enacted by parliament or, even when defined in domestic law, additional objective criteria were followed in administrative practice.[30] In fact, the legislative definition of the risk of absconding, as ground for return-related measures, has been introduced quite recently in certain jurisdictions, following courts' pronouncements reached on the basis of judicial dialogue.[31] The main issue of defining the risk of absconding in administrative practice is the lack of clarity, precision, foreseeability and transparency of such practices for the affected individuals. Furthermore, administrative acts cannot fulfil the essential requirements of domestic implementation, since the separation-of-powers requirement inherent in the rule of law is not fulfilled in this case. That is, the same authority entrusted to apply the risk of absconding has also been the author of the definition, which raises concerns regarding the respect of the rule of law.[32]

Even if the risk of absconding was transposed in a national law adopted by parliament, a third problem developed, namely that of broad definition of the objective criteria requirement. Since neither Article 3(7) nor any other provision of the Directive prescribes a list of objective criteria, Member States remain free to set their own lists, which has led in practice to the adoption of domestic lists of varied lengths. While certain factors are generally accepted as objective criteria by a majority of Member States,[33] additional criteria have been included in national legislation or followed in practice. Moreover, the compatibility of certain

[28] For instance, the term 'expulsion' is still commonly used by several Member States instead of 'return' (eg Austria and Spain). 'Public custody' is still favoured by several Member States over 'pre-removal detention' (eg France and Romania), according to REDIAL National Reports on Austria, France, Romania and Spain, available at http://euredial.eu/publications/national-synthesis-reports/; see also Chapters 2 and 14 in this volume.

[29] Spanish Immigration Act 4/2000 (Art 62) does not refer to the risk of 'absconding' either. Rather, it refers to the risk of 'non appearance': 'non presentation due to lack of residence or of identification documents'. See the REDIAL Report on Pre-Removal Detention in Spain.

[30] eg Austria; see REDIAL Report on Pre-Removal Detention in Austria.

[31] Austria, Germany and the Czech Republic introduced a legislative definition of the risk of absconding after 2014, see more in section III.A.

[32] See n 24 and CJEU judgment in Case C-528/15 *Al Chodor* ECLI:EU:C:2017:213, para 44.

[33] Such as refusal to cooperate in the identification process; use of false documentation or the deliberate destruction of documents; failing repeatedly to report to the relevant authorities; explicit expression of intent of non-compliance; existence of conviction for criminal offence; non-compliance with existing entry ban; and the violation of a return decision; see REDIAL Research Reports 2016/01 and 2016/05 (nn 8 and 15), and 2017 EMN Report (n 3) 28–29.

objective criteria with the Return Directive is highly questionable. For instance, the following circumstances were listed in 2018 as objective criteria by different Member States: illegal entry or stay (eg Estonia, France, Romania, Slovenia, Spain); lack of residence permit (eg Slovakia); lack of passport of other equivalent identification documents (eg Bulgaria, Italy); lack of sufficient financial resources (eg Italy, the Netherlands).[34] Other Member States have significantly expanded the scope of the objective criteria, by including a long list of objective criteria, in some cases amounting to as many as 15 circumstances for finding a risk of absconding (eg Italy, the Netherlands and Slovenia).[35] Such lengthy lists raise issues of compatibility with the principles of individual assessment, legality, proportionality and exceptionality of the risk of absconding which cannot be equated with the notion of irregularity. Certain Member States included among the objective criteria circumstances clearly prohibited by the Directive, as interpreted by the CJEU, such as illegal entry and stay.[36] Furthermore, other circumstances, such as lack of financial resources or of identity documents, would cover many irregularly present third-country nationals without necessarily indicating a risk of absconding, but only indicating the precarity or vulnerability of their situation. The practical result of these broad objective criteria is that of blurring the line between irregularity and risk of absconding, and reversing the logic and order set out by the Directive, namely of prioritising voluntary departure over all other forced forms of return.

A fourth problem, widespread among domestic authorities, was the automatic assumption of a risk of absconding based on the existence of one of the objective criteria, without any individual assessment being carried out. Although Article 3(7) of the Return Directive requires an individual assessment as part of the definition of the risk of absconding, which means that no objective criteria can automatically lead to the finding of a risk of absconding, several Member States have nevertheless followed a practice of presumption of a risk of absconding when certain objective criteria were found to be present.[37] Often mere illegal entry or stay led to an automatic conclusion of an existence of a risk of absconding.[38] Grounds such as criminal convictions or suspicion of criminal conviction were commonly considered as falling under the 'risk of absconding' and could automatically lead to refusal of voluntary departure and ordering removal.[39]

[34] According to data available in 2018 collected within the framework of the REDIAL Project. The domestic lists of objective criteria have been amended several times by the Member States during the 10 years of the Directive's existence.

[35] See REDIAL Research Report 2016/05 (n 14).

[36] According to Recital 6 of the Directive's preamble. For instance, Italy, see A di Pascale, 'Can a Justice of the Peace Be a Good Detention Judge? The Case of Italy', Chapter 13 in this volume.

[37] eg in Italy and the Netherlands; furthermore some objective criteria were considered in these countries as establishing a non-rebuttal presumption, see more in REDIAL Research Report 2016/01 (n 8) 18, and REDIAL Research Report 2016/05 (n 15) 15.

[38] See, in particular for Italy, the Reports cited in (n 39).

[39] Such as in Cyprus, Belgium, Spain, Germany (eg Administrative Court of Augsburg, Au 6 K 12.667, 16 January 2013), Malta (Immigration Appeals Board of Malta, judgment of 25 March 2013), see more in M Moraru and G Renaudiere, REDIAL Research Report 2016/02, 20.

This automatic decision-making appears to be more present in those Member States that viewed themselves as transit countries.[40] These practices are particularly worrying in Member States where administrative automaticity is backed up by a deferential domestic judiciary.[41]

Even when the objective and fact-based requirements were fulfilled by Member States, a fifth problem developed, namely that of different types of return measures being adopted for similar risks of absconding. This is possible due to the fact that the risk of absconding is provided by the Directive as a legal basis for five different return-related measures, thus raising the issue of gradation and demarcation of measures when a risk is identified. According to Article 7(3), in the case of a 'risk of absconding', the Member State may require the addressee of a return decision to fulfil one or more of the following obligations: (1) regular reporting to the authorities; (2) the deposit of an adequate financial guarantee; and/or (3) surrender of documents or the obligation to stay at a certain place.[42] The purpose of imposing additional obligations pending voluntary departure is to allow a period of voluntary departure in cases which would not normally otherwise qualify for such treatment. If these obligations have been breached, or if it is considered that the imposition of these obligations will not dispel the risk of absconding, or in other limited circumstances, then the third-country national can receive a period shorter than seven days for voluntary departure or even be refused the period altogether.[43] In the latter situation, but also where the obligation to return has not been complied with within the period for voluntary departure, Article 8(1) requires the Member State that has issued a return decision to carry out the removal by taking all necessary measures including, where appropriate, coercive measures, in a proportionate manner and with due respect for, inter alia, fundamental rights.

The last-resort measures that can be adopted when a risk of absconding is found are pre-removal detention and the prolongation of such detention.[44] Although the Directive does provide in the preamble that 'voluntary return should be preferred over forced return and a period for voluntary departure should be granted', the assessment of the level of risk and thus of the necessary return measure to be adopted is left to domestic assessment. In practice, similar

[40] eg Czech Republic (see M Moraru and L Janku, 'Can Strategic Litigation Rescue Asylum Seekers' Fundamental Rights? in *Utrecht Special Issue of International and European Law*, forthcoming 2020) and Romania (according to discussions during the workshops organised within the REDIAL Project up until the end of 2016).

[41] See C Demetriou and N Trimikliniotis, 'Cypriot Courts, the Return Directive and Fundamental Rights: Challenges and Failures', Chapter 5 in this Volume, and di Pascale (n 36).

[42] See Art 7(3) of the Return Directive. Since this list is not exhaustive, many of the Member States had provided additional obligations that could be imposed during the voluntary departure period. See the list in the 2017 EMN Report (n 3) 31; U Brandl, 'Voluntary Departure as a Priority: Challenges and Best Practices', Chapter 3 in this volume.

[43] See Art 7(4).

[44] See Art 15.

circumstances have not always led to the adoption of a similar return-related measure. For instance, the lack of a passport or residence permit was the legal basis for the adoption of certain obligations to be fulfilled during the voluntary departure period,[45] while other Member States adopted a pre-removal detention order, without providing additional explanations for their specific choices of measures.[46]

Ultimately, divergent interpretations of the risk of absconding have derived also from the varied configuration of domestic judicial powers in return procedures. Administrative, civil and criminal courts have certain competences to assess the risk of absconding depending on the Member States' specific allocation of judicial competences and also of the specific return measure at issue.[47] Take, for instance, the adoption and review of the pre-removal detention measure, which is subject to wide institutional diversity among Member States: a criminal judge is competent in Belgium and Spain and recently also in France, and criminal chambers in common courts in Poland; a civil judge is competent in Germany, which unlike in other jurisdictions also has the power to adopt pre-removal detention; a 'justice of the peace' (*giudice di pace*, a non-professional judge) is competent in Italy; administrative courts, with specialised chambers on immigration law, are competent in the Netherlands, Austria, Bulgaria (only within the Supreme Administrative Court) or specialised administrative courts (Sweden); and general courts are competent in Hungary.[48] The nature of the competent courts not only influences the judges' ideologies, but also the extent of their judicial scrutiny powers vis-a-vis the administration,[49] and their remedial powers. This varied European judicial design has to a certain extent contributed to the development of incoherent interpretation of the risk of absconding and remedies in cases of violations.[50]

In conclusion, the domestic implementation of the risk of absconding has suffered from delayed and incorrect transposition, resulting in a variety of domestic approaches regarding the number, content and nature of objective criteria. An additional challenge has been the diverse scope and intensity of domestic judicial scrutiny among the Member States. This has contributed to the adoption of varied

[45] eg in the Netherlands; see more in REDIAL Research Report 2016/01 (n 8) 20.

[46] In the case of *Re Rita Kumah* (Supreme Court, Civil Application no 198/2013, 29 November 2013), a Cypriot court found 'that detention is necessary for as long as there is a risk of absconding and there is a risk of absconding in this case because the applicant did not have a passport or a residence permit'. On the other hand, the Lithuanian Supreme Administrative Court has consistently held that this alone cannot be the basis for detention without carrying out an individual assessment (no A3219-858/2015, judgment of 22 July 2015).

[47] See more in Kosar and Blisa chapter in this edited volume (n 13).

[48] See *REDIAL Research Report 2016/05*, according to date available up until 2017.

[49] For instance, the Justice of Peace exercising the most limited judicial scrutiny powers, and the civil judge in Germany exercising the most extensive judicial scrutiny powers in return proceedings, see more in di Pascale (n 36) and J Bornemann and H Dörig, 'The Civil Judge as Administrator of Return Detention: the Case of Germany', Chapter 9 in this volume.

[50] See more in Kosar and Blisa (n 12).

return-related measures even though a similar risk of absconding was sometimes present.[51] Moreover, questions regarding the determination of the concrete risk of absconding and its corresponding return measure were often solved by choosing the easy route of automaticity in presuming a risk of absconding. In this context, clarification of the content and effects of the risk of absconding, and its coherent interpretation, have been achieved by national courts influenced in their decisions by the CJEU, the ECtHR, or other foreign or domestic courts. In the following sections, the main outcomes of the multidimensional judicial dialogue on the implementation of the risk of absconding notion will be assessed.

III. Judicial Dialogue in Action: Tackling Implementation Challenges

The implementation of the risk of absconding offers the opportunity to test some of the claims made by this book, namely that judicial dialogue has contributed to maintaining a balance between the two seemingly conflicting objectives of the Return Directive, ie effective return and respect of fundamental rights; filling gaps left by the EU legislator and thus ensuring a coherent application of the Return Directive; and empowering national courts to control administrative decision-making, thus ensuring the rule of law. As shown above, domestic courts across the EU faced similar questions regarding the interpretation and application of the risk of absconding: in what type of legal act should the risk of absconding be defined? What circumstances can be considered as objective criteria and how many objective criteria can be included within the risk of absconding? Is the existence of objective criteria sufficient to find a risk of absconding or should other circumstances, and which ones, be taken into consideration in the assessment? What type of return-related measure should be chosen when a risk of absconding is identified? In addition to these questions, which the competent administrative authorities too had to address, courts face an additional challenge which results from their limited powers of review and remedy in immigration cases. As mentioned above, there are varied judicial configurations across the EU, and domestic courts across the EU do not enjoy the same reviewing and remedial powers. This has led to divergent judicial decisions proliferating on similar issues regarding the implementation of the risk of absconding. For instance, in certain domestic jurisdictions, courts could not consider facts beyond those brought by the administration and third-country nationals, and could not substitute the administrative decisions with their own, but only annul the administrative decision if they found a manifest illegality in the administrative decision-making.[52]

[51] According to the case-law gathered in the framework of the REDIAL Project.

[52] See, for instance, Bulgaria: V Ilareva, REDIAL National Synthesis Report on Pre-Removal Detention, available at http://euredial.eu/docs/publications/national-synthesis-reports/BulgariaFB2.pdf.

Faced with this wide array of challenges, domestic courts resorted to various judicial dialogue techniques in the search for interpretative inspiration, including: finding solutions to conflicting norms or jurisprudential opinions; shortening the time for judicial decision-making; and enhancing the quality of judicial analyses and persuasiveness of reasoning, which can be crucial tools to strengthen judicial legitimacy against opposition from the administration or legislature.

Surprisingly, Article 3(7), which defines the risk of absconding within the Return Directive framework, has not yet formed the subject of a preliminary ruling, although the Return Directive is the EU immigration law instrument with the highest number of preliminary rulings delivered by the CJEU, close to 30 in a period of 10 years.[53] Nevertheless, the preliminary rulings delivered on other provisions of the Directive (eg scope of application, pre-removal detention), and on the notion of the risk of absconding as grounds for detention under the Dublin transfer procedure,[54] have offered salient guidelines also for the interpretation of the risk of absconding in return procedures. In addition, transnational judicial dialogue, a relatively rarely used type of judicial dialogue by domestic courts,[55] has proliferated among courts from continental legal systems in an attempt to clarify one of the requirements of the risk of absconding – 'defined by law'. This section analyses the contribution of courts and of the various types of judicial dialogue to the clarification of the objective and subjective requirements of the risk of absconding and its effects in practice.

A. The Objective Requirement: Clarification of the Meaning of 'Defined by Law' – The Ripple Effect of Judicial Dialogue

According to Article 3(7) of the Return Directive, the definition of the risk of absconding must fulfil two requirements, namely: including 'objective criteria' which are 'defined by law', which represents the objective requirement; and an individual assessment, which represents the subjective requirement. As previously mentioned, several Member States did not initially provide a definition of the 'risk of absconding' in their national legislations, but in administrative acts and jurisprudence (eg Czech Republic, Belgium, Malta, Austria, Greece).[56] Germany used to be one of these countries, and did not define the 'risk of

[53] As of June 2019.

[54] Regulation (EU) No 604/2013 of the European Parliament and of the Council of 26 June 2013 establishing the criteria and mechanisms for determining the Member State responsible for examining an application for international protection lodged in one of the Member States by a third-country national or a stateless person [2013] OJ L180, 31.

[55] See M Bobek, *Comparative Reasoning in European Supreme Courts* (Oxford, Oxford University Press, 2013); by refugee courts in particular, see Guy S Goodwin-Gill and H Lambert, *The Limits of Transnational Law: Refugee Law, Policy Harmonization and Judicial Dialogue in the European Union* (Cambridge, Cambridge University Press, 2010).

[56] According to data available until 2014.

absconding' in either return or Dublin transfers procedures until 2016.[57] In spite of its previous reticence to refer to EU secondary law and relevant CJEU jurisprudence, the German Supreme Civil Court held that the legislature had failed to fulfil the requirements set out by the Return Directive, namely to expressly provide for objective criteria in domestic legislation, instead of relying on the definition of the risk of absconding provided by the law implementing the Dublin III Regulation.[58] Following this judgment, the legislature amended section 2(14) of the Residence Act, which now includes concrete objective criteria to be taken into consideration within return procedures.[59] Prior to this judgment, the same Court obliged, in 2014, the German legislature to implement correctly Article 2(n) of the Dublin III Regulation, by defining 'risk of absconding' in the sense of Article 28 of the Regulation in a statutory law.[60] This judgment led to a cross-fertilisation of norms and judgments across the EU. This was possible due to the fact that the definition of the risk of absconding is identical under the Return Directive, Recast Reception Conditions Directive[61] and Dublin III Regulation,[62] and all three instruments legitimise the adoption of detention on the basis of the risk of absconding.

These two German judgments had ripple effects across other domestic jurisdictions which found similarly to the German Supreme Civil Court that the risk of absconding whether provided by the Dublin III Regulation or by the Return Directive had to be defined in separate national laws in order to lawfully be the ground for detention of third-country nationals. For instance, the Supreme Administrative Court of Austria,[63] and then also a Czech regional court, found that detention of asylum seekers under the Dublin procedure on the basis of a risk of absconding that was not defined in a domestic law, but solely based on objective criteria set out in consistent administrative and jurisprudential practice, is invalid. The regional court in Ústí nad Labem used these judgments as well as additional comparative reasoning. Specifically, it also assessed foreign domestic legislation (ie Belgium, Italy, Hungary, Bulgaria and Slovakia) with the aim of establishing how other legislatures interpret the requirements of Articles 2(n) and 28 of the Dublin III Regulation.[64] It found that the respective national laws contained a

[57] Up until the judgment of the German Supreme Civil Court, BGH, Decision of 18.2.2016 – V ZB 23/15, para 14.

[58] See Decision of 18 February 2016 – V ZB 23/15.

[59] Provision 2(14) Aufenthaltsgesetz was amended and now lays down seven criteria establishing the risk of absconding. For more details, see Dörig and Bornemann (n 49).

[60] BGH, Decision of 26.6.2014 – V ZB 31/14, paras 28 et seq.

[61] See Art 8(3)(b) of Directive 2013/33/EU of the European Parliament and of the Council of 26 June 2013 laying down standards for the reception of applicants for international protection [2013] OJ L180, pp 96.

[62] See Art 28(2).

[63] See judgment of Administrative Court of Austria, Verwaltungsgerichtshof, 19 February 2015, no 2014/21/0075-5.

[64] Judgment of Regional court in Ústí nad Labem of 1 June 2015, no 42 A 12/2015–78 (available in Czech at: http://nssoud.cz/files/EVIDENCNI_LIST/2015/42A_12_2015_20150615085958_prevedeno.pdf).

definition of the relevant objective criteria for assessing the risk of absconding. Following a textual interpretation of these domestic legal provisions, the court emphasised that Member States are required to adopt domestic legislative provisions to define the risk of absconding under the Dublin III Regulation. The court remarked that the Czech legislator incorrectly considered Articles 2(n) and 28(2) of Dublin III Regulation as having direct applicability, since these provisions are an exception to the general rule that EU regulations do not require transposition into national law; therefore, as with Article 3(7) of the Return Directive, the notion of the risk of absconding has to be transposed in domestic legislation. The court then turned to the analysis of Article 129(1) of the Czech Aliens Act and found that it lacked the required list of objective criteria. Furthermore, the court found that objective criteria, such as mere irregular entry and residence,[65] which were used by the Czech administration as sufficient objective criterion for detention under Dublin proceedings, were contrary to the Regulation's prohibition to detain 'for the sole reason that [the asylum seeker] is subject to the procedure established by this Regulation'.[66] It should be noted that Recital 6 of the Return Directive contains a similar prohibition of 'illegal entry and stay' as the sole legal basis for decisions being taken in return proceedings. The Czech regional court concluded that the detention order issued to the Al Chodor family was unlawful, and annulled the Foreigners Police decision to detain the family.[67]

The judgment delivered by the regional court in Ústí nad Labem in the *Al Chodor* case is quite a remarkable example of judicial comparative reasoning, assessing the judgments of two foreign supreme courts interpreting the risk of absconding, in an attempt to find a uniform interpretation of the EU legal requirement of 'defined by law' that the risk of absconding in a Dublin transfer procedure has to fulfil.[68] The first-instance court's heavy reliance on comparative reasoning might be explained by the fact that it was the first court in the Czech Republic to consider the legality of Czech detention orders on the basis of EU primary and secondary legal provisions. Another reason for the Czech court's creative reasoning could have been the sensitive political nature of the issue. In fact, the case challenged the legality of a government policy, which is traditionally seen as reserved to executive competences.[69] Recourse to additional legal sources of interpretation could have strengthened the legitimacy of the regional court's judgment towards the executive.

[65] Illegal entry and residence are also prohibited as objective criteria by Recital 6 of the Return Directive preamble.

[66] See Art 28(1) of the Dublin III Regulation.

[67] For a detailed analysis of this case, see Moraru and Janku (n 40).

[68] See Z Kühn, *The Judiciary in Central and Eastern Europe, Mechanical Jurisprudence in Transformation?* (Leiden, Brill, 2011); GS Goodwin-Gill and H Lambert, *The Limits of Transnational Law: Refugee Law, Policy Harmonization and Judicial Dialogue in the European Union* (Cambridge, Cambridge University Press 2010).

[69] See Moraru and Janku (n 40).

Nevertheless, this judicial interpretation did not convince all domestic courts.[70] In the appeal lodged by the Foreigners Police against the judgment of the regional court in Ústí nad Labem, the Czech Supreme Administrative Court favoured a broader interpretation of the EU legal notion of 'law', which, in its view, could have included not only legislation, but also other sources of law, such as judicial and administrative practice.[71] Nevertheless, having doubts about the correct interpretation of the notion of 'law', the Supreme Administrative Court addressed a preliminary question to the CJEU. The Court asked whether the absence of objective criteria in a national law leads to the inapplicability of Article 28(2) of the Dublin III Regulation.[72]

In establishing the meaning of 'law', the CJEU itself made use of judicial dialogue and referred to the ECtHR case-law for the purpose of identifying the requirements that the law must fulfil when establishing limitations to the right to liberty.[73] The Court of Justice found that 'only a provision of general application' could meet these requirements. In agreement with the first-instance Czech court and national courts from other Member States cited by the Czech court, the CJEU found that 'settled case-law confirming a consistent administrative practice on the part of the Foreigners Police Section, such as in the main proceedings' does not meet the safeguards required by Article 6 of the EU Charter of Fundamental Rights, in particular protection against arbitrariness. Consequently, detention on the basis of a risk of absconding, where the objective criteria are not set in 'a provision of general application', cannot be based on Article 28(2) of the Dublin III Regulation. The CJEU clarified that administrative practice, even if consistent and confirmed by jurisprudence, does not fulfil these requirements. Therefore Member States that adopt detention of asylum seekers in the absence of a legal provision of general application are acting contrary to EU law.

While the CJEU preliminary ruling did not have any impact in the Czech Republic, since implementing legislation was adopted a few months after the referral,[74] the *Al Chodor* preliminary ruling did generate positive spill-over effect well beyond the Czech Republic, requiring all countries operating the Dublin system and the Return Directive to define the criteria for a risk of absconding in 'a provision of general application'. This requirement has generally

[70] eg see Judgment of the Regional Court in Brno, 11 August 2015, no 33 A 40/2015-32.

[71] Provided that they possess the 'substantive' qualities of precision, foreseeability and accessibility as required by Art 5(1)(f) ECHR.

[72] Decision of the Czech Supreme Administrative Court on the suspension of national proceeding and lodging a preliminary reference to the CJEU of 24 September 2015, no 10 Azs 122/2015-88 (available in Czech at: http://nssoud.cz/files/SOUDNI_VYKON/2015/012210Azs_1500088_20150924125155_prevedeno.pdf).

[73] Specifically, compliance with strict safeguards, namely the presence of a legal basis, clarity, predictability, accessibility and protection against arbitrariness, see Case C-528/15 *Al Chodor* ECLI:EU:C:2017:213, para 40.

[74] A legislative proposal was approved by the Parliament on 11 November 2015, and came into force on 15 December 2015.

been interpreted at the domestic level as requiring definition in a domestic law. Following this judgment, the French Court of Cassation[75] and the Administrative Court of Slovenia[76] annulled detention orders issued within Dublin proceedings due to lack of domestic legislation defining the 'risk of absconding'. These courts cited the *Al Chodor* preliminary ruling as an authoritative source for their decision to find administrative detention of asylum seekers subject to Dublin procedure unlawful. Furthermore, the *Al Chodor* judgment also triggered a process of legislative codification of the 'risk of absconding' in the United Kingdom, Belgium and Cyprus,[77] and reinforced the findings of certain domestic courts that the risk of absconding, both in Dublin and return procedures, needs to be defined in legal provisions of general application, such as laws.[78]

The cases discussed here involved numerous judicial interaction techniques which led to cross-fertilisation of norms and judgments touching on the interpretation of the risk of absconding. For the purpose of clarifying whether the risk of absconding should be defined in a law or also in administrative practice, domestic courts have resorted to comparative reasoning, transnational judicial dialogue, preliminary reference and disapplication of national administrative practices in favour of a direct application of the Return Directive. Foreign and CJEU judgments empowered domestic courts to strengthen the rule of law in immigration matters by striking down non-transparent and arbitrary administrative decision-making.

B. The Objectivity Requirement – Clarification of the Content and Number of Objective Criteria

Article 3(7) of the Return Directive does not provide a common EU list of objective criteria, or an explanation of what and how many criteria a Member State could include as part of the definition of the risk of absconding. Certain Member States took advantage of the abstract definition of the 'risk of absconding', and provided for a catch-all list of objective criteria, leading to very few situations falling outside the scope of the risk of absconding.[79] Several criteria introduced by Member States appear to be irrelevant to the assessment of a risk of absconding

[75] See Cour de Cassation, judgment no 1130 of 27 September 2017 [Pourvoi n 17-15.160]. For a detailed commentary on the judgment, see Marie-Laure Basilien-Gainche, 'The French Suite. The Effect of *Al Chodor* on the Detention of Asylum Seekers for the Purpose of a Dublin Transfer', blog post available at www.asylumlawdatabase.eu/en/journal/french-suite-effect-al-chodor-detention-asylum-seekers-purpose-dublin-transfer.

[76] Administrative Court, Decision I U 1102/2016, 29 July 2016. The authorities applied by analogy the objective criteria provided for the definition of the risk of absconding as ground for pre-removal detention.

[77] See AIDA Update on the implementation of the Dublin III Regulation in 2018, available at http://www.asylumineurope.org/sites/default/files/aida_2018update_dublin.pdf.

[78] See BGH, Decision of 18.2.2016 – V ZB 23/15, para 14.

[79] See, in particular, the practices reported in France, Italy, Netherlands and Slovenia, in REDIAL Research Report 2016/05 (n 14).

(eg lack of financial resources,[80] payment of large amounts of money to smugglers for the purpose of illegally entering the territory of Member States).[81] Other problematic criteria, such as illegal entry and stay, continued as sufficient legal grounds for pre-removal detention.[82]

Member States have varied lists of objective criteria. Some of these lists are extensive, including numerous circumstances as objective criteria, whereas others include catch-all objective criteria (eg illegal entry or stay, or a criminal record). In certain jurisdictions which provide an exhaustive list of objective criteria, it suffices to satisfy a single criterion from this list to establish a risk of absconding and consequently to justify the adoption of pre-removal detention (eg Italy and Netherlands[83]). However, Article 3(7) of the Return Directive read in conjunction with Recital 6 requires that 'decisions taken under this Directive should be adopted on a case-by-case basis and based on objective criteria'. This implies that even when such objective criteria are set in national legislation, there can be no general presumption of the existence of the risk of absconding. Instead, individual situations and circumstances must additionally be taken into consideration. However, the individual assessment obligation was not included in the domestic legislation of all EU Member States. Thus competent administrative and judicial bodies could have found a risk of absconding once one of the objective criteria was found to exist.[84]

So far, the CJEU has not had the opportunity to interpret the 'objective criteria' requirement within the framework of return procedures. Nevertheless, domestic courts may find inspiration in the *Jawo* judgment, where the CJEU had to interpret the notion of 'objective criteria' within the framework of Dublin transfer proceedings.[85] In this case, any absence of the third-country national from his or her allocated accommodation without prior notification to the competent national authorities was found to entitle domestic authorities to presume a risk of absconding, but only if they had fulfilled their obligation to inform the third-country national of his or her obligation to notify the absence from or change in accommodation.

The *Jawo* as well as other preliminary rulings delivered by the CJEU in the field of the Return Directive confirm the mandatory nature of the individual assessment requirement, governing all stages of the return procedure.[86] So far, the CJEU

[80] For instance, Italy, A di Pascale, REDIAL National Report on Pre-Removal Detention, http://euredial.eu/publications/nationalsynthesis-reports.

[81] eg Germany; see Bornemann and Dörig (n 49).

[82] eg Italy, France, Slovenia, Romania, Spain and Slovakia; see REDIAL Research Report 2016/05 (n 9) 14.

[83] On the Netherlands, see G Cornelisse and J Bouwman, REDIAL Synthesis Report, first package (n 16) 2ff.

[84] ibid.

[85] Case C-163/17 *Jawo* ECLI:EU:C:2019:218.

[86] Case C-61/11 PPU *El Dridi* ECLI:EU:C:2011:268, para 39; Case C-430/11 *Sagor* EU:C:2012:777, para 41; *Mahdi* (n 15) para 70; Opinion of AG in Case C-290/14 *Celaj* ECLI:EU:C:2015:285, points 29 and 49.

rejected a refusal of voluntary departure based on an automatic finding of a risk to public policy solely on the basis of suspicion that a third-country national has committed a criminal offence or an established criminal offence.[87] The lack of identity documents was rejected as sole ground for a risk of absconding that could legitimise the prolongation of pre-removal detention.[88] On the basis of the CJEU jurisprudence and discussions during the elaboration of the Return Directive, it can be inferred that the risk of absconding shall not automatically be deduced from the mere fact that a third-country national is illegally staying on the territory of a Member State.[89]

Relying on the Return Directive and the relevant CJEU jurisprudence, national courts from several Member States have started to reverse the practice of the administrative authorities, and reinterpreted flawed national legislation in line with EU law.[90] Other domestic courts have taken a firmer position, rejecting reliance on the absence of established identity and documents. The Lithuanian Supreme Administrative Court has consistently held that this alone cannot be the basis for detention without carrying out an individual assessment.[91] The Swedish Supreme Migration Court refused to consider a refusal of voluntary departure (an objective ground for pre-removal detention under Swedish legislation) as indicating a risk of absconding sufficient to justify a detention order.[92]

Although several supreme and regional courts used the individual assessment as a parameter of legality for the risk of absconding directly on the basis of the Return Directive, the general proliferation of this approach among domestic judiciaries came only after the CJEU consistently recognised the mandatory nature of the individual assessment throughout the return procedure, and indirectly rejected certain circumstances as objective criteria. This is the case of the French courts, which although they had traditionally allowed a wide margin of discretion in decision-making to the administration, gradually started to use individual assessment as a parameter of legality for return measures adopted by the administration following the CJEU pronouncements.[93] Other national courts also rejected

[87] Case C-554/13 *Zh and O* ECLI:EU:C:2015:377.FJ.

[88] *Mahdi* (n 15).

[89] ibid, and Case C-357/09 PPU, *Kadzoev*, ECLI:EU:C:2009:741 and Proposed EU Return Directive, A6-0339/2007, 20.09.2007, Amendment 19, Art 3.

[90] See, for instance, the judgments of Slovakian courts, eg judgment 9 Sp 99/2013, see also the REDIAL Slovakian Report on Pre-Removal Detention, third package; see also the Dutch Council of State follow-up judgment to the CJEU preliminary ruling in *Zh and O* (at Raad Van State, 201407197/1/V3, 20 November 2015), which is commented in REDIAL Research Report 2016/02 (n 39) 10.

[91] No A-3219-858/2015, judgment of 22 July 2015.

[92] Supreme Migration Court (Sweden), case no MIG 2008:23 UM1610-08. The justification provided by this court was that the detention order would no longer be a last-resort measure, if refusal of voluntary departure would automatically be considered a risk of absconding, but it would be ordered in the majority of cases involving refused asylum seekers. See more in the T Quintel, *REDIAL Swedish Report on Pre-Removal Detention*, available at http://euredial.eu/docs/publications/national-synthesis-reports/SwedenFB.pdf.

[93] TA Lille, 22 July 2011, no 1104137; CAA Bordeaux, 3 April 2012, No. 11CX02996; Dutch Council of State, 10 July 2014, 201309038/1/V1; CAA Paris, 1 ch, May 310, 2013, no 12PA03323.

general statements deprived of concrete factual references to individual situations ('there is no integration in Austrian society or legal order') used to justify the existence of a risk of absconding.[94] The Council for Alien Law Litigation of Belgium (CALL) started to closely scrutinise the circumstances of return-related cases, finding different results depending on the concrete circumstances of the case. For instance, the absence of an official address in Belgium was considered sufficient proof of a risk of absconding, justifying a refusal to grant a voluntary departure.[95] In another case, CALL took a different decision, although the same objective criterion, lack of an official address in Belgium, was found applicable. The court suspended the order to leave the territory and ordered the Aliens Office to take into consideration the fact that the applicant lived in fact with his wife and two children, who resided legally in Belgium, and that this particular aspect spoke against a risk of absconding, unlike the previous case.[96] A similar change in approach was registered in Bulgaria. Although the Supreme Administrative Court had rejected the use of lack of identity documents as an automatic ground for pre-removal detention and prolongation of detention,[97] this judgment was widely endorsed only following the CJEU preliminary ruling in *Mahdi*.[98] In conclusion, there seems to be an increasing jurisprudential trend whereby courts no longer accept as justified the automatic finding of the administration of a risk of absconding under the impact of vertical judicial dialogue.[99]

This chapter does not argue in favour of more harmonisation of objective criteria as a solution to ensure more consistent assessment of the risk of absconding.[100] It argues that, first and foremost, efforts should concentrate on legislative and administrative adaptation to the red lines drawn by CJEU and domestic courts in terms of acceptable objective criteria and their assessment. Certain circumstances, such as illegal entry, stay and lack of identity documents, are difficult to maintain as objective, given the approach of the CJEU in its case-law on the risk to public policy and pre-removal detention.[101] Other criteria (eg lack of financial resources

[94] Federal Administrative Court, G307 2009115-1/2E, 28.7.2014; see the REDIAL Austrian Report on Pre-Removal Detention.

[95] CALL, no 97 083, 13.02.2013.

[96] A family seems to be widely considered as a guarantee that there is no risk of absconding.

[97] The Supreme Administrative Court of Bulgaria concluded that Recitals 6 and 13 of the Preamble to the Return Directive require the authorities to take into account several factors when establishing a risk of absconding. Among these, the Court mentioned the duration of the person's residence in Bulgaria; the categories of vulnerable persons; the existence of proceedings under the Law on Asylum and Refugees or proceedings for the renewal of a residence permit or of another authorisation offering a right to stay; the family situation; and the existence of the person's family, cultural and social ties with his/her country of origin; see case no 13868/2010.

[98] See the REDIAL Bulgarian Report on Pre-Removal Detention, third package. For a detailed assessment of the CJEU preliminary ruling in Mahdi and its impact at domestic level, see M Moraru, 'REDIAL Electronic Journal on Judicial Interaction: Articles 15 to 18 of the Return Directive 2008/115', REDIAL Research Report 2017/01, 23.

[99] See, in particular, the approach of the Austrian, Czech and French courts.

[100] A harmonisation proposal is put forward by the EC Proposal for the recast of the Return Directive, 6; although this proposal is highly criticised, see n 23.

[101] *Zh and O* (n 87) para 50; *Mahdi* (n 15) paras 40, 72.

and payment of large amounts of money to smugglers for the purpose of illegally entering the territory of Member States) seem irrelevant to the assessment of a risk of absconding. In these circumstances, the application of judicial individual assessment is not sufficient to remedy an incoherent legislative and administrative transposition of the risk of absconding; only legislative amendment can succeed. However, should harmonisation of objective criteria be followed at the EU level, three main rules should be followed. First, we should look at the common denominator of objective criteria provided across the EU Member States, instead of copy-pasting all the criteria ever provided in national legal acts. Secondly, it is necessary to ask if the criteria obtained via the common denominator method are in line with the jurisprudentially developed red lines of the CJEU. Thirdly, the remaining criteria should then be checked against normative standards, such as respect for fundamental rights and rule of law. Ultimately, an impact assessment should be carried out proving a causal correlation between a narrow or broad definition of the risk of absconding and the (in)effectiveness of returns. So far, the only proven correlation has been that between the lack of cooperation of third countries and the enforcement of returns.[102]

C. Clarification of the Effects of the Risk of Absconding – The Jurisprudential Principle of Gradualism for Choosing the Correct Return Measure

The margin of discretion recognised for the Member States by the Directive's broad definition of a risk of absconding was wrongly interpreted by the Member States not only in terms of the content and number of objective criteria, but also in terms of the effects the risk of absconding could have on the return procedure. Although the Return Directive sets out the risk of absconding as legal grounds for several return-related measures,[103] some Member States continued to prioritise pre-removal detention when a risk of absconding was identified. This was due to the fact that, at the time of its adoption, the Return Directive introduced a different model of returning irregular migrants from most of the domestic regulatory frameworks that were increasingly focused on 'securitisation' and 'deterrence'.[104]

The preliminary reference procedure has contributed to the clarification of the order in which the return measures must be adopted in the overall return procedure, thus including also those measures that could be adopted on the basis of

[102] S Mananashvili, 'EU's Return Policy: Mission Accomplished in 2016? Reading Between the Lines of the Latest EUROSTAT Return Statistics', ICMPD Policy Brief, May 2017.

[103] ie voluntary departure with obligations; shortening of voluntary departure; refusal of voluntary departure and adoption of removal order; pre-removal detention.

[104] See, in particular, Spain, Cyprus, Italy, and France; see Chapters 1, 5, 13 and 14 in this volume.

a risk of absconding. Following the preliminary references sent by Italian and French courts, the CJEU developed the principle of gradualism when deciding which return measure to adopt.[105] According to this jurisprudentially developed principle, once the return decision is issued, Member States should follow a mandatory order in the return procedure, starting from the least restrictive to the third-country national's freedom (voluntary departure),[106] followed by physical enforcement of the return (removal),[107] issue of an entry ban,[108] and the last-resort return measure, which is also the most coercive – pre-removal detention.[109] This settled mandatory sliding scale of return measures commences with voluntary return, and will allow only for a step-by-step intensification of coercion.[110] This 'gradation' of return measures was based by the CJEU on the EU law principle of proportionality, which governs the entire return procedure.[111] According to the principle of proportionality, both administrative and judicial authorities should always consider and prefer the least coercive measure available in each individual case, not least during the removal process. The CJEU jurisprudence clarified that the Directive's return model is based on novel and protective underlying principles, such as legal clarity (all irregular third-country nationals should be served with a return decision or their stay should be regularised); the principle of primacy of voluntary departure over forced return; pre-removal detention as a last resort; individual assessment of cases; and the principle of respecting *non-refoulement*, best interests of the child, family life and state of health when implementing the Directive. Following the clear pronouncement of the principle of gradualism by the CJEU, the Member States had to adopt systemic reforms of their 'expulsion' procedures, requiring changes of legal terms, definitions, order of measures, and most importantly of their 'securitisation' or 'criminalisation' approach to managing immigration.[112] In some jurisdictions, the reform took as long as a decade to align with the Directive's underlying principles,[113] while some Member States still have not achieved a correct transposition.[114]

Following the jurisprudentially developed principle of gradualism, national courts started to pay closer attention to these principles when deciding the effects of the risk of absconding; this involved: establishing voluntary departure with

[105] See *El Dridi* (n 86) paras 36–41; Case C-290/14 *Celaj* ECLI:EU:C:2015:640; *Sagor* (n 86); and Case C-329/11 *Achughbabian* ECLI:EU:C:2011:807.

[106] See Art 7 of the Return Directive.

[107] Art 8 of the Return Directive.

[108] Art 11 of the Return Directive.

[109] See, in particular, Art 15 of the Return Directive.

[110] According to *Celaj* (n 105); *Sagor* (n 86); *Achughbabian* (n 105); *El Dridi* (n 86).

[111] See *El Dridi* (n 86) para 41.

[112] See 2014 EC Evaluation of the Implementation of the Return Directive (n 8).

[113] See, for instance, the case of Spain, where the 'doctrine of fine' was effectively replaced with the removal order only in the summer of 2018. See Rotaeche (n 18).

[114] Mostly as regards the prioritisation of alternatives to pre-removal detention, see more in di Pascale (n 36); S Slama, 'Trois hautes juridictions nationales pour une directive: une interaction judiciaire en trompe l'œil', Chapter 14 in this volume; and S Sarolea, 'Detention of Migrants in Belgium and the Criminal Judge: A Lewis Carroll World', Chapter 11 in this volume.

attached obligations; limiting the voluntary departure period; refusing voluntary departure; and adopting a removal order, or detention.[115] They gradually started to scrutinise the failure of the administrative authorities to adequately assess the possibility of imposing one or more obligations as an alternative prior to adopting a coercive removal order, and quashing administrative decisions that did not respect this principle.[116] Furthermore, national courts increasingly rejected general statements, such as 'there is no integration in the society or legal order', as legitimate grounds proving a risk of absconding.[117]

A particularly sensitive challenge in the implementation of the risk of absconding was the limited reviewing and remedial powers of national courts. Certain administrative courts could not consider facts beyond those brought by administrative authorities and parties, and could not establish a different return-related measure in the place of the measure incorrectly established by the administration. The CJEU preliminary ruling in *Mahdi* empowered national courts to run an accurate and in-depth individual assessment of facts and law in order to determine the extension of pre-removal detention. To that end, the judicial authority

> must be able to take into account both the facts stated and the evidence adduced by the administrative authority and any observations that may be submitted by the third-country national. Furthermore, that authority must be able to consider any other element that is relevant for its decision should it so deem necessary.[118]

The CJEU also empowered national courts to substitute the administrative decisions on prolongation of pre-removal detention with their own decisions 'or, as the case may be, the judicial authority which ordered the initial detention, and to take a decision on whether to order an alternative measure or the release of the third-country national concerned'.[119] The CJEU preliminary ruling in *Mahdi* was interpreted by national courts across the EU as an empowerment to run an in-depth assessment of the administrative decisions ordering a pre-removal detention, and thus implicitly also a careful assessment of the risk of absconding.[120] Judicial empowerment has spread also in the Netherlands,[121] Cyprus[122] and Slovenia,[123] where courts considered they have an EU law

[115] See REDIAL Research Report 2016/01 (n 7).

[116] ibid.

[117] See eg Austrian Federal Administrative Court, G307 2009115-1/2E, 28.7.2014; for more jurisprudence see REDIAL Research Report 2016/01 (n 7) and REDIAL Research Report 2016/02 (n 39).

[118] See *Mahdi* (n 15) para 62.

[119] ibid.

[120] For more analysis of the *Mahdi* judgment and its impact in Bulgaria, see the REDIAL Bulgarian Report on Pre-Removal Detention; more widely at the EU level, see REDIAL Research Report 2017/01 (n 98). See also V Ilareva, 'The Right to Be Heard – The Underestimated Condition for Effective Returns and Human Rights Consideration', Chapter 15, in this volume.

[121] Dutch Council of State, Decision no 201408655/1/V3; see more in G Cornelisse, *REDIAL Dutch Report on pre-removal detention.*

[122] Cyprus, Supreme Court, Re. the application of Vilma Galivan Marcelino, civil application no 169/2012, 14 December 2012. See more in REDIAL Research Report 2017/01 (n 98).

[123] Administrative Court of the Republic of Slovenia, I U 1102/2016, 29.7.2016.

obligation to assess in full and also on the basis of ex officio evidence all aspects of pre-removal detention, including the requirements of the risk of absconding. Moreover, they also started to go beyond mere annulment of the administrative decisions and decide the appropriate alternatives in cases of errors in the risk of absconding assessment.[124]

It appears that, following an intensive vertical judicial dialogue with the CJEU, national courts are slowly accepting the idea of extending their judicial review beyond mere manifest error(s) committed by the national authorities when assessing the risk of absconding. Courts are increasingly approaching the principles of gradualism, individualism and proportionality as mandatory parameters of legality for the return measures adopted on the basis of the risk of absconding. While significant changes have occurred in the practice of the supreme courts of Bulgaria, Italy and Spain, there is still a long way to go before this practice is uniformly spread across courts from all levels of jurisdictions and EU countries. As pointed out by several of the authors in this volume, there is still considerable judicial resistance to this approach, which cannot be addressed solely by more harmonisation or vertical judicial dialogue, but requires transnational judicial interaction, particularly in the form of transnational trainings and exchanges.[125]

IV. Conclusions: Judicial Dialogue Strengthening the Rule of Law in the Implementation of the Risk of Absconding

This chapter has shown the development of a worrying trend among domestic administrations, which has blurred the lines between irregularity and the risk of absconding, by way of automatically presuming a risk of absconding whenever a third-country national finds herself in a situation of an irregular legal status. The broad definition of the risk of absconding, its automatic use and its transposition in administrative acts that escape parliamentary scrutiny are illustrations of a still present administrative monopoly over return procedures. This administrative control becomes particularly troublesome when it undermines judicial independence, powers and legitimacy, and endangers fundamental rights and the rule of law as mandatory principles governing the implementation of the Return Directive. Various strategies have developed in an attempt to limit the judicial scrutiny of administrative decisions finding a risk of absconding, such as: allocating competences to a new category of non-professional, honorary judges without specialisation (eg in Italy, the *giudice di pace*); limiting powers of judicial

[124] For more details see the chapters in Part II of this volume.

[125] See, in particular, Kosar and Blisa (n 13) and B Zalar, 'Impact of Judicial Dialogue(s) on Development and Affirmation of the Right to Effective Legal Remedy from Articles 13 and 14 of the Return Directive', Chapter 16 in this volume.

review of the most contentious return related measure – pre-removal detention (eg Bulgaria) or discrediting the judicial understanding of the return procedures (eg Italy, Hungary).[126]

In this context of power struggles to maintain return procedures as the prerogative of the administration, and thus resisting changes required by the Return Directive,[127] the jurisprudence analysed in this chapter shows that judicial dialogue has contributed in three main ways to the interpretation and application of the risk of absconding across the EU. First, it has helped courts to fill gaps in the EU legal definition of the risk of absconding and thus ensure a coherent application transnationally. For instance, the *Al Chodor* judgment has had ripple effects across domestic jurisdictions, leading to legislative reforms defining the risk of absconding in return procedures in national laws or a legal provision of general application.

Secondly, judicial dialogue has contributed to a de facto narrowing of objective criteria on the basis of the systematic application of individual assessment and application by analogy of the CJEU preliminary rulings as regards return proceedings. For instance, illegal entry, stay and lack of identity documents are less accepted by domestic courts as objective criteria, in particular as grounds for pre-removal detention. Moreover, a criminal record cannot automatically lead to a risk of absconding, but has to be joined by proof of a genuine and present risk.[128]

Thirdly, vertical judicial dialogue has contributed to the coherent implementation of the risk of absconding at domestic level, following common jurisprudentially crafted principles, such as: derogations should be strictly interpreted;[129] respect of fundamental rights should be ensured at all stages of return procedures;[130] the principle of proportionality should be ensured;[131] and any assessment relating to the risk of the person concerned absconding must be based on the individual examination of that person's case.[132]

In spite of these positive achievements of judicial dialogue, there still are a number of deficiencies as regards the definition of the risk of absconding in domestic legislation and its practical application by domestic administrations. Notably, the number and content of 'objective criteria' have mostly remained those existent before the entry into force of the Directive.[133] On this issue, the approach

[126] See n 20.

[127] See, in particular the long transposition of the risk of absconding in legal provisions of general application, such as laws; or the still present illegal entry and stay as objective criteria for finding a risk of absconding (e.g. Italy and Netherlands).

[128] *Zh and O* (n 87) para 50.

[129] ibid, para 42.

[130] *El Dridi* (n 86).

[131] *El Dridi* (n 86), para 41.

[132] *Sagor* (n 86), para 41; *Mahdi* (n 86) para 70.

[133] For instance Spain (see Chapter 1 in this volume), Netherlands (REDIAL National Synthesis Report on Termination of Illegal Stay (n 16) 2–4, available at http://euredial.eu/docs/publications/national-synthesis-reports/NETHERLANDS.pdf), Slovenia (REDIAL Research Report 2016/01 (n 7) 17 et seq).

taken by domestic courts has been quite conservative, as they did not address a preliminary reference to the CJEU asking for guidelines on how to interpret the requirement of 'objective criteria', nor disapplied national legislation providing numerous objective criteria that would revert the mandatory order of return stages set by the Directive. The lack of preliminary questions on the risk of absconding within return procedures could be the result of both conscious and unconscious judicial decisions. A lesser degree of EU law knowledge, a stronger orientation towards national law and deferential approach towards the decision-making of the administration may result in unawareness of certain incompatibilities or uncertainties at EU level. This orientation appears to be typical for the Italian *giudice di pace*, and to a certain extent of some of the French courts. On the other hand, the national courts' decision not to refer might be a conscious one in other countries. National judges may not refer preliminary questions as they feel quite competent to apply EU law themselves, relying on a vast body of case-law developed by the CJEU (eg Dutch courts using the individual assessment to narrow down the Dutch long list of objective criteria). In conclusion, this chapter argues that more efforts are needed from both domestic judiciaries and other state powers to remedy the domestic lists including numerous objective criteria, especially those originating from before the entry into force of the Directive,[134] along the lines of the CJEU jurisprudence.

[134] See, in particular, Spain, according to Rotaeche (n 17).

6

Cypriot Courts, the Return Directive and Fundamental Rights: Challenges and Failures

CORINA DEMETRIOU AND NICOS TRIMIKLINIOTIS

I. Introduction

This chapter will illustrate how the legal and sociopolitical context within which the Cypriot courts adjudicate renders effective implementation of the Return Directive difficult. It highlights the critical role of the courts in ensuring or undermining effective implementation and engages with gaps and weaknesses in the outcomes. The problems encountered in accessing rights under the Return Directive partly stem from the failure of judicial traditions both to learn from European and foreign domestic courts and to embrace a rights-based approach, but mostly arise from flaws in the Cypriot juridical system itself. The judicial reluctance to give primacy to the protection of fundamental rights and, in the spirit of the EU Charter, to interpret all laws transposing the EU acquis in a manner compliant with the Charter remains a key issue. In most cases the transposition of the Return Directive has brought little change to administrative policies and practices, while certain aspects of the Directive are implemented deficiently or not at all.

II. Cypriot Courts, Accession and the Return Directive

Claims to substantive rights derived from the EU Charter, regional and international law instruments (ECHR, relevant UN Conventions, etc) and the Cypriot constitution are rarely taken up; they are typically discounted in favour of a procedural approach that favours precedence over substance. In a string of landmark decisions, the Supreme Court has upheld the broad discretion of the immigration authorities to detain and deport third-country nationals, since neither the ECHR nor the constitution can guarantee the stay of a foreigner in Cyprus.[1] In most cases the CJEU jurisprudence is not referred to at all in the reasoning of the decisions; in others, courts endorse arguments that distinguish CJEU jurisprudence from the facts of the case at hand. The use of the judicial review procedure to challenge deportation and detention orders has inevitably led to a formalistic judicial approach that allows procedural obstacles to take precedence over the protection of fundamental rights.

To understand the premise of the Cypriot judicial tradition one must consider the juridical, structural and historical context within which Cypriot courts operate. The limited scope of the judicial review procedure is a stumbling block; courts tend to interpret it rather restrictively, often at the expense of substantive fundamental rights deriving from the acquis. The Administrative Court has, since its establishment in 2015, taken over from the Supreme Court the task of reviewing the actions of immigration authorities in matters pertaining to the Return Directive. There are problems with this system. First, while the supremacy of EU law is formally recognised in the fifth amendment of the constitution as well as national jurisprudence,[2] it is insufficiently implemented in practice, particularly when it comes to immigration matters. Partly due to a rigid definition of the principle of separation of powers and partly due to the nature of the judicial review procedure, the tradition emphasises maximum executive discretion over immigration matters as an expression of sovereignty. Judicial review jurisprudence, as developed by the Supreme Court and now the Administrative Court, is limited to examining the decision-making process rather than analysing the decision's merits.

The Return Directive was transposed in 2011 by incorporating most of its provisions almost verbatim into the existing immigration law ('Immigration Law') without deleting older provisions that conflicted with it.[3] The courts generally do not rank the former over the latter, even in cases of direct conflict between them. For example, Article 6 of the Immigration Law gives the Chief Immigration Officer discretion to deport non-nationals on a long list of general and vague grounds, many of which contravene the non-criminalisation and non-discrimination principles.

One has to examine this in the context of how the Return Directive and the general EU fundamental rights acquis have been integrated into the national legal and policy framework on immigration – described as the 'Cypriot migration state

[1] See *Moyo and Another v The Republic* [1988] 3 CLR, 1208; *Gnanawathie Kurumage v Republic*, 673/2007, 5 December 2008; K Paraskeva, *Κυπριακό Συνταγματικό Δίκαιο, Θεμελιώδη Δικαιώματα και Ελευθερίες* (Athens, Nomiki Vivliothiki, 2015) 566; N Trimikliniotis, 'The Proliferation of Cypriot States of Exception: The Erosion of Fundamental Rights as Collateral Damage of the Cyprus Problem' (2018) 30(2) *Cyprus Review* 43.

[2] Law No 121(1)/2006; *Organosi Agoniston Dikaiosinis v Cyprus House of Representatives*, 2/2016, 9 May 2016.

[3] Amendment 153(I)/2011 to Aliens and Immigration Law, Cap 105, *Cyprus Gazette*, I(I), A ρ 4305, 25/11/2011.

of exception' – which combines state necessity arguments with a stringent immigration regime.[4] The immigration authorities' broad powers predate Cyprus's accession to the European Union, but continue to operate as a parallel legal system that functions independently of EU law on expulsions and deportations. Even before the 1991 policy change that made Cyprus a destination for thousands of migrants, national courts were reluctant to interfere with the immigration authorities' wide margin of discretion. In an early landmark legal precedent cited in hundreds of subsequent judgments, the Supreme Court confirmed the principle that 'the right of the State to regulate the length of stay of an alien is an attribute of sovereignty'.[5] While Cypriot courts are not alone in adopting such a line, they often fail to duly consider vital aspects of EU law and jurisprudence. According to Article 6(1)(d) of the Immigration Law, 'any person convicted of murder or criminal offence for which a prison sentence of any duration has been imposed and who, due to the circumstances, is considered by the chief immigration officer to be an unwanted immigrant' is subject to detention and eventual removal. Third-country nationals convicted of an offence, no matter how minor, are denied the protection offered by the Return Directive, a practice of questionable legality grounded upon an interpretation of Article 2(2)(b) that seeks to exclude all persons convicted of an offence, even an immigration offence, from the ambit of the Directive.

III. Overview of the Judicial System and Judicial Practice

National law transposing the Return Directive does not provide for ex officio supervision by judicial authorities and, as a matter of custom, courts do not consider arguments or laws unless these have been raised or cited by the litigants.[6] They also do not question the compliance of any legislation transposing the acquis with the Directive they purport to transpose, considering this to be the task of the legislature.[7] There is no tradition of referrals to the CJEU; all requests from litigants to national courts to seek input from the CJEU have been refused on the

[4] Trimikliniotis (n 1); N Trimikliniotis, 'Migration and Freedom of Movement of Workers: EU Law, Crisis and the Cypriot States of Exception' (2013) 2 *Laws* 440 (www.mdpi.com/2075-471X/2/4/440); CM Constantinou, 'On the Cypriot States of Exception' (2008) 2 *International Political Sociology* 145.

[5] *Moyo* (n 1).

[6] A rare exception to this took place in 2018 when the Appeal Court acquitted a banker of charges relating to market manipulation on grounds raised by the Court itself rather than the litigants: *Eliades v Republic of Cyprus* and *Bank of Cyprus Public Company Ltd v The Republic of Cyprus*, civil appeals no 2/2018 and 3/2018, 12 September 2018. This decision received considerable criticism from analysts and from the Attorney General himself.

[7] *Re the application of Ioannis Hadjioannou and George Longkritis for permit to file an application for a certiorari order*, Civil Appl No 33/2018, 2 May 2018.

grounds that the issue at stake is clear (*acte claire*) and does not require further interpretation.[8]

Courts are not always involved in return procedures, as removals of third-country nationals may be (and usually are) conducted with administrative removal orders.[9] In order to challenge the legality of a removal order,[10] an application for judicial review must be filed under Article 146 of the Constitution.[11] Because removal orders are always issued in combination with detention orders, challenging the former usually involves challenging the latter as well. If challenging the length of detention, an application must be filed for a habeas corpus order under Article 155.4 of the constitution.[12] The distinction between the two procedures is not always clear and there have been several court decisions rejecting applications on behalf of detainees because they followed procedure (a) instead of (b) or vice versa.[13] The recent establishment of the Administrative Court has made matters even more complicated, because it now examines judicial review applications, whereas habeas corpus order applications continue to be examined by the Supreme Court.[14] Neither process is automatic; both must be applied for by the detainee and are costly and time consuming. This legislation is not compliant with Article 15(3) of the Return Directive, which requires an ex officio judicial review in the case of prolonged detention periods.

In 2012 (ie before the establishment of the Administrative Court) the Supreme Court, examining the habeas corpus application of Vilma Galivan Marcelino, was faced with a rather artificial argument from the authorities, based on the procedure chosen by the applicant and the Court's alleged lack of jurisdiction. The Court rejected the latter allegation on the grounds that the case concerned the legality of the detention (a matter for the judicial review procedure) and not the duration of the detention (a matter for the habeas corpus procedure). The Court ruled that 'the two ways of reviewing the legality of detention, in private and public law, converge to a degree in the framework of the scope of application of the RD aiming, in a unified manner, at the control of the legality of detention'.[15] Since the Administrative Court's founding, however, this sort of unified approach is no longer an option: the Supreme Court cannot examine judicial review applications and the Administrative Court cannot examine habeas corpus applications.

[8] *Charis Christodoulidou v Republic of Cyprus through the Public Service Committee*, Case No 12/10, 3 April 2015.

[9] Immigration Law, Art 18 PST(1).

[10] Immigration Law, Art 18 PST(3).

[11] Constitution of the Republic of Cyprus, Art 146.

[12] Immigration Law, Art 18 PST(5)(a).

[13] *Re the application of Manzoor Hussain for the issue of a habeas corpus writ*, Appl No 52/2012, 31 May 2012.

[14] Law providing for the establishment and operation of an administrative court 131(I)/2015, 21 July 2015.

[15] *Re the application of Vilma Galivan Marcelino*, Civil Appl No 169/2012, 14 December 2012.

As previously stated, the courts confine themselves to ascertaining the legality of the decision-making process and avoid evaluating the correctness of the decision.[16] If the process does not comply with a checklist contained in Article 146 of the constitution (keeping proper records, making such records available, indicating reasons for the decision, holding a due inquiry into the facts of the case), then it is annulled, the detainee is released. However, the competent administrative authority may then chose another course of action, or simply issue a new decision for detention and deportation, which is considered under the law to be a new administrative act. However, if the process complies, then the validity of the detention order is confirmed. The above rule is not strictly followed in cases of detention pending return, presumably because the judicial review and habeas corpus applications are the designated means of judicial control in these cases, in compliance with the requirements of Article 15(2) and (3) of the Return Directive. In practice, courts examining these applications are essentially looking into the facts in order to assess whether the authorities were justified in detaining the applicant or in renewing the applicant's detention. The constitutional checklist may be used, but not on its own; the grounds introduced by Article 15(1) of the Return Directive, such as less coercive measures, the risk of absconding and due diligence in pursuing the detainee's return, are also relevant.

The courts abstain from performing a thorough check of the legality of an administrative decision when the administration invokes the ground of 'public security'. In the case of *Falak Shad* the judge found that the administration's discretion as regards third-country nationals' entry stay and work is wide and it need not justify its actions when security concerns are invoked. The Court concluded that the administration is not obliged to give reasons for the deportation or refusal of entry of any person, and the Court may not get involved in what is purely an executive matter.[17] National immigration law, which was enacted long before the transposition of the Return Directive, defines an illegal migrant, inter alia, as any person who, on the basis of testimony which appears to the Council of Ministers to be adequate, may pose a threat to peace, public order or public morals or may cause hostility between citizens of the Republic or revolt against the authorities.[18] This provision appears to be in line with Article 3(2) of the Return Directive, which defines 'illegal stay' as the presence on the territory of a Member State of a third-country national who does not fulfil the conditions of entry as set out, inter alia, in the Member State's conditions of entry and stay.

The administrative powers enshrined in the Immigration Law and judicial practice do not appear to be in line with the letter or the spirit of the Return Directive. In the process of deporting 'illegal migrants' immigration authorities may detain them for up to eight days unless the detention is renewed by

[16] G Pikis *Constitutionalism – Human Rights – Separation of Powers: The Cyprus Precedent* (Leiden, Martinus Nijhoff, 2006) 128.

[17] *Falak Shad v the Republic*, Case No 763/2011, 26 July 2013.

[18] Immigration Law, Art 6(1)(z).

the Court.[19] Although still part of the law, this provision is no longer applied, as the provision introduced by the Return Directive for detention of up to 18 months is preferred by the authorities and accepted by the courts. Persons against whom a detention order has been issued have the right to be informed of the reasons for their detention unless there are public security reasons rendering the supply of such information undesirable.[20] The Court invoked public security in *Falak Shad* when the applicant sought to overrule the detention order on the grounds that it had not been justified. The Court ruled that the absence of justification in the body of a decision does not affect the legality of the detention if there is sufficient evidence in the case file. In this case it considered the national security-based reasoning on file to be sufficient justification. It added that there is no need for a prior court conviction against an applicant in order to establish a public order threat; detention in such cases should not be seen as punishment but merely as a matter for the administration's discretion. This approach infringes Article 15(2) RD, which requires that both factual and legal reasons for detention be given in writing. The risk of absconding as a justification for detention appears to be taken for granted in every case, as removal orders are invariably issued in combination with detention orders, a practice that has never been flagged by the Court as a potential infringement of the RD.

IV. Judicial Interactions

By far the most commonly cited CJEU ruling in Cypriot judgments is *El Dridi*,[21] which is used in order to determine whether or not an applicant is covered by the scope of the Return Directive. If the finding of the court is that the applicant was detained as a result of a criminal conviction, then the Directive does not apply and neither do the ceilings on detention set by Article 15(5) and (6) of the Directive. However, the courts are reluctant to extend the *El Dridi* principle to any situation whose facts are not precisely the same as those in that case. In one example, an applicant who had been convicted of illegal work and illegal stay was found to fall outside the scope of the Return Directive because his conviction was not the result of his failure to comply with a deportation order as was the case in *El Dridi*.[22] The judge ordered the applicant's release based on ECtHR case-law[23] rather than on *El Dridi*, which appears to suggest an unwillingness to endorse the principle that immigration should not be criminalised.

[19] ibid, Art 13(2).
[20] ibid, Art 13(2).
[21] Case C-61/11 PPU *El Dridi* ECLI:EU:C:2011:268.
[22] *Re the application of Laal Badh Shah*, Civil Appl No 6/2014, 11 February 2014.
[23] *Quinn v France*, Judgment of 22 March 1995 A-31; *Chahal v UK* Appl No 22414/93, Judgment of 15 November 1996.

The case of *Said Shamilovich Kadzoev (Huchlarov)*[24] has been cited by applicants to support the argument that once the maximum ceiling of detention allowed by the Return Directive is reached, then the detainee must be released.[25] In *Antoan Hazaka*,[26] a Syrian applicant who had been convicted for attempting to travel to Sweden with a false passport, and who continued to be detained long after he had served his prison sentence, applied for release from detention, arguing that the ongoing war in Syria meant there was no realistic prospect for his removal. Relying on the CJEU ruling in the case of *Arslan*,[27] the applicant argued that there was no presumption that he filed an asylum application for the sole reason of delaying or averting his return to his country of origin. The Court rejected the aplication on the ground that the applicant was not covered by the Return Directive since his detention and deportation were based on his criminal conviction.

Articles 5 and 6 of the ECHR are regularly invoked by lawyers representing detainees, and in many cases the Court may rule that the Return Directive is inapplicable (usually because the detainee has a criminal conviction) but the detainee must be released on the basis of the ECHR. In the case of *Farak Nessim*,[28] the Court relied on Article 5(1) of the ECHR and related case-law *JN v United Kingdom*[29] to rule that the reasonableness of the length of detention must be judged in light of all relevant circumstances, and if it becomes clear that deportation cannot take place within a reasonable time or the authorities are not acting with due diligence, then the detention becomes unlawful.

Sometimes the courts use the same principles to support entirely different arguments. In a 2016 Appeal Court decision,[30] the Court found that the applicant, an asylum seeker, was not covered by the Return Directive since his detention and deportation were the result of a criminal sanction against him. Referring to Article 5 of the ECHR, the Court found that the applicant failed to prove that his detention was arbitrarily long or that the authorities did not pursue the expulsion proceedings with the 'due diligence' required. They held that the reasonableness of the length of detention must be judged not only according to its duration but also in light of the surrounding circumstances, and particularly the reasons for the delay in deportation. The Court endorsed the trial court's findings that five months is not an unreasonably long time to detain a person without a passport and with a criminal conviction. A dissenting opinion by two out of the five judges found that Article 5(1) of the ECHR rendered the detention unlawful, and that the length of detention should have been examined in conjunction with circumstances such as

[24] Case C-357/09 PPU *Said Shamilovich Kadzoev (Huchlarov)* ECLI:EU:C:2009:741.

[25] *Laal Badh Shah* (n 22).

[26] *Re the application of Antoan Hazaka, asylum seeker from Syria and now at the police detention centre in Menoyia for the issue of a habeas corpus writ*, Case No 110/2013, 19 July 2013.

[27] Case C-543/11 *Arslan* ECLI:EU:C:2013:343.

[28] *Re the application of Malak Shawki Farak Nessim*, Civil Appl No 66/2016, 24 August 2016.

[29] ECtHR, *JN v United Kingdom*, Appl No 37289/12, Judgment of 19 May 2016.

[30] *Habibi Pour Ali Faysel v Republic of Cyprus through the Chief of Police and the Minister of the Interior*, Civil Appeal No 236/15, 31 March 2016.

the inaction of the administration during the detention period and their failure to pursue a speedy deportation.

In the case of *Falak Shad*, the applicant argued that Article 19(1) of the EU Charter and Article 4(1) of the Fourth Protocol to the ECHR – both of which prohibit mass deportations – had been violated, as the authorities had deported all persons involved in the incident that prompted his detention and deportation without separately examining each case.[31] His lawyer supported the argument by citing the definition of mass deportations given by the ECHR in *Becker v Denmark*.[32] The court rejected the argument, concluding that simultaneous deportation of several persons does not necessarily amount to a mass deportation, and there was no evidence that each case had not been examined separately. Generally speaking, however, the EU Charter is used less than other legal instruments, such as the ECHR, and although often invoked by lawyers representing detainees, it is usually ignored by judges, who prefer to rely on the ECHR and its related case-law.

The courts have never deliberately favoured the Return Directive over national law. Under the separation-of-powers framework, the judiciary do not look into transposition questions unless specifically directed to do so. The courts assume that national law is an accurate transposition of the Return Directive and apply it accordingly. Given that the Directive's transposition consisted of adding a series of new provisions into an Immigration Law that was already several decades old, this assumption is faulty and threatens the Directive's effectiveness. For example, one of the old provisions of the law, Article 6, sets out a long list of categories of persons defined as 'prohibited immigrants'. Another provision, Article 14, entitles the authorities to detain and deport all 'prohibited immigrants'. These provisions continue to be implemented in relation to third-country nationals who are deemed to fall outside the scope of the Return Directive.

The Immigration Law's transposition of Article 15(1) of the Return Directive does not exclude the imposition of a prison sentence for all categories of third-country nationals staying in Cyprus illegally.[33] Imprisonment is prohibited for certain specific categories of illegal immigrants but is indirectly allowed for other categories listed in Article 6, such as persons who have previously been deported,[34] persons whose entry is prohibited by virtue of any legislation in force,[35] and persons considered as illegal immigrants by virtue of the provisions of the Immigration Law.[36] This leaves room for the criminalisation and detention of migrants for the mere fact of illegal stay in Cyprus. If third-country nationals are convicted for the offence of being 'illegal immigrants' under Article 6's catch-all list, they are removed from the ambit of the Return Directive and must serve their prison sentence in the same establishment as ordinary prisoners. In theory

[31] *Falak Shad v the Republic*, Case No 763 /2011, 26 July 2013.
[32] *Becker v Denmark*, Appl No 7011/75, 3 October 1975.
[33] Immigration Law, Art 18OC.
[34] ibid, Art 6(1)(h).
[35] ibid, Art 6(1)(j).
[36] ibid, Art 6(1)(m).

the provisions of the national law that transpose the Return Directive take precedence over other provisions with which they may be in conflict, but in practice the courts never dispute the validity or operation of Article 6. An example of this is the 2010 case of an HIV-positive third-country national who was detained for the purpose of deportation under Article 6(1)(c) of the Law, which defines carriers of contagious diseases as 'illegal immigrants'. The Court found that HIV did not fit the description of a contagious disease as defined by Article 6 and ruled that discrimination on the grounds of HIV status was unlawful. However, the decision failed to challenge the validity of Article 6(1)(c) as the basis for declaring a person to be an illegal immigrant.[37]

National courts do not cite foreign domestic judgments except UK court decisions, as these are deemed to have persuasive effect on national courts.[38] In *Farak Nessim* the court referred to two English decisions, *Walumba Lumba and Kadian Mighty v Secretary of State for the Home Department*[39] and *R (A) v Secretary of State for the Home Department*,[40] in order to establish the criteria for determining whether there is a risk of absconding. Generally speaking, however, where there are precedents from national law or the ECtHR, courts are unlikely to adopt precedents from the courts of other Member States, as there is always the risk that their laws are not identical to their Cypriot counterparts. There is no tradition of endorsing the judicial rulings of other Member States in whole or in part, even when these relate exclusively to directives that apply equally to both countries.

V. Implementing the Non-Criminalisation Principle

In the case of *Hazaka*,[41] the Court accepted the authorities' argument that the applicant was not entitled to protection under the Return Directive because his removal order was based on a criminal sanction. Similarly, in the case of *Laal Badh Shah* the Court refused to use the Return Directive to invalidate the detention order in the absence of a reasonable prospect of removal, once again due to a criminal sanction that removed the applicant from the Directive's scope.[42]

[37] *Leonie Marlyse Yombia Ngassam v Republic of Cyprus*, No 493/2010, 20 August 2010.

[38] Courts of Justice Law No 14/60, Art 29(1)(e).

[39] *Walumba Lumba (previously referred to as WL) (Congo) 1 and 2 (Appellant) v Secretary of State for the Home Department (Respondent); Kadian Mighty (previously referred to as KM) (Jamaica) (Appellant) v Secretary of State for the Home Department (Respondent)* [2011] UKSC 12, 23 March 2011, available at: https://www.refworld.org/cases,UK_SC,4e2d849c2.html (accessed 21 September 2019), cited in *Malak Shawki Farak Nessim* (n 27).

[40] *R (on the application of A) v Secretary of State for the Home Department* [2007] EWCA Civ 804, UKCA (England and Wales), 30 July 2007, available at: https://www.refworld.org/cases,GBR_CA_CIV,46c98d8a2.html (accessed 21 September 2019), cited in *Malak Shawki Farak Nessim* (n 27).

[41] *Antoan Hazaka* (n 26).

[42] *Laal Badh Shah* (n 22).

Despite the fact that *El Dridi* and *Achughbabian*[43] have been cited in a number of court decisions, there has been no explicit discussion of terms such as 'gradation' and 'all necessary measures'. Little case-law has discussed the impact of CJEU jurisprudence on national criminal law sanctions under Article 8(1), nor cases that can be used to properly assess how courts interpret 'proportionality', 'non-excess of reasonable force' or 'dignity and physical integrity' under Article 8(4). Courts note that *El Dridi* and *Achughbabian* have set the legal framework for addressing the criminalisation of irregular migration and the use of national penal law in Return Directive-related matters such as detention, removal and the rights of persons. However, it is doubtful whether they have properly enforced the basic test set by the CJEU, namely: '[W]hilst, in principle, criminal legislation and the rules of criminal procedure fall within the competence of the Member States, this area of law may nevertheless be affected by EU law.' When the *El Dridi* and *Achughbabian* principles are invoked, judges tend to make subtle distinctions between the facts of those cases and the facts at hand, narrowing the scope of these landmark rulings. In a number of instances courts have appeared reluctant to make the fullest use of CJEU case-law, and the key principle of *El Dridi* that 'states cannot apply criminal legislation capable of imperilling the realisation of the aims pursued by the said directive, thus depriving it of its effectiveness' is not always followed. The CJEU expressly allows for criminal provisions punishing irregular immigrants, but subjects them to a number of limitations and conditions.[44] Cypriot courts tend to apply these limitations quite restrictively. While *El Dridi* was exclusively concerned with criminal sanctions providing for a custodial sentence in the course of the return procedure, in *Achughbabian* the Court considered Article 2(2)(b) of the Return Directive, which may only be applied to exclude from the Directive's scope of application those third-country nationals who have committed crimes unrelated to their immigration status.

In 2013, following a recommendation from the European Commission, the Parliament amended the provision of the Immigration Law purporting to transpose Article 8(1) of the Return Directive to bring it in line with the Return Directive.[45] Following *El Dridi* and *Achughbabian*,[46] Article 18OC of the Law was amended so that illegal entry or stay were no longer punishable by imprisonment. Prohibited immigrants, however, can still be sentenced to imprisonment for immigration-related offences. Article 12 of the Law stipulates prison sentences for entering or leaving Cyprus through an entry point other than an approved port; entering Cyprus by sea without a permit; and entering Cyprus by air without immediately presenting oneself to the nearest authority. Article 19 criminalises giving false statements for the purpose of remaining in Cyprus; changing a permit issued

[43] Case C-329/11 *Alexandre Achughbabian v Préfet du Val-de-Marne* ECLI:EU:C:2011:807.

[44] The provisions cannot be applied before (paras 44–45) or during (*El Dridi* judgment) the return procedure.

[45] The amendment was passed with Law 49(I)/2013 on 21 June 2013.

[46] *Achughbabian* (n 43).

under the Immigration Law; unjustified possession or use of a forged or changed permit; refusing to answer or falsely answering questions put by the immigration authorities; refusing to give the authorities documents that have been lawfully requested; resisting or obstructing the immigration authorities in the execution of their duties; failing to comply with a condition of a permit; remaining in the country after a temporary permit expires; refusing to be searched or have one's luggage searched; breaching any condition or restriction set by the Immigration Law or the Refugee Law in relation to stay; and illegal stay except where it can be proved that the person entered Cyprus lawfully before the enactment of the Immigration Law or that his or her permit expired before she/he had the chance to leave. Articles 12 and 19 can be applied to third-country nationals falling within the scope of the RD in either of two situations:

- the maximum detention period has expired and none of the countries described in the Law (country of origin, country of transit or country where the returnee wants to go) are willing to receive the returnee;[47]
- the third-country national has already been returned and has subsequently come back to Cyprus unlawfully or resides here unlawfully.

Arguing against removal, before the Supreme Court, based on the rights contained in the Return Directive has not been effective. In the case of *Asanka Ariyarathne*[48] an argument that invoked the applicant's ties to Cyprus and his right to family life was explicitly rejected. Citing the case of *Kashif v Republic*,[49] the Court decided that the 'substantial fact' at hand was the applicant's 'alien' status; his family situation alone did not guarantee him rights. The judge ruled that where third-country nationals are staying illegally, particularly in the area of removals, the sovereign right of the state takes priority. In this case, as in so many others, CJEU case-law on the Return Directive played little, if any, role in the Court's decision.

In the rare cases where they do cite CJEU case-law, courts generally take a formalistic approach, challenging administrative acts on procedural grounds. In *Asanka Ariyarathne* the Supreme Court acting in its review jurisdiction cited the Supreme Court decision in *Dejic v Republic* that upheld previous case-law:[50] an applicant cannot directly challenge detention and removal orders that do not contain procedural faults, unless he first succeeds in annulling the administrative decisions that precipitated them. For instance, an applicant must challenge a decision to reject an extension of stay or a citizenship application before he can challenge his detention or removal order.

Detention orders issued as part of a removal procedure can rarely be challenged successfully unless the removal order itself is successfully challenged.

[47] Ironically, given that this is a situation in which there is no reasonable prospect of removal one would expect the detainee to be released immediately according to Art 18 PST(6) of the Law.
[48] *Asanka Ariyarathne Kariyawasam Lokugamage v Republic*, 26 February 2014.
[49] No 1144/2008, 11.7.2008.
[50] (2008) 3 AAΔ 358; *Khatateav v Republic* (2008) 3 AAΔ 19; *Kedoum v Republic* (2005) 3 AAΔ 505.

The courts are reluctant to order the release of detainees against whom a removal order is in place, even if the Return Directive's prerequisite in Article 15(1) for removal arrangements to be in progress and executed with due diligence is not complied with. In *Laal Badh Shah*,[51] the applicant was imprisoned for illegal stay and continued to remain in detention for a year after he had served his sentence. He argued that detention is only justified when the return procedure is processed with due care and there is a realistic prospect of removal, which was not the case in his situation as he had no travel documents. The judge found that the case came under Article 18OE(2)(b) of the Immigration Law, ie the applicant was subject to a return decision due to a criminal sanction. The *El Dridi* principle was inapplicable since the applicant was given a sentence based on his illegal stay and work and not as a result of failing to comply with a return decision, as was the case in *El Dridi*. In the case of *Mohammad Khosh Soruor v the Republic*,[52] the Court upheld a detention order despite the fact that deportation was impossible and a pending case sought to challenge the removal order, ruling that the postponement of removal does not, on its own, constitute a reason for suspending detention.

The Court mentioned the *El Dridi* principle again in relation to an application from a third-country national who was declared an illegal immigrant under the Immigration Law once her employment was terminated.[53] Citing the rulings in *Dörr* and *Ünal*,[54] the Court found that the *El Dridi* principle had no application. The judge construed the principle as follows:

> [What] is prohibited [by the *El Dridi* principle] is the deprivation of liberty as a criminal measure for the noncompliance by the alien of the order of removal. Here there is no such element, neither has there been any sentence of imprisonment from the competent court for the furthering of the removal of the applicant.[55]

The principle was even more narrowly construed in the case of *Bassam Asslloum v Republic*.[56] The applicant was a Syrian national who had originally arrived in 2003 and was subsequently declared an 'illegal immigrant' after he left his job. He departed from Cyprus in 2005 and re-entered unlawfully a number of times in spite of an entry ban against him. He was arrested and detained for unlawful entry and stay and a sentence was imposed on him by the Court. He applied for asylum, as well as a habeas corpus order on the ground that his deportation to Syria was unlawful. The Court distinguished his case from *El Dridi* on the grounds that 'the [latter] sentence was imposed due to the failure of the applicant to comply with the decision to deport him', whereas in the present case the detention and deportation orders were issued after the applicant had been declared to be an illegal

[51] Civil Appl No 49/13, 24 April 2013.
[52] *Mohammad Khosh Soruor v the Republic*, Case No 1723/2011, 8 February 2012, per Judge Kranvis.
[53] *Magdalin Mensah v Republic*, Case No 5735/2013, 9 August 2013.
[54] Case C-136/03 *Georg Dörr* ECLI:EU:C:2005:340.
[55] Per Judge Nathanel.
[56] Case No 91/14, 17 July 2014, before Judge Michailidou.

immigrant on the basis of a court conviction. The court did not consider the fact that the imprisonment in the case at hand related to an immigration offence. The judge also found that the CJEU ruling in *Arslan* permitted detention pending removal.[57]

The case of *Shahin Haisan Fawzy Mohamed*[58] is rather exceptional as it restricted the blanket practice of criminalisation of third-country nationals. The Supreme Court judge considered that the offence that the Egyptian national was convicted of was minor and the time lapse did not justify removal. His asylum application had been rejected by the Asylum Service on the grounds that he had not turned up for his interview and he was subsequently deported. However, he had not been able to attend the interview as he was detained at the time. The Court also pointed out that he had been acquitted of a 2010 criminal conviction.[59] It annulled the detention and removal orders and approved the Criminal Appeal Court's reasoning that removal for a minor previous conviction – working without a permit for four years – would 'contravene the principles of good administration, good faith and justified trust to the authorities'.[60] This judgment is in line with the ruling in *Zh and O*.[61]

VI. Judicial Application of Other Return Directive Provisions: Voluntary Departure, Unaccompanied Minors and Entry Bans

While the Return Directive's purported transposition codified a procedure for voluntary returns for the first time, voluntary departures in the sense of the Directive are rarely practised. The courts regard official communications about voluntary departure as mere requests that cannot be subjected to judicial review. The Supreme Court decision in *Tatsiana Balashevich* found that the standard letter that immigration authorities customarily send to third-country nationals in irregular situations, requesting them to depart by themselves, does not constitute an executive administrative act but a mere request of no legal consequence; as such it cannot be subjected to judicial review or suspended through an interim order.[62] Since taking over in this area the Administrative Court has taken the same approach. The Court, then, does not recognise the authorities' request that an applicant depart as a voluntary return decision within the meaning of the Return

[57] *Arslan* (n 27).
[58] *Shahin Haisan Fawzy Mohamed v Republic*, Case No 1718/2010, 25 April 2013.
[59] Ποινική Έφεση 152/09, 3.6.2010.
[60] See Crim Appeal 152/09, ημερ 3 June 2010. The conviction was based on 6(1)(k) of Cap 105. The Egyptian national had worked in a sector outside of those provided for asylum seekers, and was fined CYP300 (€515.13 euro) in 2006.
[61] Case C-554/13 *ZZh* and *Staatssecretaris voor Veiligheid en Justitie* ECLI:EU:C:2015:377.
[62] *Tatsiana Balashevich v Republic*, Case No 5635/2013, 10 July 2013.

Directive, which in any case was not mentioned in the judgment. This does not seem to be in line with the Directive.

The law grants the social welfare services considerable powers when it comes to determining the best interests of unaccompanied minors and the scope of assistance given to them; the services are not monitored by any independent agency. There is no provision in either law or policy to provide children with legal advice or representation during the asylum procedure. The absence of any welfare services guidelines encourages administrative actions and court decisions that take no notice of the best-interests rule, as demonstrated by the case of *Hasnas Natalia*, involving a woman who was separated from her child because the judge refused to suspend a deportation order and entry ban.[63] The transposition of the Return Directive has actually lowered the standards for unaccompanied minors, who can now be detained for long periods without the welfare services' knowledge or support.[64]

On the subject of entry bans, the decision of *Elie Jamil El Khoury* demonstrates that the inclusion of a person in a stop list of prohibited immigrants is not judicially reviewable. The court did not refer to the rights, obligations and restrictions contained in the Return Directive; instead, it ruled that there is no right to challenge an entry ban, rendering Article 11 of the Return Directive redundant.

VII. Conclusions

When it comes to orders for the removal of third-country nationals, Cypriot judicial practice fails to meet the substantive standards set out by the principles of *El Dridi*, resulting in a body of case-law that essentially criminalises immigration offences. This is because all immigration offences, save for 'failure to comply with an order of removal', are classified by the courts as pure penal offences, excluding the operation of *El Dridi*.

The courts typically construe the 'sovereign right/prerogative' of the state in such a way as to criminalise and declare as 'illegal immigrants' anyone violating the conditions of stay under the catch-all list of grounds in Article 6 of the Immigration Law. This undermines the underlying logic of the Return Directive to the extent that it is questionable whether the prohibition of *El Dridi* is operative: in many court decisions judges construe criminal legislation in a manner that can 'jeopardise the achievement of the objectives pursued by a directive and, therefore, deprive it of its effectiveness'.[65] In addition, minor offences committed by third-country nationals (eg traffic-related offences) are used to exclude persons from

[63] *Hasnas Natalia v the Republic of Cyprus*, Case No 921/2015, 23 July 2015.
[64] Cyprus, Commissioner for the Rights of the Child, 2014.
[65] Case C-61/11 *Hassen El Dridi* ECLI:EU:C:2011:268.

the scope of the Return Directive.[66] Rights under the EU Charter and the ECHR are rarely taken up as a yardstick to assess the actions of the administration, as the courts show a tendency to endorse the wide discretion of the immigration authorities. The operative factor in a court's reasoning is the third-country national's alien status; this takes precedence over the right to family life or any ties to Cyprus, and if the alien's stay is illegal the state's sovereign right to deport comes into play. The CJEU case-law on the RD seems to play a minor role: there is often no reference to it in the reasoning of court decisions, and when it is explicitly cited, there is a tendency to distinguish the facts of the case at hand from those of the CJEU ruling, as formalism prevails over substance.

When it comes to balancing effective returns with the protection of fundamental rights, judges have generally neglected proper concern for the latter. As a rule, courts allow the executive to exercise maximum discretion in immigration control and are reluctant to implement the rights of third-country nationals that entail duties for the state.

Cyprus's judicial tradition in this field needs reform if the country is to have any hope of creating a streamlined system of networked, multidimensional law – what has been termed the 'Europeanisation of Cypriot Administrative law'.[67] To date, judicial interpretation has rendered certain characteristics of the legal system as posing obstacles to the effective implementation of the EU acquis on returns. These characteristics include the custom of not considering arguments unless they are raised by the litigants; the doctrine of separation of powers that prevents courts from questioning national laws' compliance with the acquis; and the reluctance to refer matters to the CJEU. The EU Charter is insufficiently utilised and is only rarely invoked as the measure by which the acquis should be interpreted; both litigants' lawyers and judges prefer the far more familiar ECHR, which is echoed almost verbatim in the Cypriot constitution and thus does not carry the risk of being struck down as inapplicable. The courts are happy to legitimise arguments presented by the authorities in support of a wide administrative discretion when issues of public security are invoked, and discern a risk of absconding in every return procedure regardless of the specific facts of the case. Although the de facto division of the country into north and south may partly account for these judicial trends, there appears to be an increasing shift towards criminalisation of migration through the invocation of the security threat, an argument repeatedly elaborated by the government in public discourse.

[66] For instance, in the case of *Re the application of Hamid Reza Razzaman v The Republic of Cyprus*, No 107/2014, 18 July 2014. Available at www.cylaw.org/cgi-bin/open.pl?file=apofaseis/aad/meros_1/2014/1-201407-107-2014.htm&qstring=Hamid%20and%20Reza%20and%20Razzaman.

[67] K Paraskeva, *Κυπριακό Διοικητικό Δίκαιο* (Athens, Nomiki Viovliothiki, 2017) 56.

The parallel operation of the old colonial immigration law alongside the transposed Return Directive has generated a lacuna when it comes to substantive rights derived from the Directive, the EU Charter, the ECHR and other international instruments. This is particularly acute when it comes to the detention and deportation of third-country nationals, where the discretionary powers of the immigration authorities are viewed by the courts to be 'the widest possible',[68] and are construed as 'a manifestation of sovereignty'.[69] Criminalisation, detention and expulsion, then, remain the key pillars of the 'Cypriot migration state of exception'. This is most evident in cases involving public safety, where rights granted by the Return Directive, such as the right to be informed of the legal and factual reasons for detention, are circumvented; authorities may avoid furnishing detainees with information provided they brief their administrative files. Union nationals and their third-country national partners may be deported for public order, public security or public health reasons even under the EU's free-movement acquis, but national courts take things a step further by making parallel use of the old national immigration law and circumventing the corresponding rights of the acquis.

The use of removal as a mechanism to detain and criminalise irregular migrants has been flagged by various studies as a violation that undermines the fundamental rights provided by EU law under the Return Directive. This problem is not confined to Cyprus; there are similar problems in other EU members, such as Italy[70] and France.[71] However, Cyprus fails to meet the standards set out in *El Dridi* and *Achughbabian* by a higher margin. While EU law strives to ensure that detention for committing a crime is something that is 'conceptually and legally distinct from immigration detention',[72] this distinction is not made in Cyprus, where immigration policy continues to fall under the paradigm of the 'Cyprus problem'.

[68] *Kiriak Leonov v Republic of Cyprus*, Case No 5984/2013, 24 February 2016. In Greek the word used is 'ευρύτατες'.

[69] *Moyo* (n 1) is cited in several decisions to underscore this point.

[70] R Raffaelli, 'The Returns Directive in Light of the El Dridi Judgement' (2011) 3 *Perspectives on Federalism* 32.

[71] See A. Beduschi 'Detention of Undocumented Immigrants and the Judicial Impact of the CJEU's Decisions in France' (2014) 26(3) *International Journal of Refugee Law* 333; A di Pascale, 'Can a Justice of the Peace be a Good Detention Judge? The Case of Italy', Chapter 13 in this volume; S Slama, 'Trois hautes juridictions nationales pour une directive: une interaction judiciaire en trompe l'œil', Chapter 14 in this volume.

[72] See K Costello, *The Human Rights of Migrants and Refugees in European Law* (Oxford, Oxford University Press, 2012) 257.

PART 2

Immigration Detention in the EU: The Role of Judges in Shaping Effective Standards of Control

EDITED BY GALINA CORNELISSE

7

Alternatives to Immigration Detention in International and EU Law: Control Standards and Judicial Interaction in a Heterarchy

EVANGELIA (LILIAN) TSOURDI*

I. Introduction

The use of generalised detention as a migration management tool and the abuse of alternatives to immigration (asylum and pre-return) detention as a widespread control measure, in both the return and asylum frameworks, is undoubtedly on the rise in the EU.[1] These practices contravene EU law, and notably the Return Directive and the recast Reception Conditions Directive (recast RCD),[2] both of which frame detention as the exception, establishing robust guarantees that were often absent from national legislation prior to the adoption of those instruments.[3]

International and regional human rights case-law and decisions from quasi-judicial bodies have been seminal in shaping standards on the control of immigration detention. There is a growing interrelation between the global, European (Council of Europe) and EU legal regimes in the field of human rights protection, including in what concerns the prohibition of arbitrary deprivation

* This work was supported by a VENI programme grant (project Nr. VI.Veni.191R.040) which is financed by the Dutch Research Council (NWO).

[1] For the practice of extensive recourse to detention in border areas, see eg ECtHR 14 March 2017, *Ilias and Ahmed v Hungary*, App No 47287/15; and ECRE, *The Detention of Asylum Seekers in Europe: Constructed on Shaky Ground?* (June 2017) 3–7 for an overview of the total number of persons in immigration detention for the year 2016 and for data on the infrastructural expansion of detention in the EU.

[2] Directive 2008/115/EC of the European Parliament and of the Council of 16 December 2008 on common standards and procedures in Member States for returning illegally staying third-country nationals [2008] OJ L348/98 ('Return Directive'); and Directive 2013/33/EU of the European Parliament and of the Council of 26 June 2013 laying down standards for the reception of applicants for international protection (recast) [2013] OJ L180/96 ('recast RCD').

[3] F Lutz, 'Prologue' to this volume.

of liberty. Nevertheless, while common trends are emerging, this has not resulted in uniform standards on the regulation of immigration detention. This is also the case when it comes to the distinct human rights legal regimes of the Council of Europe, with the ECHR as its cornerstone,[4] and of the European Union, with the European Charter on Fundamental Rights ('the Charter') as its main pillar.[5] The observations of Niko Krisch, that the emerging legal order is a pluralist one, and that within this pluralist order we find heterarchy rather than hierarchy,[6] apply also in the area of immigration detention.

This contribution critically analyses supranational control standards and judicial interaction within an heterarchy focusing on alternatives to immigration detention. I have chosen to focus on the legal regimes regulating both the detention of irregular migrants and asylum seekers for three main reasons. First, there are increasing links between these two policies. This is exemplified mainly through: (i) migration management initiatives in border areas which treat asylum seeking and (potential) return as part of a continuum, and increasingly use generalised deprivation of liberty policies; and (ii) policies to prolong the detention of migrants under a return obligation when they seek asylum (albeit under a different legal basis).[7] More broadly, asylum seeking is increasingly treated as a prelude to return and the imperative of an effective return policy is primed over protection obligations. Second, as will be analysed below, the EU framework on alternatives to detention is articulated more fully in the Reception Conditions Directive, a more recent instrument than the Return Directive. Third, judicial interaction between the CJEU and the ECtHR on immigration detention is aptly portrayed by a CJEU case which, while arising in an asylum framework, explicitly considers the links between asylum seeking and return.[8]

Despite the growing interest of states in implementing alternatives, there is no single legal definition of an 'alternative to detention' and therefore in practice there are different understandings of the concept. The International Detention Coalition, a civil society organisation that has been seminal in shaping government policies on alternatives to immigration detention, adopts a broad understanding of alternatives to detention conceptualising them to be '[a]ny legislation, policy or practice that allows for asylum seekers, refugees and migrants to reside in the community with freedom of movement while their migration status is being resolved or while awaiting deportation or removal from the country'.[9] Such a

[4] Convention for the Protection of Human Rights and Fundamental Freedoms, 4 November 1950, 005 CETS 1 (entered into force 3 September 1953) as amended by Protocol 14, 13 May 2004, 194 CETS 1 (entered into force 1 June 2010).

[5] [2010] OJ C83/389.

[6] N Krisch, 'The Open Architecture of European Human Rights Law' (2008) 71 *MLR* 183, 185.

[7] See subsection II.A.

[8] Case C-601/15 *JN v Staatssecretaris van Veiligheid en Justitie* ECLI:EU:C:2016:84.

[9] See International Detention Coalition (IDC) and La Trobe Refugee Research Center, *There Are Alternatives, A Handbook for Preventing Unnecessary Detention* (2011) 12. The organisation later reviewed its definition which now reads: '[a]ny law, policy or practice by which persons are not

definition serves the pragmatic aim of discussing the purpose of detention and advocating for its reduction, and a policy shift from enforcement to early engagement and collaboration with migrants.[10] Despite its pragmatic goals, this broad understanding of what constitutes an alternative to immigration detention risks creating legal confusion. For example, under this broader understanding, open reception arrangements for returnees could also be understood as an alternative to detention, as they constitute a way to manage the migration process that falls short of detention, but involves some restrictions in the freedom of movement (eg a potential curfew at a reception centre). Thus, based on a principled legal understanding, I limit my focus to what authors have described as 'the narrow sense of alternatives to detention' which 'refers to a practice used where detention has a legitimate basis, in particular where a justified ground for detention is identified in the individual case, yet a less restrictive means of control is at the State's disposal and should therefore be used'.[11] As my analysis reveals, this is also the approach that the EU has adopted.[12]

In order to ascertain the role of alternatives to immigration detention in upholding the prohibition of arbitrary deprivation of liberty I explore two human rights regimes: the global (United Nations), and that of the Council of Europe. I juxtapose judicial decisions and legal opinions emanating from UN Human Rights Committee (HRC) and the ECtHR. I trace the links between the obligation to examine alternatives to detention, the concept of arbitrariness of deprivation of liberty, and vulnerability. I reflect on the role played by the principles of necessity and proportionality. I adopt a comparative approach, distilling common trends, and highlighting exceptional approaches. I thus ascertain the role of international human rights 'judges' in controlling immigration detention and the extent to which they are interacting with each other in this process. I then outline the regulation of immigration detention in EU law, and articulate the emergence of a principled regional understanding on alternatives to immigration detention. I comment on the impact of international human rights 'judges' on EU legislation and map the fragmented legal environment which national judges face. I next turn to the interaction between the CJEU and the ECtHR on immigration detention. I conclude that despite the reality of a fragmented legal environment, all legal regimes converge (albeit through different routes) to an 'inviolable core' of the right to liberty which should inform detention decision-making at national level in the EU.

detained for reasons relating to their migration status'; see IDC, *There Are Alternatives, A Handbook for Preventing Unnecessary Detention*, rev edn (2015). See also Jesuit Refugee Service Europe, *Policy Position on Alternatives to Detention* (2012).

[10] For a detailed analysis, see A Bloomfield, 'Alternatives to Detention at a Crossroads: Humanisation or Criminalisation' (2016) 35 *Refugee Survey Quarterly* 29.

[11] C Costello and E Kaytaz, *Building Empirical Research into Alternatives to Detention: Perception of Asylum seekers and Refugees in Toronto and Geneva* (UNHCR, 2013) 10–11.

[12] See subsection II.B.

II. The Prohibition of Arbitrary Detention under International Human Rights Law and Alternatives to Immigration Detention: A Fragmented Approach

International and regional human rights law instruments, amongst others the International Covenant on Civil and Political Rights (ICCPR),[13] the ECHR, the American Declaration on the Rights and Duties of Man ('the American Declaration'),[14] and the American Convention on Human Rights (ACHR),[15] enshrine the right to liberty and security of person.[16] Personal liberty is an inalienable right which an individual cannot legitimately waive.[17] This right is qualified, meaning that while there is a presumption in favour of personal liberty, there is no absolute protection against its deprivation. As aptly put by Manfred Nowak in relation to Article 9 ICCPR: 'It is not the deprivation of liberty itself that is disapproved of but rather that which is arbitrary and unlawful.'[18] The respective legal instruments regulate powers of detention prohibiting arbitrary deprivation of liberty and providing safeguards against ill-treatment of detainees.

Alternatives to detention are part and parcel of the prohibition of arbitrary deprivation of liberty and intrinsically linked with the principles of necessity, proportionality, as well as the concept of vulnerability. They are especially important when it comes to deprivation of liberty of irregular migrants and asylum seekers. It has been observed that there is 'an uneasy tension between the universal right to liberty and the state's border control prerogatives'.[19] In the EU, irregular modes of arrival to a place of safety have led to the proliferation of mixed migration flows and have blurred the lines between border management, return and asylum policies. It is in this context that detention of irregular migrants and asylum seekers has become widespread practice. Through a set of legislative instruments adopted in 2008–2013, the EU has regulated in detail the detention framework of irregular migrants and asylum seekers.[20] Nevertheless, the non-application of

[13] International Covenant on Civil and Political Rights, New York, 16 December 1966 (entered into force 23 March 1976).

[14] American Declaration of the Rights and Duties of Man, Bogotá, Colombia, 1948.

[15] American Convention on Human Rights, San José, Costa Rica, 22 November 1969 (entered into force 18 July 1978).

[16] See respectively, ICCPR, Art 9; ECHR, Art 5; American Declaration, Art 1; ACHR, Art 7.

[17] European Commission on Human Rights, *Report Relating to the Vagrancy Cases* (19 July 1969), para 174.

[18] M Nowak, *UN Covenant on Civil and Political Rights – CCPR Commentary*, 2nd edn (Kegl am Rein, NP Engel Verlag, 2005) 210. See also HRC, *General Comment No 35* (CCPR/C/GC/35, 2014) para 10.

[19] See C Costello, 'Human Rights and the Elusive Universal Subject: Immigration Detention under International Human Rights and EU Law' (2012) 10 *Indiana Journal of Global Legal Studies* 257, 258.

[20] For the detention of irregular migrants, see: Return Directive and Proposal for a Directive of the European Parliament and of the Council on common standards and procedures in Member States for returning illegally staying third-country nationals (recast) COM(2018) 634. For the detention of asylum seekers, see: Recast RCD and Proposal for a directive of the European Parliament and of the Council laying down standards for the reception of applicants for international protection (recast)

the full spectrum of legal guarantees in practice has led to the widespread use of deprivation of liberty for some groups of irregular migrants and asylum seekers, such as those subject to border procedures or to 'Dublin transfers'.[21]

Against this backdrop, I study the role of alternatives to immigration detention in upholding the prohibition of arbitrary deprivation of liberty, a prohibition that is a constant in both the global and regional human rights protection regimes. In this section, I examine consecutively judicial and quasi-judicial decisions from two distinct human rights protection regimes: the ICCPR (section I.A) and the ECHR (section I.B). I aim to explore the links between the obligation to examine alternatives to immigration detention, the concept of arbitrariness of deprivation of liberty, and vulnerability. I reflect on the role the principles of necessity and proportionality play in this setting. The analysis reveals that in this heterarchical framework there is no uniformity either in terms of applicable standards, or in terms of (quasi)judicial reasoning. Nevertheless, common trends can be observed pointing to the existence of an 'inviolable core' of the right to liberty that national EU judges need to take to account in detention decision-making.

A. UN Human Rights Committee: Operationalising the Principle of Necessity Through Alternatives to Immigration Detention

In contrast to the ECHR, the ICCPR does not contain an exhaustive list of permissible detention grounds;[22] however, detention must pursue a specific purpose. The prohibition of 'arbitrariness' is the cornerstone of the UN system of protection of the right to liberty. As the UN HRC has highlighted:

> The drafting history of article 9, paragraph 1, confirms that 'arbitrariness' is not to be equated with 'against the law', but must be interpreted more broadly to include elements of inappropriateness, injustice and lack of predictability. This means that remand in custody pursuant to lawful arrest must not only be lawful but reasonable in all circumstances.

Furthermore, detention must be necessary in all circumstances.[23] Moreover, the HRC has found that detention may be arbitrary if the manner in which the detainees are treated does not relate to the purpose for which they are ostensibly

COM(2016) 465, as well as Regulation (EU) No 604/2013 of the European Parliament and of the Council of 26 June 2013 establishing the criteria and mechanisms for determining the Member State responsible for examining an application for international protection lodged in one of the Member States by a third-country national or a stateless person (recast) [2013] OJ L180/31 ('Dublin III Regulation').

[21] See section II below.

[22] Nevertheless, Art 11 ICCPR expressly prohibits imprisonment on ground of inability to fulfil a contractual obligation.

[23] HRC, *Hugo van Alphen v the Netherlands*, Comm No 305/1998, para 5.8.

being detained.[24] The principle of necessity is at the core of individualised detention decisions in the international human rights law framework. The necessity test would, for example, require case-by-case consideration of the likelihood of absconding based upon objective evidence or past experience. To assess the necessity or potential arbitrariness of detention measures, questions of proportionality are typically raised.[25] Proportionality facilitates the search for a fair balance between the demands of the general interest of the community and the requirements of the protection of the individual's fundamental rights.[26]

When it comes to the context of migration, the HRC has stated that detention in the course of proceedings for the control of immigration is not per se arbitrary.[27] Nevertheless, irregular entry on its own cannot justify detention.[28] In its decisions, the HRC has adopted the position that detention decisions, in general and in the immigration framework specifically, call for an assessment of whether detention would be both necessary and proportional and that these decisions should be reassessed as they extend in time. This entails an individualised assessment requiring that, after an initial period, detention would be arbitrary absent 'particular reasons specific to the individual', such as 'an individualized likelihood of absconding, danger of crimes against others, or risk of acts against national security'.[29]

Alternatives to detention play a central role in such an individualised assessment. National authorities should verify for each individual whether 'there were not less invasive means of achieving the same ends, that is to say, compliance with the State party's immigration policies, by, for example, the imposition of reporting obligations, sureties or other conditions'.[30] Vulnerability is also important; decisions should take into account the needs of children and the mental health condition of those detained.[31] Specifically, when it comes to children the HRC has found that they

> should not be deprived of liberty, except as a measure of last resort and for the shortest appropriate period of time, taking into account their best interests as a primary consideration with regard to the duration and conditions of detention, and also taking into account the extreme vulnerability and need for care of unaccompanied minors.[32]

[24] HRC, *Fardon v Australia*, Comm No 1629/2007, para 7.4.

[25] M Flynn, 'Who Must Be Detained? Proportionality as a Tool for Critiquing Immigration Detention Policy' (2012) 31 *Refugee Survey Quarterly* 40.

[26] ECtHR 7 July 1989, *Soering v the UK*, App No 14038/88, para 89.

[27] HRC, *General Comment No 35* (CCPR/C/GC/35, 2014) para 18.

[28] HRC, *A v Australia*, Comm No 560/1993, para 9.4.

[29] HRC, *FKAG v Australia*, Comm No 2094/2011, para 9.3.

[30] HRC, *C v Australia*, Comm No 900/1999, para 8.2. See also HRC, *Baban v Australia*, Comm No 1014/2011, para 7.2; HRC, *Shams and others v Australia*, Comm No 1255/2004, para 7.2; and HRC, *Zeyad Khalaf Hamadie Al-Gertanie v Bosnia and Herzegovina*, Comm No 1955/2010, para 10.4.

[31] *FKAG v Australia* (n 29) para 9.3; HRC, *Shafiq v Australia*, Comm No 1324/2004, para 7.3; and HRC, *C v Australia*, Comm No 900/1999, paras 8.2 and 8.4.

[32] See HRC, General Comment No 35, CCPR/C/GC/35, 2014, para 18 and HRC, *D and E v Australia*, Comm No 1050/2002, para 7.2; and HRC, *Jalloh v Netherlands*, Comm No 794/1998, paras 8.2–8.3.

Despite these enhanced guarantees for minors, alternatives to immigration detention are not specifically tied to the notion of vulnerability; they are linked with the requirement of an individualised assessment and the operationalisation of the principle of necessity.

B. The European Court of Human Rights: Alternatives to Immigration Detention Through the 'Back Door' of Proportionality

Unlike the ICCPR, Article 5(1) of the ECHR contains an exhaustive list of exceptions to the right to liberty and security. These exceptions should be interpreted restrictively. One of the exceptions relates directly to immigration, namely through '[t]he lawful arrest or detention of a person to prevent his effecting an unauthorised entry into the country or of a person against whom action is being taken with a view to deportation or extradition'. This provision covers two situations: pre-admission detention, and pre-deportation detention.

Prohibition of arbitrary deprivation of liberty also underpins the ECHR protection system. Article 5 ECHR does not mention 'arbitrariness' but refers instead to the concept of lawfulness. According to Article 5(1) ECHR, each detention order must be 'in accordance with a procedure prescribed by law'. Hence, in order for a given detention order to be found compatible with the ECHR, it must respect the requirements of national law. If the requirements of national law are not fulfilled, the ECtHR holds the detention to be arbitrary and thus incompatible with the ECHR. Where national law *goes beyond* the requirements of the ECHR, the ECtHR's examination will be based on the stricter requirements of national law. However, conformity with national law is not sufficient; the ECtHR has repeatedly stated that:

> It is a fundamental principle that no detention which is arbitrary can be compatible with Article 5§1 and the notion of 'arbitrariness' in Article 5§1 extends beyond lack of conformity with national law, so that a deprivation of liberty may be lawful in terms of domestic law but still arbitrary and thus contrary to the Convention.[33]

In addition, the ECtHR has specified that the notion of arbitrariness implies the absence of bad faith while deciding on detention and requires that detention be closely connected to the ground of detention invoked by the authorities.[34] Furthermore, in order to avoid arbitrary detention, the conditions and place of

[33] ECtHR 19 February 2009, *A and others v The United Kindgom* (GC), App No 3455/05, para 164. See also ECtHR 25 June 1996, *Amuur v France*, App No 19776/92, para 50; and ECtHR 4 April 2000, *Witold Litwa v Poland*, App No 26629/95, para 78.

[34] ECtHR 29 January 2008, *Saadi v United Kingdom*, App No 13229/03.

detention should be appropriate,[35] and its duration should not exceed the time reasonably required for the purpose pursued by detention.[36]

The ECtHR subjects deprivation of liberty to the requirement of necessity, with the Strasbourg Court having stated that:

> The detention of an individual is such a serious measure that it is only justified where other, less severe measures have been considered and found to be insufficient to safeguard the individual or public interest which might require that the person concerned be detained. That means that it does not suffice that the deprivation of liberty is executed in conformity with national law but it must also be necessary in the circumstances.[37]

However, according to the ECtHR, the necessity test does not apply to immigration-related detention, whether in the framework of return or preventing an unauthorised entry – a factual situation that may or may not include examination of an asylum claim.[38] The ECtHR characteristically stated in *Chahal* that:

> Article 5 para 1 (f) … does not demand that the detention of a person against whom action is being taken with a view to deportation be reasonably considered necessary, for example to prevent his committing an offence or fleeing. … [A]ll that is required under this provision … is that 'action is being taken with a view to deportation'.[39]

As poignantly observed by Galina Cornelisse, this means that the ECtHR's interpretation of the exception to the right to personal liberty in Article 5(1)(f) ECHR can hardly be regarded as a narrow one.[40] The approach to separate arbitrariness from necessity has also been criticised as leading to a false dichotomy.[41] General assumptions on proportionality cannot replace a test of necessity in each individual case.[42] The absence of a necessity test in the ECHR essentially implies that there is no obligation to consider less severe measures, ie alternatives to immigration detention, in each case. However, if *national law* establishes a necessity requirement for such detention and this is not upheld, the Court will find detention to be arbitrary and in violation of the ECHR.[43] Therefore, standards established under national law, including those adopted as part of transposition of EU Directives, are instrumental. Put simply, in practice the requirements of compatibility with the

[35] ECtHR 12 October 2006, *Mubilanzila Mayeka and Kaniki Mitunga v Belgium*, App No 13178/03.

[36] ECtHR 24 January 2008, *Riad and Idiab v Belgium*, App No 29787/03 and 29810/03.

[37] *Witold Litwa v Poland* (n 33), para 78.

[38] ECtHR 15 November 1996, *Chahal v the United Kingdom* (GC), App No 22414/93. See also *Saadi* (n 34).

[39] *Chahal* (n 38) para 112.

[40] G Cornelisse, *Immigration Detention and Human Rights: Rethinking Territorial Sovereignty* (Leiden, Brill, 2010) 295; and G Cornelisse, 'Human Rights for Immigration Detainees in Strasbourg: Limited Sovereignty or a Limited Discourse?' (2004) 6 *European Journal of Migration and Law* 93.

[41] H O'Nions, 'No Right to Liberty: The Detention of Asylum Seekers for Administrative Convenience' (2004) 10 *European Journal of Migration and Law* 149, 173.

[42] V Moreno-Lax, 'Beyond Saadi v UK: Why the "Unnecessary" Detention of Asylum Seekers is Inadmissible under EU Law' (2011) 2 *Human Rights and International Legal Discourse* 166, 184.

[43] ECtHR 2 October 2008, *Rusu v Austria*, App No 34082/02.

ECHR in the area of deprivation of liberty could vary from state to state according to what the national law in place foresees.

The above analysis does not mean that there is no place for alternatives to immigration detention in the ECHR protection system. Such alternatives, however, come into play through a different route. Namely, the Court applies the principle of proportionality to an extent by requiring good faith in the application of the detention measure, close connection to the purpose, appropriate place and conditions of detention, and a duration which does not exceed that reasonably required for the purpose pursued.[44] These proportionality considerations are intrinsically linked with the notion of vulnerability. Through the four 'proportionality criteria' mentioned above, the Court has found detention to be arbitrary in cases of unaccompanied minors, or minors held with their parents or other vulnerable individuals, as well as in cases when states did not pursue the return with 'due diligence'. The obligation of 'due diligence' has been interpreted as requiring 'sustained efforts'[45] from the part of the competent public authorities to overcome the obstacles of removal and a 'good faith' conduct on the part of the authorities.

The ECtHR has specifically referred to the obligation to examine alternatives to immigration detention in some of these cases. In *Mubilanzila Mayeka and Kaniki Mitunga*, concerning unaccompanied children detained in Belgium, the ECtHR stated that: 'Other measures could have been taken. … These included her placement in a specialised centre or with foster parents.'[46] In *Popov*, a case concerning a family with two minor children that had been place in detention, the ECtHR emphasised this, stating that:

> A measure of confinement must … be proportionate to the aim pursued by the authorities, namely the enforcement of a removal decision. … It can be seen from the Court's case-law that, where families are concerned, the authorities must, in assessing proportionality, take account of the child's best interests. In this connection … there is currently a broad consensus – including in international law – in support of the idea that in all decisions concerning children, their best interests must be paramount. … [T]he protection of the child's best interests involves both keeping the family together, as far as possible, and considering alternatives so that the detention of minors is only a measure of last resort.[47]

Vulnerability is therefore a seminal factor in the assessment of the proportionality of the detention measure, which in turn is decisive for a finding of arbitrariness and consequent violation of Article 5(1) ECHR.

Apart from cases concerning vulnerable individuals, the Court has referred to the obligation to implement alternatives to immigration detention where states did not pursue the return with 'due diligence', or where it was apparent that return

[44] *Saadi* (n 34) para 74.

[45] ECtHR 17 July 2014, *Kim v Russia*, App No 44260/13, para 50; ECtHR 12 March 2013, *Djalti v Bulgaria*, Appl No 31206/05, para. 53.

[46] *Mayeka and Mitunga* (n 35) para 83.

[47] ECtHR 19 January 2012, *Popov v France*, App Nos 39472/07 and 39474/07, paras 140–41.

would not be possible due to a breach of the principle of *non-refoulement*. In the case of *Mikolenko*, which concerned an adult male held in Estonia with a view to return, the Court took into account the fact that after his release the applicant was subject to reporting requirements. The Court thus concluded that: 'The authorities in fact had at their disposal measures other than the applicant's protracted detention in the deportation centre in the absence of any immediate prospect of his expulsion.'[48] In the case of *SK v Russia*, a Syrian applicant had initially entered legally Russia in 2012 through a business visa which he overstayed. He was later discovered by the authorities and sentenced by a national administrative court for the offence of having overstayed his visa and was held in pre-return detention in 2015 in view of his return to Syria. The Court found a violation of Article 5(1) ECHR and held that:

> [I]t should have been sufficiently evident for the national authorities already in February and March 2015 that the applicant's removal was not practicable and would remain unlikely in view of the worsening conflict in Syria. … In these circumstances, it was incumbent on the domestic authorities to consider alternative measures that could be taken in respect of the applicant.[49]

Alternatives to detention thus enter the scene through the back door of proportionality. The proportionality considerations encompassed in the ECtHR's case-law only partly counteract the lack of a necessity requirement though. Immigration detention for reasons of administrative convenience is still possible under the ECtHR, albeit limited by the proportionality considerations analysed above.

III. EU Law and the Prohibition of Arbitrary Detention: An Obligation to Implement Alternatives to Immigration Detention

The EU developed its alternatives to immigration detention policy against the backdrop of the multilevel legal obligations at international and European (Council of Europe) level analysed above. EU law contains a roadmap as to how these different levels of norms interrelate. All EU Member States are parties to the ECHR. The Charter clarifies that as far as the rights it recognises correspond to rights guaranteed by the ECHR, they should be understood to have, as a minimum, the same meaning and scope.[50] This is, however, a threshold and not a barrier: Union law may provide for more extensive protection.[51] Finally, EU Member States are

[48] ECtHR 8 October 2009, *Mikolenko v Estonia*, App No 10664/05, para 67.

[49] ECtHR 17 February 2017, *SK v Russia*, App No 52722/15, para 115. See also ECtHR 18 April 2013, *Azimov v Russia*, App No 67474/11, para 173.

[50] Art 52(3) Charter.

[51] ibid.

party to international treaties creating obligations to respect human rights, such as the ICCPR. These obligations cannot be restricted, or adversely affected by the Charter provisions.[52] This means that, where international law establishes a higher level of protection, neither obligations under the Charter,[53] nor for that matter those under the ECHR,[54] could negate it.

The Return Directive and the recast RCD regulate immigration detention in a detailed manner. Within this harmonised framework a highly sophisticated regional understanding of what constitutes an 'alternative to immigration detention' emerges. The next section provides a sketch of immigration regulation under EU law, critically assessing how international and regional human rights law, case-law and legal opinions have influenced EU law (section II.A). Thereafter, I conceptualise what an alternative to immigration detention under EU law is, also noting limitations operationalising the EU approach (section II.B). In a final subsection, I critically analyse judicial interaction between the CJEU and the ECtHR on immigration detention (section II.C).

A. Regulating Immigration Detention under EU Law: Detention as the Exception

Immigration detention practices are proliferating in the EU. It is, however, crucial to distinguish between potential poor quality of the EU legislation analysed below, and its non-implementation, or its bad-faith interpretation by Member States. Nonetheless EU legislation under negotiation at the time of writing affords greater deference to Member States, and scales back guarantees in favour of the 'effectiveness' of the return policy,[55] and in the asylum framework specifically uses detention as a sanction to dissuade secondary movements.[56] Another parallel development is the recourse to the criminalisation of irregular migration and the imposition of deprivation of liberty measures under national criminal law legislation, an issue that goes beyond the scope of this contribution.[57]

[52] Art 53 Charter. See B De Witte, 'Article 53: Level of Protection' in S Peers, T Hervey, J Kenner and E Ward, *The EU Charter of Fundamental Rights: A Commentary* (Oxford, Hart Publishing, 2014) 1523.

[53] ibid.

[54] See Art 53 ECHR.

[55] See Proposal for a Directive of the European Parliament and of the Council on common standards and procedures in Member States for returning illegally staying third-country nationals (recast) Brussels COM(2018) 634 (hereinafter '2018 Proposal') and analysis below.

[56] See Proposal for a Directive of the European Parliament and of the Council laying down standards for the reception of applicants for international protection (recast) COM(2016) 465 (hereinafter '2016 Reception Conditions Directive proposal') and analysis below.

[57] See, however, V Mitsilegas, *The Criminalisation of Migration in Europe: Challenges for Human Rights and Rule of Law* (Cham, Springer, 2016); N Vavoula, 'The Interplay between EU Immigration Law and National Criminal Law – The Case of the Return Directive' in V Mitsilegas, M Bergström and T Konstadinides (eds), *Research Handbook on EU Criminal Law* (Cheltenham, Edward Elgar, 2016) 294; Fundamental Rights Agency, *Criminalisation of Migrants in an Irregular Situation and of Persons Engaging with Them* (2014).

i. Pre-Removal Detention under EU Law

In compliance with Member States' international legal obligations, the Return Directive confirms the principle of freedom of movement of migrants subject to a return order. The Return Directive foresees that the use of detention should be limited and interpreted narrowly.[58] The 2018 Proposal erodes this guarantee by deleting the reference to the 'limited' nature of pre-removal detention.[59] The aim of detention can only be either the preparation of the return or the execution of the removal process, in particular when there is a risk of absconding, or if the individual avoids or hampers the return procedure.[60] Detention on grounds of public order or public safety is not permissible.[61] Nevertheless, in practice almost half of the Member States detain migrants on national security grounds.[62] In addition, certain Member States took advantage of the abstract definition of the 'risk of absconding' in the Directive and the absence of an EU-wide list of objective criteria,[63] and provided for a catch-all definition that does not leave sufficient margin of discretion to the competent authorities.[64]

The 2018 Proposal erodes the status quo in two ways. First, it introduces a new detention ground based on risk to public policy, public security or national security;[65] a provision of dubious compatibility with the ECHR.[66] In addition, it provides for the establishment of a border return procedure to follow up on the examination of border asylum claims.[67] In the framework of this procedure, a rejected asylum seeker who had been previously detained as part of their asylum processing may continue to be detained for an additional maximum four months.[68] These provisions, which exemplify the trends of securitisation and externalisation, if adopted, will certainly result in more extensive use of detention in pre-removal settings, putting into question its exceptional nature.

[58] Art 15 of the Return Directive.

[59] 2018 Proposal, Recital 27.

[60] Art 15(1) of the Return Directive.

[61] C-357/09 PPU *Kadzoev* ECLI:EU:C:2009:741, para 70.

[62] Namely, Belgium, Cyprus, Germany, Greece, Estonia, Finland, Hungary, Ireland, Italy, Sweden, Slovenia and UK; see European Migration Network, *The Effectiveness of Return in EU Member States: Challenges and Good Practices Linked to EU Rules And Standards – Synthesis Report* (2017) 39. Furthermore, a criminal conviction or the suspicion of having committed a criminal offence is often automatically leading to pre-removal detention, see M Moraru and G Renaudiere, 'European Synthesis Report on the Judicial Implementation of Chapter IV of the Return Directive Pre-Removal Detention' (2015) REDIAL Research Report 2016/05, 20, fn 78.

[63] Art 3(7) of the Return Directive defines the risk of absconding as 'the existence of reasons in an individual case which are based on objective criteria defined by law to believe that a person under return procedures may abscond'. For further analysis, see M Moraru 'Judicial Dialogue in Action: Making Sense of the Risk of Absconding in the Return Procedure', Chapter 5 in this volume.

[64] See in particular the practices reported in France, Italy, Netherlands, Slovenia, in Moraru and Renaudiere (n 62).

[65] 2018 Proposal, Recital 29 and Art 18(1)(c).

[66] See subsection II.C.

[67] 2018 Proposal, Art 22.

[68] ibid, Art 22(7), para 4.

Finally, the Return Directive clearly establishes that Member States may resort to detention only if less coercive measures cannot be applied effectively.[69] Thus, unlike the ECHR system but in accordance with the UN human rights treaty obligations, pre-removal detention must be necessary. This approach is compliant with the EU Charter which, in respect of international law, explicitly states that Union law may provide more extensive protection than the ECHR system, as well as international law, if this establishes a higher level of protection. As analysed above, the HRC has found that deprivation of liberty must be necessary, including in the migration context. Therefore, had EU legislation negated a necessity requirement it would have contravened Member States' international obligations under the ICCPR. The Return Directive uses the term 'to prepare the return' as a collective term for all stages of return procedures between a return decision, such as a final denial of asylum, and the issuance of an actual, executable expulsion order.[70] The *travaux préparatoires* reveal that the insertion of the term 'in particular' (instead of merely 'when') before the two necessity grounds was a mere linguistic exercise without any deliberate far-reaching consequences.[71]

In addition, the Return Directive stipulates that '[a]ny detention shall be as short as possible and only maintained as long as removal arrangements are in progress and executed with due diligence'.[72] The Directive establishes temporal limitations. The initial detention period cannot exceed six months, while in exceptional cases, this initial period can be extended for a further 12 months.[73] The latter is only possible where the removal operation is likely to last longer owing to '(a) a lack of cooperation by the third-country national concerned', or '(b) delays in obtaining the necessary documentation from third countries'.[74] However, the Directive also foresees that '[w]hen it appears that a reasonable prospect of removal no longer exists … detention ceases to be justified and the person concerned shall be released immediately'.[75] The 2018 proposal makes a significant change establishing a minimum detention period of three months.[76] This, according to the Commission, is 'in order to more appropriately reflect the period of time needed to successfully carry out return and readmission procedures with third countries'.[77] This change again undermines the exceptional nature of recourse to detention. In addition, it jeopardises the necessity guarantee since in practice it can become patently obvious that return is impossible in a period that is shorter than three months.

[69] On the obligation to implement alternatives to immigration detention, see also the following section.

[70] P De Bruycker, S Mananashvili and G Renaudiere, *The Extent of Judicial Control of Pre-Removal Detention in the EU: Synthesis Report of the Project CONTENTION* (2014) 10.

[71] ibid, 15.

[72] Return Directive, Art 15(1), second indent.

[73] ibid, Art 15, paras 5 and 6.

[74] ibid.

[75] ibid, Art 15(4); see also *Kadzoev* (n 61) paras 65–67.

[76] 2018 Proposal, Art 18(5).

[77] ibid, Explanatory Memorandum, 8.

The Return Directive also enounces a series of procedural guarantees for detained migrants that pertain both to the initial decision, and to the right to challenge the detention decision.[78] It establishes that detention should take place as a rule in specialised detention facilities; however, it recognises that Member States might have to resort to the use of prison facilities.[79] The CJEU found that recourse to prison accommodation must be truly exceptional. The fact that in Germany some federal states (*Länder*) did not have specialised detention facilities on their ground was not found to constitute sufficient excuse for recourse to prison accommodation.[80] The Return Directive contains further specifications and standards regarding detention conditions.[81] It also contains additional, albeit rather weak, guarantees specifically geared to the situation of detained vulnerable migrants.[82] However, the Directive does not fully harmonise all aspects of detention conditions.

ii. Asylum Detention under EU Law

EU asylum law regulates detention of asylum seekers in detail. According to the recast RCD, an applicant is held in 'detention' if she is confined within a particular place where she is deprived of her freedom of movement.[83] In the same manner as the Return Directive, the recast RCD establishes that detention should take place as a rule in specialised detention facilities; however, it recognises that Member States might have to resort to the use of prison facilities.[84] In any case, the definition is broadly phrased as it contains the term 'within a particular place', rather than limiting the scope to (specialised) detention facilities or prison accommodation. Thus, the protective provisions of the recast RCD on detained asylum seekers apply also in other places where they might be deprived of their liberty, such as airport transit zones, facilities at the border, 'first reception centres', etc.[85] It also echoes ECtHR case-law which found that restrictions suffered by asylum seekers held in the transit zone of a Parisian airport amounted to deprivation of liberty and therefore Article 5(1) ECHR was applicable.[86]

Detention of asylum seekers is the exception and '[a]pplicants may be detained only under very clearly defined exceptional circumstances'.[87] Seeking asylum does not constitute in itself a permissible ground for detention.[88] Instead, EU asylum

[78] Return Directive, Art 15(2) and (3).
[79] ibid, Art 16 (1).
[80] Joined Cases C-473/13 and C-514/13 *Bero and Bouzalmate* ECLI:EU:C:2014:2095.
[81] Return Directive, Art 16.
[82] ibid, Art 17.
[83] Recast RCD, Art 2(h).
[84] ibid, Art 10(1). Unaccompanied minors can never be detained in prison facilities, see ibid, Art 11(3).
[85] See also Recital 8 of the recast RCD.
[86] *Amuur* (n 33). See *Riad and Idiab* (n 36).
[87] Recast RCD, Recital 15.
[88] ibid, where an explicit reference to Art 31 of the Refugee Convention is made, as well as Art 8(1). This guarantee is restated in the recast APD, Art 16(1).

law establishes an exhaustive list of detention grounds that are linked with: the right to enter the territory; determination or verification of identity or nationality/determination of elements of the claim; protection of national security or public order; detention in the framework of 'Dublin procedures'; and finally, asylum applications filed in the framework of a return procedure.[89] I have analysed the content and scope of the six asylum detention grounds elsewhere in detail.[90] It suffices to highlight that the grounds are broadly phrased, and therefore the elements that rationalise them are the individualisation and the necessity and proportionality requirements. The 2016 RCD proposal under negotiation at the time of writing goes even further by introducing an additional detention ground 'in order to tackle secondary movements and absconding of applicants'.[91] This new ground would essentially authorise detention where an applicant has not complied with the obligation to reside in a designated place.[92] The proposed Directive in turn also significantly enlarges the cases under which an asylum seeker might be assigned to a designated residence.[93]

In view of the broadly phrased detention grounds, individualisation of the decision to deprive asylum seekers of their liberty is a crucial guarantee. Indeed, the recast RCD establishes the obligation to conduct an individualised assessment, in respect of the principles of necessity and proportionality.[94] It explicitly states that Member States need to consider whether detention is necessary or whether the same result could be achieved through a less coercive measure, ie the application of an alternative to detention.[95] As already highlighted, this goes beyond the obligations of Member States under Article 5(1)(f) ECHR, which does not foresee a necessity test, unless that is required under national law.[96] In addition, just as in the return framework, EU asylum law enounces a series of procedural guarantees for detained asylum seekers.[97] It also establishes a right to free legal aid, which is, however, circumscribed.[98] The recast RCD contains standards regarding asylum seekers' detention conditions,[99] and some guarantees specifically geared to the situation of detained vulnerable asylum seekers,[100] although without fully harmonising all aspects of detention conditions.

The analysis above revealed that in both the pre-removal and asylum frameworks the obligation to implement alternatives to immigration detention

[89] Recast RCD, Art 8(3).

[90] E Tsourdi, 'Asylum Detention in EU Law: Falling Between Two Stools?' (2016) 35 *Refugee Survey Quarterly* 7, 13–22.

[91] 2016 Reception Conditions Directive proposal, Explanatory Memorandum, 14.

[92] ibid, Art 8(3)(c).

[93] ibid, Art 7(2).

[94] Recast RCD, Art 8(2).

[95] ibid.

[96] See above, section II.B.

[97] Recast RCD, Art 9.

[98] ibid.

[99] ibid, Ar 10.

[100] ibid, Art 11, and J Pétin, 'Exploring the Role of Vulnerability in Immigration Detention' (2016) 35 *Refugee Survey Quarterly* 91.

is explicit; in addition, the instruments contain further guarantees and indications as to the content of alternatives to detention that I explore in the next section.

B. Alternatives to Immigration Detention in EU Law: The Emergence of a Regional Understanding

Within the harmonised EU framework, a coherent understanding on what constitutes an alternative to immigration detention emerges. As we have seen above, the Return Directive establishes a clear obligation to examine alternatives to detention, referred to as 'less coercive measures', before placing a migrant in detention. That Member States must examine alternative measures before resorting to the detention of returnees has been affirmed by the CJEU.[101] Unlike the recast RCD, the Return Directive does not explicitly require Member States to establish national rules concerning alternative schemes, nor does it list examples of alternatives to detention.

However, Article 7 (relating to voluntary departure) enumerates measures that could be imposed on a third-country national benefiting from a period of voluntary departure to avoid the risk of absconding. This provision highlights that:

> Certain obligations aimed at avoiding the risk of absconding, such as regular reporting to the authorities, deposit of an adequate financial guarantee, submission of documents or the obligation to stay at a certain place may be imposed for the duration of the period for voluntary departure.[102]

While Member States may apply these measures to avoid the risk of absconding, they do not constitute an alternative to detention as, at this point, the persons concerned are not liable for detention. According to a 2017 European Migration Network study, Member States do frequently employ these measures – namely reporting requirements, surrender of passports or travel documents, and accommodation in a given location (designated residence) – also as alternatives to detention.[103] Designated residence can either take the form of a specialised open centre, or could refer to smaller units, such as the Belgian 'return houses', that were initially designed for families in a return procedure and include a coaching component.[104] Bail is less frequently applied, but does exist in some Member States.[105] Nevertheless, the application of alternatives to detention in a pre-return framework at national level has not been seamless. As contributions

[101] See eg Case C-61/11 *El Dridi* ECLI:EU:C:2011:268, para 39.

[102] Return Directive, Art 7(3).

[103] European Migration Network, *Synthesis Report* (n 62) 47–48.

[104] See P De Bruycker (ed), A Bloomfield, E Tsourdi and J Pétin, *Alternatives to Immigration and Asylum Detention in the EU – Time for Implementation* (2015) 97–98.

[105] See European Migration Network, *Synthesis Report* (n 62) 48.

to this volume illustrate, certain jurisdictions continue to approach alternative measures as exceptional, instead of considering them as a mandatory step before ordering pre-removal detention.[106]

Further and more specific indications as to what constitutes an 'alternative to immigration detention' and what safeguards should accompany it can be derived from the recast RCD. As outlined in the previous section, according to EU asylum law, detention should be an exceptional measure, applicable only if a ground for detention exists and only when found necessary and proportionate after an individual examination. It cannot constitute a migration management tool applicable automatically to asylum seekers or to particular groups of asylum seekers (eg those subject to Dublin proceedings or those subject to border proceedings). Such practices are observed on the ground.[107] However, this speaks less of the quality of EU asylum law and its regulation of asylum detention, and more about its misuse or non-use by national authorities.

In order to effectively apply EU asylum law, national authorities should undertake, for every individual, both a needs and a risk assessment. The needs assessment examines the vulnerability of the individual and their eventual special reception or procedural needs.[108] The risk assessment entails an examination of whether the individual is exceptionally liable to detention. Alternatives to detention therefore come into play when an individual is exceptionally liable to detention on the basis of one of the six grounds enumerated in the recast RCD.[109] Where there is no legal basis to detain an asylum seeker, there is also no legal basis to apply an alternative to detention. The individual should simply be released. Where an individual is exceptionally liable to detention, Member States are obliged to consider whether detention is necessary or whether the same result could be achieved through a less coercive measure, ie the application of an alternative.

Alternatives to detention could entail obligations involving different levels of coerciveness. Such obligations often include restrictions on the freedom of movement, such as for example a daily curfew at the designated residence or an obligation to reside in the house of the guarantor in case of bail.[110] Their aim is to mitigate the risk factors identified by the authorities that considered that the specific individual was liable to detention. They should therefore be distinguished

[106] See eg A di Pascale, 'Can a Justice of the Peace be a Good Detention Judge? The Case of Italy', Chapter 13 in this volume; C Demitrou and N Trimlikliniotis, 'Cypriot Courts, the Return Directive and Fundamental Rights: Challenges and Failures', Chapter 6 in this volume.

[107] On the proliferation of detention and de facto detention practices for asylum seekers arriving at border areas, see ECRE, *Boundaries of Liberty: Asylum and De Facto Detention in Europe* (2017) 19–22; on the systematic reliance on administrative detention to operationalise Dublin transfers, see ECRE, *The Implementation of the Dublin III Regulation in 2018* (2019) 16–17.

[108] For greater detail, see also J Pétin, 'Exploring the role of vulnerability in immigration detention' (2016) 35 *Refugee Survey Quarterly* 91.

[109] Recast RCD, Art 8(3).

[110] For a review of practices in 6 EU Member States, see De Bruycker et al (n 104) 87–112.

from obligations that concern the totality of asylum seekers and the normal running of reception and procedural systems, such as obligations to declare the address of stay to the authorities or to remain in a specific district.

However, for a scheme to be characterised as an alternative it must 'fall short' of deprivation of liberty and constitute a non-custodial measure,[111] or it would be an alternative form *of* detention. The difference between deprivation of and restriction upon liberty is one of degree or intensity, and not of nature or substance.[112] Therefore, an examination of the implementation of each scheme is necessary before concluding whether it is, in practice, a non-custodial measure. Not only should alternatives to detention be non-custodial but they should also respect the fundamental rights of asylum seekers as enshrined in international legal instruments, the ECHR and the Charter.[113] Therefore, the implementation of such schemes should not violate the prohibition of torture, inhuman or degrading treatment, the right to human dignity, the right to private and family life and the right to an effective remedy.[114] As long as they comply with the requirements stated above, Member States are free to set up different alternatives to detention. The recast RCD mentions a number of schemes: regular reporting to the authorities, the deposit of a financial guarantee, or an obligation to stay at an assigned place.[115] The wording employed, 'such as', makes it clear that this is a non-exhaustive list which does not restrain Member States from establishing other alternatives. Moreover, Member States must not only operationalise in practice alternative schemes; they must also enact such schemes via their national rules transposing the Directive.

Even if they are not explicitly mentioned in the Return Directive, the guarantee of the non-custodial nature of alternatives to detention, and that of the respect of the fundamental rights of migrants, should also be applied in the pre-return framework. It cannot be adduced from any element in the Return Directive or the recast RCD that the EU legislator envisaged a different understanding or juxtaposition between alternatives to pre-return and to asylum detention. It is just that the earlier instrument, the Return Directive, did not make explicit these additional indications, while the more recent one, the recast RCD, does. Despite these additional indications, the implementation of alternatives to detention in the asylum framework has been problematic in practice. In Hungary alternatives have been used as a systematic migration control measure, rather than a less

[111] See recast RCD, Recital 20. The term 'non-custodial' concerns the physical liberty of the person; a non-custodial measure is one that does not dispossess someone of this liberty whether at a detention centre or at another location.

[112] See ECtHR 15 March 2012, *Austin and Others v the United Kingdom* (GC), App Nos 39692/09, 40713/09 and 41008/09, para 57; ECtHR 6 November 1980, *Guzzardi v Italy*, App No. 7367/76, paras 92–93; and ECtHR 29 March 2010, *Medvedyev and others v France* (GC), App No 3394/03, para 73.

[113] See recast RCD, Recitals 20 and 35.

[114] On the risks stemming from the application of alternatives to detention, see Bloomfield (n 10).

[115] See recast RCD, Art 8(4).

coercive means of pursuing the specific objectives linked to detention in individual cases. Throughout 2016 a designated residence was imposed in 54,615 cases, a number that raises doubts as to the individualised nature of the assessment.[116] In other cases, Member States have operationalised what are essentially alternative forms of detention, meaning deprivation of liberty in a reception centre understood as 'designated residence', rather than in a detention centre.[117] Finally, some Member States have made minimal use of alternatives to immigration detention.[118]

C. CJEU Case-Law on the Compatibility of EU Legislation on Asylum Detention with the ECHR: Deference to Member State Immigration Control Prerogatives

A concrete and legally binding obligation for the Union to accede to the ECHR is part of the TEU,[119] and a Draft Agreement on EU accession to the ECHR was adopted in 2013.[120] In December 2014, however, the CJEU found, in a highly contested Opinion, the draft agreement incompatible with the EU treaties, a finding that has delayed the accession process.[121] Pending accession to the ECHR and formalised mechanisms of cooperation between the CJEU and the ECtHR, the emerging order is 'a pluralist one, in which the relationships of the constituent parts are governed, not by legal rules, but primarily by politics, often judicial politics; within this pluralist order we find heterarchy rather than hierarchy'.[122] The CJEU must interpret EU law in conformity with the ECtHR case-law which acts as the lowest common denominator but it draws the relevant

[116] ECRE (n 1) 11.

[117] Such practice had been reported in Slovenia in 2015. In the view of the Directorate for Migration, this complete restriction to the premises of the asylum home could be considered as 'designated residence' since asylum seekers with limited scope of freedom of movement in the premises of the asylum home have exactly the same rights and duties as others accommodated in the same facility, except the right to leave the asylum home. See De Bruycker et al (n 104) 62–63, and Annex 1 Country Profiles: Slovenia.

[118] See S Slama, 'Duality of Jurisdiction in the Control of Immigration Detention: The Case of France', Chapter 12 in this volume.

[119] See Art 6(2) TEU. See also TEU, Protocol 8 and Declaration No 2 on Art 6 TEU.

[120] Draft revised agreement on the accession of the European Union to the Convention for the Protection of Human Rights and Fundamental Freedoms of 5 April 2013, Appendix I to Council of Europe, Doc 47þ1(2013)2008rev2 (hereinafter 'Draft Revised Agreement').

[121] See CJEU, *Opinion 2/13* [2014] ECLI:EU:C:2014:2454. The opinion has been the object of extensive academic commentary. See, among others, L Halleskov Storgaard, 'EU Law Autonomy versus European Fundamental Rights Protection – On Opinion 2/13 on EU Accession to the ECHR' (2015) 15 *Human Rights Law Review* 485; P Eeckhout, 'Opinion 2/13 on EU Accession to the ECHR and Judicial Dialogue: Autonomy or Autarky? (2015) 38 *Fordham International Law Journal* 955; and B de Witte and Š Imamovic, 'Opinion 2/13 on Accession to the ECHR: Defending the EU Legal Order against a Foreign Human Rights Court' (2015) 5 *EL Rev* 683.

[122] N Krisch, 'The Open Architecture of European Human Rights Law' (2008) 71 *MLR* 183, 185.

conclusions about the content of that case-law itself. There is no formal way for the ECtHR to assess the legitimacy of these conclusions and their application: the interpretation of EU law is beyond its remit. It has been rightly observed that the CJEU's references to the ECHR and the case-law of the Strasbourg court are often characterised by cryptic judicial reasoning and a lack of any comprehensive and coherent analysis of the normative weight that should be attributed to the ECtHR jurisprudence.[123]

These observations bear out also in the case of *JN*,[124] which concerned an asylum seeker who, over the span of 20 years, had launched three unsuccessful asylum applications and had committed a series of criminal offences, principally thefts, that had led to 21 convictions ranging from fines to a 3-month imprisonment. Despite the fact that a return decision accompanied by 10-year entry ban had been issued against him after the rejection of his third asylum application in 2014, Mr N had not been removed from the Dutch territory. While serving a prison sentence in 2015 for theft and failure to comply with the entry ban imposed on him, Mr N submitted a fourth asylum application. After his release from criminal detention, he was subsequently detained in his capacity as an asylum seeker on grounds of protecting national security or public order on account of the criminal offences he had committed.

On appeal from a legal action challenging his detention, Mr N advanced that his detention was contrary to Article 5(1)f ECHR on account of his lawful presence on the Dutch territory. In these circumstances, the CJEU was asked to consider the validity of Article 8(3)(e) of the recast RCD that concerns detention 'when protection of national security or public order so requires' with Article 6 of the EU Charter of Fundamental Rights that establishes for everyone the 'right to liberty and security of person'.

The CJEU addressed the interrelation between the ECHR and the EU legal order. It noted that the rights contained in the ECHR constitute general principles of EU law[125] and that according to the Charter itself, rights contained therein which correspond to ECHR rights are to have the same meaning and scope.[126] Nevertheless, it highlighted that as long as the Union has not acceded to the ECHR, that instrument has not formally been incorporated into EU law. Therefore, the starting point for the examination of the validity of EU legislation is the Charter, and namely its Article 6, and not the ECHR. Since Article 6 of the

[123] G Harpaz, 'The European Court of Justice and its Relations with the European Court of Human Rights: The Quest for Enhanced Reliance, Coherence and Legitimacy' (2009) 46 *CML Rev* 105, 109–10. For an illustration of judicial interaction between the CJEU and the ECtHR in the interrelation between the EU subsidiary protection regime and the prohibition of non-refoulement, see E Tsourdi, 'What Protection for Persons Fleeing Indiscriminate Violence? The Impact of the European Courts on the EU Subsidiary Protection Regime' in D Cantor and JF Durieux (eds), *Refuge from Inhumanity: War Refugees and International Humanitarian Law* (Leiden, Brill/Martinus Nijhoff 2014) 270.

[124] *JN* (n 8) and Case C-18/16 *K* ECLI:EU:C:2017:680.

[125] Art 6(3) TEU.

[126] Art 52(3) Charter.

Charter is a provision that contains a right which corresponds to an ECHR right, it needs to reflect the level of protection afforded by Article 5 of the ECHR. Hence, the CJEU is indirectly led to also examine the compatibility of the provisions of the recast RCD with the ECHR. Thereafter, the Court notes that the applicant's detention for the protection of national security or public order is a limitation on the exercise to his right to liberty. According to the Charter,[127] any such limitation should fulfil the following requirements: be provided by law, respect the essence of the right and be in observance of the principle of proportionality, be necessary and genuinely meet either objectives of general interest recognised by the EU, or protect the rights and freedoms of others.

The CJEU found that these limitations are compatible with the right to freedom in Article 5(1) ECHR. It held that since a return procedure can be resumed after an eventual rejection of an asylum application, it can be assumed that detention is 'still being taken' in view of deportation.[128] Hence the situation falls under the second limb Article 5(1)(f) ECHR that foresees detention 'of a person against whom action is being taken with a view to deportation or extradition'. The Court held this finding to be consistent with the ECtHR's case-law in *Nabil*.[129] Given the exhaustive enumeration of exceptions to the right to liberty and security under Article 5 of the ECHR, the grounds of national security or public order can only be validly invoked by Member States if they fall in the scope of one of the exceptions contemplated therein.[130] In *JN*, the CJEU based its reasoning on the compatibility with the ECHR on the fact that Mr N was subject to a return order and entry ban. According to Article 5(1) ECHR, each detention order must be 'in accordance with a procedure prescribed by law', and as analysed above where national law *goes beyond* the requirements of the ECHR, the Court's examination will be based on the stricter requirements of national law.

In *Ahmade v Greece* and in *RU v Greece*, the Strasbourg court stated that: 'The applicant's detention pending asylum proceedings could not have been undertaken for the purposes of deportation, given that *national law* did not allow for deportation pending a decision on asylum.'[131] These cases were issued before the recast RCD was adopted. These findings were more recently affirmed in the case of *Nabil v Hungary*. The ECtHR indeed stated in the passage mentioned by the CJEU that the 'pending asylum case does not as such imply that the detention was no longer "with a view to deportation" – since an eventual dismissal of the asylum application could have opened the way to the execution of the deportation orders'.[132] Therefore, under the ECHR the filing of an asylum claim

[127] See Art 52(1) Charter.

[128] *JN* (n 8) para 78.

[129] ECtHR, *Nabil and others v Hungary*, App No 62116/12.

[130] *A and Others* (n 33) para 171.

[131] See ECtHR 25 September 2012, *Ahmade v Greece*, App No 50520/09, paras 142–44; and ECtHR 7 September 2011, *RU v Greece*, App No 2237/08, paras 88–96 (emphasis added).

[132] See *Nabil* (n 129) para 38.

does not necessarily mean that detention cannot fall on the 'return-related' limb of Article 5(1)(f). However, national law must share this understanding. As explained above, if national law establishes stricter requirements, then the ECtHR will examine if the detention order also complied with *those stricter requirements*.

Hence in *Nabil*, the Strasbourg court went on to state that 'the detention nevertheless had to be in compliance with the national law and free of arbitrariness'.[133] Thereafter, it noted that the Hungarian authorities continued to justify detention of an asylum seeker on the basis of effecting return, without dealing with the impact of the on-going asylum procedure.[134] The Strasbourg court scrutinised closely the *national law* and found that 'to validly prolong the applicants' detention, the domestic authorities had to verify that they were indeed frustrating the enforcement of the expulsion; that alternative, less stringent measures were not applicable, and whether or not the expulsion could eventually be enforced'.[135] Highlighting that domestic courts did not duly assess whether the conditions for the continuing detention of an asylum seeker under national law were met, the ECtHR in *Nabil* condemned Hungary for a violation of Article 5(1) ECHR. Put simply, detention in that case posed problems as *national law* reflecting obligations under the provisions of the recast RCD established stricter requirements. This would be the case for every Member State because each has to apply through its *national law* the EU return and asylum acquis.

The CJEU undertook a rather selective reading of the ECtHR case-law and concluded rather hastily that since the eventual rejection of the asylum claim could lead to a continuation of the return process, detention could still fall within the realm of 'effecting return'. This is rather problematic, as the Court did not fully take into account several elements. Firstly, according to the EU recast instruments, an asylum seeker enjoys the right to stay during the examination of her claim at first instance.[136] Secondly, the Returns Directive explicitly states that asylum seekers cannot be considered as 'illegally staying' as long as their claim is pending at first instance.[137] Finally, as the referring national court made explicit, in the particular case according to national law, the return order had lapsed, thus there was no basis for a 'future' return. All these are requirements that are incorporated in the *national law* of each Member State that the ECtHR would take into account in order to decide whether a given detention order is compatible with the ECHR or not. The CJEU's approach seems to be underpinned by an extensive interpretation of what the effectiveness of the return policy entails. The Advocate General, taking a principled approach, took good notice of all these elements and

[133] ibid.
[134] ibid, paras 39–41.
[135] ibid, para 40.
[136] See recast Asylum Procedures Directive, Art 9(1) and Tsourdi (n 90) 10–13.
[137] Returns Directive, Recital 9, and Case C-181/16 *Gnandi* ECLI:EU:C:2018:465, para 40.

sought the compatibility of this ground in the other limitations of Article 5(1) instead.[138]

IV. Epilogue: Common Trends and Fragmented Standards in an Heterarchy

The fragmented standards on alternatives to immigration detention at international level are characteristic of the heterarchical nature of the global and regional human rights protection regimes. The ECtHR and the HRC are in constant interaction. Admissibility provisions ensure that jurisdictional overlap is avoided,[139] and a specific provision of the ECHR affirms that it will not constitute the basis of derogation, or limitation of human rights and fundamental freedoms ensured through other national or international legislation.[140] Nevertheless, there is no hierarchical relationship between these two jurisdictions and this has led to the emergence of fragmented standards. The ECtHR affords greater deference to its state parties than the HRC, authorising the instrumental use of immigration-related deprivation of liberty, essentially for administrative convenience, through its negation of a necessity requirement. Unlike the HRC, it has not found that states have an obligation to implement alternatives to immigration detention in every case. Nevertheless, this should not be understood as providing states with unfettered discretion as the ECtHR has circumscribed their discretion through 'proportionality type criteria'. On this basis, it has found detention to be ultimately arbitrary in cases concerning vulnerable migrants, in cases where return was not pursued with 'due diligence', or in cases where it was obvious that return would not be possible in a reasonable timeframe as it would breach the absolute prohibition of *refoulement*. Thus, alternatives to immigration detention surface through the back door of proportionality. This affirms that, apart from fragmented standards, there are also common trends, namely the prohibition of arbitrary deprivation of liberty. While the two jurisdictions take different inroads, essentially there is an inviolable core of the right to liberty under both systems.

These developments have also affected the regulation of immigration detention at the EU level. EU law foresees robust guarantees in both the pre-removal and asylum frameworks, and establishes an obligation to conduct an individualised assessment, and to implement alternatives to immigration detention. These guarantees rationalise otherwise broadly phrased detention grounds. A regional understanding on what constitutes an alternative to immigration detention emerges as a non-custodial measure that must respect migrants' fundamental rights, and

[138] See Opinion of Advocate General in *JN* (n 8), paras 116–26.
[139] See Art 35(2)(b) ECHR and First Optional Protocol to the International Covenant on Civil and Political Rights, New York, 16 December 1966 (entered into force 23 March 1976), Art 5(2).
[140] Art 53 ECHR.

only be applied where necessary and proportionate. Once more though, the law on paper has not been fully realised in practice. Certain Member States forego individualised assessments for particular groups of migrants, such as those processed at the borders, those holding specific nationalities, or those that are subject to specific type of procedures, such as 'Dublin procedures'. They classify as alternatives to immigration detention measures that as a matter of fact deprive applicants of their liberty, denying them at the same time the guarantees that detained individuals should enjoy. Other states implement alternatives as a systematic migration control measure, thus affecting thousands of migrants, whereas they should only be contemplated where a ground for detention exists. The EU legislative measures that are currently under negotiation also raise concern as they may seem to erode the exceptional nature of detention, adding new detention grounds and instrumentalising deprivation of liberty for migration management purposes. Under these circumstances, EU and national judges will have a crucial role to play in upholding the inviolable core of the right to liberty, in constant interaction, as well as with international human rights jurisdictions.

8

Scope and Intensity of Judicial Review: Which Power for Judges within the Control of Immigration Detention?

ADAM BLISA AND DAVID KOSAŘ

I. Introduction

When the Court of Justice rendered its landmark *Mahdi* judgment,[1] it caused a big splash. By unequivocally stipulating that domestic judges deciding on the extension of detention of third-country nationals under the Return Directive[2] enjoy full judicial review and may substitute the decision of administrative authorities with their own decisions,[3] the CJEU caught several EU Member States off-guard. The *Mahdi* judgment has, all of a sudden, made some of the domestic models of judicial review of immigration detention incompatible with EU law. As a result, not only Bulgaria,[4] from which the preliminary reference in *Mahdi* originally came, but also other EU Member States amended their laws or modes of judicial review.[5]

The *Mahdi* judgment also revealed that there is a huge diversity among EU Member States regarding the domestic judicial design of review of immigration detention, which may hamper judicial dialogue between the CJEU and national courts as well among the national courts in the European legal space.[6]

The legal rules covered by the European asylum and migration acquis are among the best candidates for a fruitful judicial dialogue. Domestic courts in virtually all

[1] Case C-146/14 PPU *Bashir Mohamed Ali Mahdi* ECLI:EU:C:2014:1320.

[2] Council Directive 2008/115/EC of 16 December 2008 on common standards and procedures in Member States for returning illegally staying third-country nationals [2008] OJ L348/98.

[3] See *Mahdi* (n 1) para 62.

[4] See Art 44(8) of the Law on Foreign Nationals in the Republic of Bulgaria, available at https://lex.bg/mobile/ldoc/2134455296.

[5] See eg Art 79a of the Aliens Act of 11 April 2014 (Slovenia); and Council of State, Judgment of 23 January 2015, ECLI:NL:RVS:2015:232 and Council of State, Judgment of 10 April 2015, ECLI:NL:RVS:2015:1309 (Netherlands).

[6] For the relevant literature on judicial dialogue, see G Cornelisse and M Moraru, 'Introduction', Chapter 1 in this Volume.

EU Member States have engaged with the very same definition of a refugee in the 1951 Refugee Convention for decades, and the Qualification Directive[7] made the potential for convergence even greater. Related asylum and migration directives have witnessed a similar development. However, there are also significant limits to the dialogue. The existing empirical studies show that even nations with many institutional, cultural, geographical and political similarities reach strikingly different results in refugee status determination.[8] What is striking is that this 'refugee roulette' may exist even within the same country.[9] The empirical research on third-country national detention within the EU,[10] coupled with the fact that the institutional diversity of deciding on third-country national detention among EU Member States is even greater[11] than in refugee status determination, suggest that it is highly likely that third-country nationals in the EU face a 'detention roulette' as well.

One solution how to remedy this problem is to unify the rules governing the detention of third-country nationals as well as the judicial review,[12] which is exactly what the Return Directive does. However, this chapter argues that this is not enough. Our argument is twofold. First, based on the good practices among the EU Member States, we identified five factors that may contribute to a well-functioning model of pre-removal detention control: (1) early review of lawfulness of detention; (2) the need to increase expertise of detention judges; (3) the availability of appeal against the judicial decision on third-country national detention; (4) automatic and periodic review of detention; and (5) quality legal representation for third-country nationals, including legal aid and good interpreters. Second, we argue that these five factors can reduce the detention roulette only up to a certain point and a uniform model of judicial review of third-country national detention is not a solution either. Instead we propose a comprehensive training of detention judges and other reforms that would further professionalise the national adjudication systems in this area.

[7] European Parliament and Council Directive 2011/95/EU of 13 December 2011 on standards for the qualification of third-country nationals or stateless persons as beneficiaries of international protection, for a uniform status for refugees or for persons eligible for subsidiary protection, and for the content of the protection granted [2011] OJ L337/9.

[8] See R Hamlin, 'International Law and Administrative Insulation: A Comparison of Refugee Status Determination Regimes in the United States, Canada, and Australia' (2012) 37 *Law & Social Inquiry* 933; and R Hamlin, *Let Me Be a Refugee: Administrative Justice and the Politics of Asylum in the United States, Canada, and Australia* (New York, Oxford University Press, 2014).

[9] See J Ramji-Nogales, AI Schoenholtz and PG Schrag, 'Refugee Roulette: Disparities in Asylum Adjudication' (2010) 60 *Stanford Law Review* 295; and J Ramji-Nogales, AI Schoenholtzand and PG Schrag, *Refugee Roulette: Disparities in Asylum Adjudication and Proposals for Reform* (New York, New York University Press, 2009). See also SH Legomsky, 'Learning to Live with Unequal Justice: Asylum and the Limits to Consistency' (2007) 60 *Stanford Law Review* 413.

[10] See eg the Global Detention Project data, available at www.globaldetentionproject.org; and the CONTENTION project, available at contention.eu.

[11] See section III below.

[12] In fact, independent appellate review is one of the solutions to the refugee roulette suggested by Ramji-Nogales et al, 'Refugee Roulette' (n 9).

This chapter proceeds as follows. Section II sets the stage and sketches the broader context of diversity of domestic judicial design within the EU. Section III explores various models of judicial review of detention with a specific focus on four issues: whether domestic judges decide on detention or merely review of the detention decision of an administrative authority; who is the 'detention judge' at the domestic level; differences between judicial control of detention and judicial control of return; and availability of appeal against judicial decision. In doing so, we build heavily on the chapters in this part of the book which address judicial control of detention in a specific EU Member State. Section IV discusses whether a uniform model of judicial review of detention of third-country nationals for the purpose of their return could be a solution to the existing problems. Section V concludes.

II. Broader Context: Institutional Diversity

To examine which institutional setup is the most appropriate for the proper (or ideal) functioning of the mechanism of detaining third-country nationals and returning them to the country of origin, it is necessary to provide the reader with a broader context on the institutional diversity of judiciaries in the EU Member States. The EU Member States have distinctive institutional frameworks, and these frameworks can in turn produce significantly different outcomes even when addressing the same issue such as detention of third-country nationals for the purpose of their return. Different legal systems have undeniably a lot in common due to shared legal origins, but their structure and functioning can and do change over time.[13] The resulting differences, idiosyncrasies and institutional choices matter in judicial control of detention.

Legal systems can be differentiated and categorised by various means. One of the most common ways is distinguishing between the civil and common law systems that differ, most notably, in the sources of law that are used and the organization of the judiciary. While common law systems have 'recognition judiciaries' where lawyers become judges later in their careers and their selection is merit based,[14] the judiciary in civil law systems is career based, as lawyers become judges at a relatively young age and shortly after finishing law school, and then gradually progress in the judicial hierarchy, spending very little time outside the courtroom and usually remaining in the judiciary until retirement.[15] The most

[13] T Ginsburg and N Garoupa, *Judicial Reputation: A Comparative Theory* (Chicago, University of Chicago Press, 2015) 18.

[14] This system of recruitment is sometimes also called 'lateral'; see D Kosař, *Perils of Judicial Self-Government in Transitional Societies* (New York, Cambridge University Press, 2016) 114.

[15] See ibid, 113–14; for further details on the traditional features of the career model, see JH Merryman and R Perez-Perdomo, *The Civil Law Tradition? An Introduction to the Legal Systems of Europe and Latin America*, 3rd edn (Stanford, CA, Stanford University Press, 2007) 34–38; DS Clark, 'The Organization of Lawyers and Judges' in M Capelletti (ed), *International Encyclopedia of Comparative Law*,

important difference in this regard is that judges in the career judiciaries who start at the bottom, at the courts of first instance, are to a certain degree 'rookies', while the judges in recognition judiciaries tend to be more experienced. Thus, judges in career judiciaries in general require more oversight, often in the form of de novo review on appeal, which in turn necessitates more judges in the judiciary than in the recognition judiciaries.[16] We can find significant variations and differences even within the civil or common law systems.[17] For example, the Czech judiciary is divided into civil, criminal and administrative branches, with the Supreme Court and Supreme Administrative Court at the top and with the Constitutional Court looming aside and above all.[18] In France, on the other hand, there are general as well as specialist civil courts (labour courts and elected commercial courts), criminal courts divided into three levels according to the seriousness of the offence with a special court for minors, as well as administrative courts with the Conseil d'Etat at the top.[19] Look at any other judiciary, and you will find inspirations, transplants, attempts to copy, but never a perfect, complete twin – not even in Czechia and Slovakia, countries that existed within the same state for the most of the twentieth century.

The fact that judiciaries in different countries look different is hardly surprising. What is important, however, is that the lack of convergence on separation-of-powers issues and institutional design[20] is caused by the fact that institutional design, and constitutional law in general, are often deeply rooted in the historical and cultural background of the respective countries.[21] Take France as an example again, where the separation of powers is informed by distrust towards courts which, during the French Revolution, were viewed as institutions of the *ancien régime* that stood in the way of equality between citizens,[22] while in

vol XVI: *Civil Procedure* (Tübingen, Mohr Siebeck, 2002) 164–86; or C Guarnieri, 'Appointment and Career of Judges in Continental Europe: The Rise of Judicial Self- Government' (2004) 24 *Legal Studies* 169, 169–73.

[16] Kosař (n 14) 114–15. Ginsburg and Garoupa also claim that hierarchical (eg career) judiciaries dominate in systems that emphasise social control, serving as a part of the state's apparatus governing civilians, while non-hierarchical judiciaries (eg recognition ones) serve as law-making bodies and require individual accountability; see Ginsburg and Garoupa (n 13) 18, 29–30.

[17] Note that career judiciaries can include some aspects of the recognition ones and vice versa. These 'pockets of exception' may include constitutional courts in civil law systems, to which justices are appointed on the basis of merit; see Ginsburg and Garoupa (n 13) 50–58.

[18] See Kosař (n 14) 433–34.

[19] J Bell, *Judiciaries Within Europe: A Comparative Review* (Cambridge, Cambridge University Press, 2006) 45–49.

[20] See eg Ch Möllers, *The Three Branches: A Comparative Model of Separation of Powers* (Oxford, Oxford University Press, 2013) 17–37, who examines the different approaches to the separation of powers in the USA, France, the UK and Germany and eventually concludes that *trias politica* in its pure form probably never really existed.

[21] ibid. Note, on the other hand, that in many respects, states succumb to pressure from supranational institutions to reform their institutions; see eg D Kosař and L Lixinski, 'Domestic Judicial Design by International Human Rights Courts' (2015) 109 *American Journal of International Law* 713.

[22] Möllers (n 20) 22–26.

Germany, distrust is directed rather at the legislature and the democratic process whose failure led to World War II, thus providing conditions for establishing a strong constitutional court with the task of guarding the fundamental rights and principles.[23] Translated into practice, the French Conseil d'Etat, originally set up by Napoleon, is not only a judicial body, but also an advisor to the government, thus being a blend of both executive and judicial branches.[24] Similarly, the Conseil Constitutionnel, although much more of a constitutional court nowadays, reviewing legislative acts and even hearing individual complaints, was originally designed as a council, not a court, for resolving disputes between the legislative and executive branches with former presidents of the republic as members.[25] In contrast to France, a full-fledged Kelsenian Constitutional Court (*Bundesverfassungsgericht*)[26] and a Federal Administrative Court (*Bundesverwaltungsgericht*) sit at the top of the German judiciary, both completely separated from the executive. Therefore, if we look at the institutional setup through the lens of historical roots, it may very well happen that what is uncontroversial in a certain EU Member State may be entirely unthinkable in the neighbouring one.[27]

Several implications arise from this brief overview. First, judicial review of detention in EU Member States is shaped by the respective state's institutional framework. Thus, we can find the review being delegated to civil, administrative or criminal judges, or even justices of the peace. Moreover, while judges in some countries are only controlling the lawfulness of detention, meaning that they review the decisions made by the administrative organs, in other countries it is judges who decide on detention by themselves. Second, the different institutional setups have substantial impact on the functioning of the control of detention and may in turn produce significantly different outputs, be it with regards of standard of protection, quality of decisions, or engagement in judicial dialogue within the countries and the EU. Finally, the roots and nature of these differences will influence the search for possible solutions, because they cannot be easily overcome or simply replaced with some universal 'off-the-shelf' solution. We explore these implications in the following sections.

[23] ibid, 32–37.

[24] Bell (n 19) 48–49. For a telling example of differences between jurisdictions, see ECtHR 6 November 2006, *Sacilor-Lormines v France*, App No 65411/01, where the Strasbourg Court accepted the blend of consultative and judicial functions of Conseil d'Etat, while the three dissenters from the CEE countries insisted on complete separation of these functions by creation of supreme administrative court.

[25] Bell (n 19) 49–50; for the judicial review procedure, *question prioritaire de constitutionnalité*, see Art 61-1 of the Constitution of 4 October 1958.

[26] ibid, 158–68.

[27] Yet another (German) example, the democratic principle that requires the so-called legitimacy chain (*Legitimationskette*) connecting the people with their representatives, and thus renders inadmissible for example the co-option of judges, because it breaks the chain of democratic legitimacy. In other countries, the notion that there needs to be a democratic link in the judiciary may seem outrageous. See eg EW Böckenförde, *Verfassungsfragen der Richterwahl. Dargestellt anhand der Gesetzentwürfe zur Einführung der Richterwahl in Nordrhein-Westfalen* (Berlin, Duncker & Humblot, 1998) 75; and A Tschentscher, *Demokratische Legitimation der dritten Gewalt* (Tübingen, Mohr Siebeck, 2006) 178.

III. Models of Judicial Control of Detention

In this section we build on the chapters in this volume as well as on additional sources of information on EU Member States' institutional configuration and provide an overview of the institutional convergences and differences among the EU Member States with regards to issuing pre-removal detention orders and their subsequent judicial review. Consequently, we sum up the advantages and disadvantages of the various systems and attempt to answer a question whether there is or should be any ideal model that should be pursued.

A. Who Decides? Judge Controlling v Judge Deciding

The Return Directive sets out rather vague and not very stringent requirements for the institutional framework with regard to detention orders.[28] It leaves up to the EU Member States to choose whether to entrust judicial or administrative authorities with deciding about detention. If EU Member States opt for the latter, the Return Directive requires that the lawfulness of such decision is either reviewed as speedily as possible by courts ex officio or that the third-country national is provided with the possibility to initiate the proceedings. The last institutional requirement is that the detention should be reviewed at reasonable intervals of time, again either ex officio or upon application of the detainee; should the detention periods be prolonged, such reviews are to be subject to further control by judicial authority.

The EU Member States thus have a choice, and their solutions are not uniform. Most of the EU Member States opted to put a judge in the controlling position and entrusted the administrative organs with issuing the decision on pre-removal detention,[29] but we can find significant variations in the procedure following the decision of the administrative organ. In Czechia, for example, the administrative organ orders the detention as well as its prolongation,[30] and any of these decisions are subject to judicial review only upon a suit lodged by the third-country national.

[28] Art 15(2) and (3) of the Return Directive.

[29] This is the case of Czechia, Slovakia, Slovenia, Bulgaria, Belgium, Austria or Netherlands; on Belgium, see S Sarolea, 'Detention of Migrants in Belgium and the Criminal Judge: A Lewis Carroll World', Chapter 11 in this Volume; on the other jurisdictions, see D Kosař, 'National Synthesis Report Czechia, Arts 15–18 of the Return Directive'; M Skamla, 'National Synthesis Report Slovakia Arts 15–18 of the Return Directive'; S Zagorc, 'National Synthesis Report Slovenia, Arts 15–18 of the Return Directive'; V Ilareva, 'National Synthesis Report Bulgaria, Arts 15–18 of the Return Directive'; U Brandl, 'National Synthesis Report Austria, Arts 15–18 of the Return Directive'; G Cornelisse, 'National Synthesis Report Netherlands, Arts 15–18 of the Return Directive'; all of the reports, including those cited subsequently, were compiled under the auspices of the REDIAL Project and are available at: www.euredial.eu/publications/national-synthesis-reports; see also M Moraru and G Renaudiere, 'European Synthesis Report on the Judicial Implementation of Chapter IV of the Return Directive Pre-Removal Detention', REDIAL Research Report 2016/05, 27–28. We are aware that the cited reports may not be completely up-to date and refer to them therefore only in cases we do not have more recent sources of information.

[30] Art 124(1), (7) and Art 125 of the Act No 326/1999 Coll, Aliens Act.

In Italy, on the other hand, the administrative organ orders detention and within 48 hours must submit the detention order for a review by a justice of the peace.[31]

The 'deciding' judge solution exists in Germany, where it is a judge who orders even the initial detention. The institutional setup is a projection of a constitutional tradition,[32] as Germany opted for it to safeguard the constitutionally guaranteed right to personal liberty.[33] Similarly, only a judge of instruction can order detention in Spain.[34] However, in Lithuania, Estonia or Italy, for example, although it is an administrative organ that can detain a third-country national, it can do so only for 48 hours. Only a court can order further detention after the initial 48 hours.[35] This solution in effect puts the judge in the 'deciding' position, as the 48 hours of detention by the administrative organ can be understood as a time that is necessary for submitting the case to a court and the court deciding about 'proper' detention.

B. Detention Judge

While the Return Directive stipulates that detention may be either ordered or reviewed by judicial authority, it remains silent on the attributes of the judicial authority. We also lack case-law that would define the attributes of a judicial authority according to Article 15(2) of the Return Directive, or at least according to Article 47 of the Charter of Fundamental Rights of the European Union. It could thus be said that it is largely up to the EU Member States what kind of judge they entrust with deciding about detention. For this reason, this is where the idiosyncrasies 'kick in' and we encounter significant variations among the EU Member States.

Charging the administrative judges with reviewing detention orders appears to be the most practical, and therefore also prevailing, solution.[36] The purpose of administrative judiciary in general is to review various (vertical) acts of the administrative organs that are directed at individuals. Administrative courts therefore usually decide also issues related to immigration and asylum, including

[31] A Di Pascale, 'Can a Justice of the Peace be a Good Detention Judge? The Case of Italy', Chapter 13 in this volume.

[32] For the other Member States, the reasons for choosing one or the other solution are not as clear cut. In many cases, it may have been guided simply by a mere expediency.

[33] H Dörig and J Bornemann, 'The Civil Judge as Administrator of Detention: The Case of Germany', Chapter 9 in this volume; see also Moraru and Renaudiere (n 29) 27–28.

[34] CJ Gortázar Rotaeche, 'National Synthesis Report Spain, Arts 15–18 of the Return Directive', REDIAL.

[35] I Jarukaitis and A Kalinauskaitė, 'The Administrative Judge as a Detention Judge: The Case of Lithuania', Chapter 10 in this volume; Di Pascale (n 31); and V Lapimaa, 'National Synthesis Report Estonia, Arts 15–18 of the Return Directive', REDIAL.

[36] This is the case in Netherlands, Czechia, Slovakia, Austria, Slovenia, Bulgaria, Estonia, Lithuania, and Sweden. See the relevant REDIAL reports (nn 29 and 35); Jarukaitis and Kalinauskaitė (n 35); and T Quintel, 'National Synthesis Report Sweden, Arts 15–18 of the Return Directive', REDIAL.

both return decisions and detention orders of third-country nationals. A peculiar institutional choice exists in Germany, where, according to the constitution, only a judge can decide to deprive an individual of personal liberty.[37] Although Germany does have administrative courts which usually decide matters of immigration and asylum, it is civil judges who are tasked with ordering pre-removal detention. The rationale rests in historical development of the German judiciary, because the administrative courts, established in nineteenth century, were originally part of public administration.[38] Similarly interesting is giving the power to order detention to justices of the peace (*giudici di pace*) in Italy. Justices of the peace are non-professional, honorary judges without specialisation who resolve minor disputes across jurisdictions.[39] A major disadvantage of this solution is the fact that justices of the peace are not professionals, have no special knowledge related to immigration law, and were, until 2017, paid by the case, which raises doubts they meet criteria prescribed by Article 47 of the Charter of Fundamental Rights of EU, especially those of impartiality and independence.[40] Since 2017, they are no longer paid only by the number of cases decided[41] and the quality of their decisions is scrutinised, but concerns over their independence were not dispelled.[42]

Another institutional choice is to let criminal judges order pre-removal detention.[43] At first sight, this seems to be a quite practical solution. After all, criminal judges most often decide about deprivation of personal liberty, be it in the form of pre-trial detention or sentencing to prison. Furthermore, the availability of criminal judges may be much better: there may be more criminal than administrative judges, they may be on duty and ready to issue a timely decision, and they may be closer to detention centres compared to, say, administrative courts, which may be further and less numerous.[44] On the other hand, criminal judges are not specialists in immigration or asylum law, which can result in unwanted consequences. Consider the example of Spain, where only judges of instruction belonging to the criminal division of the judiciary have the power to order detention, but due to the lack of knowledge in this area, they tend to decide in line with the request of the administration and even 'copy–paste' reasoning from the request.[45] Belgium and Lithuania opted for this scheme as well.[46] Furthermore, criminal judges may not have the power to review the return decision as well and

[37] However, see also the difference between deprivation and restriction of personal liberty, as only in the former case a decision issued by a court is required; Dörig and Bornemann (n 33).

[38] K Hailbronner and D Thym, 'National Synthesis Report Germany, Arts 15–18 of the Return Directive', REDIAL.

[39] Di Pascale (n 31).

[40] ibid.

[41] Part of their salary is still based on the productivity criteria set out by court presidents, see ibid.

[42] ibid.

[43] eg Belgium, see Sarolea (n 29).

[44] Jarukaitis and Kalinauskaitė (n 35).

[45] Gortázar Rotaeche (n 34).

[46] Sarolea (n 29).

may even have problems accessing it.[47] Finally, a hybrid model existed in France, where *juge judiciaire* (*juge des libertés et de la detention*) decided about prolongation of pre-removal detention, but a complaint against a detention order issued by administrative organ (up to 48 hours) was heard by the administrative court; due to the deficits of this solution,[48] however, it is nowadays solely a *juge judiciaire* who reviews the detention order and decides upon prolongation of detention.[49]

An important aspect of attributing the power to order detention is whether the judge ordering detention or reviewing the order is a specialist or a generalist. Generalist judges usually decide criminal, civil and even administrative law cases. This institutional framework is quite typical of common law jurisdictions.[50] In civil law jurisdictions, on the other hand, judges usually deal with either civil law cases, or criminal law ones, and, in some cases, a special branch dealing with administrative law is established as well.[51] Generalists, understandably, do not have specialisation. Even within the jurisdictions where civil, criminal and administrative jurisdiction are separated, judges who decide about detention tend not to be narrowly specialised in immigration or asylum law. The implications are clear. The administrative organs that deal solely with immigration benefit from information asymmetry.[52] Due to this fact, a judge may be required to put in an extra work and time, which she may not have, to appropriately review detention orders issued by the administrative organs. Or, the judge may simply give in and rule 'in favour' of the administrative organ, as supposedly happens in Spain.[53] There are exceptions, of course. In the Netherlands, detention orders are reviewed by specialised immigration law chambers at district courts.[54] In the UK, a bail judge specialised in immigration law oversees the cases,[55] and in Bulgaria, there is de facto specialisation at the Supreme Administrative Court.[56] Furthermore, even those judges who are de jure generalists (even within the administrative jurisdiction) often have one area that they know better than others, be it tax law, patents, or immigration and asylum law.[57]

Which solution is better? The main advantage of having specialist judges is that the quality of decisions should be much higher: not only do the judges have much more knowledge of the issue, they should also have more time for handling the

[47] See section III.C below.
[48] ECtHR, 12 July 2016, *AM v France*, App No 56324/13.
[49] S Slama, 'Duality of Jurisdiction in the Control of Immigration Detention: The Case of France', Chapter 14 in this volume.
[50] eg Bell (n 19) 305.
[51] ibid 45, 110.
[52] On information asymmetry, see K Binmore, *Game Theory: A Very Short Introduction* (New York, Oxford University Press, 2007) 102–03.
[53] Gortázar Rotaeche (n 34).
[54] Cornelisse (n 29).
[55] Immigration and Asylum Chamber of the First-tier Tribunal.
[56] Ilareva (n 29).
[57] This is the case of Czechia, where the number of administrative judges is substantially smaller than the number of civil/criminal judges, and some of the administrative judges specialise in immigration and asylum law, even though they have to deal with cases falling into other areas as well.

cases, as they do not have to spend it on deciding about issues about which they understand much less (and, as a result, have to put in much more time to study all relevant facts, jurisprudence and case-law). Furthermore, specialist judges may be much more receptive to trends in foreign case-law, which is especially relevant with respect to the harmonised pre-removal detention, and thus also much more likely to engage in horizontal, transnational and vertical judicial dialogue. On the other hand, there is a danger as well, because when only a few judges control case-law, they may also turn a blind eye to recent foreign/supranational case-law developments with no other judges available to 'rectify' this. They can thus hinder the evolution or responsiveness of national case-law, which may be detrimental to the rights of third-country nationals. Finally, having only few judges deciding one type of cases may also pose a threat to judicial independence and impartiality, because prior knowledge about which judge will probably decide a case beforehand renders her susceptible to pressure from various interest groups.[58]

C. Control of Detention v Control of Return

Closely related to the discussion of the influence of specialist or generalist judges on the quality of detention orders or reviews of such orders is the question whether the same judge reviews both the detention order and the return decision. There are several reasons to give both powers to one judge. First of all, the facts relevant to asserting legality of both decisions may not be entirely same, but they are usually to a certain degree interconnected. If review of both decisions is executed by the same judge, she does not have to do the same work twice. The second reason is that the legality of both decisions is closely linked: if the return decision is illegal, so is the detention order. This problem, however, could be solved by establishing a rule that if the return decision is overturned, the detention order is automatically voided as well. Furthermore, there is a danger that the same legal terms may be interpreted in different ways by different judges.[59]

Yet another issue, which manifests for example in Belgium,[60] and arises when the return decision and the detention order are reviewed on different tracks, is that they may miss each other completely, and while one court examines the legality of detention, the other court may have already finished the proceedings and the responsible authorities may have already executed the removal. It may seem

[58] Note, however, that immigration and asylum law is not an area of law where 'stakes are high', this danger is much more present in, for example, bankruptcy or election law; see eg A Blisa, T Papoušková and M Urbániková, 'Judicial Self-Government in Czechia: Europe's Black Sheep?' (2018) 19 *German Law Journal* 1951, 1964–65.

[59] A case-law split exists, for example, in Greece; see A Papapanagiotou-Leza and S Kofinis, 'Can the Return Directive Contribute to Protection for Rejected Asylum Seekers and Irregular Migrants in Detention? The Case of Greece', Chapter 12 in this volume.

[60] Sarolea (n 29). Note also that this problem is further amplified by uncertainty as to the scope of review.

irrelevant for the third-country national because she is out of detention anyway, but a review of the legality of the detention order may have an implication at least for claiming damages for wrongful conduct.[61] That being said, in most EU Member States, the judge who examines the legality of detention does not examine the return measure beyond acknowledging its existence.[62] Interestingly, this is so even if the judge in charge of reviewing the return decision belongs to the same court.[63] In some cases, however, judges, when reviewing a detention order, are required at least to examine whether the return decision is not manifestly unlawful.[64] Such solution respects the fact that return orders and detention orders may be issued at different times, but it does not preclude the possibility of different decisions about the same issue.

D. Is Appeal Against a Judicial Decision Available?

Although the Return Directive requires judicial review of the detention order if it is issued by an administrative authority, it does not include a requirement of an appeal *against the subsequent judicial decision reviewing such an order*, or against a judicial decision ordering detention. The EU Member States thus have full discretion as to whether the third-country national will have only one or multiple-tiered judicial review, and, consequently, there is a great diversity in their institutional choices. The approach taken by Member States varies in all three principal aspects, namely the number of appeals that can be lodged, which court deals with the appeal, and the elements that can be challenged in the appeal.

The number of appeals available to third-country nationals range from no appeal to as many as two. Slovenia, Hungary and Greece, for example, provide third-country nationals with no possibility of appeal.[65] One appeal against a judicial decision seems to be the most prevalent option,[66] while Germany and Belgium provide for two appeals.[67] The most obvious downside of providing no possibility of appeal against judicial decision is the danger of a split in case-law. Greece can serve as a good example: before the transposition of the Return Directive, the courts there disagreed about whether or not they had the power to undertake a full review of a detention order; courts disagree also about how to handle detained third-country nationals who have expressed the intention to lodge an asylum

[61] It sometimes happens in Czechia, especially in asylum law cases, that the Supreme Administrative Court reviews decisions relating to third-country nationals who are apparently already long gone.

[62] This is the case of, for example, Germany, Czechia, Slovakia, Bulgaria or Belgium; see Dörig and Bornemann (n 33), Kosař (n 29), Skamla (n 29), Ilareva (n 29) and Sarolea (n 29).

[63] Brandl (n 29).

[64] eg Italy, see Di Pascale (n 31).

[65] Papapanagiotou-Leza and Kofinis (n 59), Zagorc (n 29), B Nagy, 'National Synthesis Report Hungary, Arts 15-18 of the Return Directive', REDIAL.

[66] Czechia, Slovakia, Bulgaria, Italy, Austria, Netherlands, see Kosař (n 29), Skamla (n 29), Ilareva (n 29), Di Pascale (n 31), Brandl (n 29), Cornelisse (n 29).

[67] Sarolea (n 29), Dörig and Bornemann (n 33).

application and have not yet been transferred to the Reception and Identification Centre;[68] a split exists on the question of detaining third-country nationals after the 18-month period provided for by the Return Directive, or on the question of admissibility of objections against the conditions of detention and on who carries the burden of proof.[69] Furthermore, providing for an appeal may also foster judicial dialogue, as judges at high courts would engage with the most difficult legal issues and may be more receptive to the case-law of international courts, provided that the appellate courts are not subject to stringent time limits for issuing a decision. On the other hand, obvious downsides of an appeal mechanism are increased costs, and backlogs of cases dealing with temporary decisions.[70]

The states differ also as to which court decides about the appeal. The institutional setup in this regard is completely dependent on the organisation of the judiciary in EU Member States. Therefore, where a detention order is reviewed or issued in the first instance by an administrative court, it is usually the apex administrative court that hears the appeal, be it the Supreme Administrative Court in Czechia, the Supreme Court in Slovakia or the Conseil d'Etat in France.[71] If the first-instance review is entrusted to the civil/criminal division of the judiciary, it is usually the apex civil/criminal court.[72] One of the exceptions is Lithuania, where a general court decides in the first instance, and the Supreme Administrative Court decides about the appeal.[73] Finally, states differ also as to what can be challenged on appeal. There are basically two options: either the appeal court reviews only questions of law, or both questions of law and fact.[74] Understandably, these two options can be further modified to suit the idiosyncrasies of the respective systems. The advantages and disadvantages of both options follow from what has been said above on the question of introducing the possibility of appeal. If the aim is to safeguard the unity of case-law and fostering judicial dialogue, the appeal courts would do best with only the power to review questions of law, as they would not have to bother with factual questions. Giving appeal courts the power also to review questions of facts may, on the other hand, boost the protection of rights of the third-country nationals but, at the same time, it can prove too burdensome to engage in judicial dialogue. A compromise between these two options can be achieved by giving the appeal courts the power to annul first-instance decisions for procedural flaws and returning the proceedings before the court of first instance for completing the evidence.

[68] Some courts are of the opinion that such detention falls within the scope of the Return Directive, while others disagreed and reviewed it by analogic application of different law; Papapanagiotou-Leza and Kofinis (n 59).

[69] ibid.

[70] The latter problem could be solved by establishing a possibility of the appeal court to select for deciding only those cases that raise new or important questions.

[71] Kosař (n 29), Skamla (n 29), Slama (n 49).

[72] Dörig and Bornemann (n 33), Sarolea (n 29), Di Pascale (n 31).

[73] Jarukaitis and Kalinauskaitė (n 35).

[74] The Italian Court of Cassation can only review questions of law, while the appellate procedure in Germany includes new factual assessment; see Di Pascale (n 31), and Dörig and Bornemann (n 33).

E. The Ideal Model: Context Matters

In the previous sections of this chapter, we have shown that there is a significant diversity in the institutional choices made by the EU Member States when implementing the Return Directive and its Article 15 dealing with pre-removal detention. This diversity is a result of the significant leeway EU Member States are given by the Return Directive and procedural autonomy,[75] combined with the differences between judicial systems across the European Union, which have their roots in the history and cultures of the Member States. We have already hinted at some of the attributes above, and, in this section, we summarize them. This summary should help us, then, to elaborate on whether some institutional configurations are better than others, and if there is a uniform model that would be worthy of pursuit, ie whether there should be more convergence on institutional matters in the European Union.

Administrative judges usually have the power to review detention orders. We have already said that where an administrative branch of judiciary exists, this is a rational choice, because the usual task of an administrative judiciary is to scrutinise acts of state directed at individuals. Therefore, even if there are no specialists dealing only with the narrow area of immigration and asylum law, administrative judges are still the ones who are, in contrast to civil, criminal or other judges, the most specialised. There are, however, some drawbacks. Quite often, the administrative courts only review questions of law, and questions of fact are left out. If the goal is proper safeguard of the rights of third-country nationals, who are especially vulnerable due to their lack of knowledge of the language and the law, and sometimes even lack of proper legal assistance, a detention order should be reviewed on the basis of both law and facts at least in the first instance, and ideally on the appellate level as well. However, if we want to foster judicial dialogue, it might be preferable to task appellate courts with only reviewing questions of law, as we may assume the court would be less burdened and could use the extra resources to engage in judicial dialogue instead. Another drawback, as the case of Netherlands shows, is that the administrative courts may prove to be too deferential towards the administrative organs and may even lack the necessary speed,[76] but, as is shown below, this issue is not limited to administrative courts.

As for the other institutional choices, ie having civil or criminal judges or justices of the peace issue or review detention orders, the principal disadvantage appears to be the lack of specialisation, which is even greater than in the case of administrative judges. The most extreme manifestation of such a lack are the incidents described in relation to Spain, where some judges simply copy–paste the arguments of the administrative organs without truly reviewing them. Further

[75] See eg Case C-33/76 *Rewe-Zentralfinanz eG and Rewe Zentral AG v Landwirtchaftskammer für das Saarland* ECLI:EU:C:1976:188, and below n 85.

[76] Cornelisse (n 29).

problematic aspects include high costs and lack of speed when it comes to civil judges serving as detention judges,[77] or the fact that judges may consider control of immigration detention to be a field of secondary importance.[78] The issue with the peculiar case of entrusting justices of the peace with controlling pre-removal detention has been mentioned above, namely the fact that these judges lack expertise and that they have a motivation to decide as many cases as possible. Due to concerns over their independence and impartiality, the Italian justices of the peace are far from being a candidate for an 'ideal' model.

We can therefore say with some confidence that no currently existing model can be considered ideal, although none of them can be said to be outright bad either.[79] Each and every solution has, understandably, its advantages and disadvantages, and the underlying question thus is whether there is such a thing as an ideal model. We believe that context matters, and that the answer depends on the lens through which we examine the models. Do we want to achieve the best possible protection of third-country national rights, or do we rather prefer uniform case-law? By best possible protection, do we mean speediness of judicial review, or thoroughness? Achieving any of these (or other) goals might require different institutional arrangements, sometimes even contradictory ones. Many jurisdictions, however, exhibit good practices with respect to the mentioned goals. We identified five factors that may contribute to a well-functioning model of pre-removal detention control.

First, *time matters*. Detention constitutes an interference with personal liberty guaranteed on the international level,[80] as well as on the national/constitutional one. Therefore, the sooner it is possible to establish that detention is (un)lawful, the better. The optimal solution in this regard is, of course, to let courts, and not the administration, decide on the detention. If it is an administrative court that decides, the easiest way to guarantee a speedy review is to entrench a time limit within which the court has to reach a decision. Nevertheless, it may not be enough to give courts a deadline if they are permanently overburdened; achieving swift delivery of judgments is therefore a matter of complex institutional fine-tuning. Time matters not only for the third-country national, but for judges as well; speedy decision-making may come at the expense of quality of review and reasoning.

Second, the quality of decisions is also influenced by *expert knowledge*. The less experienced detention judges are in the area of immigration and asylum law, the less thorough their review of detention orders; this situation may not be rectified even by giving the power to review detention orders to criminal judges, who deal with criminal detention cases on a daily basis. Moreover, if detention judges lack

[77] We assume that not all of the third-country nationals challenge detention order before courts if it is issued by administrative authority.

[78] See the case of Spain above (n 45).

[79] The model that raises the most questions is the Italian one, see Di Pascale (n 31). This is not to say, however, that it is deficient or that it may not be functioning.

[80] eg Art 5 ECHR, and Art 6 of the Charter of Fundamental Rights of the EU.

sufficient expertise in immigration law, they may be reluctant to engage in vertical judicial dialogue with the CJEU and pose preliminary questions.[81] As a result, the case-law may be systematically out of tune with EU law and with the practice in other countries.

Third, even courts need *oversight*. The possibility of appeal against a judicial decision reviewing a detention order is crucial to establishing a coherent case-law and uniform approach to the relevant issues. Providing an appeal and letting the second- or third-instance court decide without a deadline and the need to review questions of fact may also foster judicial dialogue – vertical, transnational and horizontal.

Fourth, *automatic and periodic review of detention* may be the best way to safeguard the rights of third-country nationals. Reviewing detention only upon an action lodged by the detainee may unburden the courts to a certain degree, but facing a complex legal procedure coupled with lack of knowledge of the relevant language, third-country nationals may be effectively discouraged from defending their rights before courts.

Finally, *quality legal representation* matters. Even the most fine-tuned institutional framework is useless if the third-country nationals cannot access it; it is thus essential that they are provided with sufficient access to legal aid[82] and interpreters. In Italy, for example, it may prove difficult to find a senior lawyer to challenge a decision of a justice of the peace before the Court of Cassation.[83] In such a situation, third-country nationals are left in a difficult situation, even though the relevant legal rules might look great on paper.

The list of factors above does not include *judicial dialogue*, because it is not an institutional feature per se that could be entrenched by a legal act or a change of policy. It is only possible to set up a proper framework and create an environment that would enable, foster and encourage it. What is more, judicial dialogue can be to a certain degree 'self-enhancing' – introducing some institutional features may stimulate engagement in judicial dialogue, and at the same time, judicial dialogue can have a direct effect on the same and other institutional features, as well as on the output of the system, safeguarding and improving them. Thus, if we, for example, unburden and educate judges, they may engage more in judicial dialogue. Judicial dialogue, especially vertical, can then be used as a powerful defence tool against attempts to curb powers of courts.[84] Even though the institutional features with a potential of fostering judicial dialogue do not necessarily exclude other

[81] See, for example, the first preliminary reference by a Hungarian court that was rejected due to lack of jurisdiction of the CJEU (Case C-328/04 *Attila Vajnai* ECLI:EU:C:2005:596). Note, however, that this issue may apply to all the EU Member States.

[82] In Greece, no legal aid is provided in administrative cases, while in Lithuania, third-country nationals are provided with free legal aid and the decision must be announced to her in a language she understands; see Papapanagiotou-Leza and Kofinis (n 59) and Jarukaitis and Kalinauskaitė (n 35).

[83] Di Pascale (n 31).

[84] See especially the failed attempt of Czech government to limit judicial review of third-country national detention (n 98 below).

goals, they may involve some trade-offs – unburdening of appellate judges may, for example, mean not having them review questions of facts, which may decrease the standard of protection afforded to individual third-country nationals, while possibly improving the level of protection in general.

To be sure, numerous other contextual factors, such as the relationship between judges and the administration, or even the state of the public debate about immigration, may significantly influence the outcomes of a system of judicial review of third-country national detention. However, we will discuss these broader issues in the next section.

IV. More Institutional Tweaks: Towards a Uniform Model of Judicial Review of Detention of Third-Country Nationals for the Purpose of their Return?

In the previous section we exposed the broad institutional diversity in judicial review of pre-removal detention within the EU and identified five factors that improved the judicial decision-making process in this area. But these five factors, however promising, can only reduce the detention roulette. This section explores whether more unification in this area, namely the adoption of a uniform model of judicial review of third-country national detention, could further ameliorate the problem of the lack of consistency in adjudication in this area.

For now, we leave aside the constitutional limits on the ability of the EU authorities to design domestic judiciaries. It suffices to note here that, until recently, EU options for influencing the structure of domestic court systems were very limited. Moreover, the EU authorities have respected the principle of procedural autonomy of the Member States.[85] That has changed with the rule-of-law crisis in Poland and Hungary which triggered novel avenues of engaging with domestic judicial design. Most importantly, the CJEU's judgment in *Associação Sindical dos Juízes Portugueses*[86] (*ASJP*) brought domestic judicial design under its purview. The CJEU opened the door to scrutiny of domestic judicial design by creative construction of the scope of EU law, of the principle of effective judicial protection and of judicial independence as an EU law obligation.[87] While the application of the *ASJP*

[85] See eg HW Micklitz and B De Witte (eds), *The European Court of Justice and the Autonomy of the Member States* (Cambridge, Intersentia, 2012). But see M Bobek, 'Why There Is no Principle of "Procedural Autonomy" of the Member States' in HW Micklitz and B De Witte (eds), *The European Court of Justice and the Autonomy of the Member States* (Cambridge, Intersentia, 2012) 305–22.

[86] Case C-64/16 *Associação Sindical dos Juízes Portugueses* ECLI:EU:C:2018:117.

[87] M Bonelli and M Claes, 'Judicial Serendipity: How Portuguese Judges Came to the Rescue of the Polish Judiciary: ECJ 27 February 2018, Case C-64/16, Associação Sindical dos Juízes Portugueses' (2018) 14 *European Constitutional Law Review* 622.

principles to standard cases (ie not to rule-of-law-crisis cases[88]) is still unclear, this judgment made clear that the EU has competence over domestic judicial design, which may have significant spillover effects also in the area of judicial review of third-country national detention. The recent Opinion of Advocate-General Bobek in *Torubarov*,[89] which addresses the removal of decision-making powers of Hungarian administrative courts in international protection cases, shows that this is no longer a hypothetical scenario. On the contrary, the same arguments can be used, mutatis mutandis, in order to challenge the jurisdiction stripping or limiting judicial review in the area of third-country national detention.[90] Furthermore, we do not have the ambition here to determine what are the best *substantive* criteria, according to which we should select the template for the uniform model of judicial review of third-country national detention. These criteria may derive both from EU law as well as from domestic interests and may vary widely. They may include, among other things, the number of returns, compliance with fundamental rights, speediness or efficiency. What we perceive as a key criterion in this chapter is the consistency in adjudication on third-country national detention.[91] That implies the classic formula, treating like cases alike, and different cases differently. To put it bluntly, no detention roulette.

Hence, the question whether the uniform model of judicial review of third-country national detention would bring about positive results, ie whether it would further reduce the detention roulette, assumes that the EU has competence in domestic judicial design,[92] and that the key interim goal is to achieve consistency in judicial decision-making on third-country national detention. In short, our answer is that it is highly unlikely. In the paragraphs that follow we explain why.

First, a uniform model of judicial review of detention of third-country nationals may actually yield different results in EU Member States. Consider, for instance, the transplantation of the German model[93] of immigration detention to other EU Member States. Even assuming that this model works well in Germany does not mean it would work the same way elsewhere. Introducing it, for instance, in Czechia would actually have deleterious effects, as the expertise in immigration law lies with Czech administrative judges who are specialised in this area, have received a specific training over several years and have been far more exposed (and open) to EU law. Moreover, the Czech civil law judiciary is topped by the

[88] Note that the CJEU was very careful with application of the *ASJP* principles even in the *Celmer/LM* case (C-216/18 PPU *Minister for Justice and Equality v LM* ECLI:EU:C:2018:586). See the symposium on the *Celmer/LM* case, available at: https://verfassungsblog.de/category/focus/after-celmer-focus/.

[89] Opinion of AG Bobek in Case C-556/17 *Alekszij Torubarov v Bevándorlási és Menekültügyi Hivatal* ECLI:EU:C:2019:339.

[90] See also nn 98 and 106 below.

[91] This, of course, implies proper judicial reasoning that respects the accepted modalities of judicial interpretation.

[92] By doing so we also brush aside the principle of procedural autonomy. See n 85 above.

[93] This does not imply that the German model is the best. It is used merely as an example of potential pitfalls of legal transplants.

Supreme Court, which is the only apex court[94] that has not undergone a significant transformation since the Velvet Revolution. In such a situation, transplanting the German model of judicial review of detention to Czechia would yield significantly different results than in Germany. And this is, of course, just one example. In sum, each judiciary is deeply embedded in its historical, political and legal context, and any institutional transplant needs to be carefully tailored to the environment in the 'receiving' country.

Second, adoption of the uniform model might face constitutional obstacles on the domestic level.[95] Many EU Member States have strong views regarding their separation of powers and may consider certain aspects of it even a part of their constitutional identity. It is also common knowledge that there is far less convergence on separation-of-powers issues than on human-rights issues among the EU Member States.[96] Third, changing the institutional setup does not suffice and informal rules matter too. There is growing research that shows informal rules affect the functioning of the judiciary.[97] These 'informal rules of the game' are equally relevant in asylum and immigration adjudication, which is particularly prone to be affected by informal practices.

Fourth, the risk of politicisation of the courts looms large in the background. In the era of populism, immigration detention has become a politically salient issue. So far, judges, at least in those countries where they review the detention decision of the administrative authority with a lesser or greater degree of deference, have been shielded from any populist backlash.[98] Granting judges full judicial review

[94] In contrast to the Czech Constitutional Court and the Czech Supreme Administrative Court, that were established as brand new courts after the Velvet Revolution.

[95] Regarding the constitutional obstacles on the EU level, see nn 85–88 above.

[96] For a more detailed discussion of a limited convergence in separation of powers issues, see V Jackson, *Constitutional Engagement in a Transnational Era* (New York, Oxford University Press, 2013) ch 8 (see also 53 and 67).

[97] See eg G Helmke and S Levitsky (eds), *Informal Institutions and Democracy: Lessons from Latin America* (Baltimore, MD, The Johns Hopkins University Press, 2006); T Ginsburg and J Melton, 'Does De Jure Judicial Indepdence Really Matter? A Reevaluation of Explanations for Judicial Independence' (2014) 2 *Journal of Law & Courts* 187; B Dressel, RS Uribarri and A Stoh, 'The Informal Dimension of Judicial Politics: A Relational Perspective' (2017) 13 *Annual Review of Law and Social Science* 413; and S Horak, F Afiouni, Y Bian, A Ledeneva and M Muratbekova-Touron, 'Special Issue Social Networks The Dark and Bright Sides of Informal Neworks' (2018) 14 *Management and Organization Review* 439.

[98] Note, however, that courts in some countries have started to feel the backlash; among the less fortunate courts are the Hungarian, Italian or Czech ones. On Hungary, see the Opinion of AG Bobek in Case C-556/17 *Alekszij Torubarov v Bevándorlási és Menekültügyi Hivatal*; on Italy and the 'Minniti law', see eg ECRE, 'Building Fortress Italia by Introducing "A Wall of Laws"?' (14 April 2017), available at www.ecre.org/building-fortress-italia-by-introducing-a-wall-of-laws/ (last accessed 30 May 2019). In Czechia, the government attempted to limit the possibility of judicial review of detention order (and subsequent appeal against the first-instance court ruling) only to those applicants who were still in detention; the first-instance courts, however, refused to apply the law due to its unconstitutionality, and their position was later confirmed by the Constitutional Court that abolished the law even before the CJEU could have a say in the matter. See the judgment of the Czech Constitutional Court, no Pl ÚS 41/17, and the preliminary question by the Supreme Administrative Court, Case C-704/17 *DH v Ministerstvo vnitra*, which was taken back by the Supreme Administrative Court after the Constitutional Court abolished the law, but in which AG Sharpston delivered an opinion.

in immigration detention cases (or turning them into primary decision-makers in these cases) may reduce the political slack[99] and drag them to the forefront of the political arena. Judges in many EU Member States are acutely aware of this threat and feel uneasy about this development.

Moreover, by trying to fix the problems exclusively on the level of courts, we might miss something. By focusing on just one institutional player (courts), comparative studies run the risk of assuming that courts play an equally important role in the third-country national detention regime of each state. This assumption does not work even for the refugee status determination,[100] where convergence is much greater than in the law of third-country national detention. As we have shown above, there is a huge institutional diversity in judicial review of third-country national detention among Member States.[101] Most importantly, in some countries the administrative authorities decide on the detention of third-country nationals and a judge 'merely' reviews their decisions, whereas in other countries judges decide on detention without prior involvement of administrative agencies. Therefore, we cannot focus just on courts, as they are only a part of the 'detention equation'. Looking at the administrative decision-making authorities is equally important.[102] One may even wonder whether the judge is better placed to decide on the immigration detention than the administrative organ and whether she has the necessary tools.

All of these reasons counsel against expectations of high gains being brought about by a unification of the judicial review of third-country national detention. Of course, the CJEU might think otherwise and may expand[103] the *ASJP* principles[104] not only to rule-of-law crises, but also to standard fundamental rights cases,[105] such as cases concerning third-country national detention. This may, in turn, push for uniform judicial review of detention in the EU.[106] However, we think this is unlikely in the near future. It is one thing to say that the independence of Polish courts was endangered by abruptly reducing the compulsory retirement age of

[99] 'Slack', as defined by the economic theory of regulation, is the effect of information and monitoring costs that shield the actions of a regulator (in this case courts) from observation by a rational electorate. The term 'slack' was first introduced into the political economy literature by Kalt and Zupan in J Kalt and M Zupan, 'Capture and Ideology in the Economic Theory of Politics' (1984) 74 *Amercian Economic Review* 279.

[100] See Hamlin, *Let Me Be a Refugee* (n 8) 15.

[101] See section III.

[102] See mutatis mutandis Hamlin, 'International Law' (n 8).

[103] In fact, the major rationale of the CJEU's creative construction of EU law in the *ASJP* case is to expand its power in order to have a say in debates that were out of its reach beforehand. See Bonelli and Claes (n 87). This is actually a common motivation of all supranational courts who have started to engage in domestic judicial design; see Kosař and Lixinski (n 21).

[104] See above.

[105] Note that the CJEU based its reasoning in *ASJP* exclusively on Art 19 TEU, not on Art 47 of the Charter. See *ASJP*, para 28; and Bonelli and Claes (n 87) 630–31.

[106] This might happen in the judicial review of international protection, if the CJEU follows the Opinion of AG Bobek in Case C-556/17 *Torubarov*. As we showed above, the same arguments can be transplanted to the third-country national return detention (see nn 89–90 above).

judges, by packing the Supreme Court and the National Council of the Judiciary, and dismissing court presidents, and another thing to hold that detention judges are not independent, because some of them simply copy–paste the arguments of administrative organs without truly reviewing them,[107] or in general defer to the administrative authorities.[108]

That said, we believe that there are other avenues to reducing the detention roulette that we find more fruitful than the institutional unification discussed above. More specifically, we propose a comprehensive training of detention judges and other reforms that would further professionalise the national adjudication systems in this area.[109] Both of these steps have at the same time the potential to improve judicial dialogue which could then have a positive 'ripple-effect' throughout the system in the sense discussed above.[110]

As to the training, in many EU Member States immigration detention judges receive less training than judges deciding on international protection. We believe this should be changed, and immigration detention judges should receive the same amount of training with particular attention to exercises and lessons that will properly promote greater consistency. Importantly, this training should include not only substantive law, but also sessions on interviewing techniques and intercultural communication as well as sessions on judicial temperament.[111] Ideally, within each immigration court, adjudicators with particularly high and particularly low grant rates should also confer with each other and try to ascertain the cause of this phenomenon.

As to professionalisation more broadly, it is important to ensure at the domestic level that immigration detention is not perceived as a field of secondary importance.[112] In some countries there are even informal quotas for how many such cases judges must decide per month[113] and if such quotas are set too high (especially in comparison with other types of cases), the inevitable consequence is reduced time and resources devoted to immigration detention cases. Similarly, if immigration detention judges do not have comparable resources to their colleagues deciding on other disputes,[114] it inevitably decreases the quality

[107] See the case of Spain discussed above (n 45).

[108] See the situation in the Netherlands, described by Cornelisse (n 29). This is an issue also in Austria, where administrative judges are under significant political pressure.

[109] Here we rely heavily on policy recommendations aimed at reducing the refugee roulette in the USA (see Ramji-Nogales et al, Refugee Roulette (n 9) 378–89) which we adjust to the judicial review of immigration detention within the EU.

[110] See section III.E.

[111] Nevertheless, a question arises who should provide such training (EASO, national agencies responsible for training of judges, judges themselves), and it is also not unthinkable that some government would, for various political reasons, try to prevent the training to be provided to judges.

[112] See above n 78.

[113] This is the case, for instance, in Czechia.

[114] This may include, among other things, individual law clerks, enough support staff as well as quality interpreters.

of their judicial reasoning. More boldly, the EU Member States where administrative courts or justices of peace decide on or review immigration detention should ensure that administrative judges and justices of the peace enjoy the same level of judicial independence as the general judiciary, which is not always the case these days.[115]

V. Conclusion

This chapter exposed significant institutional diversity in the domestic design of judicial review of third-country national detention among the EU Member States, which may lead to a detention roulette. Subsequently, it identified five factors that may contribute to a well-functioning model of pre-removal detention control and, thus, reduce this roulette. First, review of lawfulness of detention must be conducted as soon as possible. Second, greater expertise of detention judges, irrespective of the specificities of domestic judicial design, improves detention decision-making. Third, the availability of appeal against judicial decisions on third-country national detention increases the quality of the first-instance judges' decisions as well as the overall quality of judicial review. Fourth, automatic and periodic review of detention contributes to the appropriate length of third-country national detention. Fifth, high-quality legal representation for third-country nationals, including legal aid and good interpreters, ensures that third-country nationals not only have access to judicial review of their detention, but also enjoy *effective* access to this protection.

Judicial dialogue, like a thread creating a positive ripple-effect, can play a crucial role. Some of the features mentioned above can exert a positive influence on judicial dialogue, providing necessary conditions or facilitating it. Conversely, judicial dialogue can boost and improve any of these and a number of other features, as well as the output, of judicial review of third-country national detention. Although facilitating judicial dialogue may involve some trade-offs and hypothetically lower the standard of protection from the point of view of third-country nationals, it is important both for the judiciaries themselves, who may use it as a shield against curbing of their powers, and for third-country nationals, whose rights would, if judiciaries were to suffer, necessarily suffer as well.

That said, this chapter takes a sober view of the current situation on the ground and argues that the above-mentioned five factors cannot eradicate the detention roulette; they may only reduce it. Any other institutional tweak, such as a uniform

[115] See eg Office for Democratic Institutions and Human Rights, 'Handbook for Monitoring Administrative Justice' (2013), available at www.osce.org/office-for-democratic-institutions-and-human-rights/105271?download=true; see also above the recent attempts to curb competences of courts dealing with immigration issues (n 98); and the Opinion of the CCJE Bureau, CCJE-BU(2019)3, addressing concerns about the position of the president of the Administrative Court of Vienna.

model of judicial review of third-country national detention, is also unlikely to help. Instead, this chapter proposes other solutions such as a comprehensive training of detention judges and other reforms that would further professionalise national adjudication systems in this area. Only then will third-country national detention be considered as an important field of law in the eyes of domestic judges and attract the appropriate attention, care and resources.

9

The Civil Judge as Administrator of Return Detention: The Case of Germany

JONAS BORNEMANN AND HARALD DÖRIG

I. Introduction

German law features a unique constitutional setting regarding return detention that follows from Article 104(2) of the Basic Law (Grundgesetz). In stark contrast to other legal orders,[1] this provision requires any measure of detention against the will of a person – in particular within closed facilities – to be ordered by a judicial authority.[2] Detention for the purpose of return falls within the scope of this constitutional provision.[3] Hence the civil judge is the principal administrator of return detention in Germany. This chapter will explore this unique judicial role in light of the Return Directive's implementation within the German legal order.

In contrast to a decision on the lawfulness of a return order proper,[4] the decision on whether a person will be put in detention for this purpose rests with a German civil judge. Procedurally, such a decision may issue from the hierarchical levels of the German 'ordinary' court system, involving at first instance a single judge at the local court (Amtsgericht), then on appeal a panel of three judges at the district court (Landgericht) and eventually, by way of final judicial review, a senate of five judges at the Supreme Civil Court (Bundesgerichtshof). The latter has decided a multitude of cases on return detention and exercises great influence on that area of law, deciding about 250 cases in 2017 alone.[5]

[1] For an overview, see D Kosař and A Blisa, 'Scope and Intensity of Judicial Review: Which Power for Judges within the Control of Immigration Detention?', Chapter 8 in this volume.

[2] § 415 II FamFG (Act on Proceedings in Family Matters and in Matters of Non-Contentious Jurisdiction).

[3] BVerfG (German Constitutional Court), Decision of 4.10.2010 – 2 BvR 1825/08.

[4] Which is reviewed by the administrative judicial branch; cf W Kluth, 'AufenthG § 62' in W Kluth and A Heusch (eds), *AufenthG* (2018) para 26.

[5] An overview of the decisions can be found in U Drews, '§ 5 Aufenthaltsgesetz', in H Dörig (ed), *Handbuch des Migrations- und Integrationsrechts* (2018) ch I.

Implementing the Return Directive (2008/115/EC),[6] the German Residence Act (Aufenthaltsgesetz) envisages several venues in which to detain individuals for the purpose of removal. The statute allows inter alia for detention securing deportation according to § 62(3), as well as for 'departure custody' as codified in § 62b Aufenthaltsgesetz. Furthermore, § 62a codifies procedural and organisational minimum standards concerning the execution of return detention. These provisions will be analysed in light of the Return Directive in section II below. Section III is devoted to the matter of judicial dialogue, drawing attention to the interactions of German civil judges with other judicial bodies in this context. By doing so, this chapter will analyse the effects of the Return Directive's transposition into the German legal order on national legislation and judges' interpretations of the relevant norms. It will furthermore illuminate the selective exercise of judicial interaction by German civil courts, which have created significant factual repercussions for return detention in Germany, as the preliminary reference procedures before the CJEU in *Pham* and *Bero & Bouzalmate* demonstrate.[7]

The use of detention for the purpose of removal has attracted attention within (German language) academia and practice. Carsten Hörich analysed the issue in 'Returns Following European Prerogatives', in particular reviewing the Return Directive's effects on German residence law and highlighting the shortcomings in implementation that he perceived at the time of publication (2015).[8] Maren-Kathrin Diekmann focused on the application of human rights to return procedures in Europe.[9] In a similar vein, Karin Weiss argued that return detention and humanitarian considerations are mutually exclusive.[10] It is also worth mentioning a series of studies published by the European Migration Network in 2014, analysing return detention and alternatives to return detention, inter alia specifically addressing the situation in Germany.[11]

This chapter focuses on the implementation of the Return Directive in German law until August 2019. To this end, it will employ the perspective of judicial interaction to analyse the role of the German civil judge as the administrator of return detention. Accordingly, it will allude to national statutory criteria determining the permissibility of detention and the discretion granted to judges

[6] Directive 2008/115/EC of the European Parliament and of the Council of 16 December 2008 on common standards and procedures in Member States for returning illegally staying third-country nationals [2008] OJ L348/98.

[7] Joined Cases C-473/13 & C-514/13 *Bero & Bouzalmate* ECLI:EU:C:2014:2095; and Case C-474/13 *Pham* ECLI:EU:C:2014:2096.

[8] C Hörich, *Abschiebungen nach europäischen Vorgaben. Die Auswirkungen der Rückführungsrichtlinie auf das deutsche Aufenthaltsrecht*, Schriften zum Migrationsrecht 20 (2015).

[9] MK Diekmann, *Menschenrechtliche Grenzen des Rückführungsverfahrens in Europa*, Schriften zum Migrationsrecht 25 (2016).

[10] K Weiss, 'Abschiebungs- und Zurückweisungshaft unter humanitären Gesichtspunkten oder die Quadratur des Kreises' in K Barwig, S Beichel-Benedetti and G Brinkmann (eds), *Solidarität* (2012) 388–96.

[11] cf J Grote, 'Abschiebungshaft und Alternativen zur Abschiebungshaft in Deutschland. Fokus-Studie der deutschen nationalen Kontaktstelle für das Europäische Migrationsnetzwerk (EMN)' in Bundesamt für Migration und Flüchtlinge (ed), Working Paper (2014) 59.

therein. However, it will refrain from normative claims concerning detention for the purpose of removal.[12] Against this background, the chapter will focus on third-country nationals staying illegally in the federal territory. It will exclude from its scope, first, custody to prepare deportation in light of § 62(2) Aufenthaltsgesetz, since this form of detention concerns persons who are not (yet) staying illegally on federal territory. Second, it will not focus on persons detained on the basis of Article 28 of the Dublin III Regulation, or on the basis of EU asylum law, in particular the Reception Conditions Directive. The next section will elucidate the Return Directive's implementation within the German legal order, focusing on procedures and the conditions of detention for the purpose of removal.

II. Return Detention in Germany

Under German law, the civil judge acts as the principal administrator of return detention. As demonstrated above, this follows from Article 104(2) Grundgesetz, which renders any deprivation of liberty subject to a judicial order. Per § 415(2) FamFG,[13] a person is deprived of her liberty when she is held in a closed facility against her will or under circumstances of a lack of will. However, Article 104 Grundgesetz suggests a differentiation between a *deprivation of* and a *restriction upon* individual liberty, wherein only the former must be ordered by a court.

However, one cannot always unequivocally distinguish these two types of interference from each other. The difference between deprivation and restriction derives from the intensity and duration of the detention.[14] With respect to return detention, German courts have provided clarification in two respects: first, a deportation[15] does not in itself constitute a deprivation of liberty in the sense of Article 104(2) Grundgesetz.[16] The same holds true for airport custody, which may last up to 30 days without authorisation by a judge, according to

[12] As other authors have already employed this angle of investigation; see eg M Flynn and M Flynn (eds), *Challenging Immigration Detention* (Cheltenham, Edward Elgar Publishing, 2017); A Spena, 'Resisting Immigration Detention' (2016) 18 *European Journal of Migration and Law* 201.

[13] Misleadingly, this statute goes by its historic title 'Act on the Judicial Procedure in Family Law Matters and Concerning Voluntary Jurisdiction'. Unofficial English translation available at www.gesetze-im-internet.de/englisch_famfg/index.html (last accessed 13 September 2019).

[14] See H Winkelmann, 'AufenthG § 62' in J Bergmann and K Dienelt (eds), *Ausländerrecht*, 12th edn (2018) para 8. Similarly, the ECtHR acknowledges that the 'difference between deprivation of and restriction upon liberty is merely one of degree or intensity, and not one of nature or substance' (ECtHR 6 November 1980, *Guzzardi v Italy* judgment, Series A no 39 (1980) para 93).

[15] The term 'deportation' originates from the unofficial translation of the Aufenthaltsgesetz. Throughout this chapter, it is used interchangeably with 'removal', which according to Art 3(5) of the Return Directive means the physical transportation out of a state's territory. The notion of 'return' captures the process, in its entirety, of a third-country national going back to the country of origin or transit. 'Return detention' refers broadly to custody as a measure used within the return procedure.

[16] BGH (German Supreme Civil Court), Decision of 25.6.1998 – V ZB 8/98; BVerwG (German Supreme Administrative Court), Judgment of 14.12.2016 – 1 C 11.15, para 26.

§ 15(6) Aufenthaltsgesetz.[17] Concerning the latter, the rationale for not considering airport transit a deprivation of liberty rests on the assumption that the persons concerned are in fact capable of leaving for another state.[18] Substantial arguments can be made against that view.[19] In any case, in situations where a person is effectively prevented from departure, transit becomes a deprivation of liberty and thus requires a judge's order in accordance with Article 104(2) Grundgesetz.[20]

Article 2(2)(a) of the Return Directive stipulates that Member States may decide not to apply the Return Directive to persons attempting to cross the border illegally. In line with this provision, restrictions upon an individual's liberty in transit areas pursuant to § 15(6) Aufenthaltsgesetz are exempted from the scope of the Return Directive. This effectively excludes some third-country nationals from guarantees codified therein. Accordingly, German authorities may take a person to a transit area of an airport or a place of accommodation if she has irregularly crossed an external border – *in casu* by air – and subsequently failed to obtain an authorisation to remain within the territory.[21]

As well as considering the distinction drawn by German constitutional law with regard to the severity of interference with individual liberty, the civil judge is required under national as well as EU law to take into account considerations of proportionality (section II.A) in administering procedures of return detention (section II.B) and enforcing them (section II.C).

A. Proportionality and Return Detention in Germany

The principle of proportionality constitutes the main norm of orientation for the civil judge as the administrator of return detention – to employ an apt German term, its *Leitprinzip*. The principle stems from national constitutional law,[22] but also features prominently in the EU law on return detention,[23] and in domestic provisions transposing the Return Directive. Besides the fact that measures of detention are generally subject to the principle of proportionality by virtue of the Grundgesetz, the legislature transposed the Return Directive by specifying this principle in § 62(1) first stance.[24] In line with Article 15(1) of the Return Directive,

[17] BVerfG, Decision of 14.5.1996 – 2 BvR 1516/93; BGH, Decision of 16.3.2017 – V ZB 170/16.
[18] R Fränkel, 'AufenthG § 15' in R Hofmann (ed), *Ausländerrecht* (2016) paras 24–26.
[19] See H Dörig and M Hoppe, '§ 5 Aufenthaltsgesetz', in H Dörig (ed), *Handbuch des Migrations- und Integrationsrechts* (2018) para 763. See also subsection III.A.iii below.
[20] BGH, Decision of 30.10.2013 – V ZB 90/13, para 7.
[21] BGH, Decision of 10.3.2016, V ZB 188/14, paras 10 et seq.
[22] BVerfG, Decision of 4.5.2011 – 2 BvR 2365/09, paras 98 et seq.
[23] As confirmed by the CJEU in Case C-61/11 *EL Dridi* ECLI:EU:C:2011:268, para 41.
[24] cf Kluth (n 4) para 8. The prominent positioning of the norm in para 1 resembles a result of the Return Directive's implementation. cf Winkelmann (n 14) para 1.

§ 62(1) Aufenthaltsgesetz thus determines that when 'less severe means'[25] are sufficient to serve the function of detention, a detention order is inadmissible.[26] Even though the national norm does not explicitly name potential alternatives to detention, other chapters of the Aufenthaltsgesetz offer concrete examples of measures that could serve as less severe alternatives to return detention. Judges may, for instance, consider a restriction of residence or electronic tagging a less onerous impairment.[27] If detention is ordered, proportionality demands that its duration be as brief as possible,[28] and that, in principle, detainees should be placed in specialised detention facilities.[29]

The principle of proportionality influences all stages of the procedure of detention for the purpose of removal.[30] For example, it may be disproportionate to detain a person who asserts credibly that she does not intend to evade deportation, pursuant to § 62(3) second paragraph Aufenthaltgesetz.[31] Deportation detention also cannot be ordered if the target state can reasonably be expected to be unwilling to take the person back.[32]

It must furthermore be noted that the period of three months stipulated in § 62(3) second paragraph Aufenthaltgesetz determines the upper limit of the duration of detention, not its normal duration. Thus it is left to the judge to pin down the precise period of detention that is likely to be necessary.[33] These decisions presuppose a sufficiently complete factual basis that takes account of serious factors that preclude or delay the deportation.[34] To this end the civil judge may use the PEPDAT,[35] the German central database that contains data on the time taken to obtain passports or suitable replacement documents for the return of third-country nationals.

The principle of proportionality is of particular importance in the case of minors. Whenever possible, minors, instead of being detained, should be placed in institutions for adolescents that enforce reporting obligations, or otherwise restricted in their freedom of movement.[36]

[25] In the Return Directive's wording: 'less coercive measures'.

[26] See Drews (n 5).

[27] These examples are derived from § 56 and § 56a, respectively. Possible alternatives to detention may also be deposit of travel documents or the duty to stay at a designated residence, requesting guarantees provided by a trusted person.

[28] Art 15 of the Return Directive: 'as short a period as possible and only maintained as long as removal arrangements are in progress'; § 62(1) AufenthaltsG: 'limited to the shortest possible duration'.

[29] Art 16 of the Return Directive; § 62a Aufenthaltsgesetz.

[30] *El Dridi* (n 23) para 41.

[31] BGH, Decision of 16.12.2009 – V ZB 148/09.

[32] BGH, Decision of 17.6.2010 – V ZB 13/10.

[33] BGH, Decision of 13.10.2016 – V ZB 22/16. Furthermore, there is a need to accelerate the procedure of return, in order to limit the duration in detention to a period as short as possible; BGH, Decision of 25.3.2010 – V ZA 9/10.

[34] BVerfG, Decision of 27.2.2009 – 2 BvR 538/07.

[35] The acronym stands for *Passersatzpapier-Datenbank*.

[36] BGH, Decision of 29.9.2010 – V ZB 233/10.

B. Detention Safeguarding Deportation and Deportation Custody

As the main provision transposing Article 15 of the Return Directive into German domestic law, § 62(3) Aufenthaltsgesetz determines the grounds for return detention. It is conditioned by a generic proportionality caveat, as § 62(1) highlights,[37] and stipulates that a third-country national *shall be placed in detention* by judicial order if:[38]

(i) the third-country national is legally obliged to leave the country as a result of unauthorised entry;
(ii) a deportation order according to the § 58a of the Residence Act (on terrorists and other persons posing a risk to public security) has been issued, but cannot be executed directly;
(iii) the departure period has expired and the third-country national has changed her whereabouts without providing the immigration authority with an address where she can be reached;
(iv) she was not found at the place indicated by the immigration office for reasons for which she was responsible at a time scheduled for deportation;
(v) she has evaded deportation in any other way;
(vi) there is an individualised risk of absconding as defined in § 2(14) Aufenthaltsgesetz, based on a reasonable suspicion that the third-country national wants to evade deportation by flight.

§ 62b Aufenthaltsgesetz also codifies the option of short-term departure custody, which will be considered in section II.B.vii below.

The strict 'shall' wording of § 62(3) – which suggests that judges enjoy no discretion to assess the necessity of detention – is mitigated by an exception clause, in § 62(3), second stance. This states that a competent judicial body may waive a detention order should the person concerned assert credibly that she has no intention of evading deportation (by producing a flight ticket, for example). It is the detention judge's responsibility to ascertain whether the evidence indicates that the person is genuinely willing to leave.

The grounds for detention as lined out by the national legislature in § 62(3) Aufenthaltsgesetz shall be considered below, with a particular focus on the interrelation between these national detention grounds and the Return Directive.

i. Unauthorised Entry

Under § 62(3) first stance, a third-country national is detained for the purpose of safeguarding deportation if she 'is enforceably required to leave the federal

[37] See section II.A above.
[38] cf Winkelmann (n 14) s 62.2.0.1.

territory' because she has entered German territory unlawfully (usually lacking valid travel documents such as a passport or visa).[39] According to § 50(1), read in conjunction with § 58(2) Aufenthaltsgesetz, the competent authority is obliged to enforce that person's departure from the federal territory unless there are reasons to prohibit a deportation under § 60 Aufenthaltsgesetz, giving effect inter alia to the principle of *non-refoulement*.

There must be a causal link between the unauthorised entry and the enforceable duty to leave in order to trigger this detention ground.[40] Causality presumes a temporal connection between unauthorised entry and the obligation to leave the country. This link is cut once a person files an asylum application. Applicants are permitted to stay within the federal territory during the examination of their claim, including the time it takes the Federal Office for Migration and Refugees (BAMF) to determine which Member State is responsible under the Dublin III Regulation.[41] The permitted stay is only forfeited once a final decision rejecting the application is taken, under the condition that deportation has been announced and the final decision can no longer be contested. The same holds true for the connection between an unauthorised entry and the obligation to leave the country in case an asylum application made out of (criminal) detention has not been rejected within the four-week period required under § 14(3) Asylgesetz.[42] On the contrary, a temporary suspension of deportation (Duldung) in line with § 60a Aufenthaltsgesetz only temporarily stays enforcement of the deportation, and thus does not preclude later detention for the purpose of return.[43]

This provision reflects the legal conception envisioned by the Return Directive and its interpretation provided by the CJEU. Article 2(1) of the Directive stipulates that it applies to third-country nationals who stay illegally in the territory of a Member State, while Article 3(3) defines an 'illegal stay' as one where the person 'does not fulfil, or no longer fulfils the conditions … for entry, stay or residence in that Member State'. Thus, the Return Directive explicitly foresees the detention of persons who entered illegally and are subject to a return procedure.

The Return Directive's Recital 9 clarifies that asylum seekers cannot be regarded as staying illegally in the sense of the Return Directive.[44] However, in light of the ruling of the CJEU in *JN*, an asylum application merely 'interrupts' a return procedure which potentially includes detention. So if found inadmissible, an asylum application cannot cause a return decision's suspension.[45] Throughout the application's examination, an applicant can be detained on the basis of the Reception Conditions Directive for reasons of, for example, national security and

[39] § 14 (1) Aufenthaltsgesetz. BGH, Decision of 18.8.2010 – V ZB 119/10.
[40] cf Winkelmann (n 14) para 57.
[41] BGH, Decision of 1.3.2012 – V ZB 183/11.
[42] BGH, Decision of 12.5.2011 – V ZB 309/10.
[43] BGH, Decision of 10.11.2011 – V ZB 317/10.
[44] Case C-534/11 *Arslan* ECLI:EU:C:2013:343, para 48.
[45] Case C-601/15 PPU *JN* ECLI:EU:C:2016:84, para 76.

public order,[46] and after rejection at first instance, remain in detention for the purpose of return.[47] The German Supreme Civil Court, drawing on the CJEU decision in *Arslan*, has passed a judgment concerning a person who was detained in airport custody because he had entered illegally and subsequently filed an asylum application that was rejected.[48] According to the domestic court, detention of persons who have illegally entered federal territory by air and subsequently did not file an asylum claim, or were refused protection status, are exempt from the scope of the Return Directive by virtue of Article 2(2)(a). Their detention thus falls exclusively within the scope of national law.

ii. Deportation Order According to § 58a Aufenthaltsgesetz

Another (national) ground to take a person into detention is codified in § 62(3) stance 1a Aufenthaltsgesetz. According to this provision, deportation can be requested pursuant to a deportation order under § 58a Aufenthaltsgesetz, which provides for the removal of persons who pose a 'special danger … or a terrorist threat' to the Federal Republic of Germany. In such cases, detention may be required if a deportation order cannot be executed immediately. The provision's objective is twofold: it not only seeks to secure deportation but also to ward off the threats to security specified in § 58a(1) Aufenthaltsgesetz.[49] If a deportation order has been issued, the civil courts are bound by this administrative decision.[50] However, the detention judge is required to examine whether a legal action has been taken by the third-country national against the deportation order, and to consider the status of the procedure, in her decision. A decision to order detention pursuant to this provision is also subject to the generic proportionality caveat in § 62(1) Aufenthaltsgesetz.

The German Supreme Administrative Court has ruled upon this provision's legality in light of the Return Directive.[51] However, it did not clarify whether this ground for detention falls within the Return Directive's scope or is a permissible parallel measure provided for by the national legislature based on its own competence. The Court employed cautious wording, affirming the Return Directive's 'alleged applicability' in such cases.[52] Thus it is uncertain whether this provision

[46] Art 8(3)(e) Directive 2013/33/EU of the European Parliament and of the Council of 26 June 2013 laying down standards for the reception of applicants for international protection [2013] OJ L180/96.

[47] *JN* (n 45) para 75. In Case C-181/16 *Gnandi* ECLI:EU:C:2018:465, the CJEU stated that Member States have to suspend all legal effects of a return decision, including detention for that purpose, until the resolution of the first-instance appeal against a negative decision on an application for international protection.

[48] BGH, Decision of 10.3.2016, V ZB 188/14, para 14.

[49] LG Bremen, Decision of 6.11.2017 – 10 T 569/17.

[50] BGH, Decision of 21.12.2017 – V ZB 249/17.

[51] See eg BVerwG, Decision of 21.3.2017 – 1 VR 1.17, para 32.

[52] See eg BVerwG, Decision of 22.5.2018 – 1 VR 3.18, para 40; BVerwG, Decision of 27.3.2018 – 1 A 5.17, para 24. Bolder language is applied here, stipulating that the German statute 'complies with' the Return Directive: BVerwG, Decision of 31.5.2017 – 1 VR 4.17, para 37.

is intended to implement the Return Directive,[53] or whether it constitutes a measure safeguarding internal security, explicitly exempt from the scope of EU law in accordance with Article 72 TFEU. For guidance, the Court makes references to the domestic courts of other states, namely the Conseil d'État, the Austrian Administrative Court and the Swiss Federal Administrative Court, as well as the Commission Handbook on return,[54] though it ultimately leaves this matter for the national legislature to clarify.[55]

However, the compatibility of this detention ground with those laid down by the Return Directive is doubtful. The CJEU ruled in *Kadzoev* that the 'possibility of detaining a person on grounds of public order and public safety cannot be based on Directive 2008/115'.[56] Along the lines of this reasoning, it is conceivable that § 62(3) stance 1a Aufenthaltsgesetz gives expression to national competence, effectively mitigating severe risks to national security, rather than implementing the Return Directive. It may aim at safeguarding public order even in the course of a return procedure. In any future amendments of the Aufenthaltsgesetz, the purpose of this ground of detention will require clarification from the national legislature.

iii. Unannounced Change of Residence

A third-country national's undisclosed change of residence – including to another EU Member State[57] – justifies the assumption that detention is necessary in order to effect deportation. The conditions for this detention ground are met if the period of voluntary departure has expired and the third-country national has changed her place of residence without notifying the immigration authority of an address at which she can be reached.

The immigration authority, then, must regularly inform the third-country national of her obligation to notify the authority if she wishes to leave the designated location for more than three days. She must also be told that she might face detention if she fails to comply with this obligation. This information must be provided in a language understandable to the person concerned.[58] If she fails to inform the immigration authority of her relocation and mistakenly approaches the office of public order instead, this may be taken into account by a judge assessing the necessity of return detention. If it is credibly asserted that the failure resulted from a lack of knowledge concerning the German administrative system, this may support an assumption that there is no risk of evading deportation.

[53] BVerwG, Decision of 22.8.2017 – 1 A 10.17, para 6.
[54] Commission Recommendation C(2017) 6505, 27.9.2017, App.
[55] BVerwG, Decision of 22.8.2017 – 1 A 10.17, para 6.
[56] Case C-357/09 *Kadzoev* ECLI:EU:C:2009:741, para 70.
[57] BGH, Decision of 9.3.2017 – V ZB 149/16.
[58] BGH, Decision of 14.1.2016 – V ZB 178/14.

If the third-country national has been given a time limit for voluntary departure, the reason for detention can only apply if this period has expired and the person concerned has not communicated a change of address. This is due to the fact that a third-country national need only prepare for deportation after the time limit has expired. The authority must state its efforts to determine the third-country national's residence.[59]

The detention ground for an unannounced change of residence – pursuant to § 62(3) stance 2 – implements Article 15(1)(b) of the Return Directive, exemplifying an instance in which a third-country national may be considered to have avoided or hampered return.[60] Even though a person's absence from her notified home address may indicate attempted evasion, a civil judge must take account of all the facts of the situation. For example, a single instance in which a person could not be found at her designated place of residence is not sufficient to assume a change of residence.[61]

iv. Absence

The consequences are similar in a situation in which a third-country national fails to appear on a fixed date at the location designated by the immigration authority for deportation. As a ground for detention securing return, § 62(3) third stance determines that failure to present oneself for reasons attributable to one's own responsibility indicates a risk of evading deportation. Again, as with an unannounced change of residence, a third-country national must have been informed thoroughly beforehand by the competent authority, particularly regarding the planned date of deportation.[62]

v. Evading Deportation

In a similar vein, a third-country national must be detained under § 62(3) fourth stance Aufenthaltsgesetz if she has evaded deportation 'by any other means'. This fall-back ground for detention takes in other forms of behaviour designed to foil specific deportation measures by the German authorities.[63]

vi. Risk of Absconding

Detention must also be ordered if there is a well-founded suspicion that a third-country national intends to evade deportation by absconding, according to § 62(3) fifth stance Aufenthaltsgesetz. This provision implements Article 15(1)(a),

[59] BGH, Decision of 12.5.2011 – V ZB 299/10.
[60] BGH, Decision of 29.9.2011 – V ZB 307/10, para 9, without, however, an explicit reference.
[61] BGH, Decision of 19.5.2011 – V ZB 36/11.
[62] cf Drews (n 5).
[63] BGH, Decision of 22.06.2017 – V ZB 21/17.

read in conjunction with Article 3(7), of the Return Directive, outlining a ground for detention if there is a risk of absconding. Justifications for assuming that such a risk exists are defined in § 2(14) Aufenthaltsgesetz, which results from litigation before the German Supreme Civil Court. In 2014, it obliged the German legislature to implement correctly Article 2(n) of the Dublin III Regulation, stipulating that a 'risk of absconding' in the sense of Article 28 of the Regulation must be substantiated by 'objective criteria defined by law'.[64] This need for the German legislature to amend the legal framework was retrospectively corroborated by the CJEU in *Al Chodor*, confirming with regard to the Dublin III Regulation that Member States are required to establish, in a binding provision of general application, objective criteria to this end.[65] Given the identical wording in Article 3(7) of the Return Directive, it is unsurprising that the German Supreme Civil Court confirmed the need to provide statutory explication of the risk of absconding for purposes of return detention in order to correctly implement the Return Directive.[66]

Following the judgment of the Supreme Civil Court, § 2(14) Aufenthaltsgesetz was amended and now lays down seven criteria establishing the risk of absconding. These essentially reflect the criteria developed by domestic case-law prior to the legislative specifications of § 2(14).[67] Although they 'may constitute concrete evidence', they are not in themselves decisive.[68] That means that a judge who orders detention on the ground that there is a risk of absconding is subject to the obligation to verify the circumstances of the individual case, including aspects indicating the absence of a risk of absconding. Also, a diligent German civil judge's assessment ought to go far beyond the mere fact of an illegal stay or entry in determining a 'risk of absconding'.[69]

These are the Aufenthaltsgesetz's seven criteria. First, there is a risk of absconding if the third-country national, despite having being informed of the obligation to notify a competent authority of her absence, has permanently changed her place of residence without notifying the authority of an address at which she can be reached.[70] Second, a risk of absconding is assumed if the person concerned deceives the authorities regarding her identity, in particular by suppressing or destroying identity or travel documents or claiming a false identity. Third, the same holds true if the person has failed to cooperate in the establishment of her identity and it can be concluded from the particular circumstances of the case that she intends to actively prevent her deportation. Fourth, a risk of absconding can be supposed if the third-country national has paid considerable sums of

[64] BGH, Decision of 26.6.2014 – V ZB 31/14, paras 28 et seq.
[65] Case C-528/15, *Al Chodor*, ECLI:EU:C:2017:213, para 47.
[66] BGH, Decision of 18.2.2016 – V ZB 23/15, para 14.
[67] cf Proposed Act of the German Government of 25.2.2015, BT-Drs 18/4097, 32 et seq.
[68] cf S Keßler, 'AufenthaltsG § 2' in R Hofmann (ed), *Ausländerrecht* (2018) para 36.
[69] cf M Moraru and G Renaudiere, 'REDIAL Electronic Journal on Judicial Interaction and the EU Return Policy Third Edition: Articles 15 to 18 of the Return Directive 2008/115', REDIAL Research Report 2017/01, 37.
[70] Arguably duplicating § 62(3) stance 2 Aufenthaltsgesetz, cf subsection II.B.iii above.

money to a third person so that this person will engage in activities to secure the third-country national's unlawful entry, making it likely that she will evade deportation to ensure that the expense was not in vain. Fifth, if a person explicitly expresses her intention to evade detention it is reasonable to assume there is a risk of absconding.

Sixth, the same can be deduced if the person poses a considerable risk to the life and limb of third parties or important protected rights of public security. The national legislature justified the introduction of this sixth provision by referring to an empirical finding that persons who pose a risk to security are prone to absconding.[71] Arguably, this group of persons is typically highly mobile and seeks to avoid official measures. For instance, the legislature conceives this criterion to be fulfilled with regard to persons who deal hard drugs. Thus, the provision appears to be aimed primarily at persons posing a security risk rather than indicating the likelihood of absconding. However, the legislature failed to provide sources for the alleged link between a risk to security and the probability of absconding.[72] The seventh and last criterion to establish a risk of absconding is that the third-country national has made significant preparations to evade imminent deportation which cannot be thwarted using direct force. This provision can only be applied under the condition that the person's conduct is comparable in its severity to the other reasons to presume a risk of absconding.[73] For example, if a deportee's behaviour on board an aircraft results in her ejection before the flight's departure, this may trigger this ground for assuming a risk of absconding. This behaviour need not involve physical resistance or threats; it is enough that it impedes deportation.[74]

vii. Departure Custody

The German legislature has introduced another legal basis for detention to ensure the deportation of a third-country national illegally staying on federal territory, regulated in § 62b Aufenthaltsgesetz: a short-term detention called 'departure custody' (Ausreisegewahrsam). Imposed by judicial order, it may last for no more than 10 days (until 2017, it was 4 days),[75] and requires both that the period of departure has expired and that the third-country national has exhibited behaviour that leads one to expect her to impede deportation by continually violating her statutory obligation to cooperate or deceiving authorities on her identity or nationality.

The provision on departure custody is intended to ensure the feasibility of deportation measures, in particular those deportations that require considerable

[71] Proposed Act of the German Government of 16.3.2017, BT-Drs 18/11546, 17.

[72] ibid.

[73] BGH, Decision of 15.9.2016 – V ZB 69/16.

[74] ibid, para 7.

[75] This amendment was introduced to increase efficiency of return measures, eg within the context of collective deportation via chartered flights.

organisational effort, such as collective deportation or deportation to a destination state to which flight connections do not operate regularly.[76] Departure custody may also be considered if deportation is only possible for a short period of time due to the limited validity of travel documents. A third-country national may not be taken into departure custody if she credibly asserts that she does not want to escape deportation.[77] Departure custody is also inappropriate if it is established that the deportation cannot be carried out within three months for reasons for which the third-country national is not responsible. There is a parallel here to the provision in § 62(3) third stance Aufenthaltsgesetz.

Article 15 (1) of the Return Directive implies that detention must be linked to specific conduct on the side of a third-country national that potentially compromises deportation.[78] The national provision on departure custody follows this imperative. It stipulates that the third-country national's behaviour must render 'deportation more difficult or impossible'.

C. Enforcement of Deportation Detention

The enforcement of deportation detention follows from Articles 16 and 17 of the Return Directive and is transposed by § 62a Aufenthaltsgesetz. This includes the conditions of return detention, which may be subject to the German civil judge's proportionality considerations.[79] This section will analyse the implementation of the Return Directive at national level, drawing particular attention to the need for accommodation within specialised detention facilities (section II.C.i) and the detention of minors (section II.C.ii).

i. Specialised Detention Facilities

As a rule, according to § 62a(1) Aufenthaltsgesetz, deportation detention is carried out in specialised detention facilities. If such facilities are not available, or if the third-country national poses a considerable danger to the life and limb of third parties or otherwise threatens domestic security, detention may be carried out in other custodial institutions. Detainees need to be kept separate from prisoners, hence not in ordinary prison facilities. This provision on separate detention facilities entered into force in August 2015, transposing Article 16 of the Return Directive. The exception for persons posing a security risk was introduced in July 2017.[80]

[76] Proposed Act of the German Government of 25.2.2015, BT-Drs 18/4097, 55.
[77] See Drews (n 5).
[78] *El Dridi* (n 23) para 39.
[79] cf Keßler (n 68) para 13.
[80] S Schulenburg, 'Vollzug der Abschiebungshaft von Gefährdern in „sonstigen Haftanstalten" – zum neuen § 62a I 2 AufenthG' [2017] *Zeitschrift für Ausländerrecht* 401.

The obligation to place detainees in specialised facilities in order to ensure deportation was subject to judicial interactions between the German Supreme Civil Court and the CJEU, in the context of two preliminary references under Article 267 TFEU which were both published on 17 July 2014. The first case, *Pham*, concerned the separation of persons detained for the purpose of removal and ordinary prisoners, even if the former preferred to be detained with the latter in an ordinary prison. The CJEU reaffirmed the principle that persons detained for the purpose of return are to be placed in specialised facilities, saying that a separation between these two locations of detention constitutes a substantive condition for return detention and must be observed as such.[81] Against the background of this preliminary reference, the German Supreme Civil Court ruled that an ordinary prison cannot be considered a specialised detention facility for the purpose of return.[82]

In the second procedure, joined cases *Bero & Bouzalmate*, the Supreme Civil Court asked the CJEU whether the absence of specialised detention facilities in a particular *Land* – a federal sub-entity to the German state – could justify the placement of a third-country national within an ordinary prison. The CJEU responded in the negative, confirming that Article 16 of the Return Directive imposes obligations on the Member States as such, and not on their respective constitutional structures.[83] Adhering to that judgment, the national court found detention within a prison facility to be unlawful.[84]

Taken together, this litigation has had a significant bearing on return detention in Germany. First, institutionally speaking, it has led the authorities in the *Länder* to increase efforts to set up specialised detention facilities, meaning capacities outside prison compounds.[85] Second, concerning the actual situation of detainees, it has effectuated the release of a significant number of third-country nationals from return detention due to the absence of specialised facilities.[86]

ii. Detention of Minors

§ 62a(3) Aufenthaltsgesetz ordains that the needs of minors in detention awaiting deportation must be taken into account in accordance with Article 17 of the

[81] *Pham* (n 7) para 21.

[82] BGH, Decision of 25.07.2014, V ZB 137/14, para 9.

[83] *Bero & Bouzalmate* (n 7) paras 28–30, 32. It can be questioned whether this judgment provides an instructive example of respect for Member States' constitutional identities in accordance with Art 4(2) TEU.

[84] BGH, Decision of 25.7.2014 – V ZB 137/14, paras 9 et seq.

[85] The Jesuit Refugee Service Germany compiled a summary of planned placements in specialised detention facilities for the purpose of return; see Jesuit Refugee Service Germany (ed), *Abschiebungshaft in Deutschland* (2018), available at www.proasyl.de/wp-content/uploads/2015/12/Abschiebungshaftvollzug-%C3%9Cbersicht-08_2018.pdf (last accessed 15 September 2019).

[86] cf the German government's response to a parliamentary question of 6.1.2016, BT-Drs 18/7196, including quantitative data at 6 et seq.

Return Directive. The provision makes direct reference to the Return Directive, which – from a doctrinal but also from a practical view – should be criticised.[87] However, by virtue of this transposition, detained minors must be given the opportunity to take part in age-appropriate leisure activities and, depending on the length of their stay, given access to education. Unaccompanied minors must as far as possible be accommodated in facilities that are humanly and materially capable of meeting their age-related needs. At every turn, the best interests of the child must be a top priority. The violation of these requirements can render the detention disproportionate.[88]

Cases of detained minors are very rare.[89] Judicial caution in ordering their detention – apart from humanitarian considerations – reflects an imperative flowing from Article 37b of the Convention on the Rights of the Child. According to that provision, a minor's detention can only be ordered as a measure of last resort and for the shortest appropriate period of time, wording reproduced in Article 17(1) of the Return Directive with effect within the German legal order through § 62a(3) Aufenthaltsgesetz.

III. Judicial Dialogue for the Purpose of Administering Return Detention

Informed by the implementation of return detention in Germany, in particular regarding the Return Directive's transposition, this section will analyse judicial interactions for the purpose of administering return detention. It will first selectively highlight venues for judicial interaction on return detention (section III.A). Second, it will investigate whether responsibility for administering such detention has shifted between judicial instances due to the implementation of the Return Directive and whether EU law has augmented the judiciary's power vis-a-vis other institutions (section III.B).

A. Venues for Judicial (Inter)Action in Matters of Return Detention

The role of the civil judge as administrator of return detention is defined by German constitutional law, in particular Article 104 Grundgesetz. Since detention constitutes a severe interference with – and in fact a deprivation of – individual

[87] cf W Kluth, 'AufenthG § 62a' in W Kluth and A Heusch (eds), *AufenthG* (2018) para 16, who argues that such reference presupposes a high level of knowledge on the side of persons concerned and compromises normative clarity.

[88] BGH, Decision of 7.3.2012 – V ZB 41/12.

[89] cf the German government's response to a parliamentary question of 6.1.2016, BT-Drs 18/7196.

liberty, this constitutional norm institutes solid safeguards against arbitrariness, often stronger than the requirements posed by EU law or the ECHR.[90] As such, return detention cannot be presented as a field of judicial activity in which domestic courts habitually engage in judicial interaction. However, this section will highlight instances of judicial interaction on return detention in which the Return Directive has influenced the adjudication of German civil judges. In doing so it will examine the definition of proportionality considerations (section III.A.i), the control of judicial decisions on return detention (section III.A.ii) and the separation of powers (section III.A.iii).

i. Defining Proportionality, Limiting Judicial Discretion?

The principle of proportionality provides the judge with guidance in ordering detention for the purpose of return. The principle is specifically expressed in norms of positive law such as Article 15 of the Return Directive and § 62 Aufenthaltsgesetz. Within the limits set out therein, however, judges enjoy considerable discretion in ordering return detention.[91] So while the Return Directive arguably fettered the civil judge's role as administrator of return detention by demanding statutory definition of unspecified legal notions, domestic litigation indicates the opposite: a corroboration of judicial discretion in assessing proportionality.

This is because all the grounds for detention codified in § 62(3) Aufenthaltsgesetz are coupled with a proportionality assessment undertaken by the civil judge, including the determination whether there are other, less severe means that are sufficient to secure the deportation; whether the person 'credibly asserts' that she does not intend to evade deportation; and whether deportation within the next three months is impossible for reasons beyond her control.

Another of the grounds for detention listed in § 62(3) Aufenthaltsgesetz relates to a 'risk of absconding'. The German Supreme Civil Court relied upon EU law – *in casu*, the Dublin III Regulation, and subsequently Article 3(7) of the Return Directive – to strike down the previous national legislation.[92] In its judgment, it required the legislature to clarify the 'risk of absconding' by statutory amendment.

Two aspects are noteworthy here: first, the domestic court insisted upon the obligation to implement EU law correctly, even though this might have

[90] cf D Thym and K Hailbronner, 'REDIAL National Report Germany (Articles 15 to 18)' (2017) 4, available at http://euredial.eu/publications/national-synthesis-reports/.

[91] Linking to a broader debate on the role of the judiciary in light of principles enshrined in positive law, A Stone Sweet and J Mathews, 'Proportionality Balancing and Global Constitutionalism' (2008) 47 *Columbia Journal of Transnational Law* 1; R Hirschl, 'The Political Origins of Judicial Empowerment through Constitutionalization: Lessons from Four Constitutional Revolutions' (2000) 25 *Law & Social Inquiry* 91; T Pavone, 'Revisiting Judicial Empowerment in the European Union: Limits of Empowerment, Logics of Resistance' (2018) 6(2) *Journal of Law & Courts* 303.

[92] BGH, Decision of 26.6.2014 – V ZB 31/14, paras 28 et seq, read in conjunction with BGH, Decision of 18.2.2016 – V ZB 23/15, para 14.

effectively limited its discretion in administering detention for the purpose of return. Second, the codified criteria of § 2(14) Aufenthaltsgesetz essentially reflect those developed by previous domestic case-law. Therefore, in terms of judicial discretion in determining a risk of absconding, little has changed in substance. The legislature did not incentivise new practices in administering return detention by adopting novel prerogatives. Rather, the grounds listed to substantiate a risk of absconding, such as an unnotified change of residence, flow directly from previous civil court rulings.[93] Since the legislature reaffirmed the discretionary competences of judges in this domain, the transposition of the Return Directive effectively resulted in a codification of national case-law into the German Aufenthaltsgesetz, but left the role of judges as administrators of return detention almost unaffected.[94]

ii. *Judicial Interaction as a Tool of Interpretation*

Several German courts have reviewed the legality of detention grounds securing deportation in light of the Return Directive. One example concerns § 62(3) stance 1a, which requires a detention order for the return of persons who pose a 'special danger … or a terrorist threat'.[95] The German Supreme Administrative Court sought to determine whether this provision implemented the Return Directive or merely constituted a ground for detention stemming from national law. Against the background of ambiguity, the administrative court engaged in transnational judicial interaction, discussing the findings of courts in other states,[96] and referred to the Commission's 'Return Handbook'. Although this method did not provide a clear-cut interpretation, it is an interesting example of how national courts can use findings from other legal orders to draw conclusions on the Return Directive's effects for their own purpose.[97]

In another example, the German Supreme Civil Court referred to the CJEU judgment in *Arslan*[98] for guidance on the relationship between return detention and the detention of asylum seekers. It confirmed that a person who is no

[93] For an overview, see Proposed Act of the German Government of 25.2.2015, BT-Drs 18/4097, 32 et seq.

[94] As a consequence of this codification, Keßler argues that the detention judge's discretion in assessing the facts of the case may effectively be limited: S Keßler, 'AufenthaltsG § 15' in R Hofmann (ed), *Ausländerrecht* (2018) para 36.

[95] The administrative court scrutinises § 58a Aufenthaltsgesetz, ie the legality of removals in order to avert a special danger to national security. Such a review incidentally affects the legality of the detention ground in § 62(3) stance 1a, as the former is coupled with the latter. cf BVerwG, Decision of 21.3.2017 – 1 VR 1.17, para 32; BVerwG, Decision of 22.8.2017 – 1 A 2.17; BVerwG, Decision of 22.5.2018 – 1 VR 3.18; BVerwG, Decision of 31.5.2017 – 1 VR 4.17; BVerwG, Decision of 27.3.2018 – 1 A 5.17.

[96] BVerwG, Decision of 22.8.2017 – 1 A 10.17, para 6.

[97] Since this aspect was not decisive for the outcome of the case, it did not give rise to a preliminary reference under Art 267 TFEU but instead sent a signal to the German legislature to clarify the relation of § 58a Aufenthaltsgesetz in conjunction with § 62(3) stance 1a with the Return Directive.

[98] *Arslan* (n 44).

(longer an) asylum applicant and who entered federal territory illegally is exempt from the scope of the Return Directive and may be detained in the specific situation at hand.[99]

iii. Vertical Judicial Reaction

As these examples demonstrate, German courts occasionally refer to the judgments of the CJEU or the ECtHR, but engagement with this jurisprudence is by and large reactive rather than interactive. For example, the German Federal Civil Court referred to the ECtHR judgment in *Amuur v France* solely to corroborate its finding in the context of airport custody.[100] The reference confirmed the conclusion that a restriction to liberty in airport custody could be considered on a par with a deprivation of liberty, with the duration of the interference a primary consideration. However, the court did not explain whether the 30-day maximum custody period specified by the legislature could be reconciled with the judgment cited.[101]

Another less controversial reference to ECtHR case-law was made with regard to families including minor children being detained for the purpose of removal. The German Federal Civil Court utilised Article 8 ECHR to sharpen the proportionality requirement in this regard.[102] Again, the court highlighted that this finding effectively corroborates the principle of proportionality as derived from national constitutional law.

References to CJEU judgments are often equally reactive. This can be demonstrated most aptly with a view to cases in which domestic courts considered filing a preliminary reference under Article 267 TFEU but refrained from doing so.[103] The choice[104] for a cautious approach is appropriate if domestic courts can adjudicate against the background of unambiguous norms of EU law. The determination whether EU law is sufficiently clear, forming an *acte claire*, cannot be made beyond doubt by a national court.[105] However, the latter may refrain from making a preliminary reference and may achieve a sufficient level of normative clarity by referring to CJEU judgments, as has happened on some occasions.[106]

[99] BGH, Decision of 10.3.2016, V ZB 188/14, para 14.

[100] BGH, Decision of 30.10.2013 – V ZB 90/13, para 7.

[101] But see FW Dollinger, 'AufenthG § 15' in W Kluth and A Heusch (eds), *AufenthG* (2018) para 33.

[102] BGH, Decision of 17.6.2010 – V ZB 127/10, para 38. The reference was made to the ECtHR judgment *Yilmaz v Germany* A no 52853/99 (ECtHR, 17 April 2003).

[103] BGH, Decision of 20.9.2017 – V ZB 118/17, para 13; BGH, Decision of 10.3.2016 – V ZB 188/14, para 10; BGH, Decision 18.2.2016 – V ZB 23/15, para 20. On a side note, all these judgments refer to a textbook chapter on European methods, authored by one of the judges sitting bench.

[104] See a quantitative study on 'judicial behaviour' in considering preliminary references: A Dyevre and N Lampach, 'The Choice for Europe: Judicial Behaviour and Legal Integration in the European Union' (2017) https://papers.ssrn.com/sol3/papers.cfm?abstract_id=2926496.

[105] Case C-283/81 *CILFIT* ECLI:EU:C:1982:335, paras 14 et seq.

[106] A good example for this finding is BGH, Decision of 10.3.2016 – V ZB 188/14 which refers to Case C-297/12 *Filev & Osmani* ECLI:EU:C:2013:569; *El Dridi* (n 23) para 49; and *Arslan* (n 44) para 49.

As a flipside, it is not inconceivable that domestic courts refrain from making a preliminary reference in situations where ambiguity persists but clarification is irrelevant for the decision at hand.[107] Here again, judicial interaction is limited to receptive confirmation rather than dialogue.

iv. Vertical Judicial Interaction: Preliminary Reference Procedures

This situation differs from cases in which the German Civil Supreme Court sent a preliminary reference to the CJEU. In the joined cases *Bero & Bouzalmate* and the case *Pham*,[108] delivered on the same day, judicial dialogue brought about significant factual changes with regard to return detention in Germany.

As indicated above, these cases consolidated the principle enshrined in Article 16 of the Return Directive, namely to provide specialised detention facilities separate from the compounds of ordinary prisons, in German law. The domestic court obliged the German legislature to amend the Aufenthaltsgesetz accordingly. This changed the situation of return detention in Germany significantly, inter alia causing the immediate release of detainees after the rulings in 2014. Statistics dating back to January 2016 indicate an overall reduction of persons in return detention shortly after these judgments.[109] In November 2018, the German federal government produced updated information on return detention statistics in the *Länder*, suggesting that numbers of return detentions have marginally increased since. North Rhine-Westphalia and the Free State of Bavaria both reported that, at the time of the enquiry, numbers of detainees in return detention facilities narrowly exceeded 100.[110]

B. Context of Judicial Interaction on Matters of Return Detention

Characteristically, the role of civil judges in Germany as judges of return detention is marked by the context in which it operates, ie the interrelation of civil and administrative courts at domestic level (section III.B.i) but also among the hierarchical levels of the civil judiciary, concerning in particular the questions of oversight and – possibly – remedies for unlawful detention (section III.B.ii) and with a view to constitutional warrants, the separation of powers with regard to return detention (section III.B.iii).

[107] As a case in point: BVerwG, Decision of 22.8.2017 – 1 A 10.17. See also section II.B.ii above.

[108] See section II.C above.

[109] cf the German government's response to a parliamentary question of 6.1.2016, BT-Drs 18/7196.

[110] German federal government's response to a parliamentary question in BT-Drs 19/5817 of 16.11.2018. Official statistical data only counts 'other forms of detention', which then includes return detention, see eg Federal Office of Statistics (Destatis) (ed), *Rechtspflege* (2018) 4.

i. Civil and Administrative Judges as Judges of Return (Detention)

The division of functions between administrative and civil courts in matters relating to deportation is rather clear. The administrative judge is competent to scrutinise the immigration authority's actions, in particular with regard to its conduct facilitating a deportation with due diligence. The civil judge, as a judge of detention, is responsible for ordering detention for the purpose of return. The latter's competence to assess the proportionality of detention is therefore limited insofar as a civil court cannot question the legality of a final deportation order.[111] The civil judge's examination is limited to investigating whether the removal can prospectively be carried out within a certain time period.[112]

Arguably, this division of functions between civil and administrative judges risks fragmenting the process of return and compromising effective judicial control.[113] Beichel-Benedetti has expressed concerns that civil judges – allegedly inexperienced in immigration matters – may feel overburdened when assessing all the relevant facts, particularly within the context of expedited procedures and a lack of comprehensive information.[114] He suggests that administrative courts are better equipped to judge the proportionality of return detention and should therefore assume the civil courts' role in this matter.[115]

In contrast, the principle of effective judicial control as defined by Article 19(4) Grundgesetz does not support the substitution of civil courts as administrators of detention. Rather, it guides civil judges' conduct in assessing proportionality, as illustrated by two patterns of collaboration between administrative and civil courts in matters of return. First, if a civil judge retrieves information that a return order was adopted unlawfully, the judge must inform the person concerned about venues for legal protection or file a reference to the competent administrative court.[116] Second, the German Federal Civil Court has effectively extended the civil judge's power of legality review vis-a-vis cases of detention on the ground of unauthorised entry,[117] in which the return decision was ordered by neither a competent administrative authority nor an administrative court.[118] Hence there is

[111] Kluth (n 4) para 26.

[112] See to this effect: § 62(3) second paragraph Aufenthaltsgesetz. An exception to this rule is codified in § 62(3) first stance Aufenthaltsgesetz. Since an illegal entry constitutes the very reason for detention, in this context a civil judge is obliged to conduct the relevant assessments by herself, see BGH, Decision of 16.12.2009 – V ZB 148/09.

[113] See eg M Haag, 'Abschiebehaft. Europa- und verfassungsrechtliche Anforderungen an die Anordnung und Durchführung' [2015] *Hallesche Studien zum Migrationsrecht* 1.

[114] S Beichel-Benedetti, 'Weshalb die Abschiebungshaft zu den Verwaltungsgerichten gehört' in K Barwig, S Beichel-Benedetti und G Brinkmann (eds), *Perspektivenwechsel im Ausländerrecht? Rechtskonflikte im Spiegel politischer und gesellschaftlicher Umbrüche in Deutschland und Europa* (Baden-Baden, Nomos, 2007) 314–15.

[115] ibid, 317.

[116] BGH, Decision of 25.09.1980 – VII ZB 5/80, para 19.

[117] § 62 (3) first stance Aufenthaltsgesetz.

[118] BGH, Decision of 16.12.2009 – V ZB 148/09, para 7. *In casu*, the deportation procedure was instituted by the federal police.

no indication that divided judicial scrutiny in return matters stands in contrast to the principle of effective judicial control as articulated by the CJEU in *Mahdi*.[119] Rather, the obligation to 'take into account … any facts, evidence and observations which may be submitted to the judicial authority' is not compromised by dividing responsibility between two branches of the judiciary.

ii. Controlling Return Detention

Since the civil judge acts as the administrator of return detention, her decisions are subject to control by the civil judiciary's instances of appeal. A plea to challenge a first-instance decision on deportation can be filed by either the person concerned or the immigration authority. In accordance with §§ 58ff FamFG, the court of appeal is the Landgericht. A further appeal to the German Supreme Civil Court may be possible, pursuant to §§ 70ff FamFG, even though the immigration authority may only request such an appeal with the approval of the appeals court. Quantitative data suggests that hierarchical control has significant effects on return detention, with a considerable share of first-instance decisions being annulled.[120]

In terms of intensity of control, the judge is obliged to investigate the decisive facts of the case for herself (inquisitorial procedure) according to § 26 FamFG. This factual assessment includes a third-country national's ability to stay in detention (Haftfähigkeit).[121] In principle, the procedure must include a personal hearing in line with § 420 FamFG. Judgments of the CJEU[122] and the German Supreme Civil Court[123] confirm that procedural errors may render detention unlawful only insofar as the result of the case would otherwise have been different had no errors had occurred. According to the principles laid down by the CJEU in *Mahdi*,[124] under German constitutional law judicial control must be ex officio and 'all-embracing', ie including all the relevant factual and legal considerations.[125]

Last, remedies for procedural or substantial errors – a practice German lawyers refer to as 'providing a cure' – can be granted under German law if detention was unlawful. Examples of errors include erroneously estimating the duration of detention under § 62(3) second paragraph Aufenthaltsgesetz,[126] or stating an

[119] Case C-146/14 PPU *Mahdi* ECLI:EU:C:2014:1320, para 64.

[120] Reference can be made to a private study, cited by Winkelmann (n 14) para 9: Advocacy office *Lerche Schröder Fahlbusch Wischmann's* collection of data, retrieved from cases they oversaw. Reportedly, these were marked by a high rate of second-instance nullifications of return detention orders. For further research investigation, it may be fruitful to conduct a comprehensive, impartial study on the issue.

[121] BGH, Decision of 1.6.2017 – V ZB 163/15.

[122] Case C-383/13 PPU *G & R* ECLI:EU:C:2013:553, para 45.

[123] BGH, Decision of 22.10.2015 – V ZB 79/15.

[124] *Mahdi* (n 119).

[125] Thym and Hailbronner (n 90) 3.

[126] See also section II.A above.

incorrect reason for detention.[127] Omitting the personal hearing prescribed by § 420 FamFG before ordering detention also makes the detention unlawful, and constitutes an error that cannot be retroactively cured.[128] Should a third-country national be detained unlawfully, the person concerned may claim for damages under Article 5(5) ECHR in respect of immaterial damage.

iii. Judicial Empowerment by Virtue of EU law?

The German constitution attributes a predominant role to the civil judge to order return detention. According to Article 104 Grundgesetz, only a civil judge can order detention, acting within the prerogatives of statutory law. The adoption of the Return Directive, as well as its transposition into German law, has not altered this. Even though the Directive incited several amendments to the legal framework of return detention and reduced the practice's use, the legislature refrained from limiting judicial discretion in administering return detention. This is reflected in the fact that the legislature's definition of a 'risk of absconding' codified prior case-law rather than expressing its own preferences. Additionally, the grounds for detention are subject to strict proportionality considerations that are weighed by the judge. Given all this, it is inaccurate to assume that the Return Directive directly empowers judges. Rather, the cases considered above indicate that the judiciary's constitutionally warranted dominant role within the context of detention is reaffirmed in litigation involving the Return Directive.

IV. Conclusion

This chapter illustrated the role of the civil judge as the principal administrator of return detention in Germany. It first focused on the Return Directive's implementation within the German legal order, highlighting the principle of proportionality as the guiding norm for civil judges. Then it analysed the grounds and conditions of detention for the purpose of removal in Germany, as well as their relation to the Return Directive. Next, it selected instances of judicial interaction, including the use of cross-references and preliminary references in light of normative ambiguity on the side of the German civil judge.

Concerning the judicial interaction of German domestic judges in administering return detention, two findings can be highlighted. First, such interaction – eg cross-references to other jurisdictions or preliminary references addressed to the CJEU – is rare. Second, when domestic courts did deploy the preliminary reference procedure, it created significant repercussions for return

[127] BGH, Decision of 10.6.2010 – V ZB 205/09.
[128] BGH, Decision of 4.3.2010 – V ZB 184/09.

detention in Germany. *Bero & Bouzalmate* and *Pham* serve as cases in point. Consequently, the numbers of persons in detention for the purpose of removal decreased notably.

In light of the foregoing, it can be concluded that return detention in Germany has been notably marginalised by way of judicial interaction. Considering the sensitive nature of any deprivation of liberty, however, the Return Directive's transposition reaffirmed the central role of civil judges as principal administrators of return detention, as ordained by Article 104 Grundgesetz – instituting a system of return detention that places judges at the core of decision-making.

10

The Administrative Judge as a Detention Judge: The Case of Lithuania

IRMANTAS JARUKAITIS AND AGNĖ KALINAUSKAITĖ

I. Introduction

This chapter aims to provide a general overview of the implementation of the Return Directive provisions related to pre-removal detention and alternative measures in the Lithuanian legal order, as well as analysis of the practice of Lithuanian courts as regards detention of foreigners in return proceedings, including the judicial dialogue with the CJEU and the ECtHR.[1] The Lithuanian legal landscape in this field is characterised by several features. Lithuania has so far avoided the recent waves of refugees and the ensuing consequences. That may be one reason why the detention of foreigners is not viewed as a very sensitive issue in Lithuanian society. However, some cases of asylum, notably of asylum seekers coming from Russia, have caught the media's attention.[2] Lithuania is also a transit country for foreigners who travel from Eastern and Southern countries aiming to arrive in Western Europe as their final destination. Therefore, the illegal crossing of Lithuanian borders is quite common.[3]

[1] The term 'judicial dialogue' is understood as encompassing both direct dialogue, i.e. preliminary rulings before the CJEU, and indirect dialogue, i.e. references to the jurisprudence of both the CJEU and the ECtHR and decisions of national courts of other states. However, to date, references to the practice of national courts of other states are rare in the jurisprudence of the Supreme Administrative Court of Lithuania.

[2] See, for example, the judgment of the Supreme Administrative Court of Lithuania in administrative case no eA-4718-858/2017 of 10 October 2017. The Court, evaluating the legality of a decision of the Migration Department to refuse an application for international protection, extensively relied on Directive 2011/95/EU (Qualification Directive [2011] OJ L337), as well as the jurisprudence of the CJEU (e.g. Joined Cases C-71/11 and C-99/11 *Bundesrepublik Deutschland v Y and Z* ECLI:EU:C:2012:518, para 51; and Joined Cases C-199/12, C-200/12 and C-201/12 *Minister voor Immigratie en Asiel v X, Y and Z v Minister voor Immigratie en Asiel* ECLI:EU:C:2013:720, para 43), on the notion of 'well-founded fear', and ECtHR case-law (e.g. ECtHR 28 February 2008, *Saadi v Italy*, App No 37201/06) on the standard of proof of being subjected to ill treatment.

[3] The usual conduct of such persons is as follows: once pre-removal procedures are initiated and they are detained or alternative measures are applied, they submit the asylum application. After that,

As will be seen below, various institutional and procedural factors have certain implications for the willingness of Lithuanian courts to engage in judicial dialogue with supranational courts in pre-removal detention cases. First, the relevant provisions of national law establish tight time limits for courts to deliver decisions in these cases. This has an impact on the length of reasoning of the judgments and the willingness to rely on EU law, and on the jurisprudence of supranational courts in particular. Second, these provisions are flexible: in this category of cases Lithuanian courts do not face any restrictions of their powers vis-a-vis the executive. This limits the need for exchanges with other sources of authority.

These considerations may account for the comparative lack of reliance on EU law and the jurisprudence of supranational courts by the Supreme Administrative Court of Lithuania (SACL) in the field of pre-removal detention, in contrast to other fields, eg asylum, competition or indirect taxation, where EU law has become 'the law of the land'. In these fields it is natural to find numerous references to different sources of EU law, including the jurisprudence of the CJEU, in the judgments of the SACL. If necessary, the principles of primacy,[4] and direct effect of EU law are invoked.[5] When it comes to direct judicial dialogue, the SACL is so far the champion among Lithuanian courts in terms of the use of preliminary rulings procedure.[6] In pre-removal detention cases, however, references to

if they are placed at the Foreigners Registration Centre without detention, they usually leave for Germany or Sweden. This hampers the asylum procedure as the final decision may not be taken without the foreigner present. After their return from other countries under the Dublin Regulation, the question of detention may arise again both during the period of treatment of their asylum application or if it was rejected. The Law on the Legal Status of Foreigners does not establish separate rules concerning the period of detention for asylum seekers or other foreigners; some grounds of detention (and the criteria defining the risk of absconding) overlap as well. Thus, from the point of view of EU law, some periods of detention may not come within the scope of application of the Return Directive, but from the point of view of Lithuanian legal order, the same law is applicable, and once evaluating the necessity to detain the foreigner the SACL tends to evaluate the entirety of circumstances including periods coming within the scope of the Return Directive, as well as those during which they have the status of asylum seekers.

[4] For example, in the judgment of 3 August 2017 (administrative case no eA-4316-858/2017) the SACL noted that provisions of the Law on the Legal Status of Foreigners related to voluntary departure were not fully in line with the systemic reading of para 10 of the Preamble and Arts 6–8 of the Return Directive, since they allowed voluntary departure only when the 'support of an international or non-governmental organisation is provided', although such a condition was not provided in the Directive. Here the SACL relied extensively on the jurisprudence of the CJEU, namely Case C-61/11 *El Dridi* ECLI:EU:C:2011:268; Case C-43-/11 *Sagor* ECLI:EU:C:2012:777; and C-38/14 *Zaizoune* ECLI:EU:C:2015:260. The SACL decided that there were no grounds to justify the forced removal and annulled a decision of the Migration Department ordering it.

[5] For a more detailed general overview of the practice of Lithuanian courts in the field of application of EU law, see, eg I Jarukaitis, 'Report on Estonia, Latvia and Lithuania' in G Martinico and O Pollicino (eds), *National Judges and Supranational Laws: On the Effective Application of the EC Law and the ECHR* (Groningen, Europa Law Publishing, 2010); I Jarukaitis and G Švedas, 'The Constitutional Experience of Lithuania in the Context of European and Global Governance Challenges' in A Albi and S Bordučki (eds), *National Constitutions in European and Global Governance: Democracy, Rights, the Rule of Law* (Oxford, Oxford University Press, 2019).

[6] The CJEU had received 55 references from Lithuanian courts as of the end of 2017. Of these, 21 were submitted by the SACL, 18 from the Supreme Court of Lithuania, 1 from the Constitutional

EU law and the jurisprudence of the CJEU are rare. The judgments delivered by extended chambers (typically five judges, though it can be more) of the SACL are an exception to this general trend. These usually establish the direction of court jurisprudence, and thus pay more attention to the completeness of the legal reasoning. However, most pre-removal detention cases only relate to the evaluation of factual circumstances, and thus elaborate legal arguments of interpretation are less necessary. In these cases, the principle of indirect effect of EU law, in which national law is interpreted in the light of EU law, plays a principal role.[7] The SACL usually cites the practice of the CJEU and the ECtHR to support its arguments. However, as this chapter will argue, this state of affairs does not mean that the aims of the Return Directive are not achieved. Relying on EU law or judicial discourse is not an end, but a means by which to achieve the proper delivery of justice. The following analysis of the Lithuanian regulatory system will show that it endeavours to ensure an effective return policy, while the corresponding analysis of the jurisprudence of the SACL will show that the Court takes the utmost care to protect the fundamental right to freedom and emphasises alternative measures in pre-removal cases.

The chapter is structured as follows. Section II deals with the evolution of the institutional and procedural framework in the field of detention of foreigners in pre-removal proceedings. It explains how the relevant provisions of the Return Directive were transposed into national law by the Lithuanian legislature, addresses the institutional and procedural setup of pre-removal detention and highlights national jurisprudence concerning the period of detention. Section III discusses the case-law of the SACL as regards the application of different grounds of detention. Section IV is devoted to the application of alternative measures and the principle of proportionality, and Section V offers some conclusions.

The chapter is mainly based on the analysis of the jurisprudence of the SACL, which is the last-instance court in these types of cases and is responsible for the development of court practice. Cases concerning pre-removal detention are not very frequent: the SACL only dealt with around one case every two months between 2014 and 2015.[8] This number increased in 2016–2019.[9] However, there

Court of Lithuania and 15 from other courts: Annual Report of Judicial Activity for 2017 of the Court of Justice of the European Union, 125, available at curia.europa.eu/jcms/upload/docs/application/pdf/2018-04/_ra_2017_en.pdf. This is natural given that many areas of law dealt with by administrative courts are affected by EU law.

[7] The absence of reference to provisions of the Return Directive or relevant CJEU case-law in particular decisions of a national court does not necessarily mean that the court does not have the EU law in mind when it adopts a decision.

[8] According to statistics provided by the European Migration Network in 2014, about 3000 foreigners breached rules on entry, stay or leave in Lithuania. Approximately 260 were detained for more than 48 hours and in 38 cases alternatives to detention were applied. See EMN Focused Study, *The Use of Detention and Alternatives to Detention in Lithuania*, available at ec.europa.eu/home-affairs/sites/homeaffairs/files/what-we-do/networks/european_migration_network/reports/docs/emn-studies/emn_detention_and_alternatives_to_detention_2013_en.pdf (accessed 11 September 2019).

[9] According to statistics provided by the SACL, it dealt with 47 appeals in 2016–2017 and 53 in 2018–2019.

have been a number of important case-law developments in this area. The majority of the SACL's judgments referred to in this chapter were adopted in cases of pre-removal detention, although some other judgments, notably in the field of asylum, are mentioned in order to give a more complete picture of national regulation of the detention of foreigners and to highlight their broader implications in the course of development of the jurisprudence.

II. Evolution of the Institutional and Procedural Framework of Pre-Removal Detention

In recent years, the laws relating to pre-removal detention have changed frequently. The Law on the Legal Status of Foreigners ('the Law') has been changed several times with the aim of implementing the Return Directive and providing more detailed procedures and grounds for detention in pre-removal proceedings. These frequent changes may to some extent have a detrimental effect on the development of consistent court jurisprudence.

A. General Aspects of the Implementation of the Return Directive into the Lithuanian Legal Order

The right to liberty is enshrined in the Constitution of the Republic of Lithuania. Article 20 states that 'human liberty shall be inviolable. No one may be arbitrarily apprehended or detained. No one may be deprived of their liberty otherwise than on the grounds and according to the procedures established by law.' The Constitutional Court has noted in its case-law that liberty is a fundamental natural right and may be interfered with only when it is necessary and inevitable, strictly according to requirements set out in the law.[10] The ECHR, the EU Charter of Fundamental Rights ('the EU Charter') and the jurisprudence of the ECtHR and the CJEU are relevant as well.[11]

[10] See, for example, the ruling of 5 February 1999 of the Constitutional Court of Lithuania. So far there is no court jurisprudence concerning detention of foreigners in pre-removal procedures; the jurisprudence is developed mainly in the field of criminal law. However, it is of relevance for the questions analysed in the chapter, since the provisions of the constitution are universal and do not differentiate between citizens and foreigners.

[11] In its ruling of 21 December 2006, the Constitutional Court, citing decisions of the Court of First Instance and the ECJ for the first time, noted that: 'The Constitutional Court has stated several times that the jurisprudence of the European Court of Human Rights, as a source of legal interpretation, is important for the interpretation and application of Lithuanian law. *The same should be said about the jurisprudence of the Court of First Instance and the European Court of Justice*' (emphasis added). Accordingly, the jurisprudence of the Constitutional Court of Lithuania, the SACL and the Supreme Court of Lithuania is firmly anchored in the ECHR and EU law, as well as in ECtHR and CJEU case-law.

The principle of good administration enshrined in Article 41 of the EU Charter takes a prominent place in the practice of the SACL both in general and in cases on the status of foreigners in particular. For example, in the judgment of 19 May 2014, when deciding whether the applicant was lawfully detained, the SACL referred to this principle. According to the Court, every person must be accorded the right to have his or her affairs handled impartially, fairly and within a reasonable time. The SACL, although it did not refer to specific judgments of the CJEU, noted that the provisions of the EU Charter lay down certain legal values of a general nature which can be referred to as an additional source of interpretation when deciding on the content of the principle of good administration. It also stated that this principle enshrines the right to be heard and accessibility of public services, as well as requiring that an asylum application be heard without unreasonable delay and not only in formal terms. The Court stressed that a state authority may not base its motion to detain an asylum seeker on circumstances which might be partly attributed to state activities that are incompatible with good administration (eg slow processing of the application).[12] The SACL found that there was no data in the case file indicating that the foreigner in question impeded the processing of his asylum application, and there was no basis to assume that he would hide in an attempt to avoid removal or expulsion; thus there were no grounds for detention. The Court annulled the decision of the district court that had ordered detention.[13] This judgment is important because,

[12] The foreigner concerned was initially detained for illegally crossing the border and submitted the asylum application later. At the time of the hearing of the appeal on legality of detention his application was not resolved.

[13] Judgment of the SACL in administrative case no N^{822}-70/2014 of 19 May 2014. However, this was not the first judgment where the SACL referred to the principle of good administration and the Charter in the context of the rights of foreigners. For example, in the judgment of the extended chamber in administrative case no A858-2332/2011 of 17 October 2011, the Court insisted on the obligation of migration institutions to hear a person before a voluntary departure decision is adopted, although neither the Return Directive nor the Law explicitly established such an obligation. In the judgment in administrative case no eA-2266-858/2015 of 7 July 2015 the SACL decided that the two days accorded to the person to produce additional documents, substantiating his further legality of stay upon expiry of the temporary residence in Lithuania (the foreigner failed to do it within those two days because he was not in Lithuania, and the voluntary departure decision was adopted) were inadequate, meaning the migration institution breached the right to be heard, especially as the institution was in breach of the time limits for adopting such decisions. However, in the judgment in administrative case no eA4702-858/2017 of 16 October 2017 the Court rejected the argument of the applicant that his right to be heard was breached, because he was not heard in person before the adoption of the negative decision rejecting his initial request for a temporary residence permit. (According to the relevant legislation the applicant had to fill the standardised form and to attach all the requested documents. The failure to observe that obligation led to the adoption of the negative decision.) The Court pointed out, inter alia, that the principle of good administration is not absolute but aims to ensure the adoption of reasoned decisions. Among other things, the Court extensively cited the jurisprudence of the CJEU, including Case C-277/11 *M v Minister for Justice, Equality and Law Reform, Ireland, Attorney General* ECLI:EU:C:2012:744, paras 81–82, 87–88, and the Recommendation CM/Rec(2007)7 of the Committee of Ministers of the Council of Europe on Good Administration of 20 June 2007, by which the Code of Good Administration was confirmed. Art 14 of the Code provides that: '[I]f a public authority intends to take an individual decision that will directly and adversely affect the rights of private persons, and provided that an opportunity to express their views has not been

as will be discussed, its reasoning has been applied in pre-removal detention cases as well.

The institutional and procedural framework of pre-removal detention is mainly set out in the Law on the Legal Status of Foreigners. The Law was adopted on 29 April 2004 and came into force one day before Lithuania joined the European Union.[14] The 2004 Law was much more detailed than the one it replaced.[15] This may be explained by the fact that the Law, among other things, implemented the relevant EU legal acts.[16] The previous law did not explicitly provide for the possibility to detain a foreigner in pre-removal proceedings. However, a foreigner could be detained if his identity could not be established or if he was illegally present in the country.[17] Even though Lithuania only became a member of the Schengen area on 21 December 2007, there was a need to harmonise the relevant laws in advance. The 2004 Law already established the possibility to detain foreigners in pre-removal proceedings.

Lithuania transposed the Return Directive into national law after the transposition deadline specified in Article 20, 24 December 2010. The parliament only adopted the corresponding modifications of the Law on the Legal Status of the Foreigners on 8 December 2011. They entered into force on 1 February 2012.[18] The legislature did not limit the scope of application of the Return Directive, as allowed by Article 2(2).[19] Regarding pre-removal detention, the amending Law of 2011 did not provide exact criteria related to the risk of absconding as defined in Article 3(7) of the Directive; also, its provisions on the grounds for detention were not completely in line with Article 15(1). Both deficiencies were remedied by adopting the amending law of 9 December 2014.[20] Before that, the European Commission had provided a reasoned opinion indicating that certain provisions of the Directive had not been implemented correctly in Lithuania.[21] The jurisprudence of the SACL does not explicitly address these deficiencies.

given, such persons shall, unless this is manifestly unnecessary, have an opportunity to express their views within a reasonable time and in the manner provided for by the national law, and if necessary with the assistance of a person of their choice.'

[14] Law on the Legal Status of Foreigners of the Republic of Lithuania, no IX-2206, 29 April 2004.

[15] ibid, no VIII-978, 17 December 1998.

[16] Different pieces of EU law were implemented, especially those related to the right of free movement within the EU. Some EU acts concerning the expulsion of third-country nationals and asylum (eg Directive 2001/40/EC on the mutual recognition of decisions on the expulsion of third-country nationals [2001] OJ L149/34; Directive 2003/9/EC laying down minimum standards for the reception of asylum seekers [2003] OJ L31/18) were transposed as well.

[17] Art 45 of the Law on the Legal Status of Foreigners, no VIII-978, 17 December 1998.

[18] Law amending the Law on the Legal Status of Foreigners, no XI-1786, 8 December 2011.

[19] Art 113(1)(3) of the Law on the Legal Status of Foreigners.

[20] The explanatory note No XIIP-1804 on the draft Law amending and supplementing the Law on the Legal Status of Foreigners of 12 May 2014. For a more detailed analysis of the grounds of detention and the risk of absconding, see section III of this chapter.

[21] European Commission press release, 'An Effective and Humane Return Policy: 8 Member States Have Yet to Comply with the Return Directive', 29 September 2011, available at europa.eu/rapid/press-release_IP-11-1097_en.htm?locale=en (accessed 15 September 2019).

B. The Institutional and Procedural Framework for Detention or Alternative Measures in Pre-Removal Proceedings

When it comes to implementing the provisions of Article 15(2) and (3) of the Return Directive, concerning authorities ordering the detention of foreigners and procedural guarantees, the Lithuanian legislature has chosen a mixed approach. According to the Law on the Legal Status of the Foreigners, a foreigner may be detained by a written decision of the police or any other law enforcement officer for up to 48 hours.[22] The foreigner has to be informed without undue delay about the grounds of detention, and has the right of appeal before a court and the right to free legal aid.[23]

Beyond 48 hours, detention is only possible upon the decision of a court. The legislature established an unusual jurisdictional set-up for cases concerning pre-removal detention, wherein the procedure encompasses courts from different judicial branches.[24] District courts, which belong to the general court system, decide on the detention of foreigners as first-instance courts. Their decisions may be appealed to the SACL, the final-instance court in these cases, even though it is situated in a different judicial branch.

This jurisdictional scheme was probably chosen for several reasons. First, the general competence district courts decide on detention in cases of criminal and administrative offences and thus always have judges on duty. Also, foreigners may be arrested all over Lithuania. The district court system is quite dense, whereas regional administrative courts are located in only five main cities. It could be time and resource intensive to transport foreigners to regional administrative courts. Finally, the SACL deals with migration cases, including removal decisions and asylum cases. As a result, the SACL has developed expertise in different areas

[22] Art 114(1) of the Law on the Legal Status of Foreigners. Although it is not provided directly in Art 114(1) of the Law, systemic reading leads to the conclusion that the grounds of detention are the same as those applicable beyond 48 hours, ie those provided in Art 113 of the Law. So far there is no case-law concerning the legality of detention of foreigners for the first 48 hours.

[23] Art 114(3) of the Law on the Legal Status of Foreigners.

[24] Like many European states, Lithuania has two autonomous court branches. The courts of general competence (four-level system) deal with civil (commercial, family, labour) cases and cases of criminal and administrative offences, including potential deprivation of liberty. The judgments of lower general competence courts may be appealed to a higher general competence court (depending on the nature of the case – the regional court or the Court of Appeal) up to the Supreme Court of Lithuania, which is a court of cassation. The system of administrative courts, established in 1999, has two levels: regional administrative courts and the Supreme Administrative Court, which acts as a court of appeal against the judgments of the regional administrative courts. Except for pre-removal detention cases, the jurisdictional competence of those courts is strictly separated. As a rule, administrative courts review the legality of administrative acts adopted by the executive, when they are challenged by the applicant, whereas, as will be explained further, in pre-removal cases they hear the motions, ie upon a motion of the executive they themselves adopt judicial decisions, which are the formal legal basis for detention or alternative measures.

concerning the legal status of foreigners which might be relevant in deciding whether grounds for detention exist in a particular case.

The procedure for approaching a court with a motion to detain a foreigner or apply alternative measures is described in Article 116 of the Law. If the executive institution believes there are legal grounds to detain a foreigner beyond 48 hours or to impose alternative measures, it must apply to the district court of the foreigner's location. The foreigner's presence at the court hearing is mandatory. Practice shows that state-guaranteed legal aid is available during the court proceedings.

The Law provides that the court's decision to detain a foreigner or to impose an alternative to detention must immediately be announced to the foreigner in a language that he or she understands, indicating reasons for his/her detention or for imposition of an alternative to detention. The decision becomes effective immediately. It must state the grounds for detention, the place of detention and the specific period of detention.[25]

As evidenced by case-law, foreigners are usually initially detained by officers of the State Border Guard Service or the police. If a court decides to detain a foreigner for more than 48 hours,[26] they are detained in a dedicated facility, the Foreigners' Registration Centre, a subdivision of the State Border Guard Service. Under Article 117 of the Law, the foreigner has the right to appeal before the SACL against a court decision to detain him, to extend the detention period or to impose an alternative to detention. The appeal may be filed through the State Border Guard Service, which then forwards it to the SACL.[27] The SACL examines the appeal according to the procedure established by the Law on Administrative Proceedings and must pass a decision no more than ten days after admission.[28] This short time limit cannot help but affect the content of the Court's judgments.[29]

Finally, although the Law does not establish automatic review of adopted decisions to detain foreigners, Article 118 establishes provisions concerning the

[25] Art 116(3) and (4) of the Law on the Legal Status of Foreigners.

[26] In line with the *Mahdi* judgment, once the motion (either for initial detention or its extension) is introduced, the court has several options: grant the motion and detain the foreigner for the period suggested by the institution; partially grant the motion by detaining for a shorter period; reject the request and impose alternative measures; reject the motion entirely. Case C-146/14/PPU *Mahdi* ECLI:EU:C:2014:1320.

[27] Art 117(1) of the Law on the Legal Status of Foreigners.

[28] Art 117(2) of the Law on the Legal Status of Foreigners. Once the appeal is registered at the SACL, the admission of appeal is confirmed by a separate procedural ruling of the Court stating that it satisfies all formal requirements established by the Law on Administrative Proceedings. The ruling must be adopted within three working days from the receipt of the appeal.

[29] In the flow of 'ordinary' cases the court hearings and general workload of a chamber in a given week are fixed 2–3 months before, in order to provide the parties with the opportunity to prepare for the case. Once the pre-removal appeal is complete, all procedures have to be finished within 10 days. During that period the appeal has to be sent to the other party (the executive institution) for the submission of response, the court hearing has to be organised and, finally, the judgment with full motives has to be pronounced. Also, in pre-removal cases the SACL always organises oral hearings, although it is not strictly obliged to do so.

revision of such decisions. If the grounds of detention disappear, the foreigner has the right – and the institution that initiated the detention has the obligation – to immediately request that a district court review the detention decision. Upon accepting a request, the district court must review the decision within ten days and may uphold, reverse or quash it. A further appeal can be made to the SACL as described above.

Notwithstanding the organisational difficulties facing the SACL in these cases, direct judicial involvement has its merits when it comes to the protection of the rights of foreigners. When addressing the court, the executive institution has to present clear factual and legal reasons justifying detention or alternative measures, including the relevant evidence. The individual evaluation of these arguments before an independent tribunal ensures a transparent procedure and equal arms safeguards for the foreigner, who can present counter-arguments and evidence.

C. The Period of Detention in Pre-Removal Proceedings

The provisions of Article 15(5) and (6) of the Return Directive concerning the period of detention are transposed into the Law and have been the object of several SACL judgments. In line with Article 15(5) and (6), the Law states that foreigners may not be detained for more than six months, with the exception of cases where they do not cooperate in the process of their expulsion (eg when they refuse to provide personal data or provide false information) or when the documents required for expulsion are not received. In such cases, detention may be extended for up to an additional 12 months.[30] Detention of foreigners pending a return decision, expulsion or imposing an obligation to leave Lithuania must be as short as possible, and for no longer than is needed to take the decision.[31] In practice, however, the motion of law enforcement institution is usually for up to three months' detention and later extended for another two to three months per motion. As shown by the examples below, sometimes a court decides to grant a motion to detain, but for a shorter period than proposed.

The SACL has provided several clarifications regarding the time limits of pre-removal detention. In its judgment of 15 September 2014, the Court decided that the 18-month period established by the Law on the Legal Status of Foreigners (ie the 6-month period that can be extended up to another 12 months on the basis established by law when pre-removal procedures are ongoing and/or when a decision to remove a foreigner has been taken) includes the period up to 48 hours when the foreigner has been detained by a police officer or other law-enforcement officer.[32] Thus, detention periods must be calculated from the moment of the factual

[30] Art 114(5) of the Law on the Legal Status of Foreigners.

[31] Arts 113(2) and 114(6) of the Law on the Legal Status of Foreigners.

[32] Judgment of the extended chamber of the SACL in administrative case no A^{858}-90/2014 of 15 September 2014.

detention. The Court also stated that upon the expiry of the maximum term, the foreigner must be released without delay, unless he or she can be detained on the basis of other laws (eg criminal laws). It emphasised that on matters of detention the legislature had decided not to differentiate between asylum seekers and foreigners who do not apply for asylum. In its reasoning the Court cited the provisions of the Return Directive and EU asylum law,[33] as well as the jurisprudence of the CJEU and the ECtHR.[34] In some later cases, first-instance courts repeatedly detained foreigners after their release following maximum detention terms. The SACL annulled these decisions, holding that foreigners cannot be detained again after the maximum term expires, even if there is no response from the embassies of their countries of origin.[35]

The principle of good administration has been invoked in some cases concerning pre-removal detention. For example, the SACL noted its importance in cases concerning a motion to repeatedly detain a foreigner after the maximum term had expired. The Court stressed that the fact that the embassy of the foreigner's country of origin had given no official answer regarding the repatriation certificate did not justify extending the detention for an unlimited time.[36]

In November 2015 the Law on the Legal Status of Foreigners was supplemented with a provision stating that when a foreigner who has been detained under pre-removal detention submits an asylum application, the State Border Guard Service must immediately request that a district court review the detention.[37] The same obligation arises for the institution in which the foreigner has been detained if a reasonable prospect of expulsion from Lithuania no longer exists.[38] The adoption of these amendments coincided with the rendering of the judgments of the SACL concerning the period of detention discussed above. So far there is no court

[33] Arts 4(3) and 15 of the Return Directive; Art 18(2) of Directive 2005/85/EC of 1 December 2005 on minimum standards on procedures in Member States for granting and withdrawing refugee status [2005] OJ L326/18; Art 7(3) of Directive 2003/09/EC of 27 January 2003 laying down minimum standards for the reception of asylum seekers [2003] OJ L31/18.

[34] Case C-357/09 *Kadzoev (Huchbarov)* ECLI:EU:C:2009:741; ECtHR 5 October 2004, *HL v United Kingdom* App No 45508/99.

[35] For example, the judgments of the SACL in administrative cases no A-3078-822/2016 of 23 February 2016 and no A-3054-756/2016 of 22 February 2016. Interestingly enough, these judgments do not mention the *Mahdi* judgment of the CJEU. This could probably be explained by the fact that in all those judgments the SACL referred to the judgment of the extended chamber in case no A^{858}-90/2014, in which the absolute nature of the 18-month detention period was emphasised, and thus there was no need to come up with new legal arguments. Nevertheless, the judgments do mention *Kadzoev* and Art 41 of the Charter of Fundamental Rights.

[36] Judgment of the SACL in administrative case no A-3078-822/2016 of 23 February 2016.

[37] Law no XII-2080 amending the Law on the Legal Status of Foreigners of 26 November 2015. The provision was adopted to implement the revised Asylum Procedures Directive and Reception Conditions Directive, adopted in 2013: see the explanatory note no XIIP-3291 to the draft amending the Law on the Legal Status of Foreigners of 12 June 2015.

[38] Art $118(1^1)$ of the Law on the Legal Status of Foreigners. This obligation was enshrined in the Law on the Legal Status of Foreigners in December 2014 in order to implement the Return Directive in more detail: see the explanatory note no XIIP-1804 to the draft amending and supplementing the Law on the Legal Status of Foreigners of 12 May 2014.

practice related to the application of this provision.[39] Finally, the Law provides that a foreigner must be released from detention without delay if a court quashes the detention decision or the detention period expires.[40]

III. Substantive Grounds of Pre-Removal Detention

The grounds for pre-removal detention are set by the Law on the Legal Status of Foreigners. The provisions are confusing, since Article 112 of the Law is an umbrella provision regarding the restriction of movement of foreigners,[41] while Article 113 establishes a list of particular grounds for detention. The Law states that a foreigner who is not a citizen of an EU Member State, his family member or another person who enjoys the right of free movement under legal acts of the European Union may be detained: (i) when ensuring the return of a foreigner who has been refused admission into Lithuania;[42] (ii) when a decision is taken to expel the foreigner from Lithuania or another state to which Council Directive 2001/40/EC of 28 May 2001 on the mutual recognition of decisions on the expulsion of third-country nationals applies.[43] The Law further states that when deciding on the return of a foreigner, his expulsion, the obligation to leave Lithuania or the transfer of an asylum applicant to another EU Member State responsible for examining the application,[44] the foreigner may be detained only if detention is necessary for taking or enforcing the relevant decision (ie the foreigner is hampering the taking and/or enforcement of the decision and may abscond).[45]

[39] It seems that the aim of adopting Art 118(1^1) of the Law was to implement Art 15(4) of the Return Directive. However, unlike Art 15 of the Directive, the national provision imposes the obligation to 'refer to a district court of the foreigner's place of residence with a request to review the decision to detain the foreigner', but does not directly specify the result of such a request – release from detention.

[40] Art 119 of the Law on the Legal Status of Foreigners.

[41] Art 112 provides: '[A] foreigner's freedom of movement in the Republic of Lithuania may be restricted where it is necessary to ensure national security and public policy, to protect public health or morals, to prevent crime or to safeguard the rights and freedoms of other persons.' The relation between Arts 112 and 113 of the Law has never been clarified in SACL practice. Although the Court sometimes refers to Art 112 in pre-removal cases, which would seem to be inconsistent with Art 15 of the Return Directive, it has never used a national security or public policy argument as a standalone ground for detention in pre-removal cases: when considering the necessity for detention, the Court always refers to particular grounds of Art 113. The same reference to national security is in Art 115 of the Law establishing provisions concerning alternatives to detention.

[42] Art 113(1)(3) of the Law on the Legal Status of Foreigners.

[43] Art 113(1)(5) of the Law on the Legal Status of Foreigners.

[44] As may be seen from the content of that provision, the criterion of the risk of absconding is applicable not only in pre-removal procedures of the foreigner to third states, but in procedures of transfer of asylum seekers to other EU Member States. Accordingly, provisions of Art 113(5) of the Law defining circumstances that may indicate the risk of absconding are applicable not only in pre-removal procedures, but in cases of transfer of asylum seekers to other EU Member States and, by virtue of Art 113(4) of the Law, to asylum seekers whose applications are considered in Lithuania.

[45] Art 113(2) of the Law on the Legal Status of Foreigners.

As mentioned above, in order to further implement the Return Directive, including Article 3(7), the Law was supplemented in 2014 with a list of circumstances to be considered when deciding on the risk of absconding. These are when: (i) a foreigner is not in possession of an identity document and fails to cooperate in establishing his identity or citizenship (refuses to provide personal data, provides false information, etc); (ii) the person does not have a place of residence in Lithuania or is absent from the indicated address; (iii) the person does not have a family relationship with persons residing in Lithuania or social, economic or other ties with Lithuania; (iv) the person does not possess means of subsistence in Lithuania; (v) the person has failed to comply with the obligation to leave Lithuania within the specified time limit, failed to voluntarily leave the Republic of Lithuania within the time limit stipulated in a decision to return him to a foreign state or within an extended time limit; (vi) the person fails to comply with an alternative to detention imposed by the court; (vii) the foreigner was accommodated at the State Border Guard Service without restricting his freedom of movement and has violated the rules of temporary absence; (viii) in order to escape criminal liability for illegal border crossing, the person has lodged an application for asylum pending pre-trial investigation;[46] (ix) the foreigner's stay in Lithuania may represent a threat to public policy; (x) the foreigner does not cooperate with officials of the competent institutions when his asylum application is examined.[47] One of the most common grounds of detention invoked by law enforcement institutions in court is that the foreigner hampers the taking and/or enforcement of the removal decision and may abscond. If this ground is invoked, the court ex officio analyses the entirety of the circumstances, with special attention to the past behaviour of the foreigner.

One of the most convincing indications that a foreigner might abscond is the fact that he or she has absconded before or infringed the rules of stay in the Foreigners' Registration Centre by leaving and not coming back for several days. For example, in case no A-2716-822/2016 the applicant was transferred from Sweden according to the Dublin III Regulation,[48] and applied for asylum in Lithuania.[49] The examination of his application was suspended twice because the

[46] According to Art 291 of the Criminal Code, illegal crossing of the border may be punished by fine, arrest or deprivation of liberty lasting up to two years. However, criminal responsibility is not applicable if the foreigner, who illegally crossed the border has done so with the aim of using his right to asylum. Exemption from criminal responsibility is also provided if it is established that the foreigner has illegally crossed the border with the aim of travelling to the third country, or if the foreigner has been returned to the third state, from which he had crossed the border or to the country of his citizenship. So far, there is no SACL jurisprudence in which the question of interpretation and application of Art 113(5)(8) of the Law was relevant.

[47] Art 113(5) of the Law on the Legal Status of Foreigners.

[48] Regulation (EU) 604/2013 of the European Parliament and of the Council of 26 June 2013 establishing the criteria and mechanisms for determining the Member State responsible for examining an application for international protection lodged in one of the Member States by a third-country national or a stateless person (recast) [2013] OJ L180/31.

[49] Judgment of the SACL in administrative case no A-2716-822/2016 of 15 January 2016.

applicant had departed from the Foreigners' Registration Centre for several days. Once the Migration Department adopted a decision not to grant international protection, the applicant tried to leave to another country but was apprehended at the border. The SACL took the circumstances into account, including the fact that the applicant had not cooperated in obtaining the documents for his return, and found sufficient evidence to consider that without detaining the applicant, he would attempt to hide in order to avoid his expulsion.[50]

Similarly, in case no A-3878-662/2015 the applicant had applied for asylum and had left the Foreigners' Registration Centre twice for several days while his application was being processed.[51] Initially the application was merely suspended, but eventually a decision not to grant asylum was adopted and became effective. After that the applicant left the Foreigners' Registration Centre and was detained by the district court upon a motion of the State Border Guard Service claiming he was hindering enforcement of the decision to remove him. The SACL decided that the foreigner's initial infringement of Registration Centre rules and subsequent attempt to leave the country made it necessary to detain him.

Behaviour other than absconding can also be decisive when assessing the need to detain a foreigner. In administrative case no eA-3820-624/2016 a foreigner overstayed his visa and was obliged to voluntarily leave, but did not leave the country within the set time limit.[52] The SACL found that there were grounds for detaining the foreigner: his passport had been torn (according to the applicant, in circumstances unknown to him), he refused to fill in an application for a travel document without indicating clear reasons, he had married a Lithuanian citizen during the time limit for his voluntary departure, and the Migration Department doubted the veracity of the marriage. The Court concluded that all these circumstances indicated an objective need for detention. However, the SACL did not agree with the period of detention, stating that it should be shortened from six to three months.

A consideration of the evidence plays an important role when assessing whether there is an objective need to detain a foreigner. For example, in case no N575-12/2014 the applicant had overstayed his residence permit by more than a year. The applicant claimed to have a partner, a child and a business in Lithuania. He was invited to submit additional evidence regarding his business, declared income and family, and to prove his statement that he had a family in Austria and had started to arrange his travel documents to Austria. The court pointed out in the judgment that the applicant had not submitted any documentary evidence showing he was the father of the child, nor was there any proof furnished showing

[50] The applicant claimed that at least part of his previous detention, when his asylum application was processed, was illegal; the SACL referred to the *Arslan* judgment (Case C-534/11 *Arslan* ECLI:EU:C:2013:343), and responded that neither EU law nor national legislation prohibits detention of asylum seekers.

[51] Judgment of the SACL in administrative case no A-3787-662/2015 of 2 October 2015.

[52] Judgment of the SACL in administrative case no eA-3820-624/2016 of 16 May 2016.

that he was the partner of the woman in question. The company he had established in Lithuania had been inactive for three years. Furthermore, Austria had added the applicant to the list of non-admissible third-country nationals in the Schengen Information System (SIS). Having taken all the circumstances into account, the SACL decided that the applicant's company had been established in an attempt to legalise his residence in the EU, and was therefore fictitious. The Court found that the applicant could use free movement within the EU to evade removal. Thus there was an objective need to restrict his liberty, and to keep him in detention for another 1.5 months or until his expulsion.[53]

In administrative case no A^{662}-3171/2014, the applicant was detained due to his illegal entry and stay in Lithuania. He then submitted an asylum application, which he withdrew a month later, asking to be sent to a third country. He also told authorities a different name and birth date than before. When appealing the court order to detain him, the applicant relied on Article 115(1) of the Law. The SACL decided it could not be unambiguously confirmed that the applicant's identity had been established, as he had no identity documents and had misled the officers. Furthermore, he had applied for asylum only when detained, tried to hide certain circumstances during his initial interview, and lied about his itinerary of arrival. Therefore, the SACL agreed with the district court's finding of a high probability that the applicant would abscond to other EU countries if he had freedom of movement.[54]

In case no A-3673-822/2015, the Court was called to decide whether the applicant should be kept in detention during his return procedure.[55] The applicant argued for an alternative measure, as his identity had been established and he claimed to be a minor. An independent expert gave his opinion that the applicant was over 20 years old, and likely to be 20–25 years old. The identity card was submitted by a woman who claimed to be the applicant's mother; however, there was no evidence that she was indeed his mother, or that the identity card was genuine. The SACL took into account that the identity of the applicant had not been established, that he changed his statements concerning his name and date of birth, and that according to the expert's opinion he was an adult, and concluded that his detention was necessary.

According to the Law on the Legal Status of Foreigners, vulnerable persons and families with children may be detained only in exceptional cases, having regard to the best interest of the child and vulnerable persons.[56] This provision has been interpreted by the SACL in cases including both asylum seekers[57] and migrants in pre-removal procedures. The Court stated that if a foreigner has

[53] Judgment of the SACL in administrative case no N^{575}-12/2014 of 11 April 2014.

[54] Judgment of the SACL in administrative case no A^{662}-3171/2014 of 11 December 2014.

[55] Judgment of the SACL in administrative case no A-3673-822/2015 of 22 September 2015.

[56] Art 114(4) of the Law.

[57] For an example of the former, see the judgment of the SACL in administrative case no A-1798-624/2015 of 12 February 2015; for the latter, see no A-4929-624/2016 of 21 December 2016.

ignored clear prohibitions and tried to leave the country without a valid travel document, this can justify restricting their freedom of movement or detaining them. However, when a person must take care of children, this measure can only be applied in extraordinary cases, ie when both the basis of applying the measure is extraordinary (eg threat to national security) and there is certainly no other alternative (eg the person has breached an alternative measure imposed on him). So far in all cases concerning minors the Court has ruled it inappropriate to detain the applicants, deeming it sufficient to provide accommodation in the Foreigners' Registration Centre and leave freedom of movement unrestricted.

There have also been two cases where manifestly unfounded asylum applications were submitted after a decision to return the foreigners in question was adopted. In both these cases the SACL referred to the *Arslan* judgment,[58] where the CJEU found that Directives 2003/9 and 2005/85 do not preclude a third-country national who has applied for international protection within the meaning of Directive 2005/85 after having been detained under Article 15 of the Return Directive from being kept in detention on the basis of a provision of national law.[59] For example, in case no N575-58/2014, the foreigner only submitted an asylum application after his removal procedure had begun, and during the court hearing before the SACL he stated that he had left his country of origin due to persecution by natural persons. The Court found that the applicant was abusing asylum procedures, and in order to prevent him from travelling to other EU countries there was an objective need to restrict his liberty.[60]

IV. Application of Alternative Measures and the Principle of Proportionality

Both the Law on the Legal Status of Foreigners and the case-law of the SACL give due regard to the principle of proportionality and the application of alternatives to detention.

58 *Arslan* (n 50).

59 The CJEU insisted on the necessity for case-by-case assessments of all the relevant circumstances in order to establish that the application was made solely to delay or jeopardise the enforcement of the return decision, and that it is objectively necessary to maintain detention to prevent the person from permanently evading his return. *Arslan* (n 50) para 63.

60 Judgment of the SACL in administrative case no N575-58/2014 of 10 April 2014. In a similar case, the applicant claimed he came to work to Lithuania, only submitted his application after his removal procedure had started and stated during the hearing that he was being persecuted by an organised group in his country of origin. He did not have any document proving his identity. The Court found that the applicant was abusing asylum procedure and there was a risk he would abscond, thus that there was a need to detain him: judgment of the SACL in administrative case no N575-54/2014 of 10 April 2014.

As mentioned above, the Law establishes that if a foreigner's identity has been established, he represents no threat to national security and public order,[61] and he assists the court in determining his legal status in Lithuania, the court, taking into account other circumstances as well, may decide to provide an alternative to detention.[62] The Law lists (i) regular registration at a police station; (ii) informing the territorial police of the foreigner's whereabouts through communication at a set time; (iii) entrusting the guardianship of a foreigner to a citizen of Lithuania or a relative lawfully residing there, provided that they undertake to support the foreigner; and (iv) accommodating the foreigner at the Foreigners' Registration Centre without restricting their movement.[63] When taking a decision to provide an alternative to detention, time limits must be set for their application. If the alternatives are not complied with, the responsible territorial police station must apply to the court for detention of the foreigner.[64]

The SACL has stressed several times in cases concerning pre-removal detention that detention is an *ultima ratio* measure and may be applied only when objectives established in law cannot be attained by other means.[65] In some cases the Court has reversed decisions of courts of first instance or dismissed appeals of the State Border Security Service and applied alternatives to detention instead. When deciding whether alternative measures should be applied, the SACL takes into account all circumstances of the case, such as the behaviour of the foreigner, their source of income and the stay of their family members in Lithuania. For example, in case no A-3913-822/2015, the State Border Guard Service applied to detain a foreigner because he had arrived in Lithuania illegally, and it was found that the service had already decided to return the applicant two months earlier. At the first-instance court hearing the applicant stated that he refused to return to his country of origin due to fear of persecution and had therefore changed his identity several times. He further stated that he had been detained that same year in Poland while illegally transporting citizens of Vietnam, and a pre-trial investigation had

[61] Although Art 115(1) of the Law refers to the absence of a threat to national security as a precondition for the application of alternative measures, some judgments of the SACL reveal that it does not treat such a provision as absolute. For example, in administrative case no A-3390-822/2017 of 2 March 2017, Border Control submitted a motion for detention of a group of Turkish citizens (they had already submitted asylum applications). The motion was based on the fact that the foreigners belonged to the Kurdish Workers Party (PKK) which was included in various lists of terrorist organisations. The first-instance court granted the motion and ordered detention. The SACL pointed out that the majority of documents submitted before the Court were secret, and not acceptable as evidence in administrative proceedings. Upon evaluation of the whole case file the Court stated that the evidence did not indicate a threat to national security and ordered an alternative: accommodation at the Foreigners' Registration Centre.

[62] Art 115(1) of the Law.

[63] The terminology of Art 115 (2)(5) of the Law does not properly reflect the nature of the measure, since the foreigner may not choose whether he or she wants to live in the centre or not. All foreigners living there must return to the centre before 10 pm every day.

[64] Art 115(3) and (4) of the Law.

[65] Eg the judgments of the SACL in administrative cases no A-2457-858/2015 of 8 May 2015 and A-3913-822/2015 of 21 October 2015.

been started against him. According to the applicant, he had been released on bail. The first-instance court granted the motion to detain the applicant. However, the SACL found that the identity of the applicant could be confirmed by his driving licence and a copy of his passport, both of which he had submitted. The Court also took into account – among other things – that the applicant had a source of income in Lithuania (trading cars), was living with a Lithuanian citizen with whom he was raising a child, posed no apparent threat to state security or public order, and had cooperated with state institutions during his hearing by providing exhaustive explanations and evidence. The Court concluded that the legal status of the applicant could be determined without detaining him, and he was obliged to regularly register at the territorial police station for another five months.[66]

In case no A-2457-858/2015, the applicant was obliged to voluntarily leave Lithuania once his temporary residence permit had expired. He left on the last day of the set term but returned the next morning. He had not been allowed to enter the country of destination but could not explain the exact reasons. The first-instance court decided to detain the foreigner pending a decision concerning his legal status in Lithuania. The SACL disagreed and noted that the district court had not even considered applying alternative measures to detention. The Court drew attention to the fact that the applicant was a student, and that there was no data indicating that he had hindered the process of establishing his legal status or identity. On the contrary, he had paid the fine that was imposed on him, and complied with the return decision by voluntarily departing. Thus, there was no evidence of abuse, and no reason to think he might hide or try to abscond. Furthermore the applicant was trying to legalise his stay, his claim to have financial resources had been confirmed by his brother's written obligation to regularly transfer funds, and another person had consented to allow him to stay in her apartment. The Court concluded that detention would be disproportionate, and obliged the applicant to regularly report to the territorial police station.[67]

Finally, there are instances where the SACL decided that even alternative measures would be disproportionate. For example, the Court recently upheld the judgment of the first-instance court in which it revoked alternative measures concerning an asylum seeker's family that included four children.[68] It found that the conditions at the Foreigners' Registration Centre are not favourable to minors and one of the applicants was diagnosed with depression. Because the parents were able to take care of the children and a non-governmental organisation had pledged to provide help, alternative measures were not needed.[69]

[66] Judgment of the SACL in administrative case no A-3913-822/2015 of 21 October 2015.

[67] Judgment of the SACL in administrative case no A-2457-858/2015 of 8 May 2015.

[68] See administrative case no A-5072-520/2018.

[69] Judgment of the SACL in administrative case no A-5072-520/2018 of 6 August 2018.The SACL referred, inter alia, to its earlier practice, as well as to Art 3(9) of the Return Directive, Art 11(1) of the Reception Conditions Directive (2013/33/EU, [2013] OJ L180/96) and ECtHR 19 January 2010, *Muskhadzhiyeva and others v Belgium*, App No 41442/07, para 63.

V. Conclusions

Legal provisions concerning pre-removal detention have been evolving until recently in pursuance of a proper implementation of the Return Directive, as well as directives in the field of asylum. Although the implementation of the Return Directive has not been smooth, that has not stopped the SACL developing consistent practice in this field. This pertains especially to the interpretation and application of provisions concerning the necessity and duration of pre-removal detention. Here, the SACL first takes into account the past behaviour of foreigners, in particular whether they have absconded in the past. Non-cooperation with authorities can indicate a greater risk of absconding.

The jurisprudence of the SACL reveals that it performs a case-by-case evaluation of all the relevant factors, including ex officio consideration of aspects the parties do not address. When deciding on the prolongation of detention, the Court evaluates new evidence as well as the foreigner's previous behaviour. The longer the period of detention, the higher the burden on state institutions submitting the motion for its prolongation to demonstrate that they took all necessary steps to finalise the pre-removal proceedings as soon as possible. This is especially relevant if a motion asks for detention beyond six months. In this context the principle of good administration and the Charter of Fundamental Rights of the EU play a positive part.

The application of the principle of proportionality has resulted in some first-instance court decisions being annulled and alternative measures being applied instead of detention. The SACL case-law has been followed by a shift in the approach of district courts, which have become more eager to apply alternative measures. In some cases national courts were not convinced that even alternative measures would be a proportionate response to a particular situation. With regard to the protection of vulnerable persons, the SACL has held that detention may be applied only in extraordinary cases, when it is certain that there are no other alternatives.

When it comes to judicial discourse between the SACL and the CJEU or the ECtHR in pre-removal cases, the impression is of limited interaction when compared to the practice of the SACL in other areas of law. In the majority of pre-removal proceedings, references to EU law or the ECHR are absent. This can at least partly be attributed to the short time limits for judgments and the brevity of reasoning in this type of decision. The fact that national courts have full powers of review, ie to evaluate all relevant aspects of law and fact, may also play a role. Here, one may see a certain trade-off between the speed of delivery of judgments (which is of special relevance for the third-country national and the right to freedom, as well as the requirement for speedy and efficient return procedures) and the completeness of legal reasoning as regards the reliance on EU law. In cases where EU law is part of the reasoning it largely takes the form of indirect effect, since provisions of EU law and the practice of the CJEU or the ECtHR are usually cited to strengthen the argumentation.

Overall, the jurisprudence of the SACL is in line with the objectives and provisions of the Return Directive. Over time, the Court has developed consistent practice as regards detention of foreigners, taking all relevant factual circumstances into account in order to balance an effective removal policy with the fundamental right of liberty. It responds to the requirements of the Return Directive and the jurisprudence of the CJEU, although some of the latter's judgments (eg *Mahdi*) have not yet caught its attention.

11

Detention of Migrants in Belgium and the Criminal Judge: A Lewis Carroll World

SYLVIE SAROLEA

I. Introduction

The *Alice in Wonderland* metaphor of the title reflects the pitfalls of Belgian legislation that entrust criminal judges with the control of the legality of the detention of third-country nationals. This deprivation of liberty takes place at the borders or as pre-removal detention under the Return Directive.[1] This chapter focuses on the latter measure, and it will engage with judicial dialogue, or rather its absence, between judges operating in one jurisdiction, but belonging to different branches. We will see that Belgium's choice of appointing criminal judges to review the legality of the deprivation of liberty leads to a weakening of the effectiveness of this review. This has an impact on the scope of the control and raises a risk of inconsistency in decisions that are taken in the same case by various authorities.

Three main problems must be identified. Firstly, the scope of the control exercised by a criminal judge is restricted; she is only authorised to examine the legality of the decision. This concept includes the facts with a view to assess the respect of human rights if understood largely, but excludes them if legality is interpreted narrowly. Secondly, entrusting a criminal judge with the control of the detention of foreigners, while an administrative judge assesses the legality of decisions relating to residence, leads to contradictions and inconsistencies. These are reinforced by the absence of rules on the prevalence and temporal organisation of the two interventions. No mechanism for institutional dialogue is organised between the two judges, as the criminal judge most often confines himself to referring to the

[1] See S Sarolea and P D'Huart in collaboration with National Judge B Chapaux, *Completed Questionnaire for the Project Contention National Report – Belgium* (2014) available at http://contention.eu/docs/country-reports/BelgiumFinal.pdf, See also *Revue de droit des étrangers* (RDE) no 191, Numéro special detention (2016).

decisions taken by the administrative judge when he has already ruled. Otherwise, it may lead to absurd situations of release while the removal order remains or continued detention while the administrative judge must always decide. Lastly, from a symbolic point of view, entrusting a criminal judge with the task of reviewing decisions taken with regard to migrants sends them back to a condition of guilty or at least suspicious persons. The fact that, at the same hearing, it is necessary to examine both the files of persons suspected of offences and the detention of migrants, even unconsciously, leads to mistrust or even categorical assimilation.

In the case of illegal stay in Belgium, the Immigration Office delivers orders to leave the territory as well as detention orders. The Immigration Office is not an independent administrative authority but works under the authority of the executive power (the Ministry of Immigration). The lawfulness of orders to leave the territory is monitored by an administrative body, the Council of Immigration Disputes. However, the detention orders are monitored by the judiciary: the Council Chambers (first instance), the Indictment Chambers of the Court of Appeal (three judges – second instance) and the Court of Cassation (limited jurisdiction). These courts usually deal with criminal cases, inter alia deciding on preventive detention.

The judge in charge of the preventive detention of ordinary remand prisoners thus also decides on the legality of the detention of third-country nationals in deportation proceedings. He intervenes in parallel with the administrative judge who rules on the legality of the expulsion measure itself. Their competences are complementary but above all concurrent, since no chronology governs their referral; one can decide before, at the same time as, or after the other, and the object and scope of their judicial review is distinct.

In order to highlight the particularities of the Belgian system, this chapter analyses the two controls exercised in the area of return. First, the contribution explains how the Return Directive has been implemented in domestic law (section II). Then, the role of administrative judges in reviewing the return decision is discussed (section III). This is followed by a discussion of the role of criminal judges in reviewing the detention (section IV). On this subject, it is essential to focus on the scope of the review exercised by criminal judges (distinguishing between a review of legality of detention and of its opportunity),[2] and the procedural questions raised by borrowing from the procedure for the review of pre-trial detention. This analysis leads to a critical reading of the coherence of the Belgian system and of its ability to ensure an effective remedy. The two faces of the legal framework are neither complementary nor adjusted (section V). The incongruities in the Belgian system come in even sharper relief when immigration detention is compared with pretrial detention of criminal offenders (section VII). The contribution ends with some conclusions highlighting the need for judicial

[2] Opportunity ('*opportunité*) in this sense can also be translated as 'expediency' or 'appropriateness'. In this chapter, opportunity is used to designate the review of detention that goes beyond a narrow legality review.

reform. This is all the more urgent seeing that even if EU law – ie the Return Directive – has been formally transposed into domestic law, the main pillars of the Belgian system remain largely unchanged.

II. The Return Directive in Belgian Law and Deprivation of Liberty

In Belgium, the transposition of the Return Directive in 2012 amended several articles of the Aliens Act. Article 1 of the Act incorporated new definitions, such as the concepts of voluntary return, vulnerable persons and flight risk. The Return Directive indirectly expresses a substantive rule by rejecting the option of leaving foreigners in an irregular situation. In doing so, the Directive imposes a choice on states: either regularise the stay or adopt a return decision. Subject to certain limitations, Article 6 of the Return Directive provides that: 'Member States shall issue a return decision to any third country national staying illegally on their territory, without prejudice to the exceptions referred to in paragraphs 2 to 5.' The transposition of this article led the Belgian legislator to replace the word 'may' by the word 'must' in Article 7 of the law of 15 December 1980 when it comes to issuing orders to leave the territory.

To transpose the Directive, a new Title IIIquater titled 'Provisions applicable to the return of third-country nationals illegally residing in the territory' has been inserted in the Aliens Act. These provisions govern the prohibition of entry, expulsion decisions, the method of expulsion, the special rules applicable to unaccompanied foreign minors and the information obligations imposed on the authorities. Legally speaking, Belgian law gives priority to voluntary departure over forced departure and consists, for the foreigner, in complying with the return decision within the time limit set, generally 30 days.[3] The period for voluntary departure may be extended if 'the voluntary return cannot take place within the time limit' or if the foreigner invokes 'circumstances specific to his situation, such as the length of stay, the existence of children in school, the finalization of the organization of the voluntary departure and other family and social links'.

The time limit for voluntary departure may also be shortened or waived. Several reasons may lead to a reduction or abolition of this period: failure to comply with one of the preventive measures; a danger to public policy or national security; failure to comply with a previous expulsion decision within the time limit; fraud; the lodging of more than two asylum applications, unless there are new elements in the application; and, in general, the risk of absconding. In addition to voluntary departure in the sense of departure within the prescribed period, Belgian law also mentions the voluntary return of any foreigner who makes use of

[3] Art 74/14 Aliens Act, in line with Arts 7 and 8 of the Return Directive.

'an assisted return program set up by the authorities of the host country', without attaching any special regime to it.

Regarding detention, the Return Directive did not lead to major changes in Belgian law since domestic law already stipulated that the deprivation of liberty could only occur as a last resort and may not be automatic. This principle, then, was not new. However, the principle of subsidiarity and the obligation to consider less coercive measures is more precise in the Directive and thus had an influence on the case-law. Article 15 of the Return Directive only permits detention as a measure of last resort 'in order to prepare for return and/or to carry out removal'. It may be used 'in particular where: (a) there is a risk of flight, or (b) the third-country national concerned avoids or prevents the preparation of the return or removal procedure'. It is important that this deprivation of liberty be as brief as possible and continue only if 'the removal process is ongoing and carried out with all due diligence'. Therefore:

> [W]hen it appears that there is no longer a reasonable prospect of removal for legal or other reasons or that the conditions set out in paragraph 1 are no longer met, detention is no longer justified and the person concerned is immediately released.

Detention cannot be an automatic measure; the decision to use it must comply with the principle of proportionality.[4]

These cumulative conditions are reflected in the provisions of the Aliens Act governing detention. Article 7 Aliens Act provides that:

> [T]he Minister or his delegate may, in the cases referred to in Article 74/14, § 3, deport the foreigner to the border. Unless other sufficient, but less coercive measures can be applied effectively, the foreign national may be detained for this purpose.

The Return Directive would be infringed if the authority did not respect the principle of proportionality in enforcing return. Moreover, a decision that does not set out the reasons for the deprivation of liberty in the light of the principle of subsidiarity should be considered insufficiently reasoned.[5] It is the judge's responsibility to ensure that the required gradation is respected. Thus, the mere fact that the stay was illegal following the notification of orders to leave the country and the absence of identity documents, requiring the granting of a travel document by the national authorities, is not sufficient to justify a deprivation of liberty.[6] However, as discussed below, the case-law on this point is ambiguous.

A link could be made with the case-law of the ECtHR concerning Belgian detention cases. Even though the ECtHR does generally not require that immigration detention must necessarily be a measure of last resort, the principle of proportionality has featured prominently in its case-law when ruling on the

[4] Case C-357/09 *Kadzoev* ECLI:EU:C:2009:741, para 67; and Case C-61/11 PPU *El Dridi* ECLI:EU:C:2011:268, para 41.

[5] Court of Appeal Bruxelles, acc, 7 March 2012 (2012) *Revue du droit des étrangers* 31.

[6] Court of Appeal Liège, acc, 22 April 2014, C-542.

detention of vulnerable persons. For example, in the case of a Cameroonian woman suffering from HIV, the ECtHR considered the detention arbitrary because Belgium had not considered applying less severe measures:

> The Court observes that the authorities knew the exact identity of the applicant, that she resided at a fixed address known to the authorities, that she had always attended the summonses … and that she had taken several steps … to regularise her situation. It also recalls that the applicant was suffering from HIV, that her state of health had deteriorated during her detention and that, if she had been released, she would have been dependent on emergency medical assistance …. Despite this situation, the authorities did not consider a less severe measure, such as a temporary residence permit, to safeguard the public interest of detention and avoid keeping the applicant in detention for an additional seven weeks.[7]

III. Appeal to the Administrative Judge against the Expulsion Decision

The Aliens Litigation Council is the administrative court competent to hear appeals lodged against decisions relating to asylum and residence, and decisions ancillary thereto (such as a return decision or an entry ban). It reviews the legality of these measures in the context of an action for annulment for infringement of essential procedural requirements. Where it is not automatically suspensive, the action for annulment may be accompanied by a request for suspension and a request for provisional measures.

The administrative judge exercises a marginal review of legality. He can only annul a decision affected by a defect of legality or a manifest error of assessment. He carries out an *ex tunc* examination, reviewing the legality of the decision as of the date of its adoption. If the review of legality makes it possible to cancel a decision for violation of the relevant legal provisions, defective reasons or manifest errors of assessment, it does not authorise the judge to re-examine the case and substitute his analysis for that of the administration; instead the case is referred back to the administration.

Most disputes about decisions relating to asylum and residence fall under this sole control of legality. However, these limits on the judge's powers raise questions as to the effectiveness of the remedy, specifically the appropriateness of maintaining the distinction between marginal review of legality and full review in matters involving substantive rights. This situation does not accommodate a judge reduced to exercising negative jurisdiction, because to annul is to suppress the 'evil' observed without being able to positively remedy it.[8] Thus, cancellation

[7] ECtHR 20 December 2011, *Yoh-Ekale Mwanje v Belgium*, App No 10486/10, para 124; and ECHR 19 January 2012, *Popov v France*, App Nos 9472/07 and 39474/07, para 140.

[8] '[D]uplication of proceedings before the Aliens Litigation Council should not be maintained. Any appeal should be fully contentious and in principle suspensive. The prior privilege of the

restores equilibrium, but it does not guarantee the enjoyment of the substantive right in question. In the absence of a mechanism such as the administrative loop that now exists before the Council of State in areas other than migration litigation, the applicant's rights are not recognised by means of an annulment. Migration litigation is thus characterised more by an administrative carousel mechanism than an administrative loop.[9] This means that in most cases, if the judge rules that an administrative decision infringes the law, the administration has to take a new decision. This returning of files to the administration can occur several times, with consecutive 'positive decisions' by judges.

The judge in charge of the control of the legality of the return decision issued by the administration is competent to assess its compatibility with domestic as well international and European law. The return decision is most often included in a decision refusing or terminating a right of residence. They are thus concomitant. Sometimes, however, the order to leave the territory is notified independently of the decision on the residence status of the third-country national. This is the case in the asylum procedure. The return decision is adopted by the Immigration Office, whereas the decision whether or not to grant protection is taken beforehand by the asylum authorities.

This distinction between the decision on the merits of the application for asylum and the return decision led to a preliminary reference by a Belgian judge to the CJEU in *Gnandi*.[10] During the asylum procedure, the applicant enjoys provisional asylum. This right to stay is not a right of residence. In the event of a negative decision at first instance (by the administrative authority), an order to leave the territory is issued. In the event of an appeal before the administrative judge, even one that has suspensive effect, this order is maintained, but suspended, and the third-country national receives a special residence document.

administration must, as regards the residence of aliens, be reversed, since the execution of a refoulement or removal measure necessarily entails serious damage that is difficult to repair if the measure is subsequently revoked. The principle of automatic suspension could be subject to duly justified exceptions in the administrative decision, which may, in this case, lead to an administrative référé.' See JY Carlier, 'Evolution procédurale du statut de l'étranger: constats, défis, propositions' (2011) 130 *Journal des Tribunaux* 117.

[9] On the administrative carousel, see in particular a decision of the Aliens Litigation Council that was denounced by the Council for Aliens Law Litigation (hereafter CCE, Conseil du contentieux des étrangers) (CCE, 30 November 2015, No 157.488). The CCE noted that the administration took a decision 'in identical terms' to those of an earlier annulled decision, thus violating the 'principle of *res judicata*'. Applicants who obtained the annulment of a decision of the Aliens Office following an appeal before the Aliens Litigation Council waited for several months – sometimes more than a year – before the administration complied with the judgment and ruled on their application again. The federal ombudsman has also denounced this limit to the effectivity of the rulings of the CCE, linked to the scope of its control, see Federal Ombudsman, *Régularisation médicale: Le fonctionnement de la section 9ter de l'Office des étrangers* (14 October 2016) available at www.federaleombudsman.be/sites/1070.b.fedimbo.belgium.be/files/regularisation_medicale_9ter_-_2016.pdf).

[10] Case C-181/16 *Gnandi* ECLI:EU:C:2018:465. For detailed discussion, see JB Farcy, 'L'arrêt *Gnandi*: la logique juridique sacrifiée au nom de l'efficacité des procédures de retour ?' [January 2019] *Cahiers EDEM*.

The distinction between a mere right to stay and a right of residence was accentuated in 2013 by an amendment to this document, which no longer states that the person concerned is authorised to stay during the appeal, but instead that 'the person concerned is neither admitted nor authorized to stay but may remain in the territory … pending a decision'. The Council of State rejected an application to annul this amendment, expressly noting that the Asylum Procedures Directive 'does not require States to grant a residence permit abroad on which the right to remain in the territory is conferred'.[11] The CJEU validated this interpretation. In *Gnandi* it ruled that the Return Directive and the Asylum Procedures Directives, in light of the principle of *non-refoulement* and the right to an effective remedy, do not preclude the adoption of a return decision in respect of a third-country national who has applied for international protection, immediately after the rejection of that application by the determining authority or together in the same administrative act, and thus before the conclusion of any appeal proceedings against that rejection. However, all the legal effects of the return decision must be suspended pending the outcome of the appeal. Moreover, the applicant must continue to enjoy the rights guaranteed by the Reception Conditions Directive (RCD).[12] In case of new circumstances, the situation must be reviewed.

The first question to be answered by the Court of Justice was indeed whether the Return Directive was applicable in this case. To this end, it must be examined whether, as soon as the CGRA rejects his application for international protection, the applicant is illegally residing in Belgium. In order for a return decision to be adopted, the addressee must be an illegal resident on the national territory.

According to Article 7(1) of the Procedure Directive, asylum seekers 'shall be allowed to remain' in the territory of the Member State in which they have lodged an application until a decision is adopted at first instance. Article 39(3) of the same Directive gives each Member State the possibility to extend this right by providing that the lodging of an appeal against the decision of the responsible authority in first instance has the effect of allowing applicants for asylum to remain in the territory of that state pending the outcome of that appeal. Under Belgian law, Article 39/70 of the Act of 15 December 1980 specifically grants applicants for international protection the right to remain in the territory 'during the period fixed for the lodging of the appeal and during its examination'. On the ground that he had brought a full court action before the CCE, Mr Gnandi was also issued with an Annex 35, in accordance with Article 111 of the Royal Decree of 8 October 1981, authorising him to remain in the territory. Annex 35 constitutes a 'special residence document' by virtue of which the person concerned is neither admitted nor authorised to stay but may remain in the territory of the kingdom pending a decision by the Aliens Litigation Council. This somewhat ambiguous 'status' allows a foreigner to remain

[11] Council of State, Decision of 8 March 2016, *Gnandi*, no 234.074.

[12] Council Directive 2003/9/EC of 27 January 2003 laying down minimum standards for the reception of asylum seekers [2003] OJ L31/18.

in the territory without having a legal right to stay.[13] However, this does not mean that the persons listed in Annex 35 are in illegal residence, as stated by the Council of State,[14] followed by the Court of Cassation.[15] As a result, the foreigner's stay in the territory is neither irregular nor regular.

In the *Gnandi* judgment, the Court of Justice held that such an authorisation to remain does not preclude the conclusion that the foreigner is an illegal resident as soon as his application for international protection is rejected with a decision in first instance.[16] Admittedly, the authorisation to remain in the territory of a Member State for the duration of the asylum procedure 'does not constitute a right to a residence permit', as specified in Article 7(1) of the Procedure Directive. However, in the previous *Arslan* judgment,[17] the Court of Justice had held that, in such a case, the asylum seeker authorised to remain in the territory of a Member State cannot be considered to be an illegal resident within the meaning of the Return Directive. The *Gnandi* judgment acknowledges that, in accordance with this case-law,

> an authorization to remain for the purpose of the effective exercise of an appeal against the rejection of the application for international protection precludes the application of Directive 2008/115 to a third-country national who has lodged that application until the end of the appeal against the rejection of that application.'[18]

The link between the RCD and the Return Directive had led Advocate General Mengozzi to conclude that an asylum seeker cannot be considered to be illegally residing in the territory of the Member State where he has lodged his application for international protection as long as he is granted a right to remain in that territory, whether under EU law or national law, as is the case here.[19] According to the Advocate General, under penalty of depriving the appeal of effectiveness and infringing the principle of *non-refoulement*, an order to leave the territory should only be issued once the decision to reject the asylum application has become final. As a matter of principle, this reasoning seems logical.[20] Hadn't the CJEU ruled before that an asylum seeker retains his status until a final decision has been adopted?[21] However, in *Gnandi* the CJEU chose to distance itself from the conclusions of the Advocate General. In its view, the prohibition on adopting a return decision before the outcome of the appeal 'could considerably delay the initiation

[13] Circular of 30 August 2013 repealing the circular of 20/07/2001 on the legal scope of Annex 35 to the Royal Decree of 8/10/1981 on access to the territory, residence, establishment and expulsion of foreigners, *MB*, 6 September 2013.

[14] Council of State, Decision of 25 November 2014, no 229.317.

[15] Court of Cassation, judgment of 26 April 2017, no P.17.0375.F/1. About this decision, see S Sarolea, 'L'annexe 35 réhabilitée?' [May 2017] *Cahiers EDEM*.

[16] *Gnandi* (n 10) para 59.

[17] Case C-534/11 *Arslan* ECLI:EU:C:2013:343, paras 48 and 49.

[18] *Gnandi* (n 10) para 43.

[19] Opinion of Advocate General Mengozzi in Case C-181/16 *Gnandi* ECLI:EU:C:2017:467, para 89.

[20] ibid, para 89.

[21] Case C-179/11 *Cimade and GISTI* ECLI:EU:C:2012:594, para 53.

of the return procedure and make it more complex'.[22] However, it is not clear how this would make the procedure more complex, nor how the procedure would be delayed since all the effects of the return order are, in any case, suspended for the duration of the asylum appeal. The judgment reflects a distorted view on the balance between the effectiveness of return policy and the protection of fundamental rights.

IV. Judicial Control of the Legality of the Deprivation of Liberty

As discussed above, the Aliens Act entrusts review of the legality of immigration detention to the criminal investigating courts. For these courts it constitutes a dispute that does not fit well with their main competence relating to the deprivation of liberty of suspected criminal law offenders. These courts, the council chamber and the indictments chamber sitting in criminal matters must rule on a single aspect of the return procedure – detention – without being able to decide on the stay. However, it should be noted that there is ambiguity in the terms of the law itself, seeing that the criminal court, according to section 72 of the Aliens Act, 'shall verify whether the measures of deprivation of liberty and removal from the territory are in conformity with the law'. The jurisdiction assigned to the judge may thus seem to include the legality of the removal. However, since administrative judges are specifically competent to rule on this, criminal judges rule only on the legality of the detention and not of the decision on removal from the territory.

The organisation of judicial control is a matter of national law, but it must be carried out in compliance with the Return Directive, where applicable, and with Article 5 ECHR. Article 15 of the Return Directive allows Member States to opt for exclusive jurisdiction of the judiciary to order detention or for a division of jurisdiction between the administration and the courts. In this latter case the administration takes the decision to detain the third-country national, under the supervision of the judiciary. The decision to detain must be written and reasoned, according to Article 15(1) of the Return Directive.[23] A similar requirement can be deduced from Article 5(2) ECHR, which 'requires that a person be informed, in simple language accessible to him, of the legal and factual reasons for his deprivation of liberty, so that he may discuss its legality before a court under paragraph 4'.[24] This information must be provided as soon as possible, oral communication being sufficient under the ECHR. The ECtHR considered a 76-hour delay in a case involving detention at the border excessive.[25]

[22] *Gnandi* (n 10), para 50.
[23] See also Case C-146/14 PPU *Mahdi* ECLI:EU:C:2014:1320.
[24] ECtHR 5 February 2002, *Čonka v Belgium*, App No 51564/99.
[25] ECtHR 29 January 2008, *Saadi v United Kingdom*, App No 13229/03, para 84.

In Belgium the minister or his delegate take decisions on the deprivation of liberty, as well as on its prolongation. Article 62 of the Aliens Act requires that these decisions be adequately reasoned in fact and in law. The third-country national must be informed, at the time of notification of their continued detention, about the possibility of lodging an appeal with the criminal court.[26]

Article 15(2) of the Return Directive and Article 5(4) ECHR require judicial review of deprivation of liberty. Judicial oversight must be speedy and effective, in that it must lead to release if the decision to detain turns out to be unlawful. In *Firoz*, the applicant was deprived of his liberty for the purpose of removal for almost four months, without having been able to obtain a final decision on the legality of his detention. The ECtHR condemned Belgium, finding a violation of Article 5(4) ECHR.[27]

V. The Extent of Judicial Review of Detention: A Clear Distinction in Theory

The legality of a detention is thus monitored by a judge. The scope of review is open to discussion before both the two European courts and the Belgian courts. The case-law of the ECtHR emphasises that detention review does not necessarily have to be an expediency review, but legality review can neither be understood solely as compliance with domestic law. This requires monitoring in the light of the ECHR and the general principles enshrined therein, in particular with regard to the specific purposes of the restrictions permitted by Article 5(1) ECHR.[28]

The oversight by the domestic judge also involves monitoring compliance with EU law, mainly the Charter of Fundamental Rights of the European Union ('the EU Charter') and the Return Directive. The latter clarifies the contours of judicial review by setting firm guidelines for the possibility of deprivation of liberty in the context of removal. Legality, within the meaning of the Directive, includes

[26] Royal Decree 8 October 1981, Art 75 § 3; Royal Decree laying down the regime and operating rules applicable to places located on Belgian territory, managed by the Aliens Office, where an alien is detained, placed at the disposal of the Government or maintained, pursuant to the provisions cited in Article 74/8, § 1, of the Act of 15 December 1980 on access to the territory, residence, establishment and removal of aliens, art 16.

[27] ECtHR 11 July 2013, *Firoz Muneer v Belgium*, App No 56005/10. See P d'Huart, 'Le contrôle de légalité de la détention couvre la conformité de l'éloignement à la CEDH' [January 2013] *Newsletter EDEM*.

[28] ECtHR 24 October 2012, *Mahmundi and others v Greece*, App No 14902/10. Art 5(4) ECHR does not empower the court to substitute its own assessment of all aspects of the case, including considerations of pure expediency, for that of the authority from which the decision emanates. It nonetheless calls for a review broad enough to extend to all the conditions indispensable to the lawfulness of an individual's detention in the light of para 1 (para 90). See also ECtHR 5 July 2011, *Rahimi v Greece*, App No 8687/08, paras 116, 119; ECtHR 8 February 2000, *Dougoz v Greece*, App No 40907/98, para 61.

subsidiarity, necessity and proportionality. In *Mahdi*, the CJEU adopted a broad interpretation of legality, aligning it with opportunity, and recognised the judge's power to substitute his own assessment for that of the administration.[29]

Nonetheless, the requirement of full judicial review can only be inferred from this judgment with caution, since it concerns the extension of detention and not the initial decision of deprivation of liberty.[30] This case-law could lead to a distinction between a review of legality immediately after the detention decision has been taken, and an expediency review, when the detention is extended beyond six months. The nature of any checks carried out after the first legality check and before the expiry of the six-month period of detention is not yet defined by the CJEU.

Under Belgian law, the extent of oversight is defined by the contrast between legality and opportunity. Under section 72 of the Aliens Act, the investigating courts verify 'whether the measures of deprivation of liberty and removal from the territory comply with the law without being able to rule on their advisability'. The Belgian Council Chambers are only competent to check if the detention measures and removal are in accordance with the law, without being able to decide on their opportunity. However, drawing the precise line between legality and opportunity is difficult. Indeed, the distinction between legality and opportunity is widely debated by the Belgian courts, despite the case-law of the ECtHR and the clarification provided by the Return Directive as to the role assigned to the judge. The review of legality involves in any case verification of the accuracy of the factual grounds on which the decision on deprivation of liberty is based.[31] It is not for the judge to substitute their assessment for that of the administration, which has a certain discretionary power. A corollary to this discretion is an obligation

[29] *Mahdi* (n 23). Bulgarian courts must refer a question to the CJEU for a preliminary ruling as to the nature of the review to be carried out by the judicial authority seized of a request for an extension of detention. In *Mahdi* the third-country national, who was not in possession of identity documents and who had not obtained such documents from his country of origin, had been released on the grounds that there was no reasonable prospect of removal. The Court addressed the question of whether the judge may rule on the merits of the case and exercise full judicial review, allowing him to substitute a less coercive measure for detention on the basis of 'the facts stated and evidence adduced by the administrative authority as well as any observations that the third-country national may submit' (para 53). It recalled that 'Article 15 of Directive 2008/115 is unconditional and sufficiently precise, so that no other specific elements are required for it to be implemented by the Member States' (para 54). Art 15 does not specify the nature of judicial review (para 57), which must naturally incorporate the conditions and principles set out in Art 15: the existence of a reasonable prospect of removal (para 60) and subsidiarity, particularly with regard to the risk of flight and the co-operation of the person concerned (para 61). It follows that the court must consider all the elements of fact and law (para 62). The Court added: 'Any other interpretation of Article 15 of Directive 2008/115 would result in paragraphs 4 and 6 thereof being rendered ineffective and would deprive of all substance the examination by a judicial authority which the second sentence of Article 15(3) of the directive requires, thereby jeopardising the achievement of the objectives pursued by the directive' (para 63).

[30] *Mahdi*, ibid, para 42.

[31] Court of Appeal Bruxelles, mis acc, 25 September 2012, no 3219; Court of Appeal Bruxelles, mis acc, 30 August 2013, no 2851.

to state reasons; the administration needs to justify why detention appears to be the most appropriate means of ensuring removal.[32] The motivation must refer to the particular situation of the third-country national and cannot be limited to a general and stereotyped formula. It must allow the judge to verify its adequacy against the contents of the file. This is illustrated by a case in which the Court of Cassation ruled that, given a failure by the administration to specify whether there had been a decision on the application for a residence permit, it was impossible for the Court to exercise its review of legality.[33]

Beyond review for manifest error of assessment, Belgian case-law is divided between a marginal review of legality and a broader approach, including proportionality. The first is based on the exclusion of opportunity control, which prohibits the substitution of the assessment of the judge for that of the administration. The second incorporates into legality the review of necessity and subsidiarity, which requires the judge to consider the possibility of less coercive measures. The very wording of the provisions of the Aliens Act invites him to do so by using, for all cases of deprivation of liberty, the verb 'may', thereby indicating that detention is not an obligation and should not be automatic. This wording, combined with the principles of the Return Directive, subjects the use of detention to an examination of the necessity and proportionality of detention and to an analysis of the feasibility of removal. An intermediate position consists of reviewing the detailed reasoning of the decision and requiring it to convince the judge that the administration has carried out a balancing of interests, without actually substituting the judge's assessment for that of the administrative authority.

VI. In Practice: The Ambiguities of Belgium Case-Law

Several decisions illustrate the ambiguities of Belgium case-law. For instance, in 2016, the Court of Cassation said that it does not follow from Articles 5(4) and 13 ECHR that, when carrying out a review of immigration detention, investigating courts must be able to assess the opportunity of the measure imposed. But it also said that the absence of such a review does not prevent a third-country national from submitting an arbitrary or disproportionate deprivation of liberty for review by the investigating courts.[34] Thus, the question arises: how can a court practically use those criteria, while avoiding a review of opportunity?

[32] Court of Appeal Mons, mis acc, 27 October 1995. However, see also Court of Cassation, judgment of 18 December 1996, *Revue du droit des étrangers*, 218; *contra* Court of Cassation Cass (2e ch), judgment of 24 March 1998, RG no P.98.0345.N, in the case of an alien who had voluntarily come forward to the authorities.

[33] Court of Cassation, judgment of 23 August 2006, RG no P.06.1068.F [2006] *Revue du droit des étrangers* 375.

[34] Court of Cassation (2e ch), judgment of 14 September 2016, RG no P.16.0936.F.

Thus, in a case in which the Court of Cassation exercised a limited review, it quashed a judgment by a criminal judge who had invalidated a detention measure because it was based on facts and decisions dating back ten years, and did not pay sufficient attention to positive changes in the third-country national's situation. The Court argued that the criminal judge had reviewed the opportunity and not the legality of the decision.[35] Another judgment by the Court quashed a judgment of the Indictment Chamber that a detention measure was disproportionate in view of the third-country national's behaviour. He had been issued a visa, although it had expired, and the steps he had taken showed a willingness to comply with the legislation on residence. The Court considered that the judges carried out an expediency review.[36]

On the other hand, the Court of Cassation has also ruled that if an administrative file does not mention any objective and serious element evidencing a risk of flight, release may be ordered.[37] The judiciary must be able to verify the way in which the administration has assessed the risk of absconding in the light of the criteria laid down by law. In the same vein, another Court judgment maintains that the review of legality includes verification that the risk of flight has been assessed in the light of the defendant's current situation.[38]

To justify the prohibition on substituting their assessment for that of the administration, the investigating courts sometimes refer to Article 237 of the Criminal Code, which prohibits the judge from exercising his power 'by interfering in matters attributed to the administrative authorities'. Accordingly, the judge would violate this provision if he interpreted an administrative measure 'on its merits, relevance or effectiveness'.[39] But this seems to be the wrong interpretation: Article 237 of the Criminal Code, like all provisions of criminal law, is to be strictly interpreted. This provision is found in a chapter titled 'Encroachment by administrative and judicial authorities'. It aims to protect the separation of powers and only prohibits judges from interfering 'either by making regulations on these matters, or by prohibiting the execution of orders issued by the administration'. In other words, judges are neither the legislature nor the executive. This does not prevent them from exercising the authority that is vested in the judiciary. This role is particularly important when a fundamental right, such as personal liberty, is at stake.

Furthermore, there is nothing in the Aliens Act requiring the application of this provision of the Criminal Code to the deprivation of liberty of third-country nationals in view of their removal. Since 2008, such an extensive application of criminal law is even contrary to the Return Directive. In light of the Directive,

[35] Court of Cassation (2e ch), judgment of 19 March 2013, RG no P.13.0337.N/1.
[36] Court of Cassation (2e ch), judgment of 10 June 2015, RG no P.15.0715.F/1.
[37] Court of Cassation (2e ch), judgment of 27 June 2012, RG no P.12.1028.F.
[38] Court of Cassation (2e ch), judgment of 17 December 2014, RG no P.14.1810.F.
[39] Court of Cassation, judgment of 10 June 2015, RG no P.15.0715.F; Court of Appeal Bruxelles, mis acc, 13 June 2014, no 2083.

review of the merits, relevance and effectiveness of a measure are equally necessary to ensure its legality. Thus, the obligation to consider alternative measures as an element for lawful detention implies an examination of the proportionality of the deprivation of liberty. The requirement of reasonable prospects of removal, in particular when considering the extension of the period of detention, also implies an examination of the opportunity of the deprivation of liberty.

As regards the review of the extension, the Return Directive states: 'In each case, detention shall be reviewed at reasonable intervals, either at the request of the third-country national concerned or ex officio. In the case of extended retention periods, reviews shall be subject to review by a judicial authority.'[40] Belgian law specifies in Articles 74/5 and 74/6 Aliens Act that the extension of detention is only authorised if the objective of ensuring removal is real and effectively pursued. It is subject to three conditions: (i) that the detention be limited to the time 'strictly necessary' for the execution of the removal order; (ii) that the steps towards removal be taken within seven working days of the arrest; and (iii) that the actual removal of the third-country national remains possible. The effectiveness of removal procedures must be maintained throughout the period of detention, with standards growing ever more rigorous over time.

A. Review of the Lawfulness of Detention and Article 3 ECHR

The review of legality includes conformity with fundamental rights, such as Article 3 ECHR, which prohibits removal if there is a risk of torture or inhuman and degrading treatment, and Article 8 ECHR, which protects family life. With regard to Article 3 ECHR, a judgment by the Court of Cassation concludes that the removal of an alien and the measure of deprivation of liberty taken for that purpose may result in a situation falling within the scope of this provision if there are serious reasons for fearing that, after or as a result of their removal, the alien would be in danger of being subjected either to torture or to inhuman or degrading treatment or punishment. It follows that, when an alien invokes such a risk, the investigating court must assess its existence by way of a review of legality and not of opportunity.[41] In such a case, a risk of treatment contrary to Article 3 ECHR upon return would lead to the release of the third-country national by the criminal courts.

In another case, the Court of Appeal quashed a judgment by the Indictment Chamber which found that detention was unlawful because, in the event of deportation, the third-country national would experience a significant reduction in their life expectancy. The appellate court argued that detention in this case did not

[40] Art 15(3) of the Return Directive; *Mahdi* (n 23).
[41] Court of Cassation (2e ch), judgment of 18 January 2012, RG no P.11.2130.F.

deprive the third-country national of an effective remedy. The Court of Cassation, however, considered that the judgment of the Court of Appeal did not argue convincingly that the execution of the removal order was not likely to expose the applicant to a serious risk of serious and irreversible deterioration in their state of health. In its view, the Court of Appeal had not adequately justified its decision that the non-suspensive nature of the action for annulment did not affect the regularity of their detention order.[42]

A recent case has once again illustrated the difficulties in delimiting the power of the criminal judge deciding on detention and harmonising their approach with that of the administrative judge. This is the widely reported case of removals to Sudan in January 2018 on which the Court of Cassation ruled on 31 January 2018.[43] The Court, deciding on the detention of the Sudanese nationals, rejected the Aliens Office's argument that it would only be required to examine the risk of treatment contrary to Article 3 ECHR when a foreign national had lodged an asylum application. Meanwhile the Aliens Office, with the help of Sudanese intelligence services, was seeking to identify and expel irregularly staying Sudanese nationals to Khartoum.

On 26 September 2017, the united chambers of the Aliens Litigation Council, the administrative court, warned the Aliens Office against the forced removal of Sudanese nationals in violation of Article 3 ECHR.[44] Next, the Court of Cassation ruled on the legality of the detention. In its judgment of 20 December 2017, it reversed the decision of the investigating courts ordering the release of the person concerned.[45] However, the extension of detention is subject to further appeals, and thus the detention judge can pronounce on several occasions. In this instance the indictment division ordered the person's release. It considered that the administrative file did not show an assessment of the risk that a return to Sudan would represent with regard to the requirements of Article 3 ECHR. The measure involving deprivation of liberty was therefore judged unlawful: in view of the notoriously well-known information about the particularly alarming situation in Sudan, the Secretary of State for Asylum and Migration could not envisage the removal of the third-country national without ensuring that he would not be returned to a country where he would run a real risk of being subjected to treatment contrary to Article 3 ECHR.

Since the situation in Sudan could not be ignored by the administration, the judges considered that it was their responsibility to make the necessary checks to ensure that the return of the person concerned did not entail a violation of Article 3 ECHR, irrespective of the fact that he had not applied for asylum in Belgium.

[42] Court of Cassation (2e ch), judgment of 24 June 2015, RG no P.15.0762.F.

[43] Court of Cassation, judgment of 1 January 2018, P.18.0035.F; see also JB Farcy, 'Rapatriements vers le Soudan: l'obligation d'examiner les risques de traitements inhumains ou dégradants préalablement à tout éloignement' [February 2018] *Cahiers EDEM*.

[44] CCE judgment of 26 September 2017 (GC), no 192 584, available at www.rvv-cce.be/sites/default/files/arr/a192584.an_.pdf.

[45] Court of Cassation (2e ch), judgment of 20 September 2017, RG no P.17.1232.F.

The Belgian state appealed this judgment before the Court of Cassation, arguing that the person had failed to provide any prima facie evidence of the existence of a risk of inhuman or degrading treatment in the event of his return. However, the Court of Cassation did not follow the argument put forward by the State:

> Insofar as it amounts to arguing that the [authorities] would only be required to examine the risk invoked by an alien to undergo treatment contrary to Article 3 of the Convention when he has lodged an asylum application, the plea is unfounded.

The Court recalled the obligation for the Aliens Office to verify the existence of a possible risk that the person under a removal order might face treatment contrary to Article 3 ECHR. When an appeal is lodged, the investigating courts must assess whether the authorities have carried out such a control. As the Court pointed out, such an examination falls within the scope of the review of legality, and not the opportunity of detention. Accordingly, if the Aliens Office fails to verify the existence of a risk of inhuman or degrading treatment in the event of return to Sudan, the removal order, of which the detention measure is an accessory, does not meet the legal requirements. The appeal brought by the state was dismissed. This case illustrates once again that it is impossible to strictly confine the review of the detention judges solely to the measure of detention, without reviewing the removal order itself. Another conspicuous aspect of the case is that during the litigation, no references were made to the Return Directive, in particular Articles 5 and 9, or to the case-law of the CJEU.

B. Review of the Lawfulness of Detention and Article 8 ECHR

Several judgments by Belgian courts have considered detention measures unlawful because they violated the right to family life under Article 8 ECHR. The detention of an Algerian national who was the father of four children, the youngest of whom was two months old, and who benefited, like their Moroccan mother, from a right of residence in Belgium, was thus considered disproportionate to the interference it constituted to the right to private and family life.[46] In another case, however, a Belgian court held that there was no disproportionate interference in the right to family life in the case of a woman who was five weeks pregnant and wished to marry a Belgian.[47] Another judge again considered that the obligation to temporarily return to the country of origin in order to apply for a residence permit does not infringe Article 8 ECHR, and thus detention was deemed lawful.[48]

[46] Court of Appeal Bruxelles, mis acc, 18 July 2012, no 2583.
[47] Court of Appeal Bruxelles, mis acc, 13 August 2012, no 2757.
[48] Court of Appeal Bruxelles, mis acc, 20 November 2015.

Surprisingly, in 2018, the Court of Cassation ruled in favour of a very narrow review in cases of detention of asylum seekers, explicitly referring to EU asylum law. It held that neither Article 8 of the recast Reception Conditions Directive ('the recast RCD'),[49] nor Article 74-6, § 1bis, of the Aliens Act, which transposes the recast RCD into Belgian law and is in force at the time of the administrative decision, provide that the authority which decides to keep an alien in a given place, during the examination of his application for international protection, must take into account the circumstances relating to his family life.[50]

C. Detention of Children

A new Belgian law has reintroduced the possibility of detaining families with minor children in closed centres.[51] An action for annulment has been brought before the Council of State against the new legal provisions, and by a decision of the 4 of April 2019, the Council suspended this new regulation on the basis of risks linked to the high level of noise around the airport:

> It follows from the case law of the European Court of Human Rights that the Court admits the detention of young children in a place where they are exposed to significant airport nuisances for only an extremely short period of time. In the present case, it should be noted that, pursuant to the contested Royal Decree, young children may be detained for up to one month in houses located on the site of the 127bis centre, located on the runways of the important Belgian airport of Brussels Airport. Prima facie, taking into account this time limit, the positive obligations arising from Article 3 of the Convention on Human Rights should lead the King to provide that family homes may not be located in an environment in which children are likely to be exposed to serious noise pollution. The fact that the houses are in a building zone is not likely to upset this observation.[52]

In any case, this legislation raises other issues regarding its compatibility with the EU Charter and the ECHR as well. In the past, the ECtHR has condemned Belgium in several cases concerning the detention of children, as these measures violated Articles 3, 5 and 8 ECHR. While the ECtHR has never ruled that a child can never be deprived of his liberty under immigration legislation, it has never accepted that the actual conditions of detention were in accordance with the ECHR. In addition, it uses a stringent proportionality test.

[49] Directive 2013/33/EU of the European Parliament and of the Council of 26 June 2013 laying down standards for the reception of persons seeking international protection [2013] OJ L180/96.

[50] Court of Cassation (2e ch, F), judgment of 11 April 2018, P.18.0326.F.

[51] Royal Decree amending the Royal Decree of 2 August 2002 laying down the regime and operating rules applicable to places located on Belgian territory, managed by the 'Office des Etrangers', where an alien is detained, placed at the disposal of the government or maintained, in accordance with the provisions cited in Art 74/8 § 1 of the law of 15 December 1980 on access to the territory, residence, establishment and removal of foreigners (Aliens Act).

[52] Council of State, Decision of 4 April 2019, no 244.190

Thus, in *Muskhadzhiyeva*, the ECtHR judged that in view of the young age of the children, the duration of their detention and their state of health as attested by medical certificates, the conditions in which they had been held in the closed transit centre had attained the minimum level of severity required to constitute a violation of Article 3.[53] The ECtHR recalled in particular that the extreme vulnerability of a child was a paramount consideration and took precedence over illegal alien status. The fact that the four children had not been separated from their mother did not exempt the authorities from their obligation to protect them. In *Kanagaratnam*,[54] in similar circumstances, the ECtHR reiterated that the particular vulnerability of the children, who were already traumatised even before their arrival in Belgium as a result of circumstances relating to the civil war in their home country and their flight, had been recognised by the Belgian authorities when they recognised the family's refugee status. That vulnerability had increased on their arrival in Belgium, following their arrest at the border and placement in a closed centre pending their removal.

D. Interaction between Judges

The above examples illustrate the difficulties of the interaction between control by investigating courts and control by administrative judges. How can a decision by an investigating court finding that removal violates fundamental rights be reconciled with an administrative decision ruling in the opposite direction, sometimes validated by the Aliens Litigation Council?[55] We have seen that this difficulty also results from Article 72 of the Aliens Act, which entrusts the criminal courts with the task of 'verifying whether the measures involving deprivation of liberty and removal from the territory comply with the law without being able to rule on their appropriateness'.

The majority of the case-law pronounced by criminal courts is in line with the judgments taken by administrative judges, and considers that it is not possible to diverge from these judgments on residence even if the situation has changed, for example as a result of appeals, new requests or the intervention of another authority, such as a criminal investigating judge. Thus, the Court of Cassation emphasises that neither the fact that a non-suspensive appeal is pending before the Council of

[53] ECtHR 19 January 2010, *Muskhadzhiyeva and Others v Belgium*, App No 41442/07. The applicants – a mother and her four children (aged seven months, three and a half years, five and seven years at the material time), Russian nationals of Chechen origin – arrived in Belgium, where they sought asylum. As they had spent some time in Poland, the Polish authorities agreed to take charge of them, by virtue of the Dublin II Regulation. The Belgian authorities accordingly issued a decision ordering them to leave the country. In January 2007 they were placed in a closed transit centre run by the Aliens Office near Brussels airport, pending their removal.

[54] ECtHR, *Kanagaratnam and others v Belgium*, App No 15297/09, 13 March 2012.

[55] Court of Appeal Bruxelles, mis acc, 4 April 2014, no 1279.

State or the Aliens Litigation Council,[56] nor the introduction of an application for a residence permit on humanitarian grounds subject to the Minister's discretionary power,[57] nor the fact of being a civil party against the police officers who made the arrest,[58] allows one to challenge the legality of detention.

Even if an investigating judge lifts an arrest warrant while asking the applicant not to leave Belgian territory, this is not sufficient to authorise him to remain on the territory, according to the Court of Cassation. In this case, the judges of appeal had, in accordance with Article 72 of the Aliens Act, refused to rule on the advisability of the measure of deprivation of liberty and removal from the territory, thus confirming the continuation of this deprivation of liberty, even if an investigating judge had set the plaintiff free by imposing the condition not to leave the territory.[59]

These difficulties are mainly linked to the fact that detention is a means of enforcing a removal order, aimed at an irregularly residing third-country national. The coherence problems reported are much less significant when it comes to the detention of third-country nationals who are legally residing in the territory, such as asylum seekers. An asylum seeker may be detained during the asylum procedure for various reasons: if he applies at the border; if he is found to be abusing the asylum procedure; if he presents a danger to public order; or if he is in the Dublin phase. In these cases, the judge assesses the reasons given for depriving the person of liberty: is there a risk of absconding? Is the request abusive? The judge's review concerns detention only and is generally based on more precise criteria.[60]

[56] Court of Cassation, judgment of 18 April 2007, RG no P.07.0320.F; Court of Appeal Bruxelles, mis acc, 20 Nov 2015.

[57] ibid. See also Court of Cassation, judgment of 27 July 2010, RG no P.10.1206.F.

[58] Court of Cassation, judgment of 4 Oct 2006, RG no P.06.1208.F.

[59] Court of Cassation, judgment of 12 November 1997, RG no P.97.1355.F; see also Court of Appeal Bruxelles, mis acc, 1 December 2015. The Court of Appeal, relying on the case-law of the Court of Cassation, stated that: '[A]ny conditions of residence set by the investigating judge are intended to apply only if the person concerned obtains a right of residence in the territory and do not result in the granting of such a right, this competence being vested exclusively in the administrative authority.'

[60] For instance, the Court of Cassation has judged that a decision to take into consideration a repeated asylum application by the CGRA means that the reason to detain grounded on the abuse of the asylum procedure is no longer valid. The fact that the application has been considered leads to the conclusion that there can be no question of fraud or misuse of the asylum procedure in accordance with Arts 74/6 §1bis, 9° and 12° of the Aliens Act. See Court of Cassation, judgment of 16 January 2018, P.18.0002.N. According to another Court of Cassation judgment, the automatic detention of asylum seekers at the border is illegal. The Court of Cassation considered that the only grounds for attempting to enter the kingdom to apply for asylum without satisfying the conditions of the law do not allow not for the Aliens Office to resort to placement in a closed centre in order to guarantee a possible return when it has not carried out an individualised examination of the applicant's situation: Court of Cassation, judgment of 27 December 2017, P.17.1244.F. It also ruled in an asylum case that: '[T]he Dublin III Regulation is applicable to the detention of an asylum seeker in a Member State, in particular where it does the subject of a request to take back, even if no new application for protection has been submitted has been introduced in the Member State making the request for recovery.' See Court of Cassation, judgment of 20 December 2017, P.17.1192.F.

VII. Procedural Differences in Treatment between Third-Country Nationals and Persons Subject to Criminal Proceedings

In addition to the ambiguities described above, recourse to the procedure before the investigating courts disadvantages the third-country national as they are in some respects treated worse, legally speaking, than a defendant or an accused person. Proceedings before the investigating courts on immigration detention are governed by Articles 71 et seq of the Aliens Act and the Pre-trial Detention Act. This last reference is ambiguous and generates recurring interpretation difficulties, making it hard to determine which law on pre-trial detention is applicable. Indeed, on the date the Aliens Act entered into force, the provisions on preventive detention were contained in a law of 20 April 1874 and in the Code of Criminal Procedure. The new law on preventive detention of 20 July 1990 followed the Aliens Act of 15 December 1980.

The Court of Cassation infers from this that 'the law of 20 July 1990 on preventive detention, which devotes a chapter to an appeal in cassation, has not amended article 72 of the law of 15 December 1980'.[61] Consequently, notwithstanding the entry into force of a new law on preventive detention, appeals against immigration detention are still regulated by the previous legal framework, including less favourable time limits for lodging appeals in cassation.[62] The Court of Cassation's excessively formalistic reasoning in this area reinforces legal uncertainty and creates an unjustified difference in treatment.

In addition, the Court of Cassation has refused to refer a question to the CJEU for a preliminary ruling on accelerated judicial review.[63] The question concerned the time limit within which the Court of Cassation is required to rule when it is seized with an appeal against a decision by an Indictment Chamber to detain an illegal alien. In settled case-law, as discussed above, the Court considers that the time limit of six days for lodging an appeal against preventive detention as laid down in the Act of 20 April 1874 and that the Code of Criminal Procedure applies in the case of immigration detention, and not the delays found in the new law governing preventive detention, which is 15 days.

[61] Court of Cassation, judgment of 20 September 2017, RG no P.17.0933.F.

[62] See L Denys, 'Antwoord op de noot "Wettigheidscontrole op de aanhouding van een illegale vreemdeling met het oog op verwijdering van het grondgebied"' [2013] *Rechtskundig Weekblad* 1395; JB Farcy, 'Le pourvoi en cassation en matière de privation de liberté d'un étranger demeure soumis à des règles procédurales distinctes de celles relatives à la détention préventive: un formalisme excessif ?' [2017] *Cahiers EDEM*; S Sarolea, 'Le pourvoi en cassation en matière de privation de liberté d'un étranger soumis à des règles procédurales distinctes de celles relatives à la détention préventive' [August 2016] *Newsletter EDEM*; and D Vandermeersch, 'La détention préventive de la personne présumée innocente et la privation de liberté de l'étranger' [2015] *Revue Droit Pénal* 602. See also Court of Cassation (2e ch), judgment of 10 September 2014, RG no P.14.1374.F; Court of Cassation (2e ch), judgment of 21 December 2011, RG no P.11.2042.F; and Court of Cassation (2e ch), judgment of 15 June 2016, RG no P.16.0604.F.

[63] Court of Cassation, judgment of 20 September 2017, RG no P.17.0933.F.

However, the law of 20 July 1990 should be applicable for reasons of legal certainty. Moreover, this new law did not merely amend the law of 1874 but replaced it completely, with the exception of the provisions relating to compensation in the event of inoperative preventive detention. It seems contrary to legal certainty for a judge to apply a law that has been repealed for more than 25 years. Furthermore, the application of the Act of 20 April 1874 creates a difference in treatment between two categories of persons deprived of their liberty who, according to 1980 legislation, were to be treated similarly. Although the law of 15 December 1980 provides for the alignment of the regime of detention of irregular aliens in view of their removal with that of pre-trial detention, the Court of Cassation case-law creates an unjustifiable difference of treatment.

Preventive detention refers to the deprivation of liberty of a person suspected of having committed an offence, and is subject to strict legal conditions. Although the deprivation of liberty of an illegal alien in view of their removal in no way constitutes a measure of preventive detention (recalling that illegal residence falls under criminal law, not administrative law), the 1980 law aimed to apply the latter's procedural conditions to the former with a view to 'assimilating the foreigner to a Belgian'. It also emerged from the explanatory memorandum to the Act of 15 December 1980 that the Government did not wish to follow the advice of the Council of State to completely organise the procedure in the Act because 'this would create the risk of omissions and the need to amend the Act if changes were made to those relating to remand'. The intention, then, was to apply the regime of remand while considering its possible future developments.

Moreover, whether detainees are remand prisoners or illegal aliens, in both cases they are deprived of their liberty on a preventive basis, and the lawfulness of their detention is only monitored by the judiciary a posteriori. This indicates the need for an accelerated procedure. However, according to the case-law of the Court of Cassation, foreign nationals detained in view of their removal and persons suspected of having committed a criminal offence are treated differently, to the detriment of foreign nationals. In addition to the question of time limits, there is also the fact that the Public Prosecutor's Office can appeal to the Court of Cassation against a decision of a Chamber of Indictments ordering the release of a third-country national. This difference in treatment, created by the Court against the legislative intent, is not justified and the Court should not hide behind excessive legal formalism to maintain a new 'migration exception'. The Constitutional Court could thus be seized of the question, even if it seems unlikely that the Court of Cassation would ask for a preliminary ruling, seeing that it refused to do in September 2016 on the grounds that the principle of reasonable time might be violated. In that same judgment, the Court refused for the same reason to refer a question to the CJEU for a preliminary ruling. The litigants had argued that it should ask the CJEU about the conformity of Belgian laws regulating appeal before the Court of Cassation with Articles 13 and 15 of the Return Directive, requiring a speedy judicial review. The Court refused to do so since, in its view, the reasonable time limit might be exceeded in the present case if a preliminary question were put. Moreover, it argued that European law does not determine the period within which a decision of the Court must be taken.

The first argument by the Court seems nonsensical since it results in the European judge being de facto excluded from litigation. Moreover, Article 267 TFEU on the preliminary ruling procedure does not provide for such a limitation. On the contrary, it specifies that 'if such a question is raised in a case pending before a national court concerning a person detained, the Court shall decide as soon as possible'. An urgent preliminary ruling procedure (PPU) has been set up to enable the CJEU to deal with the most sensitive questions relating to the areas of freedom, security and justice within a considerably shorter time frame, and it has been used several times in cases relating to the Return Directive. This case-law illustrates the differences in treatment of criminal offenders and migrants, the procedure applied to migrants being less protective.

VIII. Conclusions: The Urgent Need to Reform a Low-Quality Legal Framework

This chapter has attempted to illustrate the poor quality of the current legal regime regulating detention of third-country nationals in Belgium. The Belgian legal framework does not work due to the combined procedure and delimitation of judicial competences which are not interlinked or communicating. In addition to the questions that this alignment inevitably raises on the symbolic level, seeing that it implies a blurring between third-country nationals and criminal offenders, this competence is problematic in two other respects. First, the risk of conflict between the decisions of the criminal judge and those of the administrative judge is high, and such conflict undermines the transparency and coherence of the system. Second, in most situations both administrative review and judicial review have non-suspensive effect and suffer from a lack of effectiveness. To return to Lewis Carroll, Alice's rabbit is always late, and so is the criminal judge who rules on freedom when the administrative judge has already ruled. Alice finds herself in an absurd world or at least one foreign to her, like the criminal judge immersed in immigration law.

The complexity of applicable standards subjects third-country nationals and their counsels to a high degree of legal uncertainty. These defects raise questions in the face of the requirements derived from Article 5 ECHR concerning the quality of the law, which should be clear and foreseeable. With regard to the Return Directive, a particular problem is whether Belgian law provides for a speedy judicial review and the refusal of the Belgian judge to refer a question to the CJEU.

More fundamentally, these difficulties add to the inadequacy of the control exercised by the investigating courts mentioned above. The law confines the judge to a review of legality to the exclusion of opportunity, whereas the Return Directive requires such an examination, including of the proportionality of the detention.

Finally, the criminal judge is to review the legality of detention in view of removal, while the removal order itself is reviewed by the administrative judge. If it is merely a question of deciding on the subsidiarity of the use of detention, there is not much difficulty. However, if it is a question of examining, via assessing the deprivation of liberty, a violation of the right to respect for family life or the existence of a risk of inhuman and degrading treatment, the criminal court runs the risk of adopting a decision contradicting that taken by its administrative counterpart.

As stated in the invitation recently made by Damien Vandermeersch to set up a full judicial review of the detention of third-country nationals, all human beings deprived of their liberty, Belgian or foreign, innocent or presumed innocent, must have access to a full judicial remedy to verify and assess the absolute necessity of their continued detention.[64] The issue of the effectiveness of judicial control has serious ramifications for the entire field of migration law, particularly when it comes to the deprivation of liberty. This chapter has tried to demonstrate this and to argue in favour of reform of judicial oversight.

[64] Vandermeersch (n 65) 618.

12

Can the Return Directive Contribute to Protection for Rejected Asylum Seekers and Irregular Migrants in Detention? The Case of Greece

ANGELIKI PAPAPANAGIOTOU-LEZA AND STERGIOS KOFINIS

I. Introduction

Detention of third-country nationals (whether under the recast Reception Conditions Directive or the Return Directive)[1] is one of the most difficult issues of immigration law in contemporary Greece, and a permanent cause of rulings against the Greek state by the ECtHR. The increasing migration flows of recent years have only aggravated already existing dysfunctions of the system of administrative detention. Practices of automatic and systematic detention by police authorities, detention decisions usually inadequately reasoned, insufficient detention facilities, and detention of under-age immigrants at inappropriate facilities are only some of the well-documented failures of the Greek administration in this field.[2] In this framework, the role of administrative judges, who are entrusted with

[1] Directive 2013/33/EU of the European Parliament and Council of 26 June 2013 laying down standards for the reception of applicants for international protection (recast), 29 June 2013 [2013] OJ L180/96 (Recast Reception Conditions Directive), and Directive 2008/115/EC of the European Parliament and of the Council of 16 December 2008 on common standards and procedures in Member States for returning illegally staying third-country nationals, 16 December 2008 [2008] OJ L348/98 (Return Directive).

[2] See eg Amnesty International, 'Greece: Irregular Migrants and Asylum-Seekers Routinely Detained in Substandard Conditions' (27 July 2010) available at www.amnesty.org/en/documents/EUR25/002/2010/en/ (accessed 11 September 2019); Medecins Sans Frontières, 'Invisible Suffering' (1 April 2014) available at www.msf.org/invisible-suffering (accessed on 13 September 2019); Human Rights Watch, '"Why Are You Keeping Me Here?" Unaccompanied Children Detained in Greece' (8 September 2016) available at www.hrw.org/report/2016/09/08/why-are-you-keeping-me-here/unaccompanied-children-detained-greece (accessed 13 September 2019); Greek Ombudsman, 'Migration Flows and Refugee Protection: Administrative Challenges and Human Rights Issues' (April 2017) available at www.synigoros.gr/?i=human-rights.en.recentinterventions.434107 (accessed 13 September 2019).

judicial review of administrative detention of third-country nationals in the Greek legal order, is pivotal in guaranteeing the fundamental right to personal freedom of every person within the Greek territory.

Nowadays, the detention of third-country nationals pending removal is governed in the Greek legal order by Articles 30–32 of Law 3907/2011,[3] which transposed the Return Directive into Greek domestic law. Following the rejection of their asylum application, third-country nationals are considered irregular migrants and, after a return decision is issued or one that had already been issued is re-enacted, their detention is subject to the provisions and safeguards of the Return Directive as transposed by Law 3907/2011. The detention of asylum seekers is governed by the provisions of Article 46 of Law 4375/2016,[4] which provides for special terms and conditions for their detention. Actions against detention decisions, both regarding asylum seekers and third-country nationals pending removal, commonly referred to as 'objections against detention', are provided for by Article 76 of Law 3386/2005.[5]

The supranational nature of provisions governing the detention of aliens render it mandatory for national judges, when scrutinising detention decisions, to enter into various forms of judicial interaction with legal authorities beyond the boundaries of their domestic legal order. However, these interactions are not always visible. In the case of Greece, it is worth highlighting the absence of any preliminary references to the CJEU, or of any citations of the case-law of foreign domestic courts. This is particularly noteworthy as, on one hand, Greek administrative judges regularly encounter problems of interpretation of EU law when reviewing detention decisions. On the other hand, it is commonplace for administrative judges to cite jurisprudence by the CJEU or the ECtHR in order to support a particular interpretation of the relevant provisions. Moreover, we shall see that the case-law of the two European courts has an impact on the Greek jurisprudence regarding administrative detention of aliens through the gradual modification of the legislation governing the powers of judicial review.

This chapter's working hypothesis is that the reason for the limited amount of judicial interaction in the relevant Greek case-law (the lack of any preliminary references and of any citations of the case-law of foreign domestic courts) lies in the nature of the legal remedy provided for by domestic legislation and its inherent constraints. In the following pages we will try to substantiate this hypothesis, while exploring the impact that the Return Directive and the CJEU and the ECtHR

[3] Law 3907/2011 of 26 January 2011 on the establishment of an Asylum Service and a First Reception Service, transposition into Greek legislation of Directive 2008/115/EC 'on common standards and procedures in Member States for returning illegally staying third country nationals' and other provisions (Official Gazette 2011 issue A no 7).

[4] Art 46 L 4375/2016 transposes into domestic law Art 26 of the Return Directive and Arts 8–11 of the Recast Reception Conditions Directive.

[5] Law 3386/2005 of 23 August 2005 on the 'Codification of Legislation on the Entry, Residence and Social Integration of Third Country Nationals on Greek Territory' (Official Gazette 2005 issue A no 212).

jurisprudence have had on the domestic judicial review powers regarding the terms and conditions of the detention of third-country nationals.

First, we will discuss the evolution of the national legislation regarding objections against detention as the sole legal remedy available to third-country nationals in detention, through the prism of the Greek legislator's compliance with both EU law demands, and the ECHR as interpreted in the case-law of the ECtHR (section II). Then we shall examine specific issues arising in the context of the judicial review of administrative detention decisions, in order to present the scope of judicial powers when judges are scrutinising the lawfulness of these decisions and assessing the need for alternative measures (section III).

II. Overview of the Evolution of the Legislation Regarding the Detention of Third-Country Nationals and the Legal Remedies Available to them

Before the Return Directive was adopted, the administrative detention of irregular migrants pending their removal was already provided for in the Greek legal order by Article 23 of Law 4310/1929[6] and subsequently by Article 27(7) of Law 1975/1991.[7] According to the provisions of the latter law, the third-country national could be detained administratively, if there was considered to be a risk of absconding or a threat to public security, until his removal was possible. However, no judicial remedy was provided for in the law against this detention decision. The issue reached the ECtHR in the case of *Dougoz v Greece*.[8] In *Dougoz*, the ECtHR found a violation of Article 5(4) ECHR, because 'the domestic legal system did not afford the applicant an opportunity to have the lawfulness of his detention pending expulsion determined by a national court'.[9] The judgment was delivered on 6 March 2001, and the Greek legislator's reaction was immediate: on 2 May 2001, Law 2910/2001 'on the entry and stay of aliens on Greek territory' was issued. Article 44(3) of this law introduced the legal remedy of 'objections against detention' to be adjudicated before the President of the Administrative Court of the district where the third-country national was detained.[10]

[6] Law 4310/1929 of 6/16 August 1929 'on the residence and movement of immigrants in Greece, police control, passports and deportations' (Official Gazette 1929 issue A no 287).

[7] Law 1975/1991 of 21 November 1991 on the 'entry-departure, residence, employment, deportation of aliens, procedure for recognition of foreign refugees and other provisions' (Official Gazette 1991 issue A no 184). See I Papageorgiou, 'Introduction: Administrative Detention of Aliens: the Historical and Legal Framework' [2014] *Migration Law Review* 148 (in Greek); V Papadopoulos, 'The Maximum Detention Period of Third-Country Nationals – Exceeding it and Imposing New Detention on the Same Ground' [2014] *Migration Law Review* 158 (in Greek).

[8] ECtHR 6 March 2001, *Dougoz v Greece*, App No 40907/98.

[9] ibid, para 63.

[10] Both the introduction of the draft bill and the discussions at the Parliamentary Committee had taken place before the delivery of the judgment, yet while the case was under deliberation by the

This provision, which did not modify the above-mentioned terms and conditions laid down in law for the detention of irregular migrants (ie risk of absconding or threat to public security), stipulated that an administrative judge should review the 'lawfulness' of the detention. If the objections were upheld, Article 44(4) of Law 2910/2001 made it obligatory for the judge to set a maximum time limit of 30 days for the voluntary departure of the irregular migrant. Regarding the procedural rules to be followed, the law referred to Article 243 of the Administrative Procedure Code (APC), which governed the judicial review of ('objections against') the arrest and detention of debtors of the state. The latter provision provided for the appearance in person of the detainee before the judge in order for the objections against detention to be tried. However, it did not stipulate that legal assistance for the detainee was mandatory, and it did not allow for an appeal against the judgment. Thus, the administrative judge became the last-instance judge of objections against detention of third-country nationals.

Subsequently, Article 76(3) and (4) of Law 3386/2005 replaced Article 44(3) and (4) of Law 2910/2001. According to the new provisions, an administrative order of detention of an irregular migrant could be issued if there was a risk of him absconding or if he was considered a threat to public security. The maximum duration of detention could not exceed three months and the detainee had the right to lodge objections against his detention before the administrative judge. The objections could be upheld if the judge considered that there was no risk of absconding or threat to the public order or if 'he [the judge] objected to the detention'.[11] If the objections were upheld, the judge was obligated to set a time limit of 30 days to the third-country national to depart from the country voluntarily. Contrary to what Article 44(3) of Law 2910/2001 stipulated, the new law made no reference to the procedure to be followed at the hearing on the objections and contained no explicit provision giving authority to the administrative judge to review the 'lawfulness' of the detention decision. Furthermore, the explanatory memorandum to Law 3386/2005 gave no hint whatsoever about this legislative gap, which seemed to limit the scope of judicial powers of review. Inevitably, this omission caused legal uncertainty with regard to both the judge's authority to review the 'lawfulness' of the detention decision for reasons apart from those concerning matters of risk of absconding or public security and the procedure to be followed.

On the matter of the procedure, administrative judges filled the legal gap by continuing to refer to the most closely related provisions of the APC, ie the aforementioned Article 243 on the objections against the arrest and detention of debtors of the state.[12] Regarding the crucial issue of whether the judge has the

Strasbourg Court. The lack of any reasoning regarding the introduction of the new legal remedy in the explanatory memorandum to Law 1975/1991, and of any reference to it during the discussions at the Parliamentary Committee, warrant the conclusion that the provision at stake was hastily introduced as a response to a possible conviction by the ECtHR.

[11] Law 3386/2005, Art 76, para 4.

[12] See A Papapanagiotou-Leza, 'Objections to the Detention of Third-Country Nationals Pending Removal' [2007] *Dioikitiki Diki* 1099 (in Greek).

power to scrutinise the 'lawfulness' of the detention decision fully, or was limited to reviewing the substantive preconditions of detention,[13] the Greek case-law was split: certain judges were still exercising full scrutiny over the lawfulness of the detention decision, based on the explicit provision of Article 243 APC,[14] while others declined to exercise any such power.[15]

The legal uncertainty that arose from this legislative ambiguity was eventually challenged before the ECtHR. In 2009, the ECtHR ruled in *SD v Greece* that there had been a violation of Article 5(4) ECHR, because the domestic legislation did not allow for a direct review of the lawfulness of the detention of an alien detained pending expulsion.[16] The President of the Administrative Court of Alexandroupoli had previously ruled in this case that the law did not allow the release of the detained third-country national if it could be deduced from the file of the case that he had no intention or possibility to leave the Greek territory within the 30-day time limit set by Article 76 of Law 3386/2005. Based solely on that ground, the national judge rejected the objections of SD because it was indisputable that he, being an asylum seeker, would not leave the country within the said time limit. According to the ECtHR:

> [T]he applicable domestic law does not allow for a direct review of lawfulness concerning the detention of a third-country national pending removal. ... Albeit finding the return decision unlawful renders the detention decision unlawful, ex officio, courts do not review separately the lawfulness of the detention of a third-country national pending removal.[17]

The Court also pointed out the

> ambiguity of the wording of art 76(4) Law 3386/2005 seemingly stipulating that, even if objections against detention were upheld by the judge, the latter was obliged to set a time limit of maximum 30 days for the voluntary departure of the objector.[18]

Additionally, the Court found that the lodging of an action for the annulment and suspension of the expulsion decision before the administrative courts would

[13] Namely, the risk of absconding and the threat to public security; reasonable prospect of removal was not considered a precondition at the time.

[14] See President of the Administrative Court of Alexandroupoli 16/2005.

[15] See President of the Administrative Court of Athens 1687, 1921/2002, 2664/2003.

[16] ECtHR 11 June 2009, *SD v Greece*, App No 53541/07. See also ECtHR 26 November 2009, *Tabesh v Greece*, App No 8256/07, para 62; ECtHR 12 December 2013, *Khuroshvili v Greece*, App No 58165/10, paras 123–25.

[17] As the Court explains: '[T]he notion of "lawfulness" under paragraph 4 of Article 5 has the same meaning as in paragraph 1, so that the detained person is entitled to a review of his detention in the light not only of the requirements of domestic law but also of the text of the Convention, the general principles embodied therein and the aim of the restrictions permitted by Article 5 para 1. Article 5 para 4 does not guarantee a right to judicial review of such breadth as to empower the court, on all aspects of the case including questions of pure expediency, to substitute its own discretion for that of the decision-making authority. The review should, however, be wide enough to bear on those conditions which are essential for the "lawful" detention of a person according to Article 5 para 1.' *SD* (n 17) para 72.

[18] ibid, para 73.

not lead to the suspension of the detention decision. Furthermore, such a procedure would also be lengthy and Greek law (Law 3226/2004) does not provide for legal aid in administrative cases.[19] On these grounds, the ECtHR found that the Greek legal order gave no possibility to the detainee to obtain a decision on the lawfulness of his detention by a court, as required by Article 5(4) ECHR.

The Greek legislator's response was once again immediate: Article 55 of Law 3900/2010 modified Article 76 of Law 3386/2005 in order to provide explicitly for the power of an administrative judge to review the lawfulness of the detention decision when objections against it were lodged by the third-country national.[20] According to the explanatory memorandum to this law, the lack of an explicit provision providing for judicial review of the lawfulness of detention decisions 'weakens the clarity of a provision necessary for legal certainty, which affects a fundamental right, such as personal freedom, while contradicting the case law of the European Court of Human Rights'.[21] Furthermore, given that Article 243 APC had in the meantime been repealed, as detention on the ground of non-payment of public law debts was abolished, the recast version of Article 76 of Law 3386/2005 now explicitly provided for certain procedural rules (such as the immediate submission of all evidence, the possibility of oral submission of objections, the immediate delivery of the judgment, the summary reasoning of the judgment and the appearance of the detainee before the judge). For the remaining aspects of procedure, it referred to other provisions of the APC, and more specifically the provisions regarding the requests for interim measures that, inter alia, stipulate that the decision is taken in closed session and that the presence of a lawyer is not mandatory.[22]

[19] ibid, para 74.

[20] Law 3900/2010 of 17 December 2010 'Rationalization of procedures, acceleration of administrative trial and other provisions' (Official Gazette 2010 issue A no 213). This does not mean that the judge could review all aspects of the lawfulness of the detention decision ex officio. According to Art 55, para 1, 'objections must contain specific grounds [for annulment of the detention decision]'. This requirement limited the judicial power of review to the grounds raised by the objector. There are three main exceptions to that rule. According to the general principles of administrative law, judges review ex officio: (a) the competence of the administrative authority that has issued the contested administrative act; (b) the constitutionality of the law that was applied; and (c) whether the administrative act is defective on account of its legal basis. The last point is of special relevance here: in the context of objections against detention, courts should review ex officio whether the detention is ordered on the basis of an ongoing removal procedure of a third-country national and whether the maximum time limit for detention has been reached.

[21] Explanatory Memorandum to the draft law, 'Rationalization of procedures, acceleration of administrative trial and other provisions', available at www.hellenicparliament.gr/Nomothetiko-Ergo/Anazitisi-Nomothetikou-Ergou?law_id=9f66f052-b60f-49a9-9124-e79f0c49208f (accessed 13 September 2019).

[22] The entry into force of the new provisions, however, did not prevent the Strasbourg Court from ruling that, in particular cases, the third-country national in detention still did not have an effective legal remedy against detention at his disposal. The ECtHR found that the application of these provisions by administrative judges in certain cases was restrictive, especially when it came to the review of the conditions of detention as an element of the lawfulness of the detention decision. See specifically ECtHR 11 February 2016, *RT v Greece*, App No 5124/11, paras 95–100, where the Court nevertheless accepted that in principle the new rules on the objections against detention are compatible with Art 5(4) of the Convention and that there are cases of Greek courts that make full use of the judicial powers provided for in the law.

Law 3907/2011 transposed the Return Directive into the Greek domestic legal order and introduced significant changes in the law regarding the detention of third-country nationals pending removal. According to the new provisions, the detention of the irregular migrant may be ordered (i) if there is a risk of absconding, or (ii) when the third-country national concerned avoids or hampers the preparation of return or the removal process, or (iii) for reasons of national security.[23] The maximum period of detention is set to 18 months. Moreover, for the first time, the law specifies minimum conditions of detention, with distinct provisions for minors and families. Another novelty of Law 3907/2011 is that – as required by Article 3 of the Return Directive – it introduces (at Article 18(g)) express criteria for determining the risk of absconding, such as previous penal convictions, non-compliance with the obligation to return within the time limit set for voluntary departure, possession of false documents, previous cases of absconding, lack of travel or other identification papers and non-compliance with an entry ban order.

The most striking difference from the previous system of judicial review is that, under the new law, the continuation of detention is to be reviewed ex officio every three months by the competent administrative authority. If that authority decides to continue the detention, its lawfulness is to be reviewed by the judge of the local administrative court.[24] Furthermore, the law expressly calls for the review of conditions of detention by the judge, both when objections against detention are lodged and when reviewing a decision for the extension of the detention ex officio.[25] Finally, the possibility of imposing alternative measures instead of detention was introduced (indicatively, deposit of an adequate financial guarantee, the obligation to appear before the police authorities at regular intervals or the obligation to stay at a certain place). As far as the procedural rules regarding the objections against detention are concerned, Law 3907/2011 refers once more to the provisions of Article 76 of Law 3386/2005, as modified by Law 3900/2010.[26]

The detention of asylum seekers is now governed by Article 46 of Law 4375/2016.[27] This provision contains detailed arrangements for the terms

[23] We will further elaborate on these grounds below; for now, it suffices to point out that national security is not one of grounds for detention provided for in Art 15 of the Return Directive.

[24] See below, under section III.E, for further elaboration on the issue.

[25] Practically, this means that, when ruling on an extension decision, the judge has to review the detention conditions ex officio, since the detainee is not involved in the procedure. This raises, of course, the technical (but crucial) issue of how the judge can be informed on the detention conditions at a specific detention facility.

[26] There is still no ECtHR case-law on the application of these new provisions. However, several appeals have already been lodged before the Court on the ground, inter alia, of a violation of Art 5(4) ECHR because of the limited scope of the judicial power to review the lawfulness of detention, especially concerning alternative measures. See eg ECtHR 4 December 2017, *Fady Masoud Ahmed v Greece*, App No 43129/13; ECtHR 25 January 2018, *EK v Greece*, App No 73700/13.

[27] Law 4375/2016 of 3 April 2016 'on the organization and operation of the Asylum Service, the Appeals Authority, the Reception and Identification Service, the establishment of the General Secretariat for Reception, the transposition into Greek legislation of the provisions of Directive 2013/32/EC on common procedures for granting and withdrawing the status of international protection (recast) (OJ L 180/60, 29.6.2013), provisions on the employment of beneficiaries of international protection and other provisions' (Official Gazette 2016 issue A no 251). Art 46 of Law 4375/2016 transposes Art 26 of Directive 2013/32/EC and Arts 8–11 of the recast Reception Conditions Directive.

and conditions of the detention of asylum seekers, which significantly differ from the ones concerning irregular migrants pending their removal, but still refer to Article 76 of Law 3386/2005 as regards the procedural rules for the lodging of objections against the detention of asylum seekers and the judicial powers of review of the detention decision.

III. Case-Law on Detention of Third-Country Nationals

Within this context of procedural and substantive provisions that determine the limits of the judicial powers to review the lawfulness of administrative detention, administrative judges regularly come across issues that call for the interpretation of EU law or for the correct application of the case-law of the two European courts. In this section, the role of domestic judges in this judicial interaction will be examined. This will be done by focusing on case-law regarding the most controversial issues arising in the context of objections against pre-removal detention.

A. Illegal Stay

Illegal stay is defined in Article 18(b) of Law 3907/2011 as

> the presence on the Greek territory of a third-country national who does not fulfill, or no longer fulfils the conditions of entry as set out in Article 5 of the Schengen Borders Code or other conditions for entry, stay or residence under the respective legislation in force.

This definition, which literally transposes the definition of illegal stay in Article 3(2) of the Return Directive, raised questions of interpretation regarding the specific case of third-country nationals who, after being arrested for irregularly entering the Greek territory and while in custody, submit a request for asylum before the authorities of the detention centre. The latter authorities are not competent according to the Greek legislation for the recording and processing of asylum applications. In these cases, the police would usually order the transfer of the third-country national to a Reception and Identification Centre and would issue a detention decision until the transfer is effected. Given that, according to the Return Directive, the legal remedy of objections against detention is only provided for in cases of detention pending removal, and according to the Recast Reception Conditions Directive in cases of detention of asylum seekers, courts had to consider the admissibility of the objections against this specific case of detention pending transfer to a Reception and Identification Centre. Furthermore, courts had to consider the lawfulness of this decision, given the lack of a clear legal basis for the imposition of this detention.

To the question at hand, two approaches may be identified in the relevant case-law. The first approach makes use of the relevant CJEU case-law and more specifically of the *Achughbabian* case.[28] Based on an interpretation of the latter, the Court ruled that since the Return Directive does not preclude the detention of a third-country national in order to determine whether or not their stay is legal, their detention for the period from submission of the asylum application to the transfer to a Reception and Identification Centre falls within the scope of the Return Directive. This is so because during that time, the competent authorities are trying to identify the person under constraint and to determine whether that person is an illegally staying third-country national, whose release would therefore undermine the purpose of the Return Directive.[29]

According to a different approach, under the new regime of Law 4375/2016 on asylum seekers, an administrative judge held that detention of a third-country national pending transfer to a Reception and Identification Centre does not fall within the scope of the Return Directive, since detention according to the latter is only allowed where there is a risk of absconding, or avoidance of or hampering the preparation of return or the removal process. In addition, the judge ruled that the said detention also does not fall within the scope of the recast Reception Conditions Directive, since the person detained has not yet formally lodged an asylum application.[30] However, the court, citing the relevant ECtHR case-law,[31] accepted that, since detention is in any case a deprivation of personal freedom, Article 5(4) ECHR prescribes an effective legal remedy to be available also to persons in this situation. It held that in the Greek legal order, the most suitable legal remedy was the objection against detention according to Article 76 of Law 3386/2005.[32] This way the judge extended the judicial powers of review of administrative detention through the direct application of ECtHR jurisprudence.

B. Risk of Absconding – Threat to Public Order and Safety

The Return Directive lists two exhaustive reasons to detain third-country nationals pending removal. However, the Greek legislator provides for three reasons for detention: the two already provided for in the Directive and 'in case of a threat to

[28] Case C-329/11 *Achughbabian* ECLI:EU:C:2011:807, paras 31–32.

[29] See President of the Administrative Court of Thessaloniki 467/2014. In our opinion, this is not a correct reading of the *Achughbabian* case, and more specifically paras 29 and 30 where the Court of Justice ruled that: '[T]he common standards and procedures established by Directive 2008/115 concern only the adoption of return decisions and the implementation of those decisions … it is apparent that the conditions for the initial arrest of third-country nationals suspected of staying in a Member State illegally remain governed by national law.'

[30] The question whether a *formal* application for asylum is needed for a person to be considered an asylum seeker or an *informal* expression of his wish to apply for asylum suffices, is still open in the Greek legal order, since there is no settled case-law on the issue. However, Art 34(d) of the Law 4375/2016 stipulates that an asylum seeker is a third-country national 'who declares orally or in writing before any Greek authority' his wish to apply for asylum.

[31] See ECtHR 12 January 2010, *Gillan and Quinton v the United Kingdom* App No 4158/05, para 57.

[32] See President of the Administrative Court of Kavala 430/2017.

national security'. In addition, amongst the objective criteria that should be used to determine whether or not there is a risk of absconding, as prescribed in the Return Directive, Article 18 of Law 3907/2011 lists the existence of previous penal convictions, pending criminal procedures, or strong indications that a crime has been committed or will be committed by the person in custody. Given that the CJEU has already ruled that the 'possibility of detaining a person on grounds of public order and public safety cannot be based on the Return Directive',[33] a question of nonconformity of Greek law with the Return Directive is raised in this context.[34]

Greek courts have neither taken a clear and uniform stand on this issue nor made a reference to the CJEU.[35] On the contrary, it appears to be standard practice to take into account, without further reasoning, prior convictions, pending criminal procedures or other indications that the detained person may pose a threat to national or public security, either as criteria of evaluation of the risk of absconding,[36] or even as separate reasons for detention on grounds pertaining to a risk to public security.[37] However, both lines of reasoning regarding public security reasons for detention pose problems of interpretation of the relevant provisions of the Return Directive and could (or probably should) be referred to the CJEU.

C. Conditions of Detention

The question of whether or not the administrative judge has the power to review the conditions of the detention of third-country nationals has been one of the most controversial issues regarding the remedy of objections to detention. Undoubtedly, the greatest influence on the Greek case-law on this matter has been the relevant ECtHR jurisprudence, especially regarding cases brought against Greece. However, the Greek judge seems, to date, reluctant to exercise his full powers of review on the issue, even though Article 30(1) of Law 3907/2011 expressly stipulates that, for the detention or the extension of the detention of a third-country national, the availability of suitable detention facilities and the possibility to safeguard decent living conditions should be considered. Moreover, the Return Directive (Articles 16 and 17) enlists specific conditions of detention that must be secured.

In particular, some judges reject complaints invoking the conditions of detention as inadmissible on the ground that, in the context of the objections against

[33] Case C-357/09 PPU *Kadzoev* (GC) ECLI:EU:C:2009:741, para 70.

[34] See also the 2014/2231 Formal Notice according to Art 258 TFEU from the European Commission to Greece regarding possible non-compliance of the domestic legislation to the Return Directive.

[35] It is important to remember here that, since no legal remedy against decisions on objections against detention is prescribed in law, first-instance courts are also courts of last instance and thus carry the obligation, under Art 267 TFEU, to refer to the CJEU questions regarding the interpretation of EU law.

[36] See eg President of the Administrative Court of Nafplio 1/2016.

[37] See eg President of the Administrative Court of Athens 80/2015; President of the Administrative Court of Livadia 40/2016; President of the Administrative Court of Chania 41/2017.

detention, the court has no power to review the living conditions of detainees. In a rather peculiar reasoning, they do so by citing the ECtHR case-law that found a violation of Article 5(4), claiming that the domestic legal order lacks an efficient legal remedy for the review of detention conditions.[38] However, the dominant tendency of the case-law nowadays is to examine complaints about inhuman and degrading detention conditions as to their merits, usually under Article 3 ECHR and with explicit reference to the relevant ECtHR case-law. Nevertheless, the outcomes of this examination vary largely: many judges reject the complaints as unsupported by (up-to-date and detention-facilities-specific) evidence, putting the burden of proof exclusively on the detainee.[39] In other cases, judges do make use of the standards established by the ECtHR case-law on degrading conditions of detention in order to review the living conditions at a particular detention facility. However, they typically conclude that there has been no violation of the right to decent conditions of detention.[40] Finally, in some cases, judges, in view of the ECtHR case-law, order the transfer, instead of the release. Consequently, the detainee is transferred from an obviously unsuitable detention facility (usually a police station cell) to a detention centre that meets the minimum standards (according to the Article 3 case-law by the ECtHR) of decent living conditions for detainees.[41]

D. Maximum Duration of Detention

The explicit establishment in Article 15(5) and (6) of the Return Directive of a time limit of 18 months as the maximum duration of detention pending removal is a rather important substantive safeguard of the rights of third-country nationals staying illegally in a Member State. In Greece, however, there have been attempts to override this time limit. Thus, the Legal Council of the State, a body that is not part of the judiciary but has, inter alia, a consulting role for the state, issued

[38] See eg President of the Administrative Court of Kavala 430, 468/2017, citing ECtHR 22 July 2010, *AA v Greece*, App No 12186/08. It should be noted that the Greek legal system is essentially monist and Greek courts are required to set aside national legislation conflicting with ratified international treaties, such as the ECHR.

[39] See President of the Administrative Court of Athens 127/2013, who ruled that an Amnesty International report on the living conditions at the particular detention centre was out of date; see also President of the Administrative Court of Corfu 55/2016.

[40] See President of the Administrative Court of Korinthos 92/2013, who ordered the Director of the Detention Centre of Korinthos to present to the court a full report on the living conditions at the Centre, before concluding that the conditions of detention therein did not constitute a violation of human dignity; President of the Administrative Court of Thessaloniki 187/2015; President of the Administrative Court of Athens 280/2016, who ruled that the detention in a police station for a short period of time does not violate Art 3 ECHR; President of the Administrative Court of Kavala 299/2017, who ruled that the living conditions at the Pre-Removal Detention Centre of Paranesti are decent and do not violate the objector's dignity.

[41] See President of the Administrative Court of Thessaloniki 228, 284/2016.

Opinion 44/2014. In this Opinion, it argued that in cases of irregular migrants whose return decisions cannot be executed due to a lack of cooperation on their behalf, 'a restrictive measure of compulsory stay in the pre-removal detention center may be automatically imposed upon the foreign national until he/she cooperates with the competent authorities'. This measure may apply irrespective of whether or not a risk of absconding remains after the 18-month time limit has expired. According to the Opinion, this measure does not constitute detention, but rather a way to implement the alternative measure of the obligation to stay at a certain place, expressly provided for in Article 22(3) of Law 3907/2011. Accordingly, it is regarded as lawful, because

> if all irregular aliens are released … this would jeopardize the public interest and the purpose of the EU and national legislation … since this leads to an indirect 'legitimization' of their stay … while it is estimated with certainty … that this release will inevitably lead to the rapid population growth of irregular immigrants in the interior of the country, with result in adverse effects on the public order and safety.

Apart from public interest reasons, the Opinion, in a rather paternalistic way, also invoked the interests of the persons in detention 'since they are vulnerable persons, without permanent residence, without legal documents and without the opportunity to work, and they are in danger of falling into deep poverty or into the hands of illegal networks which will exploit them'.[42]

The administrative decisions ordering, in accordance with the Opinion, the compulsory stay of the third-country nationals in a detention centre after the expiry of the maximum 18-month time limit of detention have been annulled as unlawful in the majority of the cases that reached the courts. Judges ruled that this measure essentially did not differ from detention.[43] As a result, they ordered the release of third-country nationals who had been detained for more than 18 months, citing the relevant provisions of the Return Directive and the ECtHR case-law.[44] However, in a few cases judges adopted a restrictive view on the scope of the legal remedy of objections to detention and thus on the judicial powers of review of these de facto detention decisions. They rejected the objections as inadmissible due to absence of competence of the administrative judge. Their argument was that the remedy of objections against detention is only provided for in case of a detention decision and not in the case of alternative measures.[45]

[42] Legal Council of the State, 4th Division, Opinion No 44/2014, issued on 24 February 2014.

[43] On the difference between deprivation of liberty and restrictions on freedom of movement, see especially ECtHR 25 June 1996, *Amuur v France*, App No 19776/92; and ECtHR 15 December 2016, *Khlaifia and Others v Italy*, App No 16483/12.

[44] See eg the President of the Administrative Court of Athens 2258, 3114/2014. See also Papadopoulos (n 8); Theodoros Tsiatsios, *Immigration Law*, 2nd edn (Sakkoulas, Athens, 2017) 169–75 (in Greek).

[45] See President of the Administrative Court of Komotini 19/2014; President of the Administrative Court of Alexandroupoli 76/2014.

E. Ex Officio Review of the Lawfulness of Detention

Article 30(3) of Law 3907/2011 introduced automatic ex officio review, at three-monthly intervals, of whether or not the terms and conditions that allow for the detention of a third-country national are still satisfied. It also introduced judicial review of the decision for extension by the administrative judge who has the power to scrutinise its lawfulness.[46]

An important issue that arose before the courts was whether all administrative decisions (issued every three months) in favour of the continuation of the detention should undergo automatic judicial review. The prevailing (but not settled) tendency in the case-law of administrative courts claims that administrative judges are not competent to review the lawfulness of the first decision for continuation after the initial three months of detention and should thus abstain from reviewing such decisions. On the other hand, the decision to extend the detention after the initial six-month period and all subsequent decisions to continue the detention up to the maximum limit of 18 months have to undergo judicial review.[47] This, of course, does not preclude a third-country national from lodging objections against any decision on the continuation of his detention.

Decision 9/2017 of the President of the Administrative Court of Rhodes is an interesting example of the way in which administrative judges addressed their new review powers. In this case, which concerned a continuation of the detention decision after nine months, the judge cited the CJEU case-law, more specifically *Mahdi*, and referred to Article 15 of the Return Directive, read in the light of Articles 6 and 47 of the Charter of Fundamental Rights of the EU,[48] to rule that:

> [T]he decision of the competent administrative authority, upon expiry of the maximum period allowed for the initial detention of a third-country national, concerning the prolongation of detention must be in the form of a written act that includes the reasons in fact and in law for that decision.

Based on this interpretation of the relevant provisions and on the exceptional nature of the decision to extend the detention of a third-country national, the judge annulled the decision of extension on the ground that it contained no particular reasons on the necessity of the extension.

[46] See A Papapanagiotou-Leza 'Ex Officio Review of the Lawfulness of Detention Under Art 30 Law 3907/2011' [2011] *Migration Law Review* 234 (in Greek). After the initial six months of detention the judge also examines, when reviewing the continuation decisions every three months, the additional conditions for the extension of the detention set forth in Art 15(6) of the Return Directive, ie refusal to cooperate and delays in obtaining the necessary documentation from third countries.

[47] But see President of the Administrative Court of Korinthos 50/2014, abstaining from reviewing decisions to continue the detention, even after 12 months of detention, on the ground that only the decision to extend the detention after the initial 6 months may be judicially reviewed.

[48] Case C-146/14 PPU *Mahdi* ECLI:EU:C:2014:1320, para 52.

F. Minors

Detention of minors is provided for in Article 17 of the Return Directive as a last resort, when no other alternative measure is available, and for the shortest period of time possible. The Greek legislation contained similar provisions even before the transposition of the Return Directive,[49] but their actual implementation had been far from sufficient. As the Greek Ombudsman noted in 2005, the main element of the way minor third-country nationals under expulsion procedures were dealt with was 'that being a minor – which entitles one to protection according to national law and the international obligations of this country – takes second place if one is in violation of the immigration law'.[50]

The core problem the police authorities, and subsequently the competent judicial authorities, face is the lack of sufficient accommodation facilities for unaccompanied minors in Greece, which turns their detention in pre-removal detention centres into the only available solution. However, these centres lack the necessary facilities and possibilities for recreation, education, etc. Thus, the administrative judge, when trying cases of objections against the detention of unaccompanied minors, has interpreted his powers of review in a broad way, in the light of the relevant provisions of the Return Directive and the Convention on the Rights of the Child, allowing him to order either the transfer of the minor to a shelter for unaccompanied minors, when places in such a shelter are available,[51] or the termination of detention and the referral of the case to the competent Public Prosecutor for minors, in order for him to make the necessary arrangements for suitable accommodation.[52] It is rather interesting, though, that there is usually no reference to the ECtHR case-law on the issue, probably because the judge feels that the provisions of the internal Greek legal order, after the transposition of the Return Directive, are sufficient and clear enough to allow him to reach the right conclusion.

G. Health Status

The health status of the third-country national who is detained pending removal is taken into consideration by the administrative judge, in the sense that a serious

[49] Art 118 of the presidential decree 141/1991 of 30 April 1991, 'on the "Competencies and Internal Actions of the Staff of the Ministry of Public Order, and Organization of Services"' (Official Gazette 1991 issue A no 58] provided for the protective custody of minors that had disappeared voluntarily or involuntarily and for their detention in facilities different from the police station detention cells.

[50] The Greek Ombudsman, 'Administrative Detention and Deportation of Alien Minors', October 2005, available at www.synigoros.gr/resources/docs/specialreport2005.pdf (accessed 11 September 2019).

[51] See President of the Administrative Court of Larisa 48/2013 and President of the Administrative Court of Athens 3080/2014.

[52] See President of the Administrative Court of Piraeus 229/2011.

illness or disability classifies the detainee as belonging to a vulnerable group of people. Humanitarian reasons, but also the need to safeguard the constitutional right to health, call for special treatment of this group of detainees.[53] This is especially so as the health of the person concerned may deteriorate because of the conditions of his detention. Thus, for example, the President of the Administrative Court of Athens ruled that the extension of detention for over seven months of a young third-country national, who was possibly suffering from inguinal hernia, kidney and heart disease, could aggravate the state of his health and ordered his release.[54]

Equally, in the case of a third-country national who had to undergo surgery urgently due to complications caused by a fractured limb, the President of the Administrative Court of Nafplio ordered his release, on humanitarian grounds, in order to safeguard his right to health.[55] It is interesting that judges in these kind of cases do not usually refer to the Article 3 case-law of the ECtHR[56] – probably to avoid the need to assess the specific conditions of detention – but prefer to invoke humanitarian reasons for the release of the detainee. In addition, the constitutionally enshrined right of every person to the protection of their health (Article 5(5) of the Greek Constitution) may serve as the normative basis for ruling on cases concerning detainees with severe health problems,[57] thus allowing for this limited reliance on the ECtHR case-law.

H. Alternative Measures

Articles 30(1) and 22(3) of Law 3907/2011 that transposed the Return Directive introduced the possibility of imposing alternative measures to detention in the case of third-country nationals awaiting return procedures. These provisions broadened the scope of judicial powers and, at the same time, imposed on the administrative judge the burden of reviewing in each case of detention whether or not this possibility was properly examined by the administration. Administrative courts have made extensive use of these provisions, mostly imposing on third-country nationals the obligation to report regularly to the local police authorities. Thus, for example, the President of the Administrative Court of Thessaloniki

[53] Art 5(5) Greek Constitution.

[54] President of the Administrative Court of Athens 406/2015.

[55] President of the Administrative Court of Nafplio 7/2015; see also President of the Administrative Court of Komotini 654/2017.

[56] According to the Court's settled case-law, the state of health of the victim is one of the circumstances of the case that have to be taken under consideration in order to assess whether ill-treatment attains the minimum level of severity necessary for it to fall within the scope of Art 3. See eg ECtHR 10 July 2001, *Price v the United Kingdom*, App No 12402/86; ECtHR 14 November 2002, *Mouisel v France* No 67263/01, para 37; ECtHR 11 July 2006, *Jalloh v Germany*, App No 54810/00, para 67; ECtHR 28 February 2008, *Saadi v Italy*, App No 37201/06, para 134.

[57] See eg President of the Administrative Court of Nafplio 7/2015.

upheld the objections against detention of an irregular migrant, because it was not clear from the case file whether or not the possibility of alternative measures had been properly examined by the police; in that case the judge imposed on the irregular migrant the obligation to report to the local police authority at ten-day intervals.[58]

However, it is interesting that in most cases, alternative measures, as required by Article 15(1) of the Return Directive, are imposed as an *additional* (and not alternative) measure on third-country nationals who would have been released anyway because the conditions for their detention were not met (eg because there was no risk of absconding).[59] This is probably because the judge feels obliged to make sure that the preparation of the return or the carrying out of the removal process will not be hindered by his decision to release the third-country national. This approach is even more obvious in the case of the judgment of the President of the Administrative Court of Korinthos, which ordered the release of a third-country national, because the maximum time limit of 18 months of detention had expired, but still imposed on him on the same legal basis (Articles 30(1) and 22(3) of Law 3907/2011 which transpose Article 15(1) of the Return Directive) the obligation to report to the local police authority at 10-day intervals.[60]

I. Detention of Rejected Asylum Seekers

As already mentioned above, once their application for asylum is rejected, third-country nationals are considered to reside illegally in Greece (unless they have some other kind of legal residence permit). Thus, they are subject to return procedures and may be detained, under the Return Directive, on the same grounds and under the same terms as any other irregular migrant. Consequently, courts usually do not differentiate significantly between the two categories of third-country nationals who are detained pending removal.[61] However, certain specific issues arising in the context of the objections against the detention of this particular subgroup of third-country nationals may be highlighted here.

Firstly, rejected asylum seekers regularly reapply for asylum in order to delay their removal. In several cases, the administrative judges called upon to rule on the lawfulness of the detention during the examination of this new application for asylum have found the latter to be manifestly abusive, based on the relevant CJEU case-law.[62] Consequently, they have rejected the objections against the detention,

[58] President of the Administrative Court of Thessaloniki 73/2014.

[59] See eg President of the Administrative Court of Patra 18/2017; President of the Administrative Court of Komotini 45/2015; President of the Administrative Court of Athens 432/2017.

[60] President of the Administrative Court of Korinthos 461/2014.

[61] See eg President of the Administrative Court of Piraeus 271/2017; President of the Administrative Court of Komotini 1/2018; President of the Administrative Court of Thessaloniki 21/2017.

[62] Case C-534/11 *Arslan* ECLI:EU:C:2013:343.

regardless of whether it had been imposed based on the Return Directive,[63] or the recast Reception Conditions Directive,[64] on the ground that the asylum application had been made with the sole intention of delaying or even jeopardising enforcement of the return decision taken against the third-country national.

Secondly, courts tend to consider non-compliance with the time limit for voluntary return set for the third-country national in the decision rejecting his asylum application to be evidence of the risk of absconding according to Article 18(g)(a) of Law 3907/2011. The same goes for his stay in the Greek territory following the expiry of the time limit granting the right to stay as an asylum seeker. The alleged risk of absconding based on these facts then allows for the detention of the third-country national pending removal and leads to the rejection of his objections.[65] Finally, third-country nationals often express orally their will to reapply for asylum during their detention pending removal following the rejection of their initial application, which usually is not considered to be of any legal significance regarding the lawfulness of the detention decision.[66]

IV. Conclusion

The main features of the judicial review of pre-removal detention of third-country nationals since its introduction into the Greek legal order in 2001 are: (i) the legislative requirement for a swift procedure and an immediate delivery of the judgment; (ii) the lack of appeals against this judgment; (iii) the requirement to provide only brief reasons for the judgment; and (iv) the lack of specific procedural rules for the objections against detention.

Each of these features, by themselves and combined with the others, seem to play a part in shaping the way Greek administrative judges perceive their role and the scope of their powers to scrutinise the lawfulness of the detention of third-country nationals, as well as the way they use (or do not use) the available tools for judicial interaction when interpreting the provisions of the Directive.

More specifically, the lack of legal remedies against decisions on objections against detention makes the unification of jurisprudence impossible since cases

[63] See President of the Administrative Court of Trikala 6/2018.

[64] See President of the Administrative Court of Athens 370/2017.

[65] See President of the Administrative Court of Athens 843/2016; President of the Administrative Court of Piraeus 324/2017; President of the Administrative Court of Athens 385/2017. However, see President of the Administrative Court of Larisa 83/2017, whereby the third-country national had in the meantime developed family links with a Greek citizen.

[66] See eg President of the Administrative Court of Athens 602/2017. However, see President of the Administrative Court of Athens 79/2018, whereby the objections against detention were upheld, taking into consideration the expressed will of the third-country national to reapply for asylum, provided they appear before the competent authority to process their new application for asylum within a 10-day time limit. See also above (n 31) on the discussion whether a formal application for asylum is needed in the Greek legal order.

do not reach higher courts. As a result, administrative judges often follow different interpretations of the relevant legal provisions, which leads to contradictory decisions on the same legal question. This undermines legal certainty and opens the path for the lodging of applications against Greece before the ECtHR for the violation of Articles 3 and 5(4) ECHR. In light of the above, a discussion has opened on the possibility of the introduction of an appeal before the Supreme Administrative Court (Council of State) against decisions on objections against detention.

A positive development regarding the gradual unification of the case-law of first-instance judges on detention is the recent introduction of a national single electronic case-management system. As all national judgments on objections against detention are now electronically available to every judge in the country, this system allows for the interaction between administrative courts around the country. Judgments on the lawfulness of detention, which are rarely published in law reviews, are now accessible to a wide audience of judges, eventually facilitating the implicit homogenisation of the relevant case-law. This is, of course, an ongoing procedure and it is still open whether it will lead to a better understanding and interpretation of the relevant provisions.

In addition, in the absence of specific procedural rules for the objections against detention, problems arise regarding, inter alia, the permitted means of evidence,[67] the sharing of the burden of proof and the required standard of probability. Finally, summary reasoning and the requirement for immediate delivery of the judgment may sometimes prevent administrative judges from searching for new ways to expand their powers of review of detention and from inventing novel legal solutions to tackle the problems arising from the implementation of the legislative provisions on detention.

These factors may also explain the lack of any preliminary references to the CJEU, even when complex cases involving issues of interpretation of EU law arise. Regardless of the possibility of the preliminary reference being dealt with under the urgent preliminary ruling procedure provided for in Article 107 of the Rules of Procedure of the Court of Justice, judges tend to consider the procedure of preliminary reference as a rather lengthy one, in tension with the domestic requirement for immediate delivery of the judgment and the requirements of the relevant ECtHR case-law.[68] Also, the complexity of certain legal issues may be underestimated due to the requirement for summary reasoning and the absence of review of the judgments' reasoning by higher courts. Thus, despite the importance

[67] For example, currently there is no consensus on the admissibility of solemn declarations as evidence: see eg the President of the Administrative Court of Kavala 468/2017, ruling that a solemn declaration is inadmissible as piece of evidence; yet see the President of the Administrative Court of Mytilini 21/2017 and the President of the Administrative Court of Piraeus 66/2017, who adopt the opposite solution.

[68] See eg ECtHR 29 July 2010, *Karimov v Russia*, App No 54219/08, paras 125–26; ECtHR 18 February 2016, *Doherty v United Kingdom*, App No 76874/11, para 80; and ECtHR 22 November 2016, *Abdullahi Elmi and Aweys Abubakar v Malta*, App Nos 25794/13 and 28151/13, paras 117–19.

of the fundamental freedom at stake, judges prefer to avoid the time and energy-consuming procedure of preliminary references and, instead, focus on the factual circumstances of the case.

The selective citation of CJEU and ECtHR judgments by the Greek judge in order to strengthen his reasoning is the direct outcome of the above: in the absence of higher courts' jurisprudence on matters of lawfulness of the detention of third-country nationals, and limited by the requirement for swift procedures and immediate delivery of the judgment, competent administrative judges, instead of using time-consuming, vertical, direct judicial interaction techniques, prefer to refer to the already existing and easily accessible case-law of the CJEU and the ECtHR, particularly the cases directly relating to Greece.

13

Can a Justice of the Peace be a Good Detention Judge? The Case of Italy

ALESSIA DI PASCALE

I. Introduction

The reception of the Return Directive in Italy proved to be problematic and stimulated extensive reflections in Italian academic literature.[1] Implemented following a delay, the new legislative provisions introduced some correctives, but did not substantially alter the regulatory framework. Even after transposition, the Italian legal system configured return in more restrictive terms than those postulated by the Directive.

The interaction between the national judiciary and the CJEU was already established at the deadline for the transposition of the Directive, leading to the landmark decision in *El Dridi*.[2] With this judgment, the Court provided essential interpretive criteria for the Directive, which highlighted the substantial discrepancy between Italian regulations and EU rules and led to legislative reforms. However, the ensuing judicial practice on expulsion and pre-removal detention, essentially developed by justices of the peace, has not been characterised by in-depth legal analysis of the facts of the case or of the relationship of Italian law with supranational norms.

[1] See generally: C Favilli, 'L'attuazione della direttiva rimpatri: dall'inerzia all'urgenza con scarsa cittadinanza cooperazione' [2011] *Rivista di diritto internazionale* 3; B Nascimbene 'La "direttiva rimpatri" e le conseguenze della sentenza della corte di giustizia (El Dridi) nel nostro ordinamento' [2011] *Gli stranieri* 1; A Liguori, 'L'attuazione della direttiva rimpatri in Italia' [2011] *Diritto, immigrazione e cittadinanza* 3; MT Collica 'Gli effetti della direttiva rimpatri sul diritto vigente, dalla difficile compatibilità col d.lgs. N. 286/1998 al necessario intervento correttivo: un percorso davvero concluso?' [2011] *Diritto penale contemporaneo* 24 giugno; F Viganò and L Masera 'Illegittimità comunitaria della vigente disciplina delle espulsioni e possibili rimedi giurisdizionali' [2010] *Rivista italiana di diritto e procedura penale* 2; G Savio, 'La nuova disciplina delle espulsioni conseguente al recepimento della direttiva rimpatri' [2011] *Diritto, immigrazione e cittadinanza* 3; P Bonetti, 'L'éloignement de l'etranger en situation irregulière en italie après la transposition de la diretice "retour"' in C Severino (ed), *La transposition de la directive "retour", France, Espagne et Italie* (Bruxelles, Bruylant, 2015); and L Masera, 'La rétention de l'étranger en Italie après la directive 2008/115/CE' in Severino (ibid).

[2] Case C-61/11 PPU *Hassen El Dridi, alias Soufi Karim* ECLI:EU:C:2011:268.

Since 2004,[3] powers of review regarding these issues have lain within the jurisdiction of justices of the peace, lay magistrates temporarily exercising judicial duties. The structure of the judicial process aimed at protecting the rights of foreigners with regard to pre-removal detention has two phases: a mandatory phase before the justice of the peace, (*giudice di pace* or GdP) providing for a speedy review of the lawfulness of detention ordered by the administrative authority, which must end with the adoption of a motivated written decree; and a possible appeal to the Court of Cassation.

This chapter will look at the role of the judiciary in the implementation of the Return Directive in Italy, especially regarding pre-removal detention, with specific attention to relationships with European norms and jurisprudence. First, the role of the GdP within the national judicial system will be examined, with a particular focus on its competences in immigration (section II). Then, the implementation of the Return Directive in Italy, and the compatibility of Italian return policy with EU rules, will be evaluated (section III). After this, the scope of the assessment of the lawfulness of detention carried out by the judiciary (section IV) and the practice of justices of the peace will be discussed (section V). Finally, the contribution by the Court of Cassation to a proper implementation of the Directive, and its reference to supranational legal and judicial sources in securing an effective implementation in conformity with European fundamental rights will be dealt with (section VI). The Court of Cassation has carried out an important orientation role in the interpretation and application of national law with frequent references to supranational sources. By contrast, decisions issued by justices of the peace ordinarily display limited legal analysis or motivation.

II. The Establishment of Justices of the Peace and their Jurisdiction on Immigration

Following intense debate during the 1970s and 1980s over their role and functions, GdPs were introduced in Italy in the 1990s. A GdP is a lay judge in the honorary judiciary, established on the basis of Article 106 of the constitution.[4] The objective was to counter the crisis in Italian civil justice, due to an increase in the number of proceedings and organisational inadequacies, which resulted in an excessively long process as well as high costs of minor litigation. The competences assigned to GdPs were responding, with different balances, both to the need to alleviate the workload of judges and to advance conciliation-based case resolutions. The list of competences attributed to them was formed by progressive layers. In particular,

[3] See Decree Law no 241/2004, converted into the Law of 12 November 2004, no 271.
[4] Law no 374 of 1991 which came into force in 1995.

criminal and immigration jurisdictions of the GdP were established a few years later.[5] GdPs underwent significant amendment in 2017,[6] when an overall reform of the honorary magistracy was adopted.

According to the 2017 reform, a GdP is engaged in judicial practice no more than two days a week. They hold office for four years, renewable once upon their request, provided they receive a positive evaluation of activities carried out during their mandate.[7] They are appointed upon resolution of the judicial governing body and the Minister of Justice.[8] GdPs have civil, administrative and criminal jurisdiction over minor disputes and, in principle, are able to resolve smaller claims with a conciliatory approach, without the possibility of custodial sanctions.

As stressed by Legislative Decree no 116/2017, GdPs are not state employees. Under the previous regime they were paid in relation to the quantity of work carried out (number of hearings held, measures taken) without considering time spent for hearings and deliberation, or the quality of the decisions. In light of this piecework system, as well as of the renewable office, their independence and autonomy was questioned.[9] Reforms to the compensation schemes aimed to make them consistent with part-time employment, and related to evaluation of their performance. Training obligations were also strengthened. Regulations now provide for an annual stipend, alongside a variable allowance tied to annual productivity objectives set by the president of the court where the GdP is installed. Evaluation criteria include punctuality in filing measures, management of hearings, relations with the other magistrates and the proportion of measures challenged compared to the office average.

In 2004, GdPs were entrusted with immigration-related powers, including monitoring the legality of police orders on pre-removal detention and expulsion

[5] Legislative Decree of 28 August 2000, no 274.

[6] Legislative Decree of 13 July 2017, no 116.

[7] Pursuant to Art 18(5) and (6) of Legislative Decree no 116/2017, the coordinator of the office of the GdP must draw up a report on the activity performed and the GdP's capacity, diligence, commitment as well as independence, impartiality and balance. To this end, at least 20 minutes of hearing and 20 orders are examined on a sample basis.

[8] Access to the role was innovated by Legislative Decree no 116/2017: if in the past the appointment followed a competition based on qualifications and an internship of six months, the current rules provide for a ranking based on qualifications, which follows a public call, and a six-month internship followed by a suitability assessment. Only those who receive a positive evaluation of the internship will be confirmed in the ranking and may be appointed. Together with training in the judicial offices, the internship also provides for the compulsory attendance of courses lasting no less than 30 hours, organised by the school of the judiciary (Scuola Superiore della Magistratura). This school was established by Legislative Decree 30 January 2006, no 26, with exclusive competence in relation to professional updating and training of members of the judiciary.

[9] Previously, a monthly allowance of €258.23 was paid to the justice of the peace, as well as ad hoc fees for each hearing and measure adopted. With regard to immigration, they received €10 for each measure adopted. The fact that they were paid on the basis of the number of measures issued constituted an incentive to the adoption of as many measures as possible, rather than to ensure the full implementation of the right of defence: see A Di Martino et al, *The Criminalisation of Irregular Immigration: Law and Practice in Italy* (Pisa, Pisa University Press, 2013) 60.

This competence appears, however, to contrast with the accepted role of this honorary figure in the Italian system.[10] Its introduction followed a ruling by the Constitutional Court,[11] which considered the law then in force illegitimate because it did not require judicial review prior to issuing a forced expulsion order. The new competence was justified by the need to lessen judges' workload which would follow such a ruling. Assigning responsibility for decisions that affect personal freedom (eg expulsion, detention) to a magistrate without thorough legal knowledge or specific immigration expertise has affected the rights of the persons the Constitutional Court had sought to protect.[12] Such concerns were also expressed by the UN Special Rapporteur on the Human Rights of Migrants in 2013:

> The judge deciding whether expulsion and detention orders should be extended is a Justice of the Peace without any particular expertise on immigration issues. Moreover, there seem to be limited ability of these lay judges to review the detention orders on the merits: rather, the confirmation of the orders appears to be limited to formal checks, thus resulting in a lack of real judicial control over the order.[13]

In 2017, a reform of the general system of international protection was adopted that established specialised immigration and asylum law sections in the courts.[14] No revision of their jurisdiction was undertaken. Thus they retain competence to evaluate the lawfulness of expulsions, forced accompaniment to the border, pre-removal detention, and the (rarely applied) measures providing for alternatives to detention, as well as appeals against administrative expulsion.

III. Securitisation of Migration and the Implementation of the Return Directive in Italy

The implementation of the Return Directive took place in a context of progressive tightening of the Italian legal framework on immigration. Since 2002, increasingly restrictive policies have aimed to prevent and suppress irregular migration. The years 2008 and 2009 in particular saw the 'securitisation' of immigration policy, with the adoption of 'security package' measures to combat crime that included major changes to immigration laws. In 2009 the intertwining of criminal and

[10] A Caputo and L Pepino, 'Giudice di Pace e *habeas corpus* dopo le modifiche al testo unico sull'immigrazione' [2004] *Diritto, Immigrazione e Cittadinanza* 13.

[11] Constitutional Court, judgment of 15 July 2004, no 222.

[12] See especially Bonetti (n 1) 71. Such attribution must rather be framed in a repressive context aimed at tightening the fight against irregular migration. The aim was to exempt the jurisdiction of immigration from the professional magistrates.

[13] François Crépeau, *Report by the Special Rapporteur on the Human Rights of Migrants, Addendum, Mission to Italy* (29 September–8 October 2012), A/HRC/23/46/Add.3, 17.

[14] See Art 1 Decree Law no 13/2017, as converted into law by Law no 46/2017.

immigration law was strengthened through the introduction of the 'crime of irregular entry and stay',[15] which initiated criminal jurisdiction over immigration for GdPs.

In this developing context of deterrence, the return process presented several points of incompatibility with EU rules. Coercive expulsion was a measure of general application and, if immediate removal was impossible, detention was applied generally rather than as a last resort. Expulsion was commonly accompanied by a 10-year re-entry ban. On the whole, in Italy custody of irregular foreigners was characterised more than in other European countries by the prevalence of criminal and non-administrative detention.[16]

As the transposition deadline was approaching and in order to reduce the impact of the Return Directive on ongoing expulsion proceedings, the Italian Ministry of Interior adopted a circular, instructing the competent authorities how to make the internal expulsion mechanism compliant with the Directive.[17] The instructions, however, were inadequate to adjust the Italian system of expulsions, because of the structural differences with the scheme introduced by the Directive.

The Trento Court of Appeal requested a preliminary ruling from the CJEU on some of these inconsistencies, particularly the criminal sanctions for irregular migrants who received an expulsion order. Article 14(5-ter) and (5-quarter) of Legislative Decree no 1998/286 ('Single Text on Immigration'), which provides for one to five years' imprisonment for remaining on the territory in spite of an expulsion order followed by a removal order to leave within five days, was assessed in relation to Articles 15 and 16 of the Return Directive which regulate detention and define the terms and conditions thereof. The Court criticised not only the specific rule which made non-compliance punishable with imprisonment, but

[15] Art 10-bis of the Consolidated Text on immigration as amended by Law no 94 of 2009. The initial draft was limited to illegal entry, but the incriminating rule was extended to also encompass illegal stay. Detention initially envisaged was then replaced with a fine, which is nonetheless a criminal sanction. This provision passed the scrutiny of the Italian Constitutional Court (judgment of 8 July 2010 no 249) and also underwent review by the CJEU in Case C-430/11 *Sagor* ECLI:EU:C:2012:777. The CJEU pointed out that the Return Directive does not preclude Member State legislation which penalises irregular stays by means of a fine which may be replaced by an expulsion order. The Court further noted that nothing in the Directive 'precludes the removal referred to in Art 8(1) of that Directive from being carried out in the context of criminal proceedings'. In 2014 the Parliament delegated the government to repeal this criminal offence, turning it into an administrative offence. The government, however, relying on the 'particularly sensitive nature of the interests involved', decided not to revise the legislation.

[16] See L Masera (n 1) 156.

[17] Ministero dell'Interno, Dipartimento della pubblica sicurezza, Prot 400/B/2010. The Circular stated the incompatibility of the return process set in the Consolidated Text on Immigration 'which is founded on the immediate and automatic expulsion of the foreigner who stays illegally on the national territory' and the Return Directive which 'introduces a "step-by-step" expulsive mechanism'. Despite the absence of legal provisions on voluntary departure, the circular invited the authorities to draw adequate motivations in order to demonstrate that the measures were adopted on the basis of careful consideration, in accordance with the Directive. It expressly affirmed: '[T]hese reasons, to be such as to counteract the effects of the appeal, must be articulated in such a way that it can clearly emerge the compliance of the return decision with EU law.'

also 'any [other] provision of Legislative Decree no 286/1998 which is contrary to the result of the Directive'.[18] A custodial sentence was held to 'risk … jeopardising the attainment of the objective pursued by that Directive, namely, the establishment of an effective policy of removal and repatriation of illegally staying third-country nationals'. The legislation appeared therefore to be incompatible with the Directive, requiring courts and national authorities to cease to apply it, in view of its direct effect.[19] The Italian courts conformed. The Court of Cassation, on the day of the ruling, stated that the judgment, in its 'authoritative' function concerning the interpretation of EU rules, had an effect comparable to that of a *jus superviens*. It resulted in the abolition of the norm in practice.[20]

These decisions forced urgent legislative reform.[21] Nonetheless, although some specific provisions were adjusted to give effect to the *El Dridi* judgment, this did not fundamentally transform the structure of the expulsion system.[22] Doubts and criticism about the compatibility of the provisions in force with the Return Directive have continued to be raised. In particular, Italian legislation and practice are still characterised by a high prevalence of forced removal, partly because the requirements for voluntary departure are difficult to meet.

A foreigner subject to an expulsion decree can be detained in a closed facility called a CPR (ie centre for permanence before return) for the time strictly necessary if expulsion is not immediately possible through accompanying the person to the border, or the *respingimento* (rejection or push back). This can be due to the need to rescue the person, to carry out identity or nationality checks, to acquire travel documents or for lack of suitable means of transportation. In this case, administrative detention (*trattenimento*) is provisionally ordered by the police commissioner (*Questore*).[23]

Pre-removal detention is a measure of general application in practice because under the relevant law the absence of a passport establishes a risk of absconding.[24]

[18] See *El Dridi* (n 2) para 61.

[19] C Amalfitano, 'La reclusione degli immigrati irregolari per la violazione dell'ordine di allontanamento del questore non è compatibile con le prescrizioni della c.d. direttiva rimpatri' [2011] *Cassazione Penale* 2786; and D Gallo, 'La voie italienne de la criminalisation des ressortissants de pays tiers en situation irrégulière partiellement remise en cause' [2011] *Revue des affaires européennes* 433.

[20] Court of Cassation, judgment of 28 April 2011, Case *Tourghi*, no 22105. See B Nascimbene, 'Immigrazione, Corte di giustizia e norme nazionali. L'immigrazione, gli afflussi dal Nord Africa, la crisi economica' [2011] *Il Corriere giuridico* 1337. See also B Nascimbene and A Di Pascale, 'Addressing Irregular Immigration through Criminal Penalties. Reflections on the Contribution of the ECJ to Refine and Develop a Complex Balance' in N Boschiero and T Scovazzi (eds), *International Courts and the Development of International Law. Essay in Honour of Tullio Treves* (The Hague, TMC Asser Press, 2013).

[21] The reform was put in place with Law decree 23 June 2011, no 89, converted and modified by Law 2 August 2011, no 129, which amended the Consolidated Text on Immigration. See A Natale, 'La direttiva 2008/115/CE. Il decreto legge di attuazione n 89/2011 – Prime riflessioni a caldo' [2011] *Diritto penale contemporaneo*.

[22] R Raffaelli, 'Criminalizing Irregular Immigration and the Returns Directive: An Analysis of the El Dridi Case' (2011) 13 *European Journal of Migration and Law* 467.

[23] The Questore is the public official in charge of the police in the provincial capital.

[24] See Art 13(4 bis), letter A) of the Consolidated Text on Immigration.

The same law excludes the application of alternatives to detention. Presuming a risk of absconding due solely to the absence of a passport has provoked criticism, as it prevents an overall assessment of the individual situation. Nevertheless, the Court of Cassation held this legitimate in light of the discretionary power the Return Directive affords national legislatures.[25] The exercise of discretion should, however, be consistent with the principles established by the Court of Justice in *El Dridi*, which designate pre-removal detention as a measure of last resort. The practical result is that pre-removal detention is the norm in return proceedings, to the detriment of the principle of proportionality.

The European Commission has identified inconsistencies in defining a risk of absconding as a critical issue in the application of the Return Directive in the Member States. To prevent diverging or ineffective interpretations, the Commission has proposed a common, non-exhaustive list of objective criteria to determine the existence of such a risk as part of an overall assessment of the individual circumstances.[26] In particular, under the proposed new Article 6, lack of documentation to prove identity is one of the criteria that can establish a risk of absconding, but the risk is not presumed solely on this basis.

In its 2015 *Celaj* ruling, referred by the Court of Florence, the CJEU addressed the relationship between immigration and criminal law.[27] It answered the question whether a criminal sentence of up to four years imprisonment imposed for a breach of a re-entry ban by Article 13(3) of the Consolidated Text on Immigration was compatible with the Return Directive. As in *El Dridi*, *Achughbabian* and *Sagor*,[28] the CJEU reiterated that the objective of the Directive would be undermined if removal were delayed by a criminal prosecution and imprisonment. But it distinguished the circumstances of the case from cases in which illegally staying third-country nationals were subject to a first return procedure. The Court had already held that the Return Directive does not in principle preclude penal sanctions, provided that they do not undermine the objective of the Directive. It considered that these are all the more applicable against illegally staying third-country nationals who re-enter a Member State in breach of an entry ban. The Italian legislation, which sanctions a violation of a re-entry ban with imprisonment, was therefore an opportunity to examine the consequences of a repeated violation of immigration rules. Recourse to criminal sanctions, in particular providing for the detention of irregular migrants after re-entry, was thus not considered contrary to the Directive.[29]

[25] See the discussion in section V below.

[26] See Proposal for a Directive of the European Parliament and of the Council on common standards and procedures in Member States for returning illegally staying third-country nationals (recast), COM(2018) 634 final of 12.9.2018.

[27] Case C-290/14 *Skerdhan Celaj* ECLI:EU:C:2015:640.

[28] *El Dridi* (n 2); Case C-329/11 *Achughbabian* ECLI:EU:C:2011:807; and *Sagor* (n 15).

[29] See L Masera, 'La Corte di giustizia UE dichiara il delitto di illecito reingresso dello straniero espulso conforme alla direttiva rimpatri (2008/115/CE)' [2015] *Diritto Penale Contemporaneo* 5 October.

IV. Judicial Review of Pre-Removal Detention Measures

Pre-removal detention is ordered by administrative authorities, but must be promptly screened for lawfulness by a judicial authority. Article 13(2) of the Constitution provides that in exceptional cases of necessity and urgency, established by law, the public security authority may adopt provisional measures, but judicial review of any restriction of personal liberty is a constitutional guarantee.[30] Pre-removal detention represents 'a measure affecting personal freedom' for which the guarantees referred to in the Constitution must apply.[31] The fact that the initial detention is routinely ordered by security authorities rather than by a court, however, raises doubts of constitutionality.

The detention order issued by the *Questore* must be communicated within 48 hours to the GdP and, if that authority does not confirm it in the subsequent 48 hours, it is revoked. After an initial period of 30 days, detention may be prolonged for an additional 30 days. The legislature intervened in 2014 substantially reducing the reasons for prolonging detention and subordinating them to the existence of specific circumstances that make identification likely. Although not expressly referred to in the law, these circumstances implement the requirement of a reasonable return prospect, per Article 15(4) of the Return Directive, previously not foreseen. After this first extension of 30 days, the request by the *Questore* of extending detention up to 180 days[32] in total is made subject to the existence of 'concrete elements' showing that the identification of the concerned person is likely or that such delay is necessary to implement the return. In addition, specific caution must have been applied to the foreigner who has already been held in prison on a criminal charge for 180 days, in which case the detention may be extended for a maximum of 30 days, and can be extended by a further 15 days in cases of particular complexity regarding repatriation.

The change introduced in 2014 forced the *Questore* to initiate the necessary identification procedures during the criminal imprisonment, in order to prevent the detention from turning into a double penalty. The reduction of the maximum terms of detention and the increase in the burden of proof by the administrative authority, which has to demonstrate 'concrete elements' indicating the probability of identifying the foreigner or the imminence of removal, have made the current provisions more compliant with the Return Directive and the principles established by the *Mahdi* ruling.[33] But some elements, such as the failure to provide for a judicial assessment of the permanence of the risk of absconding, which the CJEU considered cannot be based only on the absence of an identity document, appear not fully in line with the requirements identified by the CJEU. The same is true of

[30] See Art 13 of the Constitution.

[31] See Constitutional Court, judgment of 10 April 2001 no 105 and judgment of 15 July 2004, no 222.

[32] Such terms were reduced to 90 days in 2014 and then re-extended by Law Decree 4 October 2018, no 113, converted by the Law of 1 December 2018, no 132, with amendments.

[33] Case C-146/14 PPU *Bashir Mohamed Ali Mahdi* ECLI:EU:C:2014:1320.

the consequent possibility of applying less coercive measures, as well as the limited scope of investigation that is essentially based on the assessment of the elements which are provided by the administration. However, the absence of a reasonable prospect of return, which prevents the further extension of detention, not only leads to the termination of detention, but also to the adoption of the order to leave the national territory within seven days. The violation of such an order results in criminal liability.

In principle, the structure of the Italian legislation appears to comply with the Return Directive which, under Article 15, requires that detention be ordered by administrative or judicial authorities, and that when it is ordered by administrative authorities, Member States provide for a speedy judicial review of the detention and the immediate release of the person concerned if the detention is not lawful. Judicial control is carried out by GdPs, who must issue a reasoned decree, to verify the lawfulness of the detention order adopted by the police. The judicial authority must assess whether the time limits and the other requirements of the law have been met (ie the substantial requirements of expulsion and the conditions that legitimise detention). Such elements, which must be indicated in the motivation of the police order, in accordance with the Directive's prescriptions, are verified ex officio. GdPs, however, basically decide ex actis, ie based on the information in the case file. In fact, the hearing takes place through fast proceedings, not open to the public, and characterised by a limited investigation. The law prescribes the presence at the hearing of the foreigner's attorney, either appointed by the person or a public defender at the state's expense. The interested party must also be promptly informed, accompanied at the hearing and must be heard by the judge if they participate in the hearing.

The GdPs' decisions on validation and extension can only be appealed to the Court of Cassation, which cannot review the merits, but only the application of law. Appealing to the Court of Cassation is a complicated and time-consuming procedure and not all lawyers can litigate before the Court. The limited number of decisions issued by the Court in relation to pre-removal detention can be regarded as an index of the practical difficulties of having access to this form of appeal.

With regard to the scope of the examination upon validation, there has been an evolution of the principles established by the Court of Cassation. Until 2013, it held that in addition to assessing the lawfulness of detention, the GdP was only competent to monitor the existence of an enforceable expulsion order, excluding any investigation of its validity.[34] Later, it revised its position. In particular relying on Article 5 ECHR, referring to the case-law of the ECtHR involving Italy,[35] the Court of Cassation acknowledged that the judicial assessment of the detention order must also be extended to the conditions of manifest unlawfulness of the

[34] See Court of Cassation, judgment of 5 December 2013 (civile sez VI), no 27331.

[35] ECtHR 1 December 2009, *Hokic and Hrustic v Italy*, App No 3449/09, and ECHR 8 February 2011, *Seferovic v Italy*, App No 12921/04.

expulsion order.[36] Article 5 ECHR permits deprivation of personal liberty with a view to deportation or extradition, but requires such detention to be lawful. The Court of Cassation saw a possible conflict in this context between Italian legislation, as previously interpreted, and the ECHR. This change of approach followed a previous decision of the Italian Constitutional Court,[37] and led the Court of Cassation to significantly expand the scope of GdP assessment. However, not all grounds of unlawfulness can lead to the annulment of detention; only those in which the violation is serious and manifest have this possible consequence.

V. The Judicial Review Carried Out by GdPs on Pre-Removal Detention

The widening of the scope of the assessment carried out by the GdP that followed these decisions of the Court of Cassation, as well as the obligation to state reasons in the validation decree and the presence of both the foreigners and their lawyers at the hearing, should in principle allow for a satisfactory assessment by the GdP. However, empirical research carried out in Italy on the decisions of GdPs in the field of removal, including judicial reviews of removal orders, immediate removal orders, pre-removal detentions orders and alternative measures to detention, has brought to light several critical issues, showing a justice administered in a rough manner, only formally compliant with the Return Directive.[38] As the final report asserted:

> Detention proceedings are usually marked with poor quality of judges' and lawyers' performance, on one side, and inadequacy of lawfulness assessment, on the other, often resulting in decisions lacking legal reasoning or omitting crucial objections raised by the defence. Judicial control looks therefore unable to comply with national and ECHR case law pushing for a thorough exam of the detention file (including the lawfulness of the deportation order entailing detention).[39]

Ordinarily, the hearings last five minutes. In many cases hearings held on the same day share the same opening and closing time. Lawyers' activity often appears

[36] See Court of Cassation, judgment of 30 July 2014 (civile sez VI), no 17407; and Court of Cassation, judgment of 5 June 2014 (civile sez VI), no 12609.

[37] Constitutional Court, judgment of 10 April 2001 no 105.

[38] The Observatory on the jurisprudence of the Justice of the peace in immigration matters (Osservatorio sulla Giurisprudenza del Giudice di pace in Materia di Immigrazione), promoted by the legal clinic of the University of Roma Tre, collected and analysed the decrees issued by the Justice of the Peace of Rome, Bologna, Bari, Florence and Naples, between 2013 and 2015, relating to the procedures for the validation and extension of the detention of foreigners awaiting expulsion. This was the first systematic research on the jurisprudence of the GdP since competence on immigration was attributed to this lay judge in 2004 and a few thousand decisions have been examined over the years of activity. See www.lexilium.it.

[39] See Monitoring Centre on Judicial Control of Migrants' Removal, *Executive Summary 2016* (1 March 2017) available at: http://www.lexilium.it/wp-content/uploads/ES_GdP2016_ENG.pdf.

unsuitable to guarantee an appropriate technical defence. Even when an adequate defence is provided, the quality of decisions remains unsatisfying due to little, if any, legal reasoning and omission of decisive facts or arguments raised by the defence. In many cases, transcripts are a template form with preset motivations, where the judge only adds a standard clause. The reasoning can be deeper and more thorough in denying a detention order, but it appears from practice that where a third-country national is considered a threat to public security or national order, the order is confirmed and requests for further investigation from the detainee's lawyer are dismissed by the judge.[40]

The Court of Cassation has progressively affirmed the need to adequately state reasons in validation and extension decrees. In one case, the GdP had authorised extending the detention of a Nigerian applicant for international protection for a further 60 days, stating only that it 'considered the existence of the conditions for granting the extension request'.[41] The Court annulled the decree, ruling it deficient in assessing the requirements for detention or the arguments made at the hearing by the defence. In another case, the Court similarly held that the decree lacked motivation, the reasoning being only the tautological statement that 'the *Questore*'s order is adequately motivated in point of fact and law'.[42] The Supreme Court therefore annulled the GdP's decrees confirming detention for two Eritrean citizens, reaffirming that measures restricting freedom must be adequately motivated and translated.

In 2015 the Court of Cassation pointed out that:

> [T]he motivation of validation of detention must ascertain the specificity of the reasons given for the request for extension of detention and their congruence with the purpose of detention required by law, namely the need for detention in order to make return possible.

The case concerned a Libyan citizen of the Tuareg ethnic group, whose detention had been ordered since his coercive accompaniment to the border was not possible and it was necessary to proceed with his identification. The detention was extended twice. The Court found that the GdP had not identified any specific situation which hindered the enforcement of return, or an actual risk of absconding or the need to acquire documents and means of transport. On the contrary, the impossibility was permanent, the Libyan embassy having declined to acknowledge him as a citizen and warned against his return, as belonging to an ethnic group strongly opposed to the government. The Court agreed with the applicant's submission that the continuation of detention had not been assessed against the only justification set by the EU legislation, effective return. The decree was annulled based both on

[40] F Mastromartino, E Rigo and M Veglio, 'Lexilium. Osservatorio sulla giurisprudenza in materia di immigrazione del giudice di pace: sintesi rapporti 2015' (2017) 2 *Diritto, Immigrazione e Cittadinanza*, available at dirittoimmigrazioneecittadinanza.it.

[41] See Court of Cassation, judgment of 7 March 2017 (civile sez VI) no 5744.

[42] See Court of Cassation, judgment of 7 March 2017 (civile sez VI) no 5650.

constitutional limits relating to the restriction of personal freedom and on the objectives of the Return Directive.[43] The jurisprudence of the Court of Cassation thus affirms that, according to constitutional and EU law, detention orders cannot be based on standardised justifications that do not engage with the facts and applicable laws. Since the 2017 reforms of the honorary magistracy, ordinary recourse to standard formulas constitutes a negative element in the evaluation at the end of a GdP's four-year mandate.[44]

Cases concerning asylum seekers subject to review by the courts, instead of by a GdP, permit closer control over the lawfulness of detention, with due regard for EU law and CJEU case-law. The Court of Rome raised the issue of whether the extension of detention, requested by the *Questore* for the purpose of examining the application for international protection, would be compatible with the principles established by the CJEU in *Arslan*.[45] The Court attempted to harmonise the provisions on the detention of asylum seekers, contained in the national legislation transposing the Asylum Procedures Directive, with the principles affirmed by the CJEU. Recalling that under Article 15 of the Return Directive the fact that an asylum application was made by a person in pre-return detention does not suffice to show that it was made merely to circumvent return and thus 'it is objectively necessary and proportionate to maintain detention', the Court concluded that the request for extension cannot be automatically set. The Court took account of the applicant's nationality, which led to the presumption that the application for asylum was not specious, and carefully examined the request for extension, noting the absence of any reasoning regarding the necessity and proportionality of detention, or on whether the application had been submitted for the sole purpose of circumventing return.[46]

VI. The Contribution of the Court of Cassation to a Proper Implementation of the Return Directive

While the case-law of the GdPs has been for the most part characterised by superficial examination of the facts, absence of legal reasoning and the confirmation of measures ordered by the *Questore* on the basis of standard formulas, the Court of Cassation has, over the years, guided the application of national legislation in accordance with the principles that inspire the Return Directive.

The contrast between the Italian system, in which pre-removal detention is a measure of ordinary application, with the system established by the Return

[43] See Court of Cassation, judgment of 23 September 2015 (civile sez VI) no. 18748, esp para 16.
[44] See section II and n 7 above.
[45] Case C-534/11 *Mehmet Arslan* ECLI:EU:C:2013:343.
[46] See Court of Rome, judgment of 10 April 2014, no 5107/2014.

Directive was brought to light in the aftermath of *El Dridi*. Recalling the principles asserted by the CJEU, the Court of Cassation pointed out that detention in view of expulsion may only be ordered if other sufficient but less coercive measures cannot be applied. Referring to the circumstances justifying detention under Article 15, the Court declared detention in the case unlawful, since it had been applied as the ordinary mode of execution of forced removal, according to national law. But since the *Questore* had failed to indicate any of the reasons foreseen by the Directive, ie a risk of absconding or that the foreigner hampers or hinders the preparation of return, the GdP should not have confirmed the police order. The Court annulled the conflicting national rules.[47]

Despite the limits placed on the application of detention by this precedent, the structure of the Italian system on return has not been questioned. Technical reasons that prevent immediate expulsion (eg lack of transport or identification) are still the main reasons for extension of detention. They do not result in a postponement of enforcement, a possibility articulated in Article 9 of the Return Directive. Alternative measures, which have to be considered under Article 15, have been only occasionally applied. This is also due to national provisions that make them applicable only where the foreigner possesses a passport or other valid ID document. This apparent contradiction has not been addressed by the Court of Cassation, which has stated that the determination of the criteria on the basis of which to scrutinise the risk of absconding is 'a necessary legislative fulfilment', envisaged by the Directive under Article 3(7). In that regard, the choice to base the existence of a risk of absconding on the absence of a passport has been considered a legitimate implementation of the Directive,[48] even though it has the effect of turning detention into a standard measure applied to those who lack documents.

The Court of Cassation has also highlighted inconsistencies and gaps in the transposition legislation. It has pointed out the need to take into account the existence of reasonable prospects of return, in accordance with Article 15(4) of the Return Directive. This requirement had not been included in the transposing legislation, for initial detention or for subsequent renewals. The Italian system was previously based on frequent short-term renewals of detention up to the maximum of 18 months allowed by Article 15, without any specific allusion to the prospects of removal. This legislative gap was reflected in GdP case-law. At the end of 2014 the need to establish a reasonable prospect of removal was introduced in relation to extension of detention, although without an express reference in the law. In a 2015 appeal by a stateless person against a confirmation of extension of detention issued by the GdP in May 2014 (before the relevant rules were amended) without assessing removal prospects, the Court of Cassation established that, when endorsing police orders, not only must manifest unlawfulness be assessed, but also

[47] See Court of Cassation, judgment of 10 July 2012 (civile sez VI) no 11583.

[48] See Court of Cassation, judgment of 24 November 2017 (civile sez I) no 28155; and Court of Cassation, judgment of 10 January 2014 (civile sez VI) no 437.

the prospects of removal. For this reason, and particularly in view of the claimant's statelessness, the Court denounced the decree's inadequate motivation.[49]

Another significant aspect on which the Court of Cassation intervened to fill a legislative gap in light of the Return Directive is the possibility of reviewing the detention measure. Review at reasonable intervals either on application by the third country national or ex officio, pursuant to Article 15(3) of the Directive, was not transposed into national law, with the consequence that many judges have not applied it. What was missing was the possibility for the foreigner to assert any new elements, suitable to make the detention unlawful, arising since the validation of the initial detention. The matter came to the attention of the Court of Cassation,[50] in an appeal against an order made by the GdP of Rome that had declared the request for the revocation of detention to be impracticable due to the absence of a procedural remedy, in consideration of the non-transposition of Article 15(3). The Court affirmed that the provision is directly applicable, even if it has not been implemented, thus overturning the ruling of the GdP on the merits.[51] The CJEU's statement in *El Dridi* regarding the precise, clear and unconditional nature of Article 15 represented an essential argument. The Court of Cassation emphasised that the GdP had erred by declaring the matter impractical for remedy under national legislation, without considering the principles delivered in *El Dridi*. According to that Court, a request for judicial review of detention is admissible in light of factual circumstances that are new or were not considered at the time of the validation or its extensions. The GdP who confirmed or extended the order must reconsider 'the current interest in detaining the foreigner according to the purposes pursued by the law and the European Directive'.[52] These two interventions confirm the Court of Cassation's attention to a correct application of the law in light of the criteria and objective of the Directive to enforce return.

Another area of significant intervention by the Court of Cassation is the affirmation of the adversarial principle in extension-of-detention procedures. Contrary to the confirmation of the initial detention, for which the law specifies that the hearing must take place with both the person concerned and a lawyer promptly notified and able to participate, nothing is foreseen for the extension

[49] See Court of Cassation, judgment of 28 September 2015 (civile sez VI) no 19201 in relation to the case of a de facto stateless woman, resident in Italy for over 20 years and mother of five children, four of whom were minors, recipient of a decree of administrative expulsion and detained. Her condition as a stateless person, however, was in clear contrast to the possibility of actually enforcing her return, pursuant to the Directive.

[50] See Court of Cassation, judgment of 29 September 2017 (civile sez I) no 22932.

[51] The decision of the Court of Cassation provided guidance on a point on which the jurisprudence of merit had taken contrasting positions. If the justice of the peace of Rome (decree 24 April 2015) had affirmed the direct applicability of the relevant provisions of the Directive, considering admissible the requests for the review of detention, the Court of Turin (decree of 16 November 2016, no 3221/2016) declared inadmissible a request for review because re-examination has not been incorporated into national law nor can it be considered directly applicable, given that the supranational norm is not sufficiently precise with regard to the deadline for review.

[52] See Court of Cassation, judgment of 29 September 2017 (civile sez I) no 22932.

procedure. The Italian legislation has, therefore, been supplemented by case-law. In particular, since 2002 the Court of Cassation has clarified that such proceedings must be carried out in full compliance with the adversarial principle. In 2016 these issues were also brought before the ECtHR which, in *Richmond Yaw and others v Italy*, condemned Italy for a violation of Article 5(1) ECHR regarding the detention of four Ghanaian asylum seekers whose detention had been extended without a full hearing.[53] The ECtHR noted that domestic case-law was clear on the need to respect the adversarial principle, even when extending a detention order. It considered that the failure to summon the persons and their counsel for a hearing amounts to a 'serious and manifest irregularity' under its case-law and that this invalidated this part of the detention.[54] Also recently, and in relation to the transposing legislation, the Court of Cassation reiterated the need to respect the guarantees of defence, consisting of the participation of the lawyer and the concerned party in the hearing, even absent an express request to be heard.[55]

VII. Concluding Remarks

Until now, the attribution of jurisdiction to the GdP has not provided an opportunity for a careful analysis of the conditions that legitimise detention, or for a thorough interaction with the rules and principles developed by the CJEU and the ECtHR. The requests for preliminary rulings from Italy with reference to the Return Directive have all been promoted by court judges, not justices of the peace. This was the case with *El Dridi*, *Sagor* and *Celaj*. A GdP raised the compatibility of some specific aspects of the system of judicial confirmation of pre-removal detention with the constitution before the Constitutional Court, but the question was dismissed as not admissible because of how it was formulated.[56] The appointment and career of a GdP does not follow the rules applicable to ordinary judges. They are not required to have undergone thorough legal preparation or have professional experience but are nevertheless faced with a complex and interdisciplinary subject, with direct consequences on personal freedom. Judging on these matters

[53] ECtHR 6 October 2016, *Richmond Yaw And Others v Italy*, App Nos 3342/11, 3391/11, 3409/11 and 3447/11.

[54] In June 2010 the Court of Cassation had declared the detention order of 17 December 2008 void on the ground that it had been adopted without a hearing and in the absence of the applicants or their lawyer. The applicants lodged actions against the Ministry of the Interior and the Ministry of Justice seeking compensation for the damage sustained in connection with their detention. Their claims were subsequently dismissed by the Rome District Court.

[55] Court of Cassation, judgment of 13 November 2017 (civile sez VI) no 26803.

[56] See Constitutional Court, order of 19 March 2010 no 109 and order of 10 April 2014 no 93. In both cases the GdP raised a question of constitutionality concerning the provision allowing hearings of validation to take place within the centres of detention. The GdP considered this contrary to the right of the defence and to the duty of impartiality of judges.

requires a proper legal background as well as effective neutrality with respect to the administrative authority which issued the measures.[57]

The Court of Cassation has ensured greater attention to compatibility with the Return Directive and European jurisprudence. The Court has been able to provide essential guidance, both recognising the direct effect of the Return Directive to fill gaps in national legislation and providing a correct interpretation of it. This was a slow evolution, due to the small number of cases brought to the Court's attention, and to the practical difficulties of reaching the Supreme Court.

Some novel developments could have a positive effect on judicial practice by GdPs. The guidelines imposed on them by the recent reform of the honorary judiciary, which place greater emphasis on the quality of their decisions and reinforce control over their activities, could result in higher-quality decisions. For example, standardised decisions can lead to a negative assessment of their performance, with repercussions on the continuation of their mandate. At the same time, the Supreme Court is interpreting the national implementing rules in light of the principles of the Directive. These clarifications, together with the Court's recent insistence on the necessity to adequately motivate judicial decrees confirming detention, may represent an opportunity for Italian GdPs eventually to engage in more comprehensive judicial control of pre-removal detention, including by referring to the supranational framework.

[57] See P Bonetti, 'Aspetti di legittimità delle norme italiane in materia di immigrazione meritevoli di un intervento legislativo' (2016) *Audizione presso la Commissione affari costituzionali del Senato della Repubblica nell'ambito dell'indagine conoscitiva sui temi dell'immigrazione*.

14

Duality of Jurisdiction in the Control of Immigration Detention: The Case of France

Trois Hautes Juridictions Nationales pour une Directive: Une Interaction Judiciaire en Trompe l'œil

SERGE SLAMA

I. Introduction

La dualité de juridiction dans le contentieux de l'éloignement[1] des étrangers en situation irrégulière[2] résulte d'une interprétation de la Constitution française par le juge constitutionnel. En effet dans une décision de 1980 sur la loi « Bonnet », qui visait à légaliser la pratique de la rétention administrative, le Conseil constitutionnel a estimé que « la liberté individuelle ne peut être tenue pour sauvegardée que si le juge intervient *dans le plus court délai possible* ».[3] Or la clause d'habeas corpus inscrite à l'article 66 de la Constitution de 1958 prescrit que l'autorité judiciaire est la « gardienne de la liberté individuelle ». Par suite, si ce « régime de détention » peut être décidé par l'autorité administrative, en revanche la rétention ne peut se prolonger au-delà d'un certain délai sans intervention d'un tel juge.

[1] Le terme générique « éloignement » ou « mesures d'éloignement » est plus couramment utilisé dans le vocabulaire français que le terme – euphémisant de la directive 2008/115 – de « retour ».

[2] Le vocabulaire français utilise l'expression « étrangers en situation irrégulière » (ESI) bien davantage que celle de « ressortissants de pays tiers en séjour irrégulier » de la directive 2008/115. Mais il s'agit bien de désigner cette catégorie – exclusion faite des citoyens de l'Union européenne et assimilés qui relèvent d'un autre régime juridique. Nous les désignons aussi par le terme de « sans-papiers ».

[3] Cons constit, déc no 79-109 DC du 9 janvier 1980, Loi relative à la prévention de l'immigration clandestine, cons 4.

Parallèlement, s'agissant de la compétence de la juridiction administrative, le Conseil constitutionnel a dégagé un principe constitutionnel[4] qu'il a déduit de la « conception française de séparation des pouvoirs ». En vertu de ce principe, à l'exception des matières réservées « par nature » à l'autorité judiciaire, relève en dernier ressort de la compétence de la juridiction administrative le contentieux des décisions prises par les autorités exécutives dans l'exercice de prérogatives de puissance publique.[5] C'est le cas du contentieux des décisions d'éloignement d'étrangers en situation irrégulière prononcées par les préfets,[6] telles que les expulsions, les arrêtés préfectoraux de reconduite à la frontière (APRF) ou, plus récemment, les obligations de quitter le territoire français (OQTF). Il faudrait donc modifier la Constitution française pour transférer l'entier contentieux de l'éloignement à un seul juge.[7]

Ce partage des compétences entre les deux ordres de juridiction dans le contentieux de l'éloignement ne devrait normalement pas interférer dans la mise en œuvre des normes européennes issues aussi bien du droit de l'Union européenne (UE) que du droit de la Convention européenne de sauvegarde des droits de l'Homme (CESDH). Un tel partage de compétences relève en effet de l'autonomie procédurale des Etats membres. En vertu des articles 55 et 88-1 de la Constitution, les normes internationales et européennes ont une valeur supérieure aux lois françaises. Cela vaut aussi bien pour le droit primaire que le droit dérivé. Toutefois, dans la pratique, la juxtaposition des deux contrôles et l'absence de coordination entre les deux ordres de juridiction exposent le système juridictionnel français au reproche d'ineffectivité des recours. Cela a été le cas par exemple de l'hospitalisation d'office, qui constitue comme la rétention une mesure privative de liberté décidée par l'autorité administrative dont la prolongation était confiée à l'autorité judiciaire. Le juge des libertés et de la détention (JLD), juge civil compétent lorsqu'une personne est privée de liberté, examinait le bien-fondé de l'hospitalisation d'office tandis que le tribunal administratif examinait, jusqu'en 2011, la légalité formelle de la décision privative de liberté. Sans remettre en cause cette dualité de juridiction, la Cour de Strasbourg a conclu à la violation de l'article 5(4) de la CESDH dès lors que les juridictions administratives refusaient de se reconnaître compétentes pour ordonner la libération d'une personne internée, même lorsqu'elles procédaient par ailleurs à l'annulation de l'arrêté préfectoral à l'origine de cette situation.[8]

[4] Il s'agit d'un principe fondamental reconnu par les lois de la République. Il y est fait référence dans le Préambule de la Constitution de 1946, qui a lui-même valeur constitutionnelle car il est cité dans le Préambule de la Constitution de 1958.

[5] Cons const, déc no 86-224 DC du 23 janvier 1987, Loi transférant à la juridiction judiciaire le contentieux des décisions du Conseil de la concurrence.

[6] Cons const, déc no 89-261 DC du 28 juillet 1989, Loi relative aux conditions de séjour et d'entrée des étrangers en France, cons 24.

[7] Cela avait été envisagé en 2007 par le président de la République Nicolas Sarkozy mais écarté par une commission présidée par un ancien président du Conseil constitutionnel : P Mazeaud, *Pour une politique des migrations transparente, simple et solidaire* (Paris, La Documentation française, 2008).

[8] CEDH, 18 novembre 2010, *Baudoin c France*, no 35935/03. Depuis cette condamnation, la loi no 2011-803 du 5 juillet 2011 a confié au seul juge judiciaire (JLD) le contrôle de la légalité, y compris formelle, de l'arrêté d'hospitalisation sans consentement.

La difficulté était la même s'agissant de la dualité des contrôles opérés, jusqu'à la loi du 7 mars 2016,[9] sur la rétention administrative qui reposait, comme le constate la Cour européenne elle-même, sur une « imbrication des compétences des juridictions administratives et judiciaires ». En effet la loi du 16 juin 2011, pourtant validée par le Conseil constitutionnel,[10] avait procédé à une « interversion » de l'ordre d'intervention des juges administratif et judiciaire. Dans le cadre de cette législation, l'étranger faisant l'objet d'une OQTF sans délai de départ volontaire (DDV) avait 48 heures pour saisir le juge administratif de la légalité de la mesure de rétention. Celui-ci devait se prononcer dans les 72 heures et était le seul compétent pour contrôler la légalité de cette mesure durant ce délai. Et ce n'est qu'à l'issue de ce délai de 5 jours (à compter du placement en rétention) que le JLD était saisi par l'administration aux fins de prolongation de la rétention. À cette occasion, ce juge judiciaire ne pouvait contrôler que les conditions de privation de liberté et ordonner – ou non – une prolongation de cette privation pour un délai de 20 jours, renouvelable une fois.

L'office du juge administratif durant le délai de 5 jours était limité. Il avait le pouvoir de vérifier la compétence de l'auteur de l'arrêté préfectoral ainsi que la motivation de celui-ci et de s'assurer de la nécessité du placement en rétention. Il n'avait, en revanche, pas compétence pour contrôler la régularité des actes accomplis avant la rétention et ayant mené à celle-ci. Il ne pouvait notamment pas contrôler les conditions dans lesquelles s'était déroulée l'interpellation, notamment sa conformité au droit interne ainsi qu'au but de l'article 5 de la CESDH. Ainsi, comme dans l'affaire *Baudouin*, ce n'est pas en soi la dualité de juridiction qu'a remise en cause la Cour dans l'arrêt *AM c France*,[11] mais le fait que le contrôle exercé par le juge administratif était « trop limité au regard des exigences de l'article 5 § 4 dans le cadre d'une privation de liberté relevant de l'article 5 § 1 f) ».[12] Durant ces cinq premiers jours durant lesquels le JLD ne pouvait intervenir, le juge administratif ne s'était pas reconnu compétent pour libérer l'étranger en cas d'irrégularité de la procédure privative de liberté.

En raison de cette condamnation, ainsi que de l'arrêt *Mahdi*,[13] la loi du 7 mars 2016 a fait sensiblement évoluer le contrôle juridictionnel sur la rétention

[9] La loi no 2016-274 du 7 mars 2016 relative au droit des étrangers en France est entrée en vigueur, s'agissant de ces mesures de rétention, au 1er novembre 2016.

[10] Cons constit, déc no 2011-631 DC du 9 juin 2011, Loi relative à l'immigration, à l'intégration et à la nationalité. cf S Slama, « Les lambeaux de la protection constitutionnelle des étrangers » (2012) no 90, avril *Revue française de droit constitutionnel* 373.

[11] Dans le considérant 40, la CEDH mentionne expressément : « l'article 5 § 4 ne va pas jusqu'à exiger une forme particulière de recours et il n'appartient donc pas à la Cour d'affirmer quelle voie de recours interne serait plus opportune qu'une autre, ni, a fortiori, de porter une appréciation sur la répartition des compétences opérée par les autorités internes entre les juges judiciaires et administratifs ».

[12] CEDH, 12 juillet 2016, *AM c France*, no 56324/13. C Palluel, « Le contrôle juridictionnel de la rétention administrative devant la Cour européenne des droits de l'homme : un contrôle au conditionnel », *La Revue des droits de l'homme [En ligne], Actualités Droits-Libertés*, 2 octobre 2016, http://journals.openedition.org/revdh/2535.

[13] Arrêt de la Cour (troisième chambre) du 5 juin 2014, *Bashir Mohamed Ali Mahdi*, aff C-146/14 PPU ECLI:EU:C:2014:1320.

administrative puisque d'une part le juge judiciaire a désormais une compétence exclusive pour contrôler le bien-fondé mais aussi la légalité de l'arrêté de placement en rétention administrative. Le juge administratif a perdu toute compétence sur cette mesure. Et d'autre part, le législateur a rétabli l'intervention dans le JLD dans les 48 heures du placement en rétention de l'étranger par l'administration[14] – ce qui paraît plus conforme à l'exigence constitutionnelle d'intervention de celui-ci dans le plus court délai possible.

En novembre 2016 la Cour de cassation a d'ailleurs précisé, dans le prolongement d'une décision du tribunal des conflits de 2015,[15] qu'il incombe au JLD de mettre fin, à tout moment, à la rétention administrative, lorsque des circonstances de droit ou de fait le justifient, et ce dans le cadre de « la recherche de la conformité au droit de l'Union de la mesure de rétention ».[16] Il s'agit là en réalité d'une application au cas particulier de la rétention administrative de la jurisprudence *SCEA du Cheneau*.[17] Afin d'assurer le respect du principe de primauté du droit de l'Union, le tribunal des conflits avait « modernisé » une jurisprudence ancienne[18] en estimant que le juge civil pouvait vérifier la conformité de cet acte administratif au droit de l'Union sans avoir besoin de poser de question préjudicielle au juge administratif (qui est normalement compétent pour apprécier la légalité d'un acte administratif).

Dans deux arrêts du 27 septembre 2017, la Cour de cassation a estimé que le transfert de l'entier contentieux de la rétention, y compris celui de la légalité de l'arrêté de placement par la loi du 7 mars 2016 au JLD, ce juge judicaire n'est toujours pas compétent, même par la voie d'exception, pour apprécier la légalité de la mesure d'éloignement dont il procède.[19] La haute juridiction n'a pas non plus admis la possibilité pour ce juge civil de renvoyer, à titre préjudiciel, l'interprétation de la légalité de ces actes administratifs individuels en cas de contestation sérieuse sur leur légalité.

[14] Article L552-1 du CESEDA issu de l'article 36 de la loi no 2016-274 du 7 mars 2016. Le JLD, qui doit se prononcer dans les 24 heures, peut prolonger de 28 jours la rétention (L.552-2). Il peut être saisi par l'administration une seconde fois pour accorder une seconde prolongation de 15 jours. La loi no 2018-778 du 10 septembre 2018 pour une immigration maîtrisée, un droit d'asile effectif et une intégration (dite « loi Collomb ») prévoit que le JLD aura désormais un délai de 48 heures pour se prononcer et que la rétention pourra être prolongée jusqu'à 90 jours. Ces modifications ont été validées par le juge constitutionnel (CC no 2018-770 DC du 6 septembre 2018).

[15] TC 9 février 2015, no 15-03986.

[16] Cass 1ère civ, 9 nov 2016, np 15-27.357. V. dans le même sens, au nom de la « bonne administration de la justice » : CA Aix-en-Provence, ord, 6 mars 2017, no 17/00186 ; CA Aix-en-Provence, ord, 7 juill. 2017, no 17/00550. V., *contra*, à propos de la légalité d'une décision de transfert prise en application du règlement « Dublin III » (CA Douai, ord, 5 nov 2016, no 16/01430).

[17] TC, 17 oct 2011, *Préfet de la région Bretagne, préfet d'Ille-et-Vilaine, SCEA du Chéneau*, no 3828 et 3829 ; Rec CE 2011, concl J-D Sarcelet.

[18] TC 16 juin 1923, *Septfonds*, no 0073.

[19] Cass 1re civ, 27 sept 2017, no 17-10.207, *Préfet du Rhône c/ Sofiane X* (s'agissant d'une OQTF). cf S Slama, « Rétention administrative : la Cour de cassation ne franchit pas le rubicond du contrôle de la légalité de la mesure d'éloignement par voie d'exception », *Lexbase public*, 20 octobre 2017.

C'est dans ce contexte jurisprudentiel et législatif que se présente la question de l'étude de l'interaction entre les juges nationaux et européens dans la mise en œuvre de la directive « retour » (DR).[20] De prime abord, on pourrait penser que les juges nationaux – administratifs et judiciaires – jouent le jeu de la primauté du droit de l'Union, en assurant le respect de la DR, à savoir l'effectivité des mécanismes assurant le « retour » des ressortissants de pays tiers en séjour régulier et la garantie de leurs droits fondamentaux. En tout cas c'est le discours tenu officiellement par ces hautes juridictions. Ainsi pour Jean-Marc Sauvé, alors vice-président du Conseil d'Etat,[21] assurait, en prenant notamment l'exemple de la DR que « grâce à un dialogue attentif et dynamique entre juges nationaux et européens, la protection des droits fondamentaux des ressortissants étrangers a été considérablement renforcée ».[22] De même dans un colloque organisé par la Cour de cassation, Anne-Marie Batut, présidente de la première chambre civile,[23] chargée en cassation du contentieux de la rétention, relevait que « le statut des étrangers, notamment dans la sphère concernant la rétention administrative, est soumis à l'influence croissante des normes internationales et européennes …, les jurisprudences de la Cour de justice de l'Union européenne et de la Cour européenne des droits de l'homme ont pour effet de renforcer la protection juridictionnelle des étrangers sur le continent européen ».[24]

Mais l'examen attentif de la jurisprudence montre que loin d'être les bons élèves européens les juridictions françaises procèdent à une interaction judiciaire en trompe l'œil. Cette instrumentalisation par les hautes juridictions françaises[25] du « dialogue » judiciaire, entre elles et avec la Cour de justice à propos de la DR, vise,

[20] Directive 2008/115/CE du parlement Européen et du Conseil du 16 décembre 2008 relative aux normes et procédures communes applicables dans les États membres au retour des ressortissants de pays tiers en séjour irrégulier, JO L 348/98, 24.12.2008. V., aussi, pour un bilan par un magistrat administratif ayant exercé des responsabilités dans un ministère : Sylvain Humbert, « Directive « retour » : quel bilan de cinq années intenses en contentieux ? » [2016] *Rev fr dr Adm* 1235.

[21] Le vice-président du Conseil d'Etat assure la présidence de cette institution rattachée à l'Exécutif, qui est à la fois conseiller du Gouvernement et juge suprême de l'Administration. Dans le cadre de sa fonction de juge suprême de l'ordre administratif, le Conseil d'Etat exerce, en cassation, le contrôle des décisions rendues par les cours administratives d'appel, à la suite des tribunaux administratifs, relativement au contentieux des OQTF.

[22] J-M Sauvé, « Le droit européen des étrangers : quelles solutions juridictionnelles pour des progrès effectifs dans la protection des droits fondamentaux ? », *Séminaire ACA-Europe*, 9 mai 2014, www.conseil-etat.fr/Actualites/Discours-Interventions/Le-droit-europeen-des-etrangers.

[23] La Cour de cassation est la cour suprême de l'ordre judiciaire. La première chambre civile a compétence, en cassation, sur les cassations à l'encontre des décisions rendues par les premiers présidents de Cour d'appel, à la suite des JLD, s'agissant de la mesure de rétention.

[24] A-M Batut, « Allocution d'ouverture » in S Gargoullaud (dir), *Le droit et les étrangers en situation irrégulière* (Paris, La Documentation française, 2017) 9.

[25] Contrairement au Conseil d'Etat et à la Cour de cassation, le Conseil constitutionnel n'est pas, à proprement parler une juridiction suprême. En revanche, avec la ratification par la France du protocole no 16 de la CESDH, il a été reconnu comme « haute juridiction nationale » au sens de ce protocole, lui permettant, le cas échéant, de solliciter l'avis de la CEDH (www.conseil-constitutionnel.fr/actualites/protocole-n16-a-la-convention-europeenne-de-sauvegarde-des-droits-de-l-homme-et-des-libertes).

essentiellement, à assurer leur marge d'appréciation et celles de l'administration, sans nécessairement assurer une meilleure effectivité des mécanismes de « retour » ni protéger effectivement les droits fondamentaux des étrangers.

On constate néanmoins que l'inclinaison de ces trois hautes juridictions nationales à assurer le respect des dispositions non transposées de la DR est variable d'un juge à l'autre (1) et qu'elles n'ont pas la même utilisation stratégique de la question préjudicielle (2).

II. Une inclinaison variable à assurer le respect des dispositions non transposées de la DR

La meilleure façon d'illustrer l'utilisation de la DR par les juridictions nationales françaises sans référence ni recours à la Cour de justice de l'Union européenne, et avant l'intervention de la Cour européenne des droits de l'Homme en 2016 dans l'arrêt *AM c France*, est d'évoquer la période pendant laquelle la DR n'était pas encore transposée dans l'ordre interne par une législation nationale.

En effet, alors même que la date pour se conformer à la DR était fixée, pour l'essentiel, au 24 décembre 2010,[26] le législateur français a pris du retard dans sa transposition. Ce n'est donc qu'avec l'entrée en vigueur le 18 juin 2011 de la loi no 2011-672,[27] voire même pour certaines de ses dispositions de son décret d'application en juillet 2011[28] que cette transposition a été – à peu près – réalisée. Or, à défaut de transposition, dès Noël 2010, la DR a commencé à être invoquée devant les juridictions par les avocats des étrangers en situation irrégulière.[29]

En règle générale, le moyen tiré de la violation du droit de l'Union européenne doit être invoqué par une des parties au litige, à savoir généralement le requérant étranger. Il existe néanmoins une différence d'approche entre le juge judiciaire et le juge administratif car si le Conseil d'Etat ne soulève pas d'office un moyen tiré de la violation d'une norme internationale ou européenne,[30] sauf dans le cas où se pose un problème de champ d'application de celle-ci ; en revanche la Cour de cassation appréhende ce moyen comme d'ordre public.[31]

[26] 24 décembre 2011.

[27] Loi no 2011-672 du 16 juin 2011 relative à l'immigration, à l'intégration et à la nationalité.

[28] Décret no 2011-820 du 8 juillet 2011 pris pour l'application de la loi no 2011-672 du 16 juin 2011 relative à l'immigration, à l'intégration et à la nationalité et portant sur les procédures d'éloignement des étrangers.

[29] L'invocation a eu lieu à la suite d'un billet publié sur notre blog appelant les avocats français à invoquer directement cette directive devant les juridictions « Le Noël des sans-papiers : invoquez directement la directive "retour" et la charte des droits fondamentaux … », *Combats pour les droits de l'homme*, 26 décembre 2010.

[30] CE, 16 janvier 1995, *Sarl Constructions industrielles pour l'agriculture*, no 112746 ; CE Ass 6 décembre 2002, *Maciolak*, no 239540 : RFDA, 2003, 694, concl P Fombeur.

[31] V, par ex, Cass, soc, 16 décembre 2008, *Eichenlaub c/Axia France*, no 05-40876. cf Cour de cassation, « Etude – L'ordre public », *Rapport 2013* (Paris, La documentation française, 2014) livre 3, www.courdecassation.fr/publications_26/rapport_annuel_tude_annuelle_36/rapport_2013_6615/etude_ordre_6618/notion_ordre_6659/ordre_public_6660/utilisation_ordre_29155.html/.

Cette période de non-transposition a donné lieu, comme nous avons eu l'occasion de le démontrer avec Marie-Laure Basilien-Gainche, à une phase de « cacophonie judiciaire » de la part des juridictions du fond – tribunaux administratifs et JLD – à propos de l'application de la DR.[32] Cette période a aussi été marquée par une remarquable répartition des rôles entre les deux juridictions suprêmes et le Conseil constitutionnel. Manifestement inspirés par Sergio Leone, ils ont alors au bon, à la brute et au truand de l'UE.[33]

A. Le bon : la Cour de cassation et la reconnaissance de l'effet vertical descendant de des articles 16-4 et 16-5 de la DR

Eu égard au caractère inconditionnel et précis des dispositions des articles 16(4) et 16(5) de la DR, leur invocabilité directe ne faisait guère de doute. D'ailleurs, la Cour de justice l'a expressément reconnu dans l'arrêt *El Dridi* en avril 2011.[34] Rappelons que le paragraphe 4 de l'article 16 prévoit que « les organisations et instances nationales, internationales et non gouvernementales compétentes ont la possibilité de visiter les centres de rétention » et en son paragraphe 5 que les ressortissants de pays tiers placés en rétention « se voient communiquer systématiquement des informations … port[ant] notamment sur leur droit, conformément au droit national, de contacter [c]es organisations et instances ».

La violation de l'article 16(5) a constitué l'un des premiers moyens soulevés devant les JLD pour obtenir la remise en liberté d'étrangers maintenus en rétention sans avoir été informé sur leurs droits.[35] Toutefois, les juges judiciaires ont répondu à ce moyen dans un ordre dispersé. Une partie des JLD et premiers présidents de cours d'appel, faisant preuve d'un véritable nationalisme judiciaire,[36] ont en effet refusé de reconnaître la moindre invocabilité – directe ou par voie d'exclusion – à ces dispositions.[37] Des réponses divergentes avaient même été données entre juges d'un même tribunal.[38]

[32] M-L Basilien-Gainche et S Slama, « Judicial Cacophony and Disharmony in the French Reception of the Returns Directive » dans L Azoulai, *Irregular Migration in Europe. Legal and Judicial Problems Raised by the Implementation of the Returns Directive*, Workshop, Centre for Judicial Cooperation, IUE Florence, 19–20 octobre 2012, https://hal.archives-ouvertes.fr/hal-00861739.

[33] V avec la même inspiration : D Acosta, « The Good, the Bad and the Ugly in EU Migration Law: Is the European Parliament Becoming Bad and Ugly? (The Adoption of Directive 2008/15: The Returns Directive) », (2009) 11 *European Journal of Migration and Law* 19. V aussi Ph Yolka, « Question prioritaire de constitutionnalité : Le Bon, la Brute et le Truand », *JCP A* no 11, 14 mars 2011, act 190.

[34] CJUE 28 avril 2011, *Hassen El Dridi, alias Soufi Karim*, Aff C-61/11 PPU, ECLI:EU:C:2011:268, pt 47.

[35] CA Douai, ord, 11 janvier 2011, no 11/00010.

[36] V en particulier CA Versailles, 20 janvier 2011, no 11-00453.

[37] V not CA Colmar, 17 janv 2011, no 00272/2011 ; CA Metz, 18 janv 2011, no /1 ; CA Versailles, ord 20 janvier 2011, no 11-00453.

[38] A Maitrepierre, « Application du droit de l'Union européenne par la Cour de cassation (juin 2011 – septembre 2012) – Chronique sous la direction de L Azoulai », *Europe* no 11, 2012, chron 3.

Saisie en cassation de l'une des premières décisions qui avait consacré l'invocabilité directe de l'article 16 (CA Metz, 28 janvier 2011), la première chambre civile a confirmé cette position. Elle a estimé que le premier président avait pu « à bon droit » jugé que ces dispositions « non transposées en droit interne », remplissaient, à l'expiration du délai de transposition, les conditions requises pour être invoquées directement par l'intéressé. La faculté reconnue aux États, au paragraphe 4, de soumettre à autorisation les visites des organisations de défense des droits de l'Homme ou encore le renvoi au paragraphe 5 au droit national, en ce qui concerne le droit de contacter celles-ci, ne suffisaient pas « à rendre conditionnelles ces prescriptions ».[39]

Cette décision de la Cour de cassation n'est pas en soi une surprise car, comme le Conseil d'Etat avec l'arrêt *Perreux*,[40] la Cour de cassation reconnaît depuis plusieurs années l'effet direct vertical ascendant de certaines dispositions de directives non transposées.[41] Dans une chronique, une conseillère référendaire à la Cour de cassation, membre de la chambre civile, souligne qu'alors même que la thèse de l'effet direct de ces dispositions a été « fort débattue » et qu'était en jeu « la remise en liberté des étrangers … (avant que leur retour n'ait eu le temps d'être réalisé) », la première chambre civile a tranché en faveur de l'effet direct de ces dispositions car

> le renvoi au droit national ne porte pas sur le principe même du droit de contacter certaines organisations ou instances, mais seulement sur les modalités concrètes d'exercice de ce droit (contact sur place, par téléphone, par voie électronique …), de sorte que le contenu des droits ainsi conférés aux étrangers par ces dispositions de la directive est clairement identifiable (droit de contacter des organisations ou instances et droit corrélatif d'information sur ce droit).

Elle fait valoir aussi que

> la faculté laissée aux États membres de soumettre à autorisation les visites de ces entités ne remet pas en cause le caractère inconditionnel de l'obligation de résultat prescrite par l'article 16, paragraphe 5, de la DR (assurer l'effectivité des droits conférés aux étrangers).[42]

La ferme prise de position de la Cour de cassation n'a pourtant pas suffi à assurer le respect de ces articles par l'administration française. Certes, l'article 67 de loi du 16 juin 2011 a bien prévu, à l'alinéa 2 de l'article L. 553-3 du CESEDA, qu'« un décret en Conseil d'Etat détermine les conditions d'exercice du droit d'accès des associations humanitaires aux lieux de rétention». Le décret no 2011-820 du 8 juillet 2011

[39] Cass 1er civ, 1er février 2012, *M Elhwary*, no 11-30 086, Bull civ 2012, no 18, et 15 autres arrêts rendus le même jour au bulletin, Actualités Droits-Libertés du 9 février 2012 par S Slama. V aussi : Cass, 1ère civ, 23 mai 2012, no 11-30091.

[40] CE, Ass, 30 octobre 2009, no 298 348 ; *RFDA* 2009, 1125, concl M Guyomar.

[41] Cass, 1ère civ 23 novembre 2004, no 03-10636 : *Bull* 2004 I, no 280 ; Cass, com, 7 juin 2006, no 03-15.118 : *Bull civ* 2006 IV no 136.

[42] Maîtrepierre, «Application du droit de l'Union européenne » (n 38).

a bien fait évoluer des dispositions de la partie réglementaire du CESEDA pour prévoir l'accès d'associations habilitées aux centres de rétention.[43] De même l'article R.533-4 de ce même code prescrivait déjà l'établissement d'un règlement intérieur rappelant les droits et devoirs des étrangers retenus. Néanmoins dans la pratique près de 18 mois après l'entrée en vigueur de ce décret, le ministère de l'Intérieur n'avait toujours pas fait en sorte que les policiers délivrent correctement les étrangers retenus, à l'occasion du placement en rétention, des informations sur les organisations et instances nationales compétentes.

Si bien que la première chambre civile de la Cour de cassation a dû intervenir une seconde fois, dans un arrêt du 13 février 2013, pour rappeler que les ressortissants de pays tiers placés en rétention doivent être informés non pas seulement de la présence d'une association conventionnée pour assurer l'assistance effective aux droits mais aussi mis en mesure de contacter *effectivement* ces différentes organisations et instances susceptibles de l'aider, même si elles n'interviennent pas dans le centre de rétention.[44]

Les dispositions du CESEDA sur l'accès des associations humanitaires aux lieux de rétention seront de nouveau modifiées par un décret no 2014-676 du 24 juin 2014. Dans une autre décision, la Cour de cassation a aussi reconnu l'effet direct des paragraphes 1, 4 et 5 de l'article 15 de la DR en rappelant que « l'assignation à résidence ne peut jamais revêtir un caractère exceptionnel ».[45]

On constate au travers de ces exemples que même si l'intervention de la Cour de cassation a été un peu tardive (plus d'un an après l'entrée en vigueur de la DR), le juge judiciaire suprême, en parfait Blondin, a veillé au respect effectif par la police de dispositions de la DR garantissant de droits reconnus aux étrangers. Le Conseil constitutionnel ne s'est pas, pour sa part, montré aussi pusillanime. Assurant à merveille son rôle de Sentenza hermétique au droit de l'Union, il n'a en rien veillé à ce que le législateur transpose correctement cette directive.

B. La « brute » : le Conseil constitutionnel ou le refus d'assurer la conformité d'une loi de transposition à la DR

Depuis sa décision de 1975 « Interruption volontaire de grossesse », le Conseil constitutionnel ne s'estime pas compétent pour assurer, dans le cadre du contrôle

[43] Article R 553-14-5 du CESEDA créé par l'article 18 du décret no 2011-820 du 8 juillet 2011. Saisi en excès de pouvoir de cet article, qui posait en réalité des restrictions à l'accès des associations aux centres de rétention, le Conseil d'Etat en a confirmé la légalité, en annulant exclusivement, au regard notamment de l'article 16 de la DR, un alinéa de l'article R 553-14-5 du en tant qu'il prévoyait que l'habilitation à proposer des représentants pour accéder aux lieux de rétention ne peut être sollicitée par les associations ayant conclu une convention avec le ministère en application de l'article R 553-14 du même code (CE, 23 mai 2012, *Gisti*, no 352534).

[44] Cass, 1ère civ, 13 février 2013, no 11-27271. cf S Slama, « Nouvelle bataille judiciaire autour de l'information des étrangers retenus et le droit de visite des ONG compétentes » in *Lettre « Actualités Droits-Libertés »*, 2 mars 2013.

[45] Cass, Civ 1re, 24 oct 2012, no 11-27.956, au Bull.

de constitutionnalité des lois, le respect des engagements internationaux de la France et ce alors même que l'article 55 de la Constitution assure la primauté des traités régulièrement ratifiés sur les lois françaises. Toutefois, sur le fondement de l'article 88-1 de la Constitution, le juge constitutionnel a accepté, depuis 2006, de contrôler s'il existe une « incompatibilité manifeste » entre une loi de transposition et des dispositions « inconditionnelles et précises » d'une directive (sans toutefois se reconnaître la possibilité de saisir la CJUE d'une question préjudicielle).[46]

Censée en assurer la transposition, la loi « Besson » du 16 juin 2011 contenait à l'évidence plusieurs dispositions incompatibles avec la DR. La Commission européenne en fera d'ailleurs, par la suite, le constat et plusieurs dispositions seront intégrées dans la loi no 2016-274 du 7 mars 2016 pour assurer une transposition plus conforme et complète de la DR.[47]

La contrariété la plus manifeste – et que les universitaires spécialistes de la question n'ont cessé de dénoncer lors de l'élaboration de la loi – est le fait que la loi de 2011 n'a pas assuré le respect de l'article 15 qui prescrit que :

> à moins que d'autres mesures suffisantes, mais moins coercitives, puissent être appliquées efficacement dans un cas particulier, les États membres peuvent uniquement placer en rétention le ressortissant d'un pays tiers qui fait l'objet de procédures de retour afin de préparer le retour et/ou de procéder à l'éloignement en particulier.

Comme l'a souligné la CJUE dans ses arrêts *El Dridi* et *Achughbabian*,[48] cela signifie que le placement en rétention doit constituer une mesure utilisée en dernier recours.

Dans son arrêt d'avril 2011, la Cour insistait en effet sur le fait que :

> l'ordre de déroulement des étapes de la procédure de retour établie par la directive 2008/115 correspond à une gradation des mesures à prendre en vue de l'exécution de la décision de retour, gradation allant de la mesure qui laisse le plus de liberté à l'intéressé, à savoir l'octroi d'un délai pour son départ volontaire, à des mesures qui restreignent le plus celle-ci, à savoir la rétention dans un centre spécialisé, le respect du principe de proportionnalité devant être assuré au cours de toutes ces étapes.[49]

A leur seule lecture, il était flagrant que les articles 44 et 47 de la loi de 2011 ne faisaient pas de la rétention une mesure exceptionnelle et elle ne favorisait pas les

[46] Cons constit, déc no 2006-540 DC du 27 juillet 2006, Loi relative au droit d'auteur et aux droits voisins dans la société de l'information.

[47] L'étude d'impact de cette loi relève notamment : « Le Gouvernement ne saurait … être indifférent aux recommandations d'autorités indépendantes et à l'émergence de préoccupations légitimes émanant de la société civile auxquelles font au demeurant écho certaines observations de la Commission européenne sur la fidélité de la transposition des directives » (*Projet de loi relatif au droit des étrangers en France : Etude d'impact*, NOR : INTX1412529L/Bleue-1, 22 juillet 2014, 59).

[48] CJUE 6 décembre 2011, *Alexandre Achughbabian contre Préfet du Val-de-Marne*, aff C-329/11, ECLI:EU:C:2011:807 ; ADL 7 décembre 2011, S Slama ; D 2012, 333, obs G Poissonnier; Droit adm, févr 2012, 46, obs V Tchen ; Europe no 2, 2012, comm 73, comm F Gazin ; Gazette du Palais, 2012, no 45, 17, comm P Henriot.

[49] *El Dridi* (n 34) pt 41.

alternatives à la rétention, notamment l'assignation à résidence. Depuis la légalisation de la rétention administrative en 1981, les autorités françaises ont en effet fait de cette privation de liberté le procédé de droit commun pour exécuter les mesures d'éloignement, phénomène qui a été amplifié en 2003 lorsque le ministre de l'Intérieur, Nicolas Sarkozy, a fixé aux forces de l'ordre des objectifs chiffrés de reconduites à la frontière. La France est encore aujourd'hui le pays de l'Union qui recourt le plus massivement à la rétention administrative.[50]

Pourtant faisant fi des évidences, le Conseil constitutionnel a jugé que « les dispositions contestées des articles 44 et 47 ne sont pas manifestement incompatibles avec les objectifs de la directive que la loi déférée a pour objet de transposer » car à ses yeux « en vertu de ces dispositions, le placement en rétention n'est possible que si l'assignation à résidence n'est pas suffisante pour éviter le risque que l'intéressé ne se soustraie à l'obligation de quitter le territoire dont il fait l'objet ».[51]

En 2013, plus d'un an après l'entrée en vigueur de la loi de 2011, seuls 1 258 étrangers avaient été assignés contre 24 176 placés en rétention. A la demande de la Commission européenne, le législateur a dû faire évoluer les dispositions validées par le juge constitutionnel car, selon l'étude d'impact de la loi de 2016, le « rapport entre les assignations et les placements en rétention … est contraire au principe de gradation qui devrait gouverner l'application des mesures de surveillance pour la préparation de l'éloignement contraint ».[52] Malgré la réforme de 2016, le rapport n'a toujours pas changé. Certes en 2017 les assignations à résidence ont augmenté en nombre (7 942 assignations « alternative à la rétention ») mais elles ne représentent toujours que 17% des 45 000 placements en rétention (dont 19 948 outre-mer).[53] Ainsi, par sa complaisance à l'égard du législateur, le juge constitutionnel français s'est montré dans l'incapacité d'assurer le respect de la DR à défaut d'avoir réellement garanti le caractère subsidiaire de la rétention.

Mais du point de vue du droit de l'Union, ce n'est pas le seul reproche qu'on puisse faire à la décision du Conseil constitutionnel de 2011. Au regard du « Manuel sur les retours » de la Commission[54] et de la jurisprudence de la CJUE, on peut aussi penser que la définition par le législateur français[55] de six cas dans lesquels il existe, sauf circonstance particulière, des « risques de fuite » de l'étranger, ce qui permet de ne pas lui accorder de délai de départ volontaire et de le placer en rétention, ne sont pas définis objectivement (pour l'essentiel ils se

[50] « La rétention est un dispositif qui ne fonctionne pas», estime la Cimade, *Libération*, 19 février 2018.

[51] Cons constit, déc, no 2011-631 DC du 9 juin 2011, Loi relative à l'immigration, à l'intégration et à la nationalité, cons 61, Constitutions, 2011, no 4, p. 581, obs V Tchen ; Constitutions 2012, no 1, 63, obs A Levade. cf P Henriot, « Les sages capitulent », *Plein Droit*, octobre 2011, no 90, 29–31.

[52] Etude d'impact (n 47) 60.

[53] Projet de loi pour une immigration maîtrisée et un droit d'asile effectif, Rapport no 552 (2017–2018) de M François-Noël Buffet, fait au nom de la commission des lois, déposé le 6 juin 2018, 201–03.

[54] Recommand de la Commission du 16 novembre 2017 établissant un «manuel sur le retour» commun devant être utilisé par les autorités compétentes des États membres lorsqu'elles exécutent des tâches liées au retour, C(2017) 6505 final, 12–13.

[55] Paragraphe II de l'article L 511-1 du CESEDA issu de la loi de 2011.

contentent de reprendre les critères préexistants dans le droit français). Pourtant le juge constitutionnel a estimé, sans motiver sa position ni analyse plus poussée de ce que constituerait une situation de risque de fuite, que « le législateur a retenu des critères objectifs qui ne sont pas manifestement incompatibles avec la directive que la loi a pour objet de transposer ».[56]

De même s'agissant de l'interdiction de retour, il a estimé qu'il n'y a pas d'incompatibilité manifeste entre les dispositions législatives adoptées[57] et l'article 11 de la DR (interdiction d'entrée). Pourtant l'article L. 511-1 III du CESEDA prévoyait, dans sa version issue de la loi de 2011, que le préfet « peut », par une décision motivée, assortir l'OQTF d'une interdiction de retour sur le territoire français alors que l'article 11(1) de la DR prévoit que, dans deux cas (si aucun délai n'a été accordé pour le départ volontaire, ou si l'obligation de retour n'a pas été respectée), les décisions de retour « sont » assorties d'une interdiction d'entrée et que, dans les autres cas, celles-ci « peuvent » être assorties d'une telle interdiction. L'article 11(3) ne permet de déroger au caractère obligatoire des deux premiers cas que pour « des raisons humanitaires dans des cas particuliers justifiés ».

Ainsi, dans ces deux hypothèses, le législateur français avait transformé une compétence liée en un pouvoir discrétionnaire sans que le Conseil constitutionnel n'y voie la moindre contrariété manifeste avec la directive transposée. Cela est d'autant plus curieux que la rédaction adoptée par le législateur était liée au fait que celui-ci craignait une censure car dans une jurisprudence antérieure le juge constitutionnel avait estimé qu'une mesure d'éloignement entraînant « automatiquement » une interdiction constituait une sanction contraire à l'article 8 de la Déclaration des droits de l'Homme et du citoyen.[58] Mais dans sa décision de 2011 ce grief est écarté car le Conseil estime que « l'interdiction de retour dont l'obligation de quitter le territoire peut être assortie constitue une mesure de police et non une sanction ayant le caractère d'une punition au sens de l'article 8 de la Déclaration de 1789 ».[59]

Sous pression de la Commission européenne, le Gouvernement français a pourtant reconnu, dans l'étude d'impact du projet de loi de 2016, que :

> si le prononcé de l'interdiction de retour est bien possible dans tous les cas de prononcé d'une OQTF, la loi ne peut, sans méconnaître la portée de l'article 11 § 1, ouvrir sans nuance un égal pouvoir d'appréciation de l'autorité compétente sur chacun de ces cas, y compris les cas de refus de délai de départ volontaire ou de non-respect de ce délai.[60]

La rédaction de l'article L. 511-1 a donc été modifiée par la loi du 7 mars 2016 afin d'assurer « l'obligation de transposer fidèlement » la DR et compte tenu de

[56] Cons constit, déc, no 2011-631 DC du 9 juin 2011, cons 48.

[57] Septième alinéa du paragraphe III de l'article L 511-1.

[58] Cons constit, déc no 93-325 DC du 13 août 1993, Loi relative à la maîtrise de l'immigration et aux conditions d'entrée, d'accueil et de séjour des étrangers en France, cons 49.

[59] Cons constit, déc no 2011-631 DC du 9 juin 2011, cons 52.

[60] Etude d'impact (n 47) 76–77.

« la volonté » du Gouvernement « d'améliorer la fidélité de notre transposition de la directive à laquelle la Commission européenne nous a invité ».[61]

La décision de 2011 n'est pas le seul cas dans lequel le Conseil constitutionnel n'a pas assuré le respect du droit de l'Union. Saisi d'une QPC portant sur les dispositions du CESEDA dont la conformité à la DR a expressément été mise en cause dans l'arrêt *Achughbabian* (l'article L. 622-1), le Conseil constitutionnel n'a pas constaté leur contrariété au principe de nécessité des peines de l'article 8 de la Déclaration de 1789. Conformément à sa jurisprudence *IVG* de 1975, il a aussi estimé qu'« un grief tiré du défaut de compatibilité d'une disposition législative aux engagements internationaux et européens de la France ne saurait être regardé comme un grief d'inconstitutionnalité ».[62] Pourtant comme le reconnaissent les services du Conseil :

> ni le requérant ni les parties intervenantes ne demandaient au Conseil constitutionnel de revenir sur cette jurisprudence [« *IVG* »]. Leur demande, telle qu'elle était formulée dans les conclusions du GISTI qui, sur ce point, étaient les plus argumentées, tendait à ce que le Conseil constitutionnel tirât les conséquences de l'arrêt de la Cour de justice en en déduisant que l'infraction réprimant l'entrée et le séjour irrégulier méconnaissait le principe constitutionnel de nécessité des peines, lequel devrait désormais être interprété à l'aune de la jurisprudence de la Cour de Luxembourg, intégrée comme élément de la constitutionnalité. Il n'y aurait plus eu de nécessité de la peine dès lors que la CJUE en interdisait le prononcé.[63]

Avec sa déclaration « surprenante »[64] d'incompétence, le Conseil n'a pas répondu au moyen « subtil »[65] développé par le GISTI[66] en préférant le « désarticulé »[67] et en le traitant « comme un *banal* moyen d'inconventionnalité ».[68]

Ces illustrations sont donc révélatrices du fait que le juge constitutionnel français, par ignorance de la matière[69] ou mauvaise volonté, ne prend pas au sérieux les

[61] « III. – L'autorité administrative, par une décision motivée, assortit l'obligation de quitter le territoire français d'une interdiction de retour sur le territoire français, d'une durée maximale de trois ans à compter de sa notification, lorsque aucun délai de départ volontaire n'a été accordé à l'étranger ou lorsque l'étranger n'a pas satisfait à cette obligation dans le délai imparti. Des circonstances humanitaires peuvent toutefois justifier que l'autorité administrative ne prononce pas d'interdiction de retour. »

[62] Cons constit, déc no 2011-217 QPC du 03 février 2012, *M Mohammed Alki B* [Délit d'entrée ou de séjour irrégulier en France], cons 3 ; *ADL* du 9 février 2012 par S Slama ; *Constitutions*, 2012, obs A Levade ; *Europe*, 2012.3 repère 3, D Simon ; *Droit pénal*, 2012.3.34 obs J-H Robert ; *Constitutions*, 2012.339, obs V Tchen.

[63] Commentaire Décision no 2011-217 QPC du 3 février 2012, www.conseil-constitutionnel.fr/sites/default/files/as/root/bank_mm/decisions/2011217qpc/ccc_217qpc.pdf.

[64] A Levade, « Directive retour et délit d'entrée ou de séjour irrégulier : l'exigence constitutionnelle de transposition des directives définitivement stérilisée dans le cadre de la QPC ? », *Constitutions* 2012.286.

[65] D Simon, « Directive retour » et sanctions pénales du séjour irrégulier. Le Conseil constitutionnel dans sa décision du 3 février 2012 refuse de censurer la loi française, *Europe* 2012.3, repère 3.

[66] Déclaration de conflit d'intérêt : nous avons participé, pro bono, à cette procédure comme expert auprès des avocats des associations tiers intervenantes.

[67] A Levade, « QPC et directive « retour » : retour en arrière jurisprudentiel ? », *JCP G* no 8, 2012, libre propos, 19.

[68] A Levade, « Directive retour et délit d'entrée » (n 64).

[69] La lecture du commentaire officiel de la décision (29), élaboré par les services du Conseil constitutionnel, montre que la question de la conformité manifeste des dispositions déférées avec l'article 11 de

griefs de violation manifeste du droit de l'Union. Mais si, en parfait *Angel Eyes*,[70] le juge constitutionnel élimine froidement les griefs de contrariété au droit de l'Union semés par les requérants et intervenants sur sa route, il est bien moins subtil que le Conseil d'Etat qui, à l'égard de la DR, s'est comporté en truand …

C. Le truand : le Conseil d'Etat ou la consécration d'une invocabilité verticale descendante d'une directive non transposée

Comme devant les juridictions judiciaires à propos de l'article 16, la non-transposition dans le délai prescrit de la DR a permis aux requérants étrangers sous le coup d'une OQTF de la contester, dès le 25 décembre 2010, en invoquant directement celle-ci, en particulier les dispositions des articles 7 et 8 régissant les conditions d'octroi d'un délai de départ volontaire (DDV). Mais là aussi les juges administratifs se sont divisés sur cette question et des solutions opposées ont pu être adoptées d'un tribunal à l'autre et même parfois, au sein même d'un même tribunal, d'un juge de la reconduite à la frontière à l'autre.

Face à de tels problèmes d'interprétations divergentes du droit de l'Union, la logique des traités européens voudrait qu'une juridiction administrative saisisse de cette « difficulté sérieuse » la Cour de justice. Mais, au sein de l'ordre administratif, les juges administratifs font preuve de davantage de discipline à l'égard du Palais Royal, leur juridiction suprême (et gestionnaire du corps des magistrats administratifs), que de la Cour de Luxembourg. Ainsi, face à cette difficulté sérieuse et nouvelle qui présente dans un grand nombre de litiges, le « réflexe » du juge administratif est d'interroger le Conseil d'Etat par la voie d'une « demande d'avis sur une question de droit », conformément à l'article L. 113-1 du code de justice administrative.

C'est ce qu'a fait le tribunal administratif de Montreuil en transmettant deux demandes d'avis à propos d'une part du caractère directement invocable, ou non, des dispositions des articles 7 et 8 de la DR en l'absence de transposition par le législateur[71] et d'autre part, de la possibilité d'exclure, par voie d'exception d'« unionité », l'application des dispositions du II de l'article L. 511-1 du CESEDA, en ce que celles-ci ne prévoyaient, à cette date, l'accord d'aucun DDV contrairement aux objectifs fixés par les articles 7 et 8 de la DR.[72]

la directive n'est pas sérieusement examinée (Commentaire Décision no 2011-631 DC du 9 juin 2011, www.conseil-constitutionnel.fr/sites/default/files/as/root/bank_mm/decisions/2011631dc/ccc_631dc.pdf).

[70] Dans la version américaine du film *Le bon, la brute et le truand*, le personnage de « la brute », interprété par Lee Van Cleef, s'appelle Angel Eyes (Sentenza dans la version originale).

[71] TA de Montreuil, 20 janvier 2011, *MJ*, no 345978.

[72] TA Montreuil, 10 février 2011, *MT*, no 1100584.

Or, dans son avis, rendu en mars 2011,[73] le Conseil d'Etat a adopté une position contrastée. Appliquant la théorie de l'acte clair, afin de ne pas procéder à un renvoi préjudiciel, il saisit cette occasion pour effectuer un véritable « vade-mecum enfin clair sur l'invocabilité des directives communautaires »[74] dans le prolongement des arrêts *Perreux* (pour l'invocabilité directe) et *Revert et Badelon* (pour l'invocabilité d'exclusion).[75] Mais s'il a reconnu l'invocabilités directe et d'exclusion de ces dispositions, il a admis dans le même temps une effet vertical descendant – pourtant prohibé par la jurisprudence européenne – dès lors qu'il est défavorable aux étrangers.

Le Conseil d'Etat fait donc une lecture constructive de la législation existante – conforme aux objectifs de la DR – avec la préoccupation principale de préserver la possibilité pour les autorités françaises de prononcer des OQTF le temps que le législateur adopte la loi de transposition. Mais pour ce faire, le juge administratif suprême estime, de manière plus critiquable, que les dispositions de la DR ne font pas obstacle à ce qu'une mesure de reconduite soit prise à l'encontre d'un étranger « dès lors que cette mesure est assortie d'un délai de retour approprié à la situation de l'intéressé et supérieur à sept jours » dans les cas prévus aux 1° [entrée irrégulière], 2° [maintien irrégulier sur le territoire] et 4° [non renouvellement titre et maintien au-delà d'un mois à l'expiration d'un titre] du II de l'article L. 511-1 – c'est-à-dire les principaux cas de reconduite à la frontière. Cette habilitation jurisprudentielle à assortir ces décisions de retour d'un délai non prévu par la loi française mais uniquement par la directive porte atteinte à notre sens, au principe de prohibition de l'effet vertical descendant, c'est-à-dire de l'impossibilité pour l'Etat d'imposer des dispositions d'une directive qu'il n'a pas transposées.[76] Certes la Cour de justice admet par ailleurs qu'il serait

> contradictoire de juger que les particuliers sont fondés à invoquer les dispositions d'une directive [inconditionnelles et précises], devant les juridictions nationales, en vue de faire censurer l'administration, et d'estimer néanmoins que celle-ci n'a pas l'obligation d'appliquer les dispositions de la directive en écartant celles du droit national qui n'y sont pas conformes.[77]

Mais cela signifie uniquement, à notre sens, que lorsqu'un particulier invoque des dispositions inconditionnelles et précises non transposées, l'administration est

[73] CE, avis du 21 mars 2011, *J et T*, no 345978, 346612, Rec Lebon ; (2011) JCP A, no 18, no 2173, obs S Slama ; (2011) *Actualité juridique Droit administratif* 1688, obs H. Alcaraz. La rapporteure au Conseil d'Etat dans cette affaire était Mme Stéphanie Gargoullaud.

[74] M Gautier, « Où l'on reparle de l'effet direct des directives communautaires » (2011) *Actualité juridique Droit administratif* 297.

[75] CE, Ass, 30 octobre 1996, *Cabinet Revert et Badelon*, no 45126 ; CJCE 19 septembre 2000, *Luxembourg c/ consorts Lintser*, aff C-287/98.

[76] CJCE 5 avril 1979, *Ratti*, aff 148/78, ECLI:EU:C:1979:110; CJCE, 26 février 1986, *Marshall*, aff 152/84, ECLI:EU:C:1986:84 ; CE Sect 23 juin 1995, *SA Lilly France*, Rec Lebon 257, concl C Maugüé.

[77] CJCE, 22 juin 1989, *Fratelli Costanzo SpA contre Comune di Milano*, aff 103/88, ECLI:EU:C:1989:256, pt 31.

tenue d'en faire application. En revanche, cela n'habilite pas une autorité nationale à se prévaloir de dispositions non transposées car cela reviendrait à sa prévaloir de sa propre turpitude.

Dans un communiqué de presse publié quelques heures après l'avis, le ministère de l'Intérieur s'est immédiatement engouffré dans la brèche en estimant que désormais « l'administration doit assortir ces arrêtés d'un délai de départ volontaire, sous réserve des deux exceptions précédemment mentionnées d'ordre public et de fraude » et, dans l'attente de l'adoption de la loi nouvelle, « des instructions précises seront données aux préfets pour que, dès à présent, un délai de départ volontaire soit accordé dans les conditions prévues par la directive ».

Et dès le 23 mars 2011, le ministre de l'Intérieur a adressé une circulaire aux préfets[78] afin qu'ils assortissent, à titre transitoire, dans l'attente de l'adoption d'une nouvelle législation, les mesures d'éloignement d'un DDV de 7 jours. Cette circulaire a été immédiatement contestée devant le Conseil d'Etat par le Groupe d'information et de soutien des immigrées (Gisti).[79]

Tordant le droit de l'Union européenne, le juge administratif a validé, en référé-suspension[80] et au fond,[81] cette instruction. Pour cela, il a considéré d'une part que le ministre pouvait prescrire aux préfets, dans l'attente de l'entrée en vigueur de la loi procédant à la transposition de la DR, « de ne pas procéder à l'exécution d'office d'un arrêté de reconduite à la frontière avant l'expiration d'un délai de départ volontaire, conforme à la directive » car, selon lui, « un tel report d'exécution revient nécessairement à laisser à l'étranger qui fait l'objet de la mesure un délai pour quitter volontairement le territoire national comme le prévoit la directive ». Selon sa lecture :

> si la circulaire ne fait état que d'un délai de sept jours révolus, cette indication, donnée à titre illustratif, n'a pas pour objet et ne pourrait avoir légalement pour effet … de priver les préfets de l'exercice de leur pouvoir d'appréciation pour déterminer, dans chaque cas au vu de la situation de la personne concernée, le délai approprié prévu par la directive pour un retour volontaire, délai compris entre sept et trente jours et susceptible, en cas de nécessité, d'être prolongé, conformément aux paragraphes 1 et 2 de l'article 7 de la directive.[82]

En raison de la prohibition de l'effet vertical descendant, il n'aurait pas dû admettre la possibilité pour une administration d'appliquer au détriment d'un administré ces dispositions non transposées. Mais, sans poser de question préjudicielle, le Conseil d'Etat s'est affranchi de cette prohibition par un tour de passe-passe juridique. Il

[78] Circulaire du 23 mars 2011, NOR : IOC/V/11/08038/C, *Conséquences à tirer de l'avis contentieux du Conseil d'État du 21 mars 2011 sur la directive « retour »*.

[79] Nous avons participé à cette procédure notamment en représentant cette association à l'audience de référé.

[80] CE, réf, 12 mai 2011, *Gisti*, no 348774.

[81] CE, 9 nov 2011, *Gisti*, no 348773.

[82] ibid.

a en effet estimé, pour justifier sa position, que la circulaire « vise à permettre aux étrangers *de bénéficier* du délai de départ volontaire prévu par les dispositions précises et inconditionnelles de l'article 7 de la DR après l'expiration du délai de transposition ». Autrement dit, cette mesure serait *favorable* aux étrangers en instance d'éloignement et, par suite, l'administration pourrait, *même s'ils n'en ont pas fait la demande expresse*, leur appliquer *d'office* le DDV de 7 jours par application directe de la DR.

En utilisant cette technique de l'interprétation conforme, le Conseil d'Etat a préservé la possibilité pour les autorités françaises d'adopter durant plusieurs mois (la DR ne sera transposée qu'à la mi-juillet 2011) des mesures d'éloignement avec la seule contrainte d'accorder un DDV de 7 jours par une application verticale descendante de la directive par l'Etat aux particuliers. Mais si le Conseil d'Etat n'avait pas admis cette possibilité, les étrangers concernés n'auraient *plus du tout* pu faire l'objet d'une mesure d'éloignement – ce qui leur était assurément plus favorable (mais aurait assurément nuit à l'efficacité du dispositif).

L'interprétation retenue est d'autant plus critiquable que la circulaire prescrivait aussi qu'un placement en rétention ou une assignation à résidence pouvaient intervenir, dans les conditions de droit commun, à l'expiration du délai de départ volontaire accordé. Or, le Conseil d'Etat a estimé qu'en apportant cette « seule précision » la circulaire n'aurait « pas prescrit de procéder au placement en rétention dans des conditions qui seraient contraires à ce que prévoit l'article 15 de la directive ». Pourtant, comme cela a été mentionné précédemment, le droit français faisait alors du placement en rétention la règle. Ce n'est qu'à titre très exceptionnel que des étrangers faisaient l'objet de mesures alternatives comme l'assignation, y compris les familles accompagnées d'enfants comme l'a montré la condamnation de la France dans l'affaire *Popov*.[83]

Même si elles ont moins défrayé la chronique, il existe d'autres illustrations dans lesquelles le Conseil d'Etat s'est arrangé avec le droit de l'Union. On pense en particulier au fait qu'avec la loi du 16 juin 2011 le législateur a maintenu la possibilité pour les préfets d'édicter, sans appliquer les dispositions de la DR, des reconduites à frontière à l'encontre d'étrangers qui, en France depuis moins de trois mois (souvent sous couvert d'un visa), soit adoptent un comportement constituant une menace pour l'ordre public, soit méconnaissent les règles relatives à la législation du travail applicable aux étrangers (travail sans autorisation, etc.) (article L. 533-1 du CESEDA). Un certain nombre de spécialistes du droit des étrangers, dont

[83] CEDH, 5e Sect 19 janvier 2012, *Popov c France*, no 39472/07 et 39474/07. Sur les résistances des autorités françaises et du Conseil d'Etat à cette jurisprudence cf A Gelblat, « La CEDH et la pratique française de rétention des mineurs étrangers : L'impossibilité pratique plutôt que l'interdiction de principe ? », *La Revue des droits de l'homme, Actualités Droits-Libertés*, 29 août 2016 ; et C Escuillié, « Un encadrement cosmétique du renvoi des mineurs étrangers arbitrairement rattachés à des adultes accompagnants », *La Revue des droits de l'homme, Actualités Droits-Libertés*, 27 février 2015, http://journals.openedition.org/revdh/1067

nous faisions partie,[84] ont estimé dès l'adoption de ces dispositions que le maintien de ce cas de « reconduites autonomes » constituait une violation de la directive « retour ».

Pourtant, saisi de cette difficulté sérieuse par la Cour administrative d'appel de Versailles, le Conseil d'Etat a, dans un avis, fait de nouveau l'application de la théorie de l'acte clair (afin de ne pas devoir renvoyer cette question à la Cour de justice) et estimé que « la directive n'est applicable qu'aux décisions de retour qui sont prises par les Etats membres au motif que les étrangers sont en situation de séjour irrégulier » (ce qui est vrai). Et par suite, il a estimé, sans motiver aucunement sa position, que

> la directive n'a pas vocation à régir les procédures d'éloignement qui reposent sur des motifs distincts, notamment la menace à l'ordre public ou la méconnaissance d'autres normes de portée générale, telle que l'obligation de détenir une autorisation de travail pour exercer une activité professionnelle.[85]

Comme l'explique un magistrat administratif, qui qualifie de « surprenante » la solution adoptée par le Conseil d'Etat dans son avis, d'une part, s'agissant du premier motif, « la méconnaissance de l'ordre public, qui peut justifier un refus de titre de séjour, implique nécessairement une irrégularité de séjour » et, d'autre part, s'agissant du second, si « la méconnaissance de l'obligation de détenir une autorisation de travail n'implique pas nécessairement une irrégularité du séjour », il n'empêche que « la décision de retour prise implique nécessairement, là encore, une irrégularité du séjour comme conséquence automatique de la méconnaissance de la règle de l'autorisation de travail ».[86]

En définitive, le législateur français a – là-aussi – fini par s'incliner et mettre le droit français en conformité avec le droit de l'Union. Avec l'article 27 de la loi du 7 mars 2016, il a en effet procédé à l'abrogation pure et simple de l'article L. 533-1 du CESEDA. Entre mi-2011 et la fin 2013, 1320 étrangers avaient fait l'objet d'une telle reconduite « autonome ».[87]

On peut aussi signaler, sur des problèmes complexes, des décisions rendues par le Conseil d'Etat, toujours sans renvoi préjudiciel, sur le caractère inapplicable de la DR aux décisions de « remise » à un autre État membre, que ce soit dans le cadre de la procédure dite « Dublin » (CESEDA, art. L. 531-2) ou dans le cas d'une remise dite « Schengen » (art. L. 531-1). Or, si dans le cas des réadmissions « Dublin », on peut approuver la solution dégagée par le Conseil d'Etat[88] (les ressortissants de pays tiers ayant déposé une demande d'asile ne sont généralement pas en séjour

[84] S Slama et Me-L Basilien-Gainche, « L'arrêt *El Dridi* : la nécessaire remise à plat du dispositif de pénalisation de l'irrégularité », (2011) *AJ Pénal* 362 ; S Slama, « Contrariété à la directive « retour » des reconduites à la frontière « autonomes » de l'article L.533-1 du CESEDA », *Combats pour les droits de l'Homme*, 6 septembre 2011.

[85] CE, avis, 10 oct 2012, *Préfet du Val-d'Oise c/ Rhabani*, no 360317, Lebon T, 630, 631, 638 et 792.

[86] Humbert, « Directive « retour » … » (n 20).

[87] Etude d'impact (n 47) 70.

[88] CE, 23 juin 2011, *Mme Tamoeva*, no 350136.

irrégulier mais des demandeurs d'asile en cours de procédure), dans le cas des remises « Schengen », sa position[89] paraît partiellement remise en cause par la décision *Affum* du 7 juin 2016,[90] en ce qu'elle juge que la DR impose que la remise soit effectuée avec diligence, ce qui implique nécessairement que les remises sont dans le champ de la directive.[91]

Du point de vue technique, on constate donc la tendance du Conseil d'Etat à privilégier le recours à la technique de l'interprétation du droit français « conforme » au droit de l'Union[92] plutôt que la censure franche de ce droit qui le rendrait inapplicable et, par suite, empêcherait toute application de la directive le temps d'adopter une loi de transposition. De longue date, comme l'avait déjà démontré en 1978 l'arrêt *Cohn-Bendit*, il privilégie aussi l'application de la théorie de l'acte clair afin de conserver une marge dans l'interprétation du droit de l'Union y compris lorsqu'il est manifestement confronté à une difficulté sérieuse d'interprétation de ce droit et lorsque les interprétations qu'il retient, sans procéder à un renvoi préjudiciel, paraissent discutables et très « arrangeantes » à l'égard des autorités nationales dans l'application du droit de l'Union. Car là aussi le Tuco administratif dégaine moins vite des questions préjudicielles que Blondin judiciaire …

III. Une instrumentalisation du « dialogue » avec le juge de l'UE

Les juges français, en particulier les juges suprêmes,[93] ne sont pas réputés comme les juges nationaux de l'Union ayant le plus facilement recours à une question préjudicielle. Comme cela a déjà été relevé, il existe au contraire une pratique assez ancienne de privilégier soit la technique de l'interprétation conforme soit l'application de la théorie de l'acte clair afin de procéder, le moins possible,

[89] CE, 27 juin 2011, *Ministre de l'intérieur, de l'outre-mer, des collectivités territoriales et de l'immigration c/ Lassoued*, no 350207, Lebon T, 818, 829 et 960. V aussi : CE, avis, 18 décembre 2013, *Préfet de Haute-Savoie*, no 371994, Rec Lebon 318.

[90] CJUE 7 juin 2016, *Sélina Affum c Préfet du Pas-de-Calais et Procureur général de la cour d'appel de Douai*, Aff C-47/15 ECLI:EU:C:2016:408, pts 79–88.

[91] Pour des développements cf l'article de Humbert (n 20).

[92] cf CE, 8 déc 2000, no 204756, *Commune de Breil-sur-Roya*, Rec Lebon 581 ; (2001) *Actualité juridique Droit administratif*, 775, note J-M Février : « il appartient aux autorités administratives nationales, sous le contrôle du juge, d'exercer les pouvoirs qui leur sont conférés par la loi en lui donnant, dans tous les cas où celle-ci se trouve dans le champ d'application d'une règle communautaire, une interprétation qui soit conforme au droit communautaire ».

[93] Dans cette partie, il ne sera question que du Conseil d'Etat et de la Cour de cassation car, comme cela a déjà été mentionné, le Conseil constitutionnel ne se reconnaît pas compétent pour poser une question préjudicielle à la Cour de justice (sous la seule réserve du mandat d'arrêt européen, en application de l'article 88-2 de la Constitution cf Cons constit, déc no 2013-314P QPC du 4 avril 2013, *M Jeremy F* [Absence de recours en cas d'extension des effets du mandat d'arrêt européen – question préjudicielle à la Cour de justice de l'Union européenne]).

à un renvoi préjudiciel. L'objectif est, pour le juge national, de ne pas encombrer inutilement le prétoire du juge européen mais aussi de se ménager une marge d'appréciation dans l'interprétation des normes européennes.[94] Ce constat général est particulièrement vrai en droit des étrangers où, depuis l'arrêt *Cohn-Bendit* de 1978,[95] le juge national, en particulier le Conseil d'Etat, a tendance à court-circuiter son obligation découlant de l'article 267 du TFUE.

Ainsi, on constate un usage stratégique, voire opportuniste, des questions préjudicielles. En revanche, une fois que le juge de l'Union est intervenu les juridictions nationales sont, dans l'ensemble, respectueuses de l'autorité de ses décisions. S'agissant de la directive « retour », deux illustrations peuvent être prises pour accréditer l'idée d'utilisation ponctuelle et stratégique de la question préjudicielle de la part aussi bien du juge judiciaire que du juge administratif. D'une part, faisant preuve d'un activisme judiciaire, les questions préjudicielles du juge judiciaire dans les affaires *Achughbabian* et *Affum* ont abouti à une remise en cause du délit de séjour et d'entrée irréguliers sur le territoire français ainsi qu'aux gardes à vue prises sur son fondement (A). D'autre part, de manière beaucoup plus ambiguë, les questions préjudicielles du juge administratif à propos du droit d'être entendu dans les procédures d'éloignement ont abouti aux (décevants) arrêts *Mukarubega*[96] et *Boudjlida*[97] qui valident, pour l'essentiel, les conceptions développées de longue date par le juge administratif français sur la portée de ce droit (B).

A. Affaires *Achughbabian* et *Affum* : un activisme du juge judicaire dans l'interaction avec la Cour de justice

La dépénalisation partielle du séjour puis de l'entrée irréguliers sur le territoire, lorsque ces incriminations constituent un obstacle à la mise en œuvre de la directive « retour », illustre les virtualités d'une interaction judiciaire constructive entre juges nationaux et Cour de justice face aux résistances des Etats. Cette interaction n'a été rendue possible que grâce à l'imagination de défenseurs des étrangers des deux côtés des Alpes, en particulier des échanges qui ont pu avoir lieu avant l'entrée en vigueur de la DR entre des avocats et des universitaires.

Lorsqu'elle a été adoptée la DR était en effet perçue par les ONG comme essentiellement défavorable aux étrangers. Certains d'entre elles avaient même dénoncé un « directive de la honte » (car elle autorise, dans certaines circonstances,

[94] cf E Neframi, *Renvoi préjudiciel et marge d'appréciation du juge national* (Bruxelles, Larcier, 2015).

[95] CE, Ass, 22 décembre 1978, *ministre de l'intérieur c/ Cohn-Bendit*, Rec Lebon 52. Daniel Cohn-Bendit avait demandé au ministre de l'Intérieur l'abrogation de son arrêté d'expulsion du territoire français édicté en 1968 en invoquant directement la directive de 1964.

[96] CJUE 5 novembre 2014, *Sophie Mukarubega c Préfet de police et Préfet de la Seine-Saint-Denis*, aff C-166/13, ECLI:EU:C:2014:2336.

[97] CJUE 11 décembre 2014, *Khaled Boudjlida contre Préfet des Pyrénées-Atlantiques*, aff C-249/13, ECLI:EU:C:2014:2431.

jusqu'à 18 mois de rétention et la rétention des mineurs, mêmes isolés). Mais son examen attentif permettait également d'y déceler un certain nombre de virtualités protectrices. En particulier, les avocats de M. El Dridi ont eu l'idée d'utiliser la directive, interprétée à l'aune des droits fondamentaux garantis par l'Union, comme empêchant la « criminalisation » du séjour irrégulier.[98] Si dans sa décision du 28 avril 2011 la Cour de justice a bien constaté que la DR, en particulier ses articles 15 et 16,

> s'oppose à une réglementation d'un Etat membre, telle que la législation italienne, prévoyant l'infliction d'une peine d'emprisonnement pour le seul motif que le ressortissant de pays tiers en séjour irrégulier demeure, en violation d'un ordre de quitter le territoire de cet État dans un délai déterminé, sur ledit territoire sans motif justifié elle ne l'a pas fait au nom des droits fondamentaux mais de l'efficacité du dispositif de « retour ».[99]

De longue date (1938), il existait en France un délit de séjour irrégulier. Avec la massification des reconduites à la frontière et des placements en rétention dans les années 1990, ce délit est devenu le support permettant, en cas d'interpellation d'un sans-papier, de le placer en garde à vue afin de préparer la procédure *administrative* d'éloignement. En effet, des dispositions du Code de procédure pénale conditionnent le placement en garde à vue à l'exigence qu'il existe à l'encontre de la personne interpellée « une ou plusieurs raisons plausibles de soupçonner qu'elle a commis ou tenté de commettre un crime ou un délit puni d'une peine d'emprisonnement ». Or, c'est précisément ce que prévoyait l'article L. 622-1 du CESEDA s'agissant du séjour irrégulier. Mais dans la pratique cette infraction pénale était instrumentalisée par les services de police et les parquets avec comme finalité principale de préparer la procédure administrative d'éloignement et non aux fins de poursuites. Ainsi, en 2009, sur 96 109 étrangers mis en cause pour infraction aux conditions générales d'entrée et de séjour, 74 050 ont été placés en garde à vue.[100] Ces mesures ont abouti à 30 270 placements en rétention pour 5 306 condamnations (597 pour la seule infraction prévue l'article L. 621-1 dont 197 à une peine de prison ferme et 50 personnes en état de récidive légale).[101]

[98] L Masera et F Vigano, membres de l'AGSI et qui ont de nombreux échanges avec les milieux juridiques français de défense des étrangers (Mirgeurop, ADDE) ont inspiré la question préjudicielle de l'affaire El Dridi. V leur article : « Illegittimità comunitaria della vigente disciplina delle espulsioni e possibili rimedi giurisdizionali » (2010) no 2 *Riv it dir proc pen* 560.

[99] V not L Masera, « Les ressorts de l'affaire El Dridi » in Gisti, *Immigration : un régime pénal d'exception* Coll. « Penser l'immigration autrement », juin 2012 ; « La rétention de l'étranger en Italie après la directive 2008/115/CE », in C Severino, *La transposition de la "directive retour". France, Espagne et Italie* (Bruxelles, Bruylant, 2015) 155–78.

[100] Etat 4001 annuel, DCPJ cité fiche thématique 15 « Les gardes à vue pour crimes et délits non routiers et le rapport « Gardes à vue / Mis en cause » de 2005 à 2010 » in Observatoire national de la délinquance et des réponses pénales, *Rapport La criminalité en France 2011*, 538.

[101] S Slama, « Confirmation de l'impossibilité de placement en garde à vue d'un ressortissant d'un pays tiers sur le seul fondement de son séjour irrégulier sans épuisement des mécanismes coercitifs de la directive » in *Actualités Droits-Libertés*, 14 juillet 2012.

Dans ce contexte, la mise en cause du délit de séjour irrégulier par la Cour de justice dans l'affaire *El Dridi* s'est répandue, dans les jours suivants la décision, comme une trainée de poudre et la contrariété de l'article L. 622-1 à la DR a été soulevée devant les JLD par de nombreux avocats entrainant des centaines de remises en liberté. Mais, là encore, les juges se sont divisés sur la position à tenir s'agissant des incidences sur le droit français de cette décision.[102] Ils ont été encouragés en cela par le fait que, contre toute évidence,[103] le ministère de l'Intérieur et la Chancellerie ont immédiatement résisté en donnant des instructions visant à minimiser l'impact de la décision du 28 avril 2011.[104] Et donc, une nouvelle fois, c'est par voie de circulaire que les autorités françaises ont cherché à entraver la mise en application de la DR conforme à l'interprétation donnée par la CJUE et ce afin de tenter de sauvegarder le dispositif français.

Dans ce contexte de nouvelle cacophonie judiciaire, une magistrate de la Cour d'appel de Paris a soulevé d'office le moyen de violation du droit de l'Union et elle a saisi, en demandant l'urgence (article 104 ter du règlement), la Cour de justice d'une question préjudicielle sur la conformité de l'article L. 621-1 du CESEDA à la DR.[105] Si l'urgence n'a pas été accordée compte tenu de la remise en liberté d'Alexandre Achughbabian, en revanche la procédure accélérée a été décidée (article 104 bis du règlement de procédure) et à la demande du gouvernement français, l'affaire a été renvoyée en Grande chambre.

Toutefois face à la levée de boucliers de certains Etats membres, la Cour de justice a tergiversé. Elle a certes confirmé la portée de l'arrêt *El Dridi* en estimant que la législation française « en cause au principal », c'est-à-dire l'article L. 621-1, en prévoyant une peine d'emprisonnement, est « susceptible de faire échec à l'application des normes et des procédures communes établies par la directive 2008/115 et de retarder le retour, portant ainsi, précité, atteinte à l'effet utile de ladite directive ».[106] Mais, elle a – en même temps – confirmé d'une part la conformité du même article L. 621-1 et des procédures de garde à vue dans une première phase d' « arrestation initiale » – qui est enfermée dans un délai « certes bref mais raisonnable » ; délai pendant lequel l'Etat peut déterminer si l'étranger

[102] S Slama, « Le printemps des sans-papiers : Directive « retour », rétention et pénalisation (les suites de l'arrêt *El Dridi*, CJUE, 28 avril 2010) », *CPDH* 9 juin 2011.

[103] cf not M-L Basilien, « Directive « retour » : la Cour de Luxembourg met en cause la pénalisation de l'irrégularité entravant l'efficacité du droit de l'UE », CPDH du 29 avril 2011 ; S Slama, « Une remise en cause profonde de la pénalisation de l'irrégularité en France », Recueil Dalloz 2011.1400 ; V Baudet-Caille, « Les peines d'emprisonnement pour séjour irrégulier dans la tourmente », Dictionnaire permanent- droit des étrangers, Bulletin no 201, juin 2011, 2 ; F Kauff-Gazin, « La directive « retour » au secours des étrangers ? : de quelques ambiguïtés de l'affaire *El Dridi* du 28 avril 2011 », Europe no 6, Juin 2011, étude 7 ; S Slama et M-L. Basilien-Gainche, « L'arrêt *El Dridi* » (n 84) 362 ; G Poissonnier, « Etranger en simple situation irrégulière : il y a urgence à légiférer » (2012) *Recueil Dalloz* 333.

[104] Ministère de la Justice, circulaire du 12 mai 2011 relative à la portée de l'arrêt de la Cour de justice européenne (CJUE) du 28 avril 2011 portant sur l'interprétation des articles 15 et 16 de la directive 2008/115/CE, dite « directive retour ».

[105] S Slama, « Pénalisation de l'irrégularité : une question préjudicielle en urgence sur l'article L.621-1 du CESEDA (CA Paris, 29 juin 2011, *A Achughbabian*) », *CPDH* 25 octobre 2011. Nous avons été impliqué dans cette affaire comme expert auprès des avocats du requérant.

[106] *El Dridi* (n 34) pt 3.

est, ou non, en séjour irrégulier. D'autre part, la Cour a rappelé la possibilité, en cas d'échec des mesures prescrites par la directive, d'infliger à l'étranger une sanction pénale d'emprisonnement dans le cas où il continuerait à séjourner irrégulièrement « sans motif justifié de non-retour ».[107]

Face à une jurisprudence aussi fuyante et arrangeante, la Cour de cassation aurait pu elle-même tergiverser. Car, une nouvelle fois, la Chancellerie a adressé des instructions développant une interprétation restrictive de l'arrêt rendu.[108] Il s'agissait là encore de maintenir, envers et contre tout, la possibilité de placement en garde à vue de sans-papiers interpellés. Une nouvelle fois les juges judiciaires se sont divisés sur les conséquences à tirer de cette décision.[109]

Après l'échec de la QPC visant à ce que le juge constitutionnel tire les conséquences, dans le cadre du contrôle de constitutionnalité, de l'inapplicabilité de l'article L. 621-1 au regard du droit de l'Union (v. supra),[110] la Cour de cassation s'est saisie de pourvois en cassation déposés par Me Spinosi, l'un des avocats d'Alexandre Achughbabian devant la Cour de justice, pour trancher dans le vif en mettant fin, dans une série d'arrêts du 5 juillet 2012, à toute possibilité de garde à vue de sans-papiers tant que « l'une des » mesures coercitives de la directive 2008/115/CE, en particulier la rétention de 45 jours, n'a pas été épuisée.[111]

Toutefois, soucieuse de ne pas interférer dans la campagne présidentielle en cours, la première chambre civile a alors temporisé en sollicitant, opportunément, l'avis de la chambre criminelle sur le point de savoir si un ressortissant de pays tiers en séjour irrégulier pouvait encore, « à la lumière des arrêts de la Cour de justice de l'Union européenne du 28 avril 2011 (*El Dridi*) et du 6 décembre 2011 (*Achughbabian*) », être placé en garde à vue sur le fondement des articles 62-2, 63 et 67 du code de procédure pénale alors que ceux-ci exigent un délit puni d'emprisonnement. Dans son avis du 5 juin 2012, la chambre criminelle a, sans chercher à ménager la chèvre et le chou, estimé qu'au regard de la jurisprudence européenne un ressortissant d'un Etat tiers en situation irrégulière mis en cause « pour le seul délit prévu par l'article L. 621-1 » ne pouvait plus être « placé en garde à vue à l'occasion d'une procédure diligentée de ce seul chef ».[112]

[107] *Achughbabian* (n 48). cf S Slama, « La Cour de justice consacre l'ubiquité du délit de séjour irrégulier, à la fois conforme et non conforme au droit de l'Union européenne selon la phase de la procédure de retour » in *Lettre Actualités Droits-Libertés*, 7 décembre 2011.

[108] Circulaire no 11-04-C39 du 13 décembre 2011 relative à la portée de l'arrêt de la CJUE « *Achughbabian* » du 6 décembre 2011 portant sur la compatibilité de l'article L.621-1 du CESEDA avec la directive 2008/115/CE dite « directive retour »).

[109] S Slama, « Mêmes causes, même cacophonie judiciaire (les suites d'*Achughbabian* – CJUE 6 décembre 2011) », *CPDH* 8 décembre 2011.

[110] Cons constit, décision no 2011-217 QPC du 03 février 2012, *M Mohammed Alki B* (Délit d'entrée ou de séjour irrégulier en France).

[111] Cass, civ, 1ère, 5 juillet 2012, arrêt no 959, no 11-30.371 ; arrêt no 965, no 11-30.530 ; arrêt no 960, no 11-19.250.

[112] Cass, crim, avis no 9002 du 5 juin 2012, *Demande d'avis formulée le 3 avril 2012 par la première chambre civile* ; *ADL* du 20 juin 2012 par S Slama et B Francos ; (2012) *Recueil Dalloz* 1551, obs G Poissonnier ; (2012) *JCP G*, act 735, obs A Levade.

La fermeté de la position de la Cour de cassation a, cette fois-ci, brisé la résistance des autorités françaises.[113] Ainsi, dès le 6 juillet 2012, la Chancellerie s'est inclinée en donnant aux Parquets des instructions contraires à ses précédentes instructions en leur demandant « d'inviter les officiers de police judiciaire à éviter de recourir désormais à une mesure de garde à vue du seul chef de séjour irrégulier ».[114] Concomitamment, le ministère de l'Intérieur a informé les préfets de ces instructions du Garde des Sceaux et leur a demandé d'en tirer les conséquences nécessaires.[115] Il a fallu attendre le début de l'année 2013 pour que la loi « Valls » no 2012-1560 du 31 décembre 2012 assure la mise en conformité du droit français au droit de l'Union par l'abrogation pure et simple de l'article L. 621-1 du CESEDA et la création de la retenue aux fins de vérifications du droit au séjour (art. L. 611-1-1).

L'effervescence a été bien moindre autour de l'arrêt *Affum*,[116] compte tenu notamment de la complexité des faits d'espèce, mêlant délit d'entrée irrégulière et transit dans l'espace Schengen. Mais cette affaire est aussi symptomatique de la résistance des autorités françaises à tirer les conséquences d'une décision remettant en cause la législation et les pratiques nationales. Elle met également en évidence l'inclination de la Cour de cassation, particulièrement de la première chambre civile, à développer une interaction avec le juge de l'UE. Non seulement elle a renvoyé à la Cour de justice la question préjudicielle ;[117] mais elle a, aussi, appliqué sa jurisprudence issue des arrêts du 5 juillet 2012 sur la garde à vue des sans-papiers aux cas d'entrée irrégulière en remettant en cause l'article L. 621-2, 2° du CESEDA.[118] Il a fallu pourtant attendre l'entrée en vigueur de la loi « asile – immigration – intégration » no 2018-778 du 10 septembre 2018 pour que cette disposition soit – enfin – abrogée.

Ces deux illustrations de l'abrogation du délit d'entrée et de séjour irréguliers à la suite des arrêts *Achughbabian* et *Affum* montrent donc l'existence d'un certain activisme judiciaire de la Cour de cassation dans l'interaction avec la Cour de justice afin d'assurer la mise en conformité du droit français au droit de l'Union,[119]

[113] S Slama, « Epilogue d'une saga judiciaire sur la garde à vue pour séjour irrégulier » (2012) *Recueil Dalloz* 2001.

[114] Circ DACG-DACS 11-04-C39, 6 juillet 2012 relative aux conséquences des arrêts de la 1ère chambre civile de la Cour de cassation du 5 juillet 2012 relatif à la garde à vue en matière de séjour irrégulier et de l'arrêt de la même chambre du 6 juin 2012 concernant l'article L.611-1 du CESEDA.

[115] Circ NOR INT/K/12/07284/C, 6 juillet 2012 relative au placement en garde à vue des ressortissants étrangers en situation irrégulière et contrôle spécifique du titre de séjour.

[116] *Affum* (n 88); (2016) *AJ pénal* 387, obs C Saas ; (2016) *Europe* no 8–9, comm 271, obs F Gazin.

[117] cf aussi Cass, civ 1ère, 12 juil 2017, *Préfet des Pyrénées-Orientales c/ M Abdelaziz X*, no 16-22.548.

[118] Cass, civ 1ère, 9 nov 2016, no 13-28.349, Bull: un ressortissant d'un pays tiers à l'Union, entré en France irrégulièrement, par une frontière intérieure à l'espace Schengen, qui n'encourt pas l'emprisonnement prévu à l'article L. 621-2, 2°, du CESEDA dès lors que la procédure de retour établie par la directive 2008/115/CE n'a pas encore été menée à son terme, ne peut, au regard des articles 63 et 67 du code de procédure pénale, être placé en garde à vue à l'occasion d'une procédure de flagrant délit diligentée du seul chef d'entrée irrégulière.

[119] Pour s'en convaincre cf dans les actes du colloque organisé par la Cour de cassation (Gargoullaud, *Le droit et les étrangers en situation irrégulière* (n 24)) les contributions de juges dans

y compris s'il s'agit de briser la résistance des autorités françaises – celles-ci se montrant dans l'incapacité de remettre en cause spontanément le dispositif existant. Sur la question du droit d'être entendu, l'attitude du Conseil d'Etat a été plus ambiguë et tend davantage à conforter la législation ou les pratiques administratives existantes ou, à tout le moins, sa propre jurisprudence.

B. *Mukarubega* et *Boudjlida*: dialogue en sourdine sur le droit d'être entendu

Ces deux affaires sont caractéristiques de techniques d'interactions avec la Cour de justice utilisées par le Conseil d'Etat visant – en même temps – à donner bonne figure tout en paraissant dialoguer avec le juge de l'UE et en veillant surtout à garder les coudées franches dans l'application des principes dégagés. En l'occurrence l'interaction est non seulement en trompe l'œil mais surtout le dialogue se réalise en sourdine.

Le principe du contradictoire préalable (*Audiatur et altera pars* ou *Audi alteram partem*) découle du principe des droits de la défense. En droit de l'Union européenne il est aussi rattaché au droit de « bonne administration »,[120] consacré sous forme de principe général du droit de l'Union et décliné à l'article 41 de la charte des droits fondamentaux pour les « affaires traitées … par les institutions, organes et organismes de l'Union ». Il se rattache aussi, peu ou prou, aux articles 47 (droit au procès équitable et au recours effectif) et 48 (présomption d'innocence) de la Charte.

Ce même principe du contradictoire préalable existe de longue date en droit français sous forme de principe général de droit comme corollaire des droits de la défense qui s'applique même dans le silence des textes.[121] Il a ensuite été inscrit dans la réglementation française par le décret « Le Pors » du 8 novembre 1983 puis généralisé par la loi du 12 avril 2000 sur les droits des citoyens dans leur relations avec les administrés. Ce principe suppose que l'administré soit invité par l'administration, préalablement à l'intervention d'une décision qui lui fait grief, à présenter des observations orales ou écrites. Toutefois, dès le début des années 1990, le Conseil d'Etat a jugé que ce principe n'était pas applicable aux arrêtés préfectoraux de reconduite à la frontière. Eu égard à la brièveté des délais de recours et de

ces affaires : D Guérin (président de la Chambre criminelle), « La directive « retour » : quelle place pour le juge pénal ? », 149–60 et M Valdès-Boulouque (Avocate générale de la première chambre civile à la Cour de cassation), « La directive retour et l'impossible pénalisation du séjour irrégulier », 162–72.

[120] L Azoulai et L Clément-Wilz « La bonne administration » in J-B Auby et J Dutheil de la Rochère (dir), *Droit administratif européen*, 2è éd (Bruxelles, Bruylant, 2013).

[121] cf CE 1944, *Dame Vve Trompier Gravier* inspiré de l'article 65 de la loi d'avril 1905. Au sein de la convention ayant élaboré la Charte des droits fondamentaux, le représentant français aurait contribué à l'inscription de ce droit à la « bonne administration » (G Braibant, *Charte des droits fondamentaux de l'Union européenne*, Le Seuil, coll. « Points essai » sous l'article 41).

jugement, il a estimé que le contradictoire pouvait, à défaut de se dérouler devant l'administration, se dérouler devant le juge.[122] Depuis, malgré les évolutions de ce contentieux, il a constamment maintenu cette jurisprudence absurde[123] et l'a même appliqué aux citoyens de l'UE et aux membres de leur famille.[124]

En droit de l'Union, la Cour de justice a admis en 2012 que le droit d'être entendu, qui découle d'un principe général de droit de l'Union, est applicable aux procédures d'asile et, surtout, il a vocation à s'appliquer « *à toute procédure susceptible d'aboutir à un acte faisant grief* » y compris « *lorsque la réglementation applicable ne prévoit pas expressément une telle formalité* ».[125] Si bien que ce droit a été rapidement invoqué devant les juges administratifs français dans le contentieux de l'OQTF dans la mesure où le prononcé d'une telle mesure de retour n'est précédée d'aucune procédure contradictoire préalable.[126] En ce sens, dès février 2013, le tribunal administratif de Lyon a rendu, en formation élargie, deux jugements reconnaissant aux étrangers le bénéfice de ce droit.[127]

Dès lors la stratégie du Conseil d'Etat a été de neutraliser la portée de ce droit, afin qu'il ait le moins d'incidence possible dans la procédure administrative précédant l'édiction de l'OQTF. Un tel positionnement permettait aussi conserver, dans sa substance, sa jurisprudence en la matière depuis 1991. L'objectif implicite était de veiller à ne pas renforcer les contraintes qui pèsent sur l'administration préfectorale lorsqu'elle édicte une mesure d'éloignement. Mais cela crée une situation paradoxale car à défaut de contradictoire préalable organisé devant l'administration avant l'édiction de l'OQTF, c'est au juge qu'il appartient de prendre en compte a posteriori les éléments que l'étranger a à faire valoir. Ce transfert du droit d'être entendu de l'administration au juge est non seulement absurde mais aussi contreproductif puisqu'il renforce le risque de censure contentieuse pour des motifs non pris en compte par l'administration alors que si celle-ci prenait la peine d'entendre préalablement l'étranger cela éviterait d'édicter inutilement une décision de retour, avec les incidences importantes pour l'étranger sur sa vie privée, familiale et professionnelle et sur ses libertés.

[122] CE, Sect, 19 avril 1991, *Préfet de police c Demir*, no 120435. cf pour une mise en perspective : S Slama, « Médiation en droit des étrangers : l'être et le néant » in P Greciano, *Justice et droits de l'homme. Les enjeux de la médiation internationale* (Paris, Mare & Martin, 2015) 287–308.

[123] CE, avis, 19 octobre 2007, *Hammou et Benabdelhak*, no 306821, Rec Lebon ; CE, avis, 28 novembre 2007, *Barjamaj*, no 307999, Rec Lebon.

[124] CE, avis, 26 nov 2008, *Silidor*, no 315441, au Lebon ; (2009) *Actualité juridique Droit administratif* 270, concl M Guyomar. La seule exception, en droit de l'éloignement, concerne les reconduites « Schengen » : CE, 24 novembre 2010, *Eddomairi*, no 344411, Rec Lebon.

[125] CJUE 22 novembre 2012, *M M c Minister for Justice, Equality and Law Reform*, aff C-277/11, ECLI:EU:C:2012:744 ; Europe 2013, comm 19, F Gazin (pts 84 et 86).

[126] En ce sens le rapporteur public Xavier Domino a fait valoir dans ses conclusions sur l'arrêt Halifa que : « La porte ainsi fermée au niveau du droit national n'a pas empêché que la question revienne par la fenêtre du droit de l'Union européenne » (X Domino, « Droit d'être entendu et OQTF : un exemple du dialogue entre les jurisprudences (conclusions) » (2014) *Actualité juridique Droit administratif* 1501).

[127] TA de Lyon, 28 février 2013, no 1208055 (citoyenne de l'UE) et no 1208057 (ressortissante de pays tiers), (2013) *RFDA* 839, concl H Stillmunkes.

Pourtant dès avril 2013, la Cour d'appel de Lyon a estimé que le droit d'être entendu issu du droit de l'UE n'oblige pas à inviter préalablement l'administré à présenter des observations orales ou écrites pour adopter l'OQTF. C'est à l'étranger sous le coup d'une mesure d'éloignement de prendre *spontanément* l'initiative de demander à être entendu, sans avoir besoin d'en être informé par l'administration.[128] D'autres CAA ont estimé que lorsque l'étranger formule une demande de titre de séjour il ne peut ignorer que le préfet peut prendre à son encontre, en cas de refus, une OQTF.[129]

Face à cette difficulté sérieuse se présentant dans un grand nombre de litiges, le tribunal administratif de Montreuil, probablement avec l'aval du Conseil d'Etat, avait prévu de lui transmettre une demande d'avis sur une question de droit sur cette question. Toutefois, deux autres tribunaux administratifs ont, conformément à l'esprit des traités, préféré adresser ce problème d'interprétation du droit de l'Union à son interprète authentique – la Cour de justice. Elle a donc été saisie de questions préjudicielles sur l'applicabilité et la portée du droit d'être entendu dans les affaires *Mukarubega* et *Boudjlida*.[130] La présidente du TA de Melun n'a néanmoins pas demandé la procédure accélérée dans ces affaires. Selon notre lecture, le coup s'est alors joué à plusieurs bandes.

Le premier ricochet a eu lieu grâce à une question préjudicielle du *Raad van State* posée parallèlement, en urgence. La Cour de justice était, en l'occurrence, interrogée, non pas sur l'applicabilité du principe général (contrairement au juge français le juge néerlandais la tenait pour acquise) mais « seulement » sur « les conséquences » attachées à sa violation lors de l'adoption d'une décision de prolongation d'une rétention. La décision,[131] rendue sur rapport du juge français (et, accessoirement, membre du Conseil d'Etat), Jean Claude Bonichot, est venue télescoper les procédures françaises.[132] En effet, dans sa décision du 10 septembre 2013, le juge européen a limité la portée concrète du droit d'être entendu en estimant que les droits fondamentaux tels que le droit d'être entendu ne constituent pas des

[128] CAA de Lyon, 14 mars 2013, no 12LY02737 ; CAA Bordeaux, 1ème ch, 4 avril 2013, no 12BX01849. cf M Clément, « Droit d'être entendu, droit de la défense et OQTF », *GDR-ELSJ*, 29 avril 2013, www.gdr-elsj.eu/2013/04/29.

[129] CAA Bordeaux, 16 juillet 2013, no 13BX00601 ; CAA Nancy, 1er juillet 2013, no 13NC00058, CAA Nantes, 27 juin 2013, no 12NT02014, CAA Marseille, 18 juin 2013, no 12MA04450.

[130] TA de Melun, 8 mars 2013, *Mme Sophie Mukarubega*, no 1301686 enregistrée sous le no C-166/13 et TA de Pau, 30 avril 2013, *M Khaled Boudjlida*, no 1300264, enregistrée sous le no C-249/13. S Slama, « Question préjudicielle sur le droit d'être entendu par l'administration préalablement à l'édiction d'une OQTF », *Actualités Droits-Libertés*, 19 mars 2013.

[131] CJUE 10 septembre 2013, *MG et NR c Staatssecretaris van Veiligheid en Justitie*, aff C-383/13 PPU, ECLI:EU:C:2013:533.

[132] Dans sa prise de position, l'avocat général Wathelet estimait, à l'inverse, que « le raisonnement de la Cour, au point 26 de l'arrêt *Distillers Company/Commission*, …, selon lequel une irrégularité de procédure n'entraîne l'annulation en tout ou en partie d'une décision que s'il est établi que, en l'absence de cette irrégularité, la décision attaquée aurait pu avoir un contenu différent, ne saurait être appliqué, par analogie, dans le cadre de mesures aussi restrictives de la liberté des personnes que la rétention » (prise de position de l'avocat général M Melchior Wathelet présentée le 23 août 2013 dans l'affaire *MG et NR*, ECLI:EU:C:2013:553).

« prérogatives absolues » et, par suite, peuvent comporter des restrictions. Ainsi, tout manquement à ce droit à l'occasion de la mise en œuvre d'une des procédures prévues par la DR n'a pas nécessairement pour conséquence d'entacher d'illégalité la décision prise et n'appelle donc pas automatiquement, s'agissant de la rétention, la remise en liberté du ressortissant concerné. Une violation des droits de la défense, en particulier du droit d'être entendu, n'entraîne l'annulation de la décision prise au terme de la procédure administrative en cause « que si, en l'absence de cette irrégularité, cette procédure pouvait aboutir à un résultat différent ». La seule méconnaissance du droit à être entendu n'entache pas, automatiquement, d'illégalité la décision administrative en cause. Le requérant doit établir que cette violation a eu un effet sur le sens de la décision. La charge de la preuve pèse sur celui-ci et non sur l'administration.

Pour justifier cette limitation de la portée du droit d'être entendu, la Cour invoque dans ses arrêts le principe de l'effet utile de la DR. A ce titre, elle rappelle, dans le prolongement des arrêts *Dridi*, *Achughbabian* et *Sagor*, que son objectif est « d'assurer des procédures efficaces d'éloignement ».

Or, comme le fit valoir Xavier Domino dans ses conclusions sur l'arrêt *Halifa*, la jurisprudence *G & R* « rejoint très fortement » la logique de la jurisprudence du Conseil d'Etat « *Danthony* ».[133] Cette source d'inspiration est d'ailleurs confirmée par le juge Bonichot lui-même. Dans un colloque à la Cour de cassation au cours duquel il était amené à faire le bilan de la jurisprudence de la CJUE relative à la DR, il relève lui-même, après avoir fait état de l'arrêt *G & R*, que cette solution « n'est évidemment pas sans rappeler la jurisprudence *Danthony* du Conseil d'État français ».[134] Faisant sien le commentaire de la chronique de droit de l'Union dans l'*Actualité juridique droit administratif*, il relève également que la décision de la Cour de justice « laisse donc au juge national l'entière responsabilité de l'appréciation de l'incidence de l'irrégularité constatée sur le sens de la décision contestée ».[135]

Par un second ricochet, le Conseil d'Etat a devancé la réponse de la Cour de justice, en estimant, dans sa décision *Halifa* du 4 juin 2014[136] que le droit d'être

[133] CE, Ass, 23 déc 2011, *Danthony*, no 335033, Rec Lebon ; (2012) *RFDA* 284, concl G Dumortier. L'arrêt Danthony est une importante jurisprudence du Conseil d'Etat (à tel point qu'elle a été intégrée dans les Grands arrêts de la jurisprudence administrative » – ouvrage de référence sur la jurisprudence administrative). Il a posé le principe selon lequel « un vice affectant le déroulement d'une procédure administrative préalable, suivie à titre obligatoire ou facultatif, n'est de nature à entacher d'illégalité la décision prise que s'il ressort des pièces du dossier qu'il a été susceptible d'exercer, en l'espèce, une influence sur le sens de la décision prise ou qu'il a privé les intéressés d'une garantie ». Cet arrêt a, depuis, ouvert tout un courant de jurisprudences qui restreint l'invocation du vice de formes en contentieux administratif (cf en dernier lieu, propos de CE, Ass, 18 mai 2018, *Fédération des finances et des affaires économiques de la CFDT*, no 414583 ; D de Béchillon, « La limitation dans le temps de l'invocation des vices de forme et de procédure affectant les actes réglementaires – Contre », *RFDA* 2018.662.

[134] J-C Bonichot, « Aux frontières du droit national : le contrôle de l'étranger sous le regard du droit de l'Union, l'acquis de Schengen et la fin des frontières intérieures » in S Gargoullaud, *Le droit et les étrangers en situation irrégulière* (n 24) 139.

[135] M Aubert, E Broussy et H Cassagnabère, « La chronique de droit de l'Union » (2013) *Actualité juridique Droit administratif* 2308.

[136] CE, 4 juin 2014, *Halifa*, no 370515, Lebon.

entendu n'implique pas que l'administration préfectorale ait l'obligation de mettre l'intéressé à même de présenter ses observations « de façon spécifique » sur la décision l'obligeant à quitter le territoire français dès lors qu'il a pu être entendu avant que n'intervienne la décision refusant de lui délivrer un titre de séjour.

Guidée par le même souci d'efficacité, la CJUE a été encore plus loin. Dans ses – très décevantes – décisions *Mukarubega*[137] et *Boudjlida*,[138] elle a en effet affaibli considérablement la substance même du droit d'être entendu lorsqu'il est appliqué en droit des étrangers.[139] Ce droit relève largement de la marge d'appréciation des Etats membres.

Ainsi, in fine, le Conseil d'Etat a pu maintenir sa jurisprudence traditionnelle privant de toute portée concrète le droit d'être entendu, même s'il découle désormais non plus d'un principe général de droit ou de la loi française mais d'un principe général de droit de l'UE …

Ces affaires sont emblématiques de la capacité du Conseil d'Etat à se ménager et à ménager à l'administration des marges de manœuvre dans la mise en œuvre des principes dégagés par la Cour de justice. Il n'oppose en revanche pas de résistance à faire siennes des interprétations portant sur des éléments procéduraux dégagées par celle-ci. Ainsi, par exemple, comme le juge de l'Union,[140] le juge administratif exige, pour le prononcé d'une OQTF, un examen cas par cas, de la situation de l'étranger afin d'assurer le respect de ses droits fondamentaux (vie privée et familiale, prohibition des tortures et traitement inhumains et dégradants, etc.).[141] De même, dans le prolongement de la jurisprudence de la Cour,[142] le Conseil d'État a admis la possibilité d'une motivation commune de l'OQTF et des mesures coercitives (obligation de présentation de l'étranger ayant bénéficié d'un DDV)[143] ou encore de la décision relative au droit de séjour et de celle de l'OQTF.[144]

[137] *Mukarubega* (n 96).

[138] *Boudjlida* (n 97).

[139] cf M-L Basilien Gainche et T Racho, « Quand le souci d'efficacité de l'éloignement l'emporte sur l'application effective des droits fondamentaux », *La Revue des droits de l'homme/ Actualités Droits-Libertés*, novembre 2014, http://revdh.revues.org/957 ; N Lepoutre, « Le droit d'être entendu avant l'adoption d'une mesure d'éloignement, un droit fondamental réduit à portion congrue », *La Revue des droits de l'homme/ Actualités droits-libertés*, 24 septembre 2018, http://journals.openedition.org/revdh/1042 ; J Schmitz, « Le principe du contradictoire à la lumière du droit de l'Union européenne : illustration en matière d'éloignement des étrangers » (2014) no 8–9 *Droit Administratif* étude 14.

[140] CJUE 6 décembre 2012, *Sagor*, aff C-430/11, ECLI:EU:C:2012:777, à propos de l'examen du risque de fuite.

[141] cf s'agissant des arrêts de principe sur le contrôle de l'erreur manifeste d'appréciation sur l'appréciation par le préfet de la situation particulière de l'étranger : CE, ass, 29 juin 1990, *Préfet du Doubs c/ Mme Olmos Quintero*, no 115687, Lebon 184. Sur l'application de ce contrôle s'agissant des interdictions de retour sur le territoire français : CE, 4 juin 2012, *Ghevondyan*, no 356505, Lebon T, 630, 638, 797 et 946 ; CE, 12 mars 2012, *Harounur*, no 354165, Lebon 83.

[142] CJUE 11 juin 2015, *Z Zh c Staatssecretaris van Veiligheid en Justitie et Staatssecretaris van Veiligheid en Justitie c IO*, ECLI:EU:C:2015:377.

[143] CE, 23 juill 2012, *Zhang*, no 359496, Lebon T, 542, 798, 893 et 946.

[144] CE, 10 oct 2013, *Fkiri*, no 359221, Lebon T, 392, 405, 482 et 491 ; RTD eur 2014.952-11, obs D Ritleng. V aussi : CE, 17 avr 2015, *Hamouchi*, no 372195, Lebon 153.

En définitive, le Conseil d'Etat n'a pas, nous semble-t-il, totalement tiré les conséquences de décisions de la Cour de justice tendant à rappeler que si les Etats membres sont libres, compte tenu de la lettre et de l'économie générale de l'article 6 de la DR, d'apprécier s'il y a lieu de constater l'irrégularité du séjour de l'étranger et, par suite, d'édicter une décision de retour, il ne devrait toutefois pas y avoir d'entre deux. Si l'Etat membre décide de de ne pas éloigner l'étranger en séjour irrégulier, il devrait le régulariser.[145] Le CESEDA prévoit certes qu'en cas d'annulation d'une OQTF, l'étranger se voit remettre une autorisation provisoire de séjour permettant un réexamen de sa situation par la préfecture.[146] Mais dans la pratique cette *limbo zone*, qu'on qualifie en France de « ni – ni » (« ni régularisables – ni expulsables ») reste fréquente.

On peut aussi s'interroger sur le point de savoir si la Cour de cassation – et le législateur français – ont totalement tiré les conséquences de l'arrêt *Madhi* qui exige lors de la prolongation de la rétention que le juge exerçant le contrôle sur cette mesure bénéficie d'un pouvoir de plein contentieux, y compris en bénéficiant d'un pouvoir de substitution de sa décision à celle de l'administration.[147]

IV. Conclusion

En conclusion, on constate que, sans constituer les arbitres ultimes de l'application de la DR, les hautes juridictions nationales, par les stratégies qu'elles adoptent jouent un rôle déterminant, en interagissant ou, à l'inverse en refusant d'interagir, avec le juge de l'Union européenne dans l'interprétation ou l'application de cette directive. Ce n'est pas l'existence d'une dualité juridictionnelle, avec l'intervention parallèle du juge administratif et du juge judiciaire, pour exercer un contrôle sur les décisions d'éloignement et de rétention, qui perturbe l'application du droit de l'Union. Surtout que depuis la loi du 7 mars 2016 la répartition des rôles est clairement définie : le contrôle de la légalité et du bien-fondé de la rétention n'appartient qu'au seul juge judiciaire (JLD) tandis que le juge administratif (TA) contrôle la légalité de l'OQTF et de toutes les décisions subséquentes (refus de DDV, IRTF, arrêté fixant le pays de destination, etc.).[148]

En revanche les hautes juridictions nationales françaises ne font toutes preuve du même activisme judiciaire pour s'assurer que les droits fondamentaux garantis

[145] CJUE 23 avril 2015, *Subdelegación del Gobierno en Gipuzkoa – Extranjería contre Samir Zaizoune*, aff C-38/14, ECLI:EU:C:2015:260, pts 31 et 32.

[146] Article L512-4 du CESEDA modifié par l'article 28 de la loi no 2016-274 du 7 mars 2016.

[147] *Mahdi* (n 13); S Slama, « Directive « retour » : la Cour de justice remodèle le contrôle juridictionnel et les modalités de prolongation de la rétention », *Lexbase Hebdo édition publique* no 340 du 17 juillet 2014.

[148] cf S von Coester et S Gargoullaud, « L'articulation des contentieux : commentaire à deux voix de la loi du 7 mars 2016 » in Gargoullaud (n 24) 93–111. Suzanne Van Coester est rapporteure publique à la section du contentieux au Conseil d'État et Stéphanie Gargoullaud est conseillère référendaire de la première chambre civile à la Cour de cassation (après avoir été en détachement au Conseil d'Etat).

par la DR et la Charte des droits fondamentaux bénéficient effectivement aux intéressés.

La Cour de cassation a plutôt joué le jeu de l'interaction judiciaire et elle a donné une pleine portée aux décisions de la Cour de justice concernant aussi bien les délits de séjour (*Achughbabian*) et d'entrée irréguliers (*Affum*) en mettant fin à la pratique des gardes à vue de sans-papiers.[149]

Fidèle à sa posture consistant à refuser à assurer le respect du droit de l'Union dans le cadre du contrôle de constitutionnalité des lois, le Conseil constitutionnel n'a pas assuré le respect de la DR, y compris lorsqu'il a été saisi de contrariétés manifestes ou lorsqu'il aurait dû tirer les conséquences de la jurisprudence de la CJUE. Enfin, le Conseil d'Etat est la juridiction qui a l'attitude la plus ambiguë et stratégique à l'égard du droit de l'union européenne et de la CJUE. De longue date, comme en témoigne déjà l'arrêt *Cohn-Bendit* de 1978, il s'évertue à se préserver des marges d'interprétation et à préserver au bénéfice de l'administration des marges d'appréciation dans l'application des normes de l'UE en droit des étrangers. Certes, officiellement, le Conseil d'Etat préconise le « dialogue des juges » – expression qui est d'ailleurs attribuée à Bruno Genevois dans ses conclusions dans l'arrêt *Cohn-Bendit*. Mais lorsqu'on analyse scrupuleusement la jurisprudence du Conseil d'Etat à propos de la DR on constate que, d'une part, il a tendance à privilégier la technique de l'interprétation conforme à un franc constat de contrariété d'une législation à une directive européenne (qui aurait pour effet de rendre inapplicable la législation en cause au détriment de l'efficacité) et, d'autre part, il a tendance user, voire même à abuser, de la théorie de l'acte clair afin de ne pas procéder à un renvoi préjudiciel à la Cour de justice afin de conserver les coudées franches dans l'interprétation de la loi française au regard du droit de l'Union.[150]

[149] Cass, civ, 1ère, 5 juillet 2012 (n 111).

[150] V, entre autres exemples en droit des étrangers de difficultés qui auraient mérité une question préjudicielle : CE, 15 janvier 2010, *Gisti*, no 334879 et CE, 19 juillet 2010, *Gisti*, no 334878 à propos de la conformité de l'article L.622-1 du CESEDA (délit d'aide à l'entrée, au séjour et à la circulation irréguliers) à la directive 2002/90/CE du Conseil du 28 novembre 2002 définissant l'aide à l'entrée, au transit et au séjour irréguliers ; CE, réf, 15 février 2013, *Anafé et Gisti*, no 365709 ; CE, réf, 20 mars 2013, *Anafé et Gisti*, no 366308 et CE, 18 juin 2014, *Anafé et Gisti*, no 366307 à propos de l'instauration d'un visa de transit aéroportuaire pour canaliser l'arrivée de réfugiés syriens au regard de l''article 3-2 du règlement (CE) no 810/2009 du Parlement européen et du Conseil, du 13 juillet 2009, établissant un code communautaire des visas (code des visas) ; CE, 1er octobre 2014, no 365054 à propos de la possibilité d'édicter une OQTF à l'encontre d'un citoyen de l'Union en raison d'un trouble à l'ordre public en raison d'un simple comportement d'escroquerie à la mendicité sur la voie publique ou encore : CE, 28 décembre 2017, *Anafé et a*, no 415291 à propos du de la réintroduction temporaire à compter du 1er novembre 2017 et jusqu'au 30 avril 2018, par les autorités françaises de contrôles aux frontières intérieures de l'espace Schengen, sur le fondement des articles 25 et 27 du règlement (UE) 2016/399 du Parlement européen et du Conseil du 9 mars 2016 concernant un code de l'Union relatif au régime de franchissement des frontières par les personnes, JO L 77/1, 23.3.2016, dit « code frontières Schengen ». V, contra, sur les droits aux conditions matérielles d'accueil des « Dublinés » : CJUE 27 septembre 2012, *Cimade & Gisti*, C-179/11. NB : déclaration de conflit d'intérêt : nous avons pris par, comme expert, à l'ensemble de ces recours.

Témoigne de cette attitude, par moments, de « gaulois réfractaire » à l'égard du droit de l'Union européenne la réaction du nouveau président de la section du contentieux, Jean-Denis Combrexelle à la condamnation, de la France, par la Cour de Luxembourg en raison du non-renvoi par le Conseil d'Etat d'une question préjudicielle en violation des obligations découlant de l'article 267 du TFUE.[151] Ce plus haut juge administratif estime en effet qu'une :

> cour suprême nationale décide, dans l'exercice des responsabilités juridictionnelles qui sont les siennes, de poser *ou non* une question préjudicielle. L'équilibre institutionnel et sans doute la sagesse commandent de ne pas cantonner le rôle des cours suprêmes à celui de l'interprétation de l'évidence.La répartition des rôles entre la Cour de Luxembourg et les juges nationaux obéit ainsi à des usages et équilibres subtils et nécessaires. Il faut les préserver. Surtout en ce moment ».[152]

Mais le Conseil d'Etat ne s'interdit pas, pour autant, le recours à l'interprétation de la Cour de justice. Mais comme en témoigne la neutralisation de la portée concrète du droit d'être entendu dans les affaires *Mukarubega* et *Boudjlida*, la jurisprudence du Conseil d'Etat – et les marges de manœuvre de l'administration préfectorale – ont finalement, dans leur substance, été préservées avant même que ces arrêts aient été rendues grâce à l'intervention des arrêts *G&R* et *Halifa*.

Dans le domaine de l'application par les juridictions de la directive « retour », plus que dans d'autres domaines, l'efficacité des procédures prévaut bien souvent sur la garantie effective des droits fondamentaux. Ce constat est d'autant plus paradoxal que le dispositif français d'éloignement des étrangers en situation irrégulière est probablement l'un des plus inefficaces en Europe.

[151] CJUE 4 octobre 2018, *Commission c France*, aff C-416/17, ECLI:EU:C:2018:811. cf P Cassia, « Camouflet européen pour le Conseil d'Etat », *Le blog de Paul Cassia*, 5 octobre 2018, https://blogs.mediapart.fr/paul-cassia/blog/041018/camouflet-europeen-pour-le-conseil-d-etat. NB : cet article a été écrit, pour l'essentiel, avant l'annonce de cette condamnation

[152] J-D Combrexelle, « Sur l'actualité du « dialogue des juges » » (2018) *Actualité juridique Droit administratif*, 1929.

PART 3

Rights and Safeguards in the Application of the Return Directive: The Role of Judges in Safeguarding Procedural and Fundamental Rights Protection

EDITED BY MADALINA MORARU AND GALINA CORNELISSE

15

The Right to be Heard: The Underestimated Condition for Effective Returns and Human Rights Consideration

VALERIA ILAREVA

I. Introduction

The *audi alteram partem* principle (from Latin, 'hear the other party') has been one of the fundamental tenets of law and justice since ancient times. The right to be heard forms an integral part of the rights of the defence.[1] Respect for the right to defence is a fundamental general principle of EU law.[2]

This chapter aims, on the one hand, to map out the main standards on the right to be heard which have been developed jurisprudentially in the context of proceedings to return illegally staying third-country nationals. Courts and judicial dialogue play an important role in filling out a gap in the Return Directive[3] as the latter does not elaborate on such standards. The chapter provides an extensive discussion on the connection between the right to be heard and the detention measure as one of the main scenarios of return proceedings in current practice. On the other hand, the chapter addresses what is seen by its author as the main problem of the application of this right in return proceedings, namely the underestimation of the role that observance of the right to be heard would play in making return proceedings effective and fundamental human rights respected. The experience of the author as a legal practitioner in the field of the Return Directive has

[1] According to the CJEU, the rights of the defence include the right to be heard and the right to have access to the file. See eg Case C-383/13 PPU *G and R* ECLI:EU:C:2013:533, para 32.

[2] *G and R* (ibid) para 32; *G and R*, Opinion of AG Wathelet, para 44; Case C-249/13 *Khaled Boudjlida v Préfet des Pyrénées-Atlantiques* ECLI:EU:C:2014:2431, paras 32–34.

[3] Directive 2008/115/EC of the European Parliament and of the Council of 16 December 2008 on common standards and procedures in Member States for returning illegally staying third-country nationals [2013] OJ L348 (the 'Return Directive').

helped to contribute with concrete material content and procedural standards to effectively hear the third-country national in return proceedings.

The structure of the contribution unfolds in answering the two main questions in the application of the right to be heard: in respect of *what* should the third-country national be heard (substantive law content of the right to be heard) and *how* should the third-country national be heard (procedural safeguards to effectively hear the person). This algorithm is preceded by an introduction to the nature and general features of the right to be heard under EU law. The last section of the chapter looks into the main stages in the application of the right to be heard. It uses the notion of the right to be heard in a broad sense to encompass both the administrative and court proceedings relating to imposing and reviewing return and detention for the purpose of removal of illegally staying third-country nationals. The right is discussed as a procedural safeguard in the context of pre-litigation administrative proceedings and as an effective remedy in the context of judicial review of the lawfulness of administrative decisions. The study of existing jurisprudence reveals the potential that judicial dialogue has in forging effective standards that correspond to the practical issues arising in the implementation of the right to be heard.

The main arguments in the chapter are based on empirical evidence and research done in the HEAR Project in respect of the legal, psychological and social aspects of the application of the right to be heard of detained immigrants pending forced return.[4] The analysis also takes note of the European Synthesis Report on the Judicial Implementation of Chapter III of the Return Directive on procedural safeguards, produced in the REDIAL Project.[5] Because the author is a practising lawyer in Bulgaria, Bulgarian case-law is at times given as supporting evidence.

II. General Features of the Right to be Heard under EU Law

The right to be heard guarantees every person the opportunity to make known his views effectively during an administrative procedure and before the adoption of a decision liable to affect his/her interests adversely.[6] The individual subject to an adverse decision should be given the opportunity to make his/her views known before a decision is taken. The purpose of this rule is to enable the

[4] Foundation for Access to Rights (FAR), 'Project HEAR: Hearing Entails Awareness and Rights' (Foundation for Access to Rights, 2016) at hear.farbg.eu. The project is implemented by FAR, a non-governmental organisation in Bulgaria. Within the framework of the project, the senior FAR lawyer conducted 30 in-depth interviews with detained immigrants in Bulgaria and documented the practices relating to the application of the right to be heard in the context of detention on immigration grounds.

[5] M Moraru, G Renaudiere and P De Bruycker (ed), 'European Synthesis Report on the Judicial Implementation of Chapter III of the Return Directive – Procedural Safeguards', REDIAL Research Report 2016/03.

[6] *G and R*, Opinion of AG Wathelet (n 2) para 44.

competent authority to duly take into account all relevant information. The individual concerned shall be able to correct errors or to submit information relating to personal circumstances that will argue in favour of the adoption or non-adoption of the decision, or in favour of it having a specific content.[7]

The CJEU has highlighted that the obligation to state reasons for a decision which are sufficiently specific and concrete to allow the person to understand why his or her application is being rejected is a corollary of the principle of respect for the rights of the defence and, in particular, the right to be heard.[8] The connection between the obligation to state reasons and the right to be heard lies in the obligation of the decision-maker to elucidate all relevant facts of the case before taking a decision. It is hardly possible to draw a full picture of the factual situation without having heard the person whom the decision is going to affect. According to Article 12(1) of the Return Directive, return decisions and, if issued, entry-ban decisions and decisions on removal, shall be issued in writing and shall give reasons in fact and in law. Article 15(2) provides that: '[D]etention shall be ordered in writing with reasons being given in fact and in law.' The ECtHR held that a decision on detention must contain elaborate reasoning and that this is one of the criteria for its lawfulness.[9]

The right to be heard should be respected even when no requirement to do so is expressly stipulated by law.[10] In his Opinion in the recent case of *Ispas*, Advocate General Bobek explained the underlying logic of this characteristic of procedural rights and, in particular, of the right to be heard under EU law:

> EU law does not always determine or establish specific procedural rules. Rather, it concentrates on the substantive side of the right or obligation. However, procedural rights are necessary to ensure the effectiveness of EU law. It is in consideration of this connection that the Court has declared that even if not expressly regulated by the provisions of EU law establishing substantive rights or obligations, respect for procedural fundamental rights, such as the right to be heard, is required. (37) In particular, the principle of respect for the rights of the defence applies when Member States act or take decisions within the scope of EU law, even if the applicable EU legislation does not expressly provide for specific procedural requirements.[11]

As an inherent element of the right to defence, the right to be heard is protected at the highest constitutional level in both EU and national law. It is enshrined in Articles 41,[12] 47 and 48 of the Charter of Fundamental Rights of the European

[7] Case C-349/07 *Sopropé* ECLI:EU:C:2008:746, para 49; Case C-166/13 *Mukarubega* ECLI:EU:C:2014:2336, paras 46–48.

[8] Case C-277/11 *M* ECLI:EU:C:2012:744, para 88.

[9] *Lokpo et Touré v Hungary*, Appl No 10816/10 (ECtHR, 20 September 2011) para 24.

[10] *M* (n 8) para 86; *G and R* (n 2) para 32.

[11] Case C-298/16 *Ispas*, Opinion of AG Bobek, ECLI:EU:C:2017:650, para 51.

[12] According to the CJEU, the legal source of the Member State's obligation to ensure respect of the third-country national's right to be heard during the return procedure is the general principle of the EU law of rights of the defence, and not Art 41 of the Charter. See eg Case C-141/12 and C-372/12 *YS and Others* ECLI:EU:C:2014:2081, para 61; *Mukarubega* (n 7) para 44; *Boudjlida* (n 2) paras 32–33.

Union ('the Charter').[13] The national constitutions of EU Member States usually enshrine the right to defence in proceedings before public authorities. For instance, German national courts rely on the national constitutional principle that guarantees the right to be heard.[14] By way of example, according to Article 56 of the Bulgarian constitution: 'Everyone, whose rights or legitimate interests are violated or jeopardized, has the right to defence. Appearing before any institution of State, every citizen may be accompanied by a defender.'[15]

The right to be heard is in principle not absolute and is subject to certain limitations. In order to be deemed lawful, any such limitations must correspond to objectives of general interest pursued by the measure in question and must not constitute, with regard to the objectives pursued, a disproportionate and intolerable interference,[16] which infringes upon the very substance of the rights guaranteed.[17] Every decision by the public authorities based on such limitations must strictly comply with all the statutory conditions circumscribing those limitations.[18]

As a matter of principle, when Member States adopt decisions on matters governed by EU law the consequences of infringement of the right to be heard are to be appraised in line with the principles of equivalence and effectiveness.[19] The principle of equivalence means that, within the remit of its procedural autonomy, each Member State may decide on the means of exercise of the rights to defence and to be heard under conditions that are equivalent to those available in similar situations governed by domestic law. The principle of effectiveness means that domestic procedural law must not make it impossible or excessively difficult to enforce rights derived from EU law. According to Recital 2 of the Return Directive, its goal is to establish an effective removal and repatriation policy, based on common standards, for persons to be returned in a humane manner and with full respect for their fundamental rights and dignity.[20]

According to the CJEU preliminary rulings in the cases of *G and R* and *Boudjlida*, 'the non-respect of the right to be heard renders a return related decision invalid only insofar as the outcome of the procedure would have been different if the right was respected'. The author of this chapter, however, concurs with the opinion of the Advocate General Wathelet delivered in *G and R*.[21] He pointed out

[13] Charter of Fundamental Rights of the European Union [2012] OJ C326.

[14] REDIAL Research Report 2016/03 (n 5) 14.

[15] In its judgment of 5 August 2014 in Case 16862/2013, the Bulgarian Supreme Administrative Court held that the right to be heard is one of the forms of the constitutional right to defence enshrined in Art 56 of the constitution.

[16] Case C-28/05 *Dokter and others* [2006] ECR I-5431, para 75; Case C-402/05 P and C-415/05 P *Kadi and Al Barakaat International Foundation/Council and Commission* [2008] ECR I-6351; Case C-27/09 P *France/People's Mujahidin Organization of Iran* [2011] ECR I-13427, paras 61–67.

[17] *G and R* (n 2) para 33.

[18] Case C-300/11 *ZZ* ECLI:EU:C:2013:363, para 51; Case C-554/13 *Zh and O* ECLI:EU:C:2015:377, para 69; *G and R* (n 2) para 69; *G and R*, Opinion of AG Wathelet (n 2) para 55.

[19] *G and R* (n 2) paras 35–36.

[20] Case C-61/11 PPU *El Dridi* ECLI:EU:C:2011:268, para 31; *Mukarubega* (n 7) para 39.

[21] See also P De Bruycker and S Mananashvili, 'Audi Alteram Partem in Immigration Detention Procedures, between the ECJ, the ECtHR and Member States: G & R' (2015) 52 *CML Rev* 569.

that the reasoning of the Court in the area of competition law, according to which a procedural irregularity will lead to annulment of all or part of a decision only if it is established that the content of the contested decision could have been different if that irregularity had not occurred, cannot be applied by analogy to measures of detention as they place such a restrictive effect on personal liberty.[22] The materiality threshold, when a fundamental human right such as the right to liberty is affected, for procedural irregularity should be lower, thereby rendering the administrative decision unlawful.

When the decision taken by the public authorities concerns pre-removal detention, proper account must be taken of the fact that the right to liberty is one of the fundamental human rights and, as such, it requires effective protection.[23] Measures that entail depriving irregularly staying third-country nationals of their liberty clearly affect them adversely.[24] Although it is not a criminal penalty, immigration detention entails deprivation of liberty and that is why it is designed to be a measure of last resort only.[25]

The conclusion of the Advocate General in *G and R* is in line with the interpretation of the right to liberty and security enshrined in Article 5 ECHR given by the ECtHR. According to Article 5(1)(f), no one shall be deprived of his liberty, save 'in accordance with a procedure prescribed by law' and in cases such as 'the lawful arrest or detention of a person to prevent his effecting an unauthorised entry into the country or of a person against whom action is being taken with a view to deportation or extradition'.

According to Article 52(3) of the Charter, in so far as the Charter contains rights that correspond to rights guaranteed by the ECHR, the meaning and scope of those rights shall be the same as those laid down by the said Convention. EU law may provide more extensive protection, but cannot descend below the established threshold of guarantees for the rights protected by the ECHR. This fully applies to the right to liberty and security enshrined in Article 6 of the Charter.

For a decision to be deemed lawful, including being imposed in accordance with a procedure prescribed by law, the ECtHR primarily requires any arrest or detention to have a legal basis in domestic law. However, this is not the decisive element in determining the lawfulness of a decision: 'In addition any deprivation of liberty should be in keeping with the purpose of Article 5(1), namely to protect the individual from arbitrariness.'[26] In other words, immigration detention may

[22] AG Wathelet cites the competition law case: Case 30/78 *Distillers Company v Commission* [1980] ECR 2229.

[23] Art 6 EU Charter; Art 5 ECHR.

[24] *G and R*, Opinion of AG Wathelet (n 2) para 53.

[25] *G and R*, Opinion of AG Wathelet (n 2) para 54.

[26] ECtHR, *Amuur v France*, Appl No 19776/92, judgment of 25 June 1996, para 50; *Saadi v the United Kingdom* Appl No 13229/03, judgment of 29 January 2008, para 67; *MA v Cyprus* ECHR 2013-IV, para 197; *OM v Hungary*, Appl No 9912/15 (ECtHR, 5 July 2016) para 41 and the case-law cited therein.

appear 'legal' under national law, but still be deemed arbitrary and, therefore, unlawful, under the ECHR.

According to Article 1 of the Return Directive:

> This Directive sets out common standards and procedures to be applied in Member States for returning illegally staying third-country nationals, in accordance with fundamental rights as general principles of Community law as well as international law, including refugee protection and human rights obligations.

Thus, interpretation of the right to be heard in the context of removal detention should also take into account that the prohibition of arbitrary detention is expressly stipulated in Article 9 the International Covenant on Civil and Political Rights (ICCPR).[27] In its General Comment on Article 9 ICCPR, the Human Rights Committee notes that an arrest or detention may be authorised by domestic law and nonetheless be arbitrary:

> The notion of 'arbitrariness' is not to be equated with 'against the law', but must be interpreted more broadly to include elements of inappropriateness, injustice, lack of predictability and due process of law, as well as elements of reasonableness, necessity and proportionality.[28]

Regarding other asylum and migration procedures eventually leading to the issuance of a return decision, in the more recent judgment in *Sacko*,[29] the CJEU reiterated that there is no absolute obligation to hold a hearing in person before the appellate authorities, if the administrative authorities had already conducted a full examination of the lodged asylum application, including by means of interviewing the applicant during the first-instance proceeding. The case concerned the nature of the right to be heard during the appeal (judicial) stage for manifestly unfounded asylum cases. The Court noted that a potential infringement of the right to effective judicial protection should be examined in relation to the specific circumstances of each case. Under Article 46 of the Asylum Procedure Directive,[30] the obligation to grant the applicant a hearing has to be assessed in the light of the court's obligation to carry out a full and ex nunc examination of the appeal. The Court pointed out that:

> [T]he characteristics of the remedy provided for in Article 46 of Directive 2013/32 must be determined in a manner that is consistent with Article 47 of the Charter, which constitutes a reaffirmation of the principle of effective judicial protection.[31]

[27] International Covenant on Civil and Political Rights (adopted 16 December 1966, entered into force 23 March 1976) 999 UNTS 171 (ICCPR), Art 9.

[28] UN Human Rights Committee, 'General Comment 35: Article 9 (Liberty and Security of Person)' (16 December 2014) CCPR/C/GC/35, para 14.

[29] Case C-348/16 *Sacko* ECLI:EU:C:2017:591.

[30] Directive 2013/32/EU of the European Parliament and of the Council of 26 June 2013 on common procedures for granting and withdrawing international protection [2013] OJ L180 ('Asylum Procedure Directive').

[31] *Sacko* (n 29) para 31.

The CJEU reached the conclusion[32] that, as long as the above requirements are respected, there might be no need for a hearing where the case does not raise any questions of fact or law that cannot be adequately resolved by referring to the file and the written submissions of the parties.[33]

As seen in the jurisprudence so far, the role of the courts and judicial dialogue are crucial in forging effective standards that correspond to the practical issues arising in the implementation of the right to be heard.

III. Substantive Law Content of the Right to be Heard in Return Proceedings

After mapping out the essential features of the right to be heard, this chapter will address the question of the substantive law content[34] of the right to be heard, namely: about *what* should the third-country national be heard? The content of the right to be heard has not been detailed by the Return Directive, but developed by the CJEU in *Mukarubega* and *Boudjlida*.[35]

In the first place, the administrative body should correctly put down the main personal identification data of the third-country national, namely, age (date of birth), names and citizenship (if any). If the essential personal data are noted incorrectly, eventual arrangements for the issuance of a travel document in the implementation of the return decision will fail.

Secondly, prior to the issuance of a return decision, the foreign national should be heard in respect of the legality of their stay, the potential applicability of the *non-refoulement* principle (existence of pending asylum proceedings or proceedings for renewal or grant of residence or stay) and the existence of a residence permit issued by another EU Member State. According to the *non-refoulement* (prohibition of return) principle, if the third-country national has entered the country (irregularly) in order to seek asylum, he/she should not be issued a return decision. Article 8 of the Asylum Procedures Directive obliges Member States, where there are indications that the immigrant may wish to make an application for international protection, to provide him/her with information on the possibility to do so. In detention facilities and crossing points, Member States shall make arrangements for interpretation to the extent necessary to facilitate access to the asylum procedure. The immigrant has the status of an asylum seeker from the date of submitting an application for international protection.[36] The ECtHR has noted

[32] *Sacko* (n 29) paras 45–49.

[33] See also ECtHR, *Döry v Sweden*, Appl No 28394/95, Judgment of 12 November 2002.

[34] The phrase 'substantive law content' is used in the context of differentiation between material (substantive) law and procedural law.

[35] Other relevant cases, though not directly related to the Return Directive, are *M* (n 9) and Case C-560/14 *M* ECLI:EU:C:2017:101.

[36] Art 3(1) of the Asylum Procedure Directive.

that if EU and international law explicitly authorise the entry or stay of immigrants pending an asylum application, an ensuing detention for the purpose of preventing an unauthorised entry may raise an issue as to the lawfulness of detention under Article 5(1)(f) ECHR.[37]

Thirdly, the personal and family situation of the individual – the best interests of children, family life, the state of health, the length of stay in the host country and belonging to a vulnerable group – should be taken into account when considering the issuance of a return decision.[38] These requirements of an individual approach and proportionality are largely found in national case-law applying the Return Directive. For example, the EU-wide effect of the CJEU preliminary ruling in *Boudjlida* led the Dutch Council of State to hold that the authorities have to hear the third-country national before taking a return decision, in particular with regard to his or her legal status in the Netherlands or another Member State, whether he or she falls under any of the exceptions to the obligation to take a return decision as enumerated in Article 6(4) and (5) of the Return Directive, and personal circumstances in the context of Article 5 of the Return Directive.[39]

Furthermore, the third-country national should be heard on the conditions of return, including on the issue of granting a time period for voluntary departure. During the initial stage of the return procedure, preference is to be given to voluntary implementation of the return obligation in line with Article 7(1) of the Return Directive, according to which the return decision shall provide for an appropriate period for voluntary departure of between 7 and 30 days. In *Boudjlida*, the CJEU noted[40] that Member States should, where necessary, under Article 7(2) of the Return Directive, extend the length of that period appropriately, taking into account the specific circumstances of the individual case, such as the length of stay, the existence of children attending school, and other family and social links. There are permissible exceptions from the rule that the third-country national shall be given a time period to voluntarily comply with the return decision, which shall be justified by the administrative body as to the reasons why no such period is granted or the granted period is shorter than 7 days.[41] In *Zh and O*, the CJEU noted that the Member State cannot refrain automatically – by legislative means or in practice – from granting a voluntary departure period in all cases:

> The correct exercise of the option to that effect provided for in Article 7, para 4 of the Return Directive requires that there must be a case-by-case assessment of whether the refusal to grant such a period is compatible with that person's fundamental rights.[42]

[37] ECtHR *RU v Greece*, Appl No 2237/08, Judgment of 7 June 2011; ECtHR *Suso Musa v Malta*, Appl No 42337/12, Judgment of 23 July 2013, para 68.

[38] *Boudjlida* (n 2) para 68.

[39] See, for example, the various national case-law cited in REDIAL Research Report 2016/03 (n 5) 12–15.

[40] *Boudjlida* (n 2) para 51.

[41] Art 7(4) of the Return Directive.

[42] *Zh and O* (n 18) para 70.

Only if no voluntary departure period has been granted in accordance with reasons provided in law, or if the obligation to return has not been complied with within the period for voluntary departure, may a Member State, which has issued a return decision against an irregularly staying third-country national, carry out the removal by taking all necessary measures including, where appropriate, coercive measures such as immigration detention, in a proportionate manner and with due respect for fundamental human rights.[43]

Last but not least comes the hearing on the proportionality of detention under Article 15 of the Return Directive. According to Article 15(1) of the Return Directive, immigration detention may be imposed only upon the cumulative presence of the following individual grounds, giving effect to the principle of proportionality: firstly, there is a risk of absconding or the third-country national avoids or hampers the preparation of return or the removal process; and secondly, less coercive measures cannot be applied effectively in the specific case. The CJEU underlines the need for gradation of the measures taken in order to enforce the return decision, a gradation which goes from the measure which allows the person concerned the most liberty, namely granting a period for voluntary departure, to measures which restrict that liberty the most, namely detention; the principle of proportionality must be observed throughout each of those stages.[44] This means that prior to imposing the heaviest measure (detention), the administrative body should hear the immigrant regarding the feasibility of alternatives to detention.[45]

IV. Procedural Safeguards to Effectively Hear the Person in Return Proceedings

The right to be heard guarantees every person the opportunity to make known his views effectively during a legal procedure.[46] The return decision and the eventual detention order are based on considerations of the personal conduct of the third-country national. At the same time, during the administrative decision-making procedure, migrants are typically in a position of dependence and subordination. Having failed to make special arrangements for the interested third-country national to be heard, the administrative body may not justifiably claim that it has carefully and impartially appraised all circumstances of the case in a manner that would allow it to produce an elaborate reasoning in the decision to be issued.

The ECtHR asserts the principle of good-faith communication between the authorities and immigrants, irrespective of whether the foreign national is lawfully

[43] *El Dridi* (n 20) paras 36–38.

[44] *El Dridi* (n 20) para 41.

[45] R Sampson, V Chew, G Mitchell and L Bowring, *There Are Alternatives: A Handbook for Preventing Unnecessary Immigration Detention (Revised)* (Melbourne, International Detention Coalition, 2015).

[46] *Boudjlida* (n 2) para 36.

present in the country or not. Thus, for example, the authorities must not intentionally mislead immigrants in order to detain them to facilitate the effectiveness of a planned operation for their removal. Such conduct on the part of administrative bodies would not be compatible with Article 5 ECHR.[47]

The Return Directive does not provide for an express list of procedural guarantees for the effective exercise of the right to be heard, but these guarantees are found in the spirit of the Directive and in the case-law and practice of Member States, the ECtHR and the CJEU. One can also identify additional procedural guarantees for vulnerable persons. Field research conducted by the author of this chapter in 2016 led to the conclusion that the procedural guarantees to effectively hear the interested third-country national are as follows: appointment of an interpreter from a language that the foreign national understands; notifying the person of the commencement of the legal procedure for the issuance of the decision in question and of the right to be heard; opportunity to use assistance provided by a defender or legal counsel; opportunity to examine the documents contained in the case-file; opportunity to give an opinion on collected evidence and to make written requests and objections; obligation of the public authority to correctly establish the facts and circumstances of the case; and opportunity to examine the explanations and objections made by the interested foreign national.[48] The above ensure compliance with the requirement stipulated in the Return Directive for decisions to be adopted on a case-by-case basis and based on objective criteria, implying that consideration should go beyond the mere fact of an illegal stay.[49]

With regard to the right to translation and interpretation, EU law contains provisions that require an interpreter to be present during the hearing of a third-country national in the context of his/her return proceedings[50] or access to the asylum procedure.[51] The national legislations of EU Member States often contain provisions on the appointment of interpreters that are more favourable than the minimum standard laid down in the Return Directive.[52] For example, according to Article 14(2) of the Bulgarian Code on Administrative Procedure,

[47] *Conka v Belgium* ECHR 2002-I (2002) 34 EHRR 54, para 42.

[48] FAR, 'Project HEAR' (2016) hear.farbg.eu.

[49] The Return Directive, Recital 6 of the Preamble. In this sense, see eg Judgment of 5 August 2011 in case no 13868/2010 of the Bulgarian Supreme Administrative Court.

[50] Art 12(2) of the Return Directive requires as a minimum standard from Member States to provide, upon request, a written or oral translation of the main elements of decisions related to return, including information on the available legal remedies, in a language the third-country national understands or may reasonably be presumed to understand. Para 3 of the same provision allows, by way of exception, the use of 'a standard form', the main elements of which are explained in generalised information sheets in at least five of those languages which are most frequently used or understood by illegal migrants entering the Member State concerned.

[51] The Asylum Procedure Directive, Recital 28. It stipulates as follows: 'In order to facilitate access to the examination procedure at border crossing points and in detention facilities, information should be made available on the possibility to apply for international protection. Basic communication necessary to enable the competent authorities to understand if persons declare their wish to apply for international protection should be ensured through interpretation arrangements.' In this sense, see also Art 8 of the Directive.

[52] REDIAL Research Report 2016/03 (n 5) 23–25.

a person who does not speak Bulgarian may use his/her native language or another language indicated by them. An interpreter is appointed in such cases.[53] As the administrative procedure for the issuance of a return-related order is initiated by the administrative body, and not by the foreign national, the costs incurred for language interpretation are to be covered by the administrative body.[54]

A necessary precondition for the exercise of the right to be heard is the fulfilment of the obligation of the public body to notify the interested third-country national of the commencement of a procedure for the issuance of a return and/or a detention decision. In order to be able to take part in the administrative process, the foreign national should be notified of its commencement and advised of his/her right to be heard. A failure to do so would mean that his/her right to defence has been restricted, because he/she has not been given an opportunity to properly organise it.[55] It is not sufficient for the administrative body to prepare a notification letter, unless action is taken to ensure that the notice is served on the party for whom it is intended.[56]

With regard to the right to assistance from a lawyer or another defender, the Return Directive does not expressly provide for a right to legal aid during the administrative phase of the process before taking the decision. The CJEU, however, notes that the irregularly staying third-country national can always engage a lawyer on his own account to assist him/her during the hearing before the competent national bodies.[57] Where this is possible, legal assistance can also be provided by lawyers working at non-governmental organisations active in this area.

In order for the third-country national to state his/her informed view in the legal procedure, he/she must firstly be given access to the documents contained in the case file relevant to their case. The right to access to documents is inherent in the right to defence as a fundamental principle of EU law.[58] The ECtHR links that access to the effectiveness of subsequent remedies, noting that 'equality of arms is not ensured if counsel is denied access to those documents in the investigation file which are essential in order effectively to challenge the lawfulness of his client's detention'.[59]

[53] In the ruling of 9 November 2011 in case no 13731/2011 of the Bulgarian Supreme Administrative Court, the Court stated that laying the signature by an immigrant under a blanket check 'I am familiar with this order in a language that I speak' without establishing that at the time of service of the act this language was Bulgarian, is not a necessary and sufficient proof of notification of the order to the addressee in a language he/she knows. The Court took into account that the order did not state the language in which its contents was brought to the attention of the foreign citizen, and there was no evidence of presence of an interpreter pursuant to Art 14(2) and (3) of the Bulgarian Code on Administrative Procedure.

[54] See eg Art 14(4) of the Bulgarian Code on Administrative Procedure.

[55] Judgment of 29 September 2008 in case 2054/of the Sofia City Administrative Court, 3; Judgment of 8 October 2014 in case 5670/2014 of the Sofia City Administrative Court, 3; Judgment of 5 August 2014 in case 16862/2013 of the Bulgarian Supreme Administrative Court.

[56] Judgment of 7 January 2013 in case 6638/2012 of the Sofia City Administrative Court, 2.

[57] *Boudjlida* (n 2) para 65.

[58] *G and R* (n 1) para 33.

[59] ECtHR *Nikolova v Bulgaria*, Appl No 31195/96, Judgment of 25 March 1999, para 58.

Article 12(1) of the Return Directive allows for the information on reasons in fact to be limited, in particular: 'in order to safeguard national security, defence, public security and for the prevention, investigation, detection and prosecution of criminal offences.' However, any such restrictions must be applied proportionally and approached individually. The administrative body should provide the reasons for the exception from the right to be heard that it has applied.[60] With regard to the application of the concept of 'risk to public policy', in *Zh and O*, the CJEU stated that:

> When it relies on general practice or any assumption in order to determine such a risk, without properly taking into account the national's personal conduct and the risk that that conduct poses to public policy, a Member State fails to have regard to the requirements relating to an individual examination of the case concerned and to the principle of proportionality.[61]

If the procedural guarantees enumerated above (right to language interpretation, right to legal counsel, right to be notified of the commencement of proceedings, and right to access the file) are present, the third-country national shall be capable of making his/her views known effectively. Then the administrative body should take into account the explanations and objections made by the foreign national and establish the relevant facts and circumstances of the case. The right to be heard requires government bodies to give proper attention to the views expressed by the immigrant and take due care in objectively examining all relevant facts and circumstances of the case in order to be able to elaborately reason their decision.[62] Elaborate reasoning within immigration detention orders which properly corresponds to the individual case at hand is a criterion for the lawfulness of these orders.

EU law[63] requires the authorities to take into consideration the special needs of vulnerable persons such as children, unaccompanied minors, persons with disabilities, elderly persons, pregnant women, single parents with children, and victims of torture, rape or other serious forms of mental, physical or sexual violence.[64] The possibility for vulnerable persons to make their views known effectively may require additional guarantees, which cannot be applied if a person has not been identified as belonging to a vulnerable group.[65]

[60] Judgment of 12 March 2012 in case 6758/2009 of the Sofia City Administrative Court, 5; Judgment of 17 May 2013 in case 1428/2012 of the Burgas Administrative Court; Judgment of 27 April 2012 in case 5255/2011 of the Bulgarian Supreme Administrative Court; Judgment of 14 July 2015 in case 15154/2014 of the Bulgarian Supreme Administrative Court.

[61] *Zh and O* (n 18) para 50.

[62] Case C-269/90 *Technische Universität München / Hauptzollamt München-Mitte* [1991] ECR I-5469, para 14; *Sopropé* (n 7) para 50; *M* (n 8) para 88.

[63] Arts 14(1)(d) and 16(3) of the Return Directive; Directive 2013/33/EU of the European Parliament and of Council of 26 June 2013 laying down standards for reception of applicants for international protection [2013] OJ L180 ('Reception Conditions Directive'), Art 21.

[64] The legal definition of 'vulnerable persons' is laid down in Art 3(9) of the Return Directive.

[65] See eg European Asylum Support Office, 'Tool for Identification of Persons with Special Needs' (EASO, 2016) ipsn.easo.europa.eu.

Both law[66] and practice[67] recognise the need for early identification of vulnerability, as a prerequisite for taking into account the special situation of these persons. On the one hand, the right to be heard is the most effective guarantee for the early identification of a vulnerability. On the other hand, during the hearing, indications might appear that additional guarantees and conditions are necessary in order to ensure that the person is effectively heard.

Thus, for example, when an unaccompanied minor declares their age, the administrative body should, inter alia, make arrangements for the appointment of a legal representative and ensure that legal assistance is provided to the child. Accordingly, under Bulgarian law, the infringement of the obligation of the administrative body to give the child a hearing during the decision-making process, if the child is 10 years old or older, is a material breach of the administrative procedure and means that the decision taken in the case is unlawful.[68] According to Article 10(1) of the Return Directive, before deciding to issue a return decision in respect of an unaccompanied minor, assistance by appropriate bodies other than the authorities enforcing return shall be granted with due consideration being given to the best interests of the child. If a decision is taken on the return of an unaccompanied child, detention, even for the shortest period, may be incompatible with the right to human dignity.[69] The ECtHR has held that immigration detention of accompanied children may also constitute a violation of the prohibition of inhumane and degrading treatment stipulated in Article 3 ECHR. The Court has emphasised the extreme vulnerability of children, which should be the primary consideration taking precedence over the status of an irregular immigrant.[70]

As a corollary, although the Return Directive does not provide for an express list of procedural guarantees for the effective exercise of the right to be heard, the two are interconnected in a symbiotic relationship whereby the right cannot exist without the safeguards. The procedural guarantees enumerated above are an indispensable condition for the genuine exercise of the right to be heard in return

[66] See eg Art 22 of the Reception Conditions Directive.

[67] See eg B Maria and G Gyulai, with contributions from project partners, *Access of Torture Survivor and Traumatised Asylum-Seekers to Rights and Care in Detention. From Torture to Detention* (Cordelia Foundation, 2016) www.helsinki.hu/wp-content/uploads/From-Torture-to-Detention-angol-WEB.pdf; Jesuit Refugee Service Europe, *Becoming Vulnerable in Detention. Civil Society Report on the Detention of Vulnerable Asylum Seekers and Irregular Migrants in the European Union – The DEVAS Project* (2010) www.europarl.europa.eu/document/activities/cont/201110/20111014ATT29338/20111014ATT29338EN.pdf.

[68] See eg Judgment of 2 February 2014 in case 358/2014 of the Bulgarian Supreme Administrative Court; Judgment of 23 November 2015 in case 15238/2014 of the Bulgarian Supreme Administrative Court; Judgment of 29 September 2008 in case 2054/2008 of the Sofia City Administrative Court; Judgment of 28 December 2015 in case 10640/2015, of the Sofia City Administrative Court; Judgment of 19 January 2016 in case 10635/2015 of the Sofia City Administrative Court.

[69] ECtHR, *Rahimi v Greece*, Appl No 8687/08, Judgment of 5 April 2011; ECtHR *Mohamad v Greece*, Appl No 70586/11, Judgment of 11 December 2014.

[70] ECtHR, *Muskhadzhiyeva and Others v Belgium*, Appl No 41442/07, Judgment of 19 January 2010; ECtHR, *Popov v France*, Appl No 39472/07, Judgment of 19 January 2012; ECtHR, *AB and Others v France*, Appl No 11593/12, Judgment of 12 July 2016.

proceedings. In this regard, the application of the Return Directive makes evident the complementarity of ECtHR and CJEU standards.

V. Stages in the Application of the Right to be Heard in Return Proceedings

As already mentioned earlier in the chapter, we use the notion of the right to be heard in a broad sense to encompass both the administrative and court proceedings relating to imposing and reviewing return and detention for removal. The right is discussed as a procedural safeguard in the context of pre-litigation administrative proceedings and as an effective remedy in the context of judicial review. In this section we look at these procedural phases as stages in the application of the right to be heard. Each return procedure relies on a shared burden of proof between the individual concerned and the decision-making administrative authority. Throughout the different stages of the return process (gradating from voluntary to compulsory measures) the division of the burden of proof changes, while the right to be heard is a key tool for establishing the relevant facts.

As a first stage, it is essential to respect the right to be heard prior to the initial decision in return proceedings.[71] The right to be heard is therefore a procedural guarantee for the lawfulness of the administrative decision issued. The right to a preliminary hearing in a pre-litigation administrative context should be distinguished from the right to be heard in the context of court proceedings. That distinction is clear from the provisions of Articles 41 and 47 of the Charter,[72] as well as being evident in the judgment of the CJEU in *Sacko*. The system of rights to defence guaranteed by the Charter requires that the rights in question be exercised separately and consecutively in the context of the different proceedings. The mere fact that judicial review is available at a later stage does not in itself remedy the infringement of the right to be heard, within the meaning of Article 41 of the Charter, committed *during* the issuing of the decision by the administrative authorities.[73]

Providing legal assistance during the administrative process means that the foreign national is better informed and such assistance is one of the preconditions for the eventual effective exercise of the right to appeal. Thus, for example, in the case of *Conka v Belgium*, the ECtHR held that the accessibility of the remedies was

[71] *G and R* (n 1) para 32; *Boudjlida* (n 2) para 36.

[72] Although Art 41 of the Charter applies to the 'institutions, bodies, offices and agencies of the Union' and does not – in and of itself – cause obligations to arise for EU Member States, the CJEU emphasises that the right to be heard and the right to good administration are inherent in respect for the rights of the defence and that the legal grounds for their observance derive from a general principle of EU law. In this relation, see eg *YS and Others* (n 12) para 68; *Mukarubega* (n 7) paras 44–45; *Boudjlida* (n2) paras 32–34.

[73] *G and R*, Opinion of AG Wathelet (n 2) paras 46–48.

undoubtedly affected by the government failing to provide any form of legal assistance to the detained immigrants both at the police station and at the immigration detention centre.[74] In this sense, the connection between the genuine exercise of the right to be heard in the administrative phase, on the one hand, and the effective implementation of the right to appeal, on the other hand, is also evident in *Boudjlida*, where the CJEU noted that:

> [T]he right to be heard before the adoption of a return decision must allow the competent national authority to investigate the matter in such a way as be able to adopt a decision in full knowledge of the facts and to state reasons for that decision adequately, so that, where appropriate, the person concerned can duly exercise his right to bring legal proceedings.[75]

The second stage in the application of the right to be heard takes place as a remedy after the issuance of the first-instance administrative decision. It relates to the right to appeal and to a speedy and fair judicial review. Access to justice is a fundamental tenet of the state of the rule of law.[76] Articles 13 and 15(2) of the Return Directive provide for effective remedies to appeal against or seek review of decisions related to return and detention. As far as return is concerned, the reviewing authority shall have the power to temporarily suspend the enforcement of return, unless a temporary suspension is already applicable under national legislation. In cases when the prohibition of torture and inhuman and degrading treatment and punishment is at stake upon an eventual expulsion, the ECtHR requires an automatic suspensive effect of the appeal against return.[77]

If the person to be returned is also placed in immigration detention, he/she has the right to be informed of the reasons for his/her detention and the rights in relation with the detention order, including the right to file a complaint.[78] According to the ECtHR:

> [B]y virtue of Article 5 § 2 [ECHR] any person arrested must be told, in simple, non-technical language that can be easily understood, the essential legal and factual grounds for the arrest, so as to be able, if he or she sees fit, to apply to a court to challenge its lawfulness in accordance with Article 5 § 4.[79]

Article 15(2) of the Return Directive provides that Member States shall immediately inform the third-country national about the possibility of contesting the detention. According to Article 5(4) ECHR and Article 9(3) ICCPR, a detained

[74] ECtHR, *Conka v Belgium*, Appl No 51564/99, Judgment of 5 February 2002, paras 43–44.

[75] *Boudjlida* (n 2) para 59.

[76] European Union Agency for Fundamental Rights and Council of Europe, *Handbook on European Law Relating to Access to Justice* (2016) www.echr.coe.int/Documents/Handbook_access_justice_ENG.pdf.

[77] See eg *Conka* (n 74) para 79; *Jabari v Turkey*, ECHR 2000-VIII, para 50.

[78] See eg Art 5 ECHR, which stipulates that: 'Everyone who is arrested shall be informed promptly, in a language which he understands, of the reasons for his arrest and of any charge against him.'

[79] ECtHR, *Abdolkhani and Karimnia v Turkey*, Appl No 30471/08, Judgment of 22 September 2009, para 136.

person is entitled to take proceedings by which the lawfulness of his detention shall be decided speedily[80] and without delay by a court and his/her release ordered immediately,[81] if the detention is unlawful. Article 15(2) of the Return Directive contains identical requirements.

In order to meet the standard of a fair trial,[82] during the court hearing the third-country national has the following rights: the right to a language interpreter; the right to be notified of the scheduled time of the court hearing and of the right to be heard; the right to assistance by a legal counsel; right to access to one's file;[83] and the right to make one's views known and to have all relevant facts and circumstances properly analysed and taken into consideration by the deciding court.[84] The right of the migrant to be heard by the court is an essential feature of a fair and equitable trial.

Thirdly, the right to be heard applies during the process of return and eventual detention for the purpose of return. It is of essential importance for the proper preparation or enforcement of removal,[85] which shall be done vigorously and with due diligence.[86] Furthermore, the right to be heard extends to conditions of detention.[87] The authorities shall put in place an effective mechanism for hearing complaints by detainees against alleged instances of ill-treatment or failure to protect them from violence by other detainees. Complainants and witnesses shall be protected against any subsequent ill-treatment or intimidation. The competent bodies shall effectively investigate the complaints.[88]

Last, but not least, the right to be heard is a key component of the obligation to review immigration detention at regular intervals. It is a procedural safeguard and a remedy upon extension of the length of detention. Article 15(6) of the Return Directive envisages two alternative substantive law conditions for extending detention, in cases where, regardless of all reasonable efforts by the authorities, the removal operation is likely to last longer owing to: (a) a lack of cooperation by the third-country national concerned, or (b) delays in obtaining the necessary documentation from third countries. The authorities shall grant the immigrant a hearing prior to assessing the existence of any of these two substantive law conditions for continuing the period of detention. Where there is no reasonable

[80] With regard to violation of the requirement for speediness under Art 5(4) ECHR, see ECtHR, *M and Others v Bulgaria*, Appl No 41416/08, Judgment of 26 July 2011; *Amie and Others v Bulgaria*, Appl No 58149/08, Judgment of 12 February 2013; *Suso Musa v Malta*, Appl No 42337/12, Judgment of 23 July 2013.

[81] Committee of Ministers of the Council of Europe, 'Twenty Guidelines on Forced Return', 4 May 2005, guiding principles 9 and 1.

[82] Art 47 Charter.

[83] *ZZ* (n 18) para 51.

[84] V Ilareva, 'Handbook on the Right of Immigration Detainees to Be Heard' (Foundation for Access to Rights, 2016) hear.farbg.eu/handbook, para 56.

[85] ibid, paras 65–66.

[86] See eg ECtHR, *Quinn v France* (1995) 21 EHRR 529, para 48; *Bordovskiy v Russia*, Appl No 49491/99 Judgment of 8 February 2005, para 50; ECtHR, *Chahal v the United Kingdom* (1997) 23 EHRR 413, para 113; ECtHR, *JN v the United Kingdom* Appl No 37289/12 Judgment of 19 May 2016.

[87] Ilareva (n 84) paras 57–64.

[88] Committee of Ministers of the Council of Europe (n 81) guideline 10.6.

prospect of removal of the third-country national, detention must be immediately discontinued.[89] With regard to the hypothesis of 'a lack of cooperation by the detainee concerned', in its judgment in *Mahdi*, the CJEU noted that its application requires a detailed examination of the factual matters and the conduct of the immigrant relating to the whole of the initial detention period. The question to be answered is whether it is likely that the removal operation will last longer than anticipated namely because of this lack of cooperation.[90] In this regard, respect for the right to be heard plays a crucial role, because an issue that should be taken into consideration is whether during the initial detention period the authorities had created the necessary conditions for proper communication with the immigrant in order to be able to receive his cooperation.

The rigorousness of the lawfulness review, exercised by the court, shall increase naturally in proportion to the length of detention. The longer an individual has been deprived of his/her fundamental right to liberty, the more solid the basis for this decision must be. Over time, the burden of proof placed on the detaining authority to demonstrate that the detention is in line with the legitimate aim of effective return increases. In this regard the right to be heard plays an extremely important role in establishing all relevant facts.[91]

It should be underlined that, in deciding on the extension of ongoing detention, there is nothing to prevent the authorities from giving the person concerned an effective prior hearing with a view to adopting the measure extending his/her detention. The hearing is not difficult to carry out, because there is no urgency – the immigrant is already being held in detention and therefore presents no risk of absconding.[92] Thus, we concur with the view of the Advocate General in *G and R* that a confirmed infringement of the right to be heard at the time of extending immigration detention under Article 15(6) of the Return Directive can in no circumstances be regarded as a 'minor' or 'limited' infringement of that right.[93] The CJEU however ruled that Article 15(2) and (6) of the Return Directive must be interpreted as meaning that, where the extension of a detention measure has been decided in an administrative procedure in breach of the right to be heard, the national court may order the lifting of the detention measure only if it considers that 'the infringement at issue actually deprived the party relying thereon of the possibility of arguing his defence better, to the extent that the outcome of that administrative procedure could have been different'.[94] The judgment in *G and R* is cited by the academic community as 'a good example of a contradiction between the case law of Luxembourg and Strasbourg'.[95] It does not seem to make the necessary differentiation between the situation when the violation of the right to be

[89] Case C-357/09 PPU *Kadzoev* ECLI:EU:C:2009:741; Case C-146/14 PPU *Mahdi* ECLI:EU:C:2014:1320, para 60.
[90] *Mahdi*, ibid, paras 84–85.
[91] ibid, para 62.
[92] *G and R*, Opinion of AG Wathelet (n 2) para 76.
[93] ibid, para 55.
[94] *G and R* (n 2).
[95] De Bruycker and Mananashvili (n 21).

heard results in prolongation of detention compared to a situation where the third-country national is not in detention, but his right to be heard has been violated.

VI. Conclusion

Law and the judicial dialogue on the right of irregular migrants in the European Union to be heard in return proceedings are in the process of development. As with every historical process, the full recognition of the right to be heard will take its time and torments. Courts (national, the ECtHR and the CJEU) have contributed to 'writing the law' on the right to be heard and its application, thus filling in the missing elaboration of such procedural norms in the Return Directive. This is evident in the judgment of the CJEU in *G and R*, in which the Court noted:

> Therefore, although the drafters of Directive 2008/115 thus intended to provide a detailed framework for the safeguards granted to the third-country nationals concerned as regards both the removal decision and the detention decision, they did not, however, specify whether, and under what conditions, observance of the right to be heard of those third-country nationals was to be ensured, nor did they specify the consequences of an infringement of that right, apart from the general requirement for release if the detention is not lawful.[96]

However, although the right to be heard is protected at the highest constitutional level in the EU and is an inherent element of the rights of the defence, the case-law of the CJEU has until now underestimated the consequences from the breach of that right on the effectiveness and lawfulness of return-related decisions. Field practice shows that returns are rendered unfeasible without properly hearing the person on the relevant facts and without a genuine communication guaranteeing the needed cooperation by the third-country national concerned. Belittling the failure to respect the right to be heard as a 'minor' breach has undermined the effectiveness of remedies against human rights violations.

The CJEU's transplantation of methodology from competition law to pre-removal detention has led to judgments that apparently contradict the case-law of the ECtHR with regard to the right to liberty. This incongruity has the potential of entailing confusion at the national level where the respect of the right to be heard has to be actually ensured. The case-law of the ECtHR can play a useful complementary role as regards the procedural safeguards needed to effectively hear the third-country national. The added value of judicial interaction between the national courts and the CJEU has been in striving to balance seemingly opposing policy objectives: effective returns and protection of fundamental rights. Currently the balance is tipped towards returns, but that does not mean that they have been made more effective.

[96] *G and R* (n 2) para 31.

16

Impact of Judicial Dialogue(s) on Development and Affirmation of the Right to Effective Legal Remedy from Articles 13 and 14 of the Return Directive

BOŠTJAN ZALAR

I. Introduction

The main question this chapter addresses is whether judicial dialogue under Article 267 TFEU has affected the development of the right to an effective legal remedy in Articles 13 and 14 of the Return Directive. In the light of the actual situation of the rule of law in the European Union,[1] and by using the *metateleological* interpretation,[2] I first address the purposes of the procedural guarantees in Articles 13 and 14 (section II). In sections III–V, I sketch the main elements of the right to an effective legal remedy based on primary EU law, the Directive and general principles of EU law. In sections VI and VII, I analyse preliminary questions and rulings of the CJEU case-law related to the interpretation of the Directive.

The legal area of return and removal of illegally staying third-country nationals is particularly relevant for this research for two reasons. First, because of the potential shift in power relations between the executive and judicial branches of

[1] See eg *State of Democracy, Human Rights and the Rule of Law: Role of Institutions, Threat to Institutions, Report by the Secretary General of the Council of Europe* (2018) esp 4–5 and 7, which concern also the problem of pushbacks of migrants and refugees and protection of their human rights; PACE Resolution 2188(2017) New threates to the rule of law in Council of Europe Member States; selected examples, 11 October 2017.

[2] See K Lenaerts and JA Gutiérrez-Fons, 'To Say What the Law of the EU Is: Methods of Interpretation and the European Court of Justice', EUI Working Papers, AEL 2013/9, Academy of European Law, Distinguished Lectures of the Academy, 26.

governments after the transfer of immigration policy from the third pillar to the first pillar which enabled individuals to invoke EU law in domestic courts against Member States.[3] The increase in EU law powers of national courts over immigration policy poses additional challenges for judicial independence. The other reason for the selection of the metateleological approach is that the case-law of the ECtHR, and in some cases also of the CJEU, shows that disputes over removal of third-country nationals often include rights-consistent interpretation of statutory laws. Adjudication under the Return Directive is not a straightforward exercise, in which judges apply a set of easily comprehensible legal provisions.[4]

In the last section, I mention some alternative modes of judicial dialogue that would be necessary or have developed informally in the international judicial community in the fields of migration and asylum, in order to comment on how judicial dialogue may contribute to better implementation of the rule of law in this field.

II. Fundamental Purposes of Articles 13 and 14 of the Return Directive

Articles 13 (remedies) and 14 (safeguards pending return) of the Return Directive are secondary EU law provisions on the right to an effective legal remedy in cases of return of illegally staying third-country nationals. The objective of the Directive is to establish an effective removal and repatriation policy, based on common standards and common legal safeguards, for persons to be returned in a humane manner and with full respect for their fundamental rights and dignity.[5] Below I reflect on what the aim of return 'with full respect for fundamental rights and dignity' actually means for the implementation of EU law with regard to the Directive.

Within these general aims, there is a fundamental purpose or a constitutional *telos* of Articles 13 and 14: 'The Union is founded on the values of respect of … rule of law and respect of human rights.'[6] In the case-law of the CJEU this goes back to the cases of *les Verts v European Parliament* from 1986 and *Kadi* from 2008. In *Kadi* the CJEU referred to *les Verts*, and stated that: '[T]he Community is based on the rule of law, inasmuch as neither its Member States nor its institutions can

[3] D Jacobson and GB Ruffer, 'Courts Across Borders: the Implications of Judicial Agency for Human Rights and Democracy' (2003) 25(1) *Human Rights Quarterly* 80.

[4] See mutatis mutandis R Ekins, 'A Critique of Radical Approaches to Rights-Consistent Statutory Interpretation' (2003) 6 *European Human Rights Law Review* 644.

[5] Recital 2 and 11 of the Research Directive, confirmed by the CJEU, see eg Case C-554/13 *Zh and O* ECLI:EU:C:2015:37, para 47.

[6] Art 2 TEU.

avoid review of the conformity of their acts with the basic constitutional charter.'[7] Next, the CJEU said that:

> [F]undamental rights form an integral part of the general principles of law whose observance the Court ensures. For that purpose, the Court draws inspirations from the constitutional traditions common to the Member States and from the guidelines supplied by the international instruments for the protection of human rights on which the Member States have collaborated or to which they are signatories. In that regard, the ECHR has special significance. … It is also clear from the case-law that respect for human rights is a condition of the lawfulness of Community acts.[8]

Concerning the scope or intensity of judicial review the CJEU clarified that the Community judicature must ensure the review, 'in principle the full review' or 'in principle a full examination' of the lawfulness of all Community acts in the light of fundamental rights.[9] Acts of authorities of the Member States, when implementing EU law,[10] must also be subject to judicial control from the standpoint of fundamental rights protection. Therefore, the underlying purpose of Articles 13 and 14 is that acts of the Member States, when implementing the Directive, must be subject to judicial control, including effective protection of human rights.

In relation to the aforementioned two elements of the rule of law, which were established by the Grand Chamber of the CJEU in 2008 and subsequently confirmed in many other cases,[11] needs to be added the interpretation of the Supreme Court of the United Kingdom in the 'Belmarsh case' of December 2004. In this case, Lord Justice Bingham rejected the view that it is for Parliament and the executive to assess the threat facing the nation, so it was for those bodies and not the courts to judge the response necessary to protect the security of the public; matters of a political character call for an exercise of political and not judicial judgments.[12] He said:

> I do not in particular accept the distinction which the Attorney General drew between democratic institutions and the courts. It is of course true that the judges in this country are not elected and are not answerable to Parliament … but the function of independent judges charged to interpret and apply the law is universally recognised as a cardinal feature of the modern democratic state, a cornerstone of the rule of law

[7] Case C-402/05 P and C-415/05 P *Kadi* ECLI:EU:C:2008:461, para 281 (citing *les Verts*, para 23).

[8] ibid, paras 283–84.

[9] ibid, paras 326, 330.

[10] See Art 51(1) of the Charter of Fundamental Rights of the EU.

[11] See eg Case C-550/09 *E and F* ECLI:EU:C:2010:382, para 44; Case C-335/09 P *Poland v Commission* ECLI:EU:C:2012:385, para 48; Case C-399/06 P and C-403/06 P *Hassan and Ayadi v Council and Commission* ECLI:EU:C:2009:748, paras 69–75; Case C-548/09 P *Bank Melli Iran v Council* ECLI:EU:C:2011:735, para 105; Case C-584/10 P, ECLI:EU:C:2013:518; C-584/10 P, C-593/10 P and C-595/10 P *Kadi* ECLI:EU:C:2013:518, paras 66–67.

[12] Opinion of the Lords of Appeal for judgment in the cause *A (FC) and Others (FC) (Appellants) v Secretary of State for the Home Department (Respondent) and X (FC) and another (FC) (Appellants) v Secretary of State for Home Department (Respondent)* [004] UKHL 456, 16 December 2004, Opinion of Lord Justice Bingham, para 37.

> itself. The Attorney General is fully entitled to insist on the proper limits of judicial authority, but he is wrong to stigmatise judicial decision-making as in some way undemocratic.[13]

Therefore, the third element of constitutional *telos* behind Articles 13 and 14 could be a requirement that judicial control, which includes effective protection of human rights in cases under the Directive, is exercised by independent and impartial judges.

In the case of *Kadi*, the Court of First Instance (CFI) of the EU followed the arguments expressed by the Attorney General in the UK 'Belmarsh case', in the sense that the question whether an individual or organisation poses a threat to international peace and security entails a political assessment and a value judgment which in principle fall within exclusive competence of the authority to which the international community has entrusted primary responsibility for the maintenance of international peace and security, the UN Security Council.[14] However, in *Kadi*, the Grand Chamber of the CJEU disagreed with the judgment of the CFI from the standpoint of constitutional guarantees forming part of the foundation of the Community.[15] The CFI's decision was also at odds with the case-law of the ECtHR. The approach used in paragraph 344 of the Grand Chamber's judgment in *Kadi* is the same as the Grand Chamber of the ECtHR used in the case of *Chahal v the United Kingdom*,[16] and referred also to the *Bosphorus* judgment.[17] The latter, where the ECtHR in paragraph 73 relied on judicial dialogue and summarised some leading judgments of the CJEU on human rights protection, was delivered two months before the CFI delivered its *Kadi* judgment.

In light of the rise of majoritarian democracy in Europe, where rights of members of minority groups can be challenged and denied, it is important to point out and examine the three elements of the rule of law also in the context of Articles 13 and 14. These are:

(a) acts of Member States against individuals, when Member States are implementing EU law, must be subject to judicial control;
(b) judicial control includes effective protection of human rights of individuals;
(c) control and effective protection of human rights must be performed by independent and impartial judges.

The third of these elements of the rule of law was confirmed by the Grand Chamber of the CJEU in *LM*, where it stated that:

> [T]he requirement of judicial independence forms part of the essence of the fundamental right to a fair trial, a right which is of cardinal importance as a guarantee that

[13] ibid, para 42.
[14] T-315/01 *Kadi* ECLI.EU:T:2005:332, para 284.
[15] *Kadi* (n 7) paras 290, 316, 322.
[16] ECtHR, *Chahal v the United Kingdom*, [GC], Appl No 2241/93, see eg paras 124–33.
[17] ECtHR, *Bosphorus Hava Yollari Turizm Ve Ticaret Anonim Sirketi v Ireland*, [GC], Appl No 45036/98, 30 June 2005.

> all the rights which individuals derive from EU law will be protected and that the values common to the Member States set out in Article 2 TEU [the Treaty on European Union], in particular the value of the rule of law, will be safeguarded.[18]

The CJEU has long considered it the responsibility of Member State courts to protect fundamental rights: for example, the Member States must, in full compliance with their obligations arising from international law and EU law, establish the grounds on which asylum seekers may be detained or kept in immigration detention;[19] it is up to the referring court to examine whether the refusal of the right of residence undermines the right to respect for private and family life from Article 7 of the Charter;[20] Member States must interpret and apply EU secondary law in a manner consistent with fundamental rights protected by the EU legal order and the other general principles of EU law;[21] when a person is not allowed to cross the border, the referring court must ascertain whether refusing to allow the person to bring claims before the court infringes the rights from Article 47 of the Charter.[22]

Thus, the main question of this chapter is whether the relationships between primary and secondary EU law on effective legal remedies and between the national law of the Member States and fundamental rights under EU law are reflected in judicial dialogue under Article 267 TFEU – and if so, in what sense are they reflected? Do these dialogues contribute significantly to the development and affirmation of the right to effective legal remedies in Articles 13 and 14?

III. Effective Legal Remedy under Primary EU Law

The second sub-paragraph of Article 19(1) TEU says that Member States must provide remedies sufficient to ensure effective legal protection in the fields covered by EU law. This provision is 'the expression of the value of the rule of law affirmed in Article 2 TEU'.[23] Therefore, it is for national courts and tribunals to ensure the full application of EU law in all Member States and judicial protection of rights of individuals also under the Return Directive.[24]

[18] Case C-216/18 PPU *LM* ECLI:EU:C:2018:586, para 48. It goes beyond the limits of this chapter to deal more thoroughly with the interpretation of the CJEU in para 54, where the CJEU links standards for judicial independence (also) to Art 267 TFEU. Those standards may be lower than standards under Art 47 of the Charter of Fundamental Rights of the EU (see paras 53, 59, 62, 79). See also Case C-64/16 *ASJP v Tribunal de Contas* ECLI:EU:C:2018:117; Case C-296/15 *Mediasanus* ECLI:EU:C:2017:431, paras 32–38.

[19] Case C-534/11 *Arslan* ECLI:EU:C:2013:343, para 56.

[20] Case C-256/11 *Dereci* ECLI:EU:C:2011:734, para 72; see also Case C-82/16 *KA and others* ECLI:EU:C:2018:308.

[21] Case C-411/10 *NS and ME* ECLI:EU:C:2011:865, paras 99 and 77.

[22] Case C-23/12 *Zakaria* ECLI:EU:C:2013:24, para 40; see also Case C-403/16 *El Hassani* ECLI:EU:C:2017:960.

[23] *LM* (n 18) para 50.

[24] See, mutatis mutandis, ibid, para 50.

In the case of *ASJP v Tribunal de Contas*, the Grand Chamber of the CJEU explained that the material scope of the second sub-paragraph of Article 19(1) TEU relates to the fields covered by EU law, irrespective of whether the Member States are implementing EU law, within the meaning of Article 51(1) of the Charter.[25] The principle of the effective protection of individuals' rights under EU law referred to in Article 19(1) is a general principle of EU law stemming from the constitutional traditions common to the Member States, enshrined in Articles 6 and 13 ECHR, and reaffirmed by Article 47 of the Charter.[26] Thus, Member States must ensure that national bodies, as courts or tribunals within the meaning of EU law, meet the requirements of effective judicial protection.[27]

Article 6(1) TEU states that the Union recognises the rights, freedoms and principles in the Charter, which have the same legal value as the Treaties. Article 6(3) TEU states that fundamental rights, as guaranteed by the ECHR and as they result from the constitutional traditions common to the Member States, constitute general principles of EU law. Insofar as the Charter contains rights that correspond to rights guaranteed by the ECHR, the meaning and scope of those rights is the same as those laid down by the ECHR, but this does not prevent EU law providing more extensive protection (Article 52(3) of the Charter).

In *Maaouia v France*, the ECtHR said that the proceedings for the rescission of an exclusion order do not concern the determination of a civil right for the purposes of Article 6(1) ECHR. The fact that the order incidentally had major repercussions on the applicant's private and family life or on his prospects of employment did not suffice to bring those proceedings within the scope of Article 6(1). The ECtHR also decided that orders excluding aliens do not concern the determination of criminal charge.[28]

One relevant question is whether Article 13(1) of the Directive accords with Article 47(2) of the Charter, since it allows appeals against decisions related to return to be decided not just by independent courts or tribunals but also by an administrative authority composed of impartial members who enjoy safeguards of independence. If this is in line with the Charter, then the next question could be: what is the actual meaning of Article 47(1) (in conjunction with Article 52(3)), which makes the right to an effective legal remedy subject to the conditions laid down 'in this Article', not in secondary EU law?[29] Article 47(1) is interpreted by the CJEU also as the right to effective judicial protection.[30]

[25] *ASJP* (n 18) para 29.

[26] ibid, para 35.

[27] ibid, para 37.

[28] *Maaouia v France*, Appl No 39652/98, 5 October 2000, paras 38–39.

[29] According to the Proposal for a Directive of the European Parliament and of the Council on common standards and procedures in Member States for returning illegally staying third-country nationals (recast) (Brussels, 12.9.2018, COM(2018) 634 final 2018/0329 (COD) (hereinafter 'the Proposal for the Return Directive – Recast') the option with administrative authority or a competent body composed of members who are impartial and who enjoy safeguards of independence is deleted.

[30] See eg Joined Cases C-584/10 P, C-593/10 P and C-595/10 P *Kadi* (n 11) para 70.

The right to an effective legal remedy is not absolute. Article 52(1) of the Charter allows limitations on its exercise under Article 47, so long as the limitation concerned respects the essence of that fundamental right, and subject to the principle of proportionality, that it is necessary and genuinely meets objectives of general interest recognised by the EU. The question whether there is an infringement of the right to effective judicial protection must be examined in relation to the circumstances of each case, including the nature of the action, the context of its adoption and the legal rules governing the matter.[31]

IV. Elements of the Right to Effective Legal Remedy under Articles 13 and 14

The right to effective legal remedy under the Return Directive is regulated in Articles 13, 14 and 15.[32] A right to effective legal remedy under Article 13(1) refers to the right of third-country nationals to seek review of entry ban, removal and return decisions, and to the right to appeal against temporarily suspending the return and entry ban decisions.[33] Based on a request by an applicant, the right to an effective legal remedy includes the possibility to obtain legal advice or representation and linguistic assistance free of charge.[34] This element of the right to effective legal remedy may be subject to conditions as set out in Article 15(3)–(6) of Directive 2013/32/EU,[35] and has to be regulated in national law.[36]

Further elements of the right to an effective legal remedy are regulated in the Directive in Article 14. During the period of voluntary departure granted under Article 7 and during periods for which removal has been postponed in

[31] ibid, paras, 101–02.

[32] In the case of *Abdida*, the CJEU states that Arts 13 and 14 of Directive 2008/115 lay down rules governing remedies available in respect of return decisions and the safeguards to be provided to third-country nationals who have been ordered to return, pending their return (Case C-562/13 *Abdida* ECLI:EU:C:2014:2453, para 40). As regards the right to effective legal remedy under Art 15 of the Return Directive, see Part II of this book. On the right to effective legal remedy under Art 15 of the Return Directive, see also: *Statement of the European Law Institute: Detention of Asylum Seekers and Irregular Migrants and The Rule of Law: Checklists and European Standards* (European Law Institute, Vienna, September 2017).

[33] Art 13(2) of the Return Directive. The Proposal for the Return Directive – Recast envisages (second subpara of Art 13(1)) a specific provision in cases where the return decision is based on a decision rejecting an application for international protection that was subject to an effective judicial review.

[34] Art 13(3) and (4) of the Return Directive.

[35] Art 53(2) of Directive 2013/32/EU of the European Parliament and of the Council of 26 June 2013 on common procedures for granting and withdrawing international protection (recast) [2013] OJ L180/60.

[36] Art 20 of the Return Directive; Art 288(3) TFEU. Art 13(3) of the Proposal for the Return Directive – Recast envisages new provisions on (automatic) suspensive effect of appeal against first-instance decisions, and time limits for conducting effective judicial remedy and for lodging an appeal against a return decision when such a decision is the consequence of a final decision rejecting an application for international protection.

accordance with Article 9 the applicants have the right to effective legal remedy in relation to:

- family unity in accordance with Article 14(1)(a);
- health care in accordance with Article 14(1)(b);
- minors have a right to access to basic education during their stay (Article 14(1)(c)); and
- vulnerable persons may claim special needs (Article 14(1)(d)).

The effective exercise of these elements of the right to a legal remedy depends also on the effective exercise of Articles 12 and 14(2).[37] Decisions that third-country nationals can challenge must be issued in writing and must give reasons in fact and in law as well as information about available legal remedies.[38] This right is not absolute and upon request the Member State must provide a translation of the main elements of decisions in a language the appellant may reasonably be presumed to understand.[39]

Article 14(2) obliges Member States to provide written confirmation in accordance with national legislation that the period for voluntary departure has been extended or that the return decision will temporarily not be enforced. Does this mean that Member States should also provide the person a written decision in case of rejection of the applications for extension of the voluntary departure and temporary suspension of the return decision despite the fact that this guarantee is not explicitly regulated in the Directive? This raises a more fundamental question: are all elements of the right to an effective legal remedy only those that are regulated in secondary law, or can fundamental rights as general principles of EU or as they are regulated in the Charter add anything substantial to the rules of effective legal remedy in the Directive?

V. Effective Legal Remedy of Illegally Staying Third-Country Nationals as a General Principle of EU Law

A starting point for answering whether fundamental rights as general principles of EU law add anything substantial to the rules for effective legal remedy in the Return Directive should be recitals 22 and 24 and Articles 1 and 5 of the Directive.[40]

[37] See mutatis mutandis Case C-402/05 P and C-415/05 P *Kadi* (n 7) para 349. See also *Abdida* (n 32) para 43; Case C-249/13 *Boudjlida* ECLI:EU:C:2014:2431, para 58.

[38] Art 12(1) of the Return Directive. See also Art 41 of the Charter and judgments of the CJEU in *Boudjlida* (n 37) paras 29, 38, 46, 58 and Case C-166/13 *Mukarubega* ECLI:EU:C:2014:2336, paras 40, 57.

[39] Art 12(2) and (3) and second subpara of Art 12(1) of the Return Directive.

[40] As a comparison to this first-step approach in the method of interpretation, see *NS and ME* (n 21) para 76.

In line with the Convention on the Rights of the Child, the best interests of the child should be a primary consideration of Member States when applying the Return Directive,[41] as should, respect for family life, per the ECHR.[42] Furthermore, the Directive respects the fundamental rights and observes the principles recognised by the Charter of Fundamental Rights of the EU.[43] Member States must respect the principle of *non-refoulement*,[44] and take due account of the health of the persons concerned.[45] Article 1 states that the Return Directive sets out common standards and procedures for returning illegally staying third-country nationals, in accordance with fundamental rights as general principles of EU law as well as international law, including refugee protection and human rights. These provisions lead towards a conclusion that Articles 13 and 14 do not provide an exhaustive list of elements of the right to an effective legal remedy.

The second step in the method of interpretation which shows that fundamental rights in procedures under the Return Directive are not protected merely by the text of Articles 13 and 14 in conjunction with Article 5 of the Directive, refers to the general approach of the CJEU according to which fundamental rights guaranteed by the Charter must be complied with where national legislation falls within the scope of EU law. EU law incorporates the fundamental rights guaranteed by the Charter.[46] This includes that where a court of a Member State is asked to review whether fundamental rights are complied with by a national provision or measure which implements EU law for the purposes of Article 51(1) of the Charter, national authorities and courts remain free to apply national standards of protection of fundamental rights, provided that the level of protection provided for by the Charter, as interpreted by the CJEU, and the primacy, unity and effectiveness of EU law are not compromised.[47] Therefore, according to the CJEU, the Member States must not only interpret their national law in a manner consistent with EU law, but must also make sure they do not rely on an interpretation of secondary legislation which would conflict with the fundamental rights protected by the EU legal order or with the other general principles of EU law.[48]

In addition, it is unrealistic to expect that the EU legislature could predict all circumstances which may raise issues of human rights protection under the Return Directive. Therefore, various elements of the right to effective legal remedy, for example the rights related to fair trial, particularly concerning limitations to procedural safeguards based on national security considerations,[49] public hearing,

[41] First sentence of recital 22 and Art 5(a) of the Return Directive.

[42] Second sentence of of recital 22 and Art 5(b) of the Return Directive.

[43] Recital 24 of the Return Directive.

[44] Second subpara of Art 5 of the Return Directive.

[45] Art 5(c) of the Return Directive.

[46] Case C-617/10 *Åklagaren* ECLI:EU:C:2013:105, para 21.

[47] ibid, para 29.

[48] *NS and ME* (n 21) para 77.

[49] According to M Moraru and G Renaudiere, 'REDIAL Electronic Journal on Judicial Interaction and the EU Return Policy (Second Edition: Articles 12 to 14 of the Return Directive 2008/115)', REDIAL Research Report 2016/04, the question on the scope of disclosure of evidence in return proceedings

independence and impartiality, reasonable time of adjudication, possibility of being advised, defended and represented, free legal aid (Article 47(2) and (3) of the Charter) and substantial rights, such as the right to respect for private and family life (Article 7 of the Charter); protection of personal data (Article 8 of the Charter; the EU General Data Protection Regulation), right to property (Article 17 of the Charter); presumption of innocence and right to defence (Article 48(2) of the Charter) and good administration, non-discrimination (Article 21 of the Charter) and protection of human dignity (Article 1 of the Charter) can be relevant and are justiciable before the administrative courts or tribunals. For example, many judgments issued by the ECtHR against the Member States concern private or family life of illegally staying applicants,[50] which are not expressly covered by the provision of Article 14(1) of the Return Directive on protection of family life (during periods of voluntary departure or for which removal has been postponed).

VI. Preliminary Rulings with Significant Links to Fundamental Rights

Since the text of the Return Directive does not regulate an exhaustive list of protected elements of the right to the effective legal remedy and this also was not an intention of the drafters of the Directive,[51] the relevant question for the purpose of this chapter is whether preliminary questions and rulings of the CJEU reflect this to any extent?

A. The Legal Nature of the Rights of the Defence and its Relation with Secondary EU Law and National Law

The case of *MG, NR* was the first to bring important interpretations of the CJEU concerning fundamental rights. The Raad van State (the Netherlands) asked two questions related to the extension of a detention measure (Article 15(6) of the Return Directive) and the general principle of respect for the rights of the

and the extent to which the objective of national security can justify derogations from the duty to state reasons in facts and law and access to fair trial and effective remedy did come up before the Croatian, Dutch, Lithuanian (no A662-1575/2013), Polish (no II OSK 2293/10, 14 December 2011), Romanian courts and before the Court of Appeal of the United Kingdom (REDIAL Research Report 2016/04, 22–23).

[50] See eg *Mehemi v France*, Appl No 85/1996/704/896, 26 September 1997, paras 24–27; *Lupsa v Romania*, Appl No 10337/04, 8 June 2006, paras 21–27; *Dalia v France*, 154/1996/773/974, 19 February 1998, para 54; *Boujaïdi v France*, Appl No 132/1996/742/941, 26 September 1997; *Maslov v Austria*, Appl No 1638/03, 22 March 2007; *Üner v the Netherlands*, Appl No 46410/99, 18 October 2006.

[51] For more on this, see F Lutz and S Mananashvili, 'Return Directive 2008/115/EC' in K Hailbronner and D Thym (eds), *EU Immigration and Asylum Law: A Commentary*, 2nd edn (Munich, CH Beck, Oxford, Hart Publishing and Baden-Baden, Nomos, 2016) 658–763.

defence (Article 41(2) of the EU Charter). The Second Chamber of the CJEU recognised that although the drafters of the Return Directive intended to provide a detailed framework for the safeguards granted to third-country nationals regarding removal and detention decisions, they did not specify whether and under what conditions observance of the right to be heard was to be ensured or the consequences of its infringement, apart from the general requirement for release if the detention is not lawful. The CJEU stated that it is settled law that the rights of the defence, which include the rights to be heard and to have access to the case-file, are among the rights enshrined in the Charter. Observance is required even where the applicable legislation does not expressly provide for such a procedural requirement.[52] However, this right may be restricted if the restrictions correspond to objectives of general interest and do not constitute a disproportionate and intolerable interference that infringes on the substance of the rights guaranteed.[53] Thus, where neither the conditions for the realisation of the right to be heard nor the consequences of its infringement are laid down by EU law, they must to be governed by national law provided that those rules are the same as those to which individuals in comparable situations under national law are subject (principle of equivalence) and that they do not make it impossible in practice or excessively difficult to exercise.[54] The task of the national court with regard to the right to an effective remedy is to review an alleged infringement of the right to be heard during an administrative procedure and to assess, taking into account specific circumstances of each case, including the nature of the act at issue, the context of its adoption and the legal rules governing the matter, whether the infringement actually deprived the party relying thereon of the possibility of arguing his defence better to the extent that the outcome of that administrative procedure could have been different.[55]

B. Relation between Effective Legal Remedy under Primary and Secondary EU Law, the Automatic Suspensive Effect of Legal Remedy and the Protection of *Non-Refoulement* in Medical Cases

In *Abdida*, the Cour du travail de Bruxelles (Belgium) asked three questions with no express reference to the Return Directive, but containing significant aspects

[52] Case C-383/13 PPU *MG, NR*, ECLI:EU:C:2013:533, para 32.

[53] ibid, para 33.

[54] ibid, para 35.

[55] ibid, paras 44, 34. In this particular aspect of the right to be heard, the REDIAL Research Report 2016/04 (n 49) mentions case-law from the Netherlands (Council of State, 201309226/1/V3, 24 June 2014), Greece (Court of Thessaloniki, 717/2015) and Belgium (CALL, 128.272, 27 August 2014), while as regards the right to be heard as a general principle of law it mentions that case-law from Greece, Belgium, Bulgaria, Slovenia, Lithuania, Austria, Germany and France use references to the judgments of the CJEU in the cases of *Boudjlida* or/and *Mukarubega*. For further elements on the right to be heard, see also section VI.B.iv and v below

of fundamental rights, including the right to effective legal remedy, in relation to Qualification Directive 2004/83, Procedure Directive 2005/85 and Reception Directive 2003/9. The CJEU decided that under the circumstances of the case those questions are relevant in the context of the Return Directive and not in the context of the other three measures. That preliminary ruling is crucial for understanding the relationship between the right to an effective legal remedy as regulated in primary EU law (Article 47 of the Charter) versus in secondary EU law. The Return Directive is to be interpreted, as stated in recital 2, with full respect for fundamental rights and dignity.[56] The remedy under Article 13(1), in conjunction with Article 12(1), to appeal against or review a decision ordering a return of third-country national, must be effective.[57] However, the Directive does not require that this remedy should necessarily have suspensive effect.[58] Article 13(1) itself does not impose that obligation, but Articles 19(2) (in conjunction with Article 5 of the Return Directive) and Article 52(3) of the Charter do.[59]

In particular circumstances, according to the CJEU, the third-country national 'must be able to avail himself' of a remedy with suspensive effect. This does not mean he should have the right to ask the first-instance court or tribunal to issue an interim measure to stop a removal procedure. Instead, a judicial dialogue has led the CJEU to follow the case-law of the ECtHR by saying that Article 47(1) of the Charter is based on Article 13 ECHR. The Court added that the ECtHR has held that, when a state decides to return a foreign national to a country where there are substantial grounds for believing he will be at risk of ill-treatment contrary to Article 3 ECHR, Article 13 ECHR requires that a remedy enabling suspension of enforcement of the removal measure should be available *ipsi iure*.[60]

This could be misleading.[61] The correct standard under which national legislation must provide automatic suspensive effect is not where there are 'substantial grounds for believing' an applicant may face 'real or serious risk' of ill-treatment or grave and irreversible deterioration in his or her state of health.[62] This is a standard of proof for protection of *non-refoulement*.[63] The standard for automatic suspensive effect is that the applicant has an 'arguable claim' in relation to Article 3 ECHR or Article 4 of the Charter. In such cases, national legislation that does not provide for automatic suspensive effect is not in accordance with Articles 5 and 13 of the Return Directive, in conjunction with Articles 19(2) and 47 of the Charter.

[56] *Abdida* (n 32) para 42.
[57] ibid, para 43.
[58] ibid, para 44.
[59] See ibid, paras 46–49.
[60] ibid, paras 51–52.
[61] For example, according to the information in REDIAL Research Report 2016/04 (n 49) following the judgment in *Abdida* the Belgian Council of Aliens Law Litigation (CALL, 156.951, November 2015) changed its jurisprudence and recognised an automatic suspensive effect to appeal against orders to leave the territory when the applicant's illness is so serious that a removal might amount to a *refoulement*, prohibited by Art 3 ECHR (REDIAL Research Report 2016/04 (n 49) 17).
[62] See *Abdida* (n 32) paras 52, 53.
[63] Art 3 ECHR, Art 19(2) of the Charter.

The *Abdida* judgment has blurred the line between two important standards for protection of fundamental rights.[64] An automatic suspensive effect of legal remedy is not conditioned by the standard of 'substantial grounds for believing the person concerned will be exposed to real risk of ill-treatment'. This refers to the material right to prohibition of ill-treatment or *non-refoulement*. Similarly, a 'very exceptional case' refers to protection of *non-refoulement* from Article 19(2) of the Charter in 'medical cases' and not to the automatic suspensive effect. The standard is characterised by the serious risk of grave and irreversible deterioration in health if the person were removed. A decision to remove a foreign national suffering from serious physical or mental illness to a country where the facilities for the treatment of the illness are inferior to those available in that state may raise an issue under Article 3 ECHR in exceptional cases, where the humanitarian grounds are compelling.[65]

Therefore, automatic suspensive effect of legal remedy is needed in all cases where third-country nationals have arguable claims in relation to Article 3 ECHR or Article 4 of the Charter. Although the aim of Article 16(3) of the Proposal for the Return Directive – Recast is to bring more legal certainty to this issue, the solution proposed is not entirely satisfactory, since it uses the standard of a 'risk to breach the principle of non-refoulement'.

In *Abdida*, the CJEU did not deal with general criteria for the establishment of an arguable claim concerning Article 4 of the Charter (or Article 3 ECHR). Under the case-law of the ECtHR, an arguable claim means that consequences of removal prohibited by Article 3 ECHR are not 'too remote'.[66] In practice, it means that when the court receives an application and knows from previous cases or information submitted by the party about poor situations in a particular country or in prisons in cases of extradition procedures, then the ECtHR would probably accept the claim as being 'arguable'.[67]

The *Abdida* judgment refers to the judgment of the ECtHR in *N v the United Kingdom* in its discussion of medical grounds for protection. However, the case-law of the ECtHR regarding seriously ill persons changed in 2016 with the judgment of the Grand Chamber in *Paposhvili v Belgium*. The new standard concerning protection of *non-refoulement* is that authorities and courts of the Member States must assess case-by-case the individual's state of health and predict how it would be

[64] *Abdida* (n 32) para 50.
[65] ibid, para 47.
[66] *Soering v the United Kingdom*, Appl No 14038/88, 7 July 1989, paras 85, 117.
[67] According to REDIAL Research Report 2016/04 (n 49) 18–20, in the case-law of other courts, too suspensive effect is granted after the courts examine whether the legal requirements for interim measures are met in each individual case (eg Czech Supreme Administrative Court, SAC 1 Azs 160/2014-25, 19 November 2014; Court of Aosta, 17 October 2012). However, in some jurisdictions suspensive effects are given also in relation to protection of private or family life (eg Supreme Court of Estonia, 22 March 2016; Supreme Administrative Court of Lithuania, SAC, AS822-768/2013, 9 October 2013) and a right to education in a primary school class (Administrative Court of First Instance of Thessaloniki, no 299/2015).

impacted by removal.[68] *Abdida* also states that the basic needs of third-country nationals who are staying illegally but cannot yet be removed should be defined in national law as required by recital 12 of the Return Directive, and refers to emergency healthcare and essential medical treatment.[69] This interpretation implicitly protects human dignity and private life.[70]

C. Requirements of 'Fair' Procedure and the Relation between National Procedural Law and EU Law

In *Mahdi*, the Administrativen sad Sofia-grad (Bulgaria) asked seven questions concerning the relationship between the Return Directive and primary EU law. Six were expressly placed in the context of fundamental rights from Article 6 and Article 47 of the Charter and the right to dignity of third-country nationals.

The CJEU said that according to recital 6 of the Return Directive, Member States should ensure that the ending of the illegal stay of third-country nationals is carried out through 'a fair and transparent procedure', and that relevant decisions should be adopted on a 'case-by-case basis and be based on objective criteria, implying that consideration should go beyond the mere fact of an illegal stay'.[71] Presumably, the CJEU (mutatis mutandis) also gives an interpretation of general requirements for fair procedure under Article 47(2) of the Charter in cases of return and removal, although it does not explicitly mention the right to a fair trial. The CJEU also reiterated that, in the absence of EU rules concerning procedural requirements, the Member State remains competent, in accordance with the principle of procedural autonomy, to determine those requirements, while ensuring that fundamental rights are observed and that the provisions of EU law relating to that measure are fully effective.[72] This includes general principles of equivalence and effectiveness.

Finally, the CJEU recognised the right of a third-country national who has no identity documents and has not obtained such documents from his country of origin, after a national court has released the person concerned on the ground that there is no longer a reasonable prospect of removal, to get 'a written confirmation of his situation'. In this respect, Member States may grant an autonomous residence permit or other authorisation offering a right to stay for compassionate,

[68] *Paposhvili v Belgium* [GC], Appl No 41738/10, 13 December 2016, para 188; for further criteria for this assessment, see paras 189–93. For further aspects of protection against *refoulement*, see section VI.B.vi below.

[69] *Abdida* (n 32) paras 54–62.

[70] Arts 1 and 7 of the Charter. According to REDIAL Research Report 2016/04 (n 49) 20, under the case-law of the Dutch Council of State, the realisation of the rights to shelter, food and clothing are conditional upon the cooperation of the third-country nationals in the return process. The exceptions are rights to necessary medical care and education of minors (District Court, the Hague, 19 May 2015).

[71] Case C-146/14 PPU *Mahdi* ECLI:EU:C:2014:1320, para 40; see also *Mukarubega* (n 38) para 61.

[72] *Mahdi*, ibid, para 50.

humanitarian or other reasons, but are not obliged to do so. The CJEU has grounded the right to get 'a written confirmation of his/her situation' in secondary EU law (Article 6(4) and recital 12 of the Return Directive).[73]

D. Concrete Elements of the Right to be Heard

In *Mukarubega*, the Tribunal administratif de Melun (France) asked two questions in relation to a return decision concerning the right to be heard as an integral part of the fundamental principle of respect for the rights of the defence, enshrined in Article 41 of the Charter. The CJEU decided that the right to be heard in the context of the Return Directive, particularly Article 6, is to be interpreted as meaning that a national authority is not precluded from failing to hear a third-country national on the subject of a return decision where, after a procedure which fully respected that person's right to be heard has determined that the person is staying illegally in the national territory.[74] The Court established that the return decision was adopted soon enough after Ms Mukarubega was heard on the subject of the illegality of her stay and that during the interview she was able effectively to present her observations on that subject.[75] Under the circumstances the obligation to hear on the subject of the return decision would have needlessly prolonged the administrative procedure, since Ms Mukarubega had already been heard on her application for asylum by the CNDA (Cour nationale du droit d'asile, National Court of Asylum) and slightly more than three months before the first return decision.[76] This standard does not relate directly to the right to defence or to be heard in court proceedings under Article 47(2) of the Charter, but rather to the general principle of good administration that applies in procedures before executive bodies. Nevertheless, important parts of the interpretation may also be applicable mutatis mutandis to the right to effective legal remedy before courts and tribunals.

In those parts of the judgment the CJEU said the right to be heard 'in all proceedings' is affirmed in Articles 47 and 48 of the Charter and in a general principle of EU law, the right to good administration.[77] The right guarantees every person the opportunity to make known his views effectively during an administrative procedure and before the adoption of any decision liable to affect his interests adversely.[78] The CJEU further explained that although the authors of the Return Directive intended to provide a detailed framework for the safeguards granted to

[73] ibid, paras 88–89.
[74] *Mukarubega* (n 38) para 82.
[75] ibid, para 81.
[76] ibid, paras 69–70.
[77] ibid, para 43.
[78] ibid, para 46; see also para 42 as regards non-applicability of Art 41 of the Charter in return procedures.

third-country nationals, they did not specify whether, and under what conditions, observance of the right to be heard was to be ensured, or the consequences of an infringement of that right.[79] Where neither is laid down by EU law, they fall within the scope of national law, provided the rules are the same as those to which individuals in comparable situations under national law are subject (equivalence) and that they do not make it excessively difficult to exercise the rights conferred by EU law (effectiveness).[80]

However, the fundamental right to be heard requires observance even where legislation does not explicitly provide for it.[81] Here the CJEU referred to the cases *Sopropé* (paragraph 38), *M* (paragraph 86) and *G and R* (paragraph 32).[82] Therefore, Member States must take account of all the CJEU's case-law concerning observance of the rights of the defence in conjunction with the Return Directive when they determine the conditions under which observance of the right to be heard is to be ensured or act upon an infringement of that right.[83]

The right to be heard as part of the rights of the defence includes:

- an opportunity to make known applicant's views effectively during an administrative procedure and before the adoption of any decision liable to affect his or her interests adversely;[84]
- an obligation of the authority effectively to take into account all relevant information;
- an opportunity of that person to correct an error or submit evidence relating to his or her personal circumstances in favour of the adoption or non-adoption of the decision, or in favour of its having a specific content;[85]
- an obligation of the authorities to pay due attention to the observations submitted by the person concerned, examining carefully and impartially all the relevant aspects and giving a detailed statement of reasons for their decision;
- reasons for a decision must be sufficiently specific and concrete to allow the person concerned to understand why his application is being rejected.[86]

Although the CJEU only makes a very general reference to Article 47 of the Charter in paragraph 43, it is reasonable to conclude that the above elements are minimum requirements for the rights to defence featured in Article 47(2).

However, the rights of the defence do not constitute unfettered prerogatives and may be restricted, provided that the restrictions correspond to the objective of

[79] ibid, para 41.
[80] ibid, para 51.
[81] ibid, para 42.
[82] ibid, para 49.
[83] ibid, para 55.
[84] ibid, para 46.
[85] ibid, para 47.
[86] ibid, para 48.

general interest pursued by the measure in question and they do not involve, with regard to the objetives pursued, a disproportionate and intolerable interference which infringes upon the very substance of the rights guaranteed.[87] Here the CJEU did not refer to the principle of proportionality in Article 52(1) of the Charter; instead, it referred to its own case-law.

E. Further Details of the Right to be Heard and Free Legal Aid

In *Boudjlida*, the Tribunal administrative de Pau (France) asked three questions with reference to Article 41 of the Charter that were very similar to those in *Mukarubega*. The CJEU repeated the interpretation from the *Mukarubega* judgment, and further found that the right to be heard had been respected in this case.[88] However, *Boudjlida* provides fresh insight into the substance of the right to be heard, which could be relevant also for effective judicial protection against return and removal decisions.

The CJEU stated that when a competent national authority is contemplating the adoption of a return decision, it must observe the obligations imposed by Article 5 of the Return Directive and hear the person concerned.[89] The person must co-operate and provide the authority with all relevant personal and family information. He must be allowed to express his point of view on the detailed arrangements for his return, such as the period allowed for departure. The authority must take into account circumstances such as children attending school and other family and social links.[90] The right to be heard does not simply require the authority to warn an illegally staying third-country national 'prior to [an] interview' that it is contemplating adopting a return decision, to disclose the evidence on which it intends to rely, or to allow the person a period for reflection 'before admitting his observations', but to give him the 'opportunity effectively to submit his point of view on the subject of the illegality of his/her stay and reasons which might' justify avoiding a return decision.[91]

The Court adds that an exception must be admitted where a third-country national could not reasonably suspect what evidence might be relied on against him or would objectively only be able to respond to it after certain checks or steps were taken with a view, in particular, to obtaining supporting documents.[92] In any event, that person has the opportunity to challenge the assessment made by the administrative authorities by bringing legal proceedings against

[87] ibid, para 53.
[88] *Boudjlida* (n 37) paras 60–63.
[89] ibid, para 49.
[90] ibid, paras 50–51.
[91] ibid, para 55; see also para 69.
[92] ibid, para 56.

a first-instance decision.[93] This proves that the right to be heard is applicable before the adoption of any decision liable to affect his or her interests adversely, that is before the first-instance administrative procedure and before the second independent (judicial) instance procedure.

The Court also confirmed that the main elements of a decision, where necessary, must be translated in writing or orally, under the conditions laid down in Article 12(2) of the Return Directive as this is a particular element of effective legal remedy directly related to Article 13 of the Directive.[94]

The Court recognised that a right to legal assistance is provided for in Article 13 only after the adoption of a return decision and solely when an appeal against it has been brought before a competent judicial or administrative authority or body composed of members who are impartial and enjoy safeguards of independence.[95] However, an illegally staying third-country national may always have recourse, at his own expense, to the services of a legal adviser when being heard, provided the exercise of that right does not affect the due progress of the return procedure and effective implementation of that Directive.[96] Perhaps the application of this standard should be applied in conjunction with the prohibition of abuse of rights in Article 54 of the Charter. In this case, the CJEU felt that Mr Boudjlida had waived his right to legal advice by going unaccompanied to the police station for his interview the same day he was invited.

Free legal assistance must be granted after a return decision has been adopted 'if requested by the person concerned'.[97] In this respect the CJEU did not refer to Article 47(3) of the Charter, which regulates free legal aid in judicial proceedings as a fundamental right. Furthermore, before the third-country national could effectively exercise his right to (free) legal assistance from the Return Directive and the Charter, he/she should be informed by the authority or by the court that such a right exists.

F. Right to Family Reunification and the Best Interests of a Child

In *KA and others*, the Raad voor Vreemdelingenbetwistingen (Council for Asylum and Immigration Proceedings, Belgium) asked nine questions concerning the use of Articles 5 and 11 of the Return Directive in respect of the right to family reunification (Article 7 of the Charter), freedom of movement of an EU citizen

[93] ibid, para 57.
[94] ibid, para 58.
[95] ibid, para 64.
[96] ibid, paras 65, 70.
[97] ibid, para 64. As regards legal aid in the context of the Return Directive only the judgment of the Austrian High Administrative Court (Ro 2015/21/2013, 3 September 2015) is mentioned in REDIAL Research Report 2016/04 (n 49) 15.

(Article 20 TFEU) and the principle of the best interests of a child (Article 24 of the Charter). However, these questions relate to circumstances where third-country nationals are already subject to valid entry bans. Therefore, after the return and entry ban decisions were taken against the third-country nationals, they filed applications for residence permits in the context of family reunification with an EU citizen who has not made use of his right of freedom of movement and establishment.[98]

At the outset, the CJEU stated that the Return Directive concerns only the return of illegally staying third-country nationals and is not designed to harmonise all rules on the stay of foreign nationals. There are no rules in it concerning how to deal with an application for residence for the purposes of family reunification that is submitted 'after the adoption of a return decision accompanied by an entry ban'.[99] Hence, the judgment's interpretation ignores the Directive.

However, if a refusal to grant a right of residence to a third-country national would undermine the effectiveness of EU citizenship because of a relationship of dependency between the third-country national and the EU citizen, since that citizen would be obliged in practice to leave the territory of the European Union, thus depriving him of the genuine enjoyment of the substance of the rights conferred by that status, Member States may use Articles 3(6) and Article 11(3) of the Directive and withdraw or suspend an entry ban, where the return decision has not been complied with and the third-country national is in their territory.[100]

Although the referring court explicitly asked whether it would be useful to refer to Article 7 of the Charter and the case-law under Article 8 ECHR, the Court chose to draw solely on Article 20 TFEU instead.[101] It further said that the Treaty provisions on citizenship of the Union do not confer any autonomous rights on third-country nationals; rather, their rights derive from those of EU citizens.[102]

Such an interpretation could provoke legal uncertainty, since in the case of *El Dridi*, which concerned the rules of detention, the CJEU stated that the Return Directive is intended to take account of the case-law of the ECtHR.[103] Furthermore, recital 22 of the Directive refers to the ECHR, particularly in respect of family life which should be a primary consideration of Member States when implementing the Directive.[104] What is the meaning of the legal provisions and case-law of the ECtHR concerning effective legal remedy if third-country nationals do not have any autonomous rights to family reunification?

[98] *KA and others* (n 20) para 32.

[99] ibid, paras 44–45.

[100] ibid, para 61.

[101] The exceptions are in paras 71 and 90, where Art 7 of the Charter and the best interests of a child (Art 24(2) of the Charter) are (only) mentioned.

[102] *KA and others* (n 20) para 50; see also para 53.

[103] Case C-61/11 PPU *El Dridi* ECLI:EU:C:2011:268, para 43.

[104] See also Art 1 of the Return Directive which refers to fundamental rights under international law and Art 5 of the Return Directive.

The CJEU in this case expressly protected only a primary and individual right of an EU citizen to move and reside freely within the territory of the Member State and to enjoy the substance of the rights conferred by virtue of his or her status,[105] since this case and interpretation of the CJEU refer to a legal situation when applications for residence permits for the purpose of family reunifications were filed only after the procedure under the Return Directive. The exception is the aforementioned option provided in Articles 6(3) and 13 of the Directive under which Member States may withdraw or suspend an entry ban.

That is why the part of the judgment that merely repeats the *Boudjlida* interpretation is important. Here, the Court reiterates that when Member States implement the Directive they must take due account of the best interests of the child, family life, the state of health of the third-country national concerned and the principle of *non-refoulement* pursuant to Article 5; the authorities must hear the person on those subjects.[106] The person has a duty of honest co-operation which means that the applicant is obliged, as soon as possible, to inform the authority of any relevant changes in his/her life. An applicant's right cannot be used to reopen or extend indefinitely the administrative procedure.[107]

Ambiguities remain. For example, according to Article 20 TFEU a third-country national who claims family reunification in circumstances where the Directive is not applicable can derive his or her right only from the right of a family member who is a citizen of the Union. How does this fit with the case-law of the ECtHR, under which illegally staying third-country nationals can autonomously claim the right to reunite with family members who are legally resident in the EU? How would this legal situation in respect of the interpretation in the case of *KA and others* fit with case-law of the ECtHR which in principle is not so restrictive, since under ECtHR case-law such an applicant is not *ipso iure* excluded from claiming the right to family reunification, particularly if he or she is a settled migrant.[108]

Also, what is the impact of *KA and others* if the illegal stay of a third-country national is for many years tolerated by the Member State and the person claims protection of private life based on Article 8 ECHR,[109] or Article 7 of the Charter? Under the particular circumstances of statelessness, the ECtHR case-law imposes a positive obligation to protect the private life of an applicant by issuing documents to authorise the applicant's stay.[110]

[105] See *KA and others* (n 20) paras 48–49.

[106] ibid, paras 102–03.

[107] ibid, para 105; see also para 107.

[108] See eg *Üner v the Netherlands*, Appl No 46410/99, 18 October 2006; *Nunez v Norway*, Appl No 55597/09, 28 June 2011.

[109] See eg *AA v the United Kingdom*, Appl No 8000/08, 20 September 2011; *AH Khan v the United Kingdom*, Appl No 6222/10, 20 December 2011; *Miah v the United Kingdom*, Appl No 53080/07, 27 April 2010.

[110] See eg *Hoti v Croatia*, Appl No 63311/14, 26 April 2018.

The CJEU decided that where the EU citizen is a minor, considerations include the child's age, his physical and emotional development, the extent of his emotional ties to each of his or her parents, and the risks which separation from the third-country national parent might entail for that child's equilibrium. The existence of a family link with a third-country national, whether natural or legal, is not sufficient, and cohabitation is not necessary to establish a relationship of dependency.[111]

The ambiguity in this part of the judgment relates to paragraphs 71, 72 and 73, where considerable importance is given to the relationship of dependence between a minor and a parent. This cannot be excluded from the assessment of the best interests of a child, but it is perhaps overemphasised. A relationship of dependency under ECtHR case-law is relevant for family reunification between adults.[112] Much like the criterion that an EU citizen must 'be compelled' to leave the EU,[113] it seems that the 'relationship of dependency' criterion takes priority over the best interests of a child from Article 24(2) of the Charter.[114]

G. *Non-Refoulement* and the Relation between Primary and Secondary EU Law on Effective Legal Remedy

In *Gnandi*, the Conseil d'État (Belgium) asked a question concerning protection of *non-refoulement* (Article 5 of the Return Directive) and the right to effective judicial protection under EU law (Article 13(1) of the Directive and Article 47 of the Charter) in relation to Belgian statutory law.[115] The CJEU decided that the sole fact that the stay of the person concerned is categorised as being illegal as soon as his application for international protection is rejected at first instance and that the return decision may, therefore, be adopted after that rejection decision or aggregated together in a single administrative act, does not infringe the principle of *non-refoulement* or the right to an effective remedy.[116] This is irrespective of any authorisation to remain pending the outcome of an appeal against that rejection.[117]

No doubt the main aim of this interpretation is to facilitate effective return and repatriation. The eventual doubt whether this interpretation will contribute anything to the protection of fundamental rights is not limited to the general point

[111] *KA and others* (n 20) para 76, second indent.

[112] See eg *Slivenko v Latvia*, Appl No 48321/99, para 97; *AW Khan v the United Kingdom*, Appl No 6222/10, 20 December 2011, para 32; *Onur v the United Kingdom*, Appl No 27319/07, 17 February 2009, paras 43–45.

[113] *KA and others* (n 21) para 74.

[114] As regards family unity in relation to the Return Directive, only judgments of the Bulgarian and Lithuanian courts are discussed in REDIAL Research Report 2016/04 (n 49) 21–22.

[115] Case C-181/16 *Gnandi* ECLI:EU:C:2018:465, para 29.

[116] ibid, para 58.

[117] ibid, para 59.

that any interpretation of the Return Directive must be consistent with the fundamental rights and principles recognised, in particular, by the Charter.[118] The doubt is to some extent diminished also when the CJEU states that Member States must ensure the full effectiveness of an appeal against a decision rejecting an application for international protection, in accordance with principle of equality of arms, which means, inter alia, that 'all the legal effects of the return decision' must be suspended during the period prescribed for bringing that appeal and, if an appeal is brought, until its resolution.[119]

The Grand Chamber reiterated its interpretation in *Abdida* and *Tall* that the remedies in Article 13 of the Return Directive must be interpreted consistently with Article 47 of the Charter, which constitutes a reaffirmation of the principle of effective judicial protection, and provides that everyone whose rights and freedoms are violated has the right to an effective remedy before a tribunal in compliance with the Article's conditions.[120] The CJEU thus confirmed that the right to effective legal remedy in Articles 13 and 14 of the Return Directive must be in accordance with the right to effective legal protection from Article 47 of the Charter. Therefore, provisions in secondary EU law on effective legal remedy do not limit the right to effective legal remedy from Article 47, despite the fact that in some cases the CJEU refers to Article 47 as a principle and not a right.[121]

The Grand Chamber also reiterated the *Abdida* interpretation that in cases of removal, if there are substantial grounds for believing that the third-country national will be exposed to a real risk of ill treatment, the right to an effective remedy must have an automatic suspensive effect.[122] Based on Articles 18 and 19(2) of the Charter the principle of *non-refoulement* is a fundamental right.[123] One level of effective judicial protection fulfils criteria from Article 47 of the Charter and thus two judicial instances are not required under EU law.[124]

VII. What Does Judicial Dialogue Reveal on Articles 13 and 14 of the Directive?

In 16 out of 23 procedures for preliminary rulings the relevant questions of national courts referred only to technical issues of detention, possibilities of various sanctions against third-country nationals or, for example, calculations of various periods regulated by the Return Directive. They concerned relations between

[118] ibid, para 51.
[119] ibid, para 61 and see further paras 62–65.
[120] ibid, para 52.
[121] For differences in methods of interpretation if a given matter concerns interpretation of a right or a principle, see Art 52(5) of the Charter.
[122] *Gnandi* (n 115) paras 54, 56. See critical comments on this interpretation at sectionVI.B.ii below.
[123] *Gnandi* (n 115) para 53.
[124] ibid, para 57; see also Case C-180/17 *X Y* ECLI:EU:C:2018:775, paras 20–44.

national statutory laws and the Directive or the interpretation of the Directive itself. Despite the fact that the CJEU has a duty to interpret all provisions of EU law which national courts need in order to decide the actions pending before them, even if those provisions are not expressly indicated in the question referred to the CJEU,[125] the Court mentioned fundamental rights in 6 out of those 16 cases, where national courts did not ask any question concerning fundamental rights. However, the CJEU in those 6 cases mentioned fundamental rights in a very general manner. In all 23 procedures the questions were germane to the issue of judicial control of the legality of administrative decisions on the return and removal of illegally staying third-country nationals.

Since the Return Directive entered into force, only 7 of 23 procedures for preliminary rulings explicitly concerned the protection of fundamental rights. Overall, out of 61 questions (in 23 procedures) around 25 questions were linked to fundamental rights issues. However, 16 of these were asked in only two cases. All questions concerning fundamental rights simply referred in a very general term to a particular provision from the Charter or to a particular general principle of EU law. Thus, no substantial dialogue between the referring courts and the CJEU on more particular aspects or problems of effective protection of fundamental rights can be identified within those procedures. Seven courts from only four different Member States have provoked interpretations concerning the fundamental rights aspects.

Two very tentative conclusions emerge from this analysis. One possible conclusion is that in the majority of cases the effective implementation of fundamental rights under the Directive does not raise serious questions of interpretation in practices of courts of the Member States. The other possible conclusion that after the EU regulatory phase of the reform on the return of illegally staying third-country nationals is over, 'all Member States now generally accept the main policy objectives of EU return policy including respect for fundamental rights'[126] is just a presumption that would need to be monitored, tested and – if necessary – addressed by judges in their respective systems of quality management in judiciaries.

Three arguments indicate that the second conclusion might be closer to reality than the first. First, those few questions concerning fundamental rights in relation to the use of the Directive were formulated by national courts in a very general manner. They were not specifically elaborated from the standpoint of particular problems or conflicting legal perspectives, although for a coherent use of fundamental rights one needs to apply the Directive together with national statutory law, case-law on constitutional rights, the Charter or general principles of EU law, the case-law of the ECtHR and other relevant international treaties, such as UN Convention of the Rights of the Child. These sources are not always easily

[125] Case C-38/14 *Extravjería v Zaizoune* ECLI:EU:C:2015:260, para 25.

[126] See the prologue to this book by F Lutz, especially the section 'The First Decade of Application 2008–2018.

reconciled for the effective protection of human rights. The second is based on the information in the REDIAL Journal that assessing ex officio the respect of procedural fundamental rights by public authorities mainly depends on the Member State's legal order and judicial organisation.[127] Although the issue of applying EU law of the court's own motion is sometimes considered the most elusive of the various rules developed by the CJEU,[128] application of EU law ex officio should at least be undisputed in relation to the right to be heard as interpreted by the CJEU in *Boudjlida* and *Mukarubega*, although some material aspect of this rule, such as the best interests of a child, would also be highly relevant in this regard. In cases where illegally staying third-country nationals do not have access to legal aid this problem adds further dimensions. The third is that preliminary rulings in *Abdida*, and particularly *KA and others*, show that the interpretations of the CJEU on fundamental rights have left ambiguities for the effective judicial protection in cases that involve issues of family reunification, automatic suspensive effect of legal remedy and *non-refoulement* in medical cases.

VIII. Conclusion

Article 267 TFEU is essential for judicial dialogue between courts of Member States and the CJEU and for the rule of law in the European Union. In 26 procedures for preliminary rulings it was essential for the judicial control of legality of administrative decisions on return and removal of illegally staying third-country nationals. Article 267 TFEU is essential also for the judicial protection of fundamental rights, including for the interpretation of requirements for judicial independence.[129] However, those seven procedures for preliminary rulings in relation to the Return Directive, which have significant links to fundamental human rights issues, are just the first step in a longer process for effective implementation of the rule of law under the Directive. Systemic approaches within judicial structures concerning knowledge and quality management of adjudicating in each Member State are needed to effectively implement every ruling of the CJEU in national case-law and to identify and deal properly with complex questions concerning protection of fundamental rights of illegally staying third-country nationals that derive from those rulings; this includes respect for the 'special significance' of the case-law of the ECtHR. In some Member States, judicial authorities have already recognised the need to develop sustainable and well-structured knowledge-management and quality-management systems that aim to improve the rule of law also from

[127] REDIAL Research Report 2016/04 (n 49) 24.

[128] See eg N Fennelly, 'The National Judge as Judge of the European Union' in A Rosas, E Levits and Y Bot (eds), *The Court of Justice and the Construction of Europe: Analyses and Perspectives on Sixty Years of Case-Law* (Berlin, Springer, 2013) 70.

[129] For the requirements of judicial independence in relation to effective legal remedy in international protection cases, see Case C-175/11, *HID and BA* ECLI:EU:C:2013:45, paras 83–105.

the standpoint of effective implementation of relevant EU law (including CJEU case-law) and ECtHR case-law before domestic courts. In some other Member States this still needs to be done. A prerequisite for the establishment of such quality-management systems is that judges are able to conduct a constructive judicial dialogue between themselves. This is not very easy given possible differences in 'powers' (ranks and knowledge) of judges and the fact that in many Member States quasi-judicial bodies (judicial councils) or even ministries are involved in the administration of justice. A clear demarcation between administration of justice, where non-judicial actors should be excluded and a system of quality management in the judiciary, where different actors, including non-judicial actors are rightfully involved, is often underestimated and blurred.

Judicial dialogue between judges of different Member States is also crucial. This is the transnational 'horizontal' judicial dialogue or cross-fertilisation between courts of different states. In a global legal context, Professor Anne-Marie Slaughter, 24 years ago, published the essay 'A Typology of Transjudicial Communication'.[130] Her three-part typology includes forms of transjudicial communications (horizontal; vertical; mixed vertical–horizontal), different degrees of reciprocal engagement (direct dialogue; monologue; intermediated dialogue) and transjudicial communication depending on functions (enhancing the effectiveness of supranational tribunals; assuring and promoting acceptance of reciprocal international obligations; cross-fertilisation; enhancing the persuasiveness, authority or legitimacy of individual judicial decisions; collective deliberation).[131] Julie Allard and Antoine Garapon mention, as forms of judicial networking, citation of foreign judgments in domestic case-law, exchange of arguments and information, ad-hoc joint forums, professional assocations of judges, syndicates, clubs etc.[132] Informal networking as judicial dialogue emerge at the margin of institutional mechanisms. Dialogues through judicial networking are not systems of court-oriented rules, systems of government by judges or the 'juristocracy' as may be said for the CJEU. The main reason, which calls for judicial dialogues of this kind at the lower levels as well, is that judges are searching for the best possible decisions.[133] Therefore, various associations and ad hoc networks of courts or judges can facilitate transjudicial transparency, cross-fertilisation and case-law dialogue.

[130] AM Slaughter, 'A Typology of Transjudicial Communication' (1994) 29 *University of Richmond Law Review* 99.

[131] From the study of Slaughter it emerges that the first literature on transjudicial communications (published by A Lester: *The Overseas Trade in the American Bill of Rights* and by AM Glendon: *Rights Talk: The Impoverishment of Political Discourse*) dates back to 1988 and 1991.

[132] J Alard and A Garapon, *Les judge dans la mondalisation* (Seuil, Paris, 2005).

[133] C Harlow, 'Global Administrative Law: The Quest for Principles and Values' (2006) 17(1) *European Journal of International Law* 211; as regards judicial dialogue at higher levels, see eg D Remy-Granger, 'How Can Interconnected Societies Contribute to Legal and Judicial Reform', Comparative Legal and Judicial Development: Towards an Agenda for Just and Equitable Society in 21st Century, 5–7 June 2000.

Due to the development of information technology, there is now a considerable proliferation of judicial networks where judges not only exchange information and experiences and discuss how to improve their services (public accountability and judicial independence), but have specialised dialogues concerning the application of particular fields of law.[134] Two examples in the fields of immigration and asylum are the International Association of Refugee and Migration Judges (IARMJ), within which the Europe Chapter (IARMJ-Europe) has around 340 members, and the Working Party on Asylum and Immigration of the Association of European Administrative Judges.

These informal exchanges are not always characterised by the concept of judicial dialogue as a 'persuasive' authority versus as a 'binding authority'. Under the methods of interpretation of EU law, and taking into account the 'constitutional status of the principle of linguistic equality' under EU law[135] for the proper use of Article 267 TFEU, a national court must, for example, be 'convinced that the matter is equally obvious to the courts of the other Member States'.[136] In the opinion of former Advocate General of the CJEU and Judge of the Supreme Court of Ireland, Nial Fennely, this is the most difficult point to resolve for national judges.[137]

Is there a substantial and transparent judicial dialogue between judges or courts of the Member States in relation to the effective protection of human rights of individuals concerned under the Return Directive? If so, it is not so much reflected in the 26 procedures described above. The IARMJ-Europe which – in close collaboration with the European Asylum Support Office – has developed a unique structure for deliberation of common training materials for judges of the Member States regarding EU asylum laws that do not yet focus on the Directive specifically. The activities of the AEAJ in this respect are limited to annual meetings of the Working Party. The European Law Institute has produced a judicial checklist concerning detention under the Directive and the ECHR, but this compilation of judicial dialogue between the CJEU and the ECtHR is limited to the right to an effective legal remedy in detention cases.[138]

The gap in transnational judicial dialogue in relation to other provisions of the Directive has been partly addressed by ad-hoc projects of the European University Institute, such as Contention, Actiones and REDIAL, which were financed by the EU Commission. The purpose was to facilitate informal dialogues among judges

[134] These are, for example: International Association of Judges (IAJ), Consultative Council of European Judges (CCEJ), European Commission for Democracy through Law (Venice Commission), the European Network of Councils for the Judiciary (ENCJ), the Association of the Councils of State and Supreme Administrative Jurisdiction of the EU (ACA-Europe) or the newly established Judicial Network of the European Union (CJEU, Supreme Courts and Constitutional Courts of the Member States of the EU).

[135] For more on this method, see Lenaerts and Gutiérrez-Fons (n 2) 8–13.

[136] Case C-283/81 *CILFIT* ECLI:EU:C:1982:335, para 16; Case C-495/03 *Intermodal Transports BV* ECLI:EU:C:2005:552, paras 39, 45.

[137] Fennelly (n 128) 77.

[138] See *Statement of the European Law Institute* (n 32) 162–258.

who participated in workshops and in the development of publications or handbooks, which have emphasised the case-law of Member States courts (and the CJEU and ECtHR) in relation to all provisions of the Directive.

However, documents such as the REDIAL journal can serve only as basic information on some fragmented parts of national case-law. In order to use judgments from other Member States, judges need full access to them; in order to have fruitful dialogue, they must be aware of one another's case-law. Thus, it seems that expectations of a 'New World Order'[139] have been overly optimistic. Informal dialogue certainly contributes to the effective implementation of fundamental rights and the rule of law. However, its impact will continue to be limited as long as leading actors within judicial systems of the Member States do not comprehend that the quality of judicial services is a complex matter that cannot be dealt with simply by monitoring the numbers of judgments upheld or quashed in appeal procedures, and that complex models of quality management must be incorporated into all major aspects of regulation of selection, promotion, evaluation, disciplinary procedure and tenure. As Judge Richard Posner put it in his book *How Judges Think*: '[J]udges are not moral or intellectual giants, prophets, oracles, mouthpieces or calculating machines. They are all too human workers, responding as other workers do to the conditions of the labour market in which they work.'[140]

[139] AM Slaughter, 'The Real New World Order' [1997] September–October *Foreign Affairs* 187.

[140] RA Posner, *How Judges Think* (Cambridge, MA, Harvard University Press, 2008) 7.

17

A Lawyer's Perspective on Access to Classified Evidence in Return Cases: A View from Poland

JACEK BIAŁAS

I. Introduction

Recently, the return of a number of third-country nationals has attracted public interest in Poland, raising the more general issue of human rights safeguards of migrants in cases featuring national security concerns. Azamat Bayduev, a citizen of the Russian Federation, was returned from Poland to Russia in August 2018 following a decision by the Minister of Interior. Shortly afterwards, he arrived in the Chechen Republic, where he was detained by local law enforcement officials. According to human rights organisations, his life and safety were at risk.[1] In another case, Ameer Alkhawlany, a PhD student at the Jagiellonian University, was returned to Iraq. According to the Internal Security Agency he contacted his friends living in Western Europe, who were Islamic radicals. He stated that return proceedings were launched after he refused to co-operate with the secret service as an informant. Neither the university authorities' interventions nor media coverage of the case prevented his expulsion.[2]

A common feature of these cases is the secrecy regarding the exact reasons why the third-country nationals were considered a threat to national security. The return decisions contained limited reasoning and the third-country nationals

[1] Amnesty International, 'Russia: Chechen Refugee Forcibly Disappeared after Being Unlawfully Deported from Poland' (2018) available at www.amnesty.org/en/latest/news/2018/09/russi-chechen-refugee-forcibly-disappeared-after-being-unlawfully-deported-from-poland/.

[2] Helsinki Foundation for Human Rights, 'HFHR Statement on Ameer Alkhawlany's Obligation to Return' (2017) available at www.hfhr.pl/en/hfhr-statement-on-ameer-alkhawlanys-obligation-to-return; Radio Poland, 'Polish MPs to Probe Iraqi Suspected of Ties with Islamic Radicals: Report' (2016) available at www.thenews.pl/1/10/Artykul/279991,Polish-MPs-to-probe-Iraqi-suspected-of-ties-with-Islamic-radicals-report.

were not informed about the evidence that motivated them. Moreover, they were returned before the courts adopted final decisions in their cases. These cases illustrate the need to look into the way in which Polish authorities guarantee the right of defence of third-country nationals. Some of these cases were also considered by national courts, which in their judgments referred to the provisions of the ECHR and the Return Directive.[3]

The Return Directive was implemented in Polish law by provisions of the Act of 13 December 2013 on Foreigners.[4] Administrative courts have delivered a number of judgments with reference to the Return Directive, several of which have concerned decisions based on national security grounds and classified evidence. Where national security is at stake, the authorities argue that providing third-country nationals with access to all the documents of the case would pose a security risk; for example, persons posing a threat to security could become familiar with the operating methods of secret services. Arguably, this secrecy could lead to abuse and does not allow for an effective defence.

The Charter of the Fundamental Rights of the EU ('the EU Charter'), the Return Directive and the CJEU jurisprudence provide guarantees of the rights of defence. According to the CJEU, in cases involving national security, the person concerned must be informed of the essence of the grounds on which a decision is based.[5] The ECHR and ECtHR jurisprudence also provide procedural safeguards relating to the expulsion of aliens. According to the ECtHR, states must review whether invoking national security as the basis for restricting a person's rights is reasonable and not arbitrary. In addition, national courts cannot carry out a purely formal examination of the administrative decision holding the person concerned to be a danger to national security.[6] The rights provided in both the EU Charter and the ECHR should be interpreted similarly.[7] In cases involving national security, the scope of the rights of defence are more narrowly construed than in other cases.

The rights of defence in Polish return cases based on national security concerns are among the most restricted in Europe. The third-country national has no chance to find out why he is considered a threat, or to ascertain the factual basis of the return decision. This chapter intends to shed light on how the Return Directive is implemented in Polish law, paying particular attention to provisions concerning the return of third-country nationals who are considered a threat to security. The chapter will elaborate on the types of judicial interaction used by the national

[3] Directive 2008/115/EC of the European Parliament and of the Council of 16 December 2008 on common standards and procedures in Member States for returning illegally staying third-country nationals [2008] OJ L348/98.

[4] Consolidated text: Journal of laws of 2018 item 2094.

[5] Case C-300/11 *ZZ v Secretary of State for the Home Department* ECLI:EU:C:2013:363.

[6] *Al-Nashif v Bulgaria*, App No 50963/99 (ECtHR, 20 June 2002); *Lupsa v Romania*, App No 10337/04 (ECtHR, 8 June 2006).

[7] Art 52(3) of the EU Charter.

courts in such cases. It will also analyse their use of the EU Charter and the jurisprudence of the CJEU, the ECHR and the ECtHR when balancing the protection of the rights of defence with national security. Until now, Polish cases concerning return and national security have not featured in procedures before the CJEU or the ECtHR. In light of serious doubts regarding the conformity of Polish law with EU law and the ECHR, which will be discussed below, it would be desirable if this changed.

This chapter is written from a lawyer's perspective. Like his client, a lawyer representing the third-country national in return proceedings involving national security does not have access to the classified documents of the case even if he has a security clearance.[8] In contrast, the courts and the authority that issued the return decision have full access. This obviously hinders effective representation and constitutes a serious imbalance in judicial proceedings, straining the equality-of-arms principle of adversarial proceedings.

This chapter discusses Polish provisions regarding return procedures in cases involving national security. It analyses the lawyers' strategy in these cases, specifically focusing on their reliance on EU law and the ECHR over national regulations that are not consistent with them. It also analyses the administrative courts' responses to the litigation strategies.

II. Implementation of the Return Directive in Polish Law

A. Overview of National Legislation Concerning Return Proceedings

The return of third-country nationals illegally entering or staying in Poland is regulated by the Act on Foreigners. The Act lists reasons for issuing a return decision, defines circumstances under which a return decision cannot be issued or enforced, contains provisions on pre-removal detention, and designates the competent authorities for handling the return procedure. According to the Act, the return decision is issued in writing and provides reasons in fact and in law, as well as information about available legal remedies. The return decision is always

[8] This contrasts with the situation in Member States such as the UK, the Netherlands and Romania, where lawyers can access some of the classified evidence to which the complainant does not have access. In Romania, lawyers' security clearance procedures take a long time, which can compromise the right to access a court as they are not nominated by the authorities. Rather, they are chosen by the applicant, who cannot be expected to know which authorised lawyers are available (see pending complaints before the ECtHR, AMN case, Romanian High Court of Cassation and Justice, file no 5473/2/2012, ECtHR App No 19943/13, available in the ACTIONES Database).

accompanied by an entry ban.[9] According to the government, mandatory issuing of an entry ban is not in breach of Article 11(2) of the Return Directive, as the latter gives Member States discretion to choose whether or not to accompany the return decision with a ban. A decision rejecting a claim for international protection is *not* accompanied by a return decision. Therefore, separate return proceedings are initiated in cases involving rejected asylum seekers; these are conducted according to the same rules as in other cases, with entry bans always accompanying return decisions.

According to the Act on Foreigners, a return decision is issued by the commander of the Border Guard station or the commandant of the Border Guard regional branch. The decision may be appealed to the Head of the Office for Foreigners, the second-instance administrative authority. An appeal generally has suspensive effect. The Head of the Office reviews the return decision, examining points of fact and of law. His decisions may be appealed before the administrative court of first instance.

Such an appeal is not automatically suspensive; the third-country national must request it. When such a request is lodged, the return decision is suspended until the court reaches a decision about it. If the court accepts the request, the suspensive effect is prolonged until the end of judicial proceedings (including any involving the Supreme Administrative Court). These proceedings can last as long as two years, raising doubts about the system's conformance with the right to a fair trial and effective judicial protection.

The administrative court of first instance conducts an *ex tunc* assessment of the decision limited to points of law. For example, it may rule that the evidentiary proceedings were defective, resulting in incorrect factual findings, but the court may not determine the facts itself. It is not bound by the appeal complaints, so it can consider all the circumstances of the case and may revoke the decision on the basis of violations of law that were not indicated in the complaints. Its judgments may be appealed to the Supreme Administrative Court. The Court must refer to all complaints and as a general rule is bound by the cassation appeal complaints.[10] Thus it cannot refer *proprio motu* to legal grounds other than those in the cassation appeal. Its judgments are final and cannot be further appealed.

The administrative courts and the Supreme Administrative Court are courts in the sense of Article 267 TFEU. The Supreme Administrative Court is a judicial body against whose decisions there is no judicial remedy under national law. Therefore it is obliged to make a preliminary reference to the CJEU in the situations provided in Article 267 TFEU.

[9] According to Art 11(1) of the Return Directive, return decisions must be accompanied by an entry ban if no period for voluntary departure has been granted, or if the obligation to return has not been observed. In other cases, return decisions may be accompanied by an entry ban.

[10] Art 183.1 of the Act on Proceedings before Administrative Courts.

B. The Law on Return Procedures in Cases Involving National Security

The Act on Foreigners contains procedural safeguards in return cases, including the right to an effective remedy before a court.[11] In general, parties to the proceedings have the right to access case files. They should be informed about this right, and their right to present their position with regard to the evidence presented by the authorities. However, there are some institutional and procedural modifications in cases involving national security. The Act provides that a return decision is issued when required for reasons of national defence or security, the protection of public safety and order, or the interests of the nation generally.[12] In such cases a period for voluntary departure is not provided.[13] The decision is immediately enforceable and an appeal to the Head of the Office for Foreigners has no suspensive effect.[14] It is also not possible to lodge a request to the administrative court for suspension. Appeal proceedings, including any before the administrative court, may only take place after the third-country national has been removed.

The Act of 10 June 2016 on Anti-Terror Activities introduced amendments to the Act on Foreigners.[15] A new Article 329a was added stating that the Minister of Interior issues a return decision to a third-country national if there is reason to suspect him of conducting terrorist or espionage activity now or in the future. The Minister's decision is immediately enforceable and cannot be suspended. In return cases involving national security, third-country nationals must be detained, and alternatives cannot be applied.[16] This provision is not compatible with Article 15(1) of the Return Directive, which requires Member States to consider alternatives before using detention in return cases. This rule was reiterated in the CJEU's jurisprudence.[17] According to the Directive, detention is particularly justifiable when there is a risk of absconding or the third-country national avoids or hampers the return or removal process. There is no provision that allows Member States to disregard the obligation to apply alternatives to detention in particular cases, even those involving national security.

The Act on Foreigners provides that the authority issuing a decision may refrain from providing its factual reasoning if this is justified for reasons related to the defence or security of the state or the protection of public safety and order.[18]

[11] See Art 331 of the Act on Foreigners.
[12] Art 302.1(9) of the Act on Foreigners.
[13] ibid, Art 315.2(2).
[14] ibid, Art 315.5.
[15] Consolidated version: Journal of Laws of 2018, item 452.
[16] See Arts 398.1 and 2 and 398a.1 and 2 of the Act on Foreigners.
[17] Case C-61/11 PPU *El Dridi* ECLI:EU:C:2011:268, para 39.
[18] Art 6.1 of the Act on Foreigners. This provision is applicable not only to return proceedings but also to other types of proceedings conducted under this Act (temporary stay permits, detention, etc). Similar provision is included in other acts concerning the entry, stay and departure of foreigners: the Act of 13 June 2003 on granting protection to foreigners on the territory of Poland, and the Act of

According to Supreme Administrative Court jurisprudence, this provision adequately transposes Article 12(2) of the Return Directive, which states that information on reasons in fact may be limited when national law allows for the right to information to be restricted. The Court states that such a restriction can help safeguard national security, defence and public safety, and assists the prevention, investigation, detection and prosecution of criminal offences.[19]

The general rule in administrative proceedings is that parties have full access to case-files and can copy them.[20] This does not apply to files containing information classified as 'secret' or 'top secret', or to files that are excluded due to important state interests; these cannot be accessed even in a limited way.[21]

Similar rules apply in return-related proceedings before administrative courts. While the Act on proceedings before administrative courts provides for a general right of access to files,[22] the law regulating state secrecy does not permit a third-country national access to classified case-files.[23] In cases involving national security, the reasons given within the judgments of the administrative courts do not contain information related to the factual grounds for which the third-country national was considered a threat. However, the court has full access to case-files, including classified ones, and is obliged to assess the legality of the decision.

All these measures deprive third-country nationals of basic information concerning the grounds of court decisions. They cannot present their position on the factual grounds leading to their return pending proceedings before administrative authorities and the court. These limitations make the Polish legal system one of the most restrictive regarding the rights of defence in the EU. Similar provisions have been adopted in countries such as Estonia and Greece. In the Czech Republic, Latvia and Lithuania, decisions should give reasons in fact and in law, but may actually be classified in full or in part. In France, Germany, Italy, Portugal, Slovenia and Spain, the parties to court proceedings have full access to case-files and decisions must contain reasons in law and in fact.[24]

The situation in Poland is worrisome as secrecy surrounding return cases may lead to situations where third-country nationals are returned without getting the chance to challenge the decision. The shortcomings of this system were disclosed by the courts in two publicised cases. In the case of the Iraqi citizen described at the beginning of this chapter, the third-country national was detained in order

14 July 2006 on entry into the territory of the Republic of Poland, stay and departure from this territory, of citizens of the European Union Member States and their family members.

[19] Supreme Administrative Court, judgment of 9 September 2016, II OSK 61/15. So far this is the only Supreme Administrative Court judgment that directly refers to Art 12(2) of the Return Directive.

[20] Art 73 of the Polish Code of the Administrative Proceedings.

[21] ibid, Art 74 § 1.

[22] Art 12a § 2 of the Act of 30 August 2002 Law on proceedings before administrative courts.

[23] Act on Protection of Classified Information of 5 August 2010, consolidated version: Journal of Laws of 2018 item 412.

[24] See J Chlebny, 'Public Order, National Security and the Rights of Third-Country Nationals in Immigration Cases' (2018) 20 *European Journal of Migration and Law* 129.

to secure his removal, which was ordered by the Border Guards.[25] Neither the authority ordering the detention and its extension nor the courts had any concrete evidence that he posed a threat to national security. Only when the appeal against the extension of the detention was brought before the Regional Court in Przemyśl did the Court demand the secret service provide material supporting their suspicions. Upon receiving the required information, the Court stated that the threat indicated by the secret service was hypothetical and that detention was therefore arbitrary.[26] However, other courts reviewing the lawfulness of the detention had confirmed the measure in the absence of any evidence of a threat. Despite the Regional Court's judgment ordering the release of the third-country national, the Ministry of Interior issued a return decision on the same day and the person was returned to Iraq.

The serious shortcomings in administrative proceedings based on classified information can be illustrated by looking at a criminal case brought against four Russian citizens of Chechen origin, charged with providing support for the Islamic State in Syria. Translated transcripts ('summaries') from telephone conversations by these individuals provided the basis for the charges brought against them. Criminal procedure law in Poland allows the parties conditional access to classified evidence. In its judgment, the Regional Court in Białystok stated that the summaries contained errors and words or phrases that were not included in the original conversations. It appeared that the conversations did not in fact refer to support for the Islamic State. In its judgment, the Court emphasised that the defendants had pointed out that the translation of their conversations was incorrect. Eventually, some of them were convicted of supporting the Caucasus Emirate in Chechnya (not ISIS in Syria as indicated by the prosecutor) and one of them was acquitted.[27] It can therefore be assumed that in the absence of the defendants' consultation by the Court, they would have been erroneously punished.

The judgment was upheld by the Court of Appeals in Białystok, which underlined the 'incorrect translation of the main evidence constituting the basis for charges'. The Court also underlined that the explanations from the defendants as to the most accurate interpretation of their conversations were crucial.[28] This case illustrates that the arrangement whereby only courts have access to secret case-files may not be sufficient to ensure that the rights of defence are observed. There may be situations in which a court is unable to verify certain facts provided by the authorities, in particular if only the third-country national concerned has knowledge of them.

[25] For more information about this case, see Helsinki Foundation for Human Rights, 'HFHR's Complaint against Compulsory Return of Iraqi PhD Student Dismissed' (2018) available at http://www.hfhr.pl/en/hfhrs-complaint-against-compulsory-return-of-iraqi-phd-student-dismissed/.

[26] Decision of the Regional Court in Przemyśl, case No II Kz 19/17 [2017].

[27] Regional Court in Bialystok, judgment of 7 August 2017, case no III K 113/16.

[28] Białystok Court of Appeals, judgment of 26 June 2018, case no II Aka 26/18.

III. Polish Lawyers' Litigation Strategy in Return Cases Involving National Security

A number of return decisions based on classified evidence have been appealed to the Warsaw Regional Administrative Court and then to the Supreme Administrative Court. In return cases involving national security, the limitations of the rights of defence are based on provisions of national law. Therefore, the lawyers' litigation strategy was to rely on supranational law – ie EU law, the ECHR, and the jurisprudence of the CJEU and ECtHR – and argue for the incompatibility of the Polish transposition of the rights of defence standards. They argued that EU law and the ECHR have priority over national law and therefore, in a situation of incompatibility, the national judge should apply the relevant provisions of the former.[29] Below, I will first discuss arguments contained in appeals based on EU law, as well as requests to the national courts to ask preliminary questions to the CJEU. Then I will present complaints based on the ECHR.

A. Reliance on EU Law Over Polish Law

The appeals were mainly based on complaints of violations of the right to be heard, a subset of the rights of defence. CJEU case-law was invoked, such as the *Mukarubega* case, according to which 'the right to be heard guarantees every person the opportunity to make known his views effectively during an administrative procedure and before the adoption of any decision liable to affect his interests adversely'.[30] The rationale of this rule as explained by the CJEU is

> to enable that person to correct an error or submit such information relating to his or her personal circumstances as will argue in favour of the adoption or non-adoption of the decision, or in favour of its having a specific content.[31]

The CJEU confirmed that the right to be heard should be guaranteed not only during administrative proceedings but also during court proceedings as indicated by Article 47 of the EU Charter, which emphasises the right to a fair legal process in all judicial proceedings.[32]

The appeals also referred to the CJEU judgments in the cases of *ZZ v Secretary of State for the Home Department* and *Kadi*.[33] In these judgments the CJEU

[29] The Constitution of the Republic of Poland of 2 April, 1997, Journal of Laws no 78, item 483, Art 91.

[30] Case C-166/13 *Mukarubega* ECLI:EU:C:2014:2336, para 47; see also Case C-249/13 *Boudjlida* ECLI:EU:C:2014:2431.

[31] *Mukarubega*, ibid.

[32] See Case C-277/11 *MM v Minister for Justice, Equality and Law Reform* ECLI:EU:C:2012:744, paras 81–82, 87, and the jurisprudence cited therein.

[33] See Case C-300/11 *ZZ v Secretary of State for the Home Department* ECLI:EU:C:2013:363; Joined Cases C-402/05 P and C-415/05 P *Yassin Abdullah Kadi and Al Barakaat International Foundation*

emphasised the need for ensuring the procedural rights of third-country nationals in cases involving national security. The Court allowed the use of secret materials, but it underlined the need to strike an appropriate balance between state security requirements and the right to effective judicial protection. It pointed out that in certain cases, disclosure of classified evidence is liable to compromise security in a direct and specific manner: in particular, it may endanger the life, health or freedom of persons, or reveal the national security authorities' investigative methods and thus compromise their work. The Court referred to Article 47 of the EU Charter and held that judicial procedure must comply with the adversarial principle to enable the person to contest the grounds on which the decision is based and make submissions on the related evidence. It concluded that the person concerned must be informed of 'the essence of the grounds' on which a decision is based, even if some evidence remains confidential.

The third-country nationals' lawyers argued that according to the CJEU jurisprudence the rights of defence were violated due to the non-disclosure of the factual reasons for the return decision, and the lack of access to the files containing information on the grounds of the decision. Therefore the third-country nationals were deprived of the right to an effective remedy before the court. Without knowing the factual basis of the return decision, they had no chance to challenge the authorities' assertion that they were a danger to national security. The lawyers emphasised that the return decision included limited reasoning, featured no information on why the third-country national was regarded as a security threat, and contained only basic information on procedure and the legal and evidentiary basis of the decision. They argued that this made judicial assessment of the latter difficult. To further support their complaints, the lawyers invoked the Commentary on the Act of Foreigners, written by a prominent judge, which argues that Polish laws that deny third-country nationals access to classified files and enable a limited provision of factual reasoning are not compatible with EU law.[34]

B. Requesting National Courts to Ask Preliminary Questions from the CJEU

The lawyers' strategy in securing the rights of defence in cases concerning classified evidence was multilayered. In addition to arguing the incompatibility of the Polish transposition of the Return Directive with EU secondary and primary law, and asking the courts to set aside incompatible national legislation, they also requested that national courts address a preliminary reference to the CJEU concerning the validity and interpretation of the relevant EU law provisions.

v Council of the European Union and Commission of the European Communities ECLI:EU:C:2008:461; cases before the Supreme Administrative Court II OSK 2586/14 and II OSK 61/15; cases before the Warsaw Regional Administrative Court IV SA/Wa 3078/17 and IV SA/Wa 2672/17.

[34] J Chlebny (ed), *Commentary on the Act on Foreigners* (Warsaw, Beck, 2015) 89.

Thus, the lawyers argued that the national court should request a preliminary ruling about the validity of Article 12(1) of the Return Directive.[35] As discussed above, this provision allows limited disclosure of the reasons for a return decision in cases involving national security. The lawyers argued that the provision seriously limits the rights of defence, contrary to Article 47 of the EU Charter and CJEU jurisprudence.

The lawyers also argued that Article 13(1) of the Return Directive needs to be clarified in the light of Article 47 of the EU Charter. In particular, they requested that the national court ask the CJEU whether these provisions permit situations in which third-country nationals are prevented from knowing what evidence supported decisions to return them.

C. Complaints of Violation of the ECHR

The third-country nationals also argued that the authorities violated procedural rights enshrined in Article 8 ECHR (covering cases concerning third-country nationals with family in Poland), Article 13 ECHR and Article 1 of Protocol 7 to the ECHR. Complaints of the violation of Article 13 ECHR were brought up in conjunction with complaints of the violation of Article 8 ECHR. The complaints also referred to the ECtHR jurisprudence on return cases involving national security.

According to the ECtHR, the ECHR guarantees that third-country nationals will not be expelled except 'in pursuance of a decision reached in accordance with law'.[36] The ECtHR has stated that 'in accordance with the law' does not merely dictate that the interference should have a basis in domestic law, but also requires it to be compatible with the rule of law. Therefore domestic law must be accessible and foreseeable, in the sense of being sufficiently clear in its terms to give individuals an adequate indication as to the circumstances under which the authorities are entitled to resort to measures affecting their rights under the Convention.[37] According to the ECtHR:

> [E]ven where national security is at stake, the concepts of lawfulness and the rule of law in a democratic society require that deportation measures affecting fundamental human rights be subject to some form of adversarial proceedings before an independent authority or a court competent to effectively scrutinise the reasons for them and

[35] National courts are not bound to address questions regarding the interpretation of EU law if the interpretation is already clear (Case C-283/81 *CILFIT and others v Ministry of Health* ECLI:EU:C:1982:335). On issues concerning the incompatibility of EU secondary legislation with EU primary legislation, however, national courts are required to address preliminary references as the invalidity of EU secondary law falls under the exclusive competence of the CJEU. See Art 267(1) TFEU.

[36] *CG and Others v Bulgaria* App No 1365/07 (ECtHR, 24 April 2008) para 72.

[37] ibid, para 39; *Lupsa* (n 6) para 32.

> review the relevant evidence, if need be with appropriate procedural limitations on the use of classified information.[38]

The Court has also indicated that within adversarial proceedings the third-country national may be represented by a special representative (following security clearance) who can challenge the executive's assertion that national security is at stake.[39] In the *CG and others* judgment, the Court found:

> [I]t [is] particularly striking that the decision to expel the first applicant made no mention of the factual grounds on which it was made. It simply cited the applicable legal provisions and stated that he 'present[ed] a serious threat to national security'; this conclusion was based on unspecified information contained in a secret internal document. … Lacking even outline knowledge of the facts which had served as a basis for this assessment, the first applicant was not able to present his case adequately in the ensuing appeal to the Minister of Internal Affairs and in the judicial review proceedings.[40]

However, ECtHR jurisprudence contains no detailed indications as to what information should be disclosed to a third-country national in order to secure his rights under the ECHR.

Relying on the standards formulated by the ECtHR, the appeals lodged before the Polish courts argued that a person faced with a return decision (or a lawyer acting on his behalf) should be allowed to acquaint themselves at least somewhat with the factual grounds for the decision. Otherwise he cannot present his point of view or challenge the arguments of the authorities.

The ECtHR judgments on which these appeals were based were decided before the ECtHR judgment in the case of *Regner v Czech Republic*.[41] In *Regner*, the Grand Chamber held that the non-disclosure of the grounds for revoking a high-profile civil servant's security clearance did not impair the essence of the applicant's right to a fair trial. The decisive arguments for the ECtHR were, first, that the national courts had unlimited access to all the classified documents, and, second, that their power of judicial review extended to all the facts of the case, beyond the grounds relied on by the applicant.

Arguably, the standard resulting from the *Regner* judgment, based on Article 6 ECHR, should not apply to migration matters.[42] However, the *Ljatifi v the Former Yugoslav Republic of Macedonia* judgment concerning the return of a third-country national referred to *Regner*. In this case the expulsion order issued by the administrative authorities had simply stated that the measure was

[38] *CG and Others* (n 36) para 40; see further *Lupsa* (n 6) para 32.

[39] *CG and Others* (n 36) paras 40 and 57; *Chahal v the United Kingdom*, App No 22414/93 (ECtHR, 15 November 1996) para 131.

[40] *CG and Others* (n 36) para 46.

[41] *Regner v Czech Republic*, App No 35289/11 (ECtHR, 17 September 2017).

[42] See ECtHR judgment *Maaouia v France*, App No 39652/98, in which the Grand Court of the ECtHR stated that Art 6 ECHR did not apply to immigration proceedings (para 38).

being taken because the applicant was 'a risk to [national] security'. The ECtHR stated that 'such a general statement, containing no indications of the facts serving as the basis for that assessment, was accepted without any further details in the ensuing judicial review proceedings'.[43] The Court noted that the national courts had confined themselves to a purely formal examination of the expulsion order as 'they did not explain, if only summarily, the importance of preserving the confidentiality of that document or the extent of the review they had carried out'.[44] Finding an infringement of the ECHR in this regard, the Court referred to *Regner*.

Applications have also been lodged to the ECtHR regarding two cases concerning the return of third-country nationals in which the administration used secret evidence. One of them, *Orujov v Poland*,[45] was communicated to the Polish government by the ECtHR on 18 January 2018. Notably, the provisions of Polish law described above are similar to the Czech laws assessed by the ECtHR in *Regner*. *Orujov* represents an opportunity for the ECtHR to clarify whether the standards developed in *Regner* also apply to the return of third-country nationals.

D. Human Rights Lawyers' Non-Judicial Strategies

In addition to litigation before national and supranational courts and efforts to reach the CJEU as a litigation forum, lawyers working for the Helsinki Foundation for Human Rights have also mobilised for changes in legislation. They recently presented proposals for the elimination of Article 6 from the Act on Foreigners, the provision stipulating the limitation of access to the reasons and evidence for return decisions. However, the authorities disagreed with their arguments and refused to modify the legislation.[46] In the face of their persistent lack of co-operation, amounting to a denial of the right of defence, the Helsinki Foundation lodged a complaint before the European Commission claiming a breach of EU law.[47]

[43] *Ljatifi v the Former Yugoslav Republic of Macedonia*, App No 19017/16 (ECtHR, 17 May 2018) para 36.

[44] ibid, para 40.

[45] Appl No 15114/17.

[46] Helsinki Foundation for Human Rights, 'Uwagi Helsińskiej Fundacji Praw Człowieka do projektu ustawy o zmianie ustawy o cudzoziemcach oraz niektórych innych ustaw (projekt z 31 sierpnia 2016 r)' (2016) available at www.hfhr.pl/wp-content/uploads/2016/09/HFPC-Uwagi-do-projektu-zmiany-ustawy-o-cudzoziemcach_12-09-2016.pdf.

[47] Helsinki Foundation for Human Rights, 'Helsińska Fundacja Praw Człowieka złożyła skargę do KE ws. przepisów przewidujących tajne materiały w sprawach cudzoziemskich' (2018) available at www.hfhr.pl/helsinska-fundacja-praw-czlowieka-zlozyla-skarge-do-ke-ws-przepisow-przewidujacych-tajne-materialy-w-sprawach-cudzoziemskich/.

IV. Administrative Courts' Responses to the Litigation Strategies

Both the Warsaw Regional Administrative Court and the Supreme Administrative Court dismissed the appeals and cassation appeals in every case described above. As their jurisprudence followed a consistent pattern, there is no need to refer to particular judgments. In each case the courts ruled that the provisions of Polish law meet the standards of both EU law and the ECHR. According to them, the administrative court has access to all the files of a case, including classified ones, and is obliged to assess the legality of the decision. The courts emphasised that they had carefully reviewed the classified files and claimed such files confirmed the authorities' conclusions on the threat posed by the third-country nationals involved.

The courts indicated that the administrative court of first instance is not bound by the arguments in a complaint and therefore may revoke the return decision based on any violations of the law, not only those indicated by the proceedings party. Procedural guarantees, then, are preserved through judicial scrutiny of the courts' administrative decisions.[48] According to this argument, because this scrutiny goes beyond the arguments of the parties, it is sufficient to secure third-country nationals' procedural rights. The administrative courts themselves claimed that the Polish model is more favourable to the rights of third-country nationals than models that involve special security-cleared lawyers, as referred to by the ECtHR in the *Chahal v UK* judgment. They argued that, as this special representative cannot contact the third-country national, his defence is not effective. Therefore the courts did not consider it necessary to refer preliminary questions to the CJEU or pose a question to the Polish Constitutional Tribunal.

The national courts also emphasised that the limitation of the parties' procedural rights resulted from the need to protect higher values such as state security and public order. These values have priority over other rights and freedoms according to Article 31.1 of the Polish constitution.[49] The courts added that a democratic state cannot be defenceless and thus it is sometimes necessary to keep information secret from parties to return proceedings. The Supreme Administrative Court has called this conclusion proportionate.

[48] This chapter is based on the judgments of the Supreme Administrative Court of 29 June 2016, II OSK 2586/14 and 9 September 2016, II OSK 61/15, and the judgments of the Warsaw Regional Administrative Court of 14 March 2018, IV SA/Wa 3078/17 and 12 April 2018, IV SA/Wa 2672/17.

[49] The Supreme Administrative Court probably referred to Art 31.3 of the constitution, which states: 'Any limitation upon the exercise of constitutional freedoms and rights may be imposed only by statute, and only when necessary in a democratic state for the protection of its security or public order, or to protect the natural environment, health or public morals, or the freedoms and rights of other persons. Such limitations shall not violate the essence of freedoms and rights.' Translation of the Article available at the website of Sejm of the Republic of Poland (lower Parliament Chamber): http://www.sejm.gov.pl/prawo/konst/angielski/kon1.htm.

The courts also argued that there are cases where EU law is not applicable. They referred to Article 4(2) TEU and Article 346(1)(a) TFEU, which provide that state security is the sole responsibility of the Member States. However, this approach is in conflict with the judgment of the CJEU in *ZZ*, in which the Court held that:

> [A]lthough it is for Member States to take the appropriate measures to ensure their internal and external security, the mere fact that a decision concerns State security cannot result in European Union law being inapplicable.[50]

The Supreme Administrative Court argued that the CJEU's findings in *ZZ* only apply to EU citizens and their family members, not third-country nationals.[51] However, this interpretation is not supported by later CJEU jurisprudence in which the Court invoked *ZZ*'s standards in a completely different matter than free movement of EU citizens.[52] Furthermore, *ZZ* refers to general safeguards contained in Article 47 of the EU Charter, applicable in all cases regarding the disclosure of secret evidence without discriminating among individuals depending on their legal status.[53]

A Warsaw Regional Administrative Court judgment in a case concerning the rejection of an asylum application on national security grounds illustrates the shortcomings of Polish migration law procedures based on secret evidence more generally.[54] The Court referred to the recast Procedures Directive,[55] which provides more detailed provisions on the rights of defence than the Return Directive. Article 23 of the recast Directive states that in cases involving national security the applicant may be refused access to the case-files. However, national law must establish procedures guaranteeing the rights of defence and Member States may grant counsellors who have undergone security checks access to classified information.

The Court stated that in Polish law the Commissioner for Human Rights (Rzecznik Praw Obywatelskich) may participate in any administrative proceeding, and his office employees who have undergone security checks have access to any classified evidence involved. Therefore the Commissioner for Human Rights may be treated as the 'special counsellor' mentioned in Article 23 of the recast Procedures Directive.

This judgment was appealed by both the Helsinki Foundation for Human Rights and the Commissioner for Human Rights. Both argued that the Commissioner's position as described by the Polish constitution and the Act on Commissioner for Human Rights does not involve being a party's representative or counsellor, nor is it restricted to protecting their subjective interests.

[50] Case C-300/11 *ZZ v Secretary of State for the Home Department* ECLI:EU:C:2013:363, para 38.

[51] Case no II OSK 1979/13 [2015].

[52] See Case C-437/13 *Unitrading Ltd* ECLI:EU:C:2014:2318, which concerns the recovery of import duties.

[53] See also Chlebny (n 34).

[54] Warsaw Regional Administrative Court case no IV SA/Wa 1612/17 [2017].

[55] Directive 2013/32/EU of the European Parliament and of the Council of 26 June 2013 on common procedures for granting and withdrawing international protection [2013] OJ L180, 60–95.

The Supreme Administrative Court agreed with these arguments but reiterated its earlier position, stating that Polish provisions on the judicial assessment of administrative decisions contain sufficient procedural safeguards in cases involving third-country nationals. The Court relied on the ECtHR judgment in *Regner*. It also stated that the EU Charter is not applicable in Poland because of the so-called Polish–British protocol provisions.[56]

However, this approach is in conflict with the judgment of the CJEU in the joined cases *NS* and *ME* in which the Court held that:

> Article 1(1) of Protocol (No 30) explains Article 51 of the Charter with regard to the scope thereof and does not intend to exempt the Republic of Poland or the United Kingdom from the obligation to comply with the provisions of the Charter or to prevent a court of one of those Member States from ensuring compliance with those provisions.[57]

Nevertheless the Supreme Administrative Court nullified the first-instance court judgment and administrative decisions. It held that while the third-country national posed a threat to state security, this threat did not amount to acts contrary to the purposes and principles of the United Nations as the administrative authorities had claimed.[58]

As discussed above, according to the Polish Code of Criminal Procedure, classified case documents are available to the parties involved, including the defendant and his representative.[59] If there is a risk of disclosure of information classified as secret or top secret, any viewing and copying of files takes place under conditions defined by the court. Access to files, documents or objects marked with the security classification must take place in the presence of a designated employee of the secret registry or secretariat, depending on the security classification. Before viewing the files the person is instructed to keep the information secret. So far, the application of these provisions has not resulted in the disclosure of secret materials, raising the question of why a similar arrangement in the area of return has been rejected by both the courts and the legislature.

V. Conclusion

Third-country nationals' lack of access to classified material in Polish return cases is inconsistent with the rights of defence, a fundamental principle of EU law.

[56] Protocol (No 30) on the application of the Charter of Fundamental Rights of the European Union to Poland and to the United Kingdom.

[57] Joined Cases C-411/10 *NS v Secretary of State for the Home Department* and C-493/10 *ME and Others v Refugee Applications Commissioner and Minister for Justice, Equality and Law Reform* ECLI:EU:C:2011:865, para 120.

[58] Supreme Administrative Court judgment of 23 November 2018, case no II OSK 1710/18.

[59] Art 156 § 4 of the Polish Code of Criminal Procedure of 6 June 1997, consolidated version: Journal of Laws of 2018, item 1987.

In its *ZZ* and *Kadi* judgments the CJEU has clearly stated that in cases involving a security risk, Article 47 of the EU Charter requires that the third-country national must be informed of the essence of the grounds on which a decision is based, as even the demands of state security cannot override the right to be heard. Polish lawyers, as well as the Commissioner for Human Rights, have argued before administrative courts that the provisions of Polish law are incompatible with EU and ECHR law. They have tried unsuccessfully to convince the courts to refer preliminary questions to the CJEU, to obtain a judgment that would result in necessary changes in national law.

Preliminary rulings concerning the right to an effective remedy would be useful not just for Poland but also in the general European context. The CJEU has not yet delivered a judgment concerning the right to defence in return cases involving national security. A judgment like this would help to unify the application of EU law in the Member States.[60]

In cases involving the return of third-country nationals and national security, Polish administrative courts mostly rely on national law, prioritising national security concerns over the right of individuals to a fair procedure. They are reluctant to use the relevant ECtHR jurisprudence, or CJEU jurisprudence interpreting provisions on the right to an effective remedy enshrined in Article 47 of the EU Charter. National jurisprudence indicates that the Polish courts' position is consistent: they feel that the provisions of national law meet the standards of EU law and the ECHR. They are generally reluctant to refer third-country nationals' cases to the CJEU; the one exception concerned the right to an effective remedy before a tribunal in a case of a Schengen visa refusal.[61] In a number of cases concerning matters such as entry refusal and the right to an effective remedy in asylum proceedings, lawyers have argued for the necessity of interpreting the relevant provisions of EU law. All these requests were dismissed by the courts.

Polish law needs to comply with the standard contained in CJEU and ECtHR case-law. At the least it should give third-country nationals the opportunity to determine the essential reasons why they have been considered threats to national safety. They should also be able to ascertain the type of evidence used to inform return decisions. That would enable them to address, and if relevant, correct, whatever behaviours led to their being considered security threats. Meanwhile, data that could threaten state security or the rights of others (eg the identity of the agent

[60] Similar issues regarding the right to defence in return cases involving national security have arisen in Germany, where the national legislation allows for return detention on the basis of national security grounds (see 1a Aufenthaltsgesetz). While referring to the similar jurisprudence of the Conseil d'État, the Austrian Administrative Court and the Swiss Federal Administrative Court, as well as the Commission Handbook on return, the German Supreme Administrative Court ultimately leaves this matter for the national legislature to clarify. See more in the REDIAL National Synthesis Report – Germany, ed Prof Dr Dr hc Kay Hailbronner and Prof Dr Daniel Thym, available at euredial.eu/docs/publications/national-synthesis-reports/Germany%20Final.PDF.

[61] Case C-403/16 *Soufiane El Hassani v Minister Spraw Zagranicznych* ECLI:EU:C:2017:960.

or a technical description of official investigative activities) should remain secret. In this way a balance can be struck between security considerations and third-country nationals' right to defence.

The law may only change if the European Commission initiates infringement proceedings against Poland and then refers the case to the CJEU. As the issue is a sensitive one for the Polish authorities, there are no prospects that they would change their position during negotiations with the Commission. Having said that, infringement proceedings could take many years and the government might be reluctant to implement the resulting judgment, which would probably accord with the *ZZ* verdict.

It is also difficult to foresee the outcome of the *Orujov v Poland* case. Polish courts have full access to classified case files, giving them significantly more competence in that area than the national courts assessed by the ECtHR in the *CG* and *Lupsa* cases. The question is how far the ECHR will apply the standard resulting from *Regner* in this case. If the *Orujov* judgment is based on *Regner*, the impact of the ECtHR on Polish law will not be significant, since Polish courts have similar access to classified documents as Czech courts. On the other hand, the case has so far strongly emphasised the procedural aspects of the right to family life, which may also be relevant in this matter.

18

The Return of the Children

CAROLUS GRÜTTERS

It is easier to build strong children than to repair broken men

Frederick Douglass (1855)

I. Introduction

This chapter focuses on the judicial dialogue on children in return procedures. In particular, the case-law of national and European courts applying the Return Directive is examined as far as children are involved.[1] The main question is whether the best interests of the child are accounted for as a primary consideration in judicial dialogues on return procedures. This concept of 'best interests of the child as a primary consideration' stems from the UN Convention on the Rights of the Child (UNCRC), which offers a universal norm on special safeguards and care of children.[2] This concept of the 'best interests of the child' plays an important role in the interpretation of the Return Directive if children are involved, indirectly through Article 24 of the Charter of Fundamental Rights of the EU ('the EU Charter'), and directly through Article 5 of the Return Directive.[3]

This chapter first contextualises the terminology regarding children (section II) and return (section III). Subsequently, in section IV, applicable legislation is clarified and placed within the context of EU policies, such as the EU Agenda for the Rights of the Child,[4] the EU Return Policy,[5] and the proposal for a recast

[1] Directive 2008/115 on common standards and procedures in Member States for returning illegally staying third-country nationals ('Return Directive').

[2] UN Convention on the Rights of the Child, adopted Res 44/25 of 20 November 1989, entered into force 2 September 1990. All Member States of the UN have ratified the UNCRC except for the USA which is only a signatory (since 1995); see www.ohchr.org.

[3] See in particular Recital 22 and Arts 5, 7, 10 and 17 of the Return Directive.

[4] Communication from the Commission to the European Parliament, the Council, the European Economic and Social Committee and the Committee of the Regions: an EU Agenda for the Rights of the Child, COM(2011) 60 final, Brussels, 15 February 2011.

[5] Communication from the Commission to the Council and the European Parliament on EU Return Policy, COM(2014) 199 final, Brussels, 28 March 2014.

of the Return Directive (Return II).[6] In section V, judicial dialogue apparent from relevant case-law of the CJEU, the ECtHR, international committees and some national courts is analysed and put into perspective. Finally, in section VI, some conclusions are drawn emphasising the increasing gap between rules and practice.

II. The Concept of a Child

The theoretically well-defined scope of 'children in return procedures' is problematic from a research perspective, since the available data (including case law) seldom reveal whether children are involved in a return procedure or that a return procedure is at stake when children are involved.

The first seemingly obvious question is: what is a child? Of course, 'child' refers to the small human creature that starts off as a baby and gradually grows up to become an adult. This description, however, raises questions. When does a child's existence actually start? And when is the child no longer a child but an adult? As far as the start is concerned one might point at the actual time of birth. That, however, would disregard the period of pregnancy and the legal notion of the unborn or stillborn child, which implies, in some cases, a starting point of the child before its birth. A Dutch appellate court ruled that even an unborn child could be placed under supervision.[7] However, a Dutch district court ruled that the rights of an EU citizen cannot be exercised by an unborn child.[8] The starting point of the child therefore seems to be depending on the legal context.

At the other end of the child-spectrum is adulthood, which seems to be less problematic to define. In legal perspective it is equivalent to attaining 18 years of age, in most countries.[9] Some legal traditions allow child marriage, ie marriages between two people of which at least one is still a minor. As a result, the minors involved become a legal adult because of their marriage; but does that stop them being a child? Even if we disregard these technical issues as of little relevance to the topic of return procedures, it leaves us with the practical problem how to determine someone's age. Based on the fact that not everyone has an authentic ID or other document to prove identity and age, practice shows several dubious

[6] Proposal for a Directive of the European Parliament and the Council on common standards and procedures in Member States for returning illegally staying third-country nationals (recast), COM(2018) 634 final, Brussels, 12 September 2018.

[7] Gerechtshof Arnhem-Leeuwarden [Dutch Court of Appeal Arnhem-Leeuwarden] 20 June 2017, 200.212.969/01.

[8] Rechtbank Den Haag (zp Amsterdam) Vz [Dutch District Court of Amsterdam] 19 November 2018, AWB 18/8339.

[9] See Art 1 UNCRC: 'A child means every human being below the age of eighteen years unless, under the law applicable to the child, majority is attained earlier.'

techniques used to assess someone's age.[10] The EU Asylum Support Office (EASO) states: 'Age assessment methods and processes differ across Member States and reliable multidisciplinary and rights-compliant age assessment processes are not always guaranteed.'[11] The UNHCR goes a step further and concludes that:

> [N]o method can determine age definitively. Most experts agree that age assessment is not a determination of chronological age but an estimated guess. Scientific methods currently available, including medical examinations based on dental or wrist bone x-rays, can only estimate age. Hence, there will always be a margin of error.[12]

Closely linked to this issue is the qualification 'unaccompanied' of a child. The UN Committee of the Rights of the Child (CRC) uses the following definition: 'Unaccompanied children are children who have been separated from both parents and other relatives and are not being cared for by an adult who, by law or custom, is responsible to do so.'[13] This suggests that a child is either accompanied or not. However, the phrase 'being cared for' raises questions as to what type or level of care suffices to change an unaccompanied child into an accompanied child. Or the other way around: what is the threshold below which an accompanied child changes into an unaccompanied child? Thus, this qualification, like the age assessment, leaves room for doubt.

The rationale for these distinctions is that the different labels (adult, (un)accompanied child or minor) come with different rights and obligations.[14] Children are – at least in the legal perspective – vulnerable persons. Article 3(9) of the Return Directive defines 'vulnerable persons' as: 'minors, unaccompanied minors, disabled people, elderly people, pregnant women, single parents with minor children and persons who have been subjected to torture, rape or other serious forms of psychological, physical or sexual violence'. Thus, children are addressed differently because they need special care and attention, for example in the form of a parent or a guardian or other legal representative. Adults, on the other hand, do not have the rights exclusively linked to children; they merely have obligations linked to 'their' children. Although the law uses the binary fiction that a person is either a child or an adult, or that a child is either unaccompanied or not, practice shows all kinds of grey areas in between, resulting in a sliding scale of rights and obligations.[15]

[10] From a medical perspective there are two highly questionable 'known' methods to asses a child's age: (1) a dental assessment, which seeks to pinpoint the development of a child's primary ('baby') and secondary ('grown-up') teeth, and (2) a bone age X-ray, which approximates the child's skeletal maturity by determining the number of active growth centres in the child's wrist bones.

[11] EASO, *Practical Guide on Age Assessment*, 2nd edn (Valetta, EASO, 2018).

[12] UNHCR, *Observations on the Use of age Assessments in the Identification of Separated or Unaccompanied Children Seeking Asylum* (Geneva, UNHCR, 2015).

[13] CRC, General Comment No 6, *Treatment of Unaccompanied and Separated Children Outside their Country of Origin* (2005) RC/GC/2005/6. See also UNHCR, *Guidelines on Policies and Procedures in Dealing with Unaccompanied Children Seeking Asylum* (Geneva, UNHCR, February 1997).

[14] Such as name, nationality, education, care by its parents, and other economic, social and cultural rights.

[15] Terminology used: foetus, baby, toddler, pre-school child, kindergartener, (very) young child, small child, minor, teenager, adolescent.

III. The Concept of Return

The second concept that needs some clarification is return. This term also has a very obvious meaning of going back to a place someone has already been or originates from. Thus, return is closely linked to an opposite movement: departure and return. Article 3 of the Return Directive provides the following definition of return:

> The process of a third-country national going back – whether in voluntary compliance with an obligation to return, or enforced – to: (a) his or her country of origin, or (b) a country of transit in accordance with Community or bilateral readmission agreements or other arrangements, or (c) another third country, to which the third-country national concerned voluntarily decides to return and in which he or she will be accepted

At first sight, this lengthy definition seems to be correct. However, it is inconsistent and at least incomplete when it comes to children. The definition is based on the assumption that a third-country national originates from outside the EU. This, however, becomes strange if applied to children who are born in one of the Member States but have no right to stay on the territory of a Member State.[16] These children are supposed to 'return', but to which country? They already are in their country of origin: in logical perspective their return is impossible.

Return is the consequence of not, or no longer, fulfilling the conditions of entry or stay in a Member State. Subsequently, the concept of return implicitly turns up in cases of rejected asylum seekers, and Dublin cases in which asylum seekers are transferred to another Member State. These third-country nationals sometimes have to wait in detention until this return or transfer can take place.

Although the Return Directive defines 'return' as the process of a third-country national going back to his country of origin, implying that the third-country national has to leave the EU, the concept of removal, ie the forced departure, is limited to 'the physical transportation out of the Member State'.[17] It might have been more consistent if this enforcement of the obligation to return had been defined as the physical transportation out of the EU.[18]

Since the purpose of 'return' in the Return Directive is to go to whatever country as long as it is outside the EU, the title of the Directive could have been clearer by using a term such as 'departure' rather than the masked term of 'return'. Subsequently, departure could have been divided into (a) voluntary departure, and (b) forced departure (instead of removal). However, Member States also differ

[16] The principle of *ius soli* – the right of anyone born in the territory of a state to the nationality of that state – is only part of national law in a restricted form in Ireland (as of 2005) and the UK (as of 1983): *ius soli* only applies if one parent of the child is a citizen, has a permanent right to reside or is legally 'settled'.

[17] Art 3(5) of the Return Directive.

[18] The proposal for a recast of the Return Directive (COM(2018) 634 final) retains these inconsistencies.

in their national qualification of a 'process of going back': terms such as expulsion, deportation, removal, extradition, repatriation, banishment and transfer can be found.[19] This chapter will use the terminology of the Directive and the term 'return' in its broadest meaning referring to the process of leaving the EU of a third-country national in all situations in which there is no (longer a) right to remain and there is an obligation to leave the EU.

IV. Relevant Sets of Rules

The topic of children in return procedures involves different legal domains. Next to the domain of the protection of children there is the domain of returning irregular staying third-country nationals. These two fields, though not completely separated from each other, have quite different perspectives. The domain of children's rights is situated in a fundamental rights-based area. The return domain, however, is positioned within the control-based approach of migration policy.

The corresponding sets of rules, ie human rights law and migration law, reflect these different approaches, considerations and correspondingly different judgments. On the one hand there is the UNCRC, treaties such as the ECHR, and the EU Charter. On the other, there is the Return Directive, an EU legal instrument which is according to its very first Recital part of a 'coherent approach in the field of immigration and asylum dealing together with the creation of a common asylum system, a legal immigration policy and the fight against illegal immigration'.[20] Nonetheless, the Return Directive is – as its title claims – primarily aimed at returning illegally staying third-country nationals.

In both sets of rules articles are included illustrating that neither of these two approaches (human rights or migration policy) can be applied in isolation. For instance, the Return Directive emphasises the importance of the principle of *non-refoulement*, the best interests of the child, family life and health, reflecting that the Directive has to respect certain boundaries: 'based on common standards, for persons to be returned in a humane manner and with full respect for their fundamental rights and dignity'.[21] Conversely, the UNCRC acknowledges that the best interests of the child shall be a primary – and not the only – consideration in all actions concerning children,[22] leaving room for the legitimate interest of the state as a competing consideration.

[19] Next to the possibility to declare a diplomat persona non grata (Art 9 of the Vienna Convention on Diplomatic Relations).

[20] The EU immigration and asylum *acquis* contains rules: on regular migration (Family Reunification Directive 2003/86, Long-Term Residents Directive II 2011/51); asylum (Dublin III Regulation 604/2013, Qualification II Directive 2011/95, Asylum Procedures II Directive 2013/32, Reception Conditions II 2013/33); irregular migration (Facilitation Directive 2002/90, Return Directive 2008/115), and borders and visas (Borders Code Regulation 2016/399, Visa Code Regulation 810/2009).

[21] Recital 2 of the Return Directive.

[22] See for instance Art 21 UNCRC on adoption, which uses instead of the phrase 'shall be of *primary* consideration' the phrase: 'shall be the *paramount* consideration'.

Problems in applying these sets of rules in the context of return procedures occur if the requested return is not effectuated by means of a voluntary departure but results in pre-removal detention.[23]

A. UN Convention on the Rights of the Child

The UNCRC is based on the idea that 'childhood is entitled to special care and assistance'.[24] Its most important concept is the 'best interests of the child'. Article 3(1) UNCRC prescribes: 'In all actions concerning children, whether undertaken by public or private social welfare institutions, courts of law, administrative authorities or legislative bodies, the best interests of the child shall be a primary consideration.' These best interests of the child are not further defined in the UNCRC although the convention lists in 54 provisions rights of children and obligations of state parties to guarantee these rights. Stalford calls the UNCRC the 'fulcrum' upon which all children's rights activities are developed and measured.[25]

Next to this core Article 3 on the best interests of the child, the UNCRC has additional rights relevant in the context of return procedures: Article 6 (development of the child); Article 9 (unity of the family); Article 10 (family reunification); Article 18 (responsibility of the parents); Article 19 (prohibition of refoulement); Article 20 (unaccompanied children); Article 22 (protection of minor asylum seekers); Article 30 (protection of children belonging to an ethnic, religious or linguistic minority); Article 37 (detention as a measure of last resort and for the shortest appropriate period of time); and Article 39 (protection of a child victim of inhuman or degrading treatment or any form of armed conflict). The tenor of all these articles is that the child is a vulnerable creature and that all kinds of measures that may seem normal applying to adults in the context of return are most of the time harmful to children and should therefore not – or only seldom – be taken.

The ratification of the UNCRC led to the establishment of the CRC.[26] The CRC has the task to examine regularly the progress made by state parties in realising the obligations undertaken in the UNCRC. In order to 'foster the effective implementation of the UNCRC', the CRC makes general recommendations, of which No 14 on the meaning and interpretation of 'the best interests of the child' is the most important.[27] These general recommendations serve as an

[23] Arts 15–18 (Chapter IV) of the Return Directive.

[24] Recital 4 UNCRC.

[25] H Stalford, *Children and the European Union. Rights, Welfare and Accountability*, Modern Studies in European Law 32 (Oxford, Hart Publishing, 2012) 32. E Del Gaudio and S Philips, 'Detention of Child Asylum Seekers in the Pursuit of State Interests: A Comparison of the Australian and EU Approaches' (2018) 36 *Nordic Journal of Human Rights* 1, 1–18.

[26] Art 43 UNCRC.

[27] CRC, General Comment No 14, *On the Right of the Child to Have His or Her Best Interests Taken as a Primary Consideration (Art 3, Para 1)* (UN, 2013).

authoritative source comparable with the Handbook of the UNHCR.[28] However, although the CRC can be seen as a committee of genuine experts, its actual power to decide issues is limited to the context of the Optional Protocol on a 'communications procedure' (ie complaints procedure), which is only ratified by a relatively small number of states.[29] Until January 2019, there have only been two decisions (formally referred to as 'adoption of views') by the CRC in which the complaint was admissible and the states involved were found in violation of the Convention.[30]

The first view (*IAM*) of the CRC concluding a violation of the UNCRC by Denmark concerns the 'return' of a Somali girl whose mother's application for asylum was rejected. The mother argued that her newly born daughter ran the risk of being forcefully subjected to female genital mutilation if she were returned to Puntland (Somalia). The CRC concluded that Denmark had failed to do what it should have done under the Convention: to consider the best interests of the child when assessing the alleged risk. Most interesting is that the CRC not only reminded Denmark that it is under an 'obligation to refrain from deporting the author and her daughter to Puntland', but also that the state is under an obligation 'to take all necessary measures to prevent similar violations from occurring in the future'. The latter is a clear instruction: change your policy.[31]

The second view (*YB & NS*) of the CRC in a communication procedure involves the meaning of *kafala* (ie Islamic foster-child) in terms of family life in the EU. This case is the reverse situation of return. In 2011 the Marrakesh Court of First Instance (Morocco) entrusted a Belgian–Moroccan married couple with the care for a child abandoned at birth. *Kafala* is not the same as adoption because *kafala* does not create any legal relationship. It is, however, comparable to fostering or guardianship. The application for a visa was rejected by the Belgian authorities, who argued that *kafala* is not an adoption and does not confer any right of residence. The authorities succeeded in delaying family reunification of the 'foster' child with its Belgian–Moroccan parents for seven years. The CRC was very clear in its view. Although the UNCRC does not explicitly oblige a state to 'recognize the right to family reunification for children in kafala arrangements … the State party is obliged to take into account the de facto ties' between the child and the carers. Subsequently, the CRC recalled its argument in

[28] UNHCR, *Handbook and Guidelines on Procedures and Criteria for Determining Refugee Status under the 1951 Convention and the 1967 Protocol Relating to the Status of Refugees*, reissued (Geneva, UNHCR, 2011).

[29] Optional Protocol to the Convention on the Rights of the Child on a communications procedure, A/RES/66/138. The UNCRC has been ratified by all countries that are Member States of the UN (197). The optional protocol on a communications procedure (the complaint protocol), however, has so far only been ratified by 40 State Parties of which 15 are EU Member States.

[30] CRC 8 March 2018, UNCRC/C/77/D/3/2016, *IAM v Denmark* (violation of Arts 3 and 19 UNCRC); CRC 27 September 2018, UNCRC/C/79/DR/12/2017, *YB & NS v Belgium* (violation of Arts 3, 10 and 12 UNCRC). In 2019 six views in Spanish cases were adopted by the CRC.

[31] CRC, General Comment No 6 (n 13).

the Danish case: '[T]he State party is also under an obligation to do everything necessary to prevent similar violations from occurring in the future.'[32]

The issue of *kafala* was also investigated in 2014 by the ECtHR in *Chbihi*, which also involved a Belgian–Moroccan couple.[33] The main difference was that in *Chbihi* the biological parents of the child were alive and entrusted the Belgian couple with their child under a personal *kafala*. In *Chbihi* the Belgian couple tried to adopt the child (which was denied), whereas the couple in the UNCRC case only wanted a residence permit for their child (which was also denied). A comparable case (*SM*) has been decided by the CJEU.[34] The case of *SM* involved a French couple resident in the UK with an official Algerian *kafala* child.[35] The CJEU decided in line with the opinion of the Advocate General with reference to *Chbihi*, that although a *kafala* child cannot be classified as a 'direct descendant' of an EU citizen, such a child may fall within the category of 'other family members'. That qualification means, according to the CJEU, that 'it is for the competent national authorities to facilitate the entry and residence of such a child as one of the other family members of a citizen of the Union pursuant to Art 3(2)(a) of that directive'.

Nevertheless, the view of the CRC that a state has violated the UNCRC has no legally binding effect: it is not a judgment. Rather, the view of the CRC is an authoritative conclusion in which the state is politely reminded that it has an obligation to refrain from acting in the way the CRC has assessed as in violation of the UNCRC.[36] Thus, phrases in the Convention such as 'the best interests of the child shall be a primary consideration' have no undisputed meaning binding to state parties of the UNCRC. Its meaning and influence therefore lies with the courts that have the power to use these views in their judicial dialogue and judgments.

The position of the CRC on the issue of detention of children has moved over time. In its first General Comment on this subject (2005) the CRC followed the literal text of Article 37(b) UNCRC: 'No child shall be deprived of his liberty unlawfully or arbitrarily … detention of a child shall be used only as a measure of last resort and for the shortest appropriate period of time.'[37] The most recent position, however, of the CRC (2017) is: '[I]mmigration detention of children should be banned.'[38]

[32] CRC, 27 September 2018, UNCRC/C/79/DR/12/2017, *YB & NS v Belgium*, paras 8–9.
[33] ECtHR 16 December 2014, 52265/10, *Chbihi*.
[34] CJEU 26 March 2019, C-129/18, *SM v UK*.
[35] By the Court of Tizi Ouzou (Algeria).
[36] M Blaak et al (eds), *Handboek internationaal jeugdrecht* (Leiden, Defence for Children, 2012).
[37] CRC, General Comment No 6 (n 13) para 61.
[38] These two so-called 'Joint' General Comments are adopted by both the Committee on the Rights of the Child and the Committee on the Rights of All Migrant Workers and Members of Their Families.

(1) Joint General Comment Nos 3 and 22: General principles regarding the human rights of children in the context of international migration, 16 November 2017, CMW/C/GC/3-UNCRC/C/GC/22.

B. European Convention on Human Rights

The most prominent set of rules in the context of human rights after the ICCPR is the ECHR.[39] In the context of return procedures two articles are of great importance: Article 3 (prohibition of torture or inhuman, degrading treatment) and Article 5 (right to liberty and security of person; and prohibition of deprivation of liberty without lawful arrest).[40] Although the ECHR has no direct effect in EU Member States, Article 6(3) TEU stipulates that fundamental rights as guaranteed by the ECHR shall constitute general principles of EU law.[41] Apart from Article 8 (right to respect for private and family life), there is no specific article that protects the right of the child. All rights in the ECHR are equally valid for adults and children. The very first mentioning of a child occurs in Protocol 7 to the Convention (1984) on equality between spouses.

If there is a serious complaint that the Convention has been violated and all domestic remedies have been exhausted, an application can be made to the ECtHR. If that application is found to be admissible, the ECtHR will examine the case on the merits. If it finds a violation of the Convention, the ECtHR even has the authority to order the payment of compensation. These options show that the ECtHR can have a substantial influence on the way authorities should implement the rights described in the ECHR.

Although the CJEU – in contrast with the ECtHR – does not decide individual cases and has no power to oblige a state to pay compensation, the authority of the CJEU in interpreting EU law prescribing which national interpretation or practice is (or is not) allowed, is – like the authority of the ECtHR – of relevance regarding the functioning of a democratic state. Both courts tend to take account of each other's judgments and sometimes refer to each other's case law, one of the many forms of judicial dialogue.[42]

(2) Joint General Comment Nos 4 and 23: State obligations regarding the human rights of children in the context of international migration in countries of origin, transit, destination and return, 16 November 2017, CMW/C/GC/4/UNCRC/C/GC/23.

See also C Smyth, 'Towards a Complete Prohibition on the Immigration Detention of children' (2019) 19 *Human Rights Law Review* 1–36.

[39] International Covenant on Civil and Political Rights, Adopted by the General Assembly of the United Nations on 19 December 1966.

[40] Art 3 ECHR: 'No one shall be subjected to torture or to inhuman or degrading treatment or punishment.' First paragraph of Art 5 ECHR: 'Everyone has the right to liberty and security of person. No one shall be deprived of his liberty save in the following cases and in accordance with a procedure prescribed by law.'

[41] The ECHR as an international treaty has direct or indirect effect in State Parties depending on the qualification of their constitutional system as monist or dualist.

[42] J Krommendijk, 'The Use of ECtHR Case Law by the Court of Justice after Lisbon: The View of Luxembourg Insiders' (2015) 22(6) *Maastricht Journal of European and Comparative Law* 812; C Eckes, 'The Court of Justice's Participation in Judicial Discourse: Theory and Practice' in M Cremona and A Thies (eds), *The European Court of Justice and External Relations Law: Constitutional Challenges*, Modern Studies in European Law (Oxford, Hart Publishing, 2014) 183–210; P Eeckhout, 'Opinion 2/13 on EU Accession to the ECHR and Judicial Dialogue: Autonomy or Autarky' (2015) 38(4) *Fordham International Law Journal* 955.

C. Charter of Fundamental Rights of the European Union

The Charter of Fundamental Rights of the European Union lists the fundamental rights of everyone under EU law.[43] Although agreed upon in 2000, it only entered into force in 2009 after the ratification of the Lisbon Treaty; since then it has been primary EU law.[44] However, it is only applicable if EU law applies. Next to Article 7 (respect for private and family life), the most relevant clause on children is Article 24 (rights of the child). The Charter contains more articles that refer to children, but these (Article 14 on education, Article 32 on child labour, and Article 33 on maternity and parental leave) are not relevant in the context of return procedures.

Article 24(2) of the Charter states: 'In all actions relating to children, whether taken by public authorities or private institutions, the child's best interests must be a primary consideration.' Although the courts are not mentioned in Article 24(2) of the Charter, they should be considered as belonging to the category of public authorities.[45] Thus, through Article 24 of the Charter, Article 3 UNCRC is implemented in EU law. Klaassen and Rodrigues argue that both the administrative body that takes a decision and the judicial body that handles the judicial review of that decision must consider explicitly the best interests of the child.[46] The CRC advocates in General Comment 14 that the best interests of the child is a threefold concept: (a) a substantive right; (b) a fundamental interpretive legal principle; and (c) a rule of procedure.[47] Nonetheless, the crucial question remains how much weight these best interests of the child should be afforded: '[I]mmigration law is an odd man out since determining that a certain situation is in the child's best interests does not mean that a right of residence exists for the child or his or her parents.'[48] Although this quote was formulated in the context of the meaning of Article 3 UNCRC and the Family Reunification Directive, the same goes for the links between Article 3 UNCRC (through Article 24(2) of the Charter) and other parts of EU law such as the Return Directive.

An important difference with the UNCRC and the views of the CRC is that the meaning and interpretation of the Charter can be requested. A national court can stay its proceedings and ask a question of EU law in the preliminary reference

[43] These fundamental rights can be found in earlier documents such as the Universal Declaration of Human Rights (1948), and treaties such as the ECHR (1950) and the European Social Charter (1961).

[44] Treaty of Lisbon, amending the Treaty on European Union and the Treaty establishing the European Community, signed 13 December 2007, in force 1 December 2009 [2008] OJ C115.

[45] S Peers, T Harvey, J Kenner and A Wards (eds), *The EU Charter of Fundamental Rights: A Commentary*, (Oxford, Hart Publishing, 2014) 687; M Klaassen and P Rodrigues, 'The Best Interests of the Child in EU Family Reunification Law: A Plea for More Guidance on the Role of Art 24(2) Charter' (2017) 19 *European Journal of Migration and Law* 191.

[46] Klaassen and Rodrigues (n 45).

[47] CRC, General Comment No 14 (n 27) paras 6–7.

[48] Klaassen and Rodrigues (n 45) 198.

procedure at the CJEU. This procedure is to ensure uniform interpretation of EU law by all Member States and is legally binding.

D. The Return Directive

The Return Directive contains a number of rules that explicitly refer to children – either as unaccompanied minors or as part of a family. The use of terminology is not very strict. The concept of *child* is used next to *minors*, who should be granted access to basic education, and *children* attending school. The Preamble contains only two considerations concerning children. Recital 21 refers to the prohibition of discrimination, ie on the basis of age. Recital 22 recalls that the Directive should be implemented in line with the UNCRC and that the best interests of the child should be a primary consideration. Also, respect for family life as described in the ECHR should be a primary consideration when implementing this Directive.

Article 3(9) defines children as vulnerable persons, which implies that children have special needs that have to be taken into account.[49] Article 5 prescribes that Member States shall take due account of (a) the best interests of the child, and (b) family life (both already considered in Recital 22 of the Directive). Interestingly, whereas the Preamble states that these aspects should be a 'primary consideration', Article 5 only instructs to 'take due account of' the best interests of the child and family life. The best interests of the child is the overarching principle that comes from the UNCRC and is applicable via both the Return Directive (through Recital 22 and Article 5) and the Charter (through Article 24).

Article 7(2) prescribes, where necessary, to extend the period for voluntary return in cases of school attending children. Article 10 again mentions the best interests of the child in the context of unaccompanied minors, although it only states that assistance shall be granted with 'due consideration' of these best interests, which is less than 'primary consideration'.

Article 16 describes in general the conditions of detention for the purpose of removal of both adults and children. Article 17(1) explicitly mentions that unaccompanied minors and families with minors should only be detained as a measure of last resort and for the shortest appropriate period of time. As was mentioned above, the CRC stated in a Joint General Comment that in fact the shortest period of time is no time at all: '[I]mmigration detention of children should be banned.'[50] Finally, the remaining paragraphs of Article 17 prescribe special accommodation for families, access for children to education, and, again, that the best interests of the child shall be a primary consideration in the context of the detention of minors pending removal.

[49] These special needs are elaborated in the context of safeguards pending return during the period of voluntary departure (Art 14).

[50] See n 37.

Overall, a number of articles of the Return Directive refer to the special needs of children and indicate that in weighing the different interests, the best interests of the child should be 'taken due account of', or given 'due consideration' or 'primary consideration'. It seems that these different types of attention suggest an increasing weight to be given to the best interests of the child. What weight, however, is unclear.[51] The CJEU has not ruled on that issue, as will become clear in section V.

E. Policy Context

The Return Directive had a 'precursor' in the Guidelines on forced return adopted by the Committee of Ministers of the Council of Europe in 2005.[52] These Guidelines deal, among other matters, with children and families in Guideline 2(5) (best interests of the child before issuing a removal order) and Guideline 11 (detention of children and families). The commentary on these Guidelines clarifies that the usage of 'best interests of the child' derives from the UNCRC. It also shows that the definitions used in these Guidelines were inspired by the European Commission's proposal for a Community return policy.[53]

In 2011 the European Commission published an EU agenda for the rights of the child.[54] The Commission stated that 'it is now the time to move up a gear on the rights of the child and to transform policy objectives into action'. The Commission further underlined the need that all policies that 'affect children should be designed, implemented, and monitored taking into account the principle of the best interests of the child enshrined in the Charter and the UNCRC'.[55] Notwithstanding these firm standpoints, the agenda does not mention the Return Directive at all. The only reference to migration is where detention for administrative purposes of children seeking asylum is addressed in its proposals for recasting the Asylum Procedure Directive. The agreement on that Directive (2013/32: Asylum Procedure II) would take another two years.

[51] See also: E Hilbrink, *Adjudicating the Public Interest in Immigration Law* (dissertation VU Amsterdam, 2017); N Ismaïli, *Who Cares for the Child? Regulating and Access in Family and Migration Law in the Netherlands, the European Union and the Council of Europe* (dissertation VU Amsterdam, 2018); Council of Europe, *The Best Interests of the Child – A Dialogue Between Theory and Practice* (Strasbourg: Council of Europe, 2016).

[52] Council of Europe, Committee of Ministers, *Twenty Guidelines on Forced Return*, adopted 4 May 2005.

[53] Communication from the Commission to the Council and the European Parliament on a community return policy on illegal residents, COM(2002) 564.

[54] Communication from the Commission to the European Parliament, the Council, the European Economic and Social Committee and the Committee of the Regions: An EU Agenda for the Rights of the Child, COM(2011) 60 final.

[55] ibid, 3.

In 2014 the European Commission published a report on the implementation of the Return Directive, its impact and possible future developments.[56] In this report the Commission underlined the need for 'more consistent and fundamental rights-compatible practices', and announced that it would publish shortly a Return Handbook and underlined the importance of relevant international standards such as those developed by the European Committee for the Prevention of Torture (CPT) and General Comment 14 of the CRC from 2013. However, there was no specific measure mentioned regarding children, nor was the detention of children addressed other than in a reconfirmation that detention of minors should only occur as 'a measure of 'last resort' and for the 'shortest appropriate period of time'.[57] Evidently, this issue is very sensitive. The Commission only mentioned that 'some stakeholders have suggested that Member States should be encouraged to include in their national law a presumption against detention of children, and to use alternatives to detention for unaccompanied minors and families with children'.

In March 2017 the European Commission published a recommendation on the interpretation of the Return Directive and the earlier announced Handbook.[58] The European Council of June 2018 further underlined 'the necessity to significantly step up the effective return of irregular migrants. … It welcomes the intention of the Commission to make legislative proposals for a more effective and coherent European return policy.'[59] Subsequently a proposal for a recast of the Return Directive was announced and presented in September 2018.[60]

The explanatory memorandum highlights that the recast does not change the scope of the Directive nor does it affect the protection of the current rights of migrants, including with regard to the best interests of the child, family life and the state of health. Thus, none of the Recitals in the Preamble or Articles concerning children is changed.

This is remarkable since both the UNHCR and the Parliamentary Assembly of the Council of Europe have on several occasions published concerns about the Return Directive.[61] Stalford criticised the 'EU's failure to include within the Directive a proper procedure for assessing the best interests of the child,

[56] Communication from the Commission to the Council and the European Parliament on EU Return Policy, COM(2014) 199 final.

[57] ibid, 18.

[58] Commission Recommendation (EU) 2017/432 on making returns more effective when implementing the Directive 2008/115, *OJ* L 66, 11 March 2017; Commission Recommendation (EU) 2017/2338 establishing a common 'Return Handbook' to be used by Member States' competent authorities when carrying out return-related tasks [2017] OJ L339.

[59] European Council conclusions, 28 June 2018, point 10.

[60] See n 6.

[61] UNHCR, *UNHCR Guidelines on Determining the Best Interest of the Child* (Geneva, UNHCR, 2008); UNHCR, *Guidelines on the Applicable Criteria and Standards relating to the Detention of Asylum-Seekers and Alternatives to Detention* (Geneva, UNHCR 2012); Parliamentary Assembly Council of Europe, *Detention of Asylum Seekers and Irregular Migrants in Europe*, resolution 1707 (2010).

despite the fact that this very principle, along with the right to family life, was promoted as a "primary consideration" when implementing the instrument'.[62] The European Parliament published in January 2019 its comments on the proposed recast Directive.[63] This report is very critical of the resistance of the European Commission to implement (in Return Directive II) ECtHR case-law on the detention of children. The report suggests amendments in line with the CRC and the Council of Europe to ban the detention of children. It argues that even the case-law of the ECtHR on the administrative detention of children leaves practically no space to detain children, reflecting an increasing consciousness that the best interests of the child are hardly ever compatible with detention.[64]

V. Case-Law and Judicial Dialogue

The available case-law somehow relevant to children in return procedures is limited. CJEU and ECtHR judgments provide a starting point. The first available case mentioning the 'best interests of the child' is a case filed in 1982 about parental rights and guardianship: a dispute between the father and the mother over their child involving foster parents and social work.[65] The question was whether it would be in the best interests of the child to return home with its natural parents or to remain in foster care. Subsequent case-law of the ECtHR in which the best interests of the child is used as a criterion to decide a case is primarily about parental differences of opinion, ie should a child return to live with the other parent?

In 1994 the ECtHR mentioned (*Hokkanen v Finland*) in its reasoning what the value and meaning under the ECHR is of the best interests of the child:

> Whilst national authorities must do their utmost to facilitate such co-operation, any obligation to apply coercion in this area must be limited since the interests as well as the rights and freedoms of all concerned must be taken into account, and more particularly the best interests of the child and his or her rights under Art 8 of the Convention.[66]

References to these interests show in the ECtHR case-law that a comparative assessment is made between the different positions of parents and that the best interests of the child, depending on their nature and seriousness, may override those of the parents: '[T]he State's obligation to reunite a parent with his child is not an absolute one, as the interests of the child's well-being may override [a] parent's interest in reunion.'[67]

[62] See eg Stalford (n 25) 80–81.
[63] Rapporteur J Sargentini of Committee on Civil Liberties, Justice and Home Affairs, *Draft Report on the Proposal for Return Directive II*, 2018/0329(COD) (Brussels, European Parliament, 2019).
[64] ibid, 81.
[65] ECtHR 8 July 1987, 9749/82, *W v UK*.
[66] ECtHR 23 September 1994, 19823/92, *Hokkanen v Finland*, point 58.
[67] ECtHR 24 April 2003, 36812/97, *Sylvester v Austria*, point 53.

Probably the first case that related to migration, *Sylvester v Austria*, was in the context of a 'return order' concerning a child under the 1980 Hague Convention on the Civil Aspects of International Child Abduction.[68] Although cross-border abduction transformed this case from a national into an international one, the essence of these type of cases is identical to the first case of 1982 mentioned above: to whom must the child be returned?

Cases directly connected with the Return Directive explicitly involving children are rare. Most cases only implicitly refer to return either as a result of a rejected asylum application or as a consequence of a Dublin transfer and usually do not mention the relevance of the Return Directive. Judicial dialogue concentrates on two issues: (a) detention of children as a last resort; (b) detention conditions of children. Whether such detention is in the context of pre-removal detention or an application for international protection is irrelevant: the best interests of the child are at stake in either situation.

A. ECtHR

In 2006, the ECtHR ruled in *Mayeka*, in which the Belgian authorities had detained a five-year-old unaccompanied girl in a transit centre in the same conditions as adults.[69] The girl stayed there for two months because she did not have the necessary travel and immigration papers, while her mother was in the process of acquiring a residence permit in Canada as a refugee. The ECtHR concluded that the girl

> was thus in an extremely vulnerable situation. In view of the absolute nature of the protection afforded by Art 3 of the Convention, it is important to bear in mind that this is the decisive factor and it takes precedence over considerations relating to the second applicant's status as an illegal immigrant. She therefore indisputably came within the class of highly vulnerable members of society to whom the Belgian State owed a duty to take adequate measures to provide care and protection as part of its positive obligations under Art 3 of the Convention. … In the Court's view, the girl's detention in such conditions demonstrated a lack of humanity to such a degree that it amounted to inhuman treatment.[70]

The important reasoning of the Court in this case is that 'the list of exceptions to the right to liberty secured in Art 5(1) is an exhaustive one and only a narrow interpretation of those exceptions is consistent with the aim of that provision'.[71] Subsequently, the ECtHR stated: '[T]he Court's case-law requires that there must be some relationship between the ground of permitted deprivation of liberty relied

[68] ECtHR 24 April 2003, 36812/97, *Sylvester v Austria*.

[69] ECtHR 12 October 2006, 13178/03, *Mayeka v Belgium*.

[70] ibid, points 55 and 58. Next to a violation of Art 3, the ECtHR also concluded a violation of the girl's right to liberty under Art 5(1) ECHR.

[71] ibid, point 96.

on and the place and conditions of detention.' In this case the Belgian legal system 'did not sufficiently protect' the girl's right to liberty.[72]

A procedurally different case was *Muskhadzhiyeva*, also against Belgium.[73] A mother with her four children had fled Chechnya and after a stay in a refugee camp in Poland, she applied for asylum in Belgium. Under the Dublin Regulation the family was detained for one month awaiting return to Poland. However, the detention conditions in the Belgian facility were still the same as in *Mayeka*, which had been decided four years earlier. Although the young children were not unaccompanied, the detention of the children was a violation of both Articles 3 and 5(1) ECHR. Thus, the Court explicitly stated that it did not make a difference for the children whether they were accompanied or not by their mother during their detention in the light of a violation of the ECHR.[74] The ECtHR reminded the Belgian authorities that they have an obligation to prevent inhuman treatment of which they know or should have known.[75]

A third detention case, *Kanagaratnam*, concerned a Sri Lankan family with three young children aged 8, 11 and 13 years.[76] This family was, after a rejection of their asylum application, detained for four months in the same Belgian detention facility mentioned in *Mayeka* and *Muskhadzhiyeva*. The ECtHR recalled that this case was the third time that Belgium was found violating Article 3 and emphasised 'that it should be borne in mind that the situation of extreme vulnerability of the child was decisive and prevailed over the status of foreigner staying illegally'.[77] The verdict of the Court is clear: 'The situation … has reached the gravity threshold required by Art 3 of the Convention to constitute inhuman and degrading treatment.'[78]

These cases illustrate the gradually changing and sharpening position of the ECtHR on the best interests of the child.[79] Another disturbing aspect is that although some five years had passed between the first (2006) and the last (2011) Belgian case, the situation in the Belgian detention facility did not.

A few months before the 2011 ruling in *Kanagaratnam*, the ECtHR had ruled in *Rahimi*.[80] This concerned a 15-year-old boy who had fled Afghanistan. After a detention period of 'only' two days the unaccompanied minor was discharged with no access to reception facilities and was left on his own. In its judgment the ECtHR underlined that it does not make a difference what the procedural background

[72] ibid, points 102–04.

[73] ECtHR 19 January 2010, 41442/07, *Muskhadzhiyeva v Belgium.*

[74] Psychological examination had found that the four children, and especially the five-year-old girl, were showing serious psychological and psychotraumatic symptoms and should be released to limit the damage.

[75] ibid, point 55.

[76] ECtHR 13 December 2011, 15297/09, *Kanagaratnam v Belgium.*

[77] ibid, point 62.

[78] ibid, point 69.

[79] Smyth (n 38).

[80] ECtHR 5 April 2011, 8687/08, *Rahimi v Greece.*

is (regular, irregular or forced migration) if children are involved: '[T]here is currently a broad consensus – including in international law – around the idea that in all decisions concerning children, their best interests must prevail.'[81] This quote was made earlier in *Neulinger & Shuruk* where the ECtHR not only referred to but also quoted Article 24(2) of the Charter.[82] In the same judgment the ECtHR also referred to the Human Rights Committee General Comments No 17 and 19 on the 'paramount interest' of the child, which is interesting since the ECtHR, so far, had only referred to the best interests of the child in detention cases. The more prominent expression 'paramount interest' had been reserved for cases on parental custody or child abduction.

The ECtHR then continues (in *Rahimi*), adding a new argument on the necessity of the measure:

> [B]y ordering the applicant's detention, the national authorities have in no way considered the question of his best interests as a minor. Moreover, they did not inquire whether the applicant's placement in the Pagani detention centre was a measure of last resort and whether they could substitute another less drastic measure in order to secure his deportation. These elements raise doubts in the eyes of the Court as to the good faith of the authorities during the implementation of the detention measure.[83]

Clearly, not just the practice in Greece was condemned but also the willingness of the Greek authorities to change this was questioned – as were the Belgian authorities in *Kanagaratnam*.

After this, a series of detention case arose in France that led the ECtHR to require better protection of children. The case of *Popov* is about the detention of a family of rejected asylum seekers.[84] The family resided in a centre that was 'authorised' for pre-removal detention of families. The ECtHR found that:

> [I]n spite of the fact that they were accompanied by their parents, and even though the detention centre had a special wing for the accommodation of families, the children's particular situation was not examined and the authorities did not verify that the placement in administrative detention was a measure of last resort for which no alternative was available. The Court thus finds that the French system did not sufficiently protect their right to liberty.[85]

This clear instruction to investigate whether there was an alternative for the administrative detention available goes even further than the literal instruction of the Return Directive on 'a measure of last resort'.

[81] ibid, point 108.
[82] ECtHR 6 July 2010, 41615/07, *Neulinger & Shuruk v Switzerland*, point 135.
[83] *Rahimi v Greece* (n 80) point 109.
[84] ECtHR 19 January 2012, 39472/07, *Popov v France*. The family received a residence permit after seven years.
[85] ibid, point 119.

The French authorities were found liable again by the ECtHR in five almost identical cases (*AB et al*) decided on the same day in 2016.[86] The main holding was threefold: (1) 'A detention measure must be proportionate to the aim pursued by the authorities, namely expulsion'; (2) 'The applicants did not present any particular risk of absconding'; (3) 'No alternative to detention had been considered.' This last argument in particular, that no alternative had been considered, is important. Apparently, it is not enough 'to limit the time of confinement'. The adjusted rule is that, in the case of children, 'other solutions, such as the assignment in a hotel, accompanied, as suggested by the applicants, by a regular check with a police station, have to be considered'.[87] This means a shift in attitude from passive prevention towards actively promoting an alternative.

The ECtHR also indicated some overly strict arguments used by the Toulouse Administrative Court on appeal in the case *AB et al.* The Court had dismissed the application for annulment of the administrative detention of the child on the grounds that the best interests of the child were not at stake 'since the decisions appealed against pertained only to the parents' personal situation'.[88] Even the request on behalf of the child to the Liberties and Detention Judge in Toulouse,[89] that the conditions of detention were incompatible with the presence of a minor child, was dismissed because: 'It is not for the judicial authority to interfere in the running of an administrative detention centre.'[90] That was the result of an earlier decision by the French Council of State in 2011 'that the construction of a separate facility accommodating families in a detention centre did not amount to the deprivation of liberty of minors'.[91] The ECtHR disagreed and referred to the *Muskhadzhiyeva*, and stated that the parent's presence with the child does not

> release the authorities from their obligation to protect the child and to adopt appropriate measures in line with their positive obligations under Art 3 of the Convention … and it is important to bear in mind that the child's extreme vulnerability is the decisive factor and takes precedence over considerations relating to the child's status as illegal immigrant.[92]

The ECtHR thus upgraded the qualification of a child from 'vulnerable' to 'extremely vulnerable'. Just before the release of the five judgments by the ECtHR in July (*AB et al*) the French law concerning the administrative detention of an

[86] ECtHR 12 July 2016, 33201/11, *RM*; ECtHR 12 July 2016, 11593/12, *AB*; ECtHR 12 July 2016, 24587/12, *AM*; ECtHR 12 July 2016, 68264/14, *RK*; ECtHR 12 July 2016, 76491/14, *RC*.

[87] *AB*, ibid, points 112–15.

[88] ibid, point 13.

[89] Tribunal de grande instance de Toulouse, Juge de la Paix.

[90] *AB* (n 86) point 14.

[91] Conseil d'Etat 18 November 2011, 352232. See also M Moraru and G Renaudiere, 'European Synthesis Report on the Judicial Implementation of Chapter IV of the Return Directive – Pre-Removal Detention', REDIAL Research Report 2016/05, 56.

[92] *AB* (n 86) point 110.

alien accompanied by a minor was changed: it is no longer allowed.[93] However, Moraru and Renaudiere mention that in practice national legislation still

> derogates from this principle in several circumstances: when the alien does not comply with a previous house arrest; absconds or hampers the execution of a previous measure; to secure an imminent departure, or when the best interest of the child requires so. In such cases, the person can be detained and the family is accommodated in separated facilities.[94]

With reference – again – to *Popov* and *Muyeka*, the ECtHR in *AB et al* then moved beyond the Return Directive to 'European Union directives regulating the detention of migrants', also implying the Asylum Procedure Directive.[95] Subsequently, the ECtHR stated that 'even constraints inherent in a place of detention, which are particularly arduous for a young child, together with the centre's conditions of organisation, must have caused the child some anxiety'.[96] In other words, the vague conditions for the detention of children in EU law should be interpreted using the more specific instructions of the ECtHR:

> The Court is of the view that such conditions, even though they necessarily represent a significant source of stress and anxiety for a small child, are not sufficient, where the confinement is for a short duration, depending on the circumstances of the case, to attain the threshold of severity required to engage Art 3. It is convinced, however, that in the case of a longer period, the repetition and accumulation of such mental and emotional aggression would necessarily have harmful consequences for a young child, exceeding the above-mentioned threshold. Accordingly, the passage of time is of primary significance in this connection for the application of this Article. The Court concludes that the permissible short duration has been exceeded in the present case, which concerns the detention of a four-year-old child lasting for eighteen days in the conditions set out above.[97]

This ECtHR judgment seems to have affected the French legislature, which decided to give more power to the Juge des libertés et de la détention (judge of freedom and detention) in cases of pre-removal detention of children.

B. CJEU

As mentioned, CJEU case-law is only indirectly connected with children in return procedures. In *KA*, for instance, the question was raised whether the best interests of the child were taken into account in a situation of a rejected application for family reunification because of an existing entry ban on the third-country

[93] REDIAL Research Report 2016/05 (n 91) 57.
[94] See n 91.
[95] *AB* (n 86) point 110.
[96] ibid, point 113.
[97] *AB* (n 86) point 114.

national adult family member.[98] In this case the Belgian Council for Asylum and Immigration proceedings was 'overruled' by the CJEU: the Council should have at least taken into account the interests of the child involved; an entry ban as such cannot exclude the best interests.

The case *Haqbin* involves an unaccompanied minor who has applied for international protection.[99] During his stay in the reception centre he was involved in a fight, held responsible and was punished for 'serious breaches of the rules relating to reception centres and serious acts of violence' with the withdrawal of material reception for the duration of 14 days. The issue at stake is whether the Reception Directive read in conjunction with the Charter allows for a sanction of exclusion from the right to material reception conditions in respect of a minor, specifically an unaccompanied minor.

The only case that was related to children and the Return Directive, *Nianga*, was removed from the register.[100]

C. National Judgments

The standard phrase of the Dutch Council of State illustrates the current 'weight' of the best interests of the child in Dutch case-law:

> Art 3 of the UNCRC has direct effect in so far as it seeks to involve the interests of the child concerned in all measures concerning children. With regard to the weight that must be assigned to the interests of a child in a specific case, the first paragraph of Art 3 of the UNCRC does not contain a standard that can be applied directly by the judge without further elaboration, in view of its formulation'. Subsequently the court states that 'the task of the judge is to check whether the State Secretary [of Justice] has sufficiently taken into account the interests of the child when weighing up his interests.[101]

This way of assessing the best interests of the child has been criticised as not being in conformity with the obligation of Article 3 UNCRC to assign the best interests of the child as the primary consideration, but merely as one of the relevant considerations.[102] The Dutch Council of State takes two disputable steps. First it reduces the *best* interests of a child to merely interests of a child, and second, it degrades the 'primary consideration' to 'take into account'.

[98] CJEU 8 May 2018, C-82/16 *KA and others* (Arts 5, 11 and 13 of the Return Directive).

[99] CJEU 12 November 2019, C-233/18 *Haqbin* (Art 20 of the Reception Conditions Directive II). At the time of writing, this case was pending.

[100] CJEU 19 May 2017, C-199/16 *Nianga* (Arts 3, 6 and 8 of the Return Directive).

[101] For instance: Afdeling Bestuursrechtspraak Raad van State [Dutch Council of State] 19 October 2016, 201604049/1/V3, ECLI:NL:RVS:2016:2727, para 3.2.

[102] D Beltman and E Zijlstra, 'De doorwerking van "het belang van het kind" ex artikel 3 VRK in het migratierecht: vanuit een bottom-up benadering op weg naar een top-down toepassing' (2013) 12(4) *Journaal Vreemdelingenrecht* 286.

An interesting Dutch 'return' case is *Howick and Lili*. This concerned a high-profile case of Armenian children that had entered the Netherlands with their mother when they were two and three years old.[103] The asylum request of the mother was rejected in 2008 and the appeal was denied in 2011. During and after this procedure the mother and her children were never placed in detention. Subsequently, the mother tried unsuccessfully to acquire another regular residence permit. In 2017 the Dutch authorities planned to return the family to Armenia. However, the morning that the Dutch Return and Departure Service arrived, the children were not at home. After an expedited procedure with a district court, the Dutch authorities enforced the return of only the mother. Thus, the mother was returned to Armenia whereas the children became unaccompanied minors in the Netherlands who need – as vulnerable people – extra care. Subsequently, the children submitted an asylum request on their own. That request was turned down. The district court annulled that decision, but was overruled by the Dutch Council of State. The children were ordered to return to Armenia. As these children had been regular guests in the media, a public outcry arose since it was apparent that in every aspect they had become Dutch children. Their intended return to Armenia was perceived by the media as a crime. In the end, under this pressure, the State Secretary of Justice gave them a residence permit.

The judgments of the district court and of the Council of State do not mention the Return Directive. Issues mentioned are the asylum request, the custody of the children and the continuous fear of these children of being picked up in order to be put on a flight back to Armenia. The case illustrates the problem in terms of relevant data: although this case is mainly about the intention of the Dutch authorities to return the family to Armenia the relevant rules are not under discussion. On the other hand, that is not that surprising. The purpose of asylum requests and regular requests for residence permits are to be safe: to remain. The issue of return, particularly if children are involved, is seen as a defeat.

VI. Conclusion

The ECHR and UNCRC, the EU Charter and Return Directive – current or recast – all suggest that children need special care. Children are classified as vulnerable persons and the best interests of the child should be a primary consideration particularly if they are not allowed to remain in a Member State and have to return to a country outside the EU. However, the situation of children who are born in a Member State and therefore cannot return since they are already 'at home' is not regulated.

[103] Afdeling Bestuursrechtspraak Raad van State [Dutch Council of State] 24 August 2018, 201806403/1/V3, ECLI:NL:RVS:2018:2816.

Although the CRC has formulated firm General Comments and the ECtHR has developed increasingly child-friendly judgments on how to treat children, the issue of children in return procedures is hard to find. Judicial dialogue on this issue is simply hard to obtain. And even when children are an issue, it seems that practice is not concerned with the best interests of the child: the children just have to follow until the point of no return.

19

Unremovability under the Return Directive: An Empty Protection?

JEAN-BAPTISTE FARCY

I. Introduction

This chapter aims to address two questions. First, the legal obstacles to removal will be analysed. Despite their irregular status, third-country nationals are not devoid of legal protection against expulsion decisions and, under certain circumstances that will be examined in this article, they may be unremovable from the territory of the Member States. In this regard, congruent judicial standards have been developed by the CJEU and the ECtHR. The second issue is that of the rights of third-country nationals who cannot be removed. According to Article 14 of the Return Directive, third-country nationals whose removal has been postponed benefit from a number of safeguards pending return. However, unless domestic law provides otherwise, the legal status of unremovable migrants is unclear as they seem to be trapped between regularity and irregularity.

In the post 'asylum crisis' context,[1] this question is highly relevant given the number of irregular entries into the European Union and the high rate of rejected asylum applications. According to Eurostat data, 516,115 non-EU citizens received an order to leave the territory of the Member States in 2017. Yet that year only 188,905 non-EU citizens were effectively returned outside of the Union.[2] Although the political priority is to increase the effectiveness of return policies, figures have remained stable over the last few years.[3] Return operations are difficult to carry

[1] D Thym, 'The "Refugee Crisis" as a Challenge of Legal Design and Institutional Legitimacy' (2016) 53 *CML Rev* 1545; M den Heijer, J Rijpma and T Spijkerboer, 'Coercion, Prohibition, and Great Expectations: The Continuing Failure of the Common European Asylum System' (2016) 53 *CML Rev* 607.

[2] Eurostat, *Statistics on Enforcement of Immigration Legislation*, data extracted in June 2018, available at: ec.europa.eu/eurostat/statistics-explained/index.php/Statistics_on_enforcement_of_immigration_legislation (accessed 5 November 2018).

[3] Commission Recommendation 2017/432 of 7 March 2017 on making returns more effective when implementing the Directive 2008/115/EC of the European Parliament and of the Council; European Commission, *On a More Effective Return Policy in the European Union – A Renewed Action Plan*, Communication to the European Parliament and the Council, 2 March 2017, COM(2017) 200 final. The rate of effective returns to third countries remains stable at around 36–37%.

out in practice since they require a lot of resources, both human and financial. Obstacles, such as the lack of travel documents, identification problems, uncooperative countries of origin or simply the high costs of return operations, impede removal. Given the limited enforceability of return decisions, the status of unremovable migrants is a question of both legal and practical relevance.

After exploring the legal impediments to removal (section II), this article assesses safeguards pending return and the rights of unremovable migrants under the Return Directive as interpreted by the CJEU (section III). Judicial interactions regarding these issues have arguably led to the development of higher judicial standards.[4] However, courts have not yet engaged with the issues of residency rights and regularisation (section IV).

II. Legal Impediments to Removal

The removal of irregularly staying third-country nationals may be postponed due to several factors. Article 9 of the Return Direction provides for circumstances under which removal is delayed. Two categories of circumstances must be distinguished. While some of them impose an obligation upon states not to remove irregular migrants, others are optional.

A. The Postponement of Removal under Article 9 of the Return Directive

Article 9(1) of the Return Directive establishes an obligation to postpone the removal of a third-country national when it would violate either the principle of *non-refoulement* or the suspensory effect of a legal remedy granted in accordance with Article 13(2). Since the principle of non-refoulement, also stated in Article 5 of the Directive under the 'General Provisions' chapter, is not defined in the Directive, provisions of the Return Directive can be read in conjunction with the Charter of Fundamental Rights of the European Union ('the Charter').[5] In particular, Article 19(2) of the Charter states that: 'No one may be removed, expelled or extradited to a State where there is a serious risk that he or she would be subjected to the death penalty, torture or other inhuman or degrading treatment or punishment.' Given the rules of equivalent interpretation set out in Article 52(3) of the Charter, the CJEU has relied on the case-law of the ECtHR to define the scope of the principle of *non-refoulement*.[6] Following the well-known *Soering* case of the Strasbourg Court, a contracting state may be held responsible for a violation

[4] Domestic case-law referred to in this article is exclusively based on the cases collected for the REDIAL project.

[5] Charter of Fundamental Rights of the European Union [2012] OJ C326/391.

[6] Case C-239/14 *Tall* EU:C:2015:824, para 54.

of Article 3 ECHR, prohibiting inhuman or degrading treatment, even indirectly for treatments inflicted in another country.[7] In the context of return, this means that states cannot, under any circumstances (the protection of Article 3 ECHR is absolute), remove a third-country national to a country where there are substantial grounds for believing that he or she will be exposed to a real risk of ill treatment contrary to Article 3 ECHR.[8] If such a risk is present, Member States have an obligation under Article 9(1) of the Return Directive not to proceed with the removal of an irregularly staying migrant.

Regarding the suspensory effect of a legal remedy, Article 13(2) of the Return Directive does not state that an appeal against a return decision necessarily has a suspensive effect. However, the CJEU has ruled that a return decision whose enforcement may violate the principle of non-refoulement must be given suspensive effect.[9] As a consequence, the removal of the third-country national concerned is automatically postponed. The finding of the Court is in line with the right to an effective remedy as interpreted by the ECtHR which requires that an automatic suspensive effect be granted in such cases.[10]

Besides the obligation to postpone removal contained in the first paragraph of Article 9 of the Return Directive, discretion is left to the Member States to decide whether removal can be postponed for other reasons. In a somewhat confusing phrasing, Article 9(2) of the Return Directive provides that Member States *may* postpone removal in other cases depending on the specific circumstances of the individual case, yet they *shall* have regard to the third-country national's physical state or mental capacity,[11] and technical reasons, such as a lack of transport capacity, or a lack of identification. The list is not exhaustive and other circumstances could be foreseen in domestic legislation.[12]

Regarding the physical state or mental capacity of a third-country national to be removed, the case-law of the CJEU has limited the scope of discretion left to Member States. Although the Court refused to grant subsidiary protection to seriously ill third-country nationals, through the application of the Charter and the principle of *non-refoulement*, it took into account the case-law of the ECtHR, in particular *N v the United Kingdom*, to rule as follows:

> In the very exceptional cases in which the removal of a third country national suffering a serious illness to a country where appropriate treatment is not available would infringe the principle of non-refoulement, Member States cannot therefore, as provided for in Article 5 of Directive 2008/115, taken in conjunction with Article 19(2) of the Charter, proceed with such removal.[13]

[7] *Soering v the United Kingdom* [GC], Appl No 14038/88, para 88. For a similar case before the CJEU, see Case C-182/15 *Aleksei Petruhhin* EU:C:2016:630.

[8] *FG v Sweden* [GC], Appl No 43611/11. Given the absolute nature of Art 3 ECHR, the protection afforded by that provision is wider than that provided by Arts 32 and 33 of the United Nations 1951 Convention on the Status of Refugees: *Chahal v the United Kingdom* [GC], Appl No 22414/93, para 80.

[9] Case C-562/13 *Abdida* EU:C:2014:2453, paras 50–52; Case C-181/16, *Gnandi*, EU:C:2018:465.

[10] *Gebremedhin v France*, Appl No 25389/05; *Hirsi Jamaa and Others v Italy* [GC], Appl No 27765/09.

[11] This obligation is also enshrined in Art 5 of the Directive.

[12] European Commission, *Return Handbook*, 27 September 2017, C(2017) 6505, 44.

[13] *Abdida* (n 9) para 48.

In exceptional cases,[14] the enforcement of a return decision entailing the removal of a third-country national suffering from a serious illness would be contrary to the principle of *non-refoulement*. Although Article 9(2) of the Return Directive allows ('may') Member States to postpone removal based on the specific circumstances of an individual case, following the *Abdida* ruling they have an obligation not to remove a third-country national who is seriously ill and whose return would lead to an irreparable harm. Based on judicial dialogue, the discretion left to Member States in Article 9(2) of the Return Directive is turned into an obligation by the CJEU in exceptional cases. By doing this, the Court ensures that EU law offers a level of protection at least similar to that of the ECHR. The CJEU indeed relies on the case-law of the Strasbourg Court in order to develop congruent, yet restrictive, judicial standards.

On this issue, judicial dialogue is not limited to interaction between the CJEU and the Strasbourg Court. It also occurs vertically between the latter and national courts. Following criticism that the ECtHR in *N* set an unduly high threshold, the Grand Chamber took the opportunity to soften its case-law in the *Paposhvili v Belgium* case of December 2016.[15] Departing from the threshold in *N*, the Court considered that 'situations involving the removal of a seriously ill person in which substantial grounds have been shown for believing that he or she, although not at imminent risk of dying, would face a real risk, on account of the absence of appropriate treatment in the receiving country or the lack of access to such treatment, of being exposed to a serious, rapid and irreversible decline in his or her state of health resulting in intense suffering or to a significant reduction in life expectancy' fall under the protection of Article 3 ECHR.[16] In deciding this case, judicial dialogue arguably took place between the ECtHR and national courts. Judge Lemmens, in his concurring opinion, acknowledged that the domestic case-law drew the attention of the Court which subsequently softened its approach.[17] According to the Belgian case-law, a risk of inhuman or degrading treatment also occurs when there is no appropriate treatment in the receiving country, even if there is no imminent risk to life.[18] Following the Grand Chamber's ruling, the CJEU has explicitly

[14] In *N v the United Kingdom* (App No 37201/06), which the CJEU refers to, the Grand Chamber ruled that unless there are 'very exceptional circumstances' where the humanitarian grounds against the removal are compelling, such as being close to death, Art 3 does not preclude removal. According to the Court, the expected deterioration of the condition of the applicant, a rejected asylum seeker suffering from AIDS, including a significant reduction in life expectancy, is not in itself sufficient to give rise to a breach of Art 3 (para 42).

[15] Criticism was expressed even by some of the Court's own judges: *SJ v Belgium*, Appl No 70055/10, concurring opinion of Judges Lemmens, joined by Judge Nussberger, and dissenting opinion of Judge Power-Forde; *Yoh-Ekale Mwanje v Belgium*, Appl No 10486/10, partially concurring opinion of Judges Tulkens, Jociené, Popovic, Karakas, Raimondi and Pinto De Albuquerque (in French only).

[16] *Paposhvili v Belgium* [GC], Appl No 41738/10, para 183.

[17] ibid, concurring opinion of Judge Lemmens, para 6.

[18] After a number of conflicting decisions between and within national courts (summarised in *Paposhvili* (n 16) paras 101–07), the Belgian Conseil d'Etat endorsed an 'autonomous' interpretation of a national provision allowing regularisation on medical grounds in order to avoid the criterion established in *N v The United Kingdom*. For a detailed analysis, see L Leboeuf, 'Le titre de séjour pour motif

adopted the revised interpretation of Article 3 ECHR.[19] Judicial dialogue should now operate among national courts across the EU so that they adapt their practice to that of the CJEU.[20]

B. Protection of Family Life

Another impediment to removal is the protection of family life and the best interests of the child. Although these grounds are not found in Article 9 of the Return Directive, Member States have a general obligation to take due account of the best interests of the child and of family life when implementing the Directive.[21]

In contrast to cases of family reunion,[22] the question here is whether the protection of family life prevents family members from being separated. When residing (regularly or not) in a host country, third-country nationals can develop family ties which would be ruptured as a result of their expulsion. Until recently, the CJEU, unlike the ECtHR, had not ruled on the protection of family life in the context of return of third-country nationals.[23] In *KA and Others* of 8 May 2018, the CJEU stated that Article 5 of the Return Directive 'precludes a Member State from adopting a return decision without taking into account the relevant details of the family life of the third-country national concerned'.[24] Member States have a duty to observe the obligations imposed by Article 5 of the Directive and hear the person concerned on that subject, even when that third-country national has previously been the subject of a return decision, accompanied by an entry ban.[25] It follows that an individual assessment needs to be undertaken in order to take due account of family life and the best interests of the child, in conformity with Articles 7 and 24(2) of the Charter.[26]

médical. Bruxelles, terminus de la ligne Strasbourg–Luxembourg' (2015) 29 *Revue de Jurisprudence de Liège, Mons et Bruxelles* 1370.

[19] Case C-353/16, *MP*, EU:C:2018:276, para 40.

[20] Unlike Belgian courts, in other jurisdictions national courts have followed the restrictive approach of the Strasbourg case-law, and thus refused to examine the accessibility of appropriate medical treatment in the home country. For instance: Raad van State (the Netherlands), 16 February 2015, case no 201409155/1/V3, and Migration Court of Appeal (Sweden), 24 March 2015, case no UM8877-13.

[21] Article 5 of the Return Directive.

[22] Council Directive 2003/86/EC of 22 September 2003 on the right to family reunification [2003] OJ L251/12, and related case-law.

[23] However, it has done so in relation to free movement rights of European citizens. See, for early cases: Case C-60/00 *Mary Carpenter* EU:C:2002:434, para 42, and Case C-109/01 *Akrich* EU:C:2003:491, para 59. See also Case C-540/03, *European Parliament v Council of the European Union* EU:C:2006:429, paras 52–59. In these cases the Court referred to the case-law of the ECtHR under Art 8 ECHR.

[24] Case C-82/16 *KA and Others* EU:C:2018:308, para 104.

[25] ibid, para 104.

[26] ibid, para 71. The CJEU previously acknowledged that Art 7 of the Charter, which states that everyone has the right to respect for his or her private and family life, must 'be given the same meaning and the same scope as Article 8(1) of the ECHR, as interpreted by the case-law of the European Court of Human Rights' (Case C-400/10 PPU *J McB* EU:C:2010:582, para 53). On the best interest of the child in return proceedings, see more in C Grütters, 'The Return of Children', Chapter 18 in this volume.

According to the ECtHR, the removal of a person from a country where close members of his family are living may amount to an infringement of the right to respect for family life as guaranteed by Article 8(1) of the Convention. When adopting a return decision, contracting states must strike a fair balance between the competing interests of the individual and of the community as a whole, which also requires an individual assessment of the case.[27] Over time, the Court has developed a number of criteria to be taken into account in the proportionality test, such as the immigration status of those involved when family life was created, the duration of irregular stay in the country, the role of the public administration and its failure to effectively remove irregular third-country nationals, whether there are insurmountable obstacles in the way of the family living in a third country, and the best interests of children.[28] Taking into account states' concerns with situations of fait accompli, the Court has ruled that in such cases the removal of a family member would constitute a violation of Article 8 only in 'exceptional circumstances'. This is most notably the case when irregular third-country nationals have children with a national or a person holding a residence permit.[29] Therefore, based on the circumstances of an individual case, private interests to live with one's close family may outweigh public interests to remove irregularly staying migrants. While such a finding is arguably not satisfactory from the viewpoint of immigration policy as it weakens its effectiveness,[30] genuine family situations cannot be ignored and overlooked indefinitely.

C. The Increasing Significance of Procedural Safeguards

Pursuant to Article 5 of the Return Directive, Member States must take due account of the best interests of the child, family life and the state of health of the third-country national concerned as well as respect the principle of *non-refoulement* when implementing the Directive. Under certain circumstances,

[27] *Gül v Switzerland*, Appl No 23218/94, para 38.

[28] These criteria are enumerated in *Jeunesse v The Netherlands* [GC], Appl No 12738/10, paras 106–09. For a critical analysis, see M-B Dembour, *When Humans Become Migrants* (Oxford, Oxford University Press, 2016) ch 6.

[29] *Rodrigues Da Silva and Hoogkamer v The Netherlands*, Appl No 50435/99; *Nunez v Norway*, Appl No 55597/09; *Jeunesse* (n 28); *Kaplan and Others v Norway*, Appl No 32504/11. Compare: *Darren Omoregie and Others v Norway*, Appl No 265/07; *Antwi and Others v Norway*, Appl No 26940/10. Due to the highly casuistic approach of the Court, its case-law lacks predictability. This increases the risk that domestic decisions may be inconsistent.

[30] D Thym, 'Respect for Private and Family Life under Article 8 ECHR in Immigration Cases: A Human Right to Regularize Illegal Stay?' (2008) 57 *ICLQ* 87, 102. Compare: C Costello, *The Human Rights of Migrants and Refugees in European Law* (Oxford, Oxford University Press, 2016) 67. Costello convincingly uses the social membership thesis to support the recognition of a legal right to stay for irregular migrants after some time.

states are prevented from proceeding with the removal of irregularly staying third-country nationals in order to protect their fundamental rights. For such rights to be enforced and be effective, procedural safeguards are granted to third-country nationals under Chapter III of the Directive. The right to an effective remedy enshrined in Article 13 ECHR also 'guarantees the availability at the national level of a remedy to enforce the substance of the Convention rights and freedoms'.[31]

An increasingly significant procedural safeguard is the right to be heard. Although it is not stated in the Return Directive, the CJEU considers the right to be heard a general principle of EU law.[32] The right to be heard guarantees every person the opportunity to make known his views effectively during an administrative procedure and before the adoption of any decision liable to affect his interests adversely.[33] As a consequence, when Member States apply the Return Directive they have the obligation to hear the third-country national prior to the adoption of a return decision. As the Court ruled in *Boudjlida*, 'when the competent national authority is contemplating the adoption of a return decision, that authority must necessarily observe the obligations imposed by Article 5 of Directive 2008/115 and hear the person concerned on that subject'.[34] Failure to hear a third-country national prior to the adoption of a return decision may lead to judicial review as national authorities have the obligation to state factual and legal reasons for that decision.[35] The right to family life and the best interests of the child can thus be upheld through procedural safeguards applicable during the return procedure. Based on the right to be heard as interpreted by the CJEU, national courts must examine whether personal circumstances have been duly taken into account before issuing a return decision. Through procedural safeguards, the Court arguably enhances the effectiveness of substantive rights in the context of return proceedings.

In this respect as well, the CJEU and the ECtHR are developing congruent standards, although there is no formal judicial dialogue. For both courts, a central component of the right to be heard, and procedural safeguards more generally, is the principle of effectiveness. For the CJEU, what matters is that third-country nationals have the opportunity to effectively submit their point of view on the subject of the illegality of their stay and offer reasons that might justify the relevant authority in refraining from adopting a return decision.[36] Yet this right is not absolute and it does not include the right to an individual interview in all

[31] *Al-Nashif v Bulgaria*, Appl No 50963/99, para 132.

[32] Case C-383/13 PPU *MG, NR* EU:C:2013:533, para 32.

[33] Case C-166/13 *Mukarubega* EU:C:2014:2336, para 46.

[34] Case C-249/13 *Boudjlida* EU:C:2014:2431, para 49.

[35] ibid, para 59. The right to be heard before the adoption of a return decision cannot be used in order to indefinitely reopen the administrative procedure (*Mukarubega* (n 33) para 71). Therefore, third-country nationals are 'subject to a duty of honest cooperation with the competent national authority' (*KA and Others* (n 24) para 105).

[36] *Boudjlida* (n 34) para 55.

circumstances.[37] Similarly, the ECtHR has ruled that, under Article 13 in conjunction with Article 8:

> States must make available to the individual concerned the effective possibility of challenging the deportation or refusal-of-residence order and of having the relevant issues examined with sufficient procedural safeguards and thoroughness by an appropriate domestic forum offering adequate guarantees of independence and impartiality.[38]

Under the influence of the case-law of the CJEU, procedural safeguards are increasingly significant and judicial dialogue is well underway with domestic courts. National decisions collected during the REDIAL project show that the right to be heard is increasingly upheld by judicial authorities across the EU.[39]

III. Safeguards Pending Return

As explained in the previous section, several circumstances can lead to the postponement of the removal of an irregularly staying migrant, pursuant to Article 9 read in conjunction with Article 5 of the Return Directive. Technically this means that while a return decision is adopted, its execution is temporarily suspended due to technical reasons or human rights obligations.[40] Since the ultimate goal remains that irregularly staying third-country nationals should be returned, the return decision is not automatically cancelled.[41] Under the Return Directive, non-removable migrants are not considered to be legally staying in a Member State,

[37] *MG, NR* (n 32) paras 39–40. A breach of the right to be heard is unlawful only insofar as the outcome of the administrative procedure at issue could have been different; Case C-560/14 *M v Minister for Justice and Equality Ireland and Attorney General* EU:C:2017:101.

[38] *Al-Nashif* (n 31) para 133. With regards to the prohibition of collective expulsion, the ECtHR ruled that 'Article 4 of Protocol No 4 does not guarantee the right to an individual interview in all circumstances; the requirements of this provision may be satisfied where each alien has a *genuine and effective* possibility of submitting arguments against his or her expulsion, and where those arguments are examined in an appropriate manner by the authorities of the respondent State' (emphasis added) (*Khlaifia and Others v Italy* [GC], Appl No 16483/12, para 248). See the contribution of Luc Leboeuf in this volume.

[39] Raad van State (the Netherlands), 20 November 2015, case no 201407197/1/V3; Corte di Cassazione (Italy), 22 July 2015, case no 15362.2015; Conseil d'Etat (Belgium), 26 June 2015, case no 231.762; The Supreme Administrative Court of Lithuania, 20 June 2013, case no A822-69/2013.

[40] Removal as such is postponed, not the adoption of the return decision. Under Art 3(5) of the Return Directive, removal is defined as 'the enforcement of the obligation to return, namely the physical transportation out of the Member State'.

[41] The European Parliament proposed to include the possibility to cancel the return decision but the amendment was rejected (European Parliament, 'Report on the Proposal for a Directive of the European Parliament and of the Council on Common Standards and Procedures in Member States for Returning Illegally', 20 September 2007, A6-0339/2007, Amendment 32). In the Netherlands, the Council of State considers that the fact that a third-country national cannot be removed to his or her country of origin does not mean that the return decision (and the entry ban, if applicable) is no longer valid: Raad van State, 3 December 2014, case no 201404098/1/V2, and 25 June 2013, case no 201208588/1/V1.

unless a Member State decides – in application of Article 6(4) of the Directive – to grant them a residence permit or a right to legal stay.[42]

Nevertheless, pending return, non-removable third-country nationals are not completely deprived of rights. Under Article 14 of the Return Directive, Member States must ensure, as far as possible, that family unity is maintained, emergency healthcare and essential treatment of illness are provided, access to basic education is granted to minors and the special needs of vulnerable people are taken into account. Compared to the initial proposal of the Commission from 2005, in which it pushed for an alignment of the safeguards pending return with those provided for in Directive 2003/9 on the reception conditions of asylum seekers, the final text of Article 14 of the Return Directive leaves a wider margin of discretion to the Member States.[43] Following concerns expressed in the course of the negotiations that references to the Reception Conditions Directive might be perceived as an upgrading of the situation of irregular migrants, and thus send a wrong policy message, a self-standing list of rights was established.[44] Yet, due to the limited level of protection offered by Article 14 of the Return Directive, the status and the rights of unremovable migrants should be primarily defined at national level, as Recital 12 of the preamble suggests. As a result, EU law possibly creates a legal vacuum that needs to be filled by domestic law. As will be discussed below, national responses differ from one Member State to another.

Unsurprisingly then, few national judgments have been reported on the implementation of Article 14 of the Return Directive.[45] Judicial interactions are also limited since the CJEU delivered only one ruling in relation to that provision. The decision of the Court in *Abdida* is, however, significant as it upholds two important safeguards for seriously ill third-country nationals: one procedural, the other substantial.[46] The Court first ruled that the right to an effective remedy requires that automatic suspensive effect be available to appeals against any order to leave the territory whose enforcement may expose the third-country national concerned to a serious risk of grave and irreversible deterioration in his state of health.[47]

[42] *Return Handbook* (n 12) 44.

[43] European Commission, Proposal for a Directive of the European Parliament and of the Council on common standards and procedures in Member States for returning illegally staying third-country nationals, 1 September 2005, COM(2005) 391 final, Article 13: 'Member States shall ensure that the conditions of stay of third-country nationals for whom the enforcement of a return decision has been postponed or who cannot be removed for the reasons referred to in Article 8 of this Directive are not less favourable than those set out in Articles 7 to 10, Article 15 and Articles 17 to 20 of Directive 2003/9/EC'; Art 4(3) of the Return Directive allows Member States to adopt or maintain more favourable provisions. For instance, in Germany reception conditions apply to those without leave to remain in the same way as to asylum seekers (see National Synthesis Report – Germany, Second Package of the REDIAL Project).

[44] F Lutz, *The Negotiations on the Return Directive* (Nijmegen, Wolf Legal Publishers, 2010) 64. During the initial debate in the Council working group, up to 21 Member States issued reservations or asked to delete the entire provision.

[45] M B Moraru and G Renaudiere, *European Synthesis Report on the Judicial Implementation of Chapter III of the Return Directive* (Migration Policy Centre, REDIAL Research Report, 2016) 36.

[46] J-Y Carlier and S Sarolea, *Droit des étrangers* (Bruxelles, Bruylant, 2016) 518.

[47] *Abdida* (n 9) para 53.

As a consequence removal is automatically suspended, pursuant to Article 9(1) of the Return Directive.[48]

The Court then considered the question of available safeguards pending return based on Article 14 of the Directive, which obliges Member States to provide for emergency healthcare and essential treatment of illness. Interestingly, the Court ruled that Member States have an additional obligation to provide for the basic needs of a third-country national suffering from a serious illness where such a person lacks the means to make such provision for himself. According to the Court:

> The requirement to provide emergency health care and essential treatment of illness under Article 14(1)(b) of Directive 2008/115 may, in such a situation, be rendered meaningless if there were not also a concomitant requirement to make provision for the basic needs of the third country national concerned.[49]

Based on this logic developed by the CJEU, the obligation to cater for the basic needs of unremovable migrants could be derived from their effective enjoyment of the other rights enumerated in Article 14(1) of the Return Directive, in particular access to education and the safeguard of family unity.[50]

While the CJEU adds another safeguard to the text of Article 14 of the Return Directive, it stresses that the right to social assistance has to be provided 'as far as possible', to the extent that the person concerned lacks the means to provide for his own needs.[51] Moreover, it is up to Member States 'to determine the form' which the provision of basic needs takes.[52] As a result, the Court only partially addresses the legal and material situation of irregularly staying migrants whose removal is postponed. Despite the Court's expansive reading of Article 14 of the Directive, the status and the rights of unremovable migrants remain largely defined according to national legislation.

IV. Limited Regularisation Prospects in Courts

Although the Return Directive provides for safeguards pending return, it does not completely fill the protection gap regarding third-country nationals whose removal cannot be enforced. The limits of EU law with respect to the status of

[48] See above.

[49] *Abdida* (n 9) para 60.

[50] ibid, conclusions of Advocate General Bot, para 149; F Lutz, 'Non-Removable Returnees under Union Law: Status Quo and Possible Developments' (2018) 20 *European Journal of Migration and Law* 28, 36. For a case of application with regards to family life: Brussels Labour Tribunal, 23 January 2015, case no 15/1/C. In the Netherlands, the Raad van State ruled that the *Abdida* case was not applicable to the situation of a third-country national who cannot be returned to Ivory Coast because his request for a laissez-passer was rejected by the embassy (15 December 2015, case no 201502872/1/V1).

[51] *Abdida* (n 9), para 59.

[52] ibid, para 61. An exact definition of 'basic needs' is still lacking under EU law. See Lutz (n 50) 36.

unremovable migrants is further reinforced by the rulings of the CJEU in *Mahdi* and *M'Bodj*. In these two judgments of 2014, the Court ruled that the issue of regularisation is left to the discretion of the Member States. Similarly, the ECtHR only recognises a right to regularisation in exceptional cases, thereby contributing to the creation of legal loopholes and limbo situations.

A. Under EU Law

As argued so far, the Return Directive contains provisions that aim to protect the rights of irregular migrants in the context of return. Under certain circumstances, Member States are prevented from proceeding with their removal as it would violate fundamental rights. In such cases, the Directive provides for safeguards pending return.

Despite this, the overriding objective of the Return Directive remains the return of irregularly staying migrants. In *Mahdi*, the CJEU ruled that:

> [T]he purpose of the directive is not to regulate the conditions of residence on the territory of a Member State of third-country nationals who are staying illegally and in respect of whom it is not, or has not been, possible to implement a return decision.[53]

In that case, a Bulgarian court asked the CJEU whether in the absence of a reasonable prospect of removal the Return Directive creates an obligation to deliver a temporary residence permit to an irregularly staying migrant. Because the Directive is concerned with the return of irregular migrants, the court considered that the latter cannot claim a residence permit on the basis of that Directive, even if a Member State cannot execute the return decision.[54] As with any irregularly staying third-country national, Member States may decide to grant a residence permit to an unremovable migrant, but they have no obligation to do so.[55]

With regards to the Qualification Directive, the CJEU ruled in *M'Bodj* that the regularisation of seriously ill third-country nationals is beyond the scope of the Directive.[56] Mr M'Bodj argued that, on the basis of Article 15(b) of Directive 2004/83 and the case-law of the ECtHR on Article 3 ECHR, individuals who

[53] Case C-146/14 PPU *Mahdi* EU:C:2014:1320, para 87.

[54] Although the absence of reasonable prospects of removal does not give rise to regularisation, it is one of the defining factors of the unlawfulness of detention. See Case C-357/09 PPU *Kadzoev* EU:C:2009:741, para 64.

[55] D Acosta Arcarazo, 'The Charter, Detention and Possible Regularization of Migrants in an Irregular Situation under the Returns Directive: *Mahdi*' (2015) 52 *CML Rev* 5, 1377. The author argues that Art 6(4) of the Return Directive should be read as an obligation in cases of non-removability. This would be in line with the overall objective of the Directive which is to end irregular stay, either through removal or regularisation.

[56] Council Directive 2004/83/EC of 29 April 2004 on minimum standards for the qualification and status of third country nationals or stateless persons as refugees or as persons who otherwise need international protection and the content of the protection granted [2004] OJ L304/12 (the Directive was recast in 2011: Directive 2011/95/EU [2011] OJ L337/9).

cannot be sent back due to the inadequacy of medical treatment in their country of origin ought to be granted subsidiary protection status. The Court, however, dismissed that argument:

> The fact that a third country national suffering from a serious illness may not, under Article 3 ECHR as interpreted by the European Court of Human Rights, in highly exceptional cases, be removed to a country in which appropriate treatment is not available does not mean that that person should be granted leave to reside in a Member State by way of subsidiary protection under Directive 2004/83.[57]

The Court did not stop there and added that a more favourable national provision cannot grant subsidiary protection to Mr M'Bodj as this would be incompatible with the Directive, given the lack of 'connection with the rationale of international protection'.[58] It follows that irregularly staying third-country nationals whose return is postponed due to their state of health cannot obtain an international protection status under the Qualification Directive, unless they are intentionally deprived of healthcare in their country of origin.[59] Although the CJEU did not find an obligation to regularise the stay of seriously ill third-country nationals, in *Abdida*, delivered on the same day as *M'Bodj*, the Court gave an ambitious reading to the safeguards pending return found in the RD.

As these two judgments reveal, the issue of regularisation falls outside the ambit of EU law as it currently stands.[60] For the CJEU, the granting of a residence permit to unremovable migrants is beyond the scope of the Return Directive, and for seriously ill third-country nationals the possibility to be granted leave to reside in a Member State by way of subsidiary protection under the Qualification Directive is extremely limited.

B. Under Human Rights Law

Before looking at national practices, let us first examine the case-law of the ECtHR on the issue of regularisation. As discussed above, the expulsion of a third-country national can raise an issue of compatibility with the ECHR, in particular

[57] Case C-542/13 *M'Bodj* EU:C:2014:2452, para 40. In this respect, the position of the CJEU is opposite to the case-law of the Belgian Constitutional Court: case no 95/2008 of 26 June 2008, case no 193/2009 of 26 November 2009, case no 82/2012 of 28 June 2012, and case no 43/2013 of 21 March 2013.

[58] *M'Bodj* (n 57) para 44. For the Court, an international protection claim must be related to the conduct of a third party and 'it cannot therefore simply be the result of general shortcomings in the health system of the country of origin' (para 35). Thus the Court finds that cases for subsidiary protection are more limited than cases falling under Art 3 ECHR, which provides for what can be labelled as a 'subsidiary-subsidiary protection' (Carlier and Sarolea (n 46) 454).

[59] See *M'Bodj* (n 57) para 36 and *MP* (n 19) para 57. The Court refers here to the ruling of the ECtHR in *SHH v The United Kingdom*, Appl No 60367/10, para 89.

[60] A notable exception is when third-country nationals can claim a derived right of residence due to their relationship of dependency with an EU citizen. See Case C-133/15 *Chavez-Vilchez and Others* EU:C:2017:354.

Articles 3 and 8. If a violation is found, contracting states are precluded from proceeding with the expulsion. In other words, the Strasbourg Court imposes a negative obligation not to expel the person concerned. Then, the question is whether the Convention could also be the source of a right to regularisation.[61]

On this question the case-law of the ECtHR calls for a nuanced answer. Admittedly, there have been a limited number of cases where the Court found a violation of Article 8 ECHR due to contracting states' refusal to grant a residence permit.[62] However, due to the exceptional nature of these cases, a right to regularisation can hardly be derived from that provision.[63] Moreover, complaints filed by unremovable migrants who considered that the denial of a residence permit constitutes a violation of human rights and human dignity have been unsuccessful. In 2005, the complaint of an Ethiopian national excluded from international protection in the Netherlands, yet non-removable on the ground of Article 3 ECHR, was declared inadmissible. According to the Court, the complaint was 'incompatible *ratione materiae* as neither Article 3 nor any other provision of the Convention and its Protocols guarantees, as such, a right to a residence permit'.[64] While states are prevented from removing third-country nationals, they do not have an obligation under the ECHR to grant them a residence status. Similarly, the fact that unremovable third-country nationals are not allowed to work in the Netherlands was considered not to raise an issue under Article 8 'as neither this nor any other Convention provision guarantees a right to work'.[65] Consequently, the negative obligation of states not to remove third-country nationals where such removal is contrary to Articles 3 or 8 ECHR is not coupled to a positive obligation to issue a residence permit or an authorisation to work.

It follows that the ECtHR is satisfied as long as applicants receive adequate protection against removal. The Court is solely concerned that the rights of

[61] D Thym, 'Residence as De Facto Citizenship? Protection of Long-Term Residence under Article 8 ECHR' in R Rubio-Marin (ed), *Human Rights and Immigration* (Oxford, Oxford University Press, 2014).

[62] *Jeunesse* (n 28); *Rodrigues Da Silva and Hoogkamer v The Netherlands*, Appl No 50435/99; *Aristimuno Mendizabal v France*, Appl No 12323/11 (only available in French); *Sisojeva and Others v Latvia*, Appl No 60654/00 and Grand Chamber ruling of 15 January 2007; *Slivenko v Latvia* [GC], Appl No 48321/99.

[63] The *Mendizabal* case concerned an EU citizen in France. Consequently, the denial of a residence permit was in clear violation of EU law. In *Slivenko* and *Sisojeva and Others*, the factual situation is very specific to Latvia where members of the ethnic Russian community lost their residence permits following the breakup of the Soviet Union, although they had lived there for years. In *Rodrigues Da Silva and Hoogkamer*, the Court granted the applicant a right to regularise her stay, considering that the authorities had indulged in excessive formalism. One explanation of the Court's reasoning in this particular case arguably relates to the fact that the applicant could have obtained a residence permit as a result of her relationship with a Dutch national (para 43). In *Jeunesse* (n 28), the Court found a violation of Art 8 in the failure to regularise the stay of the applicant, a Surinamese national who held Dutch nationality at birth. For that reason, 'her position cannot be simply considered to be on a par with that of other potential immigrants who have never held Netherlands nationality' (para 115).

[64] *Bonger v The Netherlands*, Appl No 10154/04.

[65] *I v The Netherlands*, Appl No 24147/11, para 48.

migrants under Articles 3 or 8 ECHR are not violated as a result of their expulsion per se, without consideration for their subsequent legal status (or lack thereof) in the host country.[66] Referring to the subsidiarity of its control, the Court repeatedly declares itself incompetent to rule on whether an applicant 'should be granted one particular legal status rather than another, that choice being a matter for the domestic authorities alone'.[67] As a consequence, the ECtHR implicitly admits that the legal status of non-removable migrants is outside the scope of its control. In doing so, the Court fails to offer safeguards pending return to unremovable migrants who are left without any residence permit or regularisation opportunities under domestic law.[68] As Costello notes, 'it may feed into the very precariousness the right to stay ought to protect against'.[69]

V. A Legal Void to be Filled by Domestic Law

Unremovable migrants face a conundrum: while they are protected from removal under the Return Directive or the ECHR, they do not automatically have a formal authorisation to remain on the territory.[70] Neither EU law nor the ECHR imposes a general obligation upon states to grant a residence permit (even temporary) to unremovable migrants. Yet, under Article 6(4) of the Return Directive, Member States are free to do so at any moment. Despite the European Commission's concerns about the lack of common standards,[71] the status of irregular migrants who cannot be returned and the issue of regularisation are left to the Member States.[72]

While the Commission's view on regularisation has been ambivalent over the years, Member States have used the EU arena to lament national regularisation

[66] *Dremlyuga v Latvia*, Appl No 66729/01 (in French only). The court ruled that the Convention does not go as far as to guarantee a right to a particular residence permit (permanent, temporary or other), as long as the solution proposed by the authorities allows the individual concerned to enjoy freely the right to respect for his or her private and family life.

[67] *Ahmed Ali v The Netherlands and Greece*, Appl No 26494/09, para 19; *Mehemi v France (No 2)*, Appl No 53470/99, para 55.

[68] B M Queiroz, *Illegally Staying in the EU: An Analysis of Illegality in EU Migration Law* (Oxford, Hart Publishing, 2018) 109. In this respect, the safeguards provided by the CJEU on the basis of Art 14 of the Return Directive are higher.

[69] Costello (n 30) 80.

[70] According to Art 14(2) of the Return Directive, Member States have an obligation to issue a written confirmation that the return decision will temporarily not be enforced.

[71] Communication from the Commission to the Council and to the European Parliament on EU Return Policy, 28 March 2014, COM(2014) 199 final, 8; European Commission, *An Area of Freedom, Security and Justice Serving the Citizen*, 10 June 2009, COM(2009) 262 final, 26: '[A]ll too often repatriation measures cannot be carried out on account of legal or practical obstacles. In the absence of clear rules, we should study national needs and practices and consider the possibility of establishing common standards for taking charge of illegal immigrants who cannot be deported.'

[72] The situation remains unchanged under the proposal for a recast of the Return Directive of 12 September 2018 (COM(2018) 634 final).

measures.[73] Like other admission policies, national regularisation practices may have implications for other Member States. Therefore, the development of a common immigration policy within the Area of Freedom, Security and Justice has led to an increased restriction of national regularisation mechanisms. The adoption of the Return Directive precisely embodies the idea that an effective return policy is the preferred answer to irregular migration, although regularisation remains possible in some Member States, primarily on a case-by-case basis in specific circumstances.[74] As a result, the framing of regularisation is arguably shifting from employment-based towards human-rights-based regularisations, leading to its judicialisation and depoliticisation.[75]

In order to fill the gap in the EU migration policy regarding the situation of unremovable third-country nationals, Member States have developed different responses. While the majority of them officially acknowledge when return cannot be implemented, less than half grant a temporary residence permit or a formal toleration status to the persons concerned.[76] In such cases, the authorisation to remain on the territory is valid as long as the obstacle to removal exists.[77] In countries where unremovable migrants are not granted a status, their stay is only tolerated de facto. According to a report from the European Migrant Network, Member States that grant a formal status to unremovable third-country nationals, including access to social and economic rights such as employment, consider this a good practice.[78] Two reasons explain this: first, it prevents the formation of a large group of individuals whose stay is de facto irregular and who may fall into criminality or be subject to exploitation as a consequence; second, it ensures that unremovable migrants remain in contact with the state administration, and are thus more easily found once the return decision can be enforced.[79] For third-country nationals, it means they are not 'virtually expulsed', as Spijkerboer puts it,[80] since they are granted a status, albeit temporary, to which rights are attached.

[73] See M Baldwin-Edwards and A Kraler (eds), *REGINE: Regularisations in Europe* (ICMPD, 2009) ch 7, and Costello (n 30) 99. Most commonly, those opposed to regularisation assert that it not only rewards but also fosters irregular immigration.

[74] European Migration Network, *The Return of Rejected Asylum Seekers: Challenges and Good Practices*, Synthesis Report for the EMN Focusses Study (2016) 33.

[75] A Kraler, 'Fixing, Adjusting, Regulating, Protecting Human Rights – The Shifting Uses of Regularisations in the European Union' (2011) 13 *European Journal of Migration and Law* 297. The greater involvement of the judiciary arguably makes regularisation an instrument of human rights protection rather than a tool to manage irregular immigration. See also Costello (n 30) 82.

[76] European Migration Network (n 74) 32; M Heegaard Bausager, J Köpfli Møller and S Ardittis (eds), *Study on the Situation of Third-Country Nationals Pending Return/Removal in the EU Member States and the Schengen Associated Countries* (Brussels, European Commission, 2013) 33.

[77] G Strban, P Rataj and Z Sabic, 'Return Procedures Applicable to Rejected Asylum-Seekers in the European Union and Options for their Regularisation' (2018) 37 *Refugee Survey Quarterly* 71.

[78] European Migration Network (n 74) 35.

[79] ibid, 32.

[80] T Spijkerboer, 'Ambiguities in Combatting Illegal Immigration' in P de Bruycker (ed), *The Emergence of a European Immigration Policy* (Brussels, Bruylant, 2003) 445.

From a purely legal perspective, the granting of a formal toleration status reduces grey areas and improves legal certainty, for both public authorities and the individuals concerned.

VI. Conclusion

Although the Return Directive imposes an obligation upon Member States to issue a return decision to any third-country national staying irregularly on their territory, the enforcement of that decision can be postponed due to practical or legal obstacles. Read in conjunction with the Charter and the case-law of the ECtHR, the Return Directive offers protection to irregular migrants whose removal would lead to a violation of the principle of *non-refoulement* or their fundamental rights, in particular the prohibition of inhuman or degrading treatment and the right to family life. Judicial dialogue on the legal impediments to removal has led to more protective standards, in particular for seriously ill third-country nationals. Regarding procedural safeguards, which help increase the enforcement of substantial rights, judicial dialogue is also well underway.

In cases of non-removability, Article 14 of the Return Directive provides for safeguards pending return in order to ensure that unremovable migrants are not deprived of their basic rights. In *Abdida*, the CJEU adopted an expansive interpretation of that provision, resulting in an increased level of protection. While they remain limited for now, judicial interactions based on *Abdida* could help elaborate the scope of the safeguards pending return under Article 14 of the Return Directive. In Strasbourg, the ECtHR has yet to rule on the issue of safeguards pending return. Violations of Article 3 ECHR have been found in a few cases related to destitution,[81] yet none of them concern irregular migrants.[82] In a recent decision, the Court rejected the complaint of a failed asylum seeker squatting in an indoor car park and living in poor conditions.[83] The Court not only fails to uphold the standards set by the European Committee of Social Rights,[84] but also avoids assessing the conformity with the ECHR of a non-removable third-country national's status under domestic law.[85] As a result, the status and the rights of unremovable third-country nationals remain primarily dealt with under domestic law.

[81] *Budina v Russia*, Appl No 45603/05; *MSS v Belgium and Greece* [GC], Appl No 30696/09; *VM and Others v Belgium*, Appl No 60125/11; *Shioshvili and Others v Russia*, Appl No 19356/07.

[82] Although the protection of Art 3 ECHR is absolute, the ECtHR distinguishes the situation of irregular migrants, including failed asylum seekers, from that of an asylum seeker whose application is pending. See *MSS v Belgium and Greece* [GC], Appl No 30696/09, para 251; *BAC v Greece*, Appl No 11981/15, para 39.

[83] *Hunde v the Netherlands*, Appl No 17931/16.

[84] ibid, para 37.

[85] The Court implicitly upholds the Dutch legislation which grants a temporary residence permit only to unremovable migrants who cooperate with the authorities in organising their return. See also *Khan v Germany*, Appl No 38030/12, dissenting opinion of Judge Sajo.

Under EU law as it stands, there is no general obligation to grant residency rights to unremovable migrants. According to the CJEU's case-law, the Return Directive cannot serve as a basis for regularisation. The same holds true for seriously ill third-country nationals on the basis of the Qualification Directive. The issue of regularisation thus remains largely uncharted territory for the CJEU. In Strasbourg, the ECtHR is also very cautious when it comes to regularisation. For Member States, the situation of non-removable migrants should be managed at national level only.[86] Yet, given the political priority of increasing the number of returns, regularisation opportunities are increasingly scarce. As a consequence, the interplay between EU law and domestic law leaves a gap regarding the regularisation of non-removable third-country nationals.

In order to avoid situations of legal limbo, regularisation arguably constitutes a corrective mechanism. In this regard, courts and judicial interactions could play a role in strengthening the shift towards the judicialisation of regularisation.[87] Regularisation would then increasingly become a matter of rights claims rather than administrative discretion, based on individual assessments and a fair balancing of the various interests at stake.

[86] Lutz (n 50) 49.

[87] Interestingly, in its *Return Handbook* (n 12), the European Commission recommended a number of assessment criteria regarding the conduct of case-by-case regularisations (see s 13.2).

20

The Prohibition of Collective Expulsion as an Individualisation Requirement

LUC LEBOEUF AND JEAN-YVES CARLIER

I. Introduction[1]

The prohibition of collective expulsion guarantees the right of aliens not to be expelled without an examination of their individual situation.[2] In Europe it is set out by Article 4 Protocol No 4 to the ECHR and by Article 19(1) of the European Union Charter of Fundamental Rights (EUCFR).[3] The primary objective is to prevent the expulsion of aliens as a group. The prohibition of collective expulsion is a major constraint in the enforcement of the European return policy and it has led to significant developments before the ECtHR.

However, these developments do not seem to resonate within the courts of the EU Member States, where the prohibition of collective expulsion has not instigated

[1] This chapter reflects the state of legal developments as of 10 November 2018.

[2] JFD Alba, 'Prohibition on the Collective Expulsion of Aliens (Article 4 Protocol 4)' in JG Roca and P Santolaya (eds), *Europe of Rights: A Compendium on the European Convention of Human Rights* (Leiden, Brill Nijhoff, 2012); W Kälin, 'Aliens, Expulsion and Deportation' in *Max Planck Encyclopedia of Public International Law* (October 2010), accessed at opil.ouplaw.com/home/EPIL, para 22; WA Shabbas, *The European Convention of Human Rights: A Commentary* (Oxford, Oxford University Press, 2015) 1075–80.

[3] Outside of Europe, see Art 22 (9) of the American Convention on Human Rights and Art 12 (5) of the African Charter on Human and Peoples' Rights. The International Covenant on Civil and Political Rights and the International Covenant on Economic, Social and Cultural Rights do not explicitly provide for the prohibition of collective expulsion. However, it is widely recognised at international level, as illustrated by Objectives 8 and 21 of the Global Compact for Safe, Orderly and Regular Migration, Final Draft, 11 July 2018. Both objectives mention states' commitment to upholding the prohibition of collective expulsion in the context of search and rescue operations in the seas and the enforcement of their return policies. The Global Compact intends to establish general principles and guidelines that will foster international cooperation through a holistic approach to migration, rather than a strict international legal obligation that would bind states. As the Final Draft states: 'This Global Compact presents a non-legally binding, cooperative framework that builds on the commitments agreed upon by Member States in the New York Declaration for Refugees and Migrants. It fosters international cooperation among all relevant actors on migration, acknowledging that no State can address migration alone, and upholds the sovereignty of States and their obligations under international law' (para 7). See also Annex II of the New York Declaration for Refugees and Migrants, UNGA Resolution 70/1 (19 September 2016) and J-Y Carlier and F Crépeau, 'De la "crise" migratoire européenne au pacte mondial sur les migrations: exemple d'un mouvement sans droit?', *Annuaire français de droit international* (Paris, CNRS, 2018). The Global Compacts have not been adopted at the time of writing.

major developments or controversies.[4] National courts do not appear to rely on the prohibition of collective expulsion on a regular basis. The CJEU has never been asked to interpret Article 19(1) EUCFR.[5] One might therefore be tempted to assume that the prohibition of collective expulsion does not provide fertile ground for judicial dialogue. This chapter questions and contextualises that assumption. It is suggested that the fact that national courts and the CJEU have not significantly contributed to discussions on the content and scope of the prohibition of collective expulsion does not indicate a lack of judicial dialogue in the field of European return policies. Rather, it reveals a partial yet wide overlap between the prohibition of collective expulsion and existing guarantees under EU law.

The first part of this chapter seeks to clarify the content of the prohibition of collective expulsion by reference to the case-law of the ECtHR and its relevance for European return policies. The constitutive elements of a collective expulsion in the sense of Article 4 Protocol No 4 ECHR are identified and the evolution of the case-law of the ECtHR is analysed. It is shown that a general individualisation requirement can be deduced from the prohibition of collective expulsion. The second part looks for similar guarantees under EU law. It argues that procedural and substantive EU law protections have the aggregate effect of requiring an individual examination of the situation of every alien prior to their removal from European territory. The prohibition of collective expulsion is not fully redundant with those guarantees, but it is mainly of practical relevance for cases where access to procedures is prevented. This may explain why its added value remains limited in the context of daily judicial practices.

II. The Prohibition of Collective Expulsion in the Case-Law of the ECtHR

The ECtHR has only found a violation of Article 4 Protocol No 4 in specific and exceptional circumstances.[6] The prohibition of collective expulsion used to be

[4] This finding is based on the national synthesis reports and the database set up in the context of the REDIAL Project, neither of which mention significant national case-laws on the prohibition of collective expulsion: Austria (U Brandt), Belgium (J-C Werenne and L Leboeuf), Bulgaria (V Ilareva), Croatia (Ž Zrilić Ježek), Czech Republic (D Kosar), France (J-M Favret, H Labayle and J Pétin), Germany (K Hailbronner in collaboration with D Thym), Greece (C Papadimitriou), Italy (A di Pascale), Lithuania (I Jarukaitis), Poland (J Chlebny in collaboration with BE Mikolajczyk), Spain (C Gortazar Rotaeche), accessed at euredial.eu/publications/national-synthesis-reports/ and euredial.eu/national-caselaw/. With respect to Belgium, a thorough study on the implementation of the EUCFR in the case-law of the Council for Alien Law Litigation also does not document rulings on the prohibition of collective expulsion: see M Maes and A Wijnants, 'Het Handvest van de Grondrechten van de Europese Unie: een nieuwe speler in het vreemdelingenrecht' (2016) 1 *Tijdschrift voor Vreemdelingenrecht* 6 (part I), and (2016) 2 *Tijdschrift voor Vreemdelingenrecht* 158 (part II).

[5] The case-law of the CJEU is focussed on Art 19(2) EUCFR, which establishes the principle of *non-refoulement*. See eg Case C-578/16 PPU *CK* EU:C:2017:127 (on the Dublin regulation); Case C-182/15 *Petruhhin* EU:C:2016:630 (on the European arrest warrant).

[6] At the time of writing, the ECtHR has established a violation of the prohibition of collective expulsion in seven cases.

relatively discreet in the ECtHR case-law. It seems to have gained momentum since 2010 as litigation before the ECtHR addressed the responses by EU Member States to various episodes involving a sudden increase in the arrival of migrants and refugees (such as the one that followed the Arab Spring and the incidents that regularly take place at the Spanish–Moroccan border in Melilla).

Next the constitutive elements of a collective expulsion will be highlighted based on analysis of the case-law of the ECtHR (section II.A). Emphasis will be placed on how the Court revived the prohibition of collective expulsion in the past ten years to prohibit 'push-back' policies, as well as on the concrete difficulties states face in dealing with sudden increases in the arrival of migrants and refugees (section II.B).

A. The Constitutive Criteria of a Collective Expulsion

The ECtHR has consistently defined a collective expulsion as

> any measure compelling aliens, as a group, to leave a country, except where such a measure is taken on the basis of a reasonable and objective examination of the particular case of each individual alien of the group.[7]

Following this definition, a collective expulsion has two constitutive elements: first, an alien is expelled together with a group of aliens; and second, his or her particular situation was not examined in a reasonable and objective manner.

There is no clear guidance on how large the group of aliens needs to be. In *Conka v Belgium*, a case that concerned the removal from Belgium of Slovakian Roma, the ECtHR was satisfied with a group consisting of few families (around 70 people), which it termed a 'large number of persons of the same origin'.[8] There is also no requirement of homogeneity within the group. As emphasised by a Chamber of the ECtHR in *ND and NT v Spain*, aliens who do not share a common characteristic but are expelled together, during the same period of time, may be expelled as a 'group'.[9] That interpretation is based on the relatively vague wording of Article 4 Protocol No 4, which merely states that 'collective expulsion of aliens

[7] See eg *Andric v Sweden*, App No 45917/99, ECtHR (dec) 23 February 1999; *Conka v Belgium*, App No 51564/99, ECtHR 5 February 2002. This case-law can be traced back to the decisions of the European Commission of Human Rights, eg *Becker v Denmark*, App No 7011/75, EComHR 3 October 1975; *KG v The Federal Republic of Germany*, App No 7704/76, EComHR 11 March 1977; *O and others v Luxembourg*, App No 7757/77, EComHR 3 March 1978.

[8] Conka (n 7) para 61; J-Y Carlier, 'La détention et l'expulsion collective des étrangers. Commentaire de l'affaire Conka' (2003) 14(53) *Revue trimestrielle des droits de l'homme* 198.

[9] *ND and NT v Spain*, App Nos 8675/15 and 8697/15, ECHR 3 October 2017, para 100. This case is referred to the Grand Chamber, see section II.A.iii. The Grand Chamber ruling was delivered after the editing of this chapter, and could not be included within the scope of this study. Worth noting is that the Grand Chamber focused its assessment on the applicants' conduct to overturn the ruling of the Chamber and conclude that there was no breach of Art 4 Protocol No 4. The Grand Chamber emphasised that the applicants were 'members of a group comprising numerous individuals who attempted to enter Spanish territory by crossing a land border in an unauthorised manner, taking advantage of their large numbers and in the context of an operation that had been planned in advance' (*ND and NT v Spain*, App Nos 8675/15 and 8697/15 ECHR GC 13 February 2020, para 206).

is prohibited'. It contrasts with that of another regional instrument, the African Charter on Human and Peoples' Rights. Article 12(5) of the African Charter prohibits 'mass expulsion', defined as one 'aimed at national, racial, ethnic or religious groups'.[10] It requires the group to be of a certain size ('mass', translated as 'collective' in the French version) and character ('aimed at national, racial, ethnic or religious groups').[11]

The ECtHR is concerned with the expulsion of aliens without examination of their individual situations, rather than with the numbers and cohesion of the expelled group. The size of the group and its homogeneity may point to a general policy aimed at expelling aliens collectively, but they do not suffice to conclude to a violation of Article 4 Protocol No 4.[12] ECtHR case-law mainly discusses the requirement of a 'reasonable and objective examination' of the situation of each person concerned. The approach of the Court thus seems to be pragmatic. The ECtHR assesses all relevant facts in a holistic way.

The next sections highlight the main relevant facts. For the sake of clarity, a distinction will be made between the motivation of the expulsion order (section II.A.i), circumstances surrounding the adoption and implementation of the expulsion order (section 2.A.ii) and procedural guarantees (section 2.I.iii). None of these facts are conclusive by themselves. They guide the reasoning of the ECtHR, but do not constitute strict guidelines of systematic application.

i. The Motivation of the Expulsion Order

A stereotyped motivation for an expulsion order will not in itself give rise to a violation of Article 4 Protocol No 4. According to well-established case law:

> [T]he fact that a number of aliens are subject to similar decisions does not in itself lead to the conclusion that there is a collective expulsion if each person concerned has been given the opportunity to put arguments against his expulsion to the competent authorities on an individual basis.[13]

In *MA v Cyprus*, a case involving Syrian Kurds who were expelled following their involvement in a demonstration advocating for the regularisation of their stay, identical expulsion orders were issued. But that did not suffice to establish a violation of the prohibition of collective expulsion. The ECtHR observed that the applicants' irregular stay resulted from the rejection of their asylum application, which was examined on its merits. It held that:

> [T]he fact that the deportation orders and the corresponding letters were couched in formulaic and, therefore, identical terms and did not specifically refer to the earlier

[10] Art 12(5) of the African Charter on Human and Peoples' Rights.

[11] J-M Sorel, 'Article 12' in M Kamto (ed), *La charte africaine des droits de l'Homme et des peuples et le protocole y relatif portant création de la cour africaine des droits de l'homme* (Brussels, Bruylant, 2011) 307.

[12] See section II.A.ii.

[13] *Sultani v France*, App No 45223/05, ECHR 20 September 2007, para 81; *Andric* (n 7).

> decisions regarding the asylum procedure is not itself indicative of a collective expulsion. What is important is that every case was looked at individually and decided on its own particular facts.[14]

The motivation of the expulsion order is nonetheless relevant, as shown by the ruling in *Conka v Belgium*. The ECtHR referred to the stereotyped motivation of the expulsion order as a circumstance that gives rise to a suspicion of collective expulsion. It held that 'the only reference to the personal circumstances of the applicants was to the fact that their stay in Belgium had exceeded three months' and that therefore 'the procedure followed does not enable it to eliminate all doubt that the expulsion might have been collective'.[15] Additional surrounding circumstances led the ECtHR to find a violation of Article 4 Protocol No 4.[16]

The rulings in *MA* and *Conka* show that the stereotyped motivations of the expulsion orders is a relevant fact, one that gives rise to a suspicion of collective expulsion that other circumstances may confirm or dispel. Stereotyped motivations of expulsion orders are, however, not prohibited per se. They do not suffice by themselves to establish a violation of Article 4 Protocol No 4.

ii. Circumstances Surrounding the Adoption and the Implementation of Expulsion Orders

In the ECtHR case-law, the main relevant circumstances surrounding the adoption and implementation of expulsion orders include the political context. The public acts and declarations of the authorities may establish a general policy aimed at expelling a specific group of aliens. In *Conka v Belgium*, for example, the ECtHR referred to the official declarations of the authorities.[17] A broad police operation targeting Roma people was announced, thus revealing 'a general system intended to deal with groups of individuals collectively from the moment the decision to expel them was made until its execution'.[18]

The political context was an important factor in three rulings concerning the expulsion of Georgian nationals from Russia during the autumn of 2006 following a dispute between the Georgian and Russian governments.[19] Events as documented by international organisations showed a 'routine of expulsions' as

[14] *MA v Cyprus*, App No 41872/10, ECHR 23 July 2013, para 254.

[15] *Conka* (n 7) para 61.

[16] See sectio II.A.ii.

[17] *Conka* (n 7) paras 23 and 62. The Minister of the Interior declared before the Parliament that '[o]wing to the large concentration of asylum-seekers of Slovakian nationality in Ghent, arrangements have been made for their collective repatriation to Slovakia'.

[18] Ibid, para 56.

[19] *Georgia v Russia (I)*, App No 13255/07, 3 July 2014, para 172. See also *Berdzenishvili and others v Russia*, App Nos 14594/07, 14597/07, 14976/07, 14978/07, 15221/07, 16369/07 and 16706/07, ECtHR 20 December 2016; *Shioshvili and others v Russia*, App No 19356/07, ECtHR 20 December 2016. The Georgian authorities' arrest of four Russian officers on charges of espionage escalated tensions between both countries, which had become tense following the so-called 'Rose Revolution' in 2003.

Georgian nationals were arrested en masse, detained and expelled from Russian territory.[20] Various circulars and instructions were issued by the Russian authorities to organise their swift deportation. Appeals to Russian courts were not prevented, but the guarantees provided by the Russian judicial system could not be applied in practice given the short timeframe and the number of people concerned. According to the ECtHR:

> Even though, formally speaking, a court decision was made in respect of each Georgian national, … the conduct of the expulsion procedures during that period, after the circulars and instructions had been issued, and the number of Georgian nationals expelled – from October 2006 – made it impossible to carry out a reasonable and objective examination of the particular case of each individual.[21]

These three rulings also show that the fact that a particularly large group of aliens was expelled was a relevant circumstance, as it may have indicated a general policy aimed at expelling aliens as a group. The size of an expelled group is not enough to establish a collective expulsion, but it matters within a holistic assessment of the facts.

In other rulings, the ECtHR concluded that no collective expulsion took place because the expulsion orders were issued after a proper examination of the asylum applications, in compliance with the guarantees of Articles 3 and 13 ECHR. For example, in *Sultani v France* on the expulsion of an Afghan national by collective flight, the ECtHR observed that the return decision was adopted after the rejection of the asylum application on its merits. French authorities 'took account not only of the overall context in Afghanistan, but also of the applicant's statements concerning his personal situation and the risks he would allegedly run in the event of a return to his country of origin'.[22] This ruling has particular implications for the EU practice of joint flights, which does not in itself violate the prohibition of collective expulsion.[23]

Other rulings and inadmissibility decisions follow a similar line of reasoning. They reject applications on the grounds that expulsion orders were adopted following the rejection of the initial asylum applications.[24] The ruling in *Conka v Belgium* seems to have deviated from this approach. The ECtHR established a violation of

[20] *Georgia v Russia (I)* (n 19) para 141.

[21] ibid, para 175. The African Commission of Human Rights similarly held that 'the mass expulsions, particularly following arrest and subsequent detentions, deny victims the opportunity to establish the legality of these actions in the courts', Com 279/03-296/05, *Sudan Human Rights Organisation & Centre on Housing Rights and Evictions (COHRE) v Sudan*, 2009, para 183.

[22] *Sultani* (n 13) para 83. See also *Ghulami v France*, App No 45302/05, ECtHR (dec) 7 April 2009.

[23] Council Decision 2004/573/EC of 29 April 2004 on the organisation of joint flights for removals from the territory of two or more Member States, of third-country nationals who are subjects of individual removal orders [2004] OJ L261.

[24] *Alibaks and others v The Netherlands*, App No 14209/88, EComHR 16 December 1988; *Tahiri v Sweden*, App No 25129/94, EComHR (dec), 11 January 1995; *Pranjko v Sweden*, App No 45925/99, ECtHR (dec) 23 February 1999; *Andric* (n 7).

Article 4 Protocol No 4 even though the asylum application was examined prior to the adoption of the expulsion order. It held that

> collective expulsion, … is to be understood as any measure compelling aliens, as a group, to leave a country, except where such a measure is taken on the basis of a reasonable and objective examination of the particular case of each individual alien of the group …. That does not mean, however, that where the latter condition is satisfied the background to the execution of the expulsion orders plays no further role in determining whether there has been compliance with Article 4 of Protocol No 4.[25]

This can be interpreted as implying that a violation of Article 4 Protocol No 4 can be established even where the situation of the concerned alien was individually assessed, due to the general context framing the adoption of the expulsion orders ('the background to the execution of the expulsion orders'). There is no example of this in later case-law.[26] It would therefore seem that this finding is limited to exceptional cases such as *Conka* where a discriminatory policy targeting a specific group of aliens was shown. The mere fact that a group of aliens is being expelled does not imply that a collective expulsion is taking place as long as the particular situation of each member of the group was duly taken into consideration. But the control of the Court is particularly strict when expulsions are the result of discriminatory policies that specifically target a given group of aliens.

iii. Procedural Guarantees

The primary objective of the prohibition of collective expulsion is not to impose strict procedural requirements on states; rather, it is to guarantee individual examinations, irrespective of the specific characteristics of the procedures that states may choose to apply. Some minimal procedural guarantees can, however, be deduced from the case-law of the Court on Article 4 Protocol No 4. The identification of the aliens concerned is a minimal procedural requirement that stands out. In *MA v Cyprus*, for example, the ECtHR ruled that the prohibition of collective expulsion was not infringed, on the grounds that 'the authorities had carried out a background check with regard to each person before issuing the orders and separate deportation and detention orders were issued in respect of each person'.[27]

[25] *Conka* (n 7) para 59. See the partly concurring and partly dissenting opinion of Judge Velaers, who noted that: 'The majority's doubts stem from the fact that the deportation measures were taken pursuant to an order to leave the territory dated 29 September 1999, which referred solely to section 7, first paragraph, point (2), of the Aliens Act, without making any reference to the personal circumstances of those concerned other than to say that they had been in Belgium for more than three months. To my mind, the measures taken on 29 September 1999 cannot be isolated from the earlier decisions regarding the asylum procedure. The applicants' individual circumstances had been examined on two or even three occasions and that had provided sufficient justification for the expulsions.'

[26] See nn 21 and 23.

[27] *MA* (n 14).

Other rulings refer to the lack of identification to establish a violation of Article 4 Protocol No 4. The ruling in *Hirsi Jamaa v Italy* concerned the 'push-back' policy enforced by Italian coastguards, who intercepted vessels bearing migrants in the Mediterranean Sea and sent them back to Libya. The fact that no identification took place weighed heavily in the reasoning of the ECtHR. It observed that 'the transfer of the applicants to Libya was carried out without any form of examination of each applicant's individual situation' and that 'it has not been disputed that the applicants were not subjected to any identification procedure by the Italian authorities, who restricted themselves to embarking all the intercepted migrants onto military ships and disembarking them on Libyan soil'.[28] Similarly, in *Sharifi and others v Italy and Greece*, the ECtHR condemned the immediate and automatic *refoulement*, without prior identification, of asylum seekers arriving from Greece in Italian ports.[29]

However, the issues at stake in *Hirsi Jamaa* and *Sharifi* concern far more than the identification of aliens before their expulsion.[30] The rulings condemn the systematic interception and expulsion of aliens who were prevented from accessing asylum. The emphasis placed on the lack of identification nonetheless shows the importance the Court devotes to that particular procedural guarantee. This emphasis is also found in the later ruling in *ND and NT v Spain*, which concerns the immediate expulsion of migrants intercepted at the Spanish–Moroccan border at Mellila. A chamber of the Court held that:

> [T]he issue whether there were sufficient guarantees demonstrating that the personal circumstances of those concerned had been genuinely and individually taken into account does not even arise in the present case, in the absence of any examination of the individual situation of the applicants, who were not subjected to any identification procedure by the Spanish authorities.[31]

At the time of writing, an appeal against the *ND and NT* ruling is pending before the Grand Chamber of the ECtHR. The Grand Chamber is expected to address the

[28] *Hirsi Jamaa v Italy*, App No 27765/09, ECtHR 23 February 2012, para 185. In *Hirsi*, the ECtHR also aligned the scope of application of Art 4 Protocol No 4 with that of the ECHR. It held that the prohibition of collective expulsion binds states within their 'jurisdiction' in the sense of Art 1 ECHR, ie in every situation falling under their effective control de jure or de facto. According to the ECtHR, migrants intercepted on the high seas and brought on the vessels of coastguards of a state party to the ECHR fall de jure under the jurisdiction of that state, in accordance with the Law of the Sea which establishes the duty of the flag state to exercise its jurisdiction over ships flying its flag (Art 94 of the UN Convention on the Law of the Sea). For a general theory on states' 'jurisdiction' under international human rights law, see, among others, O De Schutter, 'Globalization and Jurisdiction: Lessons from the European Convention on Human Rights' (2006) 6 *Baltic Yearbook of International Law* 185; E Lagrange, 'L'application de la Convention de Rome à des actes accomplis par les États parties en dehors du territoire national' [2008] *Revue Générale de Droit International Privé* 527; M Milanovic, *Extraterritorial Application of Human Rights Treaties: Law, Principles and Policy* (Oxford, Oxford University Press, 2011).

[29] *Sharifi and others v Italy and Greece*, App No 16643/09, ECHR 21 October 2014, paras 214–25.

[30] See section II.B.i.

[31] *ND and NT* (n 9) para 107.

relationship between Article 4 Protocol No 4 and Article 3 ECHR and clarify the relevance of the prohibition of collective expulsion for aliens who do not apply for asylum.

When it comes to identifying migrants, states have an obligation of means, not results. In *Dritsas v Italy*, a group of Greek militants who intended to attend a summit in Italy were expelled without being issued a decision stating their identity. They complained of a collective expulsion. The application was declared inadmissible by the ECtHR, which observed that the applicants refused to co-operate with the authorities and concealed their identity documents.[32] There is no violation of Article 4 Protocol No 4 when the lack of identification is attributable to the conduct of the aliens concerned.

B. The Renewal of the Prohibition of Collective Expulsion

In its earlier case-law, the ECtHR mainly relied on the surrounding factual circumstances to establish a violation of Article 4 Protocol No 4. The main focus was on the general context in which the contested expulsions took place. The prohibition of collective expulsion was mainly applied in cases where the ECtHR also established a violation of other provisions of the ECHR such as Articles 3, 5 or 13. In each case the Court appealed to the prohibition to highlight a discriminatory policy aimed at expelling a given group of aliens.

This line of case-law is exemplified by the *Conka* ruling on the expulsion of Slovakian Roma and the three rulings on the expulsion of Georgians by Russia in 2006. It closely resembles the case-law of the European Social Committee,[33] the African Commission of Human Rights[34] and the Inter-American Court of Human Rights,[35] which also give prominent weight to the circumstance that an expulsion targets a particular group based on national or ethnic origins. In situations such as this the prohibition of collective expulsion prevents the discriminatory enforcement of a return policy.

The 2010s have seen the emergence of a different yet complementary line of case-law. The ECtHR has reinvigorated the prohibition of collective expulsion with

[32] *Dritsas v Italy*, App No 2344/02, ECHR (dec) 1 February 2011. See also *Berisha and Haljiti v Macedonia*, App No 18670/03, ECHR (dec) 16 June 2005.

[33] *European Roma and Travellers Forum (ERTF) v France* (Collective Complaint No 64/2011) ECSR 5 December 2017, para 66: '[T]he Committee concludes that the administrative decisions whereby, during the period under consideration, Roma of Romanian and Bulgarian origin were ordered to leave French territory, where they were resident, are incompatible with the Charter in that they were not founded on an examination of their personal circumstances, did not respect the proportionality principle and were discriminatory in nature since they targeted the Roma community.'

[34] *Institute for Human Rights and Development in Africa, on behalf of Sierra Leonean refugees in Guinea v Guinea* (Com No 249/02) ACHR 7 December 2004, para 69: '[L]arge scale expulsions … [are] a special threat to human rights [and] the action of a State targeting specific … groups is generally qualified as discriminatory.'

[35] *Expelled Dominicans and Haitians v Dominican Republic* (Com No 282) IACHR 28 August 2014.

a view to adequately regulating European border policies. In the next two sections the concrete consequences of the evolution of ECtHR case-law will be highlighted. The focus will be on how the ECtHR relied on the prohibition of collective expulsion to guarantee access to the relevant procedures (section II.B.i), as well as on the practical difficulties faced by national administrations in dealing with sudden increases in the arrival of migrants (section II.B.ii).

i. The Right to Access the Relevant Procedure

In *Hirsi Jamaa v Italy* and *Sharifi v Italy and Greece*, the ECtHR relied on the prohibition of collective expulsion to strengthen its conclusion that 'push-back' policies violate the ECHR. It held that migrants arrested while attempting to cross the border cannot be sent back without being allowed to apply for asylum. The focus of the reasoning of the ECtHR under Article 4 Protocol No 4 lies on the procedural guarantees, which were non-existent.

In *Hirsi*, the ECtHR observed a lack of 'sufficient guarantees ensuring that the individual circumstances of each of those concerned were actually the subject of a detailed examination'.[36] It used a procedural approach to establish a violation of the prohibition of collective expulsion. Various doctrinal comments considered that the aggregate effect of the procedural guarantees established by *Hirsi*, including those deduced from Article 4 Protocol No 4, is such that states have the duty to grant access to the asylum procedure to every asylum seeker under their jurisdiction, including those rescued at sea.[37] In practical terms, it is difficult to conceive how a rigorous examination of the risk of violating Article 3 ECHR – and an effective remedy – could be guaranteed on the sea; how could it reasonably be envisaged that civil servants from asylum authorities, translators, lawyers and judges could perform their duties on a boat?

In *Sharifi*, the ECtHR followed similar reasoning. It relied on the lack of procedural guarantees to rule that the asylum seekers arrested in Italian ports when arriving from Greece and sent back without being given access to the asylum procedure were expelled collectively.[38]

The rulings in *Hirsi* and *Sharifi* give a new meaning to the prohibition of collective expulsion as an essentially procedural protection, one that guarantees access to the relevant procedure. They were adopted in a specific context, where the applicants intended to apply for asylum. But every migrant is entitled to the

[36] *Hirsi* (n 28) para 185. As underlined above, the ECtHR attached particular importance to the fact that the applicants were not properly identified before being sent back to Libya; see section II.A.iii.

[37] M Den Heijer, 'Reflections on *Refoulement* and Collective Expulsion in the *Hirsi* Case' (2013) 25 *International Journal of Refugee Law* 265; M Giuffre, 'Watered-Down Rights on the High Seas: *Hirsi Jamaa and others v Italy*' (2012) 61 *ICLQ* 728; V Moreno-Lax, '*Hirsi Jamaa and others v Italy* or the Strasbourg Court versus Extraterritorial Migration Control?' (2012) 12(3) *Human Rights Law Reports* 574.

[38] *Sharifi* (n 29).

benefit of Article 4 Protocol No 4, the scope of application of which is wider than that of Article 3 ECHR. There is nothing in the reasoning of the Court that limits the outcomes of *Hirsi* and *Sharifi* to those who risk ill-treatment. Case-law shows, however, that the extent of the applicable procedural guarantees differs depending on whether or not the migrant applies for asylum and is entitled to the additional protection of Article 3 ECHR.

ii. The Absence of Strict Procedural Guarantees

In *Hirsi*, the ECtHR acknowledged the difficulties faced by national authorities in dealing with a large influx of migrants. It emphasised that 'States which form the external borders of the European Union are currently experiencing considerable difficulties in coping with the increasing influx of migrants and asylum-seekers' and that '[it] does not underestimate the burden and pressure this situation places on the States concerned, which are all the greater in the present context of economic crisis'.[39] However, the ECtHR stated that such difficulties never justify violations of Article 3 ECHR, as this provision is absolute. It also refrained from outlining exceptions to the prohibition of collective expulsion. The fact that states face substantial difficulties controlling their borders does not justify their blocking access to asylum procedures.

The ECtHR refined that jurisprudence in *Khlaifia v Italy*:

> [W]hile the constraints inherent in such a crisis cannot, in themselves, be used to justify a breach of Article 3, the Court is of the view that it would certainly be artificial to examine the facts of the case without considering the general context in which those facts arose. In its assessment, the Court will thus bear in mind, together with other factors, that the undeniable difficulties and inconveniences endured by the applicants stemmed to a significant extent from the situation of extreme difficulty confronting the Italian authorities at the relevant time.[40]

This finding had consequences for the evaluation under Article 4 Protocol No 4. The applicants were Tunisian migrants, who were intercepted by Italian coastguards while crossing the Mediterranean Sea and brought to the island of Lampedusa. They were detained on unclear legal grounds without access to a judge in violation of Article 5 ECHR, before being sent back to their home country following a fast-track procedure. None of the applicants had applied for asylum or seemed to have had reason to do so. A Chamber of the ECtHR established a violation of the prohibition of collective expulsion on the grounds that the applicants were not heard.[41]

[39] *Hirsi* (n 28) para 122.

[40] *Khlaifia v Italy* (Grand Chamber), App No 16483/12, ECHR 15 December 2016, para 185.

[41] *Khlaifia v Italy* (Chamber), App No 16483/12, ECHR 1 September 2015, para 156. See also H Labayle and F Sudre, 'Jurisprudence de la Cour européenne des droits de l'homme et droit administratif' [2016] *Revue Française de Droit Administratif* 768 and the joint partly dissenting opinion of Judges Sajo and Vucinic, who argued: 'By labelling as "collective expulsion" Italy's attempts to police its borders during an unforeseen emergency, the majority do a grave disservice to an intentionally focused

The Grand Chamber overruled that finding. It deduced from the surrounding circumstances, including the identification procedure and the migrants' option to apply for asylum, that 'the applicants had an opportunity to notify the authorities of any reasons why they should remain in Italy or why they should not be returned'.[42] It held that:

> Article 4 of Protocol No 4 does not guarantee the right to an individual interview in all circumstances; the requirements of this provision may be satisfied where each alien has a genuine and effective possibility of submitting arguments against his or her expulsion, and where those arguments are examined in an appropriate manner by the authorities of the respondent State.[43]

The ruling of the Grand Chamber in *Khlaifia* shows that if Article 4 Protocol No 4 can be interpreted as a procedural protection and a right to access the relevant procedure, its autonomous content remains minimal. The Grand Chamber recognised that 'in an expulsion procedure the possibility of lodging an asylum application is a paramount safeguard', but it also refrained from developing additional procedural guarantees that benefit migrants who do not apply for asylum, such as the right to a personal interview. States retain a wide margin of appreciation when it comes to the return procedure. They remain free to determine how to assess the particular situations of aliens to be expelled, as long as those aliens have the opportunity to put forward arguments against their removal.

Khlaifia shows the unwillingness of the ECtHR to deduce a wide body of strict procedural guarantees from Article 4 Protocol No 4 that every return procedure must follow. This approach allows the ECtHR to give due consideration to the difficulties faced by states in dealing with surges in the arrival of migrants without affecting the absolute protection against *refoulement*. Migrants who apply for asylum must be given access to the asylum procedure and the procedural guarantees of Article 3 ECHR.[44] Those who do not apply for asylum must be allowed to

and narrow concept in international law, which is meant to apply only in the most severe of circumstances. To find a violation here misrepresents the reality of the situation faced by the Italian authorities and by the migrants in question. It necessarily dilutes a clear prohibition under international law that has its roots in the national homogenisation and genocidal policies of the twentieth century.' Others welcomed the ruling of the Chamber as setting clear procedural standards that guarantee an individual examination of the personal situation of every migrant irrespective of the introduction of an asylum application; see MR Mauro, 'Detention and Expulsion of Migrants: The *Khlaifia v Italy* Case' (2016) 25(1) *Italian Yearbook of International Law* 85 and 'A Step Back in the Protection of Migrants' Rights: The Grand Chamber's Judgment in *Khlaifia v Italy*' (2017) 26(1) *Italian Yearbook of International Law* 287; L Tsourdi, 'Refining the Prohibition of Collective Expulsion in Situation of Mass Arrivals: A Balance Well Struck?' [2017] *Cahiers de l'EDEM*, available at uclouvain.be/fr/instituts-recherche/juri/cedie/actualites/ecthr-15-december-2016-khlaifia-and-others-v-italy-gc-app-n-16483-12.html.

[42] *Khlaifia* (Grand Chamber) (n 40) para 247.

[43] ibid, para 248.

[44] On these guarantees, which stem from the requirement of a 'rigourous scrutiny' of the risk of violating Art 3 ECHR, see J Vedsted-Hansen, 'The Asylum Procedures and the Assessment of Asylum Requests' in V Chetail and C Bauloz (eds), *Research Handbook on International Law and Migration* (Cheltenham, Edward Elgar, 2014) 446. In some instances, the ECtHR also deduced the right to be given access to the asylum procedure from Art 3 ECHR, without additional reference to the prohibition of collective expulsion. See *MA v Lithuania*, App No 59793/17, ECtHR 11 December 2018.

put forward arguments against their expulsion, such as the right to family life, the best interests of the child or other humanitarian considerations. But they do not qualify for the procedural guarantees of Article 3 ECHR and states enjoy significant leeway in dealing with their situation.

The next section will discuss EU law's prohibition of collective expulsion, a protection that extends to aliens who do not apply for asylum. It will show that the harmonisation of the return procedure, as well as other procedures for obtaining residence permits on grounds such as asylum and family reunification, guarantees aliens an examination of their individual situations in conformity with Article 4 Protocol No 4.

III. The Prohibition of Collective Expulsion in EU Law

Article 19(1) EUCFR states: 'Collective expulsions are prohibited.' This is closely related to the principle of *non-refoulement*, which is set out by Article 19(2) EUCFR.[45] The prohibition of collective expulsion is, however, more than simply an expression of the principle of *non-refoulement*. As shown above in section II, the jurisprudence of the ECtHR has given the prohibition of collective expulsion an autonomous meaning, with a wider scope of application than that of Article 3 ECHR. It guarantees the right of to an individual examination of each alien's situation, irrespective of a risk of ill-treatment in the country of destination. This individualisation requirement can also be derived from Article 19(1) EUCFR because of the principle of equivalent protection established by Article 52(3) EUCFR.

The next sections will analyse the extent to which EU migration and asylum law require an individual examination of the situations of aliens before their expulsion. A thorough study of all the expressions of the individualisation requirement would go beyond the scope of this chapter, whose objective is to account for the lack of reference to the prohibition of collective expulsion in the national jurisprudence on returns. The focus will be on the main procedural and substantial guarantees, as they imply that in most cases national courts do not need to rely on the prohibition of collective expulsion to sanction a lack of individual examination. These guarantees are briefly explained in sections III.A and III.B.

[45] Art 19 EUCFR: 'Protection in the event of removal, expulsion or extradition: 1. Collective expulsions are prohibited. 2. No one may be removed, expelled or extradited to a State where there is a serious risk that he or she would be subjected to the death penalty, torture or other inhuman or degrading treatment or punishment.' See J Jaumotte, 'Article 19. Protection en cas d'éloignement, d'expulsion et d'extradition' in F Picod and S Van Drooghenbroeck (eds), *Charte des droits fondamentaux de l'Union européenne. Commentaire article par article* (Brussels, Bruylant, 2018) 445–67.

A. Individualisation as a Procedural Requirement

The right to good administration established by Article 41 EUCFR requires 'fair and impartial treatment'. It is an essential procedural guarantee that gives every person the opportunity to put forward arguments against administrative decisions that affect them.[46] The Article's scope of application is limited to 'the institutions, bodies, offices and agencies of the Union'. But it is also a general principle of EU law.[47]

The right to good administration includes the right to be heard before the adoption of an individual decision.[48] In *Mukarubega* and *Boudjlida*, the CJEU held that aliens must be heard before the adoption of a return decision, unless it is adopted following the closure of another procedure during which they had the effective opportunity to invoke the reasons to claim a residence permit.[49] In *G and R*, the CJEU ruled that the infringement of the right to be heard does not automatically negate a decision. Such a decision will only be annulled 'if, had it not been for such an irregularity, the outcome of the procedure might have been different'.[50] The alien must show precise factual and legal circumstances that would have resulted in the decision not being taken had they been put forward at an earlier stage of the procedure. With respect to asylum seekers, the right to be heard is set out by the Asylum Procedures Directive. The right to a personal interview on the first asylum application is guaranteed, buttressed by additional requirements such as the adequate training of interviewers.[51]

As well as the right to be heard, the right to good administration requires a reasoned decision. The duty to give reasons is established by Article 12 of the

[46] P Craig, 'Article 41: Right to Good Administration' in S Peers, T Hervey, J Kenner and A Ward, *The EU Charter of Fundamental Rights: A Commentary* (Oxford, Hart Publishing, 2014) 1071; F Tulkens, 'Droit à une bonne administration' in Picod and Van Drooghenbroeck (n 45) 873.

[47] Case C-604/12 *HN* [2014] EU:C:2014:302, para 49; S Bogojevic, X Groussot, and M Medzmariashvili, 'Adequate Legal Protection and Good Administration in EU Asylum Procedures: *HN* and Beyond' (2015) 52 *CML Rev* 1635-.

[48] Art 41(2)(a) EUCFR.

[49] Case C-166/13 *Mukarubega* EU:C:2014:2336, para 42; Case C-249/13 *Boudjlida* EU:C:2014:2431, para 34; H Gribomont, 'Ressortissants de pays tiers en situation irrégulière: le droit d'être entendu avant l'adoption d'une décision de retour' (2015) 219(5) *Journal de droit européen* 192. The CJEU based its reasoning on the right of defence, which is a component of the right to good administration (Case C-277/11 *M* EU:C:2012:744, para 82).

[50] Case C-383/13 PPU *G and R* EU:C:2013:533, para 38. For a critical analysis, see P De Bruycker and S Mananashvili, '*Audi Alteram Partem* in Immigration Detention Procedures, Between the ECJ, the ECtHR and Member States: *G & R*' (2015) 52 *CML Rev* 569. The *G & R* ruling concerns the right to be heard prior to the adoption of a detention order with the view to a forced removal. The reasoning of the CJEU is, however, principled. It is founded on a general interpretation of the right to be heard under EU law.

[51] Arts 14 and 15 of Directive 2013/32/EU of the European Parliament and of the Council of 26 June 2013 on common procedures for granting and withdrawing international protection (recast) [2013] OJ L180.

Return Directive.[52] It is a general requirement of EU law and is closely linked with the right to an effective remedy. In *Mahdi*, the CJEU held that this obligation

> is necessary both to enable the third-country national concerned to defend his rights in the best possible conditions and to decide, with full knowledge of the relevant facts, whether there is any point in his applying to the court having jurisdiction, and also to put that court fully in a position to carry out the review of the legality of the decision in question.[53]

In that case the CJEU ruled that the duty to give reasons also applies to decisions that extend the initial period of detention in accordance with Article 15 of the Return Directive.

The right to effective judicial protection set out by Article 47 EUCFR is another procedural safeguard for individualised decision-making.[54] Aliens are entitled to appeal against return decisions, which can have a suspensive effect when removal would violate the principle of *non-refoulement*. Appellate bodies must also have the competence to order the postponement of a removal pending their decision.[55] Aliens are entitled to minimal social protection pending their removal, as their basic needs must be covered.[56] As stated by the CJEU in *Abdida*, a postponement should also be ordered in cases where the violation of the principle of *non-refoulement* would cause a 'serious risk of grave and irreversible deterioration in [the applicant's] … state of health'.[57] The CJEU also held that Member States must define the 'basic needs' that are covered in cases of postponement, which should include 'emergency health care and essential treatment of illness'.[58]

B. Individualisation as a Substantive Requirement

EU law requires an individual examination of every asylum application. The specific profile of each asylum seeker, including vulnerabilities, must be considered

[52] Directive 2008/115/EC of the European Parliament and of the Council of 16 December 2008 on common standards and procedures in Member States for returning illegally staying third-country nationals [2008] OJ L348.

[53] Case C-146/14 PPU *Mahdi* [2014] EU:C:2014:1320, para 45. On that ruling, see DA Arazo, 'The Charter, Detention and Possible Regularization of Migrants in an Irregular Situation under the Returns Directive: *Mahdi*' (2015) *CML Rev* 1361.

[54] On the right to an effective remedy in the asylum procedure, see M Reneman, *EU Asylum Procedures and the Right to an Effective Remedy* (Oxford, Hart Publishing, 2014) 433.

[55] Arts 9 and 13 of Directive 2008/115/EC (n 52).

[56] Art 14 of Directive 2008/115/EC (n 52). On the situation faced by unremovable migrants, see F Lutz, 'Non-Removable Returnees under Union Law: Status Quo and Possible Developments' (2018) 20(1) *European Journal of Migration and Law* 28.

[57] Case C-562/13 *Abdida* EU:C:2014:2453, para 50. See also S Bodart, 'Arrêts *M'Bodj* et *Abdida*: vers une précarisation de l'autorisation de séjour pour motif médical' (2015) 4 *Journal de droit européen* 156; S Peers, 'Irregular Migrants: Can Humane Treatment be Balanced Against Efficient Removal?' (2015) 17(4) *European Journal of Migration and Law* 289.

[58] *Abdida*, ibid.

to assess the level of risk in the country of origin. The Qualification Directive requires 'the assessment of an application for international protection … to be carried out on an individual basis'.[59] A similar requirement can be found under the Asylum Procedures Directive, which requires that 'applications are examined and decisions are taken individually, objectively and impartially'.[60] The *A, B and C* ruling of the CJEU offers an example with respect to persecution based on sexual orientation. The CJEU held that:

> [T}he assessment of applications for the grant of refugee status on the basis solely of stereotyped notions associated with homosexuals … does not allow [asylum] authorities to take account of the individual situation and personal circumstances of the applicant for asylum concerned.[61]

The individualisation requirement is not limited to the assessment of the applicants' risk of persecution. It concerns all aspects of the asylum application, as suggested by the CJEU case-law on subsidiary protection and exclusion from international protection. In *Elgafaji*, the CJEU interpreted Article 15(c) of the Qualification Directive, which states that subsidiary protection must be granted to civilians fleeing a 'serious and individual threat … by reason of indiscriminate violence in situations of international or internal armed conflict'. The CJEU ruled that 'the more the applicant is able to show that he is specifically affected by reason of factors particular to his personal circumstances, the lower the level of indiscriminate violence required for him to be eligible for subsidiary protection'.[62] It established a 'scale' in which the individual situation of the asylum seeker remains relevant even in the face of indiscriminate violence. Additional considerations regarding vulnerability may lead to the granting of subsidiary protection even if the level of violence is not such that it affects every civilian in an indiscriminate way.[63] In *B and D*, the Court emphasised the need to perform an individual assessment of the behaviour of the asylum seeker in order to determine whether

[59] Art 4 of Directive 2011/95/EU of the European Parliament and of the Council of 13 December 2011 on standards for the qualification of third-country nationals or stateless persons as beneficiaries of international protection, for a uniform status for refugees or for persons eligible for subsidiary protection, and for the content of the protection granted (recast) [2011] OJ L337.

[60] Art 10(3) of the Asylum Procedures Directive.

[61] Joined Cases C-148/13, C-149/13 and C-150/13 *A, B and C* EU:C:2014:2406.

[62] Case C-465/07 *Elgafaji* ECR I-921, para 39. See also C Bauloz and G Ruiz, 'Refugee Status and Subsidiary Protection: Towards a Uniform Content of International Protection?' in V Chetail, P De Bruycker and F Maiani (eds), *Reforming the Common European Asylum System: The New European Refugee Law* (Leiden, Brill, 2016) 240.

[63] For a concrete example from Belgian case-law, see the rulings nos 195.227 and 195.228 of 20 November 2017 in which the General Assembly of the Council for Aliens Law Litigation ruled that the violence in Baghdad does not reach the level required to affect all Bagdhadis in a similar way, but those who face additional risk factors may benefit from subsidiary protection by application of Art 15(c) of the Qualification Directive. In an example of the latter, in the ruling no 201.900 of 29 March 2018 the Council for Aliens Law Litigation held that a Baghdadi family with a Sunni background, whose house was confiscated by a paramilitary group, had encountered additional risk factors.

there are 'serious reasons for considering' that he committed, incited or otherwise participated in a serious crime as defined by Article 12 of the Qualification Directive, to the extent that he is excluded from international protection. It held that 'the exclusion from refugee status … is conditional on an individual assessment of the specific facts'.[64]

The CJEU also emphasises the individualisation requirement in the field of EU migration law, including the area of family reunification. In *Chakroun*, it ruled that the sufficient resources requirement does not negate the necessity of assessing the individual situation of each sponsor: 'Member States may indicate a certain sum as a reference amount, but not … impose a minimum income level below which all family reunifications will be refused, irrespective of an actual examination of the situation of each applicant.'[65] In *K and A*, the CJEU ruled that integration tests must consider 'specific individual circumstances … such as the [applicant's] age, illiteracy, level of education, economic situation or health'.[66] All of these factors can affect an applicant's ability to present or to pass the test. In *KA and others*, the CJEU ruled that an entry ban does not justify the automatic rejection of an application for family reunification. Rather, 'all specific circumstances' must be examined.[67]

Furthermore, it follows from the very structure of the Return Directive that a return decision cannot be adopted without prior examination of the particular situation of the third-country national concerned. The Return Directive prohibits any return in violation of the prohibition of *refoulement*. It also requires that the best interests of the child, the family life and the state of health be considered.[68] At the very least this implies a requirement to assess the individual situation of each third-country national, something also emphasised by the insistence in Recital 6 of the Return Directive that return decisions be adopted 'on a case-by-case basis'. This requirement has found concrete application in the CJEU case-law on the detention of third-country nationals pending their return.[69]

The examples above show that it is inherent in the very structure of EU migration and asylum law that individual assessments of the situations of aliens

[64] Joined Cases C-57/09 and C-101/09 *B and D* [2010] ECR I-10979, para 94. See also Case C-573/14 *Lounani* EU:C:2017:71; P Chatelet, 'Statut de réfugié et lutte contre le terrorisme' [2017] *Revue des affaires européennes* 107; AM Kosińska, 'The Problem of Exclusion from Refugee Status on the Grounds of Being Guilty of Terrorist Acts in the CJEU Case-Law' (2017) 19 *European Journal of Migration and Law* 425; A Pivato, 'L'exclusion du statut de réfugié à l'aune du phénomène terroriste' (2017) 193 *Revue du droit des étrangers* 189.

[65] Case C-578/08 *Chakroun* [2010] ECR I-01839, para 48. See also Case C-558/14 *Khachab* EU:C:2016:285. See also COM(2014) 210 final and, for concrete examples of Belgian national case-law: S Sarolea and J Hardy, 'Le regroupement familial: la jurisprudence belge au croisement des sources internes et européennes' in B Renauld (ed), *Questions actuelles en droit des étrangers* (Limal, Anthémis, 2016) 7.

[66] Case C-153/14 *K and A* EU:C:2015:453, para 58.

[67] Case C-82/16 *KA and others* EU:C:2018:308.

[68] Art 5 of the Return Directive.

[69] Case C-61/11 PPU *El Dridi* EU:C:2011:268, para 39; Case C-554/13 *Zh and O* EU:C:2015:377, para 61.

must be made before their removal. EU provisions on return and the criteria that must to be met to obtain a residence permit – particularly on the grounds of asylum and family reunification – require the officials involved always to give due consideration to the specific situations of the third-country nationals concerned. In most cases a lack of individual examination violates not only the prohibition of collective expulsion but also other provisions of EU law. This may explain why national courts rarely rely on the prohibition of collective expulsion. Indeed, its value seems limited to those cases where access to the relevant procedure has been prevented.

The fact that national courts do not often rely on the prohibition of collective expulsion in their enforcement of the Return Directive can be interpreted in two ways. It may show the strength and efficiency of EU law guarantees, including the Return Directive. Prevention of access to the relevant procedure is such a fundamental breach of EU law that it only occurs rarely. On the other hand it may show that national courts lack the practical means to sanction collective expulsions. When access to the procedure is prevented as a result of a collective expulsion, access to the national courts may also be prevented. Ultimately the reality probably lies somewhere in between.

IV. Conclusion

The prohibition of collective expulsion is relatively absent from national courts' case-law on the return of third-country nationals.[70] The absence of significant national rulings on the prohibition of collective expulsion seems surprising given its wide recognition and the developments it has accrued within the case-law of the ECtHR. Thus, this chapter has reflected on the reasons why the prohibition of collective expulsion features so little in the rulings of national courts. It attempted to clarify the content of the prohibition of collective expulsion under the case-law of the ECtHR, compared to similar guarantees under EU law.

As discussed in the first part of the chapter, the case-law of the ECtHR demonstrates that the prohibition of collective expulsion is infringed by two different kinds of policies. First, discriminatory policies aimed at expelling groups of aliens without considering the individuals' personal situations are prohibited, as exemplified by *Conka* and the rulings in *Georgia v Russia* (I) and *Berdzenishvili* and *Shioshvili*. Second, 'push-back' policies that prevent access to the relevant procedure are prohibited, as illustrated by *Hirsi*, *Sharifi*, *Khlaifia* and *ND and NT*. In each of these cases the ECtHR sought to determine whether the particular situations of the aliens were examined before their expulsion. It assessed all the relevant facts, including the procedural guarantees and the circumstances

[70] This finding is supported by the case-law collected in the REDIAL Project (n 4).

surrounding the adoption and implementation of the expulsion orders. However, it refrained from imposing strict procedural requirements, such as a duty to give adequate reasons for the adoption of an expulsion order or to hear migrants individually.

The second part of the chapter showed that it is inherent in the very structure of EU asylum and migration law that an individual assessment of the personal situation of every alien must be made. Numerous procedural guarantees and substantive requirements help to guarantee this. These guarantees are stronger and more specific than the ones established by Article 4 Protocol No 4 as interpreted by the ECtHR. This may explain why national courts do not often rely on the prohibition of collective expulsion. Judges may have a natural tendency to apply the most specific rule that offers the highest level of legal certainty, as this protects their legitimacy. The prohibition of collective expulsion is therefore of little daily relevance to them, which may explain why they have not engaged in a thorough dialogue with the ECtHR and the CJEU in order to define its scope and content.

However, the prohibition of collective expulsion has not lost its autonomous meaning or usefulness. On the contrary, it can be seen as a general requirement to grant migrants access to an adequate procedure. In that sense, the prohibition of collective expulsion is a generic right that conditions the effectiveness of the whole body of more specific guarantees set out by EU law. As other chapters in this volume demonstrate, it is the definition of these guarantees that generates the most intense judicial dialogue.

INDEX

Abbreviations used in the index
AA (Aliens Act)
ACHPR (African Charter on Human and Peoples' Rights (1981))
ACHR (American Convention on Human Rights (1969))
AComHR (African Commission of Human Rights)
ADRDM (American Declaration of the Rights and Duties of Man (1948))
AF (Act on Foreigners (Poland))
APC (Administrative Procedures Code)
APD (2005) (Asylum Procedures Directive (2005))
APD (2013) (Asylum Procedures Directive (2013) (Recast Procedures Directive))
AufenthG (Aufenthaltsgesetz)
CESEDA (Entry and Residence of Foreigners/Right of Asylum Code (France))
CFR/Charter (EU Charter of Fundamental Rights (2000))
CISA (Convention Implementing the Schengen Agreement (2000))
CMW (Committee on the Rights of All Migrant Workers and Members of Their Families)
CoE (Council of Europe)
CRC (UN Committee of the Rights of the Child)
ECHR (European Convention on Human Rights (1950))
EComHR (European Commission of Human Rights)
ECSR (European Committee of Social Rights)
EP (European Parliament)
ERTF (European Roma and Travellers Forum)
EUFRA (EU Fundamental Rights Agency)
GC (general comment)
GC 6 (Treatment of Unaccompanied and Separated Children Outside their Country of Origin)
GC 14 (Right of the Child to Have His or Her Best Interests Taken as a Primary Consideration)
GG (Grundgesetz/Basic Law)
HR (human rights)
HRC (UN Human Rights Committee)
IACtHR (Inter-American Court of Human Rights)
ICCPR (International Covenant on Civil and Political Rights (1966))
ID (identity documentation)
IHRDA (Institute for Human Rights and Development in Africa)
IHRL (international human rights law)
LLSF (Law on the Legal Status of Foreigners in Lithuania (1991))
OPCP (Optional Protocol to the UNCRC on a Communications Procedure (2011))
OSCE (Organization for Security and Co-operation in Europe)
QD (Qualification Directive (2004))
RC (Refugee Convention (1950))
RCD (2003) (Asylum Reception Conditions Directive (2003))

RCD (2013) (Asylum Reception Conditions Directive (2013) (Recast Reception Conditions Directive))
RCD (2016) (Reception Conditions Directive Proposal (2016))
RD (2018) (Proposal for a Recast Return Directive (2018))
RD (Return Directive (2008))
REDIAL (REturn Directive DIALogue)
Schengen (Schengen Border Code)
TCN (third-country national)
TEC (Treaty establishing the European Community)
TFEU (Treaty on the Functioning of the European Union (2007))
UNCRC (UN Convention on the Rights of the Child (1989))

Note: The headings in the index fall essentially into two groups: subject headings and country headings. Wherever relevant the subject headings entries are picked up under the country headings. There are accordingly cross-references to countries only when most of the discussion of a particular subject relates to one or two countries where it is indexed in more detail.

www.ingramcontent.com/pod-product-compliance
Ingram Content Group UK Ltd.
Pitfield, Milton Keynes, MK11 3LW, UK
UKHW020257051026
15470UKWH00020B/387

9 781509 922956